ISSUES IN CANADIAN SOCIETY *An Introduction to Sociology*

ISSUES IN CANADIAN SOCIETY:

An Introduction to Sociology

Dennis Forcese
Associate Professor, Department of Sociology, Carleton University

Stephen Richer
Associate Professor, Department of Sociology, Carleton University

Prentice-Hall of Canada, Ltd., Scarborough, Ontario

PRENTICE-HALL, INC., ENGLEWOOD CLIFFS, NEW JERSEY
PRENTICE-HALL INTERNATIONAL, INC., LONDON
PRENTICE-HALL OF AUSTRALIA, PTY., LTD., SYDNEY
PRENTICE-HALL OF INDIA PVT., LTD., NEW DELHI
PRENTICE-HALL OF JAPAN, INC., TOKYO

Library of Congress Catalog Card No. 74-11611

ISBN 0-13-50635-2-3 (paperback)

ISBN 0-13-50636-0-4 (cloth)

1   2   3   4   5   79   78   77   76   75

PRINTED IN CANADA

Contents

Preface

To the Student and Professor

There are three deliberate design characteristics of this book which we believe are noteworthy. One is the Canadian orientation, the second is the social issues orientation, and the third is the multi-contributor format.

Canada is quite obviously not an isolated social system, to be plucked from a world setting and observed in a vacuum. Things which exist and happen in other societies — particularly U.S. society — affect Canada, often enormously. Yet, it is nonetheless vital to impart information about Canadian society as a distinguishable entity, with social norms, values, institutions, behavior, and problems which are often similar to, but equally often different from, those of other societies. In this book we have attempted to illustrate many of these features of Canadian society, not because of any silly chauvinism, but because we are committed as social scientists to knowing this nation more fully. We have tried to identify both that which is unique in Canada, and that which is comparable to other social systems.

We have approached this book by way of focusing discussion on social issues presently of importance in Canada. For our purposes this means that the starting point for the consideration of a particular area (e.g., deviance) is a concrete social issue (e.g., marihuana use). The general strategy in all the chapters is to present a social issue and ask how sociology can help us understand and analyze the problem. This approach reflects our view that what is exciting about sociology is not sociology itself, but its constant application to relevant real world issues. The more common approach is to begin with sociology and bring in social issues solely as illustrative material. Although we reject this strategy, this is not to imply a rejection of sociological concepts and theory — we subscribe to a constant process of going back and forth between concepts and theory and the social issue of concern. The key is that we use the issue as the departure point and organizing theme, rather than the discipline.

We designed this volume from a commitment to the concept of a multi-author text. We recognized from the outset that there would be problems of co-ordination of approach, concepts, and writing style, and willingly concede that these have not been altogether overcome. But we are of the view that authors who have some specialized knowledge of and commitment to a subfield of sociology are more likely to produce useful chapters than are one or two authors having to become specialists in everything.

A major difficulty which we faced was that of integrating the various chapters of the text. Two related aspects made this particularly difficult. Firstly, the very process of dividing the field of sociology into areas of specialization inevitably produces a fragmented picture of the discipline. A newcomer to the study of contemporary sociology could hardly be blamed if he drew the conclusion that the field was in reality composed of numerous 'sociologies' — the sociology of the family, of deviance, of education, of political behavior, etc. This cutting up of the field no doubt reflects wider societal trends toward differentiation and specialization. Nevertheless, it might also convey, erroneously we argue, that these 'sociologies of' are self-contained, esoteric pursuits with their unique orienting questions and conceptual tools.

The second and related problem arose from the simple fact of many authors contributing to the text rather than one or two. How could we minimize discontinuity and at the same time reap the benefits of having acknowledged specialists writing original chapters in their own areas?

We have addressed these problems in several ways, the four principal ones being an attempt to ensure that the different authors use fundamental concepts in the same way; that each chapter follow the same general format; that each part of the book be preceded by an introduction; and that the book as a whole be organized in a logical, systematic fashion.

The first was not as difficult as we initially feared. There was fairly high uniformity among the contributors in the meaning attached to various basic concepts. Where such consistency of usage did not exist we ourselves undertook to make appropriate changes. Although the book is organized into various subfields, then, the standardization of concepts serves to indicate, we hope, that the perspective of sociology transcends specific areas and that each 'specialist' is simply applying the same basic models and concepts to his area of interest.

In addition to this, he is organizing his chapter in the same way as his fellow contributors. Consistent with our approach to the discipline, each author was given the following set of instructions as to format:

(1) Select one or more dominant Canadian social issues in the substantive area. Present a general discussion of the issue(s) in layman-like prose.

(2) 'Translate' the issue into sociology using the appropriate concepts.

(3) Discuss and explicate the major models or theories which have been applied to the problem.

(4) Bring in any empirical findings which have tended to support and/or reject these.

This format not only has the function of integration, however, but serves as well to introduce the reader to the *method* of sociology. These four steps represent the way in which many sociologists typically go about their research. One first may be motivated by one or more social issues or problems, whether these be drug use, urban blight, delinquency, or any other social problems. The next step is to place the problem in a sociological perspective: formulate the issue in terms or concepts intrinsic to the discipline. We then search previous works for one or more models or theories which might guide us in asking questions, collecting data, and in analysis. The data and analysis in turn feed back to our original model or theory — lending credence to it, refining it, or perhaps leading to its total rejection. In short, the sociological method is a constant cycle, a continuous interplay between social issues, models, and empirical facts. The chapters in this text reflect this interaction.

We have also written introductory remarks for each part of the book. These are intended to place the chapters in context, and indicate the manner in which they interrelate. In addition, we provide selected and annotated reading suggestions for each part, with works salient to each chapter.

Finally, the layout of the book reflects a logical evolution. We begin with basic concepts, introduced in a narrative fashion. We build on these concepts in Chapter Two where we take up the topic of socialization, a topic which we view as central to the sociological perspective. We end this first part of the book with a brief demographic profile of Canada, providing the broad background information necessary to utilize fully the chapters which follow.

The second and third parts of the book are devoted to two broad themes: issues of inequality and issues of industrialization. The two are of course related, as we attempt to establish in our part introductions. But the specific issues emphasized by the contributors to this volume do cluster about one or the other of these two principal themes.

We conclude the book with two chapters on sociology in Canada. The first is an account of the development of sociology in Canada, and the influences upon that development. Anglophone and Francophone sociology are distinguished in this chapter, in large part by the extent to which they have grown up in response to social issues. The final chapter invites the student and the teacher to explore the nature and meaning of university education in sociology. The chapter is intended to be provocative and is an exposition of considered opinions on questions of teaching content and style, student evaluation, the role of the university, and the place of sociology. It invites dissent as much as agreement.

There is no doubt that this volume could have been lengthier; it is not our claim that the book is completely comprehensive in its demonstration of things sociological. But the chapters survey a wide range of behaviors and societal factors and do, we believe, illustrate the interests and aspirations of sociologists in Canada.

D.F.
S.R.
Ottawa

1 : FOUNDATIONS

Introduction to Part One

What is Canadian society? It is easy enough to define Canada in the political or geographical sense; a nation of more than 22 million people, a vast territory with sufficient resources to provide us with food, shelter, and luxury goods. We call ourselves Canadians and we speak of Canadian society, but few of us would be satisfied to claim that we fully understand Canadian society, or that Canadian society is simply a matter of approximately 22 million people who by birth or by choice happen to live above the 49th parallel of North America.

We might think that we knew something about Canada as distinct from the United States, China, or any other nation of the world; yet we would also probably recognize that there could be no straightforward description of Canada and its peoples once we exceed political and geographical definitions. Conventionally we try to deal with some of the Canadian diversity when we distinguish the French Canadian from the English Canadian; the Westerner from the Ontarian; the Roman Catholic from the Protestant or the Jew; the wealthy from the poor. This book attempts to understand that which distinguishes Canadians from one another, as well as from the peoples of other societies. The object is to begin to understand human beings, human behavior, and human societies in general, and Canadians, Canadian behavior, and Canadian society in particular. Such is the subject matter of sociology.

In Chapter One of the book we introduce many of the concepts which are universally used in modern sociology. The chapter is intended to acquaint the reader with the necessary peculiarities of a specialized vocabulary such as grows up in any discipline. The concepts introduced have been restricted in number to those which are most commonly and basically used, so as not to boggle the mind, but also to illustrate that such terminology is used in sociology only in aid of more precise communication and shared meaning. There was a day in the discipline's development, perhaps not altogether past, when intellectual creativity was confused with the invention of new concepts. But over the years more productive notions of originality have been established, and many of the concepts once offered to the discipline have become obsolete and been abandoned.

The first chapter also contains a brief description of the principal theoretical orientations of sociology. These have been sketched very briefly and certainly are not to be viewed as fully satisfactory and exhaustive summations of complex theoretical approaches. The sketches are intended to provide, however, a basic appreciation of the major emphases of the several sociological theories which we believe to be most widely employed, and which occur in subsequent chapters.

In Chapter Two we describe what we take to be a fundamental interest of social scientists: childhood socialization, or human learning. It is quite simply our belief that no sociologist can hope to understand human behavior and society without coming to grips with socialization. Thus we find that the major theoretical orientations of the discipline all incorporate as fundamental an approach to human learning.

In our discussion of socialization, we take deliberate care to point out that the analysis of social learning is not synonymous with an emphasis upon statics or non-change in human societies. Whether societies are simple or complex, traditional or modern, socialization relates generations and is a key to both continuity and change. Human beings are creatures of their societies and their social experiences. We all learn attitudes, beliefs, values, norms, and behaviors; some orient us to change, others to social stability. Therefore, a sociologist must be concerned with the manner in which individuals are socialized and how that socialization varies with social context. Socialization, social change, and social structure are inter-dependent fields of study.

In Chapter Three we outline some of the basic structural features of Canadian society. We deal with the elementary: people. Demographic factors such as population size, births, deaths, immigration and emigration, ethnic and religious composition, and urbanization, are outlined over the time-span of this century. These population inputs are the basis of the complex Canadian social structure.

Recommended Readings: Annotated

Baldwin, Alfred, *Theories of Child Development.* New York: John Wiley and Sons, 1967.

This is a good sourcebook on psychological and sociological approaches to childhood socialization, although it omits the symbolic interactionist model. The book is not adequate for definitive study, but serves as a suitable introduction.

Berger, Peter, *Invitation to Sociology: A Humanistic Perspective.* New York: Doubleday, 1963.

More than any other book which we know, this little paperback volume comes to grips with the nature of sociological assumptions as they relate to a humanistic conception of social life and human freedom. The book illustrates the soul of sociology.

Kalbach, Warren, and Wayne McVey, *The Demographic Bases of Canadian Society.* Toronto: McGraw-Hill, 1971.

The authors have compiled in tables and narrative the information which sociologists find most pertinent among demographic data on Canada. The data are from the 1961 Census.

Thomlinson, Ralph, *Sociological Concepts and Research.* New York: Random House, 1965.

For a good and lucid exposition of the basic sociological concepts, and the basic research techniques, there is no better first reading.

CHAPTER ONE

A Sociological Perspective

Dennis Forcese and Stephen Richer
Carleton University

Man and Environment

In the Kalahari desert of South-West Africa, a woman pokes among the
scant undergrowth for edible roots, digging with a pointed wooden stick,
while her mate sets off to hunt with his bow and poison-tipped arrows. In
rural Mexico, a woman squats pounding cornmeal with a stone mallet,
while her mate drives a small herd of goats from an enclosure towards an
open field for grazing. In a small Portuguese village, a woman sits at a
table preparing assorted vegetables for the evening meal yet hours away,
while her mate slowly works his small boat across the Atlantic Ocean to
his traditional fishing grounds in the Grand Banks. In Edmonton, a
woman closes the door behind her school-bound children, contemplating
a cup of coffee, while her mate edges his automobile through traffic-
clogged streets to a downtown office building. Or, as increasingly occurs,
she may bundle the children into a second car, heading for school or day-
care center, and then herself set off for the office. These few examples
from a multitude of human situations and behaviors in a multitude of
human societies share a commonalty: the human biological organism.
They also reflect variables: the precise nature of the behaviors and the
conditions of existence. Each of the persons in our examples would be
able to offer some explanation for his way of life.

Human beings have not wanted for explanations of human behavior.
The intervention of natural and supernatural spirits, gods, extra-
terrestrial beings, the moon, sun or stars, climate, human nature, and
instincts have all separately and severally been invoked to explain why
men and women are what they are, and do what they do. Resort to such

explanations is not uncommon today, among so-called 'civilized' no less than among so-called 'primitive' peoples.

But unique to the contemporary world is the extent to which human beings believe that they can control their destiny, and understand their behavior, not by invoking some unobservable force, but additionally, or instead, by studying the conditions which affect humankind. One such perspective is that of sociology, and its emphasis upon environment. Sociologists emphasize the extent to which the human being is shaped by and is the product of environmental factors. This is not to say that we fail to recognize the importance of biological factors in determining behavior. Much work has been done by psychologists establishing the importance of biological factors in cognitive and social development (Jensen, 1969; Eysenck, 1970). But no science of behavior can do justice to all facets of human existence. A basic process of science is abstraction – each science looks at behavior with the aid of a particular set of concepts which act as 'reality filters.' Both physiological psychologists and sociologists, among others, study human behavior. The difference between the two sciences lies not in the subject matter or in degrees of error or truth, but in the different conceptual glasses with which we look at the world. The conceptual approach of sociology reflects the basic assumption of *environmental primacy*. Thereby biological factors are relatively ignored in sociological explanations; they are viewed as givens to be put aside in favor of environmental variables. Conversely, in physiological psychology, biological factors receive attention at the expense of other variables. The givens of one science are thus the important research variables of another. Sociologists, then, emphasize the *social environment*. This includes other men and women, the manner in which they interact, what they manufacture, from physical objects such as tools, clothing, and shelter to symbolic objects such as language, stories, and beliefs. Thus, the sociological viewpoint is, in a sense, that man and his behavior must be explained in some considerable part by reference to the conditions which man himself creates, and having created, passes on to succeeding generations. Put differently, *man acts upon his environment, and is acted upon by his environment.* Man is both the producer and the product of his social relations and organization – his *society* – and his language and tools – his *culture*. The biological organism *homo sapiens* can only be understood within such an ongoing socio-cultural setting. This is a key premise of many of the social and behavioral sciences, including sociology.

Men live in groups, and insofar as can be testified by physical anthropologists and archaeologists, they always have. To be sure, these groups interact with or are affected and limited by the physical conditions of geography and climate. A people such as the Shoshone

Indians of Southern California, or the Barren-land Eskimo of Canada, quite obviously have faced a harsh natural environment, as contrasted, for example, to the conditions experienced by pre-European contact Polynesians of the South Pacific or the aboriginal inhabitants of the North-West coast of North America, the Kwaikuital Indians. In that the environment differed, so too did the human response. What also differs is the extent to which that response might exploit, or be subject to the physical environment.

To take our initial examples, our Bushmen inhabit an arid and forbidding territory, and their lives are a continual struggle for the means of sustenance. Food is to be had, but not altogether predictably, and certainly not whenever desired; the animals migrate, and so too the Bushmen. Our Mexican family will have the advantage of horticulture; they occupy a territory which permits some controlled production of foodstuffs, such as corn, and forage for domestic animals. However marginally by Canadian standards, they are able to respond to environmental conditions in a manner permitting a somewhat more predictable and secure subsistence – and they are *sedentary,* not *nomadic.* Similarly, the Portuguese family may have vegetables grown in a small garden, or purchased in a local market with the income from months of fishing off the Grand Banks. The environment which they exploit is enormous in scope, and relatively lucrative. Finally, our Canadian family, heirs to a machine technology and a complex division of labor, will not produce their own foodstuffs. Others do so for them, in a complex system of specialized work, transportation, and monetary exchange. The environment is exploited for its agricultural and mineral wealth not by our Edmonton couple but by others in the society; and the environment's harsher features, such as the cold Alberta winters, are effectively tolerated and even ignored in snug and often overheated buildings.

Significantly, whatever our societal example, mankind is heir to his ancestors' responses as much as to the physical context. For a given people such responses consist of some manifestation of a potentially indeterminate number of specific forms of organization of communication (language), and organization of effort and resources, including rules of conduct, distribution of food, and development and utilization of tools (technology). Insofar as we do not deal with a hypothetical genesis or first generation, human beings are born into such an ongoing system or pattern of responses – a socio-cultural environment – as much as they are into a physical environment. Indeed, most anthropologists insist that even before the emergence of *homo sapiens,* our biological ancestors were interacting in group situations, perhaps using crude tools, and generally affecting one another (and affecting continued evolutionary selections, probably in the adaptive value of forebrain development). (Geertz, 1964)

Human beings are endowed with a unique biological capacity for extensive and complex learning behavior, as contrasted with the instinctual responses of animals which vary little from birth. Human beings learn and they learn within social settings. They learn words, attitudes, rules of behavior, and behaviors.

Succeeding generations acquire the features of preceding generations, for they are both casually and deliberately taught such features. Human beings are *socialized* and made aware of that which exists around them: other people and objects, the pre-established organization and dispersion of such people and objects, and the value which is placed upon them (see Chapter Two).

Socialization

All sociologists emphasize that the human infant inherits a socially, as well as a physically, defined environment. From birth the infant is subjected to the influences of his parents, siblings, aunts, uncles, peers, acquaintances, and as well, chance encounters. The behavior of these persons is governed by the prevailing social definitions of appropriate behavior, as well as the idiosyncracies of personality arising from biological character and individual experience. There are social *norms, shared or collective rules of behavior,* which prompt a mother to nurse the infant or not, to fondle the infant more or less, to swaddle the infant or not, to respond with anger or not to the infant's demands. By responding, and by the nature of their responses, the parents are more or less restraining the child and shaping the child's expectations and behavior.

Throughout childhood, one is *socialized* — taught how to respond and taught the limits of response. The normative system of the family, the church, the peer group, the school, and the larger society all contribute to this learning process. These components of the social environment are inherited by the child, in the sense that they are there when the child is born. They thereby limit the range of expression which theoretically is permitted the malleable human infant. And, insofar as the child learns these pre-existing modes of behavior, they persist and are passed on to succeeding generations. The *socialization* process insures such continuity, not the absence of variation and change, but quite simply, continuity.

Thus, for example, children learn the behavior deemed appropriate and believed inevitable for the sexes. The Bushman boy observes male hunting interest and behavior, avidly taking in the stories of the hunt, and sharing the vicarious excitement which the men recall in their tales.

He practices with his own weapons, on ant-hills, beetles, and small beasts of prey. The little girl is similarly expected to engage in female activities. She will accompany her mother as she collects wood for the fire, or tubers for the meal, and as soon as physically able, will assist in these tasks — as well as the care of younger children (see Chapter Eight).

This learning process is effected in part because of the human infant's physical dependence upon adults; for instance, shelter, protection, sustenance cannot be acquired independently by the human infant. The means to existence are provided by parents, as are affection and examples of appropriate behavior. *The parents and other members of the family are the first persons whom the child observes, responds to, and imitates.* Of course, as the child grows older, the number of persons with whom he or she interacts increases. And, in simple societies such as that of the Bushman, all members of the band have contact with the infant. But it remains the case, that insofar as the child remains within the institution of the family, the interaction with parents and siblings is pre-eminently influential. On the basis of parental responses the child gradually learns words, attitudes, and applied behaviors, and forms a self-image and a personality, which will be elaborated as learning proceeds outside the context of the family unit. To take the example of language, as the infant of our Edmonton couple emits sounds, certain sounds are favored and responded to by parents, such as anything approximating 'mamma' or 'dada,' and with smiles, laughter, and generally increased attention, such sounds are rewarded and encouraged, where others are ignored. Similarly, to sketch a typical middle class Canadian family setting, the infant, particularly once mobile, begins to learn to distinguish objects to which he or she has legitimate access; toys are made available, while handling books, vases, radios, or sundry other items elicits parental shrieks and admonishments.

The child's conformity to norms of behavior is initially, and always to some extent, secured by the imposition of threatened or real sanctions. The persons in a position to impose sanctions are, for most infants, their parents. The first experience a child has of power and authority is within the family unit. *Power, the ability to control the behavior of others irrespective of their wishes,* is in the hands of the parents. This is so not only because of their superior strength and control over necessary resources such as food and shelter, but also because they are assumed by other adult members of society to have a right to such control within limits defined by the laws of the state. This *right to exercise power comprises legitimation and hence we speak of legitimate power* or *authority.* Thus, in Canada, parents are understood to have the right under law to control the behavior of their children, and indeed, are deemed responsible for that behavior until the child is eighteen years of age. Thereby parental control is recognized as right and proper by other members of Canadian society, and as such, is legitimated (see Chapter Seven).

Additionally, in the case of our Mexican or Portuguese example, there is the legitimation of formal religion, in the institution of the Roman Catholic Church and its assertion of the God-given rights and obligations of parents to protect, care for, and control their children. Our Mexican mother or father will not often invoke the authority of the state, but of God and the Church.

The sanctions applied by persons in power, such as parents, are both positive and negative — *rewards* or *punishments*. As such sanctions are applied to a child, he comes to associate them with certain behavior and thereby will come to anticipate them. Such anticipation will come to mean that in rather short order behavior eliciting rewards, such as desirable foods or affection, will occur frequently, whereas behavior eliciting punishments will tend to occur less frequently. As our folklore would have it, there is some blend of the carrot and the stick as the child grows and adjusts to the social environment which he had no hand in choosing.

Social Structure

The enormity of the reward or the punishment will be a function of social *values*. *Values are the shared definitions of importance attached to forms of behavior and to objects in a society by members of that society*, and are themselves learned. Societal *norms are rules or expectations of compliance to the values of some social groups*. The greater the value attached to a given mode of behavior, the more urgent is compliance.

It is rarely the case that a society is perfectly homogeneous in norms and values, particularly a complex society. Among simple *hunting and gathering* peoples, such as our Bushmen, there is a uniformity of expectations. The society is small, and the people live in small bands of six to fifteen persons. They are related by kinship ties and norms of mutual dependence and responsibility. The conceivable possibilities and toleration of alternative behaviors is slight when compared to a complex society such as Canada. In a modern industrialized society such as Canada, large in territory and population, and consisting of peoples whose origins are to be found in the societies of the whole world, there are numerous conceivable and tolerable expressions of behavior — to such an extent that the boundary norms and values are difficult to identify.

However, even for complex societies, it is possible to identify a dominant societal value emphasis which might distinguish one society from another. If by a *society* we mean *a collectivity or group of persons sharing a commonly defined territory and perpetuating and sustaining itself across several generations,* one can note behaviors and attitudes which occur more often and are viewed by members of the society as conventional or normative. But within a society there is always variation among social groups in the extent to which they hold given values and conform to given norms. Different ethnic groups, for example, or different social classes within Canada, will attach different values to behavior such as thrift, hard work, cleanliness, to take those examples. Accordingly, violations of a societal norm of hard work would be reacted to quite differently in a middle class as opposed to lower class setting; sanctions would be more probably invoked against the middle class offender than against the lower class offender. Or, to take another Canadian example, we know that Canadians of different ethnic groups, and of different social classes, have varying attitudes towards formal education (see Chapters Five and Six). For example, a person of Icelandic descent in Manitoba manifests very positive values regarding education, as do persons of German Mennonite descent. For both ethnic groups the number of students completing university education is disproportionately high (Forcese, 1964; Siemens, 1965). In this manner, values and norms vary with one's ethnic group and social class status. *Social class status* refers to one's position in a *stratification system,* an institutionalized hierarchy of social rank by power, prestige, and economic possession. Where many people have approximately the same social status and way of life, and thereby comprise a *stratum,* we may speak of a *social class* (see Chapter Four).

Every individual is associated with several *status positions.* We may speak of one's status relative to a society's system of stratification — i.e., *a social class status* — or relative to any salient societal institution. For example, in relation to the institution of the *nuclear family, that family consisting of the mating couple and any children,* one might have the status of father; in relation to the institution of the *extended family, consisting of all relations,* that same individual will have the social statuses or positions of son, uncle, and nephew (see Chapter Eight). In relation to an occupational institution he might have the status of accountant in a firm, like our Edmonton man, working his way to his downtown office.

Each such status or position is associated with an appropriate predefined *role involving rights and obligations.* The norms and values which we have been discussing do not exist in disorder; rather they are clustered into *roles* or *definitions* of *expected behavior appropriate to a given social status.* Accordingly, a person is expected to behave differently as a son than as a father, than as an accountant. It is the *association of such predefined roles which makes up institutions,* such as the family, or the large formal organizations or bureaucracies consisting of ranked occupational statuses and roles which pervade our society (see Chapter Ten).

Institutions are highly resistant to change. Consider that an institution is comprised of roles, norms, and values and that there is a continuity in these across generations by means of socialization. Consider further that such institutions, insofar as they have changed, have done so over a very long period of time, gradually adapting to changing physical and economic conditions to achieve a compatible relationship with this larger environment. The family has changed since its inception in the distant pre-historical past; in Canada, for example, the family tends to emphasize *nuclear* or *conjugal* rather than extended ties, and as a unit, consumer rather than productive economic functions, although not exclusively (see Chapter Eight). But in contrast, our Bushman, Mexican or Portuguese families will be thoroughly involved in relations with kin. They will live in close physical association, often in the same shelter or house, and will participate collectively in protecting and caring for children. In addition, the family as an extended group and *all* its members will be engaged in securing the means to subsistence. Even children will be involved in producing foodstuffs, clothing, and income, rather than acting to consume a plethora of short-lived consumer items such as would be found in the home of our Edmonton couple.

But the unit of organization consisting of a mating pair and any offspring — *the nuclear family* — is fundamental. And the values and norms of a family, although specific to historical periods and societies, are slow to change because the parents are the initial and principal agents who socialize succeeding generations.

Insofar as institutions generally, and not just the family, consist of pre-established roles, *the complex of inter-related institutions known as social structure* is very slow to change. In Canada, as we have previously noted, the parents are initially responsible for regulating the behavior of their children and ensuring their conformity to informal and formal (legal) community expectations. Other members of the family, neighborhood, and community may also intervene. As the child matures, and particularly in larger population centers in modern complex societies, formal agencies come to assume more of the regulatory functions. In Canada, for example, *the maintenance of conformity to societal norms,* or *social control,* is to a large extent delegated to agencies such as the police, the courts, and penal institutions. In addition, in complex urban societies as opposed to rural societies, the norms tend to be increasingly formalized in statutes or laws (see Chapters Nine and Eleven).

It is the case that the larger the population and the more complex the social organization, the greater the role of such formal agencies of control. Yet, most individuals, through their day-to-day behavior, are complying with norms which they have learned in childhood, and sanctions are infrequently brought to bear. We will have learned to be 'upright citizens.'

In this manner, most people come to take their own way of life for granted as right, normal, part of 'human nature.' This is quite understandable, given the structure of socialization and interaction in societies such as Canada. But it leads to unfortunate misperceptions of the way in which people in other societies live. *Ethnocentrism is the attitude that only our way of life is right and normal* (including the Canadian feature of gradual social and political change), and that of other cultures and societies — including subcultures within our own society — is aberrant. The behavior which other people have learned is judged in terms of our own learned behavior, values, and norms, and in that it is different, it is judged to be inferior.

Thus, if our Edmonton mother were suddenly removed to the Kalahari Desert, she would be apt to recoil in horror and disgust from the activities and living conditions of her Bushman counterpart. The diet would be revolting, the lean-to shelter dirty and inadequate, and the people generally 'ignorant and savage.'

Often we are explicitly taught views of other peoples which are grossly erroneous. Such *stereotypes are oversimplified and usually derogatory summations of the character of a group of people,* such as, for example, the Jew as 'money-lender,' the Negro as 'natural athlete,' the Italian as a laborer excelling in brick-laying, and so on. These stereotypes, which we learn as we learn other attitudes, are important aspects of prejudice and discrimination. *Prejudice refers to attitudes which pre-judge a group of people, and discrimination refers to the behavior derived from such pre-judgment which affects this group of people.* Such pre-judgment and discriminatory behavior may be to the advantage or the disadvantage of a group (see Chapter Six). For example, our view that Lilliputians are incapable of education may be associated with discriminatory behavior on our part, such as failing to provide adequate educational opportunities for Lilliputians. Or, we might believe all Lilliputians to be geniuses and thereby insure that they invariably attend college and receive every educational opportunity. In this manner, the prejudicial attitude and discriminatory behavior become self-fulfilling — *a self-fulfilling prophecy.*

In precisely such a manner, Canadians are inclined to the prejudicial attitude that Indians and Metis are 'lazy' and ineducable, while middle class urban Canadians are expected to attain high educational and occupational levels (see Chapters Five and Six).

Models of Behavior and Society

Whatever the variation in emphasis and nuance, most sociologists would have the preceding concepts in common. It is also the case that from such common ground, there is a divergence in the features of human society which sociologists would emphasize in explaining aspects of social behavior. Their divergent emphases are several, and defy concise summation. But it is possible to identify those which in our view are most widely represented in sociology. We characterize these emphases as *models* for they *are systematically organized or inter-related concepts and assumptions which are taken to represent social behavior*. These models or perspectives are the point from which a sociologist will derive statements of relationship between social factors which he seeks to verify or prove to be features of social behavior. The *proposed statements of relationship or hypotheses* are the objects of empirical inquiry or research, and insofar as they do come to be researched, are the genesis of much of the factual information which sociologists seek to acquire in order to describe and to account for behavior patterns.

It has been our experience that most sociologists work with aspects of each of the major theoretical models of sociology and find merits as well as drawbacks in each. Only a minority of sociologists are truly and unequivocally committed to a single model, because any such model is an incomplete representation of reality, and entails distorting assumptions. But each does highlight features of social interaction, and thereby may be profitably, albeit cautiously, used in sociological analysis.

One model of analysis in sociology is known as *structural-functionalist systems theory*. The most influential contributor to this model has been Talcott Parsons, with works running to several volumes, perhaps the best known of which is *The Social System* (Parsons, 1951). Proponents of this model have emphasized the structural aspects of social life: the stable or slowly changing character of complex human institutions. Structural-functionalists have traditionally analyzed societies in terms of the *functions* of societal items, these items being interdependently arranged to comprise a *social system*. An item of behavior, an artifact of culture, a role, a norm, a value, or an institution, is *functional* insofar as it contributes to the maintenance or persistence of a social system or society. Put otherwise, something is functional, even social change, if it enhances the probability that a society will persist. Conversely, an item is *dysfunctional* if it detracts from the maintenance of the social system. Such functions or dysfunctions may be recognized and intended by members of a society – *manifest functions* – or unrecognized and unintended – *latent functions* (Merton, 1957).

For example, the practice of our Bushman hunters in killing only what they and their fellows can consume might be viewed as functional, for it preserves the game on which the band depends for existence. Contrast this to the behavior of the sports hunter. Perhaps our Edmonton accountant indulges in sports hunting, and were he and numerous others to fly into the northern territories and hunt and kill caribou for the pleasure of it, (or even for furs and income as in the historical North American practice), depleting the foodstuffs upon which Eskimo bands depend, the behavior might be deemed dysfunctional.

As the above examples may illustrate, there is a level of analysis difficulty, which complicates precise functionalist analysis. Items may be analyzed in the context of the social subgroup, the society as a whole, or the society as contrasted to other societies. Thereby, to speak of something as functional or dysfunctional is a very relative matter, and dependent upon a carefully specified frame of reference: that is, functional for whom and in what context? For example, gambling may be functional for some people because it alleviates tensions and provides a hope for greater prosperity. Yet, for many, it may also be dysfunctional insofar as it seriously diverts income which is needed for support and perhaps dysfunctional also because gambling may divert an individual from more effective means of improving his life situation.

Structural-functionalists have concentrated on the inter-relationships of the components of society. The interaction of individuals, groups, and institutions comprises systems of behavior of considerable persistence. Functional analysis has attempted to explain and account for this persistence.

Other sociologists, however, are less impressed with persistence than with *change.* Given social structure and socialization, it is perhaps less remarkable that societies persist than that they change at all. The process of social change is dealt with by structural-functionalists largely by reference to dysfunction and discontinuities in the socialization process. But another school of social theorists, those emphasizing *conflict,* claim that inherent in human interaction is a potential for conflict which precipitates change. Some sociologists, such as Lewis Coser, are both functionalists and conflict theorists. Coser argues that conflict is itself functional, in that it helps establish group boundaries and may dissipate tensions (Coser, 1956). A Marxist rather than funtionalist influence characterizes the work of other sociologists who associate themselves with a conflict approach to social analysis. For example, departing from orthodox Marxist literature, Ralf Dahrendorf views modern societies as characterized by a struggle for positions of legitimate power (Dahrendorf, 1959). Others, such as Johann Galtung or Irving Zeitlin, develop analyses which incorporate the Marxist thesis of economic condition and conflict and apply it to contemporary social problems, such as metropolitan domination of hinterland, (Toronto vis-à-vis rural Ontario and Western Canada) or relations between nations (the United States vis-à-vis Canada, or London, England vis-à-vis pre-Confederation Newfoundland) (Galtung, 1971: Zeitlin, 1972).

Marx and Engels in effect argued that conflict was necessary for social evolution or progress. Only in the destruction of a form of society, such as capitalism, could humanity move forward to a superior level of social organization, communism. The destruction and loss of life that might be engendered during the period of conflictual transition, would be viewed as necessary and desirable.

An emphasis upon conflict between groups, such as social classes, ethnic groups, or nations, as a characteristic and dynamic factor in human society is the distinguishing feature of the conflict model. The conditions and outcomes of conflict, and conflict as a mechanism of social change, are analyzed, as are, of course, the institutional obstacles to such change.

Both the functionalist and the conflict perspectives look at the systemic properties of human behavior: that is, behavior within groups bounded by institutions. But the study of human behavior also allows an emphasis upon perceptual inputs. The *symbolic interactionists* have emphasized in their model that human behavior is determined by mutual perceptions. Interacting individuals respond to what they believe to have occurred, or their *definitions of the situation,* and these definitions may differ. But insofar as individuals act on the basis of these perceptions or definitions, symbolic interactionists would emphasize, as W.I. Thomas put it, that a situation is real if it is real in its consequences (Thomas, 1931).

Individuals exist in a social environment — they respond to the behavior of others around them. They form impressions of others, and impressions of what others think of them. The *looking-glass self* concept of Charles Horton Cooley represents the fact that everyone is affected by an image of self which he believes others hold (Cooley, 1922). Our own self-image is an adaptation to other personalities and our impression of the way in which others react to our personality. If we believe that others perceive us as ugly, or stupid, we may come to believe ourselves ugly or stupid. If others emphasize that we have violated a norm, then we may come to view ourselves as norm violators, or *deviant.* Or, as it is frequently put, people are stigmatized or *labelled.* In time, that self-perception or *self-image* may become self-fulfilling, insofar as the person acts in keeping with his image and thereby influences others to do likewise (see Chapter Nine).

There is evidence, for example, that Canadian children succeed, or not, in our school system, partly as a result of their self-images. Their images, in turn, are dependent upon teacher attitudes, I.Q. scores, testing, and the like. Thereby, a student may come to be viewed as 'stupid' and a school failure, and/or a 'trouble-maker,' and will come to share that image, and behave accordingly (Forcese and Siemens, 1965).

Accordingly, our relationship with others is dependent upon perception and changes in perception. Language, of course, is the principal medium of this symbolic interaction in human societies. Such perceptual exchanges are, as we shall discuss in the next chapter, an integral part of the socialization process and are operative throughout the lifetime of an individual.

The emphasis upon perception has points in common with another body of thought known as *exchange theory*. Like symbolic interactionism, this orientation assumes the operation of mental processes as actors relate to their environment: calculated decision-making is part of the model. Like symbolic interactionism, the approach also implies putting oneself in the place of others as mutually satisfying exchanges are consummated (Singelmann, 1972).

Exchange theorists place their major emphasis upon social interaction as a continual process of reward and punishment. Persons exchange both goods and symbols, including expressions of approval and disapproval. Behavior more frequently occurs when it generates rewarding behavior on the part of other actors (Homans, 1961; Blau, 1964).

For example, we can imagine our Edmonton household, and the interaction which occurs, as a series of exchanges between parents and child. Set the table, and the child earns a penny; finish your carrots, and the child earns ice-cream; put on your pyjamas, and the child earns a story. In each instance, the parents reward the child in exchange for co-operation, obedience, and conformity (Richer, 1968).

When we incur punishments or negative sanctions, we reduce the behavior which incurred such sanctions; just as when we are rewarded, we seek to maximize such reward by repeating the behavior which attracted it. Thereby compliance or conformity is in considerable part related to the system of sanctions in a society. Moreover, as we discuss in the next chapter, the system of sanctions is intrinsic to socialization, itself a key to conformity.

Conclusions

In subsequent chapters the concepts and the orientations or models which we have sketched will all be utilized as we consider various aspects of Canadian society and behavior. *Additional concepts will also be introduced, and defined when they appear.* Parts II and III of this volume tend to emphasize the structural features of Canadian society, i.e., those institutionalized patterns of groups and behavior which tend to persist in this country. These analyses should be approached with an awareness that within these structural constraints, which are by no means uniform across the nation, Canadians are learning how to behave. Accordingly, even if one prefers a structuralist emphasis, it is important to recognize that such an emphasis is incomplete without a contiguous awareness of socialization. Socialization is the specific topic of the next chapter.

References

Blau, Peter, *Exchange and Power in Social Life*. New York: John Wiley and Sons, 1964.

Cooley, Charles Horton, *Human Nature and the Social Order*. New York: Charles Scribner's Sons, 1922.

Dahrendorf, Ralf, *Class and Class Conflict in Industrial Society*. Stanford: Stanford University Press, 1959.

Eysenck, H.J., *The Biological Basis of Personality*. Springfield, Ill.: Charles C. Thomas, 1970.

Forcese, Dennis, 'Leadership in a Depressed Primary Industry: A Social Description of the Fishermen of Lake Winnipeg.' Unpublished Master's thesis, Winnipeg, University of Manitoba, 1964.

Forcese, Dennis, and Leonard Siemens, 'School-Related Factors and the Aspiration Levels of Manitoba Senior High School Students.' Winnipeg, University of Manitoba, 1965.

Galtung, Johann, 'A Structural Theory of Imperialism,' *Journal of Peace Research,* I (1971), 81-117.

Geertz, Clifford, 'The Transition to Humanity,' in Sol Tax (ed.), *Horizons of Anthropology.* Chicago: Aldine Publishing Co., 1964, pp. 37-48.

Homans, George, *Social Behavior: Its Elementary Forms*. New York: Harcourt, Brace and World, 1961.

Jensen, Arthur R., 'How Much Can We Boost I.Q. and Scholastic Achievement?' *Harvard Educational Review,* XXXIX (1969), 1-123.

Merton, Robert, *Social Theory and Social Structure,* (revised and enlarged edition). New York: The Free Press, 1957.

The Oxford Universal Dictionary. New York: Oxford University Press, 1955.

Parsons, Talcott, *The Social System*. New York: The Free Press, 1951.

Richer, Stephen, 'The Economics of Child Rearing,' *Journal of Marriage and the Family,* XXX (1968), 462-466.

Siemens, Leonard B., 'The Influence of Selected Family Factors on the Educational and Occupational Aspiration Levels of High School Boys and Girls.' Winnipeg, University of Manitoba, 1965.

Singelmann, Ken, 'Exchange as Symbolic Interaction,' *American Sociological Review*, XXXVII (1972), 414-423.

Thomas, W.I., *The Unadjusted Girl*. Boston: Little Brown and Co., 1931.

Zeitlin, Irving, *Capitalism and Imperialism*. Chicago: Markham Publishing Company, 1972.

CHAPTER TWO

Socialization: Becoming Canadians

Dennis Forcese and Stephen Richer
Carleton University

Continuity

Several years ago Peter Berger concisely summarized what we take to be the viewpoint and the subject matter of sociology when he noted that we are concerned with both 'man in society' and 'society in man' (Berger, 1963). Perhaps 'man in society' is the more obvious: each human being inherits an ongoing social environment and has no choice in the matter. By virtue of birth, each of us is obliged to exist in a society which pre-existed our lifetime and which, even as adults, we have had little or no hand in shaping. This inherited social baggage means that we have been subject to numerous restraints upon the full range of behavior which is potentially ours by virtue of our biological qualities. These restraints are vested in the complex structure of cultural items, including thought systems and language, the norms and values, the roles and institutions, and the people which make up Canadian or any society. In time we may come to have some effect upon our social environment, or aspects of it, particularly other individuals; but the fact that we are essentially subject to the boundaries of that environment from birth remains true. This fact need not eliminate all conception of human volition; but the structural restraints are a fundamental fact of life.

Not only are we heirs to a long-evolving social environment, it is also the case that we are taught the features of that environment and taught to accept that environment as right and natural. The environmental characteristics come to be our own not through some process of biological osmosis but through socialization. We come to be creatures of our society as our parents before us, sharing a language, attitudes, values, norms, behavior traits, which we largely come to take for granted. In this sense we may speak of 'society in man,' for we will have internalized the attitudinal and behavioral repertoire of a society. *Internalization* need not be taken to suggest that human beings are shaped such that behavior is robot-like and internally programmed, not subject to conscious intellectual scrutiny, and to a continued system of sanctions. We continue to respond to rewards and punishments through our lifetime (Scott, 1971); we may continue to evaluate alternative conceptions of being, provided we have learned to value such intellectual activity. We are subject to continued socialization through our lifetime. But the concept of internalization does denote that we learn to conform to a social environment such that much of our behavior becomes almost reflexive, and we accept most features of that environment as legitimate, desirable and altogether admirable, unless we have been taught otherwise. Thus, for example, a person might grow up and have been socialized in Winnipeg, satisfied that it was the 'heart of the continent' in more than an approximate physical sense, and that the winsome ballad of 'The Red River Valley' was for and about Manitobans and not Texans. Such unquestioning acceptance is a typical outcome of socialization.

Change

Although the social structure which confines us, and the socialization experience which we undergo, ensure a continuity in societal existence, it must be recognized that both social structure and the processes of socialization relate to social change as well as to societal persistence. A social structure consisting of perfectly integrated values, norms, roles, and institutions, such that they are all perfectly complementary, is unlikely in the extreme. So too is it unlikely that a society can ever utterly isolate itself from extra- societal contacts and communications which introduce intellectual and technological innovations. Rather, in virtually all societies, and certainly Canada, there are contradictory structural demands upon individuals, and external contact, which permit different and sometimes contradictory socialization experiences. Such structural differentiation and varied socialization render societies always subject to some conflict, accommodation, and change. Indeed societies so homogeneous, controlled, and isolated as not to change have rarely been approximated in human history, and then most nearly so in isolated hunting and gathering societies (such as the Tiwi of Australia).

Social change is a part of virtually every society because of a range of external and internal factors. No contemporary society is completely isolated from other societies, although the extent of contact and communications may vary. Accordingly, a variety of contacts among societies will constantly introduce new factors into a society, often bringing about substantial change. Conflict among societies, the *diffusion* or spread of cultural items such as technological devices and art forms, and the migration of peoples, all introduce inputs which will affect and change a society.

Similarly, within the society, the contradictions and conflicts among groups, including variations in learning, *demographic shifts,* whether migrations of peoples or variations in the birth and death rates, innovations, whether technological or in thought and art forms, will bring about changes in a social system. In some societies, such as our own, change is in a sense built in because of the high value which is attached to technological and intellectual innovation or creativity. Additionally, in any society there will be some *culture drift* that makes for change; that is, simply the imperfect transmission of societal features because of imperfect communication and socialization.

Further, just as sociologists do generally agree that we begin to account for continuity by reference to socialization, we may begin to account for change by reference to socialization without discounting other factors, such as the economic and technological. If new attitudes come to exist and perhaps prevail, such as the attitude towards Western Canadian political separatism, or new behaviors, such as with regard to cohabitation and procreation, these must in some sense be related to learning or socialization as well as to the socio-economic changes which constitute the setting within which socialization occurs.

Canadian Heterogeneity and Socialization

In Ottawa, a clock and counting device tick off a constant estimate of births in Canada. In Port-aux-Basques, Calgary, Trois-Rivières, Kamloops, Dawson City, Antigonish, Biggar, Fredericton, Brandon, Hamilton, Charlottetown, and across the span of the nation, infants are born and acquire the *ascribed status* and citizenship rights of 'Canadians.' What these infants shall become as adults, in terms of attitudes, skills, memberships, occupations — whatever predispositions they have and *achieved statuses* they might earn — will to some extent be circumscribed by the fact that they are born in a politically defined entity known as Canada. They will be subject to Canadian laws, Canadian histories, and not least, Canadian climates, all varying with region or province. They will share a parliamentary form of government, and judiciary, and in a less clearcut sense, a system of distribution and consumption of resources. They will also come to realize that they have in common the Canadian Broadcasting Corporation. But they will not all share the same language, customs, values, consumer opportunities, religion, ethnic background, or generally, the same opportunities, aspirations, and attitudes. For although Canada may be viewed as a distinct nation and society, it is no less the conspicuous case that Canada is a nation consisting of diversity or heterogeneity. Canadians have long remarked upon this diversity. We are often inclined to speak of our 'ethnic mosaic,' consisting of immigrants and their descendants from the nations of the world, all proud of their background and to some extent seeking to maintain that background in language, custom, art, and history. The Scots in Nova Scotia, *les Canadiens* in Quebec, the English Loyalists in Ontario, the Ukrainians of the Prairie provinces, the Chinese of British Columbia, to single out but a few, are persisting subgroups with persisting subcultures within Canadian society. (See Chapter Three.)

We are equally aware when we reflect upon it of the regional loyalties which make up Canada, in part a function of physical topography, and often congruent with patterns of ethnic settlement, and reinforced by a federal system of government which ensures some measure of regional political autonomy. The Maritimes are often viewed and view themselves as a distinct region, as does Quebec, *une nation,* Ontario, the Prairies, British Columbia, the Yukon and Northwest Territories, and generally the northern areas of the provinces.

The people of these regions and their political representatives in turn often perceive distinct economic interests which coincide with the regions, as indeed there are. The extractive economies of the Maritime provinces, and to a still significant extent, Quebec, the agricultural economy of Saskatchewan and Manitoba, the oil-rich extractive economy of Alberta, resource-rich British Columbia, and the commercial and industrial heartland of South-central Ontario and metropolitan Montreal are easily distinguishable. That these economic bases affect the infant born in one region or another is all too evident, even before birth in the nature of prenatal care, and subsequently, shelter, education, and eventual occupation and income.

These diversities will also come to be reflected in differences in each of our Canadians' attitudes and perceptions, from subtle and innocuous variations in slang vocabulary, such as between the conventionally North American 'hamburger' in Ontario and the Winnipeger's 'nip,' to attitudes of hostility, such as some Ontarians direct to French Canadians, and vice versa, or Prairie farmers direct to the 'eastern establishment' of Ontario, and in particular, Ottawa and Toronto. Behavioral variations will also be manifested, not only in the previously noted educational and occupational spheres, but also in matters such as political preference, with the regions of Canada repeatedly showing marked patterns of political choice, such that they become characterized as Liberal Quebec,

Tory Ontario, the socialist Prairies (or federally, the Conservative Prairies) and Socred Alberta and British Columbia.

Compound such diversity by recognizing that within ethnic, linguistic or regional sectors of Canada, we may discern additional subgroupings, such as, for example, by religion, rural-urban residence, and more especially, social class. To recognize such diversity is to recognize simply that to speak of Canadian society is misleading insofar as it is taken to imply a uniformity of condition and experience, a matter of disquiet not only for the politician, but also any social scientist in quest of straightforward generalizations about Canadian society.

In fact, to state the obvious, to begin to approach and understand Canada one must understand the diversity which is in fact the preoccupation of the bulk of the work in this volume. But also, we must begin from some appreciation of how Canadians learn to be Canadians, *Canadiens,* Capers, Ontarians or Westerners. Our infants will learn the subloyalties, attitudes, and behaviors which we have outlined. Our infants will be socialized, and thereby, there will be a Canadian continuity, which is in fact a continuity of diversity.

For example, contrast two hypothetical Anglophone Canadians: one socialized in a community in North End Winnipeg, consisting of persons sharing a Ukrainian linguistic background, Eastern Orthodox religion, lower-middle class family status, and educated in a Western-Canadian public school system; another socialized in a community in Westmount, Montreal, consisting of persons sharing an Anglophone linguistic and ethnic background, Anglican religion, upper-middle or upper class family status, and educated in private Eastern-Canadian schools. Both have been born and socialized in a national society known as Canada, and will have shared certain features of that society — the mass media, a legal system, the larger environment, formal education in the English language, approximately similar curriculum content — but the impact of their commonalities will have been attenuated by the differences in environmental inheritance and experience.

Political Socialization: An Illustration

That a society persists even given a multiplicity of socialization inputs indicates that despite diversity, there is some commonality. Over the short run the conflicts within a society may be held in bound through the exercise of coercion, but over the long run, a society's persistence depends upon the voluntary compliance of the population. Such compliance occurs when people accept a society and the power relations within it as *legitimate*. Such legitimacy is learned, and this learning process relates to the matter of political socialization.

If we analyze contemporary societies we cannot escape considering the effort expended upon generating some consensus and legitimacy. The central government of any society persists — is allowed to govern — insofar as it is tolerated by the population, or a significant sector of that population. A society has a distinctive and persistent social and political identity insofar as people are socialized to accept and to some extent manifest that identity. Where this is lacking, it may have to be created. Thus, for example, a principal problem for many new nations is the creation of a sense of nationhood from a hodge-podge of regional, ethnic, and tribal loyalties.

In a not-so-new nation such as Canada, *political socialization* is no less important. Particularly, given the cleavages characterizing Canada, the process of generating a sense of legitimacy for a national government is all the more problematic. With provincially controlled educational systems, variations in curricula may generate or perpetuate signficantly different conceptions of reality and significantly different loyalties. Quebec's relations with the Anglophone provinces are only the most obvious example.

In Canada, as in other societies, children are socialized such that they come to manifest certain attitudes to the exercise of power. Initially, within the context of the family, the child first and most markedly experiences a power relationship — that of his parents over him. The nature of the relationship is important. There are data which suggest, for example, that very authoritarian parents will shape a child to have cynical, suspicious attitudes to office holders, and yet also, a high probability of conformity, particularly given a strong political leader (Adorno, 1950; Langton, 1969). Thus, basic predispositions to authority will be produced within the family, before a child ever attends school.

Once the child is in school, the state begins to exert a more direct influence. Before school attendance, family influence will have been moderated by the socialization impact of the mass media — government controlled and supported. But in the school system, a child is systematically exposed to symbols of authority. The stories which he is told by teachers, and in the texts which are used, present a point of view which the child is required to learn. Respect for political leaders, such as the Prime Minister, for example, is taught. The role and actual office holders are presented in an idealized fashion. One outcome is that such leaders come to be viewed by children as benevolent and paternalistic. (Dawson and Prewitt, 1969; Hess and Torney, 1968) Conceptions of the social collectivity are taught children by means of easily grasped symbols meant to be representative of the society: the American eagle, the British lion, or the Russian bear are all symbolic expressions of collective valor and strength. The Canadian beaver would seem at best to be of dubious worth as a collective symbol, but surely at the least is expressive of the middle class Canadian value of hard work. Additionally, symbols such as national flags are used to represent the permanence and legitimacy of the collectivity. Similarly, historical figures are mythologized, and presented as idealizations of national virtues. The songs which are taught — including national anthems — contribute to the process. So too, class-room activities are important. Electing class officers, student governments, mock parliaments, all socialize children to take for granted a certain kind of political relationship and process.

When one considers that in Canada, regional variations in education have realized different political socialization inputs, some contemporary Canadian political conflicts are put in better perspective. For example, the symbolic import of the historical figure of Louis Riel is quite different for Anglophones in Ontario and Manitoba, than it is for Francophones in Quebec. Similarly, the symbolic and emotive import of the historical event of the Battle of the Plains of Abraham is obviously different for Anglophone Canadians than it is for Francophones. One could continue at some length, considering the differing meanings associated with the monarch, linguistic rights, and generally, complex and sophisticated histories which clearly have varied between Quebec and Anglophone Canada. (Royal Commission on Bilingualism and Biculturalism, *Education*, 1968)

Let us take as an additional example the presence of simple symbols in Canadian schools. Such symbols serve effectively to orient children to political systems. (Dawson and Prewitt, 1969) Schools in different regions of Canada utilize different symbols. Thus, had one attended public school in Manitoba during the 1950's and 1960's, one would have learned loyalties derived from the symbols encountered in Manitoba schools — symbols principally oriented to Canada's ties with the United Kingdom. Classrooms usually contained a portrait of the Queen, for example, and the school day might begin with 'God Save the Queen.' Music or singing period in the schools depended upon the original little red book, a song book. The favorite tunes included 'The Maple Leaf Forever' with its images of the brave singing men of the Northwest Mounted Police; but as or more often, children were directed to the stirring sentiments of 'The British Grenadiers.' One hardly need stress that such content would not have been a feature of Francophone schools in Quebec.

Given regional diversities in the content of political socialization, it would seem that as measured against the criterion of a national political consensus, Canada has been characterized by an ineffective system of political socialization. The educational system, its control constitutionally guaranteed the provinces, has not operated to counter-influence regional allegiances as effectively as has been done in nations of centralized government or a federal nation of greater central powers such as the United States. Rather, in effect there have been efficient subsystems of political socialization, which have been constitutionally facilitated. In addition, Canadians have been systematically exposed via the mass media and the school system to the political symbols of other nations, principally the United States and the United Kingdom. Our children have in many instances a greater knowledge of American or British folk heroes and political leaders than they do of Canadian: Davy Crockett rather than Radisson; George Washington rather than John A. Macdonald; the King or Queen rather than the Prime Minister. The socialization process has thereby contributed to regional loyalties within Canada, and to extra-national loyalties. Thereby the venerable problem of 'Canadian identity' has persisted.

The Content of Socialization

Bearing in mind the diversity which we have stressed in the Canadian experience, we may summarize in a more abstract fashion the general features of socialization. The major learning in socialization involves the culture of the society or group concerned. The primary components are represented by concepts previously noted — roles, norms, and values. As a point of departure, we may say that the actor learns four salient aspects of culture: (1) a general set of norms to some extent independent of specific social positions; (2) roles affiliated with specific positions; (3) at a more abstract level, general orientations characteristic of particular roles and clusters of roles; and (4) the dominant values of the group. The first of these can be treated rather quickly, the other three deserve more extensive treatment.

Norms not Related to Particular Positions

There are norms which one would be hard pressed to allocate to any particular social position. If middle class society is taken as a point of reference, one is not supposed to use physical force to settle disputes or take one's clothes off in public. Such norms transcend specific social positions; indeed they are usually codified in the legal system of a society as formal law. In one sense they may be viewed as the set of norms embodying the role of citizen. In various subgroups of a society one may find similar non position-related norms. For example, in Canadian prisons, whatever position an inmate is occupying, whether 'trustie' or maximum security, he is constrained by the norm of 'no ratting.' (Mann, 1968) Such generally applicable norms are an integral part of the content of socialization.

Roles

Role learning is a more complicated phenomenon than might initially be apparent. A person, in learning a particular role, must inevitably learn the other roles which interlock with or complement his own. This will become clear if one thinks of a role as composed of two components — rights and duties. The rights of a social role outline what privileges the actor can claim by virtue of occupying that social position, even if the claim is an ideal definition rather than fully realizable. The teacher, for example, can claim in our society some modicum of respect and attention. The duties of a teacher include the competent transmission of factual knowledge and a 'fair' (or *universalistic*) judgment of his students. The role complementary to the teacher's is that of student. The interlocking character of these two roles can be seen if we look at the rights and duties of the student's role. The former consist of being taught competently and receiving a fair evaluation of his performance. His duties, on the other hand, include being attentive in class and displaying some minimum respect for the teacher. As can be seen, the complementarity is expressed in the fact that *the rights of one role are the duties of the other.* Indeed, one may view the structure of society as a vast network of such interlocking roles. Apart from this network, an individual further comes to learn that his behavior in a social position will determine in large measure the extent to which he may claim various rights. If the student is noisy and inattentive he is not fulfilling the duties aspect of his role, increasing the likelihood that its rights will be denied him. It should be noted that the opportunities for each role occupant to deviate successfuly from role duties or obligations are by no means equal. If the teacher is biased towards a particular student (utilizes *particularistic standards*) there are few formal sanctions available to the student which might bring the teacher's behavior back in line. On the other hand, the institution of education provides the teacher with several sanctions to utilize if student obligations are unfulfilled. Isolation, poor grades, and expulsion are three such sanctions. Each, of course, is routinely resorted to in Canadian schools, especially the sanction of poor grades.

General Role Orientations

Talcott Parsons has provided us with a conceptual framework for classifying roles and clusters of roles. He argues that roles exhibit a range of alternative normative patterns. These may be described in terms of five *pattern-variables,* each constituting an option for action on the part of individuals. Parsons suggests that the nuances of these variables must be learned during socialization.

Three of the more useful of these variables are *diffuseness-specificity, affectivity-affective neutrality,* and *universalism-particularism.* The first refers to the range of obligations required towards another actor. If the range of obligations is very wide (such as the role of father vis-à-vis son) we speak of a diffuse role. On the other hand the role of teacher vis-à-vis student is more specific in nature. The second variable refers to the degree of affect or emotion permitted in the role. Some roles, such as mother or father, allow considerable display of affection, while others, such as doctor, prohibit such displays. The expectations attached to the doctor's role are those of *affectively neutral* behavior regarding his patients. Finally, *universalism-particularism* refers to the extent of objectivity of judgment the role demands. If the expectation is that the actor or role incumbent judge everyone according to the same set of standards, we speak of his obligations as universalistic. A teacher's role is an example here. A student is evaluated by a teacher on the basis of general standards of performance. This would be contrasted to particularism, where a student might be judged on the basis of his ethnic group membership, or family membership, rather than against all his peers in a classroom.

A fourth pattern-variable relates to *ascription* and *achievement.* This pair provides a classification of roles according to whether the quality of an actor (*who* he is) is important, or whether his performance is important (*what* he does). To illustrate, some social positions require qualitative judgments in recruiting actors to membership. This is true, for example, of beauty contest winners, who are successful by virtue of ascribed physical attributes. On the other hand, attaining the status of Schenley award winner in football depends predominantly on performance or achievement.

The final pair of polar types involves the extent of *self* versus *collectivity* orientation. Some roles require one to be interested in the other person to the virtual exclusion of interest in one's self. The doctor is expected to display a collectivity orientation — he is not expected to tell a man critically injured in an automobile accident that unless he has a certain amount of money for fees he will not be treated. On the other hand, it is perfectly appropriate for a man selling vegetables to get the best price he can in the bargaining process.

Parsons suggests that these role orientations appear time and again in societal life. The actor must be alert to recognize the correct orientation in any given social relationship. To give the reader an idea of the developmental progression of role orientation learning, it is useful to point out the major stages as we have them from Parsons' discussion. (Parsons and Bales, 1955; Baldwin, 1967: ch. 18) It will be noted that Parsons relies heavily on the Freudian framework, and attempts really to modify it to fit a more sociologically oriented approach. Without subscribing to the Freudian stages of personality development, we can take the explication as illustrative of the development of role orientations.

For Parsons (and Freud) the major developmental stages are the *oral, anal, oedipal-latent,* and *adolescent.* In the former (roughly through the first year) the child is in a state of oral dependency; the only relevant actors are himself and his mother. However, it is doubtful whether the child even differentiates these two roles; Parsons speculates that they are merged. Hence, there is no role orientation learning in this stage. In the anal phase the notable occurrence is the increasing demands made on the child to take on certain responsibilities for himself. The drama of toilet training serves the function of revealing to the child that he is an entity somewhat independent of his mother. The withholding or presentation of feces is uniquely under his control — he becomes a semi-autonomous being; the roles of mother and infant are distinctly separated. Parsons argues that this differentiation in the child's mind is mainly along the axis of diffuseness-specificity. The child's orientation to his mother is diffuse. He does everything and anything to please her. On the other hand, the child learns that his mother's orientation to him is specific. She feeds him, cares for him via a series of specific tasks. She is also, the child learns, involved with numerous other duties outside the child's own needs and demands. These involve caring for other members of the family. In short, to the child the mother's relationship to him has become a specific slice of a larger commitment. His own orientation remains diffuse, however, — she is his only concern. Parallel with this, one might discern a differentiation along the axis self-collectivity. The child is self-oriented — his needs are of total concern. His mother, on the other hand, exhibits a marked collectivity orientation; her role dictates that her family come first. It is suggested, then, that this is the first exposure of the child to the difference between roles which are self- and collectivity-oriented.

In the oedipal stage the child learns that he cannot always behave in an affective manner. Prior to this stage expressions of emotion (anger, love, etc.) were rarely held in check. As the child grows older, however, self-control is increasingly demanded. Affective neutrality emerges as an alternative to affectivity. As with the previous two distinctions, this difference appears often among adult roles, some of which allow emotional displays, some of which prohibit such behavior.

When the child enters school there begins a gradual shift from particularistic to universalistic evaluation, and from ascription to achievement. The orientation of his family is characterized by particularism; the fact that he is their son is taken into account by parents in judging behavior. In school, however, the child for the first time finds himself competing exclusively on the basis of universalistic standards. The fact that he is Daddy's son has no bearing on the outcome of the competitive process. A function of the school is thus to wean the child away from the particularism of the family so that he can eventually participate in the universalistic roles characteristic of the work world. (Parsons, 1959)

Emphasis on achievement rather than ascription is parallel with this development, although qualitative attributes such as sex and age are perhaps more important at the elementary level than during adolescence, where the pressures of occupational choice increase the importance of performance as a dominant aspect of the student role.

In sum, then, these distinctions which emerge in socialization form the basis for later distinctions in adult roles. It should be noted that *Parsons uses these pattern-variables not only to characterize role orientations but also to describe values, institutions, and occasionally total societies.* For example, the institution of the family (relative to other institutions) is characterized by particularism, affectivity, diffuseness, quality, and a relative tolerance of self-interested orientations. Education, on the other hand, tends toward the obverse of these variables. Similarly, some societies and subgroups within societies tend to be more particularistic than others in their allocation of rewards. Nepotism and other forms of particularism are the basis for political power in some areas, while in others positions are attained via successful competition on universalistic grounds.

Societal Values: Canadian Society and the Pattern-Variables

An example of the application of the pattern-variables to entire societies is the work of S.M. Lipset and his rather speculative comparison of Canada, the United States, the United Kingdom, and Australia (Lipset, 1963; 1964; 1968). Emphasizing that Lipset's work must be viewed as tentative rather than factual, we may note his analysis as an example of the manner in which the pattern-variables have been used to characterize the dominant action choices of a society. These action choices are here taken to indicate differences in value emphasis.

Lipset suggested that one could discern distinct variations in learned values in the four nations — a function of differing structural conditions over their histories. For example, according to Lipset, Americans and Australians are more universalistic than are Canadians or Englishmen;

Canadians and Britons are more collectivist-oriented than are Americans or Australians. Lipset also suggested an additional pattern-variable: *egalitarianism-elitism. Egalitarianism* was taken to mean an emphasis upon individual opportunity, while *elitism* referred to a preference for hierarchical authority and privilege structures. Lipset considered Canada to be less egalitarian than either the United States or Australia, although more egalitarian than Britain.

Generally, Lipset determines his Canadian pattern-variable scores by pointing to what he calls Canada's 'counter-revolutionary' or 'loyalist' origins, in opposition to the American Revolution. He suggests, too, that from the outset Canada was characterized by greater government participation in economic development, as in the building of the Canadian Pacific Railway. Additionally, Lipset perceives a greater regard by Canadians for 'law and order' as opposed to the United States. This he relates also to historical experience, with American frontier individualism and lawlessness contrasted to the controlled expansion through the Canadian West, under the watchful supervision of the Northwest Mounted Police. (Such a characterization does conveniently obscure features of Canadian history which are less than pacific, such as the Seven Oaks Massacre or the Riel Rebellion, to take but two examples. But the general difference in frontier expansion to which Lipset refers does seem to have been a feature of North American history.)

But such illustrations do not constitute measurement. Lipset never adequately operationalizes (measures) the pattern-variables. Rather than employ consistent measures, he uses information such as the historical experiences noted above, or data such as the lower rates of Canadian as opposed to American criminal deviance, to lend credence to his arbitrary assignment of the pattern-variable scores. Thereby his work is ultimately one man's judgments, very much open to criticism. (Horowitz, 1973; Romalis, 1973) The point to be taken, whatever the inadequacies of Lipset's measurement of the pattern-variables, is that the variables have been used for societal analysis to characterize nation-wide learned value emphasis and behavior tendencies.

Societal Values: The Kluckhohn Approach

Florence Kluckhohn has suggested another way in which societies and subgroups within them may be delineated according to their dominant value patterns. These may be conceived of as providing answers to what Kluckhohn sees as universal human problems. She argues that there is a limited number of common human problems for which all peoples at all times must find some solution. She discerns five crucial problems, the various solutions to which reflect essential value differences among human societies. (Kluckhohn, 1960)

Firstly, each society must come to grips with the *character of human nature*. Is man basically evil, good, or a combination of these? It was Hobbes' contention that man's inherent cruelty and hedonism necessitated a powerful web of social control embodied in the state, otherwise the 'war of all against all' would become a reality (Hobbes, 1881). Kluckhohn suggests that American society, by virtue of its puritanical origins, has essentially adopted this view of man as basically evil, though perhaps perfectible. It should be noted that when we talk of American society or Canadian society, we are in reality referring to the middle classes of these nations, who, of course, reflect the 'dominant' value orientations of the society concerned. As we have suggested, there is considerable variation in values *within* any given society, partially explaining the difficulty of many groups in attempting to rise to the middle classes.

The second problem concerns *the relation of man to nature*. Is man dependent on nature, is man in harmony with nature, or does man control nature? In American and Canadian middle class society the solution appears to be the last — man must master nature, he must utilize her resources, he must bend her to his will. In contrast, some societies have adopted the first of these orientations. Passive reaction to the whims of nature is argued to characterize the Spanish-American culture in the southwest part of the United States. Here a distinct fatalism pervades, — the world is God-given and hence immutable, what will be will be. A similar argument has been advanced in relation to rural societies in general, where there is a dependence on environment as opposed to a mastery orientation. (Rosen, 1959; Richer and Laporte, 1971)

A third aspect concerns *the temporal focus of human life* — does one orient oneself to the past, the present, or the future? Some societies, such as ancient China, revered the past, two manifestations of which were ancestor worship and a strong family tradition. On the other hand, other societies appear to have embraced a present orientation. The job of day-to-day living seems to pre-empt considerations of the past or future; today is important, let tomorrow take care of itself. It has been suggested that a modal value orientation of the American lower classes is a present rather than a future emphasis. (Riessman, 1962) The Canadian and American middle class, however, embody a distinct future orientation. Progress, change, a 'new and better tomorrow' are the touchstones of this way of life.

Fourthly, *what kind of human activity is preferred* — being, being-in-becoming, or doing? A being orientation reflects an expression of the spontaneous human personality; a virtually uninhibited surrender to basic needs and impulses characterizes this category. Kluckhohn offers the patterning of fiesta activities in Mexican society as a manifestation of this preference. The being-in-becoming solution is also concerned with the 'basic' human being, but emphasizes at the same time the notion of development. The being value is thus a relatively stagnant posture, the human being *as is* is unquestionably accepted. Not so being-in-becoming, which reflects as well a concern with growth, with advancement. The doing orientation is characteristic of Canadian and American society. 'What the individual does, and what he can or will accomplish, are almost always the primary questions in the American's scale of appraisal of persons.' (Kluckhohn, 1960: 309)

Finally, we must consider *man's relationship to other men*. Here do we emphasize individual autonomy, a collateral relationship, or a lineal relationship? The former gives primacy to individual autonomy, as opposed to the subjugation of the individual to the social order. *Collaterality emphasizes man's links with collateral groups* — those which extend laterally from his own position (e.g., his extended family — brothers, sisters, cousins, friends, etc). *Linearity emphasizes man's links with his social group through time.* The notion of heredity of social positions is a manifestation of this orientation.

Both the Canadian and American middle classes appear to emphasize an individualistic orientation. Family ties are secondary to individual mobility in society. To leave one's family to go away to school or to seek advancement in the occupational sphere is perfectly legitimate. (Taylor, 1968)

The modal value orientations of North American society could be described as individualistic, future directed, mastery over nature, doing, and conceiving of man as inherently evil (although capable of being converted). One, of course, must introduce a modicum of caution here. Firstly, although there is a fair amount of evidence that these orientations form the typical American pattern, the evidence that Canadians also espouse these values is less than conclusive. A large-scale study of value orientations in Canada has yet to be undertaken. Therefore, although the approach presented may be an apt appraisal of Canadian society, the preceding statements are best seen as a set of hypotheses about Canadian society, rather than a set of empirically based findings. A second cautionary note concerns the limitation alluded to earlier: that the values discussed are characteristic of the middle classes of North America. In this sense they are 'dominant' values. As we move further up or down the class ladder, however, these values would be hypothesized to grow more and more divergent. For example, here is a description of the 'culturally deprived' child in the lower classes of American society:

... on the liability side of the ledger are: traditionalism, pragmatism, and anti-intellectualism; limited development of individualism, self-expression and creativity; frustration and alienation; political apathy; suggestibility and naivete; boring occupational tasks; broken, overcrowded homes. On the asset side are: the cooperativeness and mutual aid that mark the extended family; avoidance of the strain accompanying competitiveness and individualism; equalitarianism, informality and warm humor, the security found in the extended family and in a traditional outlook.*

These value orientations are markedly different from those characteristic of middle class individuals.

Relative lack of future orientation in the American lower classes has been empirically documented by Hyman (Hyman, 1953), while fatalism among lower class Australian high school students was observed by Katz (Katz, 1964). Danziger points out the strong collateral orientation of South African minority groups (Danziger, 1963). Finally, data on Canadian secondary school students reveal striking differences between English and French Canadians with regard to ambition, value accorded occupational success, and desirable attributes of a job. French students are much higher on the first two items, while interesting differences emerge on the latter variable. Specifically, French Canadians are more likely to value income as opposed to prestige in a job, less likely to value freedom of action, and much more likely to value 'helping others.' (Breton, 1972) This latter finding may be interpreted as a manifestation of a collateral as opposed to individualistic value orientation.

In short, where a group is located in the structure of society has a large bearing on the values the group possesses and hence transmits to its members. This, of course, raises a whole series of questions about achievement potential in Canadian and American societies. Such value analysis questions the extent to which we can claim that middle and lower class children compete on an 'equal' basis in our predominantly middle class school systems. Indeed, as discussed in Chapter Five, numerous data illustrate that the competition is anything but equal. Also, value analysis suggests that to some extent the problems of the impoverished in our society may be related to value orientations which are incompatible with the dominant, middle class orientations. Similarly, such value analysis offers insight into the difficulties encountered by immigrant groups in Canadian and American cities. These and other similar questions will appear again in later chapters where we consider stratification and mobility (Chapter Four), deviance (Chapter Nine), and urbanization (Chapter Eleven).

*Frank Riessman, *The Culturally Deprived Child* (New York: Harper and Row, 1962), p. 48.

How Learning Occurs — The Process of Socialization

We turn now to the problem of the process of socialization. How does society become 'internalized' so that the actor is able to participate with a minimum of conflict in his social milieu? There is no simple answer to this question. In fact, the field includes a variety of concepts, the important ones being imitation, identification, role-taking, and reinforcement. Role-taking appears to be virtually synonymous with identification, so the latter term will be dropped as we attempt to present a coherent picture of the socialization process.

The several approaches to socialization which we shall discuss are, in our view, complementary rather than rival explanations. Each illustrates an aspect of the overall process of socialization. Thus, although the exchange theorist would emphasize reinforcement and the symbolic interactionist would emphasize role-taking, we suggest that each is an aspect of the learning process and the primacy of one or the other is not empirically or theoretically established.

Imitation

A common process in acquiring new knowledge is imitation. Says Philip Slater,

> ... Social learning takes place almost entirely through imitation. This imitation has been variously conceived and explained, but the core is always the same — we learn to act like human beings (no matter how 'inhuman' this may at times seem), or like members of a given society or subgroup, or like males or females, or like teenagers or adults, by observing how other members of these social categories behave and mimicking them. We even learn how to be individualists or nonconformists by imitating other individualists and nonconformists, which accounts for the paradoxical fact that individuals of unconventional persuasions cluster together to form their own conventions.*

While we have all observed this kind of behavior, however, reducing all social learning to imitation is not satisfactory. It is perhaps true that general norms and values can be acquired through something akin to imitation. By hearing and observing his father around the house, a boy might embrace the value of getting ahead in one's occupation. But simple imitation will not convey the notion of the complementarity of roles, which is the essence of societal functioning. The actor must not only know the appropriate behavior for each social position he occupies

*Philip Slater, 'Social Bases of Personality,' in N.J. Smelser (ed.), *Sociology* (New York: John Wiley and Sons, 1967), p. 589.

(e.g., son), but must also know where his role fits into a whole system of roles (behavior of son to mother, son to father).

Also, an imitation approach to learning does not by itself answer the question of why imitate. Why should the actor imitate other actors? In short, the approach lacks a motivational rationale for the actor's behavior. We shall address this problem when we consider reinforcement theory.

Role-Taking and the Self — The Approach of G.H. Mead

Perhaps the most insightful analysis of exactly what occurs in the course of socialization is Mead's discussion of empathic role-taking. For Mead, interaction with others creates a self-identity in man that is at the same time a societal identity. A major component of an actor's personality is the dictates, values, and expectations of society as transmitted from the actor's circle of socializers (parents, other siblings, teachers, peers).

The process central to Mead's argument is what he terms 'role-taking.' The basic difference between infrahuman and human behavior is that while the former involves automatic, non-reflective responses to cues, the latter involves responses to *interpreted* stimuli. Let us look at a hen-chick 'interaction' as opposed to human interaction:

> ... when a mother hen clucks, her chicks will respond by running to her. This does not imply, however, that the hen clucks *in order* to guide the chicks, i.e., with the *intention* of guiding them. Clucking is a natural sign or signal — rather than a significant (meaningful) symbol — as it is not meaningful to the hen. That is, the hen (according to Mead) does not take the role, or viewpoint, of the chicks toward its own gesture and respond to it, in imagination, as they do. The hen does not envision the response of the chicks to her clucking. Thus, hen and chicks do not share the same experience.

> ... Human beings, on the other hand, respond to one another on the basis of the intentions or meanings of gestures. This renders the gestures symbolic, i.e., the gesture becomes a symbol to be interpreted; it becomes something which, in the imagination of the participants, stands for the entire act.

> Thus, individual A begins to act, i.e., makes a gesture; for example, he draws back an arm. Individual B (who perceives the gesture) completes, or fills in, the act in his imagination; i.e., B imaginatively projects the gesture into the future: 'he will strike me.' In other words, B perceives what the gesture stands for, thus getting its meaning. In contrast to the direct responses of the chicks, the human being inserts an interpretation between the gesture of another and his response to it.

... The imaginative completion of an act — which Mead calls 'meaning' and which represents mental activity — necessarily takes place through *role-taking*. To complete imaginatively the total act which a gesture stands for, the individual must put himself in the position of the other person, must identify with him. The earliest beginnings of role-taking occur when an already established act of another individual is stopped short of completion, thereby requiring the observing individual to fill in, or complete, the activity imaginatively.*

For Mead, then, human interaction is anticipation of others' reactions to our behavior, as well as the adjustment of our own behavior to the expectations of others. Because the symbolic meaning of various gestures must be shared by all in a society or subgroup in order for role-taking to occur, Mead terms human communication 'symbolic interaction.' Such interaction obviously implies a common language for its participants.

Mead's position, then, is that the formation of the child's social 'self' is a continual process of seeing himself as others see him. He has no social existence apart from his perception of others' attitudes towards himself. We are what we think others think we are. If the reader does not accept this, he might try to conceive of the emergence of his own self-image independently of the attitudes of others toward him. This exercise will, we predict, prove fruitless.

According to Mead the self emerges in three fairly distinct phases:

PREPARATORY STAGE

Here the child simply imitates overt activity (as discussed previously). He may copy his mother's cigarette smoking by inserting a stick in his mouth. No role-taking occurs here, although imitation is a preliminary to such activity.

PLAY STAGE

Here the child plays at various roles. Simple complementarity of role-learning takes place as the child plays 'mother,' 'nurse' and other distinctive societal roles. The key point is that in playing these roles the child begins to put himself in the place of others and act back towards himself. For example, a little girl will often pretend that she is the mother and her doll is herself. The doll is invariably naughty and receives several spankings, just as the child herself is treated by the mother when norms are violated. This we term 'simple' complementarity of roles because the child plays various roles one after the other, with no sense of a network of roles. As Meltzer says, 'He has, as yet, no unitary

*B.N. Meltzer, *The Social Psychology of George Herbert Mead* (Center for Sociological Research, Western Michigan University, 1964), pp. 12-14.

standpoint from which to view himself, and hence, he has no unified conception of himself. In other words, the child forms a number of separate and discrete objects of itself, depending on the roles in which it acts toward itself.' (Meltzer, 1964: 16)

GAME STAGE

Here the child obtains a unified self. He is not only able to take the role of particular actors in his social environment but can eventually see himself from the standpoint of a *group* of actors, or as Mead terms it, 'the generalized other.' Mead suggests that children's games are a main vehicle in instilling in the child this generalized group perspective. In the game of baseball, for example, the actor must not only know his own role (first baseman) but also its relationship to each other position in the game (complex complementarity). He must also know the overall values of sportsmanship and fair play which pervade the contest. In short, he must see himself through the eyes of the entire group. This implies that there are several 'generalized others' that the child internalizes; as many as there are groups that are salient for him.

Mead suggests that the self is composed of two entities: *the 'me,'* which includes all the generalized and specific others in the actor's social environment; and *the 'I,'* which is the impulsive tendency of the actor. Every act for Mead begins with an impulse initiated by the 'I' which is in turn followed by a consideration of the social consequences of the act by the 'me.' (Freud's notion of Id, Ego, and Superego is close to this formulation.) Mind for Mead is essentially a process of constant internal conversations between the 'I' and the 'me.' For example, an actor about to steal a bike (the initial 'I' impulse) will then perceive this intention in the light of possible reactions of his family, his peer group, and perhaps his teacher or religious group, (the 'me'). Again, then, the essence of social behavior is a constant process of viewing our actions and potential actions through the eyes of others.

Agencies of Socialization: Family, School, and Peers

The extent to which the picture of himself transmitted by various significant others is consistent and clearly articulated will determine whether or not the actor will posses high or low self-knowledge. Further, if the picture is a positive one he will enjoy a relatively high level of self-esteem; if negative, his self-esteem will be low. These dual components of the self will in turn have a substantial effect on his probability of success in later life. For example, the recent study of Canadian secondary students finds that those who manifested low self-knowledge were more likely to be without an explicit career goal. Further, those who displayed a low sense of personal *efficacy, i.e., believed they had little control over their own destinies,* were less likely to have formulated a career goal, less likely to want to finish high school and to go on to post-secondary school, and, when a career *was* selected, less likely to have chosen a high status occupation. (Breton, 1972)

This variation in self-knowledge and self-esteem implies that not everyone is socialized in the same way. Indeed, this follows inevitably from the notion of the social self arising through interaction with significant others in one's social environment. The nature of one's family, the kind of school one attends, the peers one interacts with will have a large effect on exactly what is learned. There is evidence, as suggested earlier, that lower class families tend to transmit a present rather than a future orientation to their children. The day-by-day struggle for survival pre-empts considerations of the future, and focuses attention on the present. Further, studies of Canadian and American families have revealed that there is a large difference between upper and lower class families in the quality of interaction. Persuasion via free-flowing discussion tends to characterize parent-child interaction in upper class families, while more authoritarian techniques of control are more often found in lower class homes. (Seeley *et.al.,* 1968; Garigue, 1968; Kohn, 1959)

Apart from the family's position in the stratification system, one may also look at the consequences for socialization of internal structural variations of families. For example, regarding authority structure within the family, Canadian adolescents whose participation in family decisions was relatively low were found to exhibit low personal efficacy, greater dependence on others in decision-making, and lower desire to complete high school and continue to post-secondary school. (Breton, 1972)

The Meadian 'significant other' framework would also imply that children will have different values and self-conceptions depending on the size and completeness of their families. Indeed, adolescents from *large as opposed to small Canadian families* are lower on personal efficacy, more dependent in decision-making, and less likely to exhibit high educational aspirations. Further, the particular position of the child within the family appears relevant for the aspirations he will manifest. Specifically, oldest children are more likely than younger children to plan to finish high school, to want to proceed to post-secondary school, and to select high status occupations. The interpretation offered is that oldest children are more likely to receive the cognitive stimulation provided by extensive contact with adults. (Breton, 1972)

Finally, *parental absence* apparently affects adversely such phenomena as educational aspirations and vocational decision-making. That is, the child lacking stable and persisting contacts with both parents will tend to aspire to lower educational and occupational levels. (Breton, 1972)

As societies industrialize, however, the *school's responsibility* as a major socializing agent increases at the expense of the family's. While the child's development is still shaped largely by family factors, there is increasing evidence that the school and its personnel play a significant part. Thus, in Canada, the provincially administered school systems can contribute to a marked regional variation in socialization.

The school must be viewed as an important part of the child's interpersonal environment. Here he is assigned grades, allocated a program of study and supported or rejected in his activities by teachers, principals, and guidance counsellors. All of these have consequences for his self-conception; in complex interaction they may confirm already established conceptions, provide contradictory evaluations, enhance or impede self-knowledge. Evidence exists showing that students in terminal as opposed to post-secondary high school programs have relatively low educational and occupational aspirations. Students who have failed manifest the same pattern. Students who were placed in their program by the school as opposed to choosing it themselves exhibit low personal efficacy, high dependence in decision-making, and low vocational competence. (Breton, 1972)

The nature of the student's surrounding *peer group* is also found to be important. If a student is in a school with a large proportion of middle class students, his aspirations are elevated, regardless of his own social class. The interpretation is that his middle class peers are carriers of and hence diffusers of achievement values learned in their own family environments. (Breton, 1972)

Perhaps most directly relevant to Mead's framework is the set of findings with regard to parent, school personnel, and peer support for a student's plans. If an actor's self-conception is derived from others' attitudes towards him, it follows that the goals he sets for himself will reflect others' appraisals of his potential success. Indeed, whether parents encourage or discourage education, or certain occupational choices, has a profound effect on a child's intentions. (Siemens, 1965) The same is true of teacher and peer encouragement, although the effects are less pronounced (Forcese and Siemens, 1965). In the area of leisure pursuits, such as athletic activities, it appears that peers have a more significant influence (Coleman, 1961).

Reinforcement Theory

Although we have outlined in detail the process which according to Mead characterizes social learning, as well as summarizing some supporting empirical data, we have still not answered the question of 'why.' Why should the child react to the image which his parents, teachers or peer group have of him? This issue came up at the beginning of this section when simple imitation was discussed. Although we put it off at that point, we must deal with it here. The major shortcoming of Mead's approach is its failure to provide a rationale for role-taking. Here is where the behaviorist or exchange theory approach to learning can contribute. Most applicable is *operant conditioning*. The principles of this approach have been derived mainly from animal experiments and involve the pairing of a behavior *(operant)* with a reward *(reinforcement)*, or punishment. The more closely the reward or punishment follows the behavior, the more effective the learning, and there is an increase in the frequency of the behavior which has been reinforced. Once learned, a behavior will persist even where it is only intermittently rewarded; in fact, if reinforced infrequently, learned behavior tends to be very persistent. In addition, people generalize and learn to recognize the environmental features associated with previously experienced rewards, and also to recognize similar conditions. These environmental stimuli then come to elicit the behavior which had been previously reinforced. There is abundant research evidence supporting operant learning principles, most of the research having been conducted by psychologists. A counterpart to psychological behaviorism can be found in the sociological exchange model, especially that of George Homans. (Homans, 1961)

In order to relate the interactionist and behaviorist models, we suggest that the reinforcement of role-taking by parents and other significant actors in the child's environment is the specific learning mechanism which produces behavior. As for the nature of the rewards utilized, they range from gestures such as nods and smiles, to words and compliments, to material items. (Homans, 1961) In addition, Parsons, a non-behaviorist, argues that in the family setting anxiety reduction is a major reward (Parsons, 1955). In his view, anxiety reduction by the manipulation of love as a reward appears to be a major technique in producing desired role behavior. The child thus sees himself from his parents' perspective, adjusting his behavior accordingly through fear of loss of love. It would seem that in general the attainment of approval from significant others is a salient motivating force in human society. Coleman documents this for adolescents by showing how the great importance attached to peer recognition influences the extent of investment of energy in various athletic and academic activities (Coleman, 1961). Although material rewards are obviously also successful motivators, they may not have the same potency.

It should be noted as a concluding comment that many symbolic interactionists would be considerably uneasy about attempting to add to their formulation by utilizing behaviorist principles. Although Mead intended his work as an increment to the behaviorist model, his followers tend to view this approach as extremely inappropriate for the understanding of human behavior. To the Mead group the crucial distinction between animal and human behavior is that man has language which enables him to share common symbols. It is by virtue of this that man is able to think, indeed to put himself in the place of another and reflect on the appropriate behavior from that person's perspective. The common meaning of a person raising his arm enables us all to interpret this as the beginning of the act of striking. In short, for Mead social behavior inevitably involves internal behavior — the process of mind. In contrast, behaviorists for the most part have chosen to ignore all internal behavior (e.g., thinking) — only overt behavior is recognized as the relevant domain of study. (However, Homans and other exchange theorists who depend upon behaviorist findings do place emphasis upon cognitive and symbolic activity.) (Homans, 1961)

Some Answers to Sociological Determinism

At this point the reader may be experiencing a vague uneasiness about the way the discussion has proceeded. He may be asking himself where is man — where in this sea of norms, roles, and institutions is the individual, the ultimate source of action? Is he really, as may have been conveyed in the discussion, a passive reactor to social pressures, mechanically playing out the various roles accorded him by various groups? One could easily dismiss this question by simply classifying it as irrelevant. It could be argued that the perspective presented in the foregoing pages only reflects an orienting model, a set of assumptions sociologists use to look at reality. As such, they serve a heuristic function, and must be judged solely by their capacity to suggest interesting questions and to organize reasonably well (at least as well as other models) what we know about human behavior. However, we do believe that at the level of subjective meaning, if not at the level of scientific procedure, the question is relevant, and therefore merits some kind of answer. We offer two.

Social Contract and Exchange Theory

In all of the preceding discussion there has been an implicit assumption about the relationship between society and the individual. *The assump-*

tion has been that of 'societal primacy,' which is simply that society as an entity has always existed, and that man the individual, as far back as one wishes to go, has always been confronted by webs and networks of social control.

Not all philosophers and social scientists accept this formulation, however. An extremely popular notion was that provided by John Locke. For Locke, society was the conscious creation of individuals who were inherently free, who existed in a state of natural simplicity, but who perceived that for the good of everyone a society should be set up. In short, men set up a social contract, which was essentially an agreement to respect the rights of others, a contract enforced by civil government. (Locke, 1821)

Several contemporary American sociologists, notably George Homans, Peter Blau, and James Coleman, have found this kind of formulation much more appropriate than the societal primacy notion in attempting to understand human behavior. Coleman, for example, argues that postulating a set of norms and values to begin with does not at all solve the Hobbesian problem: ' ... sociologists have characteristically taken as their starting point a social system in which norms exist, and individuals are largely governed by these norms. Such a strategy views norms as the governors of social behavior, and this neatly bypasses the difficult problem of order that Hobbes posed.' (Coleman, 1964) Coleman goes on to argue that norms arise out of the interaction of men, each seeking to maximize his own self-interest. He then shows how particular norms become adopted, which is essentially a process of bargaining — of achieving a compromise representing the optimum rule, given the interests of all concerned. Both Homans and Blau have adopted similar positions as they attempt essentially to deduce societal characteristics (e.g., norms, values) beginning with a group of rational men, each attempting to further his own ends. (Homans, 1961; 1964; Blau, 1964)*

This position has been argued to characterize the whole tenor of American sociology, which has been described as 'voluntaristic nominalism:' ' ... the assumption that the structure of all social groups is the consequence of the aggregate of their separate component individuals and that social phenomena ultimately derived from the motivations of these knowing, feeling and willing individuals.' (Wolff, 1959) Given our previous discussion of American middle class values this is not a novel idea. As may be recalled, Kluckhohn suggests that American society is characterized by the value of individualism as opposed to either a collateral or lineal orientation. That many American sociologists also embody this principal value is not surprising.

*The difference between these two approaches is that Blau's man is close to the rational man of economic theory, while Homans' approximates the man of operant conditioning.

What is surprising is that this view of man and society is often used by its more vigorous adherents to explain the *origins* of social life itself. In the beginning, then, there was ostensibly a collection of non-social men who got together and set up, through a process of extensive bargaining, a system of order we call society. This formulation, however, does not hold up under empirical evaluation. Specifically, it is incompatible with what anthropologists have discovered about so-called 'primitive' tribes. As Slater has pointed out, ' ... anthropological investigations, however, have shown us the extraordinary social complexity of many such "primitive" societies, and the manifold rules of comportment with which their inhabitants are afflicted.' (Slater, 1967: 549) Indeed, the web of social control encompassing primitive man was perhaps more stifling than that engulfing our own behavior. The higher visibility of deviance character-istic of small communities, as well as the highly developed and intense religious life characteristic of pre-industrial groups, made them ex-tremely close-knit, constraining units. (Vallee, 1968) As far back as the available historical data permit us to go, then, man has always been a societal animal. As Slater goes on to say:

> Locke's notion of the relation between individual and society is based on a common error — the tendency to view a whole as developing historically from its parts. A complex structure, however, arises not from its current constituents but from a simpler structure. (Slater, 1967: 555)

The thought of an individual existing independently of society is thus unacceptable. This is not to say, of course, that behavior of the kind discussed by Coleman does not occur. To imply that it is non-normative, though, is inaccurate. While bargaining structures are common occur-rences, they tend to reflect the existence of more general societal norms which in fact legitimize the behavior.

For example, one easily recognizes the behavior of two horse traders as that characterized by each participant attempting to maximize his own self-interest. To a large extent, though, this behavior has been legitimized by a cluster of norms which specify appropriate behavior for bargainers trying to arrive at a deal. This same behavior would be grossly inappropriate in a doctor-patient relationship.

Similarly, the parent-child relationship may often appear to be a free-wheeling bargaining process (Richer, 1968). Let us assume, for example, that in a particular family it is in the interest of the parents to get their ten-year-old child to bed as early as possible so that they can have as much time to themselves as feasible. Let us also assume that it is in the interest of the child to stay up as late as he can. Finally, let us say that there is as yet no bed-time rule established in the family. Through a process of discussion and bargaining the time finally arrived at is 9:30, somewhat later than the parents would have liked but nevertheless earlier than the child's preference.

This would seem, then, to be an instance of the emergence of a norm via each party acting in their own self-interest and arriving at a satisfactory compromise. We would argue, though, that the bargaining did not really occur in a normative vacuum. While the particular outcome was not societally decreed, the bargaining occurred within certain normative limitations. The child did not in all likelihood argue for 2:00 in the morning, nor did his parents begin by suggesting 6:30 in the evening. They both brought with them to the session certain preconceived notions about the *range* of acceptable bed-times in their society. While specific norms may emerge out of self-interested interaction, then, one might always point to higher level norms within the context of which bargaining occurs. While man does indeed have the 'freedom' to engage in self-seeking behavior, he must do so within the permissible limits set by his community.

Conflicting Norms

Peter Berger has argued that one way out of social determinism is to conceive of society as 'a stage populated by living actors.' He suggests that like actors in a play *we* and only we may decide precisely how our various roles are to be played:

> ... the dramatic model of society at which we have arrived now does not deny that the actors on the stage are constrained by all the external controls set up by the impresario and the internal ones of the role itself. All the same, they have options — of playing their parts enthusiastically or sullenly, of playing with inner conviction or with 'distance,' and, sometimes, of refusing to play at all. *

In other words, although surrounded by social expectations and demands, we may exercise our own discretion as to which roles we play in earnest, which we play in a relatively mechanical way, and which we tend to ignore.

We agree with Berger, but would carry his point further. We would suggest that this differential allocation of time and energy among roles is not only possible but is in fact *inevitable,* because of the way society is structured. A discussion of the concepts of role conflict, role-set conflict, and multiple role conflict will make the point clear. *Role conflict,* the generic term here, occurs when a particular role or role-set contains

---

* Peter Berger, *Invitation to Sociology*, p. 138. Copyright © 1963 by Peter L. Berger.

demands for behavior which are to some extent incompatible with one another. One example is the role of professor. On the one hand he is expected to transmit knowledge competently and then objectively evaluate his students on their mastery of this knowledge. On the other hand, he is expected to be fairly close with students, both in discussing their problems and in trying to attract students to his discipline. These two conflicting expectations are often the source of discomfort for many professors. One solution is to avoid wherever possible getting too close to one's students, thus allowing relatively painless fulfillment of the evaluator segment of his role. The other solution, of course, is to minimize his evaluator role, perhaps by not giving exams or assignments, thus permitting him to engage fully in building close relationships which are likely to produce committed students. In any event, the point is that some kind of rational decision must be taken on this issue to allow the professor to function properly.

Following Merton, an actor's *role-set* is that complement of role relationships which persons have by virtue of occupying a particular social status (Merton, 1963). The role-set of a teacher thus consists of relationships with students, principal, parents, and other teachers. Needless to say, though, there will usually not be perfect consensus among these actors as to how the teacher should play his role. Students may have one group of expectations, the principal a somewhat different set, colleagues a third set, and parents still a fourth conception. When incompatible demands are made on an actor by members of his role-set we term the result for the actor *role-set conflict*. In Mead's terms, which of these significant others does the teacher choose in guiding his conduct?

Finally, the concept *multiple role conflict* accrues inevitably from the fact that all of us occupy more than one social position. We are both teachers and husbands, students and sons. Some of us could probably count a dozen or more distinct social positions that we simultaneously occupy, all with somewhat different roles attached to them. The role of sociologist implies for its proper fulfillment many hours spent in research, in building up the fund of knowledge in the discipline. The role of father implies attention to one's children — hours spent playing catch, going to movies, attending ball games, and more. These two spheres, work and family, are often in conflict for the actor's time, a situation we term 'multiple role conflict.' Both of these 'generalized others,' — that composed of occupational dictates and that of family responsibilities, cannot always be satisfied. The actor throughout his daily life must make thousands of decisions directed at solving this inevitable problem of conflicting roles. His very survival in society demands that he be calculative, innovative, and ingenious.

This is essentially our answer to sociological determinism. *Paradoxically, the very cultural and structural factors which apparently constrain our individuality also give rise to it,* for each man, in the ways in which he resolves his role conflicts, emerges as a unique entity. As W.J. Goode has pointed out in an article entitled 'A Theory of Role Strain,' *social behavior is in large measure a series of 'role bargains'* (Goode, 1960). Since the actor cannot possibly meet all of the demands made on him to the satisfaction of all those in his social environment, he must constantly be weighing and evaluating the advantages and disadvantages of allocating his time and energy to various roles. His behavior is thus essentially strategic and internal — it is a cognitive process in the Meadian tradition.*

As Berger said, then, we alone decide how we are to play our roles. Some we will play with great commitment and sincerity, some we will only pretend to play, giving the illusion of self-involvement in order to make others believe we are committed. The range of strategies is limited only by our ingenuity in presenting acceptable performances. (Goffman, 1959)

Society, then, is not a prison, nor social behavior a routinized reaction to decreed roles. The structure of society itself, by virtue of its complex web of interlocking and often conflicting roles, *demands* that we plan, plot, and strategize; in short, that we become individuals.

Conclusions

When discussing socialization it is all too easy to slip into the error of viewing societies as uniform and little changing. Because socialization is obviously the means to social continuity across generations, we can be led to ignore that it is also the means to discontinuity, for conflicting attitudes and behavior, and new forms of social organization, are themselves established in societies through learning.

Socialization must also, therefore, be viewed as a means to social change and individual autonomy. If people learn to accept features of some society, so too they learn to challenge features of a society, or to desire and accept altered conditions. Moreover, people are more or less able to adapt to social change depending upon their learning experi-

---

*It might be noted here that such behavior cannot be explained through Stimulus-response principles. As soon as one postulates man as calculative, as choosing between at least two alternative modes of, say, role allocation, one cannot predict the outcome in terms of pure conditioning. The model is too simple for the *human* animal. The psychologist might say that the actor would go where the reward was greater, but the process of arriving at which was in effect greater is a cognitive one, not a mechanistic reaction to overt stimuli.

ences. Difficulty in adjusting to change is far greater in a society whose members have been taught to expect an unchanging rhythm of existence, such as in peasant agrarian societies, than where people have been socialized to expect and to accept wide-ranging social, demographic, and technological changes, such as in Canada, the United States, or any industrialized nation. Thereby, *the adaptation to change is a function of socialization.*

There is another reason why socialization does not make for uniformity. Quite simply, socialization inputs are never perfectly consistent and homogeneous in a society. Few societies, least of all modern complex societies — even with their massive communications technologies — ever even approximate fully centralized control over each and every agency of socialization. Such control would more nearly permit of homogeneity of output such as that visualized in the fearful literature discussing totalitarianism. In some real sense, *human freedom is realized through heterogeneity,* where a society includes a variety of life styles and subcultures.

In a society such as Canada, taken as a whole, one cannot fail to recognize that several socialization inputs co-exist: the family, ethnic subcultures, religious organizations, social classes, regional subgroupings, a wide range of occupational situations, variously owned and controlled mass media, and constitutionally sanctioned provincial systems of formal education. The multi-ethnic, multi-denominational, multi-regional inputs into Canadian socialization experiences assure that in fact there is no prototypical 'Canadian.'

References

Adorno, T., *et.al., The Authoritarian Personality.* New York: Harpers, 1950.

Baldwin, Alfred, *Theories of Child Development.* New York: John Wiley and Sons, 1967.

Berger, Peter, *Invitation to Sociology.* New York: Doubleday, 1963.

Bijou, S.W., and Donald M. Baer, *Child Development,* vol. 1. New York: Appleton-Century-Crofts, 1961.

Blau, Peter, *Exchange and Power in Social Life.* New York: John Wiley and Sons, 1964.

Breton, Raymond, in collaboration with John McDonald and Stephen Richer, *Social and Academic Factors in the Career Decisions of Canadian Youth.* Department of Manpower and Immigration, Ottawa, 1972.

Coleman, James S., 'Collective Decisions,' *Sociological Inquiry,* XXXIII (1964), 166-181.

——, *The Adolescent Society.* New York: The Free Press, 1961.

Danziger, K., 'The Psychological Future of an Oppressed Group,' *Social Forces,* XLII (1963), 31-40.

Dawson, R., and K. Prewitt, *Political Socialization.* Boston: Little Brown and Co., 1969.

Forcese, Dennis, and Leonard Siemens, *School-Related Factors and the Aspiration Levels of Manitoba Senior High School Students.* Winnipeg, the University of Manitoba, 1965.

Garigue, P., 'The French Canadian Family,' in B. Blishen *et al., Canadian Society.* Toronto: Macmillan, 1968, pp. 151-166.

Goffman, Erving, *Presentation of Self in Everyday Life.* New York: Anchor, Doubleday, 1959.

Goode, W.J. 'A Theory of Role Strain,' *A.S.R.,* XXV (1960), 483-496.

Hess, R., and J. Torney, *The Development of Political Attitudes in Children.* New York: Doubleday, 1968.

Hobbes, Thomas, *The Leviathan.* Oxford: James Thornton, 1881.

Homans, George, *Social Behavior, Its Elementary Forms.* New York: Harcourt, Brace and World, 1961. (Rev. ed. 1974)

——, 'Bringing Men Back In,' *A.S.R.,* XXIX (1964), 809-818.

Horowitz, I.L., 'The Hemispheric Connection: A Critique and Corrective to the Entrepreneurial Thesis of Development with Special Emphasis on the Canadian Case,' *Queen's Quarterly,* LXXX (1973), 327-359.

Hyman, H.H., 'The Value Systems of Different Classes: A Social Psychological Contribution to the Study of Stratification,' in R. Bendix and S.M. Lipset (eds.), *Class, Status and Power.* New York: The Free Press, 1953, pp. 426-442.

Katz, F.M., 'The Meaning of Success: Some Differences in Value Systems of Social Classes,' *Journal of Social Psychology,* CLXII (1964), 141-148.

Kluckhohn, Florence R., 'Variation in the Basic Values of Family Systems,' in N.W. Bell and E.F. Vogel (eds.), *The Family.* Toronto: Macmillan, 1960, pp. 304-315.

Kohn, M., 'Social Class and Parental Values,' *A.J.S.,* LXIV (1959), 337-351.

——, 'Social Class and the Exercise of Parental Authority,' *A.S.R.,* CXXIV (1959), 352-366.

Kuhn, Manford, 'Kinsey's View of Human Behavior,' *Social Problems,* II (1954), 119-125.

Langton, K., *Political Socialization.* New York: Oxford University Press, 1969.

Lipset, S.M., 'Canada and the United States: A Comparative View, ' *C.R.S.A.,* I (1964), 173-185.

——, *Revolution and Counterrevolution: Change and Persistence in Social Structures.* New York: Basic Books, 1968.

——, 'Ideology and Mythology: Reply to Coleman Romalis (and other critics),' in A. Effrat (ed.), *Perspectives in Political Sociology.* Indianapolis: Bobbs-Merrill, 1973, pp. 233-265.

——, *The First New Nation.* New York: Doubleday, 1963.

Locke, John, *Two Treatises on Government.* London: 1821.

Mann, W.E., 'The Socialization Process,' in W.E. Mann (ed.), *Canada: A Sociological Profile.* Toronto: Copp Clark, 1968, pp. 89-91.

Mead, George H., *Mind, Self and Society.* Chicago: University of Chicago Press, 1943.

Meltzer, B.N., *The Social Psychology of George Herbert Mead.* Center for Sociological Research, Western Michigan University, 1964.

Merton, Robert K., *Social Theory and Social Structure.* Glencoe, Ill.: The Free Press, 1963.

Parsons, Talcott, 'The School Class as a Social System,' *Harvard Educational Review,* XXIX (1959), 297-318.

Parsons, Talcott, and R.F. Bales, *Family, Socialization and Interaction Process.* New York: The Free Press, 1955.

Richer, Stephen, 'The Economics of Child Rearing,' *Journal of Marriage and the Family,* XXX (1968), 462-466.

Richer, Stephen, and Pierre Laporte, 'Culture, Cognition and English-French Competition,' in J. Elliott (ed.), *Immigrant Groups.* Scarborough: Prentice-Hall of Canada, 1971, pp. 141-150.

Riessman, Frank, *The Culturally Deprived Child.* New York: Harper and Row, 1962.

Romalis, Coleman, 'A Man of His Time and Place: A Selective Appraisal of Lipset's Comparative Sociology,' in A. Effrat (ed.), *Perspectives in Political Sociology.* Indianapolis: Bobbs-Merrill, 1973, pp. 211-231.

——, 'Political Values and Sociological Analysis: Some Further Reflections,' in A. Effrat (ed.) *Perspectives in Political Sociology.* Indianapolis: Bobbs-Merrill, 1973, pp. 267-274.

Rosen, Bernard, 'Race, Ethnicity and the Achievement Syndrome,' *A.S.R.,* XXIV (1959), 47-60.

Royal Commission on Bilingualism and Biculturalism, *Education* (Vol. II). Ottawa: Information Canada, 1968.

Scott, John F., *Internalization of Norms.* Englewood Cliffs: Prentice-Hall Inc., 1971.

Seeley, J.R., Alexander Sim, and E. Loosley, 'Family and Socialization in an Upper Class Community,' in B. Blishen *et.al., Canadian Society.* Toronto: Macmillan, 1968, pp. 109-139.

Siemens, Leonard B., *The Influence of Selected Family Factors on the Educational and Occupational Aspirations of High School Boys and Girls.* Winnipeg, The University of Manitoba, 1965.

Singleman, Ken, 'Exchange as Symbolic Interaction,' *A.S.R.,* XXXVII, 4 (1972), 414-423.

Slater, Philip, 'Social Bases of Personality,' in N.J. Smelser (ed.), *Sociology.* New York: John Wiley and Sons, 1967.

Taylor, N., 'The French Canadian Industrial Entrepreneur and his Environment,' in B. Blishen *et al., Canadian Society.* Toronto: Macmillan, 1968.

Vallee, Frank, 'Kabloona and Eskimo in the Central Keewatin,' in B. Blishen *et al., Canadian Society.* Toronto: Macmillan, 1968, pp. 563-573.

Wolff, Kurt, 'The Sociology of Knowledge and Sociological Theory,' in L. Gross (ed.), *Symposium of Sociological Theory.* New York: Harper and Row, 1959.

CHAPTER THREE

Canada: Profile of a People

John de Vries and Dennis Forcese
Carleton University

Introduction

The bases for many of the observations and generalizations of sociology are to be found in demographic data. In broad form, these data outline major social changes in Canada, as reflected in rates of birth, death, immigration, emigration, and the subsequent religious and ethnic composition of regions of Canada. In turn, these factors affect social-ization, income, prestige, power, education, and the social class member-ship of Canadians.

Previously we considered 'becoming Canadian' from the perspective of childhood socialization in Canada. We emphasized that there exists in Canada a diversity of socialization experiences, related to region, ethnic group membership, religion, social class, and other factors. In this chapter we wish to take up more precisely the composition of Canadian society, in an attempt to summarize some of these diversities.

It should be clear that although we may well emphasize socialization when considering the attitudes and behaviors of the people of Canada, many Canadians have been socialized in societies other than Canada. For generation after generation from the inception of Canadian society, becoming Canadian was not a matter of being socialized in Canada from birth through adulthood, rather, we all, or our parents, or our grandpar-ents, or our great-grandparents, or their parents or grandparents before them, were immigrants to Canada. Ultimately, of course, only the native peoples who preceded European colonization would be excepted from this statement. Thereby, at any given time in Canadian history, becom-ing Canadian has been a matter of choice and not of birth for thousands of people who gradually adapted to and helped shape Canadian society.

The immigrants and the native peoples who have contributed to Canadian society have been socialized in socio-cultural systems often radically different from the middle class Canadian model which we sketched in the previous chapter. What the immigrants have learned in their societies of origin has been brought with them as much or more than any physical baggage. And in varying degree, what they have learned has been passed on to their children, even when the children have been born in Canada. Thus we may often speak of viable subcultures within the larger Canadian society. Generally, however conventional a point it may be, we must not lose sight of the fact that Canada, whatever its characteristic commonalities, is an amalgam of native born, immigrants, and their children. The diversity which this amalgam represents is briefly outlined in the pages which follow.

Views on Population Change

It is obvious, even trivial, to point out that no society can exist without a population and that the rate of population change is a critical constituent of a society. In this chapter we are interested in the changes in Canadian population over time. Basically this means that we are interested in births *(fertility)*, deaths *(mortality)*, immigration and emigration, and the manner in which these result in population decrease over time, population increase over time, or a stable population size (*zero population growth* or ZPG).

Since the size and the growth of a society's population are such fundamental characteristics, it is understandable that they have been the subject of a great deal of discussion. Indeed, we find statements about desirable population size, or desirable growth rates, throughout the traditions of western civilization, beginning with Plato and Aristotle.

Basically, the arguments may be divided into the 'optimistic tradition' and the 'pessimistic tradition.' The optimistic tradition stresses the positive aspects of population *increase,* sometimes for political reasons, sometimes for economic reasons, sometimes for religious reasons. On the other hand, the pessimistic tradition argues for a *zero growth rate.* The pessimistic argument is usually one which states that resources are insufficient to support a *larger* population than is currently being sustained, or that such a situation will be reached very soon. Ironically, there are *no* cases in the known literature where a *negative* growth rate is advocated, not even for a short period of time. Rather, the pessimistic tradition advocates zero population growth, to be attained as quickly as possible.

Although the pessimistic tradition does go back to Plato's *Republic* (where a constant population of 5,040 is advocated), the best known early discussion within this tradition is undoubtedly that by the Reverend Thomas Malthus. His *Essay on the Principle of Population* was originally published anonymously in 1798, followed by subsequent revisions and amendments in 1803, 1824, and 1830. In many ways, the *Essay* was little more than a summary of points which others in the pessimistic tradition had already made before him, but, as Hutchinson states, it should be regarded as ' ... not so much a sudden advance as it was a natural development and synthesis of current trends of thought....' (Hutchinson, 1967: 154)

The basic arguments presented in the *Essay* are: (1) Human populations, if left unchecked, tend to increase *geometrically,* that is, have a constant growth *rate.* For example, his observations on the United States' population censuses for 1790, 1800, 1810, and 1820, led him to estimate an annual growth rate of 2.8 per cent or a 'doubling time' of about twenty-five years. (2) Food and other resources cannot be expected to increase faster than at an *arithmetic* mode of growth, that is, increase by a fixed *amount* per year. (3) Consequently, in the long run population will outstrip resources. (4) When this level is reached, 'the actual population will be kept equal to the means of subsistence by misery and vice....' (Hutchinson, 1967: 155)

As a consequence of this argument, the obvious conclusion is that population growth must be checked before the 'laws of nature' produce their own checks. Malthus saw essentially two main categories of checks: (1) *preventive checks,* which would relate to reducing fertility; and (2) *positive checks,* which would have the effect of increasing mortality. The former would include sexual abstinence, and the latter would include war, famine, and pestilence. In other words, the two types of checks refer respectively to the reduction of the number of births and the increase of the number of deaths, the relationship of the two constituting the basic demographic formula for population change in those cases where the effects of immigration and emigration could be disregarded.

Contrasting with Malthus' sombre calculations have been the attitudes of persons in the 'New World,' apparently blessed with limitless space and resources. Thus, for example, optimism has characterized the outlook of successive Canadian governments. In Canada, occupying a vast and sparsely inhabited territory, governments have tended to encourage population increases through births and through immigration. During the seventeenth, eighteenth, and nineteenth centuries, it was thought perfectly proper and desirable that Canadians have large families; propagation was encouraged by the church and by the state. In Quebec, for example, large families were encouraged by politicians and by the Roman Catholic Church, not only from religious motives, but as a means of maintaining the French presence in North America and in a sense subverting or overcoming the British conquest. But even in Anglophone Canada, population increase was a political priority. The government of the newly confederated nation of Canada under the leadership of John A. Macdonald urged population expansion into the frontier regions or territories of British North America. Quite apparently natural increase alone would not secure a population sufficient to such expansion. Accordingly, in a race to occupy the territories before the United States, the Macdonald government encouraged immigrants who wished to settle in the Canadian West. Macdonald's famous 'national policy' was built not only around the national railway, but also the immigrants who were to use that railway in the move to settle the Canadian frontier.

Population Increase in Canada: Immigration

A peak period of immigration to Canada in the twentieth century was during the decade preceding World War I. For example, in 1913, 400,870 people entered Canada. The period from 1921 to 1930 also witnessed a large influx of immigrants. (See Table I.) In 1928, for example, a total of 166,783 people immigrated to Canada. Then, from a figure of 104,806 immigrants in 1930, the number dropped off dramatically to 27,530 in 1931, and 11,277 by 1935. The Depression was upon Canada and the world, and immigrants were no longer being sought by Canadian governments unable to find employment and adequate food and shelter for those already living in the country. Particularly, in the Canadian West, the territory to which earlier governments had sought to attract immigrants, the 'dirty thirties' were years of suffering and hardship. The space was still there, but no one wanted it.

Not until the post-World War II period did immigration to Canada pick up again. In 1939 the figure was 16,994, and reached a low point of 7,576 in the war year of 1942. But in 1946, 71,719 immigrants entered Canada, and in 1948, 125,414. This influx was a reflection of the post-war changes in Europe, with refugees and war-brides turning to North America. Similarly, the termination of European colonization in Africa and Asia left Canada, along with Australia, New Zealand, and the United States, as attractive alternatives to Europe. The post-World War II figures peaked in 1957, largely due to the Hungarian uprising and the refugees it produced; in 1957, 282,164 people entered Canada.

Table I: Immigrant Arrivals, 1913-1972*

1913	400,870	1933	14,382	1953	168,868
1914	150,484	1934	12,476	1954	154,227
1915	36,665	1935	11,277	1955	109,946
1916	55,914	1936	11,643	1956	164,857
1917	72,910	1937	15,101	1957	282,164
1918	41,845	1938	17,244	1958	124,851
1919	107,698	1939	16,994	1959	106,928
1920	138,824	1940	11,324	1960	104,111
1921	91,728	1941	9,329	1961	71,689
1922	64,224	1942	7,576	1962	74,586
1923	133,729	1943	8,504	1963	93,151
1924	124,164	1944	12,801	1964	112,606
1925	84,907	1945	22,722	1965	146,758
1926	135,982	1946	71,719	1966	194,743
1927	158,886	1947	64,127	1967	222,876
1928	166,783	1948	125,414	1968	183,974
1929	164,993	1949	95,217	1969	161,531
1930	104,806	1950	73,912	1970	147,713
1931	27,530	1951	194,391	1971	121,900
1932	20,591	1952	164,498	1972	122,006

*Sources: *Canada Year Book 1972* (Ottawa: Statistics Canada, 1972), p. 222.

Quarterly Immigration Bulletin, December, 1972, (Department of Manpower and Immigration).

Reproduced by permission of Information Canada.

Population Increase in Canada: Births and Deaths

It is a general feature of human societies that births and deaths are most numerous in pre-industrialized social systems. In such societies many children are born, and many die at birth or in infancy. Generally, too, the life expectancy at birth is modest, approximating an average of thirty years. However, with the improvements in nutrition, sanitation, and health care which have been associated with industrialization, the death rate declines sharply. And, in the history of the Western industrialized nations, the birth rate also declines, although less dramatically.

Both the stage of high births and high deaths, and that of low births and low deaths, are approximately static in population size in the sense that births and deaths more or less cancel each other. Quite literally, fertility and mortality are in balance. This is quite in contrast to the

Figure 1: Stages of Demographic Transition

Stage	Level of Social Organization	Birth Rate	Death Rate	Rate of Population Increase
1	simple and traditional societies	high	high	static
2	contemporary underdeveloped societies	high	low	rapid
3	contemporary industrialized societies	low	low	gradual

experience of many 'developing' nations of the world today. In these societies, medical and sanitary technology has been readily imported from the industrialized nations, drastically reducing the death rate, while the birth rate has remained at the high pre-industrial or traditional society level, supported by the traditional social values associated with many children. In such a situation, the population size increases rapidly, and has given rise to the much used expression 'population explosion.'

Canada has come to approximate Stage 3 of the 'demographic transition,' as have other industrialized societies. In the absence of immigration, a perfect realization of Stage 3 would constitute zero population growth. Canada is not at that point, but relative to the situation of the underdeveloped nations, fertility and mortality in Canada are in approximate balance, with the prospect of only gradual natural increase. Within Canada there have been variations by province. For example, Quebec until recently manifested a high birth rate, but now reports the lowest birth rate in the nation. (Table II)

If we break down the fertility by provinces, it is apparent that the least industrialized regions of Canada are those presently experiencing the highest birth rates; that is, the Yukon, the Northwest Territories, and Newfoundland. Conversely, Quebec, Ontario, and British Columbia are experiencing the lowest birth rates, and the lowest rates of natural increase.

Over time, the general profile in Canada has been one of a gradual decline in the birth rate, from a rate of 29.3 per 1,000 population in 1921, to 20.1 in 1937. Parallel to this decline, the death rate moved from 10.6 per 1,000 in 1921 to 9.6 in 1938. But the war and post-war period marked an increase in the Canadian fertility rate, to a high of 28.9 in

Table II: Annual Live Birth and Death Rates per 1,000 Population by Province, 1931-1971*

	1931		1941		1951		1961		1971		
	Births	Deaths	Births	Deaths	Births	Deaths	Births	Deaths	Births	Deaths	Natural Increase
Newfoundland	23.3	13.4	27.3	12.5	32.5	8.3	34.1	6.6	24.5	6.1	18.4
P.E.I.	21.3	10.4	21.6	11.9	27.1	9.2	27.1	9.3	18.8	9.0	9.8
Nova Scotia	22.6	11.6	24.1	12.0	26.6	9.0	26.3	8.3	18.1	8.5	9.6
New Brunswick	26.5	11.4	26.8	11.3	31.2	9.4	27.7	7.9	19.2	7.8	11.4
Quebec	29.1	12.0	26.8	10.3	29.8	8.6	26.1	7.0	14.8	6.8	8.0
Ontario	20.2	10.4	19.1	10.4	25.0	9.6	25.3	8.2	16.9	7.4	9.5
Manitoba	20.5	7.7	20.3	8.9	25.7	8.7	25.3	8.0	18.2	8.1	10.1
Saskatchewan	23.1	6.6	20.6	7.2	26.1	7.7	25.9	7.7	17.3	8.0	9.3
Alberta	23.6	7.2	21.7	8.0	28.8	7.6	29.2	6.7	18.8	6.5	12.3
B.C.	15.0	8.8	18.4	10.4	24.1	10.0	23.7	8.8	16.0	8.1	7.9
Yukon	10.0	16.5	14.4	13.4	38.0	9.4	38.1	6.4	27.5	5.7	21.8
N.W.T.	15.7	11.8	26.3	25.6	40.6	17.8	48.6	11.4	37.0	6.6	30.4
Canada	23.2	10.2	22.4	10.1	27.2	9.0	26.1	7.7	16.8	7.3	9.5

*Sources: John Porter, *Canadian Social Structure*, (1967), p. 47. Reprinted by permission of The Canadian Publishers, McClelland and Stewart Limited, Toronto, the Carleton Library Board, and Information Canada.

Data for 1971 from *Vital Statistics Preliminary Annual Report, 1971*, Cat. 84-20 (Ottawa: Statistics Canada, 1973). Reproduced by permission of Information Canada.

Table III: Emigration to the United States, 1961-1972*

Year	Entering United States from Canada			Canadian-born Entering from Elsewhere 4	All Canadian-born 5 = 3 + 4
	All Persons 1	Not Canadian-born 2	Canadian-born 3 = 1-2		
1961	44,470	13,158	31,312	726	32,038
1962	44,272	14,703	29,569	808	30,377
1963	50,509	15,189	32,320	683	36,003
1964	51,114	13,763	27,351	723	38,074
1965	50,035	12,516	37,519	808	38,327
1966	37,273	9,566	27,707	651	28,358
1967	34,768	12,039	22,729	713	23,442
1968	41,716	14,527	27,189	473	27,662
1969	29,303	11,107	18,196	386	18,582
1970	26,850	13,384	13,466	338	13,804
1971	22,709	—	—	—	13,128
1972	18,596	—	—	—	10,776

*Sources: *Canada Year Book 1972* (Ottawa: Statistics Canada, 1972), p. 232 (for 1961-1970). Reproduced by permission of Information Canada.

1972 Annual Report, U.S. Immigration and Naturalization Service, Tables 13-14 (for 1971-1972).

1947. From that year and the so-called 'baby boom,' a gradual decline again set in, with the 1971 fertility rate at 16.8. By 1971 also, the mortality rate was down to 7.3 per 1,000 population.

Emigration

Throughout Canada's history, emigration has been a relatively small component among the demographic factors which affect changes in population size. The main streams have traditionally been migration to the United States (both on the part of native-born Canadians and of people who had earlier immigrated to Canada), and 'return migration' of Western European immigrants (that is, the return to their countries of origin of people who had earlier immigrated to Canada). Since Canada, like most nations, does not account systematically for the people who decide to settle in another nation, we must rely upon United States data on people entering the United States from Canada in order to estimate Canadian emigration. Table III shows the number of Canadian-born persons entering the United States from Canada and elsewhere, and all persons entering the United States from Canada, for the years ended June 30, 1961-1972.

The number of emigrants leaving for the United States has been declining through the 1960's, from a total of 44,470 in 1961, with a maximum in 1964 of 51,114, to a low in 1972 of 18,596. This decline in the second half of the 1960's in part reflects changes in American immigration policies which have become more restrictive for people born in the Western Hemisphere, as contrasted to the privileged position which previously obtained for those emigrating from Canada. Note that the number of persons entering the United States from Canada, but who are *not* Canadian-born, does not show the drastic decline which we indicated for native Canadians. (Table III)

Net Population Increase

When we aggregate the information on births, deaths, immigration, and emigration, we note that Canada had a rapidly increasing population through the first half of this century. Table IV summarizes the total Canadian population size at the time the Censuses are taken in Canada on June 1 of years ending in '1,' that is, every decade. It should be noted that part of the increase from 1941 to 1951 was due to the accession of Newfoundland in 1949.

We can see that the decades following the Second World War brought the largest numerical increases in the Canadian population; as we have previously noted, this is to a large degree due to post-war immigration,

Table IV: Population, Showing Numerical and Percentage Changes, Canada, 1901-1971*

Year	Population	Numerical Increase	Change over Past Decade (%)
1901	5,371,315	538,076	11.1
1911	7,206,643	1,835,328	34.2
1921	8,787,949	1,581,306	21.9
1931	10,376,786	1,588,837	18.1
1941	11,506,655	1,129,869	10.9
1951	14,009,429	2,502,774	21.8
1961	18,238,247	4,228,818	30.2
1971	21,568,311	3,330,064	18.3

Note: Newfoundland is not included in these figures until 1951.

*Source: *1971 Census of Canada,* Vol.1, Bulletin 1.1-2, Table 1 (Ottawa: Statistics Canada, 1973). Reproduced by permission of Information Canada.

Table V: Components and Rate of Population Increase, Canada, 1956-1969*

Year	Births	Deaths	Natural Increase	Net Migration	Population Increase
1956	28.0	8.2	19.8	4.6	24.4
1957	28.2	8.2	20.0	12.9	32.9
1958	27.5	7.9	19.6	8.7	28.3
1959	27.4	8.0	19.4	4.2	23.6
1960	26.8	7.8	19.0	3.1	22.1
1961	26.1	7.7	18.4	2.2	20.6
1962	25.3	7.7	17.6	1.3	18.9
1963	24.6	7.8	16.8	1.9	18.7
1964	23.5	7.6	15.9	3.1	19.0
1965	21.3	7.6	13.7	4.7	18.4
1966	19.4	7.5	11.9	7.0	18.9
1967	18.2	7.4	10.8	8.7	19.5
1968	17.6	7.4	10.2	6.4	16.6
1969	17.6	7.3	10.3	5.0	15.3

*Source: *Canada Year Book 1970* (Ottawa: Statistics Canada, 1971), p. 215. Reproduced by permission of Information Canada.

combined with the high birth rates of the late 1940's and early 1950's. Closer inspection of the annual *rates* of increase shows, however, that the rate of population increase in Canada has been declining. (Table V)

For example, in 1956 the population increase was 24.4 per 1,000 population, or 2.4 per cent per year. By 1969 it was 15.3 per 1,000, or 1.5 per cent per year. Contrast this with developing societies, where the rate of population increase is usually between 2.5 per cent and 3 per cent per year.

The increases in population vary enormously period by period, and province by province. For example, as one might expect, there are enormous increases in the population of the Prairie provinces at the end of the nineteenth century and early in the twentieth century. In the period 1901 to 1911 Saskatchewan showed a percentage increase of 439.5, the highest in Canada, as compared with a percentage increase of 34.2 for that period in Canada as a whole (Kalbach and McVey, 1971: 23; Table VI). Recalling that *the percentage increases for the western provinces and the territories are a reflection of smaller population bases,* the

Table VI: Province with the Decade's Highest Percentage Population Increase, and Percentage Increase by Decade for Canada, 1851-1971*

Decade	Province with Highest Increase	Percentage Increase	Percentage Increase for Canada
1851–1861	Ontario	46.6	32.6
1861–1871	Nova Scotia	17.2	14.2
1871–1881	Manitoba	146.8	17.2
1881–1891	Manitoba	145.0	11.8
1891–1901	British Columbia	82.0	11.1
1901–1911	Saskatchewan	439.5	34.2
1911–1921	Alberta	57.2	21.9
1921–1931	British Columbia	32.4	18.1
1931–1941	Northwest Territories	29.1	10.9
1941–1951	Yukon	85.1	18.6
1951–1961	Yukon	60.8	30.2
1961–1971	Northwest Territories	51.3	18.3

*Sources: Reprinted from *The Demographic Bases of Canadian Society* by Warren E. Kalbach and Wayne W. McVey, by permission of McGraw-Hill Ryerson Limited.

Statistics for 1961-1971 are from *Census of Canada, 1971* (Ottawa: Statistics Canada, 1973). Reproduced by permission of Information Canada.

table prepared by Kalbach and McVey is illustrative of the pattern of growth by provinces in Canada (Table VI).

The table is almost a mirror reflection of the history of Canadian settlement. First, the growth in the mid-nineteenth century of Ontario; then, by the last quarter of the century, the expansion into the Canadian West is well under way, and for two decades Manitoba experiences the highest rate of increase. By the last decade of the century, gold is attracting people to British Columbia. The first decade of the twentieth century belongs to Saskatchewan, in a period of enormous growth in Canada's 'wheat bowl.' Then, from 1911 to 1931, Alberta and British Columbia experience the greatest increase, as Western settlement fills in. From 1931 onwards, the greatest percentage increases are in Canada's 'last frontier,' the northern territories. For the last decade, 1961-1971, it is again the Northwest Territories which reveal the highest percentage increase, 51.3 per cent.

Ethnic Composition and Mother Tongue

Thus far we have been speaking of immigration without distinguishing the origins of the immigrants to Canada. As is well known, the immigrants have come from many nations, and in different periods of Canadian history, different nations have tended to provide the bulk of immigrants to Canada. Each successive wave of immigrants has tended to settle in a distinct region of the nation, consistent with the pattern of settlement which we considered in the previous section.

Thus, the conventionally distinguished multi-ethnic society, or 'mosaic,' which constitutes Canadian society may be broken down by distinguishable regional clustering. For example, the bulk of immigrants to Canada from Eastern Europe and the Ukraine entered the country at the end of the nineteenth century and in the early twentieth century. This was the period of expanding settlement in the Canadian West, with the aid and encouragement of the Canadian government. Consequently we find today that persons of Ukrainian origin tend to be found in Manitoba, Saskatchewan, and Alberta. (Table VII) The last decade has seen continuing immigration from the United Kingdom and other Commonwealth countries, but also American immigration, with settlement tending to cluster in urban Ontario. Also, a large number of Italian and Portuguese immigrants have settled in Ontario. (Tables VIII and IX)

Of those who have immigrated to Canada, 71.1 per cent have entered the country since 1946 (Table X): that is, 2,341,945 persons. The province chosen for settlement by the greatest number of immigrants is Ontario, with 1,326,255 immigrants since the end of World War II. (Table X) Only in the province of Saskatchewan do we find that fewer

Table VII: Numerical and Percentage Distribution of the Population by Ethnic Groups, for Canada and Provinces, 1971*

Ethnic group — Groupe ethnique	Canada	Newfoundland — Terre-Neuve	Prince Edward Island — Île-du-Prince-Édouard	Nova Scotia — Nouvelle-Écosse	New Brunswick — Nouveau-Brunswick	Québec	Ontario	Manitoba	Saskatchewan	Alberta	British Columbia — Colombie-Britannique	Yukon	Northwest Territories — Territoires du Nord-Ouest
					Numerical distribution — Répartition absolue								
Total	21,568,310	522,105	111,640	788,960	634,560	6,027,765	7,703,110	988,245	926,245	1,627,875	2,184,620	18,390	34,810
British Isles — Britannique	9,624,115	489,570	92,285	611,310	365,735	640,045	4,576,010	414,125	390,190	761,665	1,265,460	8,945	8,785
French — Français	6,180,120	15,410	15,325	80,220	235,025	4,759,360	737,360	86,510	56,200	94,665	96,550	1,225	2,275
German — Allemand	1,317,195	2,375	955	40,910	8,405	53,870	475,315	123,065	180,095	231,010	198,310	1,555	1,330
Hungarian — Hongrois	131,890	105	15	755	365	12,565	65,690	5,400	13,825	16,240	16,600	195	120
Italian — Italien	730,820	500	110	3,770	1,385	169,650	463,095	10,445	2,865	24,805	53,795	160	245
Jewish — Juif	296,945	365	55	2,530	1,030	115,990	135,190	20,010	2,195	7,325	12,180	35	30
Native Indian — Indien nord-américain	295,215	1,225	315	4,475	3,915	32,840	62,420	43,035	40,470	44,540	52,215	2,580	7,180
Netherlands — Néerlandais ..	425,945	670	1,245	14,845	5,365	12,590	206,940	35,300	19,040	58,565	70,535	515	340
Polish — Polonais	316,425	280	110	3,265	690	23,975	144,115	42,700	26,910	44,325	29,545	245	270
Russian — Russe	64,475	35	10	245	105	4,065	12,580	4,040	10,030	10,235	22,990	70	60
Scandinavian — Scandinave ..	384,790	1,185	275	4,030	3,605	8,825	60,225	35,110	59,105	98,430	112,125	1,000	900
Ukrainian — Ukrainien	580,655	175	130	2,315	605	20,330	159,880	114,410	85,920	135,510	60,145	610	635
Asian — Asiatique	285,535	1,655	385	4,825	2,370	40,685	112,780	9,575	7,460	25,660	79,760	155	225
Other and unknown — Autres et inconnus	934,170	8,560	440	15,470	5,965	132,985	491,500	44,510	31,930	74,895	114,405	1,100	12,410

Percentage distribution — Répartition en pourcentage

Total	100.0	100.0	100.0	100.0	100.0	100.0	100.0	100.0	100.0	100.0	100.0	100.0	100.0
British Isles — Britannique	44.6	93.8	82.7	77.5	57.6	10.6	59.4	41.9	42.1	46.8	57.9	48.6	25.2
French — Français	28.7	3.0	13.7	10.2	37.0	79.0	9.6	8.8	6.1	5.8	4.4	6.7	6.5
German — Allemand	6.1	0.5	0.9	5.2	1.3	0.9	6.2	12.5	19.4	14.2	9.1	8.5	3.8
Hungarian — Hongrois	0.6	—	—	0.1	0.1	0.2	0.9	0.5	1.5	1.0	0.8	1.1	0.3
Italian — Italien	3.4	0.1	0.1	0.5	0.2	2.8	6.0	1.1	0.3	1.5	2.5	0.9	0.7
Jewish — Juif	1.4	0.1	—	0.3	0.2	1.9	1.8	2.0	0.2	0.5	0.6	0.2	0.1
Native Indian — Indien nord-américain	1.4	0.2	0.3	0.6	0.6	0.5	0.8	4.4	4.4	2.7	2.4	14.0	20.6
Netherlands — Néerlandais ..	2.0	0.1	1.1	1.9	0.8	0.2	2.7	3.6	2.1	3.6	3.2	2.8	1.0
Polish — Polonais	1.5	0.1	0.1	0.4	0.1	0.4	1.9	4.3	2.9	2.7	1.4	1.3	0.8
Russian — Russe	0.3	—	—	—	—	0.1	0.2	0.4	1.1	0.6	1.1	0.4	0.2
Scandinavian — Scandinave ..	1.8	0.2	0.2	0.5	0.6	0.1	0.8	3.6	6.4	6.0	5.1	5.4	2.6
Ukrainian — Ukrainien	2.7	—	0.1	0.3	0.1	0.3	2.1	11.6	9.3	8.3	2.8	3.3	1.8
Asian — Asiatique	1.3	0.3	0.3	0.6	0.4	0.7	1.5	1.0	0.8	1.6	3.7	0.8	0.6
Other and unknown — Autres et inconnus	4.3	1.6	0.4	2.0	0.9	2.2	6.4	4.5	3.4	4.6	5.2	6.0	35.7

Note: British Isles includes English, Irish, Scottish and Welsh. Scandinavian includes Danish, Icelandic, Norwegian and Swedish.

Source: *Census of Canada, 1971*, Cat. 92-744, Table 1 (Ottawa: Statistics Canada, 1974). Reproduced by permission of Information Canada.

Table VIII: Immigrant Arrivals, by Citizenship, 1968-70*

Country of Citizenship	1968	1969	1970	Country of Citizenship	1968	1969	1970
	No.	No.	No.		No.	No.	No.
Australia	3,380	3,074	2,916	Morocco	1,428	377	290
Austria	787	504	431	Netherlands	3,312	2,529	1,947
Belgium	742	722	454	New Zealand	1,126	913	969
Britain and colonies	41,466	37,105	30,281	Norway	448	324	248
Central America	70	116	153	Pakistan	723	1,120	1,129
Ceylon	123	205	207	Poland	1,250	980	874
China	5,259	5,272	3,465	Portugal	8,841	8,031	8,700
Czechoslovakia	9,653	4,721	1,411	Rhodesia	12	12	2
Denmark	1,061	633	470	South Africa	948	678	734
Egypt	1,948	1,471	986	South America	2,146	3,945	4,368
Finland	806	758	681	Spain	1,683	995	912
France	6,020	3,995	3,292	Sweden	389	288	281
Germany	5,942	3,880	3,000	Switzerland	1,926	1,531	1,520
Greece	8,157	7,134	6,506	Trinidad and Tobago	2,444	5,610	4,811
Haiti	599	708	987	Turkey	621	423	319
Hungary	715	626	541	U.S.S.R.	221	145	136
India	3,963	5,939	6,324	United States	19,059	21,474	23,183
Ireland, Republic of	1,871	1,503	1,324	Yugoslavia	6,402	5,241	6,701
Israel	1,503	868	816	Other African	409	451	539
Italy	21,232	10,884	8,731	Other Asian	6,808	6,198	6,512
Jamaica	3,477	4,124	4,932	Other European	20	623	549
Japan	628	698	785	Stateless	1,792	1,810	1,642
Lebanon	1,314	985	1,021	Other	1,013	1,561	1,202
Luxembourg	16	12	10				
Mexico	221	335	421	Totals	183,974	161,531	147,713

*Source: *Canada Year Book 1972* (Ottawa: Statistics Canada, 1972), p. 226. Reproduced by permission of Information Canada.

Table IX: Intended Province of Destination of Male and Female Immigrants Admitted to Canada, 1968-70*

Province or Territory	1968			1969			1970		
	Males	Females	Total	Males	Females	Total	Males	Females	Total
Newfoundland	505	501	1,006	421	411	832	310	320	630
Prince Edward Island	84	92	176	95	87	182	97	88	185
Nova Scotia	1,031	926	1,957	1,085	1,082	2,167	1,015	992	2,007
New Brunswick	518	507	1,025	599	640	1,239	555	515	1,070
Quebec	18,414	17,067	35,481	14,129	14,101	28,230	11,867	11,394	23,261
Ontario	48,419	47,736	96,155	42,720	43,868	86,588	40,207	40,525	80,732
Manitoba	4,712	4,011	8,723	3,083	3,297	6,380	3,007	2,819	5,826
Saskatchewan	1,852	1,705	3,557	1,209	1,283	2,492	836	873	1,709
Alberta	6,738	6,465	13,208	5,657	5,617	11,274	5,313	5,092	10,405
British Columbia	11,120	11,376	22,496	10,902	11,051	21,953	10,939	10,744	21,683
Yukon and N.W.T.	110	85	195	107	87	194	111	94	205
Canada	93,503	90,471	183,974	80,007	81,524	161,531	74,257	73,456	147,713

*Source: *Canada Year Book 1972:* (Ottawa: Statistics Canada, 1972), p. 228. Reproduced by permission of Information Canada.

Table X: Population Born Outside Canada, by Period of Immigration, for Canada and Provinces, 1971*

Province	Total	Immigrated prior to 1946		Immigrated 1946–1971[a]	
		Number	Percentage	Number	Percentage
Canada	3,295,530	953,585	28.9	2,341,945	71.1
Newfoundland	8,940	1,410	15.8	7,530	84.2
Prince Edward Island	3,705	1,335	36.0	2,370	64.0
Nova Scotia	37,190	12,785	34.4	24,405	65.6
New Brunswick	23,730	9,590	40.4	14,145	59.6
Quebec	468,925	97,375	20.8	371,550	79.2
Ontario	1,707,395	381,155	22.3	1,326,235	77.7
Manitoba	151,250	69,415	45.9	81,835	54.1
Saskatchewan	110,690	77,950	70.4	32,740	29.6
Alberta	282,260	117,430	41.6	164,830	58.4
British Columbia	496,660	184,250	37.1	312,415	62.9
Yukon	2,545	535	21.0	2,005	78.8
Northwest Territories	2,245	355	15.8	1,890	84.2

[a] Includes the first five months only of 1971.

*Source: *1971 Census of Canada*, Cat. 92-761, AP-10, Table I, p. 2 (Ottawa: Statistics Canada, 1973). Reproduced by permission of Information Canada.

Table XI: Population by Mother Tongue by Province, Canada, 1971*

	English	*French*	*German*	*Indian and Eskimo*	*Italian*
Canada	12,973,810	5,793,650	561,085	179,825	538,360
Newfoundland	514,520	3,635	515	1,620	175
P.E.I.	103,105	7,360	140	145	35
Nova Scotia	733,560	39,330	2,000	2,710	1,495
New Brunswick	410,400	215,730	1,110	2,725	755
Quebec	789,185	4,867,250	31,025	21,050	135,455
Ontario	5,971,570	482,045	184,880	28,590	344,285
Manitoba	662,720	60,550	82,720	31,665	7,265
Saskatchewan	685,920	31,605	75,885	26,020	2,045
Alberta	1,263,935	46,500	92,800	29,920	15,570
British Columbia	1,807,250	38,035	89,020	18,550	91,030
Yukon	15,345	450	565	1,030	75
N.W.T.	16,305	1,160	425	15,800	175

*Source: *1971 Census of Canada*, Advance Bulletin, Cat. 92-758, AP-7 (Ottawa: Statistics Canada, 1972). Reproduced by permission of Information Canada.

immigrants have entered since 1946 than prior to 1946; 70.4 per cent of immigration to Saskatchewan occured before World War II. The other Prairie provinces, Manitoba and Alberta, have experienced 54.1 per cent and 58.4 per cent of their immigrant settlement since 1946, distinctly lower than any other area of Canada except Saskatchewan. New Brunswick follows with a post-war percentage of 59.6.

Another picture of the ethnic distribution of Canadian society can be obtained by looking at the reported 'mother tongue' for Canada and the provinces. 'Mother tongue' refers to the language a person first learned in childhood and which is still understood by the person. (Continued understanding, however, cannot be taken to mean constant or frequent language usage.)

English and French are, of course, the two principal mother tongues reported (Table XI). Across all the provinces, these two languages are the mother tongue of the great majority of Canadians: English in all provinces except Quebec, and French in Quebec. There are large groups of people of French mother tongue in the provinces adjacent to Quebec: Ontario and New Brunswick. Of other European mother tongues, German, Italian, and Ukrainian are the largest for the entire country. The German and the Italian represent substantial immigration *after* World War II, while the Ukrainian represents earlier immigration.

We find that patterns vary from province to province, in accordance with the immigration histories of the provinces. Thus, Ukrainian is concentrated to a large degree in the Prairie provinces (there are more people of Ukrainian mother tongue than of French mother tongue in Manitoba, Saskatchewan, and Alberta), while Italians are concentrated in Quebec and Ontario. Similarly, Germans as well as many small groups are concentrated in Ontario. An exception to this pattern are the Chinese, Japanese, and other Asiatic mother tongues which tend to be concentrated in British Columbia. The largest Indian and Eskimo populations as indicated by mother tongue are to be found in the Prairie Provinces collectively; Manitoba has the largest population, followed by Ontario, Alberta, Saskatchewan, Quebec, British Columbia, and the Northwest Territories.

Religion

To a large extent the ethnic and linguistic distributions which we have been considering are reflected in the settlement patterns of Canadians of various religious denominations. For example, Roman Catholics have the highest proportions of the total populations of Quebec, New Brunswick, and areas of Ontario adjacent to Quebec (also southeastern Ontario and northern Saskatchewan). Conversely, Protestants are in the majority in Newfoundland, Nova Scotia, Ontario, the Prairie Provinces, and British Columbia. (See Figures 2 and 3.)

If we consider religion to be stated denomination of membership, without any reference to actual religious activity, we find in 1971 that 20,638,735 Canadians indicate a religious affiliation. Or, to put it conversely, only 929,575 Canadians unequivocally state that they are affiliated with no religious denomination. Interestingly, this last figure represents a tenfold increase over that of 1961 (94,763), reflecting undoubtedly some increased secularization, but for the most part, probably a reflection of less insistent census questioning in 1971 regarding religious affiliation. (Table XII)

The Protestant religions, when aggregated, constitute numerically the greatest religious affiliation in Canada, as they have from the conception of the nation in 1867. Of these, the single largest denomination is the United Church (United Church and Methodist), followed by the Anglican Church. (Table XII) If we do not aggregate the several Protestant denominations, the single largest religious affiliation in Canada is the Roman Catholic, with 9,974,895 in 1971, approximately two-and-a-half times as large as the United Church affiliation.

If we consider the distribution of persons by religion in the provinces,

Figure 2: Protestant Denominations in Canada by Census Divisions, 1971*

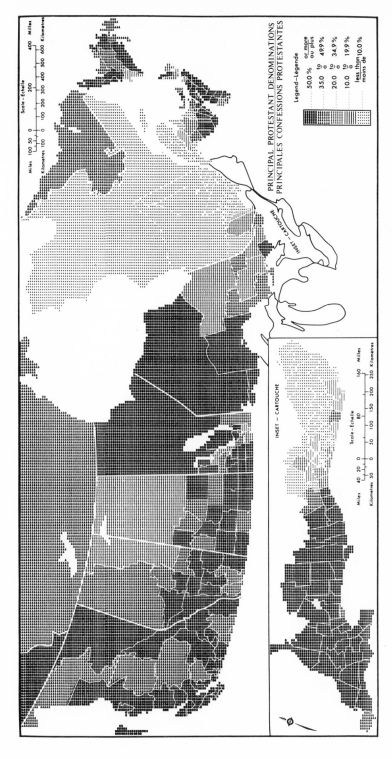

*Source: *Census of Canada, 1971* Advance Bulletin, Cat. 92-763, AP-12 (Ottawa: Statistics Canada, 1973). Reproduced by permission of Information Canada.

Table XII: Population by Religious Denomination, for Canada, 1921-1971*

Religious denomination	1921	1931	1941	1951	1961	1971
Canada(1)	8,787,949	10,376,786	11,506,655	14,009,429	18,238,247	21,568,310
Adventist	14,200	16,058	18,485	21,398	25,999	28,590
Anglican	1,410,632	1,639,075	1,754,368	2,060,720	2,409,068	2,543,180
Baptist	422,312	443,944	484,465	519,585	593,553	667,245
Buddhist	11,316	15,921	15,676	8,184	11,611	16,175
Christian and Missionary Alliance	283	3,560	4,214	6,396	18,006	23,630
Christian Reformed	(2)	(2)	(2)	(2)	62,257	83,390
Churches of Christ, Disciples	13,125	15,831	21,260	14,920	19,512	16,405
Confucian	27,185	24,253	22,282	5,791	5,089	2,165
Congregationalist	30,788	(3)	(3)	(3)	(3)	(4)
Doukhobor	12,674	14,978	16,878	13,175	13,234	9,170
Free Methodist	—	7,740	8,805	8,921	14,245	19,125
Greek Orthodox(5)	170,069(6)	102,529	139,845	172,271	239,766	316,605
Hutterite	(7)	(7)	(7)	(7)	(7)	13,650
Jehovah's Witnesses	6,689	13,582	7,007	34,596	68,018	174,810

Jewish	125,445	155,766	168,585	204,836	254,368	276,025
Lutheran	286,891	394,920	401,836	444,923	662,744	715,740
Mennonite(8)	58,874	88,837	111,554	125,938	152,452	168,150
Methodist	1,161,165	(3)	(3)	(3)	(3)	(9)
Mormon	19,657	22,041	25,328	32,888	50,016	66,635
Pentecostal	7,012	26,349	57,742	95,131	143,877	220,390
Presbyterian	1,411,794	872,428	830,597	781,747	818,558	872,335
Roman Catholic	3,399,011	4,102,960	4,806,431	6,069,496	8,342,826	9,974,895
Salvation Army	24,771	30,773	33,609	70,275	92,054	119,665
Ukrainian Catholic	(6)	186,879(10)	185,948(10)	191,051(10)	189,653(10)	227,730(10)
Unitarian	4,943	4,453	5,584	3,517	15,062	20,995
United Church	8,739	2,021,065	2,208,658	2,867,271	3,664,008	3,768,800
Other	138,555	151,689	158,337	196,720	277,508	293,240
No religion	21,819	21,155	19,161	59,679	94,763	929,575

(1) Exclusive of Newfoundland prior to 1951.
(2) Figures not available.
(3) Included with 'United Church.'
(4) Included with 'Other.'
(5) Includes those Churches which observe the Greek Orthodox rite, such as Russian Orthodox, Ukrainian Orthodox and Syrian Orthodox.
(6) 'Greek Catholic' and 'Greek Orthodox' combined under 'Greek Church.'
(7) Included with 'Mennonite.'
(8) Includes 'Hutterite' prior to 1971.
(9) Assigned alternately to Free and Wesleyan Methodist.
(10) Includes 'Other Greek Catholic.'

*Source: *Census of Canada 1971*, Cat. 92-724, Vol. I, Part 3 (Bul. 1.3-3), p. 9-1 (Ottawa: Statistics Canada, 1973). Reproduced by permisssion of Information Canada.

Table XIII: Percentage Distribution of the Population by Religious Denomination, for Canada and Provinces, 1961 and 1971*

Province	Anglican	Baptist	Lutheran	Presbyterian	Roman Catholic	United Church	Other(1)
				1961			
				Percentages based on geographic totals			
Canada	13.2	3.3	3.6	4.5	45.7	20.1	9.6
Newfoundland	28.5	0.2	0.1	0.5	35.7	21.4	13.5
Prince Edward Island	5.8	5.7	0.1	12.2	46.1	26.2	3.9
Nova Scotia	18.1	13.7	1.6	5.6	35.3	22.2	3.6
New Brunswick	11.4	15.7	0.3	2.3	51.9	14.3	4.0
Quebec	3.7	0.3	0.4	1.1	88.1	2.9	3.4
Ontario	17.9	4.0	3.9	7.9	30.0	26.3	9.9
Manitoba	13.8	1.9	6.9	3.2	22.9	29.3	22.0
Saskatchewan	10.2	1.7	10.3	2.7	26.3	32.0	16.7
Alberta	11.8	3.2	9.2	4.2	22.4	31.5	17.8
British Columbia	22.5	3.0	6.2	5.5	17.5	31.0	14.3
Yukon	30.9	4.9	6.0	5.6	27.2	17.2	8.3
Northwest Territories	38.5	0.8	2.1	1.3	42.9	8.2	6.2

1971

Percentages based on geographic totals

Canada	11.8	3.1	3.3	4.0	46.2	17.5	14.0
Newfoundland	27.7	0.2	0.1	0.6	36.6	19.5	15.4
Prince Edward Island	6.2	5.7	0.1	11.7	45.9	24.9	5.5
Nova Scotia	17.2	12.7	1.5	5.1	36.3	20.6	6.6
New Brunswick	10.9	14.0	0.3	2.1	52.2	13.4	7.1
Quebec	3.0	0.6	0.4	0.9	86.7	2.9	5.5
Ontario	15.8	3.7	3.5	7.0	33.3	21.8	14.8
Manitoba	12.4	1.9	6.6	3.1	24.6	26.0	25.5
Saskatchewan	9.4	1.6	9.8	2.2	27.9	29.6	19.4
Alberta	10.5	3.1	8.2	3.5	24.0	28.1	22.7
British Columbia	17.7	3.0	5.5	4.6	18.7	24.6	25.9
Yukon	25.3	4.7	5.0	3.8	25.4	16.9	18.9
Northwest Territories	36.4	1.1	2.1	1.3	41.3	8.6	9.1

(1) Includes 'No religion.'

*Source: *Census of Canada 1971*, Advance Bul., Cat. 92-763, AP-12 (Ottawa: Statistics Canada, 1973). Reproduced by permission of Information Canada.

Figure 3: Roman Catholics in Canada, by Census Divisions, 1971*

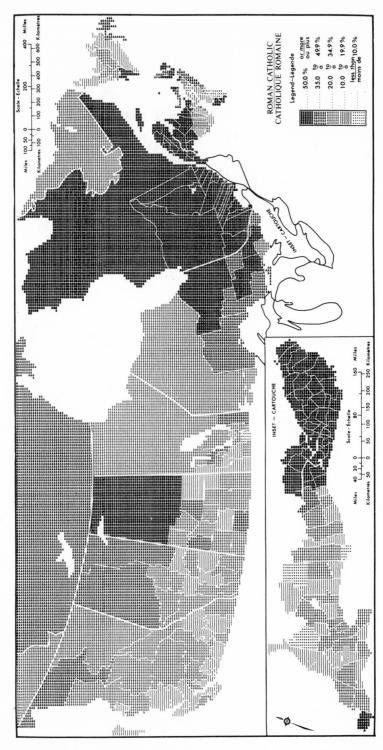

ROMAN CATHOLIC
CATHOLIQUE ROMAINE

Legend–Légende

	50.0 % or more ou plus
	35.0 to à 49.9%
	20.0 to à 34.9%
	10.0 to à 19.9%
	less than moins de 10.0%

INSET – CARTOUCHE

Scale – Echelle

Miles 100 50 0   100   200   300   400 Milles

Kilometres 100 0 100 200 300 400 500 600 Kilomètres

INSET – CARTOUCHE

Scale – Echelle

Miles 40 20 0   80   160 Milles

Kilometres 50 0 50 100 150 200 250 Kilomètres

*Source: *Census of Canada, 1971* Advance Bulletin, Cat 92-763, AP-12 (Ottawa: Statistics Canada, 1973). Reproduced by permission of Information Canada.

Table XIV: Rural Population as a Percentage of the Total Population, 1871-1971*

1871	80.4	1911	54.6	1951[a]	43.3
1881	74.3	1921	50.5	1951[b]	38.4
1891	68.2	1931	46.3	1961	30.4
1901	62.5	1941	45.7	1971	23.9

[a,b] Until 1941 the census definition of rural was 'unincorporated area.' In 1951 this definition was changed to denote places with less than 1,000 population. For 1951[a] the figures represent the earlier definition; for 1951[b], the later definition.

*Sources: John Porter, *Canadian Social Structure*, (1967), p. 54. Reprinted by permission of The Canadian Publishers, McClelland and Stewart Limited, Toronto, the Carleton Library Board, and Information Canada.

Percentage for 1971 calculated from *Census of Canada, 1971,* Bul. 1.1-9, Cat. 92-709, 1973.

Table XV: Population by Rural and Urban Residence, Canada and Provinces, 1971*

	Urban	Rural
Canada	16,410,785	5,157,525
Newfoundland	298,800	223,305
Prince Edward Island	42,780	68,860
Nova Scotia	447,405	341,555
New Brunswick	361,145	273,410
Quebec	4,861,245	1,166,520
Ontario	6,343,630	1,359,475
Manitoba	686,445	301,800
Saskatchewan	490,630	435,610
Alberta	1,196,255	431,620
British Columbia	1,645,405	530,215
Yukon	11,220	7,170
Northwest Territories	16,830	17,480

*Source: *Census of Canada, 1971,* Bul. 1.1-9, Cat. 92-709 (Ottawa: Statistics Canada, 1973). Reproduced by permission of Information Canada.

and we do not aggregate the Protestant denominations, the largest affiliation in all but the Western provinces is Roman Catholic. The largest proportion of Roman Catholics is in Quebec, with 86.7 per cent; the only other province with a majority of Roman Catholics is New Brunswick, with 52.2 per cent in 1971 (Table XIII). In the provinces of Manitoba, Saskatchewan, Alberta, and British Columbia, the United Church constitutes the denomination with the largest number of reported members.

Urban and Rural Residence

We have previously remarked upon the settlement of immigrants in the large metropolitan centers of Canada, especially Toronto and Montreal. It is also the case that native-born Canadians have tended to congregate in cities. In all societies of the modern world, especially the industrialized societies, a conspicuous process is that of urbanization (see Chapter Eleven). It is the case that the world-wide trend is toward city-living. In Canada, an increasing proportion of the population has come to reside in our cities, to the point where today most Canadians live in metropolitan areas (Table XIV).

As can be seen from Table XIV, each decade since Confederation has witnessed a decline in the proportion of the Canadian population who reside in rural as opposed to urban areas. Today, about three-quarters of the population have an urban residence (Table XV). In every province, urban centers dominate numerically, with the exception of Prince Edward Island and the Northwest Territories. In each province, there is at least one urban area considered a Census Metropolitan Area (CMA), constituting a numerically significant proportion of the total provincial population (Table XVI). As will be discussed in subsequent chapters, especially Chapter Eleven, this dominance extends beyond a matter of mere numbers and reflects a pervasive influence upon the nature and quality of life in Canadian society.

Conclusions

The demographic profile which we have sketched comprises the population skeleton of Canadian society and its complex organization. Just as a general awareness of socialization is fundamental, so too is an awareness of basic population features. These features, and other demographic data, will be integrated into subsequent chapters which discuss the social inter-relationships which make up Canadian society.

Table XVI: Metropolitan Areas, 1971*

Province	City	M.A. Population	Province Population	M.A. as % of Province
Newfoundland	St. John's	131,814	522,104	25.25
Nova Scotia	Halifax	222,637	788,960	28.22
New Brunswick	St. John	106,744	634,557	16.82
Quebec	Montreal	2,743,208	6,027,734	58.17
	Hull	149,230		
	Quebec City	480,502		
	Chicoutimi	133,703		
Ontario	Toronto	2,628,043	7,703,106	63.90
	Hamilton	498,523		
	Ottawa	453,280		
	St. Catherines–Niagara	303,429		
	London	286,011		
	Windsor	258,643		
	Kitchener	226,846		
	Sudbury	155,424		
	Thunder Bay	112,093		
Manitoba	Winnipeg	540,262	988,247	54.67
Saskatchewan	Saskatoon	126,183	926,242	28.85
	Regina	140,734		
Alberta	Calgary	403,319	1,627,874	55.23
	Edmonton	495,702		
B.C.	Vancouver	1,082,352	2,184,621	58.51
	Victoria	195,800		

*Source: *Census of Canada, 1971,* Cat. 92-708, Vol. 1 (Ottawa: Statistics Canada, 1973). Reproduced by permission of Information Canada.

References

Canada Year Book 1970. Ottawa: Queen's Printer, 1971.

Canada Year Book 1972. Ottawa: Queen's Printer, 1973.

Census of Canada 1971. Ottawa: Information Canada, 1973 (Bulletins specified in Chapter).

Hutchinson, E.P., *The Population Debate.* Boston: Houghton Mifflin, 1967.

Kalbach, Warren, and Wayne McVey, *The Demographic Bases of Canadian Society.* Toronto: McGraw-Hill, 1971.

Porter, John, *Canadian Social Structure.* Toronto: McClelland and Stewart (The Carleton Library), 1967.

Quarterly Immigration Bulletin. Ottawa: Department of Manpower and Immigration, Dec., 1972.

United States Immigration and Naturalization Annual Report. Washington: U.S. Immigration and Naturalization Service, 1972.

2 : ISSUES OF INEQUALITY

Introduction to Part Two

Since the end of World War II, no topic has received as much sociological attention as that of social stratification. Without any prior instruction on our part, four of the authors contributing to this volume, quite independently, were moved to treat of the issue of social inequality, the issue expressive of social stratification in Canada and every society of the world. Social inequality is a complex issue. The four chapters in this section approach the issue from the inter-related perspectives of role inequalities, educational inequalities, ethnic inequalities, and political or citizenship inequalities. The distinctions, of course, are analytical; each is a reinforcing facet of the total picture of stratification or institutionalized inequality in Canadian society.

It is with some chagrin that sociologists may today look back at the North American development of the discipline and find that institutionalized social inequality was ill-studied until after the Second World War. It is conventional today to acknowledge that Karl Marx has had an enormous impact upon modern sociology; yet that impact has been only within the past thirty years. It seems to us that the North American mythology which described a land of plenty, with freedom of opportunity, universal affluence, and no social classes, if not accepted by early sociologists, at least was not really challenged. To be sure, there was the early community work of the Lynds in Middletown (Lynd and Lynd, 1929; 1937) and later that of Warner in Yankee City (Warner, 1941; 1945). But these works, containing a study of social class and inter-related ethnic factors, were pioneering and precisely illustrative of the lack of sustained attention to stratification. They came to be venerated after the war.

In Canada, as in the United States, people who were otherwise quite capable of recognizing differences in the life styles of their fellow citizens, tended to insist that whatever these material differences, we were all still middle class. The traditionally legitimated class distinctions of Europe, with its continuity with a feudal past, were absent in North America — although less so in Canada in the absence of a revolutionary national genesis. Therefore, distinctions in social rank, short of extremes, were more difficult to identify, while their very existence was denied in American and Canadian ideologies. It is characteristic of class stratification, as opposed to feudal estate systems such as those of Europe in the Middle Ages, or caste stratification systems such as that of traditional India, that the distinctions among strata are in no way clearly and identifiably demarcated. The absence of such demarcation permits the persistence of a myth of classlessness. And it hinders sociological examination of stratification in that less than perfect measurements have to be devised, such as occupational ranking scales, wherein what we take to be social class is an operational artifact of our measurement. Thus, where we conventionally speak of lower, middle, and upper classes, these strata are not clearly identifiable and conscious groups in the Marxian sense of social class, but rather, are aggregates of persons so classified by sociologists by virtue of some shared socio-economic features.

The absence of explicit public awareness of *systematic* and *institutionalized* inequality in Canadian society was also associated with the work ethic and to some extent Protestant individualism. The notion that differences in income and life style were attributable to individual effort, or the lack of such effort, mitigated against a recognition of systematic and inherited inequalities. Success or failure was a reflection upon the individual, and not the social system; even the Great Depression did not altogether destroy this myth. Given this prevailing and shared attitude, insofar as people were aware of real differences in wealth, such differences were not attributed to systemic features; subsequent generations could still succeed with hard work and a little luck.

It is perhaps fair to say, however simple, that once past the distraction of the war, many Canadians refused to forget the 'dirty thirties.' The myth of equality of opportunity may not have withered away, but from the war it was scarred. Moreover, clearly, sociologists had discovered stratification, and soon data from the United States and from Canada were to make clear to some of the academic community that inequality was not only present, but persistent and inherited. In Canada, almost singlehandedly, the work of John Porter established social stratification as the pre-eminent area of specialization within Canadian sociology. After several papers, his book *The Vertical Mosaic* (Porter, 1965) pointed up the differential advantage of Canadians as a function of the accident of their ethnic background, with the privileged Anglo-Saxon 'charter group' dominating the Canadian stratification hierarchy. A spate of works, their number continuing to grow, have joined Porter's, documenting the links among factors such as ethnic background, income, education, and social status.

Chapter Four is in this tradition. Gilbert and McRoberts discuss the several inputs which make up institutionalized inequality in Canada, particularly from the perspective of opportunities for social mobility or changes in social status. The chimera which has teased social philosophers and sociologists for centuries — the possibility of the ideally egalitarian and classless society — is evaluated in the chapter, and is a principal device whereby the authors contrast the reality of stratification in Canada with the breadth of what is theoretically possible in human relations.

Gilbert and McRoberts begin by sketching the theoretical origins of the study of stratification. They outline the work of Karl Marx, Max Weber, and the elitists, such as Vilfredo Pareto. They go on to distinguish differentiation or the division of labor in societies from institutionalized inequalities or social stratification. Data are presented which indicate that Canada is a markedly stratified society, with inequalities of condition and opportunity.

In Chapter Five, Guy Rocher specifically examines the part which the Canadian formal educational systems have had in contributing to and perpetuating social inequality. Formal educational systems in North America were supposedly designed to implement the fullest possible social opportunity for citizens. By educating oneself, one could achieve the profession and status to which one aspired. Yet, sociological research has conclusively demonstrated that the extent to which a child desires such education, and the extent to which the child is capable of attaining the performance levels expected by those in the school system, vary by social class. Lower class children have lower educational and occupational aspirations, do less well in school, are less likely to graduate from high school and go on to college, than are middle class children. This is so even when we eliminate any variable impact of intelligence. Inequalities in educational opportunity by ethnic groups are also considered, especially those between French Canadians inside and outside Quebec, and English Canadians.

Inequality demonstrated and related to the schools, Rocher turns the coin and considers the role of the educational system in effecting social change. The school system does afford some opportunities for social mobility for individuals, although it fails to alter the stratification system. He also notes that it is within the school system that many innovative challenges to the status quo are nurtured, and equalitarian ideologies sustained. He suggests that the convictions of educators and students are important inputs to social change in Canada.

Frank Vallee, in Chapter Six, takes up the matters of ethnic identity and institutionalized inequality vested in ethnic distinctions. The chapter, informed by a breadth of comparative illustrations, considers the conflict generated in multi-ethnic societies such as Canada. In the course of the analysis, it is made clear that the ethnic relations characteristic of Canadian society are in no sense uniquely Canadian. Perhaps more than any other, Vallee's point is that the strains and conflicts associated with ethnic group relations are a function of perceived inequalities, with disadvantaged or minority ethnic groups striving to redress a system of economic distribution to their advantage.

Vallee begins by reviewing the misunderstandings associated with the very concepts of ethnicity and ethnic groups. He then turns to a general description of the manner in which multi-ethnic societies such as Canada came to exist, and how they differ. The relations of ethnic groups to systems of inequality, including the Canadian, are examined in terms of how they are maintained and how they change. In this context, the alternative and complementary theoretical perspectives of the conflict, structural-functionalist and social psychological models, are appraised, and illustrated with Canadian information.

He then concludes with a discussion of the arguments and counter-arguments which have been posed in Canada for the maintenance of ethnic pluralism versus ethnic assimilation and a homogeneous sense of 'Canadianism,' noting that in Canada, although there is some evidence of a sentiment favoring 'multi-culturalism,' there is no satisfactory indication of any consensus on the part of Canadians.

The several themes related to inequality are brought together in Mildred Schwartz's keystone chapter dealing with citizen rights and inequality. A distinguishing feature of the chapter is its reference to policies or political actions which might cope with the inequalities in Canadian society. In the most fundamental sense, inequality in Canada is a political problem — a problem of citizenship — in that any rectification will involve the exercise of power. As William Gamson has noted, the exchange between those wielding legitimate, formal power or authority, and a public and its influence, is the inevitable dynamic of society. The shared discontent of the Canadian public coping with institutionalized inequalities, therefore, is the key to any social change which might act to alter the prevailing structure of inequality in Canadian society.

Schwartz works in the Weberian tradition introduced in Chapter Four. She emphasizes that inequality is not simply economic in nature. In particular, she focuses upon equality as a political issue, with politics viewed as fundamentally related to the distribution of scarce values. Power is the central concept in her analysis.

She discusses the meaning and impact of force, power and authority, and collective goals. The collective goals she explores relate to citizenship rights, and are political, civil, and social. The issue is the degree of equality of such rights in Canada.

Specific examples which she discusses include voting rights, representation in government (political rights), religious expression, linguistic expression (civil rights), access to educational institutions and social services (social rights). The extent and the manner in which these rights have been attained in Canada is the principal consideration of the chapter.

References

Gamson, William, *Power and Discontent*. Homewood, Ill.: The Dorsey Press, 1968.

Lynd, Robert, and Helen Lynd, *Middletown: A Study in American Culture*. New York: Harcourt, Brace and World, 1929.

——, *Middletown in Transition*. New York: Harcourt, Brace and World, 1937.

Warner, W. Lloyd, (with P.S. Lunt), *The Social Life of a Modern Community*. New Haven: Yale University Press, 1941.

——, *The Status System of a Modern Community*. New Haven: Yale University Press, 1942.

Warner, W. Lloyd, (with Leo Srole), *The Social Systems of American Ethnic Groups*. New Haven: Yale University Press, 1945.

Recommended Readings: Annotated

Breton, Raymond, *Social and Academic Factors in the Career Decisions of Youth*. Ottawa: Department of Manpower and Immigration and Information Canada, 1972.

To date, this is the most extensive published analysis of the social factors which affect the aspirations of young people in Canada, and thereby, their mobility.

Clement, Wallace, *The Canadian Corporate Elite: An Analysis of Economic Power*. Toronto: McClelland and Stewart, (The Carleton Library), 1975.

The concentration of economic power in Canada, and its impact on equality of condition and opportunity for Canadian citizens, is thoroughly explored and documented in this work.

Curtis, James, and William Scott (eds.), *Social Stratification in Canada.* Scarborough: Prentice-Hall of Canada, 1973.

The book examines the several facets of stratification in Canada. Included are papers on occupational structure, education, politics, ethnic groups, and the measurement of social status.

Dosman, Edgar, *Indians: The Urban Dilemma.* Toronto: McClelland and Stewart, 1972.

This book is a current account of different approaches to changing the system of inequality and injustice facing Canadian Indians. Chapter Eight is especially relevant.

Elliott, Jean (ed.), *Minority Canadians: 1. Native Peoples and Minority Canadians; 2. Immigrant Groups.* Scarborough: Prentice-Hall of Canada, 1971.

These two volumes assemble numerous essays describing the indigenous and immigrant ethnic groups which make up the Canadian multi-ethnic society.

Jencks, Christopher, *Inequality: A Reassessment of the Effect of Family and Schooling in America.* New York: Basic Books, 1972.

A contentious work, Jencks' book re-examines the accumulated data which relate social background variables to educational and occupational achievement. He argues that the American school system, even with recent reforms, has not reduced the degree of inequality in American society.

Harp, John, and John Hofley (eds.), *Poverty in Canada.* Scarborough: Prentice-Hall of Canada, 1971.

This collection of papers, including the work of sociologists, anthropologists, and economists, provides theoretical and empirical information regarding impoverished Canadians.

Kahl, Joseph, *The American Class Structure.* New York: Holt, Rinehart and Winston, 1957.

The reader wishing information about the nature of stratification in the United States can find no better single volume source, containing both data and analytical insight.

Manzer, Ronald, *Canada: A Socio-Political Report.* Toronto: McGraw-Hill Ryerson, 1974.

In this work, Manzer marshals a wealth of current data, and explores the extent to which the Canadian political system has permitted the satisfaction of what he considers basic human needs.

Porter, John, *The Vertical Mosaic.* Toronto: University of Toronto Press, 1965.

This is simply the most important work in Canadian sociology. Porter explores the institutionalized inequalities of Canadian society, and in particular the powers and privileges of Canada's elites.

CHAPTER FOUR

Differentiation and Stratification: The Issue of Inequality

Sid Gilbert, University of Winnipeg
Hugh A. McRoberts, Carleton University

Theoretical Overview

In sociology a persisting issue has been the nature of inequality and the nature and possibility of a 'classless' society. Traditional and contemporary social theorists have had uniquely distinct views depending upon their conception of class. The *Marxists,* with their emphasis upon the economic determination of social inequalities would answer 'yes,' a classless society is possible. Since, for them, classes were determined by private property, the abolition of private property would lead to a classless society. The *elite theorist* response to Marxian analysis was to note that in any society there had to be some ruling or governing body, and that this necessitated inequalities in political power. Similarly, Weber categorized inequalities as economic, political, and social and pointed out that even if economic inequalities were eliminated there might still be political and social inequalities.

The more contemporary debates surround the *functional theory of stratification.* The functionalists attempt to argue that stratification is functional to society and, therefore, necessary.

Pre-Marxist Views

Before Marx, discussion of the issue of social inequalities was largely carried on by theologians, philosophers, and economists. Their explanations of social inequalities had reference to the supernatural; to natural or biological differences among men; or to an ethical theory such as *utilitarianism* which has as its central premise seeking the greatest happiness for the greatest number.

91

Lenski indicates that the Hebrew prophets of the eighth century B.C., Amos, Micah, and Isiah, denounced a social order based upon extreme inequalities, luxury, and self-indulgence and demanded reform based upon their conception of a god who demanded justice, ethical behavior, moral and spiritual conformity. On the other hand, social inequalities have also been explained or justified by reference to the supernatural. In India, about 200 B.C., the Laws of Manu, a religious document, essentially posited social inequalities as divinely ordained. (Lenski, 1966:4-5) Similarly, the Greek philosophers, Plato and Aristotle, differed over the necessity of social inequalities. However, instead of appealing to the supernatural, they treated social inequalities as naturally, that is, biologically determined, ' ... I am myself reminded that we are not all alike; there are diversities of natures among us which are adapted to different occupations' (Plato, 1947: 128). Given these biological differences Plato advocated a division of labor based upon a differential distribution of power and authority but at the same time also favored the communal ownership of property, equality of material possessions, and equality of opportunity. Aristotle, however, took the position that all men were 'by nature' unequal, and hence, there was a natural rank order among men. In fact, Aristotle defended slavery and private property ownership and his position was, therefore, more supportive of social inequalities. We can contrast these approaches with a more sociological approach which stresses the relationship between social inequalities and social factors.

Marx on Social Class

The basis of Marx's theory of social classes and class conflict is rooted in his *thesis of historical materialism.** For Marx, society was dichotomized into two important segments: the mode of production and the superstructure. The *mode of production* was comprised of the *means of production,* that is, the resources, raw materials, technology and accompanying skills, and the (social) *relations of production,* which encompassed the division of labor, or occupational specialization, the system of ownership and the distribution of rewards, and the legal expression of these relations of production. The *superstructure* was composed of religion, ideology, and the state.

Social classes fit into this scheme as part of the relations of production

---

*This thesis is called 'historical materialism' because: it represents a theory of social change or evolution (i.e., historical); and it identifies the material or economic conditions of life as the underlying cause of this change (i.e., materialism).

and were viewed as largely determined by the means of production. Before going into the criteria Marx established for classes certain preliminary points should be made. First, Marx did not coin the term 'class,' nor discover the existence of classes, nor discover the conflict of classes. Marx himself makes the point:

> ... And now as to myself, no credit is due to me for discovering the existence of classes in modern society or the struggle between them. Long before me bourgeois historians had described the historical development of this class struggle and bourgeois economists the economic anatomy of the classes. What I did that was new was to prove: 1) that the *existence of classes* is only bound up with *particular historical phases in the development* of production, 2) that the class struggle necessarily leads to the *dictatorship of the proletariat*, 3) that this dictatorship itself only constitutes the transition to the *abolition of all classes* and to a *classless society* . . . *

Secondly, the term class was used by Marx in a far different sense than it is used today. Today *sociologists use class to mean institutionalized group differences in styles of living, wealth, income, education, occupation, and esteem or prestige*. In other words, the term class is used in the *distributive* sense, that is, as a characteristic that applies to each member of the class. Individuals have more or less of something, and in the research process sociologists measure this commodity, process or value, and place the individuals on a continuum. This ranking is then cut at certain points and the resulting groupings are usually referred to as classes. However, when created in this manner *the groupings are statistical artifacts*. They are a construct, a heuristic device in the head of a researcher as opposed to a real entity. In contrast, Marx used the term class in the *collective and political* sense. He was talking about properties of the class as a whole. (Jordan, 1971: 23) For example, when he said that the *proletariat* or workers were revolutionary, he meant that the proletariat as a class was revolutionary and not that each and every member of the proletariat was revolutionary. When class is used in this manner, in the collective sense, it denotes a real entity — an entity having causal efficacy. It does not simply denote a statistical artifact when used in this collective sense.

This distinction between using class in the distributive sense as opposed to using class in the collective sense leads to a distinction between a theory of *social stratification* and a theory of *social change*. As Dahrendorf (1959:19) has indicated, a theory of social stratification is a

---

*Karl Marx and Frederick Engels, *Selected Works* (New York: International Publishers, 1969a), p. 679.

description of society at a particular point in time, while a theory of social change would deal with a law of evolution. Since Marx used class as an analytical category, not a descriptive one, his theory of class and class conflict really represents a theory of social change and not a theory of social stratification.*

> Marx did not wish to formulate a universal theory of social class valid always and everywhere. His explicitly stated intention was to construct a theory applicable to an historical stage of social evolution and thus universal but only within a certain time-space or cultural region. (Jordan, 1971: 24)

Marx formulated his theory of social classes and class conflict based upon nineteenth century capitalism. We should not be surprised if this theory is less than adequate when treated as a universal theory of social stratification as it is in many introductory texts (Rossides, 1968; Reissman in Smelser, 1967, to cite just two) and in more advanced texts also (Barber, 1957; Lenski, 1966). Nevertheless if we reformulate Marx's theory as many have done we can create a reasonably accurate theory of stratification in nineteenth century capitalist societies.

Having made these three preliminary points, (1) that Marx did not discover classes and class conflict, (2) that Marx used 'class' in the collective sense as opposed to present sociological use in the distributive sense, and (3) that the theory of classes and class conflicts can more appropriately be considered as a theory of social change, we can now examine exactly what constitutes a Marxian class. The first criterion is *a common relationship to the means of production.* Ownership of the means of production (private property) is a prime determinant of class. We can contrast this with the present determinants of class. Source of revenue, that is, occupation and size of income, are major determinants of class status in modern usage. Marx, however, rejects source of revenue and size of revenue as determinants of class. Instead, he maintains that it is the organization of the productive system, and more importantly, the ownership versus non-ownership of the means of production, or private property, that constitutes a necessary condition for class formation. Thus Marx distinguished the *proletariat,* or workers, and the *bourgeoisie,* the owners of capital, the means of production. Speaking of the workers, Marx, in the *Poverty of Philosophy,* said:

---

*Those who argue this way usually point out that if Marx was interested in *describing* the existing distribution of goods he would have utilized and emphasized more of a multi-class model than a two-class model. Although there is evidence of a multi-class model in the historical writings of Marx, (i.e., 'The 18th Brumaire of Louis Bonaparte' and 'The Class Struggles of France 1848-1850'), the *emphasis* is clearly on a two-class model which is more suitable to an explanation of social change.

The domination of capital created the common situation and common interests of this class. Thus, this mass is already a class in relation to capital, but not yet a class for itself.*

and in another passage

'Vulgar' common sense turns class differences into differences in the size of one's purse, and class conflict into a quarrel between handicrafts. The size of one's purse is a purely quantitative difference, by which two individuals of the *same* class may be *brought into conflict*. It is well known that the medieval *guilds* opposed each other on the basis of *handicraft differences*. But it is equally well known that modern class differences are not in any way based upon handicraft differences, and that, on the contrary, the division of labor produces very *diverse* occupations within the *same* class. (1969b: 208)

This relationship to the means of production is only a necessary but not a sufficient condition for the existence of a class for itself. Common relationship to the means of production creates a *class in itself* but *not for itself*. A class for itself has two more defining characteristics.

The second criterion is *class consciousness*. By virtue of sharing the same relationship to the means of production *the working class has certain 'objective' interests in common and becomes aware of its opposition to the dominating class*. Therefore, a class manifests class consciousness and social cohesion: an awareness of (1) its common relationship to the system of production, its common interests and (2) its common opposition to an exploiting class. The conditions that facilitated this class consciousness among the proletariat were the alienating aspect of the division of labor, the increasing concentration of the workers in factories and in urban areas, the resulting ease of communications between them, and an increase in the size of the working class.

The third criterion of a class for Marx is *political action*. The proletariat enters into a conflict with the dominating class. In this regard, Marx noted in *The German Ideology:*

The separate individuals form a class only in so far as they have to carry on a common battle against another class ... (1947: 48-49)

In *The 18th Brumaire of Louis Bonaparte,* Marx stated that:

In so far as millions of families live under economic conditions of existence that separate their mode of life, their interests and their culture from those of the other classes, and put them in hostile opposition to the latter, they form a

*From *Karl Marx: Selected Writings in Sociology and Social Philosophy,* T.B. Bottomore and Maximilien Rubel (London: C.A. Watts, 1956). We have used the Penguin Books edition, 1969b, p. 195.

class. In so far as there is merely a local interconnection among these small-holding peasants, and the identity of their interests begets no community, no national bond and no political organization among them, they do not form a class. (1969a: 172)

The existence of a 'community' and a 'national bond' refers to the criterion of class consciousness or social cohesiveness previously mentioned. Here we are concerned with the criterion of political action. *Marx maintained that all class struggles were political struggles.* Only when a class organizes and engages in political activity does it finally become a class for itself – a Marxian class; a class competing for power. In gross terms, then, the above represents the characteristics of a Marxian class. To further develop these and other matters germane to the Marxian theory of class and class conflict, the details of the revolutionary process should be mentioned.

It is in the 'Preface to a Contribution to the Critique of Political Economy' that Marx (1969a) most explicitly formulates the materialist conception that underlies the conflict of social classes. Marx notes that at a certain stage of evolution the material forces of production come into conflict with the existing relations of production. Or in other terms, technology comes into conflict with the property relations, in this case, bourgeois ownership of property.

In *Capital* Marx (1967) puts forward a *labor theory of value,* taken over from Ricardo but modified. Here Marx argues that the value or price of a commodity represents only the labor expended in its production. Capitalists make a profit because by virtue of their position as employers they are able to extract more labor from the worker than that for which they pay him. This surplus represents their profit. To Marx, it also represents exploitation of one class by another. Furthermore, as the system develops, the large capitalists beat the small capitalists, and capital and wealth become increasingly concentrated. This increasing concentration of capital, and increasing mechanization (the new technology), means that the demand for labor is reduced. In other words, capital or machines replace the worker. In addition, the supply of workers is increased because now women and children are drawn into the productive process. The result is an *industrial reserve army* – an army of unemployed. This increases competition for jobs and lowers the wages of those employed. Marx suggested that it also brought into being a class, a revolutionary class, a universal class (the proletariat), who would be the 'grave-diggers' of capitalist society. But prior to revolution, the result of these changes is increasing poverty, or as Marx called it, *pauperism.* This process is referred to as the *Law of Increasing Misery.*

In the 'Manifesto of the Communist Party,' Marx (1969a) goes into greater detail on how this process of class struggle begins as individuals confront the industrial bourgeois, then factory workers, then local trades people. At this stage they do not attack the bourgeois themselves, but they attack and destroy factories and machines. At this stage they also attack the landowners, the non-industrial bourgeois, the petty bourgeois.

Then with increasing misery, increasing size, increasing concentration in factories and cities, increasing communication, an ever-expanding union of workers is formed. Class consciousness and political cohesiveness develop. The struggle intensifies, becomes violent, and a segment of the ruling class cuts itself adrift and joins the proletariat. The final outcome is the overthrow of the bourgeoisie.

Marx believed that a *classless* society would emerge out of the revolution rather than merely a society with a new elite. The proletariat was to be the new general representative of a society in which the bourgeoisie had historically represented all the evils of society. In short, you have one liberating class, *par excellence,* overcoming one oppressing class.

MARX IN RETROSPECT

There are a number of ways to evaluate a theory, such as internal consistency, logical adequacy, external consistency, and experience. In evaluating Marx's theory of class and class conflict, we suggest that the criterion of experience be applied. That is, examine the predictions based on the theory and consider whether or not these predictions have been falsified or have been confirmed. On the whole if we produce a box-score of Marx's predictions we arrive at the following:

Incorrect	*Correct*
1. the law of increasing misery	1. the increasing concentration of capital
2. the polarization of classes	2. the pervasiveness of class conflict
3. revolution in capitalist society	3. the importance of technology in social change
4. disappearance of intermediate classes	4. the correspondence between economic and political power
5. classless society	

Most of the incorrect predictions can be directly traced to Marx's failure to estimate correctly the role of technology in generating new positions. Although he recognized that on the one hand industrialization increased the demand for labor and on the other increased the supply of labor, he overemphasized the latter process. We now know that industrialization creates a far greater demand for labor than was originally supposed: but not manual labor. Industrialization necessitates labor in the sense of skilled, trained, educated labor. It opens up a whole new range of positions requiring greater technical training. Hence the outcome was not a huge industrial reserve army as Marx prophesied but a large middle class, who were rewarded appropriately for their increased technical knowledge. Thus in our view the main flaw in Marx's law of increasing misery appears to be his incorrect assessment of the effect of industrialization upon the occupational structure.

MARX AND STRATIFICATION

Although we have been dealing with Marx's theory of social classes and class conflict as a theory of social change rather than a theory of social stratification, it is possible to interpret Marx's work, or to use it, as a theory of social stratification. However, one should then not be surprised if many problems and deficiencies occur. In the first place, Marx examined a capitalistic society, and therefore if we ask of his theory 'Who gets what and why?' we should expect the answer to be applicable only to capitalist societies. Secondly, the two questions: 'Who gets what and why?' and 'What provides the impetus for structural change in a society?' are not the same questions. Hence, a poor answer to the first question may be a good answer or at least a better answer to the second question.

In any case, if one had to transform the Marxian theory of social classes and class conflict into a theory of social inequality the results would resemble the following:

(1) In capitalist society goods are distributed on the basis of power.
(2) The most important (not the only) source of power in capitalist society is economic.
(3) Therefore, those with economic power receive the rewards and surplus produced by the society.
(4) They receive a disproportionate share of the society's production because they exploit those who do not possess economic power.
(5) The economic elite prevents the oppressed majority from realizing their true situation by creating and supporting: (a) an ideology of individualism; (b) a social structure that resists redistribution of power and hence a redistribution of rewards or surplus.

Classes, Parties, Status Groups

It has always been said that the German sociologist Max Weber wrote his major works in reaction to Marx. Weber's disagreement with Marxist theory centered on four essential topics: a greater separation of political and economic power; capitalism versus bureaucracy as the prime cause of alienation; the emphasis on the independence of ideas as opposed to Marxian historical materialism; and the goodness of socialism. Many have treated Weber's writings on power and stratification as a refutation of Marx but they are more appropriately labelled as a modification and an extension of the Marxian approach. Whereas Marx emphasized economic power, Weber separated political from economic power and introduced social power.

For Weber a society is differentiated into three important sectors: economic, political, and social. The distribution of economic power in a society creates *classes;* the distribution of political power in a society creates *parties;* and the distribution of social power in a society creates *status groups* (Weber, 1968). Making this distinction we can see why Weber is pessimistic about socialism. If economic power, that is property differences, were eliminated there would still be a differentiated system based upon political and social power. The political bureaucracies of a socialist society would be just as alienating as the economic bureaucracies of a capitalist system.

Diagramatically, the Weberian framework can be presented as in Figure I.

Figure 1: Weber's Classification of Power

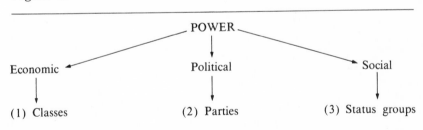

First, *Weber agrees with Marx that classes are economically determined and that property and lack of property are the basic categories of all class situations.* However, instead of treating property and the absence of property as a dichotomy as Marx does, Weber treats property as a continuum of a range of economic situations. Weber, then, is using class in the *distributive* sense rather than in the collective sense as does Marx. Furthermore, Weber differentiates between 'economically conditioned' power and power *per se.* Individuals may seek power not only to enhance themselves economically but also for its own sake. Weber also disagrees with Marx about the inevitability of political action on the part of the proletariat. Marx, it is remembered, stated that the increasing misery of the workers would lead to class consciousness and eventually, inevitably, revolution. Weber, however, maintains that communal action *may* result from class interests, but not *necessarily*. Furthermore, that action is not necessarily directed against the bourgeoisie. In the light of experience Weber seems to have made the more appropriate analysis regarding this particular point. Economic interests did not give rise to massive communal actions by social classes in capitalist societies.

Weber's famous statement regarding political power is that 'parties live in a house of "power."' Parties then, for Weber, represent collectivities struggling for political power. They are competing for social domination. They *may be* founded on classes or status but they need not be. Again this position may be contrasted with the Marxian position that defined classes in terms of political action.

Status groups are formed by the distribution of *social honor*. But on what basis is social honor awarded? Although Weber does not answer this question clearly and unambiguously he does give some suggestions, beginning with the suggestion that honor or prestige are linked to economic position.

> ... class distinctions are linked in the most varied ways with status distinctions. Property as such is not always recognized as a status qualification, but in the long run it is — and with extraordinary regularity.*

But in addition persons are accorded honor by virtue of their particular style of life, education, birth or family background, or occupation. Groups of such individuals may come to be distinguishable as strata or status groups. Such a style of life might include the avoidance of work or pursuit of economic gain, endogamous marriages, and exclusive rituals.

Weber, it can be seen, has *not* elaborated a new and comprehensive theory of social stratification. Instead he has made a number of useful distinctions which when added to the modified Marxian approach discussed above begin to develop a more universal approach to the distribution of social inequalities. Weber's conception of power as heterogeneous, ubiquitous and residing in all organizations rather than merely economic organizations indicates that *the distribution of power, either economic, political, or social, may be the key independent (causal) variable in a theory of the distribution of material and social inequalities.* We can now see that even if private property ownership is abolished and economic power is held by the people in common through the state,

*Max Weber, 'Class, Status, Party,' in H.H. Gerth and C. Wright Mills (eds.), *From Max Weber* (New York: Oxford University Press, 1968), p. 187.

differences in the political power of groups, occupational or otherwise, may lead to material or social inequalities. Thus the society would be 'classless' in the Marxian sense but not 'partyless' in the Weberian sense and not devoid of social inequalities.

Elite Theorists

Another critique of Marx is that of the elite theorists who attack Marx's prediction of a classless society on the political level by noting that in any society there has always been a ruling or governing class and a non-governing class. Therefore, a classless society is impossible. They also disagree with Marx's treatment of the ruling class as closed to those whose origins are not in the ruling class. Thirdly, the elite theorists note that the change in society is cyclical rather than revolutionary.

PARETO

Pareto (1970), like Marx, made a basic division in society. Marx's distinction was an economic one between the bourgeoisie and the proletariat — the owners and the workers. Pareto's division was between the *elite, those who had achieved the pinnacle of success* in their field of endeavour, and the *non-elite* or the *masses*. This distinction was largely a political one. Pareto further divided the elite into the *governing elite* (those who exercised political power) and the *non-governing elite*. It was Pareto's contention that, contrary to the Marxian position that the ruling class was closed, it was open and that there was a circulation of the more talented or gifted individuals from the non-elite to the elite.

In addition to refuting the Marxian position of the closed ruling class, Pareto's concept of the *Circulation of Elites* represents an attack on the Marxian notion of an inevitable revolution and a revolution by the masses. Instead, Pareto is suggesting that social change is cyclical rather than revolutionary. The general state of society is such that the elite can maintain their rule by (1) force and fraud, and (2) the circulation of elites (or the co-opting of the more talented members of the lower class or non-elite).

The elite need these new members for two basic reasons according to Pareto. First, the elite have a tendency to decline in quantity. They do not reproduce themselves in proportion to the general increase in the population. Secondly, the elite have a tendency to decline in quality as well as quantity. That is to say, according to Pareto they lose the psychological characteristics that are necessary to stay in power such as the requisite ruthlessness. Therefore, the elite must strengthen itself by admitting the members of the non-elite that have these desirable psychological characteristics.

MOSCA

Mosca (1970) also utilized a two-fold division but in different terms: a division between the ruling class and the ruled — the masses. Again in contradiction to Marx, Mosca and the elite theorists in general are approaching the problem of a classless society from the political side. The elite theorists were emphasizing political power as opposed to Marx's emphasis on economic power.

Mosca was basically contending that in any society, regardless of the economic and political structure, whether it be feudalism, capitalism, monarchy, oligarchy, democracy, or even a dictatorship, a distinction can always be made between the rulers and the ruled. Why? First, according to Mosca, because the masses are incapable of ruling themselves. Secondly, because a minority is organized and able to exert power over the unorganized masses. Thirdly, because man has an innate need to be governed.

What is the nature of this ruling class? First, it is a minority and is organized. Secondly, as does Pareto, Mosca notes that members of the ruling class do share certain psychological characteristics, such as ambition, capacity for hard work, and intelligence. However, Mosca does not emphasize these psychological characteristics as much as does Pareto. Also Mosca recognized that to a certain extent these are *socially produced* and are not just innate attributes.

Another characteristic of the ruling class is that it maintains itself. The best way to become a member of it is to be born into it. The nature of this class is also revealed when Mosca deals with the relationship between the ruling class and the masses, or deals with the rise and fall of elites. A ruling class rules because it is able to dominate the major 'social forces' operating within a particular society. A 'social force' is an activity or function important for the maintenance of a particular society. New elites develop when new social forces develop, and, if these elites are not admitted to the ruling class they constitute a revolutionary threat. Thus, in explaining the rise and fall of elites, Mosca does not deal exclusively with psycholgical characteristics or the loss of psychological characteristics by the elite as did Pareto. Notice that this position is not very far from some contemporary writers. Porter (1965) would call these elites dominating the major social forces 'functionally specific' elites, Keller (1968) would call them 'strategic' elites and Galbraith (1967) has referred to one such elite as the 'technostructure.'

Mosca's notion that the elites control the major 'social forces' in a society is similar, but *not identical,* to Marx's position on class interests. But it is broader — taking into consideration not just economically determined interests but moral and religious interests. These would be independent social forces and not just a reflection of the economic structure as Marx maintained. Finally, the ruling class governs by what Mosca refers to as a *'political formula'* — *or an ideology that legitimates its rule.* This can be based upon the supernatural or upon concepts which appear to be rational.

Perhaps Mosca's major contribution was the conception that individual freedom or civil liberties as we refer to them today, are safeguarded by the existence of countervailing forces in a society. Mosca considered as superior the political system that best insures, as he called it, 'juridical defense' or *de facto* justice, not just formal justice as stated in laws and constitutions. The best system was one that clearly separated the social forces in society so that no one class held all the power. In this way, the power of each elite checked the power of the other elites. Based on this theory Mosca advocated a separation of: (a) temporal or secular authority, (b) ecclesiastical authority, (c) economic power, (d) military power. The consequences of any concentration of these forces is repression by a more powerful oligarchy. Given the above statement, we can see why Mosca would oppose the Marxian position. This pluralism of elites as the safeguard of individual rights has become a contemporary issue and will not be dealt with any further here. Suffice it to say that those who follow the Marxian position stress a unification of elites under the dominant economic elite and those who follow a pluralistic position stress a system of countervailing elites with no one dominant on all issues.

MICHELS

Another elite theorist, Robert Michels, makes a similar case. Michels formulated the *Iron Law of Oligarchy* which may be captured in the phrase 'Who says organization, says oligarchy' (Michels, 1966: 365). Michels' basic point was that *the need for organization,* be it in a political party, a church group, or a state, *necessitates some form of hierarchical decision-making arrangement where some members, a minority, exercise authority on behalf of the group.* Thus, inequalities in political power are inevitable.

Overview

The elite theorist critique and the Marxist position need not be seen as mutually exclusive theoretical frameworks. Instead, much of the elite analysis could be accommodated within a Marxist position and can actually serve to remedy and round out the Marxian theory of class and class conflict. For example, the elite position can illustrate why the proletariat did not become the grave-diggers of capitalist society. They indeed did become a social force with their own elite which was accommodated within the existing economic structure.

But apart from its contribution in this regard the elite perspective is valuable in analyzing the distribution of goods and services in diverse societies. It may be the case that before a truly egalitarian society can emerge much more must be considered than the economic system. In other words, abolition of private property is likely only a necessary but not a sufficient condition for complete equality of condition. The distribution of political power must also be considered.

As we have seen, Marx's concern was with economic inequalities, Weber conceptually separated economic from political and social inequalities and Mosca, Pareto, and Michels discussed the necessity for certain political inequalities within any society. We now turn to the more contemporary debate surrounding the *functional theory of stratification* which leads us directly to the development of a conceptual framework for discussing stratification, inequalities, and differentiation in Canada.

The Functional Theory of Stratification

The Davis-Moore article, 'Some Principles of Stratification' (1970) presents the functionalist case. Their argument proceeds as follows: Certain positions in society are functionally more important than others and require special skills for their performance. However, society only has limited talent available to fill these positions and the conversion of this talent to skill requires special training which involves sacrifices. Therefore, differential rewards are necessary to encourage people to fill these positions and hence stratification results, i.e., *stratification is both functional and inevitable.* Notice that stratification is defined as inequality: 'If the rights and prerequisites of different positions in a society must be unequal, then the society must be stratified, because that is precisely what stratification means.' (Davis and Moore, 1970: 370).

Melvin M. Tumin (1970) has pointed out that there are some important difficulties encountered in such a theory. First, the concept of certain positions being functionally more important may be called into question. Secondly, the stratification system provides built-in obstacles to the discovery of talent and, therefore, may be viewed as dysfunctional; people from lower strata do not have the same opportunity for training. Thirdly, in some cases it is not the person who is undergoing training who must sacrifice, but his or her parents. A fourth defect Tumin sees is that the theory has neglected alternative motivational schemes such as intrinsic work satisfaction and social duty. Fifthly, when Davis and Moore state that differential rewards constitute strata they fail to realize that it cannot be demonstrated that it is unavoidable that differential prestige and esteem shall accrue to positions which command differential rewards in property and power. Finally, when Davis and Moore conclude that stratification is functional and inevitable they neglect the point that the only items which society must distribute unequally are the power and property necessary for the performance of the different tasks. In other words, if these are viewed as necessary to execute the responsibility of the position (as resources not rewards) then no prestige and esteem need follow. Historically, however, power and property have tended to produce prestige and esteem. But this cannot establish the inevitability of the phenomenon.

Wesolowski (1966) notes another defect of the functional theory as expressed in the Davis and Moore article. He states the functionalist thesis in three points:

(1) stratification is a functional necessity and therefore is inevitable;
(2) stratification is a functional necessity because society needs a mechanism to motivate people to occupy positions which are socially important and require training;
(3) stratification does this — it insures that the most qualified people fill these positions. (Wesolowski, 1966: 64)

Wesolowski states that Davis and Moore eventually withdrew the third point because of the criticism of Tumin and others. These criticisms Wesolowski summarizes as follows:

(a) ascribed statuses are overlooked;
(b) not all those who have equal ability have equal opportunity to acquire training;
(c) not all those who have equal training have equal opportunity to acquire these positions.

Therefore, Wesolowski concentrates on the core of the theory as expressed in points 1 and 2 above. The core of the functional approach is a theory of motivation that states that striving for high income and high prestige is an indispensable and principal motive which drives people to seek the positions. Yet, this is obviously not true of societies where statuses were ascribed or inherited. The question then becomes: does it hold true where statuses are achieved? The answer is 'no.' According to behavioral psychology people will not automatically seek material goods and prestige. Their motives depend on their socialization. In addition, authority or power may be a sufficient reward by itself, rather than material gain and prestige.

Other comment is offered by Buckley (1961). He notes that Tumin's critique of the Davis and Moore article dealt with content only, whereas he points out a basic conceptual flaw. The basic issue, Buckley contends, is that the functional theory of stratification would be more correctly considered as a theory of 'certain aspects of social differentiation and hierarchical organization.'* *Davis and Moore have incorrectly identified stratification as different positions (differentiation) whereas most sociologists would treat stratification as the existence of strata that persist over several generations,* continuing ' ... to occupy the same relative positions and to receive the same relative amounts of material ends, prestige, and power.' (Buckley, 1961: 479) The strata have a historical continuity implying 'stratum permanence' and 'hereditary inequality' and not merely the achieved inequality emphasized by Davis and Moore.

Buckley points to a distinction between stratification and differentiation that Davis and Moore have missed.

> If we can agree that the term 'social strata' refers to social groups or collectivities, and not positions, and that stratification refers to the existence of strata in a society, then perhaps we should logically insist that stratification be defined in terms of groups or collectivities, not positions. (Buckley, 1961: 481)

Social stratification would, therefore, be the existence of a graded hierarchy of continuous social groups rather than as Davis and Moore hold the existence of a graded hierarchy of social positions.

Some Analytical Distinctions

The debate surrounding the functional theory of stratification is fruitful in that it leads to a number of conceptual distinctions which clarify preceding debates and show that some of the participants in these debates have been arguing at cross purposes. These distinctions reveal that there have been logically separate dimensions associated with 'stratification' which tend to be empirically related.

SOCIAL DIFFERENTIATION
First, we must consider *social differentiation* as a distinct issue. Although actors can be differentiated on a number of bases the differentiation referred to here is *role differentiation or the division of labor.* In every society, actors perform different occupational tasks in connection with the production, distribution, and consumption of a society's goods and services. Associated with these tasks are certain performance expecta-

*Walter Buckley, 'Social Stratification and the Functional Theory of Social Differentiation,' in S.M. Lipset and N.J. Smelser (eds.), *Sociology: The Progress of a Decade* (Englewood Cliffs: Prentice-Hall Inc., 1961).

tions, certain behavioral norms and some level of authority necessary to discharge the responsibilities of the position. At the same time there have tended to be differential rewards associated with these positions. This is the problematical aspect. We maintain that *there is no necessary connection between the degree of differentiation and the extent or necessity of social inequalities.* In fact, in western societies where social inequalities are firmly established there are numerous complex, highly technical positions which go relatively unrewarded with regard to income. The position of the academic is a good example of this. These people are typically paid considerably less than persons with similar or even less training working in government or the private sector. Critics are usually willing to concede the fact that these positions may go relatively unrewarded in a material sense but have a high prestige or non-material reward component. This prestige or subjective reward depends upon the value structure of the particular society. We would contend that the values held by individuals are the result of their socialization and that furthermore, there is nothing inherent in human nature compelling individuals to differentially evaluate differentiated tasks and positions. In other words, people learn to make these invidious distinctions. Under a different structural system, different normative and value orientations, this differential evaluation need not occur. In any case, *social differentiation does not imply the necessity of material inequalities.*

SOCIAL INEQUALITIES

A separate analytical topic relates to the nature, the extent, and the consistency of the social inequalities themselves. Social inequalities may take various forms. They may be material (income or wealth) or non-material (esteem, prestige, social honor). Following Weber, *the forms of inequality may also be classified as economic, political or social.* In addition to the nature of the inequalities a researcher may be interested in the extent of the inequalities, either *cross-sectionally* (at one point in time) or *longitudinally* (over several time periods). Finally, one may be interested in the extent to which these inequalities overlap. Ranking high on certain dimensions may be associated with ranking high on other dimensions. Or these separate forms of inequality may be only loosely related. This is referred to as the consistency of the various dimensions of inequality.

STRATIFICATION

A third separate topic is the extent of stratification in a society. *We define stratification as the intergenerational persistence of social status, not as the existence of material inequalities.* Thus a society may have inequalities but as long as there is full equality of opportunity to become unequal it is not a stratified society. It only becomes stratified when strata perpetuate themselves, that is, when a son's adult social status is determined by his origin status (his father's social status). An unstratified society, in these terms, would be one where a son's origin status does not determine adult status. On the other hand, the greater the correlation between a father's social status and a son's adult status, the greater the stratification.

Theoretical Summary

In answer to the question presented at the beginning of this chapter concerning the possibility of a classless society we can now see that various social theorists have had divergent opinions depending upon their conception of class. Marxists, who emphasize economic causes of social inequalities, would answer in the affirmative. If private property were abolished and everyone shared the same relationship to the means of production a classless society would emerge. In the light of the Weberian modification to the Marxian position and in the light of the elite theorist critique it is evident that in any society there still must be some differential distribution of political power and thus at least this one kind of social inequality.

Stratification in Canada

Out of the controversy surrounding the functional theory emerged a number of useful distinctions between social differentiation, social inequality, and social stratification. These distinctions will form the basis of a conceptual framework which will be developed and applied in analyzing Canadian society.

We will first discuss social differentiation in the context of the Canadian labor force. Secondly, we will look at the three main forms of inequality: power, income, and prestige. Finally, we will examine the nature of opportunity in Canada as it relates to the formation of strata in Canadian society.

Social Differentiation in Canada

Within the context of modern industrial societies, the form of social differentiation may, in a sense, be regarded as a nucleus around which stratification occurs. It is not, however, as we have noted above, the stratification system itself. To consider it to be so would be to make an error of the same sort as confusing the building in which a bureaucracy works with the bureaucracy. All this is not to say that the study of the forms of social differentiation is not relevant to the study of stratification, but rather to point out as emphatically as possible that they are not stratification in and of themselves.

The major aspect of social differentiation with which we will be concerned is the *structure of the labor force*. There are two reasons for this. First, the major way in which work is accomplished in a modern industrial society, with the significant exception of housework, is through paid participation in the labor force. Secondly, due to the close association between income, prestige, and power, and occupation within the labor force, occupation has for most members of society, with the exception of the extremely wealthy, become probably the best single indicator of a person's position in the class structure.

Since the beginning of this century, there have been three major changes in the structure of the Canadian labor force:

(1) The increasing rate of labor force participation by women;
(2) The decline in agricultural employment;
(3) The decline of the blue collar worker sector and the corresponding growth of the white collar sector.

We will now look briefly at each of these changes.

Table I presents the labor force participation rates by age and sex for Canada from 1901 to 1961. The data show a very clear increase in the gross participation rate for women throughout the period from 14.8 per cent in 1901 to 26.3 per cent in 1961. This increase is perhaps more striking when we consider that in the same period the male participation rate dropped by almost ten percentage points and that the major factors in this drop would tend to have an equal effect on both males and females. As can be seen from the male portion of the table, the major changes in male participation occur in the age group 14-19 and the age group of 65 and over. The change in the former group is a function of increasing participation rates in education, and of rising minimum school leaving ages. This clearly affects both males and females within this age range to much the same degree. The change within the latter age group is a function of the increasing application of a compulsory retirement age of 65. Again there is little reason to believe that this change would have a differential impact on males and females.

Figure 2 shows the growth of the male and female labor forces during the period from 1901 to 1961. As can be seen, the rate of growth of the female segment of the labor force has been considerably more rapid than that for males. Indeed, this difference is such that in the period 1951 to 1961 more females have entered the labor force than men. Thus, the increase in female labor force participation is apparently a long-term trend.

Given this increasing participation on the part of females, the interesting question becomes one of where they are fitting into the division of labor. Table II shows the changes by selected occupational categories in female participation. The data show a slight decline in female participation in both the manufacturing and service sectors, coupled with a slight rise relative to males in the transportation and communication industries. In general, however, these changes have been

Table I: Percentage Distribution of the Labor Force, by Age and Sex, 1902-61*

Year	Total, both Sexes [a]	Total	Under 20	20–24	25–34	35–64	65 and Over
			Males				
1901	100.0	85.2	—	—	—	—	—
1911	100.0	85.1	—	—	—	—	—
1921	100.0	83.0	10.3	9.9	20.3	38.7	3.7
1931	100.0	81.4	9.0	10.6	18.8	39.0	4.0
1941	100.0	79.8	7.9	10.2	19.3	38.5	3.9
1951[b]	100.0	77.7	6.3	9.3	19.2	39.0	3.9
1961[b]	100.0	73.6	5.3	8.1	18.2	39.1	2.9
1951[c]	100.0	77.8	6.3	9.3	19.3	39.0	3.9
1961[c]	100.0	73.7	5.4	8.1	18.1	39.1	2.9
			Females				
1901	100.0	14.8	—	—	—	—	—
1911	100.0	14.9	—	—	—	—	—
1921	100.0	17.0	4.3	4.3	3.8	4.1	0.4
1931	100.0	18.6	4.1	5.2	4.3	4.6	0.4
1941	100.0	20.2	3.8	5.2	5.3	5.5	0.5
1951[b]	100.0	22.3	3.9	5.0	5.2	7.8	0.4
1961[b]	100.0	26.4	4.0	4.4	5.3	12.1	0.6
1951[c]	100.0	22.2	3.9	5.0	5.2	7.7	0.4
1961[c]	100.0	26.3	4.1	4.5	5.2	12.0	0.6

[a] Ages 10 and over for 1901-31; ages 14 and over for 1941-61.
[b] Excludes Newfoundland.
[c] Includes Newfoundland.

*Source: Denton, *The Growth of Manpower in Canada* (Ottawa: Queen's Printer, 1967), p. 54, Table 18. Reproduced by permission of Information Canada.

Figure 2:   Growth of the Labor Force, 1901-1961*

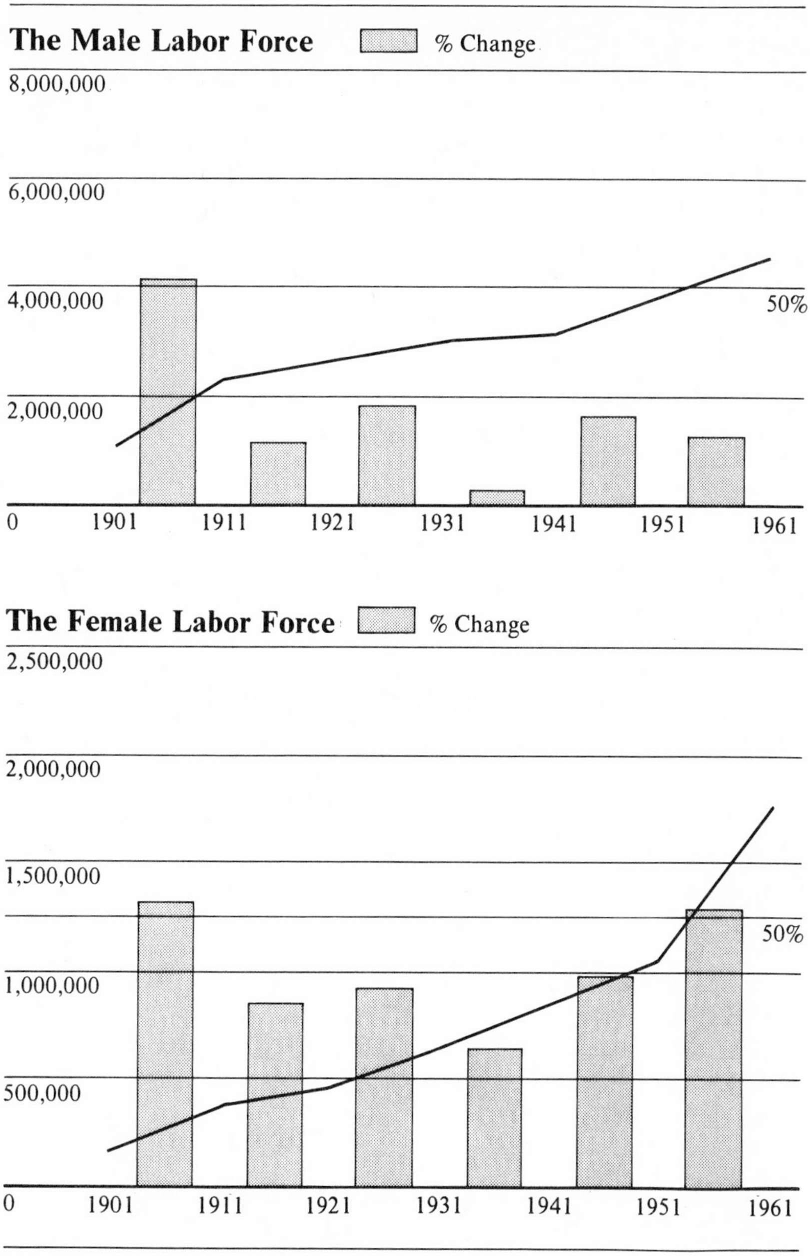

The Male Labor Force   % Change

The Female Labor Force   % Change

*Source: Department of Labour, *Manpower Trends in Canada* (Ottawa: Queen's Printer, 1965), pp. 8-9. Reproduced by permission of Information Canada.

**Table II: Percentage Female Labor Force Participation by
Selected Occupational Categories, 1901-1961***

	1901	*1961*
White collar	20.6	41.3
Professional	42.5	43.2
Clerical	22.1	61.5
Sales	10.4	36.7
Manufacturing	24.8	16.8
Transportation and communications	1.4	7.9
Service	68.6	57.1

*Source: Department of Labour, *Manpower Trends in Canada* (Ottawa: Queen's Printer, 1965).
Reproduced by permission of Information Canada.

small. When we look at the remainder of the table it becomes abundantly clear where women have been absorbed into the labor force: it has been in the white collar sector where the growth in female participation has been of the order of 100 per cent from 1901 to 1961. Further, it is clear that while women have made considerable inroads into the selling occupations and have come to dominate clerical occupations, they have in sixty years made no significant inroads into the professional occupations. This has occurred, as well, despite the previously noted differential rate of increase in labor force participation.

In short, it is clear that in the Canadian labor force there is a marked sexual component to the division of labor, and that women who work are predominatly allocated to white collar, non-professional roles. The reasons why this allocation occurs are not at this point in time either clear or generally agreed upon; however, we may to some extent attribute these effects to both differential socialization with respect to achievement, and to different norms governing labor force participation.

Table III shows that there has been a sharp decline in the proportion of the labor force engaged in agriculture in the period from 1931 to 1961. Overall, the decline has been from 28.8 per cent in 1931 to 10.2 per cent in 1961. However, it will be noticed that most of the change has occurred in the period from 1941, when the proportion in agriculture was 25.8 per cent of the labor force, to 1951 when the proportion was 15.9 per cent. These changes represent the final phases of a rural-urban shift which saw Canada begin this century with 65 per cent of its population living in rural areas and with 40 per cent of its labor force engaged in agriculture, and move to a point where 70 per cent of its population in 1961 is living in urban areas, and 10 per cent of the labor force is engaged in agriculture.

Table III shows that two groups in the labor force have undergone substantial changes in the period from 1931 to 1961. The white collar group has increased from 24.4 per cent of the labor force in 1931 to 38.6 per cent of the labor force in 1961. When we look at the changes within

Table III: Labor Force[a] by Occupational Group, 1931-1961*

	1931	1941	1951	1961
Occupational Group		*percentages*		
White Collar	24.4	25.2	32.5	38.6
Managerial and proprietary	5.6	5.4	7.5	7.9
Professional	6.1	6.7	7.4	10.0
Clerical	6.6	7.2	10.9	12.9
Commercial and financial	6.1	5.9	6.7	7.8
Manual	33.8	33.4	37.6	34.9
Manufacturing and mechanical	11.5	16.0	17.4	16.4
Construction	4.7	4.7	5.6	5.3
Laborers[b]	11.3	6.3	6.7	5.4
Transportation and communication	6.3	6.4	7.9	7.8
Service	9.3	10.5	8.6	10.8
Personal	8.3	9.3	7.3	9.3
Protective	1.0	1.2	1.3	1.5
Primary	32.5	30.6	20.1	13.1
Agriculture	28.8	25.8	15.9	10.2
Fishing and hunting	1.2	1.2	1.0	0.6
Logging	1.0	1.9	1.9	1.3
Mining	1.5	1.7	1.3	1.0
Not stated in census	—	0.3	1.2	2.6
Total	100.0	100.0	100.0	100.0
All occupations, number (000's)	3,922	4,196	5,215	6,342

[a] 1931-1951, 14 years of age and over; 1961, 15 years of age and over. Includes Newfoundland in 1951 and 1961, but excludes Yukon and Northwest Territories for all years.
[b] Except in agriculture, fishing, logging, and mining.

*Source: John Porter, *Canadian Social Structure,* (1967), p. 93, Table E6. Reprinted by permission of The Canadian Publishers, McClelland and Stewart Limited, Toronto, the Carleton Library Board, and Information Canada.

this group, two points become clear. First, most of the growth is confined to two categories of workers, the professional workers, and the clerical workers. Secondly, most of the change has occurred since 1941.

The data in Table IV show that, while all categories of the service sector of industry (this sector tends to employ more white collar than blue collar workers) have shown a growth of 87 per cent in the period from 1946 to 1963, the secondary manufacturing sector has shown a growth of only 44 per cent in the same time period. When we consider this in conjunction with the slight decrease in the proportion of manufacturing and mechanical workers from 1951 to 1961, then the suggestion that there is a trend towards a decline in blue collar workers and an increase in white collar workers, due to a much higher relative rate of growth in the service sector vis-à-vis the secondary manufacturing sector, gains support. While Canada is not yet a 'service economy,' work by Bell (1968) and others would suggest that this is the direction in which industrial economies will tend to proceed. These data may be

Table IV: Changes in Employment by Industry, 1946-1963*

	Number of Persons Employed		Amount of Change	
	1946[a] *(000's)*	*1963 (000's)*	*Number (000's)*	*%*
Goods producing	2,809	2,883	74	+1
Primary	1,371	819	−552	−40
Secondary	1,438	2,064	626	+44
Service producing	1,858	3,482	1,624	+87
Transportation and communication	344	455	111	+32
Public utilities	33	85	52	+158
Trade	573	1,019	446	+78
Finance, insurance, real estate	124	254	130	+105
Other services	784	1,669	885	+113
All industries	4,666	6,365	1,699	+36

[a] Excluding Newfoundland.

*Source: John Porter, *Canadian Social Structure,* (1967), p. 93, Table E6. Reprinted by permission of the Canadian Publishers, McClelland and Stewart Limited, Toronto, the Carleton Library Board, and Information Canada.

indicative of the early stages of such a shift within the Canadian economy.

These, then, are the major changes which have taken place in the structure of the division of labor within the Canadian social structure. While such changes do have implications for both the structure of inequality of condition and the structure of inequality of opportunity in Canada (most notably in the rising importance of education as a criterion for occupational incumbency (Bell, 1968; Porter, 1965) it should be noted that they are also distinct from them. Stratification is more concerned with the structures of inequality for which the division of labor provides a context and it is to these structures that we will now turn our attention.

Equality of Condition and Equality of Opportunity

While the previous discussion has focused on differences in the occupational structure, stratification is, by definition, rather more concerned with differences between people and with how these differences are maintained and perpetuated. But it should be clear to the reader that by inequality we mean something beyond mere difference.

In the study of social stratification in the broad sense in which we employed it at the outset of this chapter, we are especially concerned with inequalities with respect to the allocation of the scarce and desirable resources of the social system. As we pointed out previously, these can roughly be divided into three broad categories: power, prestige or honor, and income or wealth. When we speak of inequality of condition in a society, it is differences with respect to these variables to which we refer. If we were simply to leave our discussion at this point we would be in a good position to commence an empirical examination of the degree of inequality of condition — many would say degree of stratification — in society at any given point in time. However, such an approach is, by definition, static; it can at best produce a snapshot, or a series of snapshots, of the degree of *inequality of condition* at a point or points in time. To equate these with the study of stratification, however, is to ignore one of the fundamental aspects of society. Society exists in a historical context.

The question can then be raised as to whether the inequality of condition which we observe in the snapshots is merely the result of differential individual effort and ambition being rewarded in a 'fair' fashion or whether those inequalities, to state the opposite case, are passed on from generation to generation in a system where the rewards and failures of the father are truly visited on the son and upon his sons. Then we are talking of a different type of inequality, *inequality of opportunity*.

Equality of opportunity is effectively the degree to which, under universalistic criteria, individuals have an equal chance to attain desired occupational roles. The exact nature of what constitutes, or ought to constitute, the specific content of the set of universalistic criteria involved in the attainment process varies to some degree from society to society. However, in Canada it is generally agreed that the criteria ought to be based on a combination of ability and effort. If we accept that ability is more or less randomly distributed throughout the social system, then the degree to which there is or is not equality of opportunity must be ultimately a function of either overt departures from universalism or differential distribution of motivation or effort. This then is the other dimension of what we refer to in our narrower definition of stratification − equality of opportunity; or, in other words, we are also looking at the degree to which classes (*cf*. Buckley, 1961) − in either the collective or distributive senses of the term − are continuous in their membership across generations and become strata.

To ignore this would be to ignore an essential aspect of stratification. Clearly, there is a very great difference between a society which is highly differentiated with respect to goods and resources and has little or no equality of opportunity, and a society in which considerable inequality of condition continues to prevail and in which there is at the same time a relatively high degree of equality of opportunity. To associate the study of stratification only with the distribution of goods and resources in a static sense is to ignore this crucial point which can make a difference as great as night and day in the consideration of a particular social system.

This is not to suggest that the issue of the degree of inequality of condition is unimportant or ought to be ignored. The two notions − equality of condition and equality of opportunity − are very much related, as the typology in Figure 3 shows. Indeed, a knowledge of both is necessary in order adequately to define the stratification system of a given society.

Figure 3:   A Typology of Distributive Systems

Equality of Opportunity	Equality of Condition	Type of Society
low	high	communal
low	low	stratified
high	low	meritocratic
high	high	egalitarian

By *communal* is meant a social system such as that found in some early societies where there is little difference in the distribution of resources in the society, and where, at the same time, there is little possibility of mobility. Role allocation is almost entirely ascriptive. By *stratified* is meant a social system which is similar to a modern industrial society, where there is a relatively high degree of inequality in the distribution of resources, and where the life chances of an individual are still quite closely linked to the status of his family. A *meritocracy* refers to a society in which, while the distribution of resources remains highly unequal, the individual's life chances are relatively independent of his family's status. The *egalitarian* system would be one in which the resources and goods of the society are relatively evenly distributed, and in which the allocation of occupational roles is relatively independent of one's family's status. (See also Svalastoga, 1965: 36-70.)

The static approach which is solely or mainly concerned with the degree of inequality of condition will, as suggested, fail to make a distinction between the 'stratified' society and the 'meritocratic' society and between the 'egalitarian' and the 'communal.'

Canadian society is, in company with most modern industrial societies, clearly a 'stratified' society. That is, it is a society which, as we will show later, has as a major feature a marked degree of inequality, in terms of the distribution of its scarce and desirable resources, and it is a society in which the opportunities which one enjoys are very much a function of one's social status. While there have been some policy initiatives which have attempted to alleviate the effects of inequality of condition in Canada (e.g., medicare, taxation policy), in general, any attempts to attack this area directly have been diverted or diluted. (See Maslove, 1972 on this.) And, except for educational expenditures, there has been scant effort to improve equality of opportunity.

INEQUALITY OF CONDITION: THE DISTRIBUTION OF POWER

In turning to Canadian society to illustrate the three major forms of inequality of condition we will begin by looking very briefly at one aspect of the concentration of economic power as but a single example of the inter- and intra-institutional distribution of power in Canadian society.

In the traditional nineteenth century capitalistic enterprise, the ownership, control, and day-to-day management of the firm were not infrequently fused into one role. However, as discussed by Gordon in Chapter Ten, with the increasing complexity of industrial production, the day-to-day running of the operation was more and more delegated to managers. At the same time, the increasing size of the industrial corporation meant that it became more and more difficult for the individual owner, or entrepreneur, to raise from his own resources or even borrow the necessary capital to expand or found an enterprise. As a result, ownership became in some measure separated from control. Today we operate with what is effectively a three tier system:

(1) the owners, who are generally shareholders and who individually own very little — and frequently know less — of the enterprise;
(2) the board of directors, who are in theory the creature of the shareholders, and who, taking direction from the shareholders, are responsible for the major trends of corporate policy;
(3) the working management, who oversee and direct the day-to-day operations of the firm.

Hence, in the modern corporation it is the case that, in theory at least, the three functions are entirely separate. In general, the owners are widely spread throughout the upper level of the economy and have little direct interest in the corporation as long as their investment continues to be a paying proposition. Further, they are frequently too isolated to act even if they do wish to become concerned, a state of affairs which is encouraged by boards of directors who are frequently loath to divulge lists of shareholders to anyone. In general, then, owners have little say in making the broad policy decisions which shape the economy.

The working management have a somewhat greater influence on policy-making but two points are worthy of note: First, their outlook is inevitably to some degree focused to a relatively specific concern for policy as it affects only their own firms. Secondly, those managers who operate at the level where their decisions have a major influence on broader policy, in fact are frequently made board members. Hence, if we focus on boards of directors as the locus of the concentration of economic power, we will not go too far wrong.

Probably the best study to date of this concentration of power through directorships in Canada is to be found in Porter's *The Vertical Mosaic* (1965: 231-263). Here Porter was able to demonstrate that ' ... 907 individuals residing in Canada shared between them 1,304 (81 per cent) of the directorships in the dominant corporations as well as 118 (51 per cent) of the directorships in the nine chartered banks and 78 (58 per cent) of those in the life insurance companies.' (1965: 234) There is, then, a relatively small group of men who control, and whose collective decisions effectively shape, the Canadian economy. These are the economic elite.

When we use the term 'collective decisions' we do not mean to imply that these men actively conspire in their decision-making. Such a notion — although cherished by some — is a bit too far fetched. What we do mean is that in their decision-making these men are aware of each other, each others' institutions, and in a general way they are aware of the common interests and goals shared by all the institutions of which they are a part. This is the sort of environment in which price fixing (both illegal and perhaps costly) is unnecessary and where a system of price leadership (both legal and less risky) functions in its place. In this sort of situation, legislation such as the Combines Investigation Act stands as part of a meaningless charade in which government, through the legislation, gives the appearance of imposing strong controls on the economy and the business community responds by appearing to be appropriately upset.

In *The Vertical Mosaic* Porter extensively documents, using both case studies and large amounts of other data, the relationships — both in terms of decisions and in terms of kinship ties and friendship ties — between the various power holders in Canadian society. He shows, among other things, that in general, these people come from the same schools and universities, the same socio-economic and ethnic-religious background, and tend to belong to the same clubs and voluntary organizations.

INEQUALITY OF CONDITION: THE DISTRIBUTION OF INCOME

The second type of reward associated with occupational roles is monetary income. Unlike power, income is what might be called a 'pure' reward. By this, we mean that while with respect to some roles at least a minimal differential amount of power is necessary for their performance, in the case of monetary rewards, there is probably no need for differentials in order to necessitate the carrying out of the role. Thus, in examining a society we can establish an absolute condition of comparison and state very precisely within the limitations of the data, the degree to which there is or is not equality of condition with respect to economic rewards.

Within the broader context of the meaning of equality of condition, it is useful at this time to comment on the meaning of the phrase, 'the scarce and desirable resources of a society.' It should be made very clear that, when we are talking about classes and stratification, we are talking only about the distribution of public or social resources. These can and must be distinguished from the many 'private' rewards which are not infrequently associated in a differential fashion with different roles. These rewards (for example, intrinsic job satisfaction, happiness, security, etc.) are functions of the individual psyche and the way in which an individual approaches a role. While such reactions are primarily socially conditioned, we would argue that they do not form part of the direct distribution system of society and, as such, their distribution lies outside the scope of the discussion of inequality.

The second point which needs to be made concerns the relationship of economic rewards to the two other main types of social or public rewards. Economic rewards can, in some measure, be converted into either or both power and prestige. This is particularly so if the economic rewards can be maintained inter-generationally. In addition, of course, in our present society it is most frequently the case that those positions which command large incomes also command considerable power and prestige. There is, we would argue, no general causal component present in the relationship. However, it should be noted, as Marx does, that, in general, money can be used to compel both private and public rewards in other forms. For this reason, and because income is certainly the main determinant of the whole of a person's material conditions of life, we would regard equality of income as the minimal necessary condition for any socially meaningful state of equality of condition.

Given these considerations, the examination of the distribution of income in a society ought to serve as not only a direct measure of the degree of economic inequality, but as well as a very strong indication of the general degree of equality of social condition within that society. It should be noted that this indicator is relatively conservative, in that it ignores the question of accumulated wealth, the ability of the wealthy to conceal income, the regressive nature of the Canadian tax structure, (i.e., the poor pay proportionately more taxes than the rich), and finally, the fact that those in the higher income groups make a disproportionate use of the social services provided by the system.

Table V presents the average median incomes of Canadian family heads for the years 1951 to 1961. These figures are adjusted for changes in the value of the dollar (constant dollars) and are further adjusted for changes in the consumer price index. Thus, these figures may be seen as comparable measures of real income.

Table V: Actual and Constant Dollar Average Incomes of Canadian Males by Year, 1921-1961*

	1921	1931	1941	1951[a]	1961
Actual Income	1,057	927	993	2,127	3,679
Constant Dollar Income	1,486	1,649	1,915	2,563	3,679

[a] 1951 figures are medians, not averages.

*Source: Jenny Podoluk, *Incomes of Canadians* (Ottawa: Queen's Printer, 1968), p. 242. Reproduced by permission of Information Canada.

Table VI: Cumulative Income Distribution by Quintiles for Selected Years*

(Cumulative percentage of total family incomes — wages and salaries)

Population by Income Quintile	1931		1951		1961	
Lowest						
1	5.3	(5.3)[a]	8.0	(8.0)	5.0	(5.0)
2	16.6	(11.3)	21.9	(13.9)	19.0	(14.0)
3	33.9	(17.3)	39.8	(17.9)	37.0	(18.0)
4	57.4	(23.5)	62.4	(22.6)	59.0	(22.0)
5	100.0	(42.6)	100.0	(37.5)	100.0	(41.0)
Highest	100.0		100.0		100.0	

[a] The figures in brackets represent the percentage share of Total Family Income (Wages and Salaries) received by each quintile.

*Source: Jenny Podoluk, *Incomes of Canadians* (Ottawa: Queen's Printer, 1968). Reproduced by permission of Information Canada.

In looking at these data, we see that there has been a considerable improvement in the aggregate condition of the Canadian family with respect to real income. This is evidenced by an increase of $1,349 in real income in the period 1951 to 1961, an increase of 38 per cent.

However, in Table VI we have data which reveal the unequal distribution of income in Canada. The cumulative family income distributions in Table VI show the percentage of population for each of five levels or quintiles of income.

Thus, we note that the lowest income quintile of Canadians received only 5.3 per cent of all family income in 1931, 8 per cent in 1951, and 5 per cent in 1961. If we were to estimate a condition of perfect equality of income, and contrast it to the actual income distribution it would appear as the 45° line in Figure 4. In a condition of perfect equality, 20 per cent of the population would receive 20 per cent of the aggregate Canadian incomes, 40 per cent would receive 40 per cent, and so on. In Figure 4, the degree to which the actual income curve sags below the estimated line of equality is the degree of inequality in the income distribution.

These data very strongly suggest that the changes in *relative* condition with respect to the distribution of income have been so small as to be considered negligible. Clearly, in the four decades which have passed since 1931, the progress which we in Canada have made towards achieving equality of condition has been pitifully small (see Maslove, 1972).

Figure 4:   Lorenz Curves on Income for Canada, 1931, 1951, 1961*

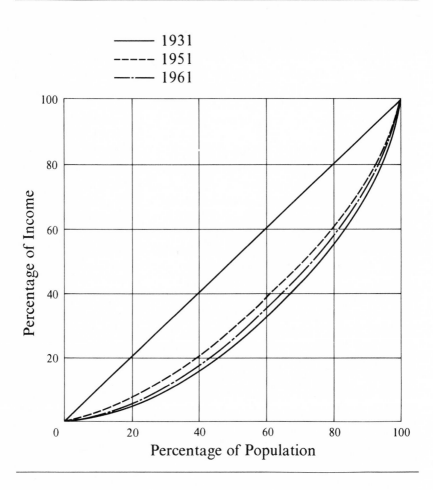

*Source: Table V.

INEQUALITY OF CONDITION: THE DISTRIBUTION OF PRESTIGE

Of the three basic types of rewards, prestige is perhaps the most difficult to pin down in terms of a general definition. This is in part due to the fact that prestige is so very highly inter-correlated with wealth and power that, except in cases of inconsistency, its independent effect is hard to locate. It is clear that a role which carries with it high income and great power, will, in general, carry with it high prestige, and conversely, a role which has little income and little power has, in general, low prestige. This may indeed lead one to the conclusion that prestige is merely an artifact of power and wealth and is not an independent reward. However, there are positions in our society which may be high in terms of both wealth and power but which are lower in status than positions which carry with them much less power and income.

Prestige is an attribute of a role, not of an individual. By this we mean that, while an individual may by his behavior in a role add or subtract from the prestige accorded to him in that role, there is a general level of prestige which members of a society are prepared to accord to the occupants of a role, regardless of their particular personalities.

Thus, if we see prestige in this way we may define the prestige of a position as being the rank of that position in a generally socially agreed upon hierarchy of positions. This implies that we can determine the prestige of a position within a social system simply by asking a representative sample of the members of that system to rank positions according to prestige. The resultant ranking is a prestige ranking and the fact that it will for most positions resemble very closely the ranking which we would get if we ranked positions with respect to power and wealth need neither surprise nor disturb us. Indeed as Weber, who introduced the threefold decomposition of status into wealth, power, and prestige notes in his discussion:

> For all practical purposes, stratification by status [prestige] goes hand in hand with a monopolization of ideal and material goods or opportunities, in a manner we have come to know as typical. (Weber, 1968: 181)

It is very likely the case, when the prestige of a position is being considered, that the amount of power and wealth associated with it are major factors in making a determination. However, the fact that a consideration of these two factors alone as determinants of social status would result in a significant number of positions being allocated to status levels to which on the basis of observable social behavior they do not belong encourages us in the belief that prestige is a separate and distinct element in the determination of status level.

In dealing with the other dimensions of social status, we have conceived of the occupational role as the major source of distribution and for the same reasons we will continue to do so in looking at prestige.

In Canada, there has been only one major study of occupational prestige; this was done in 1964 by Pineo and Porter (1967). Their study was based on a national sample of 793 Canadians and looked at the prestige of 204 occupations. The study was a replication, with some innovations in method, of two studies done in the United States in 1947 and 1962.

Table VII presents the results of this study by major Census classification (1961 Canadian Census Classification). Table VIII shows an alternative way of classifying occupations into major groupings.

The very high correlations between the result of the Canadian study and those arrived at in the United States in both 1947 and 1963 strongly suggest that these rankings are highly stable over time and among

Table VII: Occupational Prestige Scores by Major Census Classifications*

Census Major Occupation Group	Number of Titles	Mean Score
		High
Owners and managers	27	60.38
Professional	46	64.11
Clerical	14	37.46
Sales	11	36.99
Service and recreation	23	37.17
Transport and communications	13	41.72
Farmers and farm workers	6	34.98
Loggers and related workers	3	27.87
Fishermen, trappers and hunters	2	23.50
Miners, quarrymen and related workers	5	33.12
Craftsmen, production process workers	43	36.55
Laborers (not elsewhere specified)	3	21.47
		Low

*Source: Peter Pineo and John Porter, 'Occupational Prestige in Canada.' Reprinted from *The Canadian Review of Sociology and Anthropology,* 4:1 (1967), by permission of the authors and the publisher.

represented exclusively by economic interests in the possession of goods and opportunities for income, and (3) is represented under the conditions of the commodity or labor markets. (These points refer to 'class situation,' which we may express more briefly as the typical chance for a supply of goods, external living conditions, and personal life experiences, in so far as this chance is determined by the amount and kind of power, or lack of such, to dispose of goods or skills for the sake of income in a given economic order. The term 'class' refers to any group of people that is found in the same class situation.)*

and

A 'class' is any group of persons occupying the same class status. The following types of classes may be distinguished: (a) A class is a 'property class' when class status for its members is primarily determined by the differentiation of property holdings; (b) a class is an 'acquisition class' when the class situation of its members is primarily determined by their opportunity for the exploitation of services on the market; (c) the 'social class' structure is composed of the plurality of class statuses between which an interchange of individuals on a personal basis or in the course of generations is readily possible and typically observable. †

The degree to which the incumbents of the occupations within the classes created by Blishen and other writers are in fact more like each other in terms of prestige, income, and education than they are like most of the members of the other classes, is then the degree to which these classes can be seen as indications of classes as Weber defined them.

Inequality of Opportunity

In our typology, we have designated as stratified any society in which there exists both significant inequality of condition and significant inequality of opportunity. We have said that Canada is a stratified society and in the previous section we have discussed inequality of condition and its occurence in Canadian society. We will now turn to an examination of the second condition of a stratified society, the degree of inequality of opportunity.

A situation of equality of opportunity has been defined as one under which each and every individual has an equal opportunity to become unequal. It is usually assumed that, in a system in which there is substantial equality of opportunity, rewards will be the simple outcome

*H.H. Gerth and C. Wright Mills (eds.), *From Max Weber* (New York: Oxford University Press, 1968).

†Max Weber, *Theory of Social and Economic Organization,* trans. by A. Henderson and T. Parsons. Copyright © Macmillan Publishing Co., Inc., 1947.

of ability and effort. Such a system has been given the label 'meritocracy' by author Michael Young, and we have carried his label over into our typology. (Young, 1958)

The meritocratic ideal has been the panacea of most Western industrial nations since the beginning of the twentieth century. However, the result has only been to produce a series of relatively highly stratified societies. The reasons for this are clear. Like the economic notion of the open market, equality of opportunity is a simple concept, which is, however, very difficult to operationalize. To begin with, equality of opportunity makes the assumption that ability is relatively equally distributed between social groups such as classes, religions, ethnicities, and races.

But, it would appear to be the case that, quite literally, from the moment of conception, some have a better chance to become unequal than others. Further, it would appear that there is a direct linkage between the point of social origin of a person and the degree to which his chances to become unequal differ from the societal mean. When one compounds the initial class related differences in biological ability which relate to dietary and health care factors with the even more important differences, also class related, in terms of resources for education, attitudes to work and education, and access to information about occupations, it should not be surprising if one finds that even within the context of a meritocratic ideal, a stratified society could result. Further, if this meritocratic belief is countered by an economic system which lays some emphasis on the inheritance and transmission of family resources, then the development of a stratified society can firmly be predicted.

Within the Canadian context, the presence or absence of belief in the meritocratic ideal is itself a point of debate. However, it could be argued that the general emphasis on universalistic evaluation and on achievement found in most industrial societies encourages at least minimum subscription to the notion of meritocracy. However, with respect to the issue of whether or not Canada is a stratified society, the presence or absence of such beliefs is not of great importance.

In examining Canadian society, we will first look at data on occupational mobility which will suggest very strongly that Canada is a society in which there is a marked degree of inter-generational occupational immobility. Secondly, we will look at data on educational achievement which will suggest strongly some of the sources of inequality of opportunity in Canada.

Occupational Mobility

The study of occupational mobility is the study of the extent to which the occupation of a son is similar to, or different from, that of his father. The argument in simplest terms is that the greater the degree of inequality of opportunity in a society, the greater the probability is that fathers and their sons will have similar occupations or occupations which, in the Weberian sense, place them in the same social class. This does not however mean that no sons should be in the same class as their fathers. Clearly even under a system in which there was to be equality of opportunity some sons would in fact be able to earn entrance into occupations at the same class level as their fathers. If we assume that both motivation and ability will be randomly distributed with respect to social class in a society in which there is equality of opportunity, we can in fact argue that in such a society the probability of a son being in the same social class as his father will be independent of his father's social class.

The only Canadian national study which gives occupational data which are suitable is the Pineo-Porter study of occupational prestige mentioned previously. McRoberts (1971) used these data in looking at occupational mobility in Canada, and found that in Canada there is more status inheritance than independence for all occupational levels.

Professional and managerial occupations have the greatest level of inheritance. Farming has the second highest level of inheritance, but it is clearly a declining occupation with a relatively high exit rate and a relatively low entrance rate. This can been seen, first, from the fact that while farming accounted for 40 per cent of the father's generation of occupations, it accounted for only 18.8 per cent of the son's occupations. The categories of middle level white collar workers and lower level workers both show inheritance with the middle level occupations showing slightly more than the lower level occupations. The general pattern for both is one of slight upward mobility.

The source of much of this inequality of opportunity can be traced back into the educational system: it is in the educational system that individuals are given the training which constitutes for most the prerequisite for entrance into an occupational level. Once the educational process is complete the individual has a set of credentials which place (except for those with very high educational attainment) very definite ceilings on his occupational prospects. As explored by Rocher in the following chapter, it is primarily in the educational process that the status advantages of the father are passed on to the son.

Social Class and Education

If we wish, then, to examine the sources of the stratification process we must look at the educational structure which gives access to the occupational structure. In case there is any doubt that there are substantial inequalities in educational opportunity the following findings by Sewell are worth quoting:

> Using such measures of socioeconomic status as parental income, father's and mother's educational attainment, and father's occupation — either singly or in combination — we found enormous differences in educational opportunities among the various socioeconomic groups and between sexes. These differences are great regardless of what socioeconomic indices are used and regardless of how restrictively or broadly opportunity for higher education is defined — whether it is taken to mean college entry, college graduation, professional or graduate study, or simply any kind of formal education beyond high school.
>
> Even when we control for academic ability by dividing our sample into fourths according to the student's scores on standardized tests, we find that higher SES (Socio-Economic Status) students have substantially greater post-high school educational attainment than lower SES students.*

In Canada two studies, one for all of Canada by Breton (1972) and the other for Ontario by Blishen and Porter, suggest very strongly that, if students' educational plans are a useful proxy for actual educational attainment, then in Canada, educational achievement is at least as closely bound up with social class as it is in the United States. Table X, which is drawn from the Blishen and Porter study, shows the distribution of educational plans of students in Ontario by their fathers' occupations, controlling for the students' mental ability (i.e., mental ability equal). The results are striking. The proportion of students of high socio-economic status and low mental ability who plan to go on to university is equal to (for males) and larger than (for females) the proportion of students of low socio-economic status and *high* mental ability who plan a university education.

In looking for the reasons for such educational inequalities, what must be remembered is the fundamental class nature of educational institutions. Educational institutions are, both in their origins and in their present forms, middle class. Their management tends to be from the upper-middle class, their staff from the lower-middle class, and their intention is to teach the values and skills of the middle class. What this means is that education tends to become defined in almost purely academic terms, with the emphasis being on both the learning of the elements of middle class culture — the humanities — and on the development of abstract skills — the sciences. The result of this is that

---

*W.H. Sewell, 'Inequality of Opportunity for Higher Education,' *American Sociological Review*, XXXVI (1971), 795.

other types of skills tend to be valued downward and perhaps to be considered as being of both lesser importance and lesser value. Work done in Ontario by King (1970) and in Canada by Richer (1972) tends to suggest, in schools where both academic and non-academic programs are taught, that the non-academic students are considered to have lower prestige than the academic students. Further, King's work suggests that the non-academic students take considerably less part in the other activities of the school than do the academic students.

Using the justification of more efficient usage of resources, most provinces in Canada have adopted one version or another of a streaming system which separates, often as early as grade nine, those students with primarily academic skills and interests from those whose interests or skills theoretically suit them to a more vocational or practical education. The chief difference between those streams in formal terms is that the students in the academic stream are being prepared for further education at the post-secondary level, leading ultimately to jobs in middle and senior management and the professions, while those in the vocational/practical stream are normally considered to terminate their education upon leaving high school. On the surface, such a system would seem to be perfectly reasonable. In a society with a highly complex division of labor, it would be foolish indeed to presume that a common education beyond a basic level is even a desirable, let alone a necessary, policy.

Table X: Percentage Grade 12 Students Wanting to Graduate From University by Socio-economic Status, Mental Ability and Sex*

| | Socio-economic Status | | | | | |
| | High | | Middle | | Low | |
Mental Ability	*Male*	*Female*	*Male*	*Female*	*Male*	*Female*
High	77	56	55	42	46	30
Middle	51	46	53	35	34	22
Low	46	36	35	12	21	13
Number	205	176	431	383	675	690

*Source: Reprinted with the permission of B.R. Blishen and John Porter, from their study of Ontario High School Students.

Table XI: Student's Program By Father's Occupational Status*

				Status			
Program	*I*	*II*	*III*	*IV*	*V*	*VI*	*Total*
5–year	86	83	74	69	56	51	65
4–year	14	16	26	30	43	49	35
Number	(178)	(212)	(289)	(534)	(1,021)	(299)	(2,530)

*Source: Reprinted with the permission of B.R. Blishen and John Porter, from their study of Ontario High School Students.

Hence, it is both reasonable and apparently efficient to suggest that some differentiation between those seeking a primarily theoretical training and those seeking a more practical training should occur. However, let us look at the result of such policies.

Table XI presents the distribution of grade twelve students by program, and by fathers' occupational status, for the province of Ontario. In Ontario the five-year program is normally considered to be university preparatory and the four-year program to be terminal. As the data very clearly show the status system of the larger society is transferred and exists in microcosm in the Ontario high school. The students from higher socio-economic backgrounds are found disproportionately in the five-year programs and the students from the lower levels of the socio-economic hierarchy are clearly over-represented in the four-year programs. The factors operating to produce this type of outcome are many and complex. However, some of the relevant considerations will be mentioned briefly:

Differential Valuation of Academic Activity There is some evidence (Kohn, 1969) that families of different socio-economic backgrounds place a differential valuation on both the content of formal education and on the value of education in the job market. (Hyman, 1966) Thus, we might expect, as the lower class family tends to place a lower valuation on education, that more of their children would be found in non-academic terminal streams.

Differential Preparation There is some evidence to suggest that the middle and upper class child begins school better prepared than his lower class counterpart and that, in general, all education does is to accentuate the differences. As academic performance is one of the criteria used in assignment to programs, it is not surprising to find that there are more lower class students in terminal programs.

Differential Adherence to Middle Class Norms It is a fairly well established sociological fact that different socio-economic groups have different norms concerning what is correct deportment and dress for a given situation. Further, it is in some measure the case that if there is a 'middle Canada' the secondary school teacher is their ideal type. These people are, in general, well intentioned and try to be fair, but they find the deviations from middle class norms concerning what is correct deportment and dress which the lower SES students represent just a little bit frightening. It is suggested that while their reaction to this may not take the form of active discrimination it may take the form of a cheerful willingness to let the effects of the first two differences take their course as smoothly and quickly as possible.

Early Entry into the Labor Force The plight of many Canadian families is economically marginal enough that, even when all other conditions are favorable, there is a very real chance that, for many lower SES students, *the* paramount consideration must still be to get into the labor force as early as possible in order to add a further pay cheque to the family resources.

It will be noted that ultimately the source of each of these difficulties lies in the family or origin of the student. Further, it will be noted that each of these problems is directly related to the class position of the student's family. Thus, in large measure, the school can be seen as a gate-keeper to the class structure or perhaps more correctly as a sorter in which the inequalities of birth are clarified and sorted out. It is a place where people are allowed to find their 'level.'

Conclusions

Inequality of opportunity and inequality of condition are obviously inter-dependent. As we have argued, they need not be associated theoretically, but empirically, in Canada, they are. Thereby we speak of Canada as a stratified society. The persisting inheritance of differences in income and wealth, power, and prestige which exist in this country are perpetuated precisely because of the nature of the channels of achievement in Canada. The educational system is not equally efficient in educating or developing the talents of persons of all social classes. That is, from existing conditions of inequality as manifest in economic strata, disadvantages are passed on across generations of Canadians, with children heirs to their father's social status. Rather than break down such inequality of opportunity, the educational system serves to maintain it.

In saying this we do not wish to imply that a more open opportunity structure would reduce in any way inequalities in income or status. Opportunity serves only the principle of meritocracy. If we seek a more egalitarian society we must be prepared to envisage fundamental changes in our social, political, moral, and economic structures.

References

Barber, Bernard, *Social Stratification.* New York: Harcourt, Brace and World, 1957.

Bell, D., 'The measurement of knowledge and technology,' in Sheldon and Moore (eds.), *Indicators of Social Change.* New York: Russell Sage Foundation, 1968.

Blau, P.M., and O.D. Duncan, *The American Occupational Structure.* New York: John Wiley and Sons, 1967.

Blishen, B.R., 'A socio-economic index for occupations in Canada,' in Blishen *et al., Canadian Society* (3rd ed.). Toronto: Macmillan, 1968.

——, 'The construction and use of an occupational class scale,' in Blishen *et al., Canadian Society.* Toronto: Macmillan, 1961.

——, 'Social class and opportunity in Canada,' *Canadian Review of Sociology and Anthropology,* VII. 2, 1970.

Breton, R., *et al., Social and Academic Factors in the Career Decision of Canadian Youth.* Ottawa: Queen's Printer, 1972.

Buckley, Walter, 'Social stratification and the functional theory of social differentiation,' in Seymour Martin Lipset and Neil J. Smelser (eds.), *Sociology: The Progress of a Decade.* Englewood Cliffs: Prentice-Hall Inc., 1961.

Dahrendorf, Ralf, *Class and Class Conflict in Industrial Society.* Stanford: Stanford University Press, 1959.

Davis, Kingsley, *Human Society.* New York: Macmillan, 1948.

Davis, Kingsley, and Wilbert E. Moore, 'Some principles of stratification,' in Melvin M. Tumin (ed.), *Readings on Social Stratification.* Englewood Cliffs: Prentice-Hall Inc., 1970.

Duncan, Otis Dudley, 'Social stratification and mobility: problems in the measurement of trend,' in Eleanor B. Sheldon and Wilbert E. Moore (eds.), *Indicators of Social Change.* New York: Russell Sage Foundation, 1968.

Galbraith, John Kenneth, *The New Industrial State.* Boston: Houghton Mifflin Company, 1967.

Glass, D.V. (ed.), *Social Mobility in Britain.* London: Routledge, Kegan Paul, 1954.

Hodge, *et al.,* 'A comparative study of occupational prestige,' in Bendix and Lipset (eds.), *Class, Status and Power.* New York: The Free Press, 1966.

Hyman, H.H., 'The value systems of different classes,' in Bendix and Lipset (eds.), *Class, Status and Power.* New York: The Free Press, 1966.

Jordan, Z.A., *Karl Marx: Economy, Class and Social Revolution.* London: Michael Joseph, 1971.

Keller, Suzanne, *Beyond the Ruling Class.* New York: Random House, 1968.

King, A.J.C., and R. Ripton, 'Teachers and students: a preliminary analysis of collective reciprocity,' *Canadian Review of Sociology and Anthropology,* VII, 1, (1970).

Kohn, M.L., *Class and Conformity.* Homewood, Ill.: The Dorsey Press, 1969.

Koklo, G., *Wealth and Power in America.* New York: Praeger, 1962.

Lenski, Gerhard E., *Power and Privilege.* New York: McGraw-Hill, 1966.

Marx, Karl, *Karl Marx: Early Writings,* T.B. Bottomore (ed.). New York: McGraw-Hill, 1964.

——, *Capital Vol I and III.* New York: International Publishers, 1967.

——, *Karl Marx and Frederick Engels: Selected Works.* New York: International Publishers, 1969a.

——, *Karl Marx: Selected Writings in Sociology and Social Philosophy,* T.B. Bottomore and Maximilien Rubel (eds.). Middlesex: Penguin Books, 1969b.

Marx, Karl, and Frederick Engels, *The German Ideology.* New York: International Publishers, 1947.

Maslove, Allan M., *The Pattern of Taxation in Canada.* Ottawa: Information Canada, 1972.

McRoberts, Hugh A., 'Explorations in Canadian Occupational Mobility.' Master's thesis, Carleton University, 1971.

Michels, Robert, *Political Parties.* New York: The Free Press, 1966.

Mosca, Gaetano, 'The Ruling Class,' in Marvin E. Olsen (ed.), *Power in Societies.* New York: Macmillan, 1970.

Nosanchuk, T.A., 'A note on the use of the correlation coefficient for assessing the similarity of occupational rankings,' *Canadian Review of Sociology and Anthropology,* IX, 4, (1972).

Pareto, Vilfredo, 'Elites and force,' in Marvin E. Olsen (ed.), *Power in Societies.* New York: Macmillan, 1970.

Parry, G. *Political Elites.* London: George Allen and Unwin, 1969.

Pineo, P.C., and John Porter. 'Occupational prestige in Canada,' *Canadian Review of Sociology and Anthropology,* IV (1967), 24-40.

Plato, *The Republic in Man and Man: The Social Philosophies,* Saxe Commins and Robert N. Liscott (eds.). New York: Random House, 1947.

Porter, John, *The Vertical Mosaic.* Toronto: University of Toronto Press, 1965.

Reissman, Leonard, 'Social stratification,' in Neil J. Smelser (ed.), *Sociology: An Introduction.* New York: John Wiley and Sons, 1967.

Richer, S., 'Educational plans in comprehensive and in single programme schools,' in Breton *et al., Social and Academic Factors in the Career Decision of Canadian Youth.* Ottawa: Queen's Printer, 1972.

Rossides, Daniel W., *Society as a Functional Process: An Introduction to Sociology.* Toronto: McGraw-Hill, 1968.

Sewell, W.H., 'Inequality of opportunity for higher education,' *A.S.R.*, XXXVI (1971), 793-809.

Svalastoga, Karre, *Social Differentiation.* New York: David McKay, 1965.

Tumin, Melvin M., 'Some principles of stratification: a critical anaylsis,' in Melvin M. Tumin (ed.), *Readings on Social Stratification.* Englewood Cliffs: Prentice-Hall Inc., 1970.

Weber, Max, 'Class, status, party,' in H.H. Gerth and C. Wright Mills (eds.), *From Max Weber.* New York: Oxford University Press, 1968.

——, *Theory of Social and Economic Organization* (trans. by A. Henderson and T. Parsons). New York: Macmillan, 1947.

Wesolowski, Wlodzimierz, 'Some notes on the functional theory of stratification,' in Reinhard Bendix and Seymour Martin Lipset (eds.), *Class, Status and Power.* New York: The Free Press, 1966.

Wrong, Dennis H., 'The oversocialized conception of man,' *American Sociological Review,* XXVI (April, 1961), 183-193.

Young, Michael, *The Rise of the Meritocracy.* London: Thames and Hudson, 1958.

CHAPTER FIVE

Formal Education: The Issue of Opportunity

Guy Rocher
University of Montreal

Introduction

A complex and diversified system of education constitutes one of the peculiar traits of modern industrial society. The industrial, technological, and scientific revolution of the nineteenth century has created a growing number of new jobs and new occupations which require various types of general or specific training. Modern industry calls for a great variety of skilled and semi-skilled workers, various levels of technicians and clerks, as well as research people in its laboratories. Similarly, public services have grown tremendously, requiring specialized public servants in all kinds of areas — from public administration, engineering, natural and physical sciences to the more modern social sciences like economics, sociology, political science, demography, and anthropology. The development of health and welfare services, both public and private, which has accompanied urbanization, has also created new positions in hospitals, welfare services, public and private clinics, and convalescent homes.

One of the consequences of the creation of these new occupations has been the development of a more and more complex educational system. Primary education has become progressively generalized; the traditional rural one-classroom school has been replaced by central schools, and bussing children from home to school and back home has become the rule; after the last world war, secondary education became more and more generalized as well as more diversified; vocational and technical schools multiplied to meet the requirements of the labor force in various areas; higher education grew as it had never done in the past. The idea that children needed to be educated as thoroughly as possible so that they could earn a living in the new industrial society became plain common sense in the Western world.

At the same time, requirements for entering old as well as new occupations rapidly increased. Jobs which required only an elementary school education a few years ago are now open only to people who have completed high school and sometimes even college. Competence is judged foremost by a diploma.

In this context, the relationship between education and society has changed and become extremely complex. In the pre-literate or traditional society, education was part of daily life within the structures of family and kinship. In modern industrial society, new types of institutions (nurseries, kindergartens, schools, colleges, universities of various sorts) have replaced the family and kinship in at least part of their socializing function.

It is impossible to deal here with all the problems linked to the new relationship between education and society. We will focus on one of them, which is particularly important and which has been the subject of many discussions and much research: economic and social inequalities with regard to the educational system.

The Equalitarian and Democratic Ideology

Because it has become so vital to the industrial society as well as its members, the educational system comes necessarily to be related to a great variety of values, value judgments, aspirations and expectations. As a matter of fact, the educational system is built on values and value judgments, of which it is a reflection. Each society has its own image of what is and what its educational system should be or, one might more precisely say, there are several such images in each society, more or less conflicting and more or less contradictory. These images are the expression of judgments on the society as a whole, of wishes and hopes for oneself and for the society to which one belongs, of frustrations that one suffers for oneself or for those one loves. It is in that sense that one can say that the educational system becomes part of various ideologies.

This is particularly clear in modern society. Thus, since the beginning of this century and still more *since the end of the Second World War, the ideology of a democratic and equalitarian educational system has become dominant in the Western world.* This ideology has been expressed in various arguments, such as reports by royal commissions, official programs for curricula proposed or imposed by departments of education, speeches by politicians, and writings of experts on education.

Summarizing the content of this ideology is not easy. But we can at least introduce it here by proceeding to underline three of its main traits.

First, *democratizing the system of education means making education not the privilege of the few, but bringing it to every citizen as his right, a right which is guaranteed by official public declarations and documents, such as a constitution or a law.* This means simply that the educational system is open to any citizen without discrimination of race, religion, sex, age, or income.

This right of every citizen to formal education has been expressed still more firmly as an obligation: in practically every country in the world, and especially those of the Western world, the state has taken upon itself the authority to enforce compulsory education for all children up to a certain age, generally fourteen or fifteen years old. The ideological basis of compulsory education is that the state must protect the right of each child to receive an education, even against the will or the authority of the parents.

Secondly, because of his right to an education, *each citizen is now called upon to share in the public financial support of the educational system.* Education is not secured solely or mainly by private institutions any more as was the case for a long time when the churches directly assumed the responsibility of educating the people. Today, in nearly all countries of the world, the State has taken the responsibility of supporting or financing a public network of schools, as well as sometimes a parallel network of private institutions, and each citizen is called upon to contribute to this financing, through a system of taxation.

In some countries, the state has refused to subsidize private institutions, in the name of educational democracy. This is the case in the United States, and was the case for a long time in France. However, generally speaking, most states have reached some kind of agreement with private institutions or with some groups of private citizens, and have agreed to assume a part or even sometimes the whole of their expenses.

Thirdly, *the most important trait of the democratization of education is probably the equality of opportunities for all.* Theoretically speaking, one of the main objectives of the modern democratic society is to eliminate the various factors of inequality which still exist and which inhibit groups or categories of citizens who have fewer chances than others of benefiting from the educational system. At least, this is the official ideology of the democratic society. It is the image it wants to create of itself and it is the objective it aims to realize. But, precisely because it is an ambitious and difficult objective, it is clearly far from being realized. The questions that are being raised more and more strongly are: 'Is the democratic modern society fair to all its groups of citizens?' and 'Are all groups or classes or categories of citizens treated on an equal footing, especially in terms of educational accessibility?' These questions are becoming increasingly the focus of much research and discussion among social scientists.

The Thesis of Social Reproduction

In North American society, it has generally been taken for granted, for quite a long time, that the school was the normal channel of mobility open to all citizens who were willing to use it, since it was available to all without any kind of discrimination. Thanks to its educational system, North American society was regarded as having no closed class system, but as being, on the contrary, a society where social stratification was largely open and where more social mobility was possible. With a general system of education, what Vilfredo Pareto has called the 'circulation of elites' was possible and, in fact, partly realized. One did not need to be born within the ruling class in order to accede to a position of power, influence or wealth.

More recently, this view of an open society, which was shared by most American sociologists for many years, has come to be more and more seriously questioned. *Many sociologists, both American and European, have recently supported the thesis that the educational system is not a channel of social mobility, but rather a factor of stagnation of the stratification system.* This point of view had already been expressed by Robert and Helen Lynd in their pioneering study of Muncie, Indiana, published in 1929. They described the ways in which the school served to inhibit the educational aspirations of children from the lower social classes. Since then, the sorting process of the educational system, which plays against the lower class children who are more or less forced either to drop out or to go into the vocational and technical classes or schools, has been described by some other sociologists, like Warner, Havighurst and Loeb (1944), as well as August B. Hollingshead (1949). This view of the educational system has been expressed still more strongly by critical philosophers and sociologists, like Paul Goodman (1962) and E.Z. Friedenberg (1959).

In France, the thesis of social reproduction was developed by two sociologists, Bourdieu and Passéron (1970). According to these authors, the educational system is not an agent of social change. In industrial society, its action has been rather to the advantage of the middle classes and the social groups which are already privileged and which have always been so. *On account of the cultural as well as the economic obstacles with which it opposes the mobility of the lower classes, the system of education reproduces indefinitely existing social inequalities, and can even create wider discrepancies and more inequalities.* Bourdieu and Passeron founded their thesis on an empirical study of the social origins of French students at the Faculté des Lettres of the University of Paris (1964).

The thesis of social reproduction brings up the problem of the relationship between the educational system and society, not in a static but in a dynamic way. The fundamental question that it raises is the following: Is the system of education a factor of social change, as has long been thought, or does it simply reflect or even amplify the actual system of social stratification?

This is precisely the topic that will be dealt with in this chapter. In the first part, we will bring to light the main inequalities that contradict the official equalitarian democratic ideology and that are related to the role of the school in modern society: social class inequalities, regional differences, racial and ethnic discrimination, cultural disparities. In the second part, we will try to assess the role of education with regard to social change in the modern industrial society.

Social Inequalities

Socio-Economic Inequalities

A few years ago, having access to high school was far from being as general as it is now. Table I shows the rapid and drastic change which has taken place over the last decade throughout Canada. While 66 per cent of Canadian 14- to 17-year-olds (male and female) were enrolled in grade nine in 1960-61, 98 per cent (male) and 97 per cent (female) were to be found in grade nine in 1970-71. The percentage increase has been marked for each province, and for girls as well as boys.

Table II provides similar information, still more refined. It gives us the 'retention rate' (adjusted for interprovincial and international movement of population), that has been calculated for 1960, 1965, and 1970. This rate compares the enrollment in grade eleven to the enrollment of the same age group in grade two, nine years earlier. For Canada as a whole, the retention rate has jumped from 50 to 80 per cent over a period of ten years, a most remarkable increase indeed.

On account of this increase, starting in the 1950's and still more in the 1960's, inequalities of educational opportunity have been measured more and more in terms of unequal access to higher education. In this respect, a great many studies undertaken in different countries all converge towards the same conclusion: upper class children have more chances of completing high school and entering college than lower class children. This conclusion is valid for Canada as well, as far as can be judged from the available data.

For instance, the Canadian sociologist John Porter analyzed class differences with regard to the educational system (1965). Tables III, IV, and V, reproduced from his book, illustrate class inequalities in Canada. We see from Table III that the father's occupation has a strong influence on the children's chances of getting access to higher education. In Table IV, it is the influence of the father's level of education that is shown, and in Table V, the influence of the family income.

These three variables (the father's occupation, the parents' level of education, the family income) are generally regarded as the three main factors that determine the socio-economic status of the family and its members. It is clear from the three tables that these three variables all

Table I: Grade 9 Enrollment for Canada and Provinces, Selected Years*

	1960 – 1961		1965 – 1966		1970 – 1971	
Province	*M*	*F*	*M*	*F*	*M*	*F*
	%		%		%	
Newfoundland	50.8	52.9	55.0	55.1	62.5	66.1
Prince Edward Island	50.3	68.6	68.8	78.1	76.9	94.8
Nova Scotia	53.9	68.7	66.5	71.6	76.8	85.8
New Brunswick	55.8	63.6	65.2	72.4	81.6	85.7
Atlantic Provinces	53.6	60.0	63.2	67.8	74.4	80.8
Quebec	43.9	43.9	75.3	72.7	98.7	98.1
Ontario	83.1	82.9	98.9	93.1	107.5	103.2
Manitoba	70.2	69.9	83.5	80.9	93.5	91.8
Saskatchewan	74.9	78.8	85.5	86.1	90.2	93.2
Alberta	85.2	84.5	92.0	88.8	99.0	96.6
British Columbia	83.2	84.6	93.0	89.7	99.0	96.4
Western Provinces	79.4	80.6	89.4	87.0	96.5	95.1
Canada	66.1	66.8	85.4	82.4	98.5	97.1

*Source: *Education in Canada, 1973* (Ottawa: Statistics Canada, 1973), p. 338. Reproduced by permission of Information Canada.

Table II: Retention Rate for Canada and Provinces, Selected Years*

Province	1960–1961 %	1965–1966 %	1970–1971 %
Newfoundland	38.1	46.3	65.6
Prince Edward Island	33.5	55.4	64.2
Nova Scotia	47.4	62.3	69.7
New Brunswick	44.0	55.0	68.2
Atlantic Provinces	43.1	55.2	67.8
Quebec	34.2	61.3	81.1
Ontario	57.0	69.9	81.7
Manitoba	61.4	75.4	81.2
Saskatchewan	56.3	70.7	78.4
Alberta	67.1	74.1	84.2
British Columbia	71.2	75.8	84.0
Western Provinces	64.5	74.2	82.7
Canada	49.8	66.6	80.0

*Source: *Education in Canada, 1973.* (Ottawa: Statistics Canada, 1973), p. 358. Reproduced by permission of Information Canada.

Table III: Percentage Distribution of University Students' Parents by Occupational Level, 1956*

Occupational Level	Students' Parents	Total Labor Force
Proprietors and managers	25.7	8.3
Professionals	24.9	7.1
Clericals and sales	12.3	16.5
Skilled and semi-skilled	21.1	30.6
Agriculture	10.9	15.7
Laborers	5.1	20.5
Total	100.0	100.0

*Source: John Porter, *The Vertical Mosaic,* Chapter VI, Table XXII. © University of Toronto Press 1965.

Table IV: Percentage Distribution of Arts and Science Students by Fathers' Educational Level, 1961*

Highest Level of Education of Parents	Students' Parents	Family Heads Aged 35–65 in Total Population
Elementary school	26.5	53.7
Some high school	24.0	25.8
High school graduate	19.8	12.8
Some university	9.1	3.2
University graduate	20.6	4.6
Total	100.0	100.0

*Source: John Porter, *The Vertical Mosaic*, Chapter VI, Table XXV. © University of Toronto Press 1965.

have the same influence, always playing against the underprivileged and in favor of the children who belong to upper class families.

These class differences are both reflected in and reinforced by regional or geographic inequalities. For instance, important differences exist in the large industrial cities between the schools that are to be found in the

Table V: Percentage Distribution of University Student Families and All Canadian Families, by Family Income Groups, 1956*

Family Income ($)	Student Families	All Canadian Families
10,000 and over	15.2	3.3
7,000–9,999	12.2	8.4
5,000–6,999	21.3	18.7
4,000–4,999	14.8	15.7
3,000–3,999	17.5	22.9
2,000–2,999	11.6	17.0
Under 2,000	7.4	14.0
Total	100.0	100.0

*Source: John Porter, *The Vertical Mosaic*, Chapter VI, Table XXI. © University of Toronto Press 1965.

Table VI: Failure Rate of Grade I Students in Selected Districts of Montreal, 1965-1966*

District	Total Grade I Students	Failure Rate (%)
St–Henri	900	16.4
Pointe St–Charles	381	15.2
Centre–Ville	238	15.5
Mile–End	737	11.5
Centre–Sud	1,317	18.5
Hochelaga	1,605	10.5
Rosemont	1,443	5.0
Montreal Catholic School Board	18,299	9.3

*Source: Pierre Bélanger and Guy Rocher (eds.), *Ecole et Société au Québec* (Montreal: HMH, 1970), p. 342.

underprivileged areas and the schools of the middle class suburbs. These differences have already been brought to light in the United States, especially by Patricia Sexton (1961; 1967) and James B. Conant (1959). In Canada, a study undertaken a few years ago in Montreal by the Catholic School Board* shows that the proportion of first-grade children who fail differs greatly from one district to another in the same city. One can see from Table VI that in the districts of Montreal defined as 'underprivileged,' the number of children who fail their first year of primary school is much higher than both in Rosemont, a relatively middle class district, and in the total population of children attending the schools of the Catholic School Board.

The same differences can be observed from one city to another. The rate of school retention is much higher in residential cities and towns than in working class cities and towns. This is well illustrated in Table VII. In the city of Outremont, which constitutes a middle class enclave within the metropolitan area of Montreal, the proportion of 20- to 24-year-old men and women who still go to school is much higher than in working class cities like Oshawa and Hull, where the proportion of young men and women of the same age who are still in school is very low.

*Quoted in *Ecole et Société au Québec*, edited by Pierre W. Bélanger and Guy Rocher, (Montreal: HMH, 1970), pp.341-342.

Table VII: Percentage of Population at School, Aged 20-24, for Selected Cities, 1961*

City (Population 30,000+)	20-24 Year Olds at School (%)	
	Male	Female
Outremont	37.3	18.0
Saskatoon	21.8	11.8
Vancouver	19.6	8.3
Port Arthur	16.9	5.0
Trois-Rivières	16.0	5.9
Winnipeg	14.9	5.0
Toronto	13.3	6.5
Montreal	11.0	4.2
Oshawa	10.5	2.7
Hull	6.3	3.3

*Source: *Census of Canada, 1961* (Ottawa: Statistics Canada). Reproduced by permission of Information Canada.

Why the Socio-Economic Inequalities?

All the inequalities that have just been described call for an explanation. Where do they come from? How are they maintained? Why are they transmitted from one generation to another?

In order to answer these questions, it will be useful to start from another disparity which is related to those we have just described. All the studies in Europe as well as in North America have proven the existence of a high correlation between the socio-economic status and the I.Q. of children. Children who grow up in underprivileged urban districts or in rural areas far away from the urban centers have a lower mean I.Q. than other children. For instance, a broad survey made in France in 1944 by a group of psychologists and social scientists clearly demonstrated these disparities (Institut national d'études démographiques, 1950; 1954). Many studies have come to the same conclusion in the United States.* In

*See especially A.L. Baldwin, Urie Bronfenbrenner, D.C. McClelland, J.L. Strodlick, *Talent and Society* (Princeton, N.J., Van Nostrand,1958); J.S. Coleman *et al., Equality of Educational Opportunity,* (U.S. Dept. HEW, 1966); C. Jencks, *Inequality,* (New York, Basic Books, Inc., 1972); G.S. Lesser, G. Fifer, D.H. Clark, 'Mental abilities of children from different social-class and cultural groups,'*Monog. Soc. Res. Child Develop.,* 1965.

Table VIII: Distribution of Grade 7 Students according to I.Q., in Selected Districts of Montreal, 1963-1964*

District	Higher Third %	Middle Third %	Lower Third %
St. Henri/Pointe St–Charles	24.0	30.0	46.0
Centre–Ville	19.0	36.0	45.0
Mile–End	21.0	33.0	46.0
Centre–Sud	24.0	32.0	44.0
Hochelaga	29.0	32.0	39.0
Rosemont	38.0	35.5	26.5
Montreal Catholic School Board	34.2	33.3	32.5

*Source: Pierre Bélanger and Guy Rocher (eds.), *Ecole et Société au Québec* (Montreal: HMH, 1970), p. 340.

Canada, the same correlation has been observed in Montreal. The research undertaken by the Catholic School Board, mentioned earlier, brought to light the difference between the I.Q. of lower class children and upper class children, shown in Table VIII. Moreover, this relation between I.Q. and socio-economic status is to be found again in the relationship between school achievement and socio-economic status. Lower class children have lower grades, less academic motivation and are more likely to fail, even in their first years in school, than upper class or middle class children.

This question has recently been the object of passionate debate among American social scientists, following an article by Jensen (1969), who supported the view that I.Q. is heritable and therefore largely stable. I.Q. cannot be increased, according to Jensen, by a change of environment or by special educational programs. Jensen applied his conclusions to the black population. But his reasoning also applied to lower class white children. As opposed to Jensen's, the viewpoint most generally held by social scientists is that intelligence is a product of both heredity and environment, and that a change of environment or special educational programs can upgrade the I.Q. of children (Senna, 1973).

For our purposes, three main conclusions have come out of that debate. First, it is clear that *I.Q. is not intelligence as such, but rather a measurement by specific tests of a type of mental or intellectual activity.* Second, the mental ability measured by I.Q. tests is *less familiar and less natural to lower class children* than it is to upper class or middle class children. Third, it is precisely this very type of intellectual activity that is *valued at school and that is assessed in the classroom.*

The type of intellectual activity that is favored by the school is very largely verbal. It is based on the manipulation of abstract and general concepts which call for a certain capacity to use language and symbolic communication. It is more and more generally believed that there lies probably one of the main advantages that upper and middle class children have in school. They have been better initiated in their families to the manipulation and use of abstract thought, to the type of language that is most valued in the classroom, and to the patterns of reasoning that are generally used by educators. A study made in Halifax, N.S. by Barbara Clark (1971) among the population of underprivileged black children showed that a pre-school program helped these children to develop the intellectual capacities and aptitudes that lead to school achievement and to better grades.

Some sociologists, psychologists, and linguists have supported the view that language deficiencies, or what some have rather called language differences, are responsible for the fact that working class children have less success in school, drop out in greater numbers and are so weakly represented in higher education (Williams, 1970).

Still more broadly, it has been pointed out that the school is a reflection of the spirit, the culture, the aspirations of the middle class. Therefore, working or lower class children have more difficulty in adapting to the school climate than middle class children. To most of the lower class children, the school climate always remains foreign, to the point where they feel almost marginal and more or less unwelcome in the schools. This viewpoint has been expressed in the United States by sociologists like Cohen (1955), Friedenberg (1959), Conant (1961) and Riessman (1962); it has also been presented by British sociologists like Halsey, Floud and Martin (1956), and by French sociologists like Bourdieu and Passeron (1964), and Baudelot and Establet (1971).

For people living in underprivileged districts of the cities, or for lower-working class people, as well as for those living in rural areas, especially in remote areas, sending their children to a college seems practically impossible. There is a kind of *socio-cultural distance* between themselves and higher education. The economic obstacles or the geographic distance appear to be still more serious because of the socio-cultural distance through which they are perceived. Therefore, the educational and professional aspirations of the parents for their children are still weaker and lower, because they do not think it possible for their children to have access to higher education. Because of the attitude of their parents, the children themselves are not motivated to enter higher education. They rather feel that this is something for 'the others,' i.e., those who are both economically and intellectually fit for advanced studies. Lower class children do not enter higher education because they do not aspire to do so; they do not aspire to enter higher education because they do not think they are fit for advanced studies; they do not think they are fit for higher education because they have never been told that they can have access to higher education.

This is the vicious circle that is sometimes called a 'self-fulfilling prophecy.' The self-fulfilling prophecy is quite a common phenomenon in social life: things happen because people think they will happen the way they do and because people expect or want them to happen the way they do. The difference between the educational and vocational aspirations of middle or lower class children is a nice case in point.

One could add that the teachers also contribute to the self-fulfilling prophecy. In many subtle and more or less conscious ways, they tend to discourage the lower class children from aspiring to higher education. They operate a discreet but efficient selection: they push to higher education only the lower class children who have a very high I.Q., who are totally motivated and whose parents support the children. Consequently, fewer lower class children than middle class children will be supported by their teachers in their aspirations to higher education.

Whether or not the teachers themselves come from middle class families is immaterial. The significant fact is that the middle class becomes their class of reference with regard to the values they possess, the norms they follow, and the aspirations they have for their students. More broadly, the image of the society and of the conditions for one to succeed in that society come directly from the ideology of the middle class.

Racial and Ethnic Inequalities

The racial inequalities in the access to education have been amply illustrated in research in the United States. James Conant (1961), Patricia Sexton (1961), and many others have shown how the American blacks and the Puerto Ricans have never benefited from the same educational services as the white population. The buildings, the quality of the equipment, the teachers, the curricula have long been of lower quality for the blacks. Therefore, only very few black children could compete with white children at college entrance examinations and tests. More recently, the same kind of discrimination has been brought to light with regard to the Chicanos, the Mexican Americans.

Racism of one kind or another has not been completely absent from the Canadian educational scene. One case has been reported by Hobart and Brant, a sociologist and an anthropologist, with regard to the

Eskimos of the Western Canadian Arctic. After several months of field work in 1963, 1964, and 1965, they drew a comparison between the treatment of the Eskimos in Greenland by the Danish Government and the Eskimos of the Canadian Arctic. Here is how they summarize the situation of the Canadian Eskimos:

> The Canadian Government has almost completely ignored the Arctic during most of the twentieth century ... There was no systematic provision of education for Eskimos until 1959 ... The educational system which has come into existence in the Western Arctic, at first under mission auspices and, since 1952, increasingly under Federal auspices, contrasts as sharply with the Greenland system as have the Danish and the Canadian Arctic administrative philosophies. The educational system in the Western Arctic is characterized by these features: continuous use of non-native teachers, in the past predominantly clergy, changing to lay teachers today; throughout its history, instruction given wholly in English; establishment and heavy utilization, from the beginning, of residential schools, with latter-day emphasis upon large units; curriculum almost entirely oriented to the southern Canadian culture and value system; and minimal attempts to produce text materials appropriate to the Arctic ... Obviously, much of contemporary Eskimo education in the Western Canadian Arctic is inappropriate, and perhaps even dis-educative from the standpoint of preparation for the life children will lead as adults.*

Similar conclusions have been reached by several other anthropologists who have worked among the Eskimos. †

Moreover, in a young and complex country like Canada, which is bicultural in its origins and which has become multicultural as a result of successive waves of immigration, one can also expect to find ethnic inequalities. The greatest disparity is to be found between the French Canadians and the British-born Canadians. This disparity was investigated at the end of the nineteenth century by the first Canadian sociologist, Léon Gérin.‡ Using the census data up to 1891, Léon Gérin showed that the educational level of French Canadians was much lower than that of British-born Canadians. A remarkable difference could be

---

*C.W. Hobart and C.S. Brant, 'Eskimo Education, Danish and Canadian: A Comparison.' Reprinted from *The Canadian Review of Sociology and Anthropology*, 3:2 (1966), by permission of the authors and the publisher.

†See especially the chapters by J. Ferguson, G.J. Uranos and Margaret Stephens, John and Irma Honigman, and Frank J. Vallee, in *Native Peoples*, edited by Jean Leonard Elliott, (Scarborough, Ontario, Prentice-Hall of Canada, 1971).

‡ Léon Gérin's analysis has been summarized and discussed by Guy Rocher, 'La sociologie de l'éducation dans l'oeuvre de Léon Gérin' in *Ecole et Société au Québec*, edited by Pierre W. Bélanger and Guy Rocher (Montreal: HMH, 1970).

observed within Quebec, where the districts with an Anglophone majority had a much higher average educational level than the districts with a Francophone majority. Outside of Quebec, in Ontario and New Brunswick, the districts where a significant proportion of Francophones were to be found had a lower level of education than the others.

Léon Gérin explained this phenomenon by the manner in which children were trained and educated in their families. According to him, the Anglophone families helped develop initiative, craftsmanship, respect for knowledge, a love of work, and competitive individualism. In the French Canadian families, togetherness and belongingness were more developed, at the expense of personal ambition and competitiveness.

Seventy years later, a similar analysis was undertaken, using the data of the 1961 Census (Rocher, 1965). It appears from this study that *in the 1950's, the French Canadians still had a much lower level of education than the British-born Canadians, that they were ill-equipped, intellectually and professionally, for the industrial society in which they lived.* There appears therefore to have been a continuity in time, both in the disparity between French- and English-speaking Canadians, and in their attitudes towards education. But an important change has taken place since 1961. The so-called 'quiet revolution' which started about that time brought with it a drastic change in the educational and professional aspirations of the French Canadian population.

However, if it is less acute, the problem of ethnic disparities has not been solved. It is still there and needs to be understood. The explanation of the phenomenon which was given by Léon Gérin (1964) was 'culturalist' in the sense that he was explaining the lack of interest in education among French Canadians through the cultural climate in the family and kinship, and the types of inter-personal links that it developed and maintained. More recently, another explanation was provided by the sociologists Jacques Dofny and Marcel Rioux (1964). They present the hypothesis that the French Canadians can be regarded as what they have called an 'ethnic social class.' According to them, it is not enough to define the French Canadians as an ethnic group, because it does not provide us with the right concept to analyze and understand their behavior and attitudes. The social class concept, they say, applies very well to the French Canadian group, and what we already know of class behavior and attitudes may help us understand the French Canadians. As a matter of fact, this type of analysis was made more or less explicitly by American sociologists speaking of the black population. Like the American blacks, the French Canadians constitute an under-privileged economic group whose labor force serves mainly economic interests which are linguistically and culturally foreign to them. The long-standing lack of interest of the French Canadians in education, their slow integration into the industrial society, their refusal to accept modern culture, show a behavior typical of an underprivileged social class, which feels alienated from the economic advantages and benefits of the industrial capitalistic society.

This line of analysis does not necessarily contradict Léon Gérin's. On the contrary, the two can be fused together. The familistic behavior described by Léon Gérin can be regarded as one aspect of the general attitudes of the French Canadians when defined as an ethnic social class.

The French Canadians Outside Quebec

The foregoing explanation is probably valid for the Quebec French Canadians, but the situation of the French Canadians outside Quebec is different enough to call for other elements of explanation. What has just been said is probably not untrue of the French Canadians living in Ontario or New Brunswick, and Léon Gérin as well as Dofny and Rioux do not seem to question the validity of their explanation, both for the French Canadians outside Quebec and for those living in Quebec.

On the other hand, the context within which the French Canadians in Quebec and those living outside Quebec have to function is so different that it is hard to believe that other elements of explanation should not be added in order fully to understand the behavior of the French Canadians outside Quebec. As a matter of fact, a study recently made in Ontario shows that the lower level of education of the French Canadians living in that province is closely related to the meaning that the public school has for them and the threat they think it represents for themselves and their culture.* As is well illustrated by this research, *no other ethnic group in Ontario finds itself in a situation as conflicting as the French Canadians.* For the latter, the public school is in open contradiction with both their national identity and their fundamental values. This is why the French Canadians in Ontario have a lower level of education, not only than the British-born Canadians, but also than practically all the other ethnic groups in Ontario.

Indeed, some ethnic or religious groups in Canada voluntarily restrict the formal education of their children. This has been the case with the Mennonites, a religious group which has a strong internal cohesion and tends at the same time to isolate itself from the rest of society. The Mennonites, at least the traditional groups, do not allow education

Report of the Royal Commission on Bilingualism and Biculturalism, Vol. II, (1968), pp.80-94.

beyond the age of fourteen, that is, only up to the age of compulsory education. They believe that after the age of fourteen, their children must be withdrawn from school in order to avoid being submitted to a pernicious influence and being cut off from their religious community (Kurokawa, 1971). One could also mention the case of other anabaptist sects, like the Hutterites and Amish, who cut themselves off still more drastically from the rest of society, to a point where they may refuse to send their children to public school.

These attitudes differ greatly from those of the French Canadians, in that they reflect an explicit rejection of school and what it represents in modern society. As to the French Canadian group of Ontario, the research reported above has underlined an ambivalence towards public school: the French Canadians would like to see their children get more education, as they value education; but at the same time, they want to resist the cultural influence of the school on their children.

The Educational System and Social Change

The first part of this chapter was devoted to some of the main social, economic, and cultural inequalities related to the school. This leads to the general conclusion that serious rigidities are built into the social system of modern societies. The industrial capitalistic society is not as open as the official ideology says it is.

On the other hand, it must be recognized that this is only one aspect of the relationship between education and society. One must not ignore the other side of the coin, i.e., the extent to which the educational system can bring some social changes and the conditions under which the changes can take place. We will now look at three aspects of the educational system that can be regarded from this other angle: the school as a channel of social mobility, the spirit of educational reforms, and the role of student movements.

The School as a Channel of Social Mobility

It is true, as we have illustrated above, that the culturally, socially or economically privileged social classes are disproportionately represented in the educational system as we approach higher education; but it is also true that *a certain proportion of lower class children have access to colleges and universities*. This is clear from Tables III, IV, and V. The parents of about half the students registered in Canadian colleges and universities in 1956 were clericals, skilled and semi-skilled workers, farmers, laborers, i.e., below the occupational level which most of these students could expect to achieve (Table III). Seventy per cent of the students registered in the Arts and Science faculties of Canadian universities in 1961 had achieved a higher level of education than their parents (Table IV). The family income of 35 per cent of Canadian university students in 1956 was under $4,000 per annum.

Of course, these figures are not proportionate to the distribution of the total labor force or to the distribution of income among Canadian families. Had the general population been 'normally' represented in higher education, 54 per cent of the university students would have come from families with an income of less than $4,000, instead of 35 per cent, and only 15 per cent would have had parents in the two upper educational levels (proprietors and managers, professionals) instead of 50 per cent. But this fact, which reflects the process of social reproduction discussed earlier, must not hide the other fact that there is a certain amount of social mobility through education which brings some fluidity to the system of social stratification.

On the whole, the obstacle of social class to higher education is therefore not absolute. Some other factors must also be taken into account, which can help a certain proportion of lower or working class children enter higher education. Three main factors may break the social class barrier: *a high I.Q., strong motivation on the part of the student, high educational and professional aspirations on the part of the parents and the student*. When these three factors meet, lower and working class children have a chance of staying in school as long as they can or as they wish.

Indeed, in many cases more intelligence, work, and energy may be necessary for lower and working class children to achieve the same educational level as middle class boys and girls. They have to break more resistance and overcome more obstacles. But the fact remains that for these children, the school really is a *channel of upward mobility* in terms of educational achievement, occupational level, and income. And the number of lower and working class children who have benefited from this type of mobility has increased enormously over the last three or four decades, and again since the figures just quoted were calculated. This can be interpreted as a contribution of the educational system to the greater fluidity of the class system in modern industrial societies, especially North American societies.

On the other hand, a very important distinction must be made here between the individual level and the societal level. It can be said that the educational system plays the role of the channel of individual mobility for a certain proportion of young men and women, but the *overall system of social class and social stratification is not modified at all*. For instance, Spady (1967) has shown that in the United States, the absolute number of undergraduates and graduates from the working class has increased steadily over the last few years, but that the same trend can also be observed at the same tempo for middle class children. Therefore, there are more working class children at the college and university level, but the representation of the working class compared with the middle class remains the same. This means that more individuals have been mobile, but that the system has not changed. Although no specific study has been made of the same phenomenon in Canada, it is most probable that the same conclusions can be reached for this country.

Social mobility at the individual level may therefore conceal the stability or the stagnation of the social structure, as well as the process of social reproduction that still goes on. Because it brings some satisfaction to a certain proportion of the lower and working class, this type of mobility can also serve to justify a policy that favors the status quo of the society and that blocks the social, economic or political changes that the State should undertake or at least support or encourage. In that sense, the greater fluidity of the social stratification system for individuals can at the same time be an obstacle to change for the society as a whole.

The Spirit of Educational Reforms

A second aspect of the dynamic role of the educational system in society needs to be underlined. On the one hand, it is generally said that the school is essentially conservative and that the educational system is an agent of social reproduction. On the other hand and at the same time, it is precisely in the educational institutions, especially at the level of higher education, that one finds the most radical questioning of current values, present social structures, and established ideologies. Thus, the educational institution appears as the main place where some cultural changes take place in modern society.

Particularly since the last world war, education in industrial societies as well as in developing societies has been the object of many studies, inquiries, seminars, and symposiums, all of which were aimed at operating more or less drastic changes in the content as well as in the pedagogy of teaching at all levels, and adapting the educational system to the needs and the spirit of modern society. A systematic analysis of all these works has not yet been made, but it is most certain that one could extract out of them an ideology of change which, if fully realized, would modify not only the system of education but the system of modern society as well.

This ideology of educational reform has been characterized mainly by two basic principles which have served as the main guidelines of thought. The first was the *democratization of education*. All the reforms which were proposed were inspired by the principle that secondary education must be open to all, and that post-secondary education must be open to all those who are able to enter it. Put in different terms, this principle might be expressed in the following way: *each student should have the opportunity to benefit by an education which corresponds to his capacities, his tastes, and his interests, and he should be able to pursue his studies in the field or fields in which he is interested as far as he can or will go.* This principle was based on the ideology of 'equal opportunities for all' and on the confidence that this principle could be implemented. In practice, this meant the organization of a public system of education at all levels, free education for all and at all levels, and a system of scholarships for those who needed more help than just free education. Moreover, the democratization of education called for reforms of the school itself, in order to make the educational structures more flexible, to modify the pedagogy and to organize the counselling of students.

The second basic principle was probably less explicit and less general-ized than the first, but it was probably more important than the first. Put in simple terms, it was a proposal to *develop to their utmost all the capacities and aptitudes of each student.* The traditional system of education in Western societies aimed at the exclusive development of intelligence, and only a certain type of intelligence. The proposed reforms tried to broaden this concept of intelligence and to put forward a more general and more global training with the view that the traditional concept of intelligence was too limited and that it needed to be much more diversified. For instance, the general trends of the educational reforms of the last few years have all been focused on a greater freedom of expression, more spontaneity and creativity on the part of the student, more imagination in his work. Following this line of thought, all the reforms proposed have aimed at the liberation of resources which have not been exploited enough in the human being up to now.

Of course, these principles for educational reform could not be implemented completely or perfectly. It is not easy to persuade a large body of teachers and professors to modify the teaching and training methods to which they themselves were submitted and which they have been practising for several years. It is not easy to change the mentality or the expectations of parents with regard to the school, nor to convince the administrators of the educational system to undertake difficult transfor-mations of the same system. One can say, therefore, that educational reform has met with serious resistance on the part of various groups: teachers, parents, students, administrators, as well as public opinion in general.

And yet, in spite of this resistance, one must recognize that the proposed reforms have been partly implemented. And where they have been implemented, they have sometimes clearly contributed to significant changes, not only in the educational system, but in society as a whole. For instance, Stephen Richer measured the consequences of some pedagogical changes. He spent several hours in a primary school in urban Canada, observing the interactions between the children and their teachers in teacher-centered classrooms and in student-centered classrooms. He concludes:

> The open classes (student-centered) are relatively successful in elevating working-class interaction primarily by virtue of this capacity to elicit greater *student* initiation of relationships with the teacher. Such an atmosphere appears much more compatible with their life style than does the traditional closed classroom (teacher-centered).
>
> In sum, the study documents lower than chance teacher interactions for working class children in closed classrooms, and higher than chance interactions in open settings. In the educational literature open classes have typically been advocated on philosophical and/or pedagogical grounds. This paper suggests that such learning environments may have an additional unanticipated consequence; namely, enhancing the probability of success of working-class children in our schools. (Richer, 1974)

More generally speaking, one can say that educational reforms and the spirit they reflected have had some impact on public opinion and sometimes social policies. They have become the object of public discussions, which is at least a way of not denying the need for them. And, as often happens, even those who were opposed to the reforms were progressively influenced by the new spirit and the new mentality which inspired them. Even though it is a far cry from what might have taken place, one can say that an important educational reform has begun, that the spirit of the schools as well as of the colleges has changed, that the objectives of education have been questioned and re-evaluated, that the role and the function of teachers and professors have changed and that, on the whole, many new ideas have circulated in the educational milieu.

Marcel Fournier (1973) has analyzed the changes that the introduction of the teaching of the social sciences has brought about in the political climate and social policies of Quebec. He traces part of the so-called 'quiet revolution' which took place in Quebec in the 50's and still more in the 60's to the role played by the Faculty of Social Sciences at Laval University in the 30's and 40's.

On the whole, it is hard to find another sector of modern society where more drastic reforms have been proposed, and where the established structures and the current ideology have been questioned to the same extent. Compared to education, the rest of society has changed rather slowly and very little in the last two or three decades. Thus, one can say that the educational system has served as a kind of laboratory where current social values and social attitudes have changed most rapidly and to the largest extent. In this manner, the system of education has served as an indirect agent of social change and has played the role of a dynamic element in modern society.

Student Movements

The third factor of change in the educational system, which has recently been more visible than the first but not necessarily more efficient, is the political action of the student movements which took place in almost all Western societies in the last decade, and in a good number of countries outside the Western hemisphere. Groups and associations of more or less radical students and sometimes teachers or professors have attacked the existing educational and social structures, the established ideas, the current policies, the established order and power. They have questioned altogether the system of education as it is now, as well as the type of society that it reflects and to which it is supposed to prepare the labor force with various levels of qualifications.

More generally, an increasing gap has been created between what has been called *a student 'counter-culture'* and the dominant culture of the adult society. The counter-culture has especially *attacked the main taboos of our culture and civilization, the useless constraints of that society, and the too exclusively rational conception of life which has been the dominating ideology of the Western world.* It is first in this counter-culture that new forms of personal freedom, free expression of feelings, liberation from social and economic constraints, and rejection of established authority have found expression.

But the counter-culture is a designation that is somewhat misleading. As a matter of fact, it is not a culture that applies to all youth. It is a culture that has been found especially in colleges and universities, and somewhat also in high schools. In other words, it is a culture or a subculture that is peculiar to a part of the student population.

The counter-culture that originated in the colleges and universities has been a factor of social change, both on the campuses and outside. Through this counter-culture and the student movements, a certain number of students have contributed to the creation and diffusion of new ideas, new attitudes, and have actively contributed to a change in society. This is particularly the case with 'young radicals,' whose psychology Kenneth Keniston (1960; 1968) has tried to investigate and whom he has helped make better understood, in demonstrating that their behavior was perfectly 'normal,' contrary to what has too often been said.

Some social psychological studies have shown that young men and women who pursue advanced studies have a general tendency to adopt more 'liberal' attitudes and sometimes more 'radical' attitudes (Feldman and Newcomb, 1970). That is why the universities of the past as well as the present have often been the mainspring of social criticism, political activism and change of ideas and ideologies. A good number of studies have pointed out the role of student movements in the past and recently (Lipset, 1971). Moreover, some historical periods have been marked by greater student agitation than others. We have recently lived through a period of that sort, where student organizations have been numerous, highly politicized and active in the defense of various causes.*

Indeed, the efficiency of these student movements has been relative. In France, the student protests of 1968 constituted an important historical break with the past and they were surely instrumental in the opening of a new era in the history of French universities. † In some South American countries, like Argentina, Brazil or Chile, student movements have often played a dominant political role both in universities and in the political life of the country.‡ From what we know, it seems that student movements were very active and important in the cultural revolution in China, from 1966 to 1970.

On the other hand, the student movement in the United States, although active and fairly well organized, has been rather slow in influencing American internal and external policy, especially with regard to civil rights, the Vietnam war and the policy of the United States in its relationship with communist countries. In Canada, it is hard to say that student movements have had a real impact on university policies, still less on Canadian policy. And yet, some recent studies have shown the active role of student movements in the history of the last decade in Quebec.**

---

*On the sources and history of student activism in the United States recently, see especially, Hal Draper, *Berkeley: The New Student Revolt,* (New York, Grove Press, Inc., 1965); Michael V. Miller and Susan Gilmore (eds.), *Revolution at Berkeley: The Crisis in American Education,* (New York, Dell, 1965); S.M. Lipset and S.S. Wolin (eds.), *The Berkeley Student Revolt: Facts and Interpretations,* (Garden City, N.Y., Doubleday, 1965).

†On the French student movement, see especially Alain Touraine, *La société post-industrielle,* (Paris, Denoël, 1968); *Le mouvement de mai ou le communisme utopique,* (Paris, Seuil, 1968).

‡See, for example, S.M. Lipset and A. Solari (eds.), *Elites in Latin America,* (New York, Oxford University Press, 1967), especially Part III.

**For instance, Paul R. Bélanger and Louis Maheu, 'Pratique politique étudiante au Québec,' *Recherches Sociographiques,* XIII, No.3 (Sept.-Dec., 1972), 309-342.

Conclusion

One general conclusion which comes out of all that has been said here is surely that the relations between education and society are far more complex than is generally assumed. It is surely not true to say that society is what education makes it. But one cannot say either that education simply reflects what society is. There is between the two a network of interactions that is exceedingly complex. The educational system is the mirror of a society, its social stratification, its culture, its dominant ideologies, its political structure. But it is also the main place where society and culture are discussed and questioned, and where the roots of social criticism are generally to be found. It is therefore true to say at the same time that the educational system is conservative and that it is the seedbed of the social changes to come.

References

Baudelot, Christian, and Roger Establet, *L'École Capitaliste en France*. Paris: François Marpero, 1971.

Bélanger, Pierre W., and Guy Rocher (eds.), *Ecole et Société au Québec*. Montreal: HMH, 1970.

Bourdieu, Pierre, and Jean-Claude Passeron, *Les Héritiers*. Paris: Editions de Minuit, 1964.

——, *La Reproduction*. Paris: Editions de Minuit, 1970.

Clark, Barbara S., 'Pre-school Programs and Black Children,' in Jean Leonard Elliott (ed.), *Immigrant Groups*. Scarborough: Prentice-Hall of Canada, 1971, ch. 8.

Cohen, Albert K., *Delinquent Boys*. Glencoe, Ill.: The Free Press, 1955.

Conant, James B., *The American High School*. New York: McGraw-Hill, 1959.

——, *Slums and Suburbs*. New York: McGraw-Hill, 1961.

Dofny, Jacques, and Marcel Rioux, 'Social Class in French Canada,' in Marcel Rioux and Yves Martin (eds.), *French-Canadian Society*. Toronto: McClelland and Stewart, (The Carleton Library), 1964, pp. 307-318.

Feldman, Kenneth A., and Theodore M. Newcomb, *The Impact of College on Students*. San Francisco: Jossey-Bass Inc., 1970.

Floud, J., A.H. Halsey, and F.M. Martin, *Social Class and Educational Opportunity*. London: Heinemann, 1956.

Fournier, Marcel, 'L'institutionnalisation des sciences sociales au Québec,' *Sociologie et sociétés*, 1 (May, 1973), 27-57.

Friedenberg, E.Z., *Coming of Age in America*. New York: Random House, 1965.

——, *The Vanishing Adolescent*, Boston: Beacon Press, 1959.

Gérin, Léon, 'The French-Canadian Family: Its Strengths and Weaknesses,' in Marcel Rioux and Yves Martin (eds.), *French-Canadian Society*. Toronto: McClelland and Stewart, 1964, pp. 32-57.

Goodman, Paul, *Compulsory Mis-education.* New York: Knopf, 1962.

Hobart, C.W., and C.S. Brant, 'Eskimo Education, Danish and Canadian: A Comparison,' *Canadian Review of Sociology and Anthropology,* III, 2 (May, 1966), pp. 57 and 64.

Hollingshead, August B., *Elmstown's Youth.* New York: John Wiley and Sons, 1949.

Institut national d'études démographiques, *Le niveau intellectuel des enfants d'âge scolaire,* 2 vols. Paris: Presses Universitaires de France, 1950 and 1954.

Jensen, A.R., 'How much can we boost I.Q. and scholastic achievement?' *Harvard Educational Review,* XXXIV, 1, Winter-Spring, 1969.

Keniston, Kenneth, *Young Radicals, Notes on Committed Youth.* New York: Harcourt, Brace and World, 1968.

——, *Youth and Dissent: The Rise of a New Opposition.* New York: Harcourt, Brace, Jovanovich, 1960.

Kurokawa, Minako, 'Mennonite Children in Waterloo County,' in Jean Leonard Elliott (ed.), *Immigrant Groups.* Scarborough: Prentice-Hall of Canada, 1971.

Lipset, S.M., 'Youth and Politics,' in R.K. Merton and R. Nislet (eds.), *Contemporary Social Problems,* 3rd edition. New York: Harcourt, Brace, Jovanovich, 1971, pp. 743-791.

Lynd, Robert S., and Helen Lynd, *Middletown: A Study in American Culture.* New York: Harcourt, Brace and World, 1929.

Porter, John, *The Vertical Mosaic.* Toronto: University of Toronto Press, 1965, especially Chapter VI.

Report of the Royal Commission on Bilingualism and Biculturalism, Vol. 11. Ottawa: Queen's Printer, 1968.

Richer, Stephen, 'Middle Class Bias of Schools: Fact or Fancy?' *Sociology of Education,* Fall, 1974.

Riessman, Frank, *The Culturally Deprived Child.* New York: Harper and Row, 1962.

Rocher, Guy, 'Carences de nos ressources humaines et évolution des besoins,' in *L'utilisation des ressources humaines: un défi à relever,* 1965 Conference of L'Institut Canadien des Affaires Publiques. Montreal: Les Editions du Jour, 1965, pp. 69-80.

Senna, Carl (ed.) *The Fallacy of I.Q.* New York: The Third Press, 1973.

Sexton, Patricia Cayo, *Education and Income: Inequality of Opportunity in the Public Schools.* New York: Viking Press, 1961.

——, *The American School, A Sociological Analysis.* Englewood Cliffs: Prentice-Hall Inc., 1967.

Spady, William, 'Educational Mobility and Access: Growth and Paradoxes,' *American Journal of Sociology,* LXXIII, No. 3 (November, 1967), 273-286.

Warner, W. Lloyd, Robert G. Havighurst, and M.D. Loeb, *Who Shall be Educated?* New York: Harper and Row, 1944.

Williams, Frederick (ed.), *Language and Poverty.* Chicago: Markham Publishing Co., 1970.

CHAPTER SIX

Multi-Ethnic Societies: The Issues of Identity and Inequality

Frank G. Vallee
Carleton University

Introduction

Premier Amin of Uganda orders the expulsion of thousands of Asians from his country; in Northern Ireland the casualty list from Protestant-Catholic strife exceeds 500; black athletes threaten to boycott the Olympics if Rhodesia is invited to participate; ominous rumblings are heard from the ranks of black workers in South Africa; a new stand is taken by American Indians at Wounded Knee, the site of Custer's Last Stand; in Canada, hundreds of French-speaking students in Cornwall go on strike and demand a completely French High School.

It takes little time and ingenuity to glean scores of examples of group conflict from the mass media on a given day, for conflict is a normal condition in human society, just as normal as co-operation. Groups or categories of people in conflict represent a variety of types of interest — class against class, left wing versus right wing, denomination against denomination, male against female, black against white, and on and on. *Of much interest to sociologists is conflict which pits against one another groups based on ascription.* Membership in such groups is determined primarily, if not entirely, by the attributes with which one is born — e.g., skin color, sex — and by descent or family connections.

We hasten to insert that sociologists are interested not only in conflict among ascriptive groupings. Other processes, such as co-operation, integration, and symbiosis (mutual dependence) also claim their attention. In fact, until recent years much sociological study of ascriptive groupings concentrated on anything but conflict, for it was widely assumed that such groupings were losing much of their significance under conditions of modernization, that communal boundaries, based on race and ethnicity, were dissolving. However, today we are forced to examine this assumption in the face of evidence from all over the world of nationalistic movements, many of them struggles of ethnic minorities to maintain themselves or develop autonomously. Communal boundaries continue to divide some people from others in political states on every continent.

It appears that the ideal of the ethnically homogeneous state wherein individuals are treated primarily as 'citizens' outside the context of their ascriptive attributes, is a rare specimen. This ideal derives from a stage in European history where the nation-state, in which political boundaries coincide with cultural ones, was regarded as the most desirable. However, modern states are typically heterogeneous with reference to ethnicity. In some cases this heterogeneity is of much importance, in others it is of minimal significance. The object of this chapter is to explore the ways in which ethnicity figures in the fate of modern societies, with frequent reference to Canada. Of special interest to us is how social scientists go about the job of explaining how ethnic goups and multi-ethnic societies are maintained and changed. Some issues and policies also come in for brief comment.

Definitions

What do we mean by 'race,' 'ethnic,' 'minority' and other terms already used but not defined? In the topic under discussion definition is more than an academic exercise in taxonomy, for much confusion in argument and analysis is caused by the use of the same word to mean different things and of different words to mean the same thing. Everyone knows of the special difficulties of social science, as compared with physical science, because of its dependence on words and concepts in everyday use. Nowhere in the many fields of social science is this difficulty greater than it is in race and ethnic relations studies. Look, for instance, at the varied use of the term 'race.'

In English and many other European languages (e.g., *race* in French; *razza* in Italian; *Reize* in German) the term is often, perhaps most often, used to denote a group of people which is dintinctive in some clear-cut way, through one or a combination of language, culture, and physical appearance. Thus people speak of the English race, the French-Canadian race, the Gypsy race, and the like, using the term synonymously with the French *nation* and the German *Volk*. This usage is still very common.

One reads in the recent reports of the Royal Commission on Bilingualism and Biculturalism of the two Founding Races of Canada — the French and the English.

Another common popular usage of the word is with respect to physically distinct *categories*. One hears of the Yellow Race, the Black Race, the White Race, The Red Race, as though these were actual groups of people whose personalities and cultures coincided with their color. Such usage suggests the underlying belief that the most important individual and group traits are inherited biologically. Thus the emphasis on *line of descent*. In this view, people are born into their 'race,' whether this is taken to mean a cultural or biological grouping. The etymology of the word is instructive in this respect. Shipley gives the following as one root of the word:

> '*Race:* lineage, seen in Italian *razza,* is from Old High German *reiza,* a stroke, a line, as it marks the direct line of descent.' (Shipley, 1959: 294)

In contrast with the popular usage of the term race, anthropologists and biologists attempt to be specific and unambiguous in their definitions, a recent one of which is cited:

> [Race is] . . . 'an anthropological classification dividing mankind (HOMO SAPIENS) into several divisions and subdivisions (or subraces). The criteria for labeling the various races are based essentially on physical characteristics of size, the shape of the head, eyes, ears, lips, and nose, and the color of the skin and eyes. The hereditary characteristics, such as skin color (widely used as a criterion of race), are not exclusive to any racial group, but overlap from one racial category to another. The characteristics used in classification are determined on a statistical basis, that is, according to frequency of occurrence, with a high percent of certain characteristics in each classification . . . '*

By this definition a race is a statistical category and not a group in the sociological sense. Physical characteristics, such as skin color, often do provide a basis for the processes of status allocation and group formation, but these processes are social and psychological and are not determinted by biological make-up as such.

Another term which is sometimes used synonymously with race in its sense of a distinct group, is *ethnic*. The Greek root of this term *(ethnos)* is usually translated into English as people or nation, but without the latter's connotation of citizenship in a state. A double confusion arises in

*From *A Modern Dictionary of Sociology* by George A. Theodorson and Achilles G. Theodorson. Copyright © 1969 by George A. Theodorson, with permission of Thomas Y. Crowell Company, Inc., publisher.

Canada over the use of the term 'nation.' In French (*la nation*) the term refers to a group which shares a common culture, whether or not they are citizens of the same state. In English the word is sometimes used synonymously with state, so that nationality means the same as citizenship. Thus, when some Canadians define Canada as being composed of *deux nations,* others assume that they mean two states.

A secondary denotation of 'ethnic' in Western European languages is that of non-Christian, outsiders. This helps account for the vestige of pejorativeness attached to this term to this day in some countries. For instance, many Canadians of Anglo-Saxon origin regard other origins (Ukrainian, Chinese, German, etc.) as 'ethnic,' a term which they would not apply to themselves. It is noteworthy that in 1972 Gérard Pelletier, Secretary of State in the Federal Government of Canada, made a plea that people abolish the word ethnic and substitute the word cultural for it, so that one would speak of cultural rather than of ethnic groups in Canada. Pejorative or not, the term enjoys widespread usage in everyday speech as well as in social science. Because it is a central concept in this chapter, it is imperative that we consider its definition rather closely.

One problem with definitions of the term 'ethnic' in social science is the number and variety of criteria used. All definitions of ethnicity and ethnic group include references to distinctive cultural traits, such as language and customs, as a necessary element. The trouble is that culture is made up of so many traits in so many spheres of life. Which of these should be included, and which excluded, when defining ethnicity and ethnic group?

Many definitions state that the ethnic group may be based on distinctions in religion, nationality, language, life-style, physical appearance. Does this mean that the Jehovah's Witnesses, say, are an ethnic group? Do the people who live in Hippie communes, with their distinctive life-style, form an ethnic group? One can think of many such subcultures which one would not call ethnic groups. What is needed is a definition which permits us to distinguish ethnic from other subcultures.

The crucial importance of *descent* is what distinguishes ethnic from other subcultures. People in Hippie communes, radical religious cults, model railroad clubs, and the like, do not qualify as an ethnic group because descent is not a key criterion for membership in them. One reason for the oft-noted overlap between ethnicity and social class is that in both cases it is affiliation with a particular family which provides the initial definition of the individual's ethnic and social class status.

It is advisable to define ethnicity as an attribute before going on to define the various groupings and processes which have an ethnic referent. In our usage, ethnicity refers to descent from ancestors who shared a *common culture or subculture manifested in distinctive ways of speaking and/or acting.* This common culture may have been carried by many different kinds of grouping, such as religious, political, geographical, but in all cases the *kinship networks are crucial bearers of the culture.*

The question of which descent lines are used as bearers of the attribute of ethnicity is an empirical one. One would expect that where descent is traced matrilineally, for example, the attribute of ethnicity would be traced through the mother's mother's mother's, and so on, line of descent. Special problems arise where descent is traced bilaterally and multilaterally. In such cases the observer learns what norms govern the passage of ethnicity. In our own society, descent is traced multilaterally, but there is a bias in favor of male lines. Surnames are passed down the male line, and surnames are regarded as key symbols of ethnic identification although not always reliable ones. In Canada and certain other countries, the chief criterion used both officially and unofficially to establish ethnic origin is descent from male ancestors. For instance, in the Canadian census the question concerning origin is asked in the following way:

> Of what nationality was your first male ancestor who came to this continent? (*Census of Canada, Instructions to Enumerators*)

The definition of ethnicity above, like all definitions, is in some ways over-inclusive and in other ways under-inclusive. It is over-inclusive in that not all persons in a given line of descent identify with or are identified with the ethnic affiliation of that line. It is under-inclusive in that some persons who are not in a given line of descent may identify with and be identified with the ethnic affiliation of that line of descent.

The introduction of the terms 'identify with' and 'are identified with' invites us to recall the two-sided coin aspect of ethnicity, the subjective aspect of how a person thinks of himself, and the objective or external aspect of how a person is labelled by others. When a person identifies with ethnicity 'A' and is recognized by others as affiliated with 'A,' both sides of the coin are similar and there is congruence. However, congruence is not automatic. For instance, a person might want to identify with a particular group, but have his bid rejected. Or perhaps more often, a person might be labelled or defined as belonging to a certain category when he does not identify with that category. For instance, many White Americans and Europeans, upon their arrival in Hawaii, discover they are labelled as *haoles* (pronounced *howleys*), which can be translated as 'White Stranger who will never be one of us.' Now quite independently of how the person feels, he is forced to accept that definition of himself for many purposes and come to terms with it. He cannot will that definition of himself out of existence.

The matter of ethnic identification, especially the subjective aspects of it, is one of the more complex issues in social science and attempts to study it in a scientific way are fraught with difficulties. One reason for these difficulties is that observers tend to oversimplify reality and seek to find how people respond to certain ethnic labels, as though there were a fixed connection between a particular label and a particular person. Identities are fluid. For instance, in one situation a person might feel strongly conscious of being a Franco-Ontarian vis-à-vis a Québecois; in another, the same person might feel strongly Francophone vis-à-vis Anglophone Canadians; in still another the same person might feel strongly Canadian vis-à-vis Americans and include in his 'we-group' those who in another situation are regarded as part of the 'they-group.' Again depending on the situation, it behooves a person to present himself as being linked with one or another category.

In this listing of definitions of important terms for our purposes, the final one to consider is that of *ethnic group*. The term ethnic group is applied very loosely in both everyday speech and social science. Often it is used with reference to what in social science is more properly called a social *category*, which is

> ... a plurality of persons who are not organized into a system of social interaction ... but who do have similar social characteristics or statuses. (Theodorson and Theodorson, 1969: 384)

In order for a social *category* to become a social *group* the people in it must develop a sense of *we-feeling or common identity*, which should be the basis for some meaningful interaction and solidarity. One could add that a social group which is more extended than a small family or small association would have some sort of organization or structure, no matter how informal. Thus we say that *an ethnic group is made up of people who share ethnicity (as previously defined), who share some sense of peoplehood or consciousness of kind, who interact with one another in meaningful ways beyond the elementary family, and who are regarded by others as being in the one ethnic category.* The latter point is important to keep in mind. We take into account not only the subjective feeling of being in an ethnic group, but also the way in which membership is recognized or not recognized by others. Needless to say, ethnic groups as so defined are of many different stripes and varieties, a topic which is taken up in the next section.

A multi-ethnic society is, for our purposes, *a political state which contains more than one major ethnic group as defined above.* The qualification 'major' is made in order to exclude states which have one large dominant group and one or more very small ones which are of only peripheral significance in the country as a whole.

The most important basic terms for the purposes of this chapter have been defined. Other terms will be defined and discussed as they arise in the ensuing analysis of the establishment, maintenance of, and change in multi-ethnic societies. This analysis will benefit from a few notes on research approaches to the study of ethnicity, or at least a few of the major ones.

Approaches to the Study of Ethnicity

There are three main approaches used in studying ethnic groups and multi-ethnic populations. These are not so much competing approaches as they are complementary to one another. One may be termed the *ethnographic* approach. In it the attempt is made to present an exhaustive account of the history, culture, and social organization of a particular ethnic group. The format followed is similar to that used for generations by anthropologists in the study of cultures. In this type of study, relations between ethnic groups usually command some attention, but the main thrust is in the direction of treating the group studied as if it were detached from other ethnic groups. The emphasis is on how the elements of culture and social organization *within* the group are related to one another, and how historical factors account for changes in the group. Perhaps the most familiar studies of this kind on the Canadian scene are those of small, religiously based communal groups, such as the Hutterites (Bennett, 1967). However, there are studies of larger-scale and less clearly bounded groupings which feature this anthropological approach. A notable recent one is the massive program of study of French Canadian groupings in Quebec and the Maritimes, excerpts from which have been published recently. (Tremblay and Gold, 1973)

Another approach to note takes as its central interest the relations *among* ethnic groups, usually in specifically defined communities and regions. The emphasis in such studies is on processes, such as competition, co-operation, symbiosis, conflict which involve exchanges across ethnic boundaries. A notable example is that of Frederik Barth's (1969) collection of studies in ethnic group relations in various parts of the world. On the Canadian scene, apart from Hughes' classic works, a good example of the use of this approach is that of Jackson in his study of conflict and accommodation in an Ontario community. (Hughes, 1943; Jackson, 1966)

Finally we mention the approach that takes the society as a whole (almost always defined as the political state) as its universe of study and asks, in effect, what does the attribute of ethnicity mean, how is it used in sorting people out, in the society? In this approach it is usual to feature comparisons of many ethnic groups and categories on a number of dimensions: political behavior, economic standing, occupational distribution, measures of segregation, and the like. (Vallee *et al.*, 1957) In this way it is hoped a general picture of the significance of ethnicity for a society can be drawn. Ideally it is within the context of such a general picture that studies employing the first two approaches may be placed.

There are many other approaches used in studies which have a bearing on ethnicity, but to go into them in detail would consume too much space. For example, there are studies of immigrant adjustment (Richmond, 1967); of comparisons between groups in terms of specific items like child-rearing, stereotyping, values (Berry and Wilde, 1972); of perceived social distance between ethnic categories, and many others. (Taylor *et al.*, 1972) However, we have selected for comment only what appear to us to be the major approaches to societal-level studies where ethnicity is a major focus.

How Multi-Ethnic Societies Get Established

A number of authors have documented the ways in which multi-ethnic societies began (Lieberson, Schermerhorn, Banton). Some became that way through internal divisions, or *fission,* to use a term from anthropological analysis. This process means simply the emergence of subgroups based on kinship which over a long period evolve into substantial tribes which, however, maintain contact with one another and for some purposes may be regarded as in the same social system. Most of the anthropological examples are from pre-modern Africa. The process is to be found in the Biblical myths concerning brothers, each of whom becomes patriarch and ancestor of a distinctive tribe (e.g., Ham, Shem, and Japhet).

However, the great majority of multi-ethnic societies of ancient and modern times were established through contact of previously separate groups which came to share the same social and geographical space. In discussing this matter we shall concentrate on a few examples where contact has led to the development of modern multi-ethnic states.

The first kind of historical situation is exemplified in the expansion of imperialist powers into neighboring or overseas territories. The best-known cases come from European expansion, although the same process occurred in both the Far East and the Near East. One result of such expansion was the subordination of native or aboriginal people by the incomers. Two main subtypes or varieties of such expansionist situations may be distinguished. In the first place, we have colonies established for economic profit or military advantage, but where there is little or no settlement of immigrants of the imperial power. A number of instances may be cited: the Dutch and French in the South Pacific; the British in the West Indies; the Japanese in Korea.

In the second place we have the invasion of large numbers of settlers who displace the native population and claim the land as their own, founding what are in effect new societies, with the invaders becoming 'chartered members.' Familiar instances are the settlement of Europeans in North America; the British in New Zealand and Australia; the British and Dutch in southern parts of Africa. The invaders and their descendants come to dominate the colonies and then become hosts to subsequent waves of immigrants. The latter may be 'imported' in groups to work plantations or mines, or come as individuals or families seeking a better living. In any case, the waves of immigrants add to the ethnic and in many cases the racial heterogeneity.

Shifts in political boundaries as a result of wars and their aftermaths have often thrown together into one state ethnic groups which were previously in different states, or have split into different states ethnic groups which were formerly within the same political boundary. This process is a particularly familiar one in European history, but it has gone on, and still goes on, in other parts of the world, most notably in Africa and the Pacific.

Wars and predatory expansion are not the only causes of new combinations of ethnic groups which were formerly separate. The process of federation, the linking up into political units of previously separated units, such as is going on now in Western Europe and the Caribbean, is a response to pressures other than war, just as was the confederation of units into what is now Canada.

Many societies developed their multi-ethnic character through combinations of these processes. The United States began as a frontier-contact society, involving the taking over of Indian lands, its Anglo charter-group hosting incoming slaves and free immigrants, spreading landward against its territorial boundaries to absorb Spanish-Americans, and hopping overseas and intervening land space to include Hawaii and Alaska with their variety of ethnic groups. Canada, too, combined a number of processes in developing its multi-ethnic character: one European group, the French, and another, the English, tussling for sovereignty over what they considered 'empty space' (the Indians did not regard it as empty!). Hughes makes some interesting observations on the concept of 'empty space: '

> But what is an empty country, region, or even a vacant lot? The Romans made country empty by conquering the natives, and setting up their own kind of agriculture. The European colonizers of the 15th, 16th and 17th centuries were generally met by natives when they landed in a new, to them,

country; to these Europeans much of the New World was empty. A vacant lot may be populated with boys playing ball, until some one with a land title, a building permit, some capital and a bull-dozer turns up. To the builder the site has been vacant.*

The James Bay Region is a contemporary case in point. Eventually, the Europeans concluded their dispute, one side winning the tussle, both sides supplanting native groups in much of the country and acting as hosts to subsequent waves of immigrants, the federating process going on in the meanwhile.

Types of Multi-Ethnic Society

From these various movements of boundaries and populations, different types of multi-ethnic society emerge. The literature on race and ethnic relations provides examples of the wide range of types, of which we discuss only a few, keeping in mind our special interest in Canada in a comparative perspective.

In one type, distinctiveness among constituent ethnic groups is maintained, with rather rigid barriers between them. The dominant group controls the key institutions, and has a monopoly over arms and the agencies of enforcement. There are not many such regimes in their 'pure' form. The most frequently cited example and the closest to the pure form of this type is South Africa. Elaborate arrangements are required to keep the groups segregated from one another: pass laws, laws against marriage across racial lines, separate facilities of all kinds, residential segregation, are the most obvious means of maintaining such a multi-ethnic society. If such a regime lasts long enough to acquire a religiously sanctioned legitimacy from enough people in all sectors, the coercive means of maintaining it may give way (in theory, at least!) to the kind of self-regulating caste system which India was said to be in the past. This type of multi-ethnic system occurs in places where physical distinctions among groups are pronounced.

In another pure type, distinctions are maintained among the constituent groups, but the latter are regarded as, at least officially, equal to one another in rights, and these rights are officially recognized at least in the regions they occupy, for in this type it is usual for the groups to be clustered territorially and for the practise of their distinctive religion and/or language to be statutorily guaranteed. Switzerland is the standard example of this type which is most often cited. A striking feature of Switzerland is the at least rough coincidence between ethnic boundaries

*E.C. Hughes, 'Colonies, Colonization and Colonialism,' a paper delivered to the American Ethnological Society, April, 1973.

and territorial boundaries, although, of course, there is intermingling across ethnic lines, especially in the cities.

Of the many types of multi-ethnic society, the third and final one we mention is that in which the ethnic categories and groups are distributed widely and interspersed one with the other, although geographical clusters of particular groups occur. It is less common for statutory guarantees fostering the maintenance of particular groups to occur in this type of society than it is in the type mentioned above. Australia is a good illustration of this type.

Many modern states are mixtures of the latter two types. Canada is a case in point. Coincidences between ethnic and territorial boundaries, in which special guarantees of language rights apply, are found only in Quebec, which is the extent to which Canada resembles the Switzerland model. Otherwise its ethnic groups are dispersed in varying degrees over the country, with several notable clusterings, such as the Icelanders around Gimli, Germans around Kitchener-Waterloo, Scottish in Cape Breton, and so on. However, no special rights are accorded these groupings in their 'territories.' That is, they are not *officially* recognized and given statutory rights as ethnic groups. An exception to this statement concerns the Indians, who have a special status deriving from the Indian Act and whose reserves can be regarded as ethnic-territorial units.

One important point in considering types of multi-ethnic society is the extent to which certain regions are the 'homelands' for large numbers of particular ethnic groups. In other words, territoriality is important when we consider how the groups relate to one another in the state as a whole. Where there is coincidence between ethnic and territorial boundaries, the likelihood of strong ethnic solidarity is enhanced, for it implies that there is a low rate of interaction between members of different ethnic groups.

The *number* of major ethnic groups is another important characteristic to consider. Where there are only two, the chances of polarization are enhanced. The Flemish- and French-speaking groups in Belgium; the Protestants and Catholics in Northern Ireland; the Watutsi and Bahutu of Africa, are examples of dual societies. Where there are more than two major groups, chances of polarization and partitioning are reduced. In Canada English-French dualism is balanced by a plurality of other groups, although in certain regions, like New Brunswick and Quebec, the dualism is quite pronounced and the chances of polarization quite high.

A final point on this topic has to do with the ways in which multi-ethnic societies are internally stratified. Theoretically it is possible to construct or at least to imagine a society where ethnic distinctions are maintained and where the groups are equal to one another in status, prestige, and power. But, empirically, ethnic groups tend to be arranged in some sort of hierarchy, or system of stratification, in multi-ethnic societies. That is, multi-ethnic societies tend to be vertical rather than horizontal mosaics, to use the imagery of John Porter. No wonder there is stress and strain in multi-ethnic societies! The concern in the remainder of this chapter will be with systems of inequality in which ethnicity is an important factor.

Types of Ethnic Group

Ethnic groups differ from one another on many dimensions, such as visibility and primary bases of group formation (e.g., religion, language, color, etc.). (Elliott, 1971) We note only the more obvious factors to take into account in a typology of ethnic groups. One factor is whether or not the group is a minority. Now *minority* is another term which is used in more than one sense. On the one hand it is used to mean *a group which is smaller in number than another group.* On the other hand it is used to mean *subordinate or inferior status.* A group can be a majority in terms of numbers but a minority in terms of status. An obvious example is the situation of the blacks in South Africa and Rhodesia, numerically a majority but of minority status. The English in the Province of Quebec are a numerical minority but not a status minority unless, of course, certain rights that they have long enjoyed (e.g., schooling in their own language) are withdrawn. (Bill 22, recently passed in the Quebec Assembly, is perceived by many Anglophones as threatening the withdrawal of such a right — education in the English language).

The sheer fact of numbers in itself must be qualified by the fact of distribution of the ethnic group's population. In the overall Canadian population, those of Italian origin form only about 2 per cent, but more than half of these live in rather large concentrations in the cities of Toronto and Montreal. Such concentration permits the development and maintenance of many ethnic group institutions, such as parishes, clubs, mass media, special shops, etc.

The phrase minority *status* is used in at least three ways: for a group which is statutorily deprived of certain rights which others have; for one that is low in education and income; for one that is looked down upon. Usually these three aspects are correlated. However, a group may be low in prestige, high in income and education, and curtailed in some rights, such as in standing for political office or in the practise of their faith. Middleman minorities may be cited as an example. A *middleman minority* is one which performs certain functions, usually in trade and commerce, and is situated socially between the dominant and sub-ordinate groups. This role has been performed by Jews in many European countries, Chinese in Southeast Asia, Asians in some African countries.

Another important variable which serves to differentiate one ethnic group from another is degree of *closure* (Neuwirth, 1969). A completely closed group would form a wholly independent society and thus would not qualify as an ethnic group in our terms. In other words, by definition there are no completely closed ethnic groups, because the latter are always part of a larger society. However, some groups do maintain a high degree of autonomy. Consider the Hutterites in Canada, for instance, voluntarily segregated, very much self-sufficient in their agri-cultural communities, taking care of most of their own needs, arranging for marriages within the Hutterite group (endogamy). In a case like this the cultural and social boundaries of the group coincide and are obvious to all. At the other extreme, consider the Dutch in Canada. They are interspersed throughout the occupational system, have a relatively low rate of endogamy, send their children to public schools, and except for a few rural communities in Ontario with a strong commitment to a religious denomination, are residentially dispersed. They do have some Dutch-Canadian associations, patronized especially by immigrants, but this is the extent of the formal structuring among them. It is questionable whether or not we should refer to the Dutch of Canada as an ethnic *group,* in the sense defined above.

If we take a combination of criteria, such as extent to which a group's members marry outside *(exogamy)* or within *(endogamy)* the group; extent to which a group is segregated from others in occupation and residence; extent to which a group has its own set of institutions and resources, such as schools, churches, newspapers, we get a measure of the extent to which the group is 'closed' and distinctive. In Canada the groups that score highest on most criteria seem to be the native peoples, the French, Jews, Ukrainians, and Italians. Those that score lowest are the Scandinavians and most others of Western European origin.*

---

*This conclusion is tentative and based on varied sources. In no publication could we find brought together the data for different ethnic groups on *combinations* of more than two measures of homogeneity and segregation which would permit us to rank groups on their degree of closure. Volume IV of the *Report of the Royal Commission on Bilingualism and Biculturalism* (1970: 300) ranks twenty-nine groups according to rates of endogamy, mother tongue retention, and religious affiliation. Raymond Breton (1960; 1964), in his study of immigrants in Montreal, shows how a number of ethnic groups differ in terms of their affiliations within their own groups, knowledge of one or both official languages, educational level, and institutional completeness. Vallee (1969 and forthcoming) provides a comparison of the French outside Quebec with a number of other groups in terms of endogamy, occupational homogeneity, and residential segregation. It should be pointed out

There is another important way in which ethnic groups differ from one another and that pertains to the prevailing orientation of group members towards the society. In a much-quoted article written more than a generation ago, Wirth (1945) presented a scheme in which distinctions were drawn between four types of ethnic group goals or orientations, as follows: assimilationist, pluralist, secessionist, and militant. Most members of an ethnic group where the assimilationist goal prevails are not much interested in maintaining ethnic distinctiveness and are more concerned with gaining acceptance as individuals on the terms set out by the majority group. To use a familiar imagery, they want their ethnicity to melt in the societal pot. The pluralist orientation is the label applied to those who seek to maintain some degree of ethnic group distinctiveness, with one's own and other groups linked in a kind of mosaic. On the other hand, the secessionist orientation carries the concern with maintaining group distinctiveness to the point of rejecting membership in the society, in effect seeking to set up a separate society. Finally, the militant orientation refers to the view that one's own ethnic group should dominate others in the society. A modification of this scheme with reference to minority ethnic groups in Canadian society has been suggested by Elliott (1971: 8).

Needless to say, in order for an ethnic group to be characterized as primarily assimilationist, pluralistic, secessionist, or militant, it is not necessary that all members be oriented in the one way. Within the ranks of a given group, more than one of the orientations mentioned may co-exist among the various segments that make up the group. This is obviously the case with several groups in Canada, especially the Francophones of Quebec.

If it is obvious that more than one orientation may be found in a given group at any one time, it is also obvious that orientations change over time, for contacts among ethnic groups occur in an historical context. In another classic formulation which deals with changes over time, Park (1964: 189-195) set out a model more than a generation ago which he called the Race Relations Cycle. He argued that contact between ethnic groups passes through phases marked by competition and conflict, accommodation and, ultimately, assimilation. Particular ethnic groups may be viewed as being at one or another stage of this process, depending chiefly on how long the group has been settled in the society, for Park's formulation had particular reference to immigrants. For example, to tie back into Wirth's scheme, a group could be primarily

---

that a group which has a high closure score in one setting (a particular city, for instance) could have a lower score in a different setting (another city, or the country as a whole, for instance).

pluralistic at one stage, wanting to maintain distinctiveness but wanting at the same time to be accepted and esteemed by other groups, then shift towards a more assimilationist outlook as acceptance and esteem are gained. The Irish in both the United States and Canada are often cited as examples of this shift.

This formulation of Park's has been widely criticized for a number of reasons, the most important of which is the idea of ultimate assimilation as an inevitable result of ethnic group contact in modern society, which view mirrors the melting-pot ideology of the United States. We now realize that assimilation is only one of the probable outcomes of ethnic group contact, others being pluralism and secession. However, modified versions of Park's original model are useful in helping us think our way through the complexities of multi-ethnic societies, especially when we move beyond the simple classification of types of ethnic group and of multi-ethnic society to consider changes in those groups and societies. (Lyman, 1968: 16-22)

It will be recalled that our aim is to deal with the ways in which sociologists approach the study of ethnicity and how they set about the job of explaining the structures and processes involved in contact between ethnic groups. The stage has been set for such a discussion, which opens with an examination of some of the everyday ways of looking at and explaining happenings in multi-ethnic societies.

Folk or Layman Models

In this section we shall look at different ways of explaining how multi-ethnic societies, in which there is unequal status and prestige between ethnic groups, are maintained. By 'ways of explaining' we mean theories and conceptual schemes, or models, used by social scientists as well as by laymen. In the latter case we refer to what have been called 'folk' or layman theories which have wide circulation in a society, although the bearers of them hardly, if ever, think of their ways of explaining as theories. Nevertheless, if a way of explaining something is based on a set of propositions and assumptions about what makes the world tick, we may refer to it as a theory, even though it has not been formalized. Many so-called scientific theories are elegantly stated folk theories or at least have counterparts in the non-scientific domains of a society, and lend an aura of rightness or legitimacy to popular ideas. To avoid confusion, we shall hereafter use the term *model* as a synonym for the term 'way of explaining,' because although all theories employ models, not all models are theories in the strict sense. (Forcese and Richer, 1973: 37-51) In this section we look at four such models which we label as follows: the Racial; the Faulty Ethnic Group; the Faulty Individuals; and the Rotten Society.

One common view put forward to explain how boundaries are or should be maintained between ethnic groups in systems of inequality is based on the notion that psychological and cultural endowments are inherited. This is called the *racialist* view and is especially common where racism is practised, in those places where visibly distinctive physical properties, such as skin color, serve as role signs. (Banton, 1967) From time to time a scientific finding is presented to support this view which is, however, rejected by the great majority of biological and social scientists.

A variant of this view, often used in conjunction with it, is that God ordained that breeding populations be kept separate and unequal. This could be because of some ancestral curse, for example, the mark of Cain, or because of the relegation or promotion of people in their various incarnations. The chief point to keep in mind here is that these views, whether supported by science or religion, imply a notion of fixed boundaries which must remain so even though changes in other aspects of life, for example, modernization, are accepted. Another implication is that it is not the fault of any particular individual or set of individuals now living that their genes are what they are or that some remote ancestor sinned. It is a matter of *fate* and nothing can, or ought to be, done about it.

Another view which uses the notion of inheritance, but without its biological or religious connotation, is that systems of ethnic inequality are maintained because the oppressed groups pass on from generation to generation certain behavioral and cultural habits which reduce the chances of gaining in prestige or standard of living. This may be called the *Faulty Ethnic Group* model. The important factors in this model are related to group properties, which are viewed as determining individual life chances. Because this unhappy condition is not a result of genetic inheritance, nor is it divinely ordained, something can be done about it without tinkering with the major institutions of the society. For example, children from such depressed groups may be rescued and brought up by boarding schools or in foster homes where they may be socialized in the right way. Much of the thinking which informed the policies of government and church groups with reference to native peoples in Canada was based on this notion of the faulty culture from which people should be rescued.

A more recent trend has been to intervene in the process of passing faulty behavior and attitudes from generation to generation and try to change the way of life of whole groups through various schemes, such as community development, or by trying to move populations and disperse them among people whose good behavior and attitudes would perhaps prove infectious. This common view has received a certain degree of support from the social science community, as we shall see in the next section when we discuss the *Culture of Poverty* model.

A view which is closely related to the Faulty Culture one but differs from it in that it focuses on individuals as such, may be called the *individualism-voluntarism* model, which has considerable ideological support in North America. According to this view, systems of inequality among ethnic groups arise and are maintained because of individual differences which just happen to get clustered in certain parts of the population, for example, among French Canadians or Spanish Americans. Any individual can make it, if he has the gumption and the luck. He might have to overcome prejudices and other obstacles, but the system is open to talent and rewards effort. Perhaps some tinkering with the society's institutions is tolerated or advocated among those who hold this view — open discrimination outlawed, ghetto schools improved — but the social system is basically good as is evidenced by the fact that we all know at least one Indian, some Italians, many French Canadians, a few Negroes, even a Gypsy who have made it.

This view receives little support from social scientists, the majority of whom reject the individualism-voluntarism model as having little explanatory power when it comes to accounting for systems of inequality in which ethnic factors are important.

Finally, we mention a layman model which finds a fair degree of support among social scientists. We call it the *Rotten Society* model. According to it, ethnic inequalities arise and are maintained because the society is pervaded by a spirit of hate and ethnocentrism and exploitation. To some this is because the society has an unjust economic system, the working of which requires that some sections of society exploit other sections. To others, if the economic system is unjust it is not because of its inherent structure but because the spiritual values of people are decadent. It follows that effectively to change the situation, something like a moral or social revolution — or both — is required.

The extent to which one or the other way of explaining ethnic inequalities is dominant among a population is a question for empirical research, although common sense suggests that certain models are more likely to be held in one rather than other sections of a society. For example, one would hardly expect the Rotten Society model to be embraced by large segments of the dominant ethnic group.

The folk or layman ways of explaining the maintenance of vertical mosaics mentioned above are not the only ones, but we believe that they are the ones most deserving of discussion. They should be kept in mind when we consider those models which are most common in social science, the topic of the following section.

Social Science Models

Let us think of types of social science model as fitting somewhere along a continuum, at one end of which we find those that feature factors of an *impersonal* nature and at the opposite end of which are those of an intensely *personal,* subjective nature. At the impersonal end of the continuum are those models which make few assumptions about sentiment and motivation and which regard processes like migration, segregation, economic adaptation as the result of *aggregates of individual decisions* in response to pressures in the physical and social environments rather than as a result of collective planning or decision-making. Attention is more or less confined to demographic, ecological, economic, and geographical factors in these models. At the personal end of the continuum are those models which focus on sentiments and motivations as the major factors to study, being concerned with psycho-dynamic processes and states. Towards the middle of such a continuum lie the models which concentrate on social and cultural factors, taking into account both impersonal and personal factors in various mixes.

Looking first at models which favor impersonal variables, those who use them remind us that much of what happens in the maintenance of, or change in, multi-ethnic societies can only be adequately understood against the background of factors which act as constraints within which social and psychological processes operate. We refer to such factors as population distribution and trends, market forces, industrialization, and the like. Space does not permit an extensive treatment of such factors and so we shall present only a few examples of their relevance for ethnic group matters.

We have already indicated the importance of relative population size and clustering, or its opposite, dispersal. For a given society or region we ask: are the numerical proportions between ethnic groups changing through different rates of natural increase and migration? In Canada, for example, this is a question of more than academic interest to those French Canadians who are concerned about the small addition to their ranks through immigration and the declining birth-rate. Concern about race relations in Britain only became sharp when the number of black immigrants rose steeply. The very large-scale movement of American blacks into the cities of the north has had a formidable effect on relations between the races. Huge ghettos added a new dimension to the picture of American life.

Most models which attempt to explain the volume and direction of population flow, view migration and settlement as primarily responsive to market forces, such as demands for labor, shortage of land, and the like. These are large-scale processes which are not 'directed' from a central individual or institution.

At local levels analogous market processes occur which are not centrally directed, although various agencies — planning boards, municipal governments, real estate dealers — exercise some power and influence over outcomes. An example with implications for ethnic relations in Canada pertains to the French outside the Province of Quebec. French migrants from Quebec to New England and to some Canadian provinces, tended to settle near rivers. In the case of farmers, this tendency was understandable in the light of patterns of Quebec farming. But what is not commonly realized is that migrants to towns and cities also tended to settle near rivers, not because of any traditional farming patterns but because these migrants went mostly into industries which were located by riversides. The settlement of industries near rivers was because of the locational advantage provided by rivers as means of transport, source of power, and convenience of waste disposal. During the past several decades the locational advantage of rivers for industry has diminished or disappeared, because of changes in transportation and sources of power. Land use patterns have changed accordingly and urban riversides are now much desired as park and recreational land, sites for high-rise apartments, hotels, art centers, and the like. Old neighborhoods in these settings are being 'renewed,' re-zoned, in most cases virtually wiped out. The French in these places had developed local enclaves, centered on the church, school, and other institutions. Because they are over-represented in the working class and low income categories, many have little choice in relocating, but relocate they must as a result of market and political pressures. The old neighborhood, focal point for French social interaction, is lost to the group with important consequences for the maintenance of its boundaries. (Robert and Vallee)

In microcosm the situation described illustrates how relatively impersonal forces set constraints on developments in the social sphere. However, we should be aware of the dangers of attributing too much explanatory or predictive power to such models. Let us consider, for example, the ways in which the processes of industrialization and economic growth, usually described in terms of impersonal factors such as market forces, geographical location, and the like, have been linked to ethnic group relations.

Until recently it was widely assumed that industrialization and economic growth would mark the end or at least the diminution of differences among ethnic groups and the relevance of ethnicity. It was assumed that industrialization would encourage thinking in terms of universalistic and achievement criteria and that thinking in terms of particularistic, ascriptive criteria would fall into disrepute. Further, it was assumed that as standards of living rose among deprived groups in developing societies, discontent would wane and that they would have less reason for resentment against dominant groups. As a matter of fact, examples of some of the most impressive strengthening of ethnic group boundaries, some of the most violent expressions of resentment against other ethnic groups, are to be found in multi-ethnic societies with the most remarkable rates of economic growth and industrialization. Reasons for this apparently unexpected finding will be given in the subsequent discussion of models which focus on sociological and psychological variables.

Suffice it to say at this point that ways of thinking which highlight the kinds of impersonal factors mentioned, if carried to extremes as ways of explaining and predicting what happens in ethnic relations, suffer from making too few assumptions about social and psychological processes, treating the latter either as given or as of minor significance. As we move along the continuum from impersonal to personal models we encounter those that put social and psychological processes center-stage and treat the kinds of variables just discussed as part of the background.

Conflict Models

Those social scientists who see as most crucial the political and economic *interests* which different groups have in maintaining or changing the status quo, give prominence of place to *conflict* as a process in society and to *power* as a key factor. This approach to the study of multi-ethnic societies directs the observer to look for the political and economic standing of different ethnic groups relative to one another, to see how these groups fare with reference to decision-making over their own lives and over society. The stress is on what are usually called 'material' interests. Always in the background and at times in the foreground, is the coercive machinery of the society, controlled by the advantaged. It is not taken for granted in these models that those whose interests are in conflict actually perceive the situation in that way. For example, the disadvantaged may be lulled by a false consciousness into accepting the status quo. Whatever resentment is generated amongst them might be directed towards targets other than the advantaged or the system as a whole, say, towards *other* disadvantaged groups, or towards scapegoats, or towards foreign countries and ideologies. The means used by the dominant groups to maintain the system insure that institutional control is vested with them, in some cases by wholesale exclusion of the lower status ethnic groups, in others by co-opting elite members of disadvantaged groups on a selective basis into some decision-making bodies, usually in token capacities.

In the conflict perspective, much attention is focused on deliberate attempts by disadvantaged groups to change the distribution of power and prestige, for it is assumed that those who dominate the society will not initiate any meaningful changes without pressures from below. These pressures are conveyed by *social movements* of protest. More precisely, the pressures are conveyed by organizations and their spokesmen who channel the collective protest and make it manifest in many different ways. It is typical of such movements, at least in North America, to have as an initial goal the attainment of a better deal for their members considered as individuals and families, to have, that is, a 'civil rights' approach. The favorite terms used in this connection are *integration* and *equality*. The depressed ethnic or racial group is usually supported by people from outside the group who are interested in gradual reform. Where, as is so often the case, no significant gains are made compared with gains made by other groups, there is a shift in emphasis away from individual civil rights and integration, and towards collective rights and group autonomy, an extreme form of which is political separation. Leadership of the movement becomes more militant. Support of outsiders fades in significance, with those interested in gradual reform dropping out or being rejected, those interested in radical reform or revolution remaining in or joining. Words and deeds which are regarded as shocking during the civil rights phase, now appear as moderate and reasonable. Counter-protest movements gain in strength, a concern with law and order taking precedence over concern with the demands of the protesters.

The oversimplified pattern just sketched has been used to describe black protest movements in the United States. (Yetman and Steele, 1971) Obvious parallels in Canada can be seen in recent developments in Quebec independentist movements (Bergeron, 1971): the growing militancy of the Acadians, especially in North-Eastern New Brunswick (Poulin, 1972), the shift in emphasis from individual to collective rights and group autonomy among Indians (Dosman, 1972). What the outcomes of communal conflict are likely to be depends on so many variables that it would require a separate chapter to discuss adequately. The chief point to make here is that those who favor the conflict model pay special attention to the strains in society and direct their research attention to concrete situations where these strains are manifested. They tend also to pay special attention to the historical dimension of the groups and situations they study.

It should be obvious that the conflict model is most suited to describing means of maintaining the status quo or potential change in situations where the gaps between the advantaged and disadvantaged are very wide, in terms of access to valued resources and societal decision-making. It is also useful in analyzing actual change in those situations where the gaps are closing, that is, where the previously disadvantaged groups are gaining ground on the advantaged, perhaps through industrialization and economic growth. Social scientists have discovered that outbreaks of open conflict in multi-ethnic societies are most likely to happen where formerly depressed groups begin to make political and economic headway (Schermerhorn, 1970: 389), because only under such conditions is the extent of their deprivation actually perceived by them. This matter will receive more attention when we deal with social psychological factors.

In studies of systems of inequality in multi-ethnic societies, some social scientists employ a notion of conflict which pertains not so much to interests and power as it does to conflicting cultural traditions and values. A simplified statement of this approach is that groups are where they are — high, medium, low — in the hierarchy primarily because the cultural traditions of some groups are more congruent than the cultural traditions of others with the needs of modern industrial society. This way of explaining matters lends itself more to showing how things stay as they are rather than how they change, because traditions and values are by definition long-lasting, slow to change.

For example, it has been argued, although not so much in recent years, that French Canadians are over-represented in the lower classes because their culture rewards the kind of activity which keeps people tied to the extended family, the religious congregation, and the quest for spiritual rewards in the afterlife. The culture shapes their personalities in such a way that they are at a disadvantage compared to English Canadians, and thus it is not surprising that they are low on the socio-economic totem pole. (Richer and Laporte, 1971) Like the blacks in Nova Scotia (Potter and Hill, 1966; Clairmont and Magill, 1970), or the Indians in the North (Nagler, 1972), they are not sufficiently suffused with the Puritan ethic which impels people towards individualism, achievement, and self-interest. Their life-style does not equip them to meet the demands of an advanced industrial society. Indeed, their culture is in conflict with the demands of such a society. A variant of this view will be found in the literature on the Culture of Poverty (Lewis, 1966), which emerges through the transmission by poor people from generation to generation of norms and values which run counter to the norms and values of the dominant groups. The majority of conflict theorists reject this kind of explanation, arguing that it turns attention away from the structure of power and of political-economic interests in the society and puts the finger on the 'defective' culture of the group about which, presumably, not very much can be done. (Valentine, 1968)

One problem with focusing on interests to the relative neglect of other factors has been touched upon: that is, the problem of whether or not the actors *perceive* their interests in the same way as the observer. Another is the decreasing utility of the concept when it is broadened to include other than 'material' interests. People have emotional as well as material vested interests. These emotional interests could run counter to what the observer feels are the material interests. For instance, the conservatism of people in the most depressed groups has often been noted. This conservatism may be interpreted either as a cultural pattern, a value shared by people in the particular lowly group, or as a fear of acting out of line lest the weight of the dominant group be brought to bear in retaliation. The conflict theorist would tend to the latter kind of interpretation in explaining how multi-ethnic systems of inequality are maintained. The fear-of-reprisal factor in the apparent conservatism of depressed groups has been noted in the literature on Chavez' attempts to mobilize Chicano (Mexican-American) grape-pickers against the growers (Grebner *et al.*, 1970). An interesting example from the Canadian scene is Valentine's analysis of some of the factors impeding the development of a co-operative among Metis people in Saskatchewan. One such factor was the dependency relationship which the Metis had with the free-enterprise traders, and the fear of arousing the disfavor of the latter, for they controlled the local economy. (Valentine, 1954) The latter kind of interpretation draws attention to the constraints within which the depressed ethnic group operates, because of its powerlessness, and questions the utility, or indeed the validity, of an approach that pays much heed to cultural values which are particular to the group being studied or which are shared with other groups in the society.

Those who favor the conflict approach in the study of ethnic relations often deny that there is a basic consensus at the level of values and societal identification between groups which underlies their conflicts of interests. Actually, this is a matter for empirical testing in specific cases. To take the matter of consensus about societal identification, we may ask: to what extent do Francophones of Quebec think of themselves primarily as 'Canadians,' their Frenchness or 'Quebecness' being of a lower order of identity? As we pointed out on page 167, it is one of the most difficult tasks in social science to measure locus and strength of identity. Quite apart from technical difficulties in this kind of research, there is the lack of fixity, and a great fluidity of identification, depending on situational factors. But, suppose we take as an approximation to the true picture the findings of the Groupe de Recherche (1963) in their study of attitudes towards separatism in the Province of Quebec, the chief finding of which was that only 13 per cent were avowed separatists, putting Quebec ahead of Canada, while 64 per cent were anti-separatist, presumably putting Canada ahead of Quebec. Does this permit us to conclude that there is consensus between Francophone Quebeckers and other Canadians on this basic matter of identification? Perhaps this is not a fruitful question. Perhaps it is best to ask the following question: among people of actual or potential influence in the Francophone middle and upper classes, is there consensus on this matter of identification? Obviously, there is not, for a minority of that category opts for the separatist solution, but it is a minority of people with actual or potential influence who may mobilize sentiment among substantial parts of the Francophone population. The point of most importance here is that it is not so much a matter of what degree of consensus there is at a given time, but rather a matter of how different segments of a group (intellectuals, workers, white collar, etc.) define basic values and societal indentification.

Conflict models are often contrasted with the structural-functional way of looking at society, it being charged that in the latter view conflict is neglected or down-played in the attempt to demonstrate the existence of norms and values that cut across the whole society and serve to integrate it. The extent to which this contrast is a valid one and some of the implications for the study of ethnic group relations of using one or the other model will be examined in the following section.

Structural-Functional or System Models

An outstanding feature of the structural-functional or social system way of thinking about society, is the use of the notion of a system of *interdependent parts,* which tend towards integration. By parts is meant the elements that go to make up a social-cultural system, such as roles, statutes, collectivities, institutions, norms, values, beliefs. If parts get out of kilter, certain mechanisms come into play which tend to restore the status quo, either in its previous form or, more usually, in a slightly changed form. These mechanisms are only rarely perceived by people for what they are: that is, most of what the actors do in the social drama contributes, without their knowing it, to the continuity of the society and its development.

In this perspective, even conflicts may be viewed as contributing to the development of societal institutions and a common culture. A familiar example in many sociology texts is that of labor-management conflict. Wrangling and stoppages of work appear to be disruptive in particular cases, but they often result in new legislation or new forms of arbitration which are perceived as benefiting the society as a whole through improved means of formal conflict management. In this perspective, conflict is 'put in its place' as just another process, rather than being regarded as a matter of central importance. In fact, more attention is given to integrative processes and relationships, such as exchange, symbiosis and the like. These are seen as fulfilling needs which must be satisfied in order for a given unit (e.g., the society, the association, the family, the individual) to persist and develop in its environment. The stress is on the underlying consensus which binds people together, despite the more superficial differences which divide them.

Sociologists who use this model usually operate at a high level of abstraction with concepts which are far removed from everyday experience. Furthermore, they often take as their chief reference points such global units as 'American Society,' 'Canadian Society,' 'Post-Industrial Society,' although the structural-functional approach is applicable to units at both micro and macro levels.

In fact, the structural-functional way of looking at things is especially appropriate to the study of particular ethnic groups, each considered as an isolate, in the *ethnographic* style mentioned on page 168. In this kind of endeavour, the group can be considered as a kind of organism with boundaries. Questions can then be phrased in terms of what kinds of needs must be met in order for this 'organism' (the ethnic group in question) to persist as a distinctive social and cultural entity. Attention is focused on how the parts mesh together: how beliefs and values are passed on in the socialization process; how mutual support reinforces the value of belonging to the group; how social networks keep people oriented to one another rather than to outsiders; how distinctive customs reinforce the beliefs, and so on.

It is obvious that the structural-functional approach with reference to the study of particular ethnic groups is more useful where the groups are clearly demarcated from others, for example, the Hutterite communities, than it is where the groups are dispersed and heterogeneous, for example, the Ukrainians in Canada. For those groups which are very much dispersed geographically and quite heterogeneous, the approach is less useful.

With reference to studies of multi-ethnic *societies,* this approach is most useful in analyzing stable situations of long standing where the different ethnic groups that make up the society have developed ways of co-existing without the need of blatantly obvious means of coercion. Such situations do exist — perhaps less commonly than in the past — where over the years ways of dealing with one another have evolved through the process of accommodation, where friendly avoidance (good fences make good neighbors!) makes conflict unlikely, where the different ethnic groups are not in competition for the same scarce resources. The latter type of situation is best exemplified in those places where different ethnic groups have a *symbiotic* relationship with one another. In sociology the term symbiosis means a

> relation of mutual dependence between unlike and distinct groups within a community that works to their mutual advantage. (Theodorson, 1969: 429)

An example of symbiosis would be a community or region where one ethnic group concentrates on agriculture, another on manufacturing, the latter buying the former's produce with the earnings from sales within and outside the community or region. Another example is the mutual dependence that was developed between white fur traders on the one hand and Indian trappers and transporters on the other. To the person primarily interested in how people get linked into symbiotic networks of interdependence, the question of whether or not such relations are exploitative is beside the point. If the people in the situation define it as to their advantage, there is consensus that stretches across ethnic barriers and we have a socially symbiotic relation between groups based on their specialization in the division of labor.

Actually, this type of situation is rare in modern industrial society. Most of the examples of it in the literature are from non-industrial and rural localities. (Barth, *op. cit.*) This is not to say that there is no occupational specialization by ethnic origin in the division of labor of modern industrial states. The data for distribution of occupations by ethnic origin for Canada are clear on this point. Some groups are much over-represented in some sectors of the division of labor, which is one reason for the coincidence between social class and ethnicity. Table I gives a kind of profile of over- and under-representation of people of various origins in the male labor force, derived from the 1961 Census of Population in Canada. The clustering of particular groups in particular categories gives a rough idea of their degree of specialization. As a matter of fact, ethnic origin is one of the better 'predictors' of where people are likely to be placed in the labor force in Canada. (Hall, 1971)

But does this picture of the niches occupied by different ethnic groups imply social symbiosis as described above? We should say not, for there is no evidence that the people occupying the less favorable niches feel

Table I: Occupation of the Male Labor Force, by Ethnic Origin (%), Canada, 1961*

	All origins[a]	British	French	Dutch	German	Hungarian	Italian	Jewish
All Occupations	100.00	100.00	100.00	100.00	100.00	100.00	100.00	100.00
Managerial	10.23	12.15	7.62	7.93	8.29	6.34	6.58	39.38
Professional and technical	7.58	9.34	5.92	6.92	6.09	8.44	2.80	13.66
Clerical	6.90	8.22	6.71	5.17	5.02	4.21	3.68	6.79
Sales	5.59	6.56	5.22	4.51	4.40	3.08	3.16	14.15
Service	8.51	9.18	7.68	6.71	6.37	8.89	8.47	2.55
Transport and communication	7.54	7.96	8.90	6.63	6.24	4.17	4.74	2.82
Farmers and farm workers	12.18	10.73	10.79	22.50	21.00	17.56	2.67	0.45
Loggers	1.68	1.00	3.29	0.64	0.71	0.60	0.58	0.01
Fishermen, trappers and hunters	0.76	0.88	0.51	0.53	0.33	0.04	0.05	0.01
Miners and related work	1.38	1.18	1.54	0.76	1.29	2.00	1.65	0.03
Craftsmen and production workers	28.79	25.54	31.40	29.58	32.52	34.85	43.73	15.62
Laborers	6.25	4.63	7.46	6.12	5.59	7.97	19.25	1.09
Not stated	2.61	2.63	2.96	2.00	2.15	1.85	2.64	3.44

All Occupations	Polish	Russian	Scandinavian	Ukrainian	Other European	Asiatic	Indian
	100.00	100.00	100.00	100.00	100.00	100.00	100.00
Managerial	9.17	15.16	9.34	7.14	8.98	21.44	1.15
Professional and technical	6.73	8.36	5.93	5.83	6.79	9.62	1.05
Clerical	5.16	4.53	4.49	5.65	4.93	5.40	1.03
Sales	3.84	5.96	4.41	3.52	3.59	5.23	0.86
Service	7.30	5.62	6.88	7.32	11.41	24.54	7.80
Transport and communication	4.82	5.33	6.39	6.43	4.18	3.22	3.74
Farmers and farm workers	14.01	19.91	22.89	22.96	12.79	5.69	19.08
Loggers	1.01	1.25	1.83	0.66	1.76	0.48	11.65
Fishermen, trappers and hunters	0.09	0.09	1.22	0.10	0.36	1.49	17.62
Miners and related work	2.47	1.20	1.69	1.76	2.52	0.26	1.12
Craftsmen and production workers	35.06	24.22	27.58	29.57	33.57	16.61	17.69
Laborers	7.53	5.85	5.02	6.87	7.18	4.19	14.29
Not stated	2.81	2.52	2.33	2.19	1.94	1.83	2.92

[a] Including those of ethnic origin categories not given in the Table.

*Source: *Census of Canada 1961, Cat. 94-515* (Ottawa: Statistics Canada). Reproduced by permission of Information Canada.

that the division of labor has advantages for them.* Looking at the set of data presented in Table I, the person who favors the conflict approach would pay special attention to the constraints within which those in the less favorable slots must live and how these constraints are manipulated by the advantaged, for he would assume a conflict of interest between the advantaged and disadvantaged. He would be less concerned with how people in the situation define it, less concerned with how their cultural values and societal networks predispose them to this or that sector of the work force, than with the question of what *power* factors (for instance, control over resources and facilities) operate to maintain this kind of division of labor.

On the other hand, the person guided by the structural-functional approach would be much concerned about how people in the situation define it, how their cultural values and social networks predispose them in one direction and another, and, perhaps of most importance, concerned about the extent to which the 'ethnic' factor in the division of labor contributes to, or impedes, the goals of a modern industrial society.

It is not the argument here that one approach is inherently better than the other one in the study of ethnic groups and multi-ethnic societies. Suggestions as to the appropriateness of this or that approach have been made with reference to different kinds of research problems. It is obvious that the structural-functional perspective is most appropriate where a total-system analysis is called for, or where the time-perspective is a long one, so that what appear to be disastrous conflicts at a given time may be seen as temporary disruptions in the long run. The conflict perspective is, as we have said, most appropriate to the study of situations where the differences between the ethnic groups is pronounced in terms of their access to resources and rewards in short-term time periods.

An important point we are trying to get across is the notion that the choice of this or that approach is not only a matter of academic import: it has important implications for the conclusions people come to about ethnicity as a factor in society. The favoring of a conflict or a structural-functional approach to the study of, say, English-French relations in Canada makes a difference as to what one looks for in the way of data, how one interprets the data, and the conclusions one derives from them.

Comparing the approaches, we are led to another conclusion: the

---

*Roseborough and Breton report on differences between Canadians of English, French and 'Other' origins with respect to how they view economic and political advantages of ethnic groups in Canada. While the French manifest most dissatisfaction relative to the English, the *level* of dissatisfaction or satisfaction seems to be neither high nor low among the less advantaged. (Howard Roseborough and Raymond Breton, 'Perceptions of Relative Economic and Political Advantages of Ethnic Groups in Canada,' in Bernard Blishen, *et al,* (eds.), *Canadian Society: Sociological Perspectives,* 3rd Edition (Abridged) Toronto: Macmillan, 1971, pp. 401-425.)

conflict approach makes fewer assumptions than the structural-functional about *psychological* processes. It will be recalled that we set out to look at models of studying ethnicity in terms of a kind of continuum from those which were most impersonal at one end to those that were most personal at the other end. We have now come to the 'other end' where we take account of social-psychological interests in ethnicity.

Social-Psychological Models

From a research point of view, the most difficult aspects of ethnicity and ethnic-group relations to deal with are the subjective ones. It is easy enough to determine many objective facts about ethnic groups and categories: their demographic characteristics, voting patterns, associational life, and so on. These are matters of *behavior,* what people do, the positions they are in. The deeper we go into matters of *feelings,* the more slippery and rocky the research path grows. This does not deter researchers from travelling the path. In fact, if one were to assess the volume of research output, measured in terms of number of articles on different ethnicity-related topics, the psychologically oriented projects would probably outnumber those oriented in the direction of other social sciences by a healthy margin, at least in North America. In this short space we cannot even begin to do justice to the corpus of literature produced by those, mostly but not entirely of the professional psychologist category, who direct their attention to subjective matters like identity, motivation, stereotyping, prejudice, cognitive mapping, and socialization. What we shall do is confine comments to those matters of psychological import which bear most closely on the societal aspects already discussed.

On the topic of how and why systems of inequality are maintained, there is a vast literature on the dynamics of stereotyping and prejudice, concerned mostly with how difficult it is for stigmatized groups to narrow the gap between themselves and the dominant groups because of the heavy weight of misunderstanding and dislike bearing down upon them. An oversimplified version of the once very common views on this subject goes as follows.

During the process of socialization, children pick up from their parents and peers, from their school books and mass media, *stereotypes* of what their own and other ethnic groups are like.

> A stereotype refers to those folk beliefs about the attributes characterizing a social category on which there is consensus.*

*Marlene Mackie, 'An Explication of Stereotypy,' paper presented at the Annual Meeting of the Canadian Sociology and Anthropology Association, St. John's, Nfld., June, 1971, 32 pages. The quote is from page 8. This paper attempts to clear up the confusion surrounding stereotyping and prejudice.

These stereotypes, or much oversimplified views of what groups are like, provide the bases for unfavorable judgments, or prejudices, and these in turn are unlikely to change unless there is personal contact with the targets of prejudice. It was widely assumed that personal contact, as well as the presentation of 'correct' information, especially about ethnic minorities, would help reduce prejudice and the discrimination which is often based upon it. Furthermore it was commonly assumed that tendency to be prejudiced was related directly to personality type, rigid and authoritarian personalities being most prone to both stereotyping and prejudice. Proper socialization of a liberal kind, coupled with greater mixing of people of different groups and education campaigns to show how really decent are the stigmatized groups would certainly improve the ethnic relations scene in a significant way.

We now know, from the result of many studies, that things are not that simple. For instance, tendency to stereotype is not closely linked with tendency to have unfavorable views, or prejudices, about other groups. (Gardner *et al.,* 1970) Under certain conditions, for instance, where people are forced to interact across ethnic boundaries, dislike actually increases. Deliberate attempts to 'educate' people out of their prejudices sometimes backfire and alienate the targets of the program. At this point in the evolution of the research enterprise into prejudices, simplistic notions have been thrown out and more rigorous methods and techniques applied than was the case in the past. One consequence is a lack of clear guidelines for persons interested in reducing prejudice.

One interesting development in recent years is not so much the change in attitudes about *other* groups, but the change in attitude towards *one's own* group. We refer here to the movement to re-define previously stigmatized traits as desirable. The most obvious case of such re-definition is caught up in the phrase, 'Black is Beautiful.' The objective of such a movement is to purge members of the group of the self-doubt and self-hate which sometimes accompanies their being stigmatized. Some positive affirmations of pride in one's group are to be found among Indians and Inuit in Canada. For example, some Inuit spokesmen are striving to get rid of the term Eskimo — a word not known in their own language — and substitute for it the term Inuit. This process of re-definition of self has received little careful research attention, compared with how people define other groups, although the former is of great importance in the study of change.

Another psychological concept which is particularly important in the study of change has already been mentioned: the concept of *relative deprivation*. According to Theodorson, the term was first used by Stouffer in his classic study of *The American Soldier*. Theodorson's definition of the concept follows:

Deprivation or disadvantage is measured not by objective standards but by comparison with the relatively superior advantages of others, such as members of a *reference group* whom one desires to emulate. Thus the mere millionaire can feel relatively disadvantaged among his multimillionaire friends, as can the man with only a small yacht, or a one-star general, and so forth. (Theodorson, 1969: 343)

Again, there is an enormous literature on the topic of relative deprivation and the kinds of outcomes it engenders — aggression, withdrawal, scapegoating — for the concept is often linked in a cause-and-effect chain with another psychological concept, not discussed here, that of frustration-aggression. Within the confines of this chapter we mention only a few varieties of relative deprivation, those most relevant to the topic of change in multi-ethnic societies with marked inequalities between groups.

In a study of how relative deprivation causes civil strife, Gurr (1969) identified four general patterns of conditions which are labelled as follows: Aspirational Deprivation or the revolution of rising expectations; Decremental Deprivation; Progressive Deprivation; and Persisting Deprivation. The first pattern, that of the revolution of rising expectations, when people are encouraged to believe that things will get much better for them, but where, for whatever reasons, their hopes are dashed, would seem particularly applicable to the native people in some parts of Canada and the French in Quebec and New Brunswick.

The second pattern, that of decremental deprivation, has to do with the loss of advantages which have been held in the past. Poor whites in the southern states, who have seen the blacks gain, could perceive that gain as a loss for them. There is no research evidence for this, but it could be argued that as previously 'minority' groups gain in status — the French in the public service of Canada, the Indians in some localities — the most threatened members of the majority groups would be those whose advantages were being sacrificed.

The third pattern, that of progressive deprivation, in which a period of marked improvement in the lot of a depressed group is followed by a period of slump, is one most often associated with revolutionary movements. Good things have been sampled, but no further eating is allowed, because there is a short supply or because it has been discovered that to eat the good things people need sound teeth and the teeth of a particular group are not sound — they do not have the 'facilities.' The case of the Francophones in Quebec comes to mind here.

The final pattern, that of persistent deprivation, is one where for a long period the expectations of the group have been relatively stable and their means of achieving these expectations have also been stable. Sporadic outbursts are likely from a depressed group, which, if that group is strong enough, may alter the system of inequality, but which, if it is not strong enough to wield much power on the larger scene, will make little long-term difference in its position. The native peoples of Canada and the blacks in Nova Scotia come to mind as perhaps the most likely candidates for the dubious honor of being persistently deprived.

Some research has been carried out on the perception of inequalities as between ethnic groups in Canada. We have already referred to the Roseborough and Breton study on page 181 and in the footnote on page 190. In another study, the same authors report on differences between French, English, and Others within a large business organization in terms of how they assess their positions in that organization. Although not couched specifically in terms of relative deprivation, that concept has a bearing on the kind of explanation they suggest for one of their findings:

> We have seen above that French workers are as likely to be satisfied with their job situation, even though they are objectively in a lower occupational status (on the average). There is little evidence to show that this is due to differences in values and goals. Moreover, it seems that it can hardly be attributed to better opportunities. One possible explanation could be derived from the fact that French and non-French live in segregated communities and as a result compare their lot with that of other workers within their own communities ... That is, it takes an objectively lower social standing to make him fare advantageously in relation to the people with whom he compares himself.*

This is an example of one area of convergence in theory and research between psychology and sociology with special relevance to systems of ethnic inequalities, that area covered by concerns with aspirations and expectations, reference groups, relative deprivation, and status inconsistency.

If time and space permitted we could extend the discussion to other areas of convergence in which psychological variables are of special relevance to sociological studies of ethnicity, for example, the study of ethnic identity, culture, and personality. These topics have been only fleetingly touched upon here, not because they are unimportant, but because we decided to select only a few topics to illustrate the relevance of social-psychological variables, or the 'subjective' side of the ethnic relations coin.

*Raymond Breton and Howard Roseborough, 'Ethnic Differences in Status,' in Blishen, *et al, Canadian Society* (Toronto: The Macmillan Company of Canada Ltd., 1961), p. 465.

Social Policy and Ethnicity

As we have seen, there are many multi-ethnic states today. In some, the ethnic dualism or pluralism as the case may be is not defined as a key problem; in others it is. Where it is, the trend is towards official government intervention in both a goal-attainment and conflict-management role. Even a cursory review of the various kinds of intervention and of the policies which accompany intervention (e.g., integration in the U.S.A., assimilation in Australia, segregation in Rhodesia, nationality recognition in the U.S.S.R.) is well beyond our terms of reference. We confine our brief remarks to highlights of Canadian policies.

Many policy areas have implications for ethnic groups in Canada. Some of the more obvious areas are bilingualism and biculturalism, multiculturalism, and the affairs of the native peoples. Less obvious perhaps, but still of great importance to ethnic groups, is immigration policy. Even less obviously related to ethnicity are policies of regional and economic development, yet these do have direct implications, because many of the most depressed groups are in the least developed areas: blacks in Nova Scotia, Acadians in New Brunswick, Indian, Metis and Inuit in the North. In our remaining comments we touch only on three policy areas most directly related to ethnicity: bilingualism and biculturalism, multiculturalism, and the native peoples.

We set out to discuss these policy areas in terms of their degrees of inclusiveness, from those that *directly* involve a few groups (Indians, Inuit, Metis) to those that involve all. This is not to set an order of precedence of importance of policy areas, for the moral and societal significance of a policy area does not necessarily coincide with the numbers of groups and individuals involved in it. It is simply that the logic of the scale of inclusiveness is a convenient one to follow here.

Issues involving the native peoples are very much in the public eye. Underlying the arguments over specific issues − aboriginal rights, unfulfilled treaties or the validity of treaties, the taking over with little or no compensation of native territories − are strong sentiments of past and present injustices and the feeling that the dominant society would like to to see these people disappear as a distinct group, that is, become assimilated. Native movements are directed towards more autonomy and control over their own lives, as well as towards social and economic equality. Although their numbers are small and they are scattered widely throughout the country, mostly in economic backwaters, their social power is growing as they become better organized at regional and national levels and put their challenges before courts and legislatures.

The government response appears to be shifting towards accepting the idea of native autonomy.

Policies are in a state of flux, being thrashed out in negotiations between spokesmen of native groups and government, under the influence of court decisions about native rights. This is an extremely complex subject for a number of reasons. A very important one is that there is not just a single category of native in the country. For official, statutory purposes there are on the one hand those of 'registered' Indian status, members of bands, who come under the Indian Act, which means that they have certain rights and services from which those of Indian ancestry who do not come under the Act are excluded. The Inuit (Eskimo) are a special case. Although they have a distinct identity of their own, they are regarded as a tribe of Indians for certain purposes, but not for others. For example, no treaties were negotiated with them, they do not hold land collectively, as in the case of Indian bands on reserves. Their official status is not very clear.

The chief basis for inclusion or exclusion is that of *descent*. With certain exceptions, in order to be classified as of Indian status, one's male parent must be of that status. An Indian woman who marries a non-Indian loses her official status and her descendants are not eligible for that status. She and her descendants might identify both socially and culturally with the Indian group, but be excluded from it officially. Like others, this issue is being fought in the courts and is too complicated to explore here. (Cumming and Mickenberg, 1972) We point out only that the prevailing opinion among status Indian spokesmen is that the patrilineal rule should remain in force, providing a simple way of controlling entry into group membership and a way of restricting that membership. Anthropologists have frequently pointed out the function of unilineal descent (tracing through one line for social purposes) in sorting people out into discrete segments.*

The prevailing view of the non-status people of Indian ancestry appears to be that membership should be decided by descent through either male or female line, and that another criterion should be strength of identification with one's Indian traditions and culture. On this issue we see actual or potential conflict between the interests of two sections of the one category as well as between the idea of *collective* rights and *individual* rights, and how the movement towards equality for women can get tangled with the movement towards group autonomy and development.

*Cf. e.g., Paul Bohannan, *Social Anthropology* (New York: Holt, Rinehart and Winston, 1963). See especially Chapter Nine.

Another set of issues with relevance to policy in Canada involves the congruence in some respects and conflict in other respects between two thrusts: that towards *bilingualism* and *biculturalism,* on the one hand, and that towards *multiculturalism,* on the other hand. As with any other state, Canada has its burden of internal problems — economic, political, social — but it shares with only certain other states the problem of maintaining unity between two segments, each of which has a world-encompassing international language as a mother tongue. For many Canadians, the most pressing problem is that of 'keeping Quebec in Confederation' by official and public recognition that the French are not just another ethnic group, that they are a charter group and have the right to French language education, government services, and French language media wherever in Canada they form a significant part of the population. The argument is that the French in all of Canada should have the same language rights as do the non-French in Quebec.* It is perhaps ironic that within Quebec there is a strong movement to reduce these very non-French rights. †

The main point to make here is that large sections of the Canadian population do not subscribe to the view that Canada is primarily defined by a dualism between English and French and that the French have special rights outside Quebec. (Vallee and de Vries)

The few surveys available on this topic show that in Quebec and the Maritime Provinces, the 'special' status of the French is acknowledged by the majority of non-French, but that in parts of Ontario, in British Columbia and, particularly in the Prairie Provinces, the non-French tend to regard the French in their midst as one among many ethnic minorities of more or less equal status.‡

To cite only one survey by way of illustration of this point, Table II represents the distribution of responses to a question on the right of the

---

*Book 1, General Introduction, 'The Official Languages,' *Report of the Royal Commission on Bilingualism and Biculturalism,* (Ottawa: Queen's Printer, 1967).

† *The Commission of Inquiry on the Position of the French Language and Language Rights in Quebec.*

‡The chief source upon which the following statements are based is the Canadian Institute of Public Opinion (CIPO), some of whose polls have included questions pertaining to French language rights and bilingualism. During the past decade or so the following polls have included questions relevant to the topic: 305 (Nov., 1963); 312 (June, 1965); 334 (March, 1969); 353 (May, 1972); 359 (May, 1973). Another survey whose findings support the conclusions about regional and mother-tongue differences in attitudes to French language rights is 'A Study of Interethnic Relations in Canada,' The Social Research Group (Le Groupe de Recherche Sociale), unpublished report to the Royal Commission on Bilingualism and Biculturalism, Ottawa, 1965, 355 pages.

French-speaking citizens to deal with officials in their areas in the French language. In the national sample of 709, the majority (55 per cent) approved of these French rights. However, if we break the sample down by region and mother tongue, we find a disproportionate share of approval accounted for by French mother-tongue respondents and by non-French monther-tongue respondents in Quebec and the Maritimes. In fact, on the Prairies, only 22 per cent of English mother-tongue respondents approve. In the table we give the regional break-down by English mother-tongue only, because the number of French respondents outside Quebec and of other mother-tongue (non-French, non-English) respondents outside Ontario and the Prairies is too small to warrant inclusion by region.

We cannot conclude from evidence we have that all of those who do not favor special rights for the French are in favor of *multiculturalism,* for some would be in favor of a strong Canadian identity in which specific ethnic identities are washed out in a process of assimilation. In any case, there is certainly a lack of consensus, not only as between different ethnic groups, but also as between different regions of the country, on this issue. (Schwartz, 1967)

The argument in favor of assimilation, implying a single strong Canadian identity, may be advanced on two grounds. First, it can be argued that an ethnically plural society always runs a strong risk of internal conflict which drains social energy from society-wide tasks.*

The second ground upon which the maintenance of strong ethnic solidarities is attacked has to do with equality. Porter (1972) has put the case for the costs in terms of individual mobility chances of a policy of encouraging the maintenance of distinct ethnic subcultures. He points out that the more official recognition is given to ethnic groups, and the more that status ascription by descent is used as a key criterion for sorting out people, the lower is the likelihood that real equality of opportunity and life chances in the occupational sphere will be achieved in Canada.

And so the debates go on, between the 'liberal' assimilationists, that is, those who want but would not force assimilation, and the pluralists. We conclude with a rather trite, but true, observation: whatever the policies are, they have to be implemented in a real world in which much of what happens is beyond the control of planners and policy-makers. In this

---

*Cf. e.g., Arend Lijphart, 'Cultural Diversity and Theories of Political Integration,' *Canadian Journal of Political Science*, IV,1 (March, 1971); Eric Nordlinger, *Conflict Regulations in Divided Societies*, (Cambridge, Harvard University Center for International Affairs, 1971).

Table II: Response to CIPO Poll 334, March 1969, by Region and English Mother Tongue*

Question 12:   'As you may know, the Federal Government is planning a bill on language rights by which all areas where 10% of the population is French-speaking, these citizens should have the right to deal with Federal officials in their area in their own language. Do you approve of this idea or not?'

	Canada	*Maritimes*	*Quebec*	*Ontario*	*Prairies*	*Brit. Col.*
All Mother Tongues						
Approve	55 (396)	57 (37)	85 (170)	52 (133)	25 (30)	38 (26)
Disapprove	36 (258)	34 (22)	8 (16)	39 (98)	70 (84)	54 (38)
Qualified and don't know	9 (55)	9 (6)	7 (13)	9 (23)	5 (7)	8 (3)
English Mother Tongue						
Approve	45 (187)	58 (35)	71 (10)	50 (101)	22 (20)	43 (21)
Disapprove	47 (194)	32 (19)	14 (2)	43 (86)	71 (63)	49 (24)
Qualified and don't know	8 (33)	10 (6)	14 (2)	7 (15)	7 (6)	8 (4)

*Source: Canadian Institute of Public Opinion, Toronto, made available through Social Science Data Archive, Carleton University, Ottawa.

chapter, we have tried to show what some of the real world variables are, to provide a perspective which takes into account the demographic, psychological, and social-cultural constraints within which policy-making goes on.

References

Banton, Michael, *Race Relations.* London: Tavistock Publications, 1967, especially Chapter One.

Barth, Frederik (ed.), *Ethnic Groups and Boundaries: The Social Organization of Cultural Differences.* Boston: Little, Brown, 1969.

Bennett, John W., *Hutterian Brethren: The Agricultural Economy and Social Organization of a Communal People.* Stanford: Stanford University Press, 1967.

Bergeron, Léandre, *History of Quebec: A Patriot's Handbook.* Toronto: N-C Press, 1971. (See especially the section on 'Recent Events,' p. 216f.)

Berry, J.W., and G.J.S. Wilde, *Social Psychology: The Canadian Context.* Toronto: McClelland and Stewart, 1972.

Clairmont, Donald H., and Dennis W. Magill, *Nova Scotian Blacks: an Historical and Structural Overview.* Halifax: Institute of Public Affairs, Dalhousie University, 1970, especially Part II.

Cumming, Peter A., and Neil H. Mickenberg (eds.), *Native Rights in Canada.* Toronto: Indian-Eskimo Association of Canada and General Publishing Company, 2nd Edition, 1972.

Dosman, Edgar J., *Indians: The Urban Dilemma.* Toronto: McClelland and Stewart, 1972. (See especially Chapter Eight.)

Elliott, Jean Leonard (ed.), *Minority Canadians,* Vol. I, 'Native Peoples,' Vol. 2, 'Immigrant Groups.' Scarborough: Prentice-Hall of Canada, 1971. (See Introduction to either volume for the typology.)

Forcese, Dennis, and Stephen Richer, *Social Research Methods.* Englewood Cliffs: Prentice-Hall Inc., 1973, pp. 37-51.

Gardner, R.C., D.M. Taylor, and M.J. Feenstra, 'Ethnic Stereotypes: Attitudes or Beliefs,' *Canadian Journal of Psychology,* XXIV, 5 (1970), 321-324.

Graham, Hugh D., and Ted R. Gurr (eds.) *Violence in America: Historical and Comparative Perspectives.* New York: Praeger, 1969, esp. pp. 462-471.

Grebner, Leo, Joan W. Moore, and Ralph C. Guzman, *The Mexican-American People: the Nation's Second Largest Minority.* Glencoe, Ill.: The Free Press, 1970, esp. pp. 443-512.

Gzowski, Peter, 'This is the True Strength of Separatism,' article in *Maclean's Magazine,* November 2, 1963, pp. 13-18. (Uses data gathered by Le Groupe de Recherche Sociale, Montreal.)

Hall, Oswald, 'The Ethnic Division of Labour Revisited,' in Richard Ossenberg (ed.), *Canadian Society: Pluralism, Change and Conflict.* Scarborough: Prentice-Hall of Canada, 1971.

Hughes, Everett C., *French Canada in Transition.* Chicago: University of Chicago Press, 1943.

——, 'Colonies, Colonization and Colonialism.' Paper presented to the *American Ethnological Society,* April, 1973.

Jackson, John D., 'French-English Relations in an Ontario Community,' *Canadian Review of Sociology and Anthropology,* III, 3 (August, 1966). Reprinted in Jean Leonard Elliott (ed.), *Minority Canadians,* Vol. 2, 'Immigrant Groups.' Scarborough: Prentice-Hall of Canada, 1971.

Lewis, Oscar, 'The Culture of Poverty,' *Scientific American,* CCXV, 4 (October, 1966).

Lyman, Stanford M., 'The Race Relations Cycle of Robert E. Park,' *Pacific Sociological Review.* II, 1 (Spring, 1968), 16-22.

Nagler, Mark, 'Minority Values and Economic Achievement: The Case of the North American Indian,' in Mark Nagler (ed.), *Perspectives on the North American Indians.* Toronto: McClelland and Stewart, 1972, pp. 131-141.

Neuwirth, Gertrud, 'A Weberian Outline of a Theory of Community: Its Application to the "Dark Ghetto,"' *British Journal of Sociology,* XX (1969), 148-163.

Park, Robert Ezra, *Race and Culture.* New York: The Free Press (Paperback Edition), 1964.

Porter, John, 'Dilemmas and Contradictions of the Multi-Ethnic Society.' Paper presented to the *Royal Society of Canada,* Section II, St. John's, Newfoundland, June, 1972.

Potter, Harold, and Daniel Hill, *Negro Settlement in Canada,* unpublished report to the Royal Commission on Bilingualism and Biculturalism. Ottawa: Queen's Printer, 1966, p. 35.

Poulin, Pierre, 'Fin de l'à-plat-ventrisme,' *L'Acayen,* 1, 1 (April, 1972,) 3-7.

Richer, Stephen, and Pierre Laporte, 'Culture, Cognition, and English-French Competition,' in Jean Leonard Elliott (ed.), *Minority Canadians,* Vol. II. Scarborough: Prentice-Hall of Canada, 1971, pp. 141-150.

Richmond, A.H., *Postwar Immigrants to Canada.* Toronto: University of Toronto Press, 1967.

Robert, E. André, and Frank G. Vallee, *Within and Outside the Bilingual Belt: The French Outside Quebec.* Publication date expected to be 1974.

Schermerhorn, R.A., *Comparative Ethnic Relations: A Framework for Theory and Research.* New York: Random House, 1970.

Schwartz, Mildred, *Public Opinion and Canadian Identity.* Berkeley: University of California Press, 1967.

Shipley, Joseph T., *Dictionary of Word Origins.* Ames, Iowa: Littlefield, Adams and Co., 1959.

Taylor, Donald M., Lise M. Simard, and Frances E. Aboud, 'Ethnic Identification in Canada: a Cross-Cultural Investigation,' *Canadian Journal of Behavioral Science,* IV, 1 (January, 1972).

Theodorson, George A., and Achilles G. Theodorson, *Modern Dictionary of Sociology.* New York: Crowell, 1969.

Tremblay, Marc-Adélard, and Gerald Gold, *Communities and Culture in French Canada: Elements in an Ethnology of French Canada.* Toronto: Holt, Rinehart, and Winston, 1973.

Valentine, Charles A., *Culture and Poverty: Critique and Counter-Proposals.* Chicago: University of Chicago Press, 1968.

Valentine, Victor F., 'Some Problems of the Metis in Northern Saskatchewan,' *Canadian Journal of Economics and Political Science,* XX (1954), 89-95.

Vallee, Frank G., Mildred Schwartz and Frank Darnell, 'Ethnic Assimilation and Differentiation in Canada,' *Canadian Journal of Economics and Political Science,* XXIII (November, 1957), 540-549.

Vallee, Frank G. and John de Vries, 'Issues and Trends in Bilingualism in Canada,' to appear in Joshua Fishman (ed.), *Advances in the Study of Multilingual Societies,* The Hague: Mouton (forthcoming).

Wirth, Louis, 'The Problem of Minority Groups,' in Ralph Linton (ed.), *The Science of Man in the World Crisis.* New York: Columbia University Press, 1945. Reprinted in the Bobbs-Merrill Reprint Series in the Social Sciences, S- 318.

Yetman, Norman R., and C. Hoy Steele (eds.), *Majority and Minority: The Dynamics of Racial and Ethnic Relations.* Boston: Allyn and Bacon, Inc., 1971. See especially Part VI, 'The Black Revolution and Beyond,' pp. 521-621.

CHAPTER SEVEN

Politics: The Issue of Citizenship

Mildred A. Schwartz
University of Illinois at Chicago Circle

Basic Concepts of Political Experience

Equality as a Political Issue

Item: If you become ill, and happen to live outside one of the large, metropolitan centers, it is highly likely that when you find a physician, he will have a patient body potentially twice as large as his colleagues in major cities, be older on the average, and less likely to have specialized training. For example, in data presented to the Royal Commission on Health Services, the 1961 ratio of physicians to population was 1 to 578 in Toronto, but 1 to 1,201 for non-metropolitan areas in Ontario. According to the Commissioners,

> Several factors lure the newly fledged professional to the urban areas rather than the rural: the less adequate diagnostic and treatment facilities in rural areas, lack of professional contacts, generally lower standards of living and the lack of amenities. (Royal Commission on Health Services, 1964, I: 246)

If the Commissioners had asked whether there were any political explanations for this distribution, they could have found these without much difficulty. The political element in the provision of health services relates to decisions about the numbers and kinds of people permitted to acquire medical skills. These decisions contribute to a set of collective goals delineating who should be included in the medical profession, and less directly, who should have access to medical attention.

Item: The chances of surviving the birth process are more precarious, both for mother and child, in Newfoundland than all other provinces. In 1961, for example, out of every 1,000 births, 37 babies would be dead.

For every 100,000 live births, 88 mothers would die. If we use Ontario as a contrast, infant mortality was 23 and maternal mortality 38. (Dominion Bureau of Statistics, 1963) Were these differences the result of comparatively poor personal health practices, or perhaps the cumulative effects of genetic dispositions? Whatever the answers, political factors were also at work here, in this case the consequence of a lack of political power. On the assumption that collectively, the families of these mothers and babies wanted to improve their life chances, they could not do this because they lacked the means to mobilize the necessary resources. They probably did not have the knowledge to locate the roots of their limited life chances, and even if they did, they did not have the power to influence those institutions which could improve their situation. Evidence that differentials in infant and maternal mortality have declined are some indication that power shifts have also taken place.

Item: A manufacturer looking for new business opportunities decides to locate in an area where the level of unemployment has generally been high. Local conditions seem to guarantee an adequate supply of labor along with relatively low labor costs. The company seeks out this location to enhance its competitive position, increase profits, and generally maintain the organization's existence. Such a move seems desirable on economic grounds. The economic rationale underlying it, however, is closely tied to political considerations. For example, the predecessor of Georgetown Seafoods, Limited, of Prince Edward Island, was started with massive financial support from the provincial government, and when the firm went bankrupt, it was sold to another private company at much below cost. The original decision to promote the fish processing plant was the government's, anxious to find additional employment and income for its constituents. The failure of the first company and the subsequent financial losses that had to be absorbed were directly compounded by the government's over-eagerness to stimulate the economy, regardless of cost. (Mathias, 1971: 15-42)

These illustrations, which on first sight may have little in common, are intended to arouse a broader recognition of what constitutes political experience.* And by looking for the shared elements in the three examples, we can also confront the affinity between politics and the issue of equality. It is customary to see politics as concerned with legislative bodies, with the making, interpreting, and enforcing of laws, with

---

*Since this chapter was written, Ronald Manzer (1974) has published a book on the social and political conditions of Canada that complements the approach used here. Our major concept is citizenship: his is needs. The former leads to an emphasis on social structural factors, growing out of the theories of Marshall, Rokkan, Marx, and Parsons. The latter is more psychological, and builds on the work of the psychologist Maslow. There remain many similarities in the topics covered, and Manzer, given the scope of a book, is able to provide much more detail and empirical evidence.

leadership, parties, elections, and so on. It is true that these make up much of the substance of political life, varying of course with the society in which they occur. But they do not get to the heart of the essentially political issues, or to the recurring political processes. Therefore we must begin by examining the bearing that these political essentials have on the issue of equality in Canadian society.

The fundamental political issues are those that involve collective decisions directed to achieving collective goals. One prominent set of goals in all social systems has to do with regulating the allocation of what is collectively valued. This in turn sounds, superficially at least, like a very general description of the economic system. It is certainly possible to interpret our introductory examples as placing an unusual emphasis on the economic. The approach was deliberate, as a recognition of parallels in the ways the political and economic systems operate, and the mutually reinforcing influences between the two.

Politics, in the sense we use it here, is not synonymous with government or the state. It is any action involving the 'collective pursuit of collective goals.' (Parsons, 1966: 72) It may take place in trade unions, business corporations, universities, and even in institutional areas not normally thought to have political content, such as religion or the family. While this is a definition most congenial to sociologists, it has also come to be shared by many political scientists. (Bachrach, 1967: 72-75)

Power – The Central Concept

Power is a central concept in the study of politics, but its very importance has led to a confusing number of usages. Rather than attempt to review the variety of usages, it is sufficient here to point out that *power may be viewed as an attribute of individuals or as a property of a social system.* William Gamson, reviewing these two perspectives as they have appeared in the literature, notes that the achievement of personal goals has generally been seen as threatening and conflict-laden, while the achievement of collective goals has been viewed as almost benign. He sees them instead as intertwined, arguing that 'both the benign and the threatening emphases among students of power concern a single relationship between *authorities'* and those affected by decisions, whom Gamson calls *'potential partisans.'* (Gamson, 1968: 2) *The perspective presented here will often stress the social systemic aspects of power,* but not as a way of avoiding issues of conflict. It will see the definition of collective goals as a means for delimiting which resources are valued, and hence subject to socially meaningful scarcity.

The individualistic perspective on *power* includes the famous definition of Max Weber that it is *'the probability that one actor within a social relationship will be in a position to carry out his will despite resistance.'* (Weber, 1947: 152) This is a definition that has surprisingly little to do with the content of politics, since it does not touch on the existence of collective goals. Gamson also includes studies of elites in this individualistic category, as exemplified by the work of Vilfredo Pareto (1935), Gaetano Mosca (1939), and C. Wright Mills (1956).

In addition to recognizing power as an individual resource, it is often useful to focus on power as an attribute of social systems. This is a perspective adopted by Parsons (1967: 308), Clark (1968: 3-126), Etzioni (1968: 314) among others. Clark puts it most simply when he says *power involves the ability to 'select, change, and to attain the goals of a social system.'* (Clark 1968: 46)

The new concern with ecology can be used to illustrate the various aspects of power. Where pure air and water become scarce resources, the ability to insulate oneself from the effects of pollution can be crucial. We can expect protective responses from those with the purchasing power to find pleasanter environments, and also with the knowledge to judge the effects of pollution on their well-being. Thus the better educated and more prosperous, normally least affected by pollution, often express most concern, as was recently found in a study of Hamilton, Ontario (Winham, 1972: 401) Power is manifested where such people display concern about pollution, playing the role of Gamson's 'potential partisans.' This potential becomes mobilized where people organize, enlist the support of the mass media, and engage in various techniques to press for control measures from industry and government. Power takes on an even more systemic character where it is considered in terms of binding decisions made with respect to environmental control. For example, in situations where the conflict between environmental protection and continued industrial growth is recognized, decisions must be made on the priority of goals, and the costs people are willing to pay for their achievement. In the case of Hamilton, the mayor is quoted on his defence of the city's transactions with two steel mills: 'There's an awful lot of talk these days about ecology. Our greatest problem in this city isn't ecology. It is unemployment. This deal will help ease that problem.' (Winham, 1972: 389) In other words, priority is assigned to the maintenance of the quality of material life, regardless of the costs to the environment.

The Use of Force

Weber distinguished the exercise of power in general from that inherent in the life of the state by reserving for the state monopoly over the *legitimate use of force.* (Weber, 1947: 156) Agencies other than the state, including those to whom the state makes such delegation, can of course use force in order to insure that their wishes are followed, but where they are not entitled to do so, sanctions in turn can be mobilized against them. To the extent that the arrogation of force cannot be halted, as in the case of guerilla bands or vigilante groups, then the authority of the state itself hangs in precarious balance. For those to whom force is given as a sanctioning authority, its use is the ultimate weapon, though often reluctantly employed. This reluctance stems from the resources that must be committed — if you take out your army today, and do your worst, what can you do tomorrow? Force expended is gone, and the threat of force is no longer of the same potency. Your enemies are dead, injured, or intimidated. If they are not, you have no alternative but to continue using force until you or they capitulate. The cost may be greater than the user can bear. For such reasons, force is preferred as threat rather than as action, but it still must be a real threat.

The dilemmas of power as these pertain to the use of force were never more critical in Canada than following the crisis of October, 1970. James Cross, British trade commissioner, and Pierre Laporte, Quebec minister of labor and immigration, were kidnapped by cells of the Front de Libération du Québec (FLQ). The FLQ had emerged in the 1960's as a group dedicated to the separation of Quebec and prepared to demonstrate its purpose through acts of violence. Prior to the kidnappings, violence had been directed against property, especially that which symbolized attachment to Canada (letter boxes were a favorite target), and while lives had been lost, this had been the result of property destruction. (Morf, 1970) Terrorism entered a new phase with the kidnappings, and more stringent responses seemed in order. When the ordinary measures of the city and provincial police forces seemed inadequate, Premier Robert Bourassa called in the army. This was followed by the imposition of the War Measures Act by an Order-in-Council of the federal government. Both of these were extraordinary steps at a time when the country was not at war and when there had not been previous indications of the threat of large-scale insurrection. Force was being met with force, and in the outcome, Pierre Laporte would die, while the kidnappers of James Cross would be permitted to leave the country and seek sanctuary in Cuba. Debates on the government's use of force will continue for a long time, but the implications require pause. Whether we agree with him or not, Guy Rocher has made several telling points in his assessment of the events.

> I do not share the analytical methods or ideology of the FLQ, but it has proved an important sociological truth: terror can be phenomenally and devastatingly efficient ...

> The government has entered into revolutionary warfare, and that is a serious mistake. Even a moral mistake. One day, sooner or later, we will realize that, instead of condemning revolutionary war it walked straight into it. It played

the same game and gave extra power to the FLQ's action. The FLQ wanted to create a state of war and the government was completely taken in. (Translated by Saywell, 1971: 149)

Legitimate Power or Authority

By legitimacy, sociologists generally refer to a situation where the order of existence is considered right and proper, and deserving of support. With respect to authority, this means that the governed recognize the right of the rulers to rule. Without that recognition, a ruler has no legitimate claims to rule, imposing his will instead by the constant exercise of force. (Lipset, 1960: 64)

This definition of legitimacy can be applied to the Canadian state and the allocation of political authority within it. The division of powers between the central government and the provinces was spelled out in the British North America Act and designed to insure a strong central government. These intentions were eroded through interpretations of the Judicial Committee of the Privy Council, and also through changing circumstances. (Laskin, 1967: 395-401; Fletcher, 1968: 140-158; Lower, Scott *et. al.,* 1958) Quebec separatism represents the most recent and sharpest challenge to the traditional division of powers, and with it, to the legitimacy of the political community. (Hagy, 1969: 229-238) But many people, while rejecting separation, have argued for a redefinition of the place of Quebec in the Canadian state.*

The terrorism of the FLQ raised anew the issue of provincial versus federal authority. According to a document prepared by sixteen leading members of the Quebec community early in the crisis,

> The destiny of two human lives, the reputation and collective honour of our society, the obvious danger of a political and social degradation that this society is presently facing, all this makes it clear to us that *the responsibility for finding a solution and applying it quite rightly lies primarily with Quebec.* (Cited in Saywell, 1971: 77) (Emphasis added)

Alternatively, as the events of October unfolded, there was a feeling among some groups that the mediation of third parties was required, a technique often helpful in settling disputes generally (Dahrendorf, 1959: 229-230). This was inauspiciously discussed in terms of the formation of a 'provisional government.' From one interpretation, this meant that the Quebec government had already lost its claim to legitimacy. From another, it meant that the advocates of a provisional government were

---

*For example, see the various interpretations in J. Peter Meekison, *Canadian Federalism: Myth or Reality.* (Toronto: Methuen, 1968), pp. 337-412.

abandoning all commitment to democratic forms of representative government, and hence advocating the most illegitimate alternative. (Saywell, 1971: 145-148)

In the face of the uncertainty generated by the FLQ violence, doubts about how the two kidnapped men might be saved and what these events meant as preludes to more general unrest, the imposition of the War Measures Act was largely approved. One indication of this comes from a poll conducted by the Canadian Institute of Public Opinion even prior to the news of Pierre Laporte's murder. The question asked a sample of 556 adults, 'Frankly, do you feel that the governments in Ottawa and Quebec are being too hard and tough on the FLQ kidnappers, so far, or not tough enough?' In the country as a whole, 37 per cent answered 'not tough enough' and 51 per cent 'about right.' In Quebec, the comparable figures were 32 and 54 per cent respectively. (Canadian Institute of Public Opinion, Gallup Poll Report, October 19, 1970) Yet, as Breton has observed with regard to the War Measures Act,

> A measure which results in a high proportion of useless arrests of innocent victims is likely to generate a lot of mistrust, as well as a measure with a diffuse rather than a specific target. A measure which is clearly disproportionate to the severity of the danger will, at least as an after-effect, throw doubt on the trustworthiness of the authorities. The War Measures Act appears to have involved useless arrests, a diffuse target, and to be somewhat disproportionate.*

Aside from those directly concerned in Quebec, anxiety about the consequences of the War Measures Act was centered mainly in the universities and among the NDP. Protection of the individual in his relations with the state is one way of defining civil liberties. (Tarnopolsky, 1966) Civil liberties, in turn, are related to the maintenance of legitimacy by contributing to the predictability and trustworthiness of political authorities. The War Measures Act cannot be judged solely in terms of its immediate effects, but must be viewed with respect to its long-run consequences for the operation of political authority. (Borovoy, 1971: 99-117)

According to Max Weber, there are three bases of legitimate authority: traditional, charismatic, and rational-legal. (1947: 324-362) The *traditional* claim to authority derives from appeals to established ways of doing things, orderly laws of succession, prescribed claims to office. Its prototype is captured in the cry, 'The King is dead, long live the King.'

---

*Raymond Breton, 'The Socio-Political Dynamics of the October Events.' Reprinted from *The Canadian Review of Sociology and Anthropology*, 9:1 (1972), p. 52, by permission of the author and the publisher.

The *rational-legal* claims to legitimacy are those that give authority to the office of ruler, rather than to his person. They are satisfied by adherence to recognized rules and procedures both for gaining and exercising office. Legitimacy based on a *charismatic* claim comes from the person of the ruler. The original meaning of charisma, the gift of grace, embodies the special nature of this form of leadership. It is revolutionary, breaking with traditions, although often calling on support from a purer past. It is personal, requiring of the leader the ability and force to solve critical problems without regard to established organizations. Since such leaders represent a break with the past, their legitimacy has a paradoxical element. It comes from the promise of solutions to problems, and it survives only as long as the leader is able to deliver on his promises.

In a political system such as Canada's, those elected to office operate in a rational-legal milieu, and consequently are bound by the requirements of an ongoing organization. At the same time, there is always a tendency to make personalized and even emotional appeals to voters; in other words, electoral politics often have some charismatic elements. Where the right to vote is widespread, we can expect to find recurring tensions between the nature of charismatic leadership and the demands of party organization. (Bendix, 1960: 440) Weber's pure type of charismatic leader, when he is found in a political context, is likely to be the founder of a new movement. A particularly good example is the case of the late William Aberhart, first premier of a Social Credit government in Alberta.

William Aberhart began his career as a high school teacher and in addition founded the Calgary Prophetic Bible Institute for the propagation of a fundamentalist form of Protestantism. By the time he was exposed to Social Credit theories, he had already built a large personal following in Alberta, aided by his effective use of radio in the transmission of his religious message. His interest in Social Credit developed while Alberta was suffering the worst effects of the Great Depression, when personal and social distress was widespread. He saw in social credit the solution to most worldly problems, and as people listened to him, the relation between religious and political salvation became unmistakable. Aberhart's imposing presence, his skill as an orator, the persuasive conviction of his manner were all irresistible. In addition to possessing these prototypical charismatic qualities, he was a resourceful organizer, building up a dedicated following that would be translated into a political movement able to win the first election it contested. (Irving, 1959) The break with the kind of politics practiced by the two older parties was sharp, introducing virtually one-party government. As a result of his strong personal appeals, Aberhart's followers were inspired with the conviction, 'Mr Aberhart will find a Way. If we all stand behind him we can build a new world under his leadership.' (Irving, 1947: 136) To those puzzled by Social Credit doctrines and how they could be applied, the reply was, 'You don't have to know all about Social Credit before you vote for it; you don't have to understand electricity to use it … all you have to do is push a button and you get the light.' (Macpherson, 1962: 152)

In general, *what is politically legitimate is not merely, or even necessarily, what is legal, but what is acknowledged by those who accept the authority.* It is not, then, a body of rules or precepts, although it may be bolstered by them. It is a principle of social organization, a social value that can be attached to a variable number of individuals or offices, even within the same society. But to have any meaning, it must be accepted by sufficient numbers to give the claimants the support needed to exercise authority. Total acceptance is not required, but enough so that the ultimate threat in the case of the state, the use of force, need not be constantly dissipated in keeping large numbers of dissidents from triggering recurring revolts.

Equality as a Collective Goal

Equality as the goal of a political system has impressive precedents. Indeed, democracy can be described as a system whose central ideal is equality. (Bachrach, 1967: 83; Mayo, 1960: 70) The rallying cry of the French Revolution gave equality a central place with the values of liberty and fraternity. The American Declaration of Independence affirms equality as self-evident, associated with certain inalienable rights, among them being life, liberty, and the pursuit of happiness. Aside from such generalities, it is not too clear just what these words mean in practice. In the case of the French and American Revolutions, and many others that were to follow, the stirring words often remained just that, never to be realized through the efforts of ordinary men. The implicit irony in these fine-sounding proclamations was not often evident to the actors involved, but it hardly escapes us. For example, when Thomas Jefferson presented the argument of natural equality, he was not at the same time able to find acceptance for his thesis that this was inimical to the continuation of slavery. From these precedents, it is not surprising that equality should mean different things to different people. (Rees, 1971) Since it is apparent that inequalities can be found in a great variety of individual and group attributes, it is necessary to decide which are the crucial social and political arenas.

Of the arenas in which equality is crucial, primacy is most often given to the economic. This is especially so for those who work from a Marxist perspective. For example, in a recent work by Charles Anderson, social inequality is presented as synonymous with inequality in income and wealth. 'Economic inequality sets the conditions for differences in health, education, work, leisure use, life style, and power, though these factors influence economic position in return.' (Anderson, 1971: 101) Without denigrating the importance of economic factors, we believe that narrow and exclusive concentration on them obscures the power dimension of such issues as who has access to valued resources, how these are distributed and by what means, and with what effect.

Another approach to equality has been suggested by the British sociologist, T.H. Marshall, who in turn takes off from the economist Alfred Marshall. The earlier Marshall was moved by human suffering and poverty, but found the solutions offered by socialism unacceptable. The problem he posed, quaintly outmoded in its language, and some might argue, narrowly prejudiced in outlook, nevertheless has the beginnings of an important question. Addressing the Cambridge Reform Club in 1873, he said,

> The question is not whether all men will ultimately be equal — that they certainly will not — but whether progress may not go on steadily, if slowly, till, by occupation at least, every man is a gentleman. I hold that it may, and that it will.*

It is T.H. Marshall's interpretation of what he sees as the sociological thesis underlying this statement that is of interest to us.

> It postulates that there is a kind of basic human equality associated with the concept of full membership of community — or, as I should say, of citizenship — which is not inconsistent with the inequalities which distinguish the various economic levels in society. (Marshall, 1965: 76)

It is not necessary to agree with Alfred Marshall's conclusions to accept this approach. T.H. Marshall himself questions the compatibility between his concept of citizenship and the inequalities of a social class system found under capitalism. The major value of looking at equality in terms of *citizenship,* in any case, is that it gives us a way of viewing equality that takes in the full range of *politically relevant* themes relating individual and group interests to the social system.

We will follow Marshall in distinguishing three kinds of citizen rights: social, political, and civil. *Political* rights are those that enable community members to participate in the exercise of political power. This means that citizens can hold office in the crucial decision-making bodies and

*Quoted in T.H. Marshall, *Class, Citizenship and Social development,* p. 74. © 1963 by T.H. Marshall.

that they can freely choose those that sit on those bodies. *Civil* rights are associated with individual freedom — freedom of speech, of belief, the right to justice, and perhaps more culture-bound, the right to hold property and conclude legal contracts. By *social* rights Marshall means those that give the individual the 'right to a modicum of economic welfare and security and the right to share to the full in the social heritage and to live the life of a civilized being according to the standards prevailing in the society.' (Marshall, 1965: 78)

It is important to recognize that *all* these rights must be present before we can speak of 'equality,' since they define the minimal limits of citizenship, of full membership in a political community. In any given society, we can expect that groups may enjoy different rights, gaining access to them at different historical periods, and that the struggle to obtain these rights can involve varying degrees of overt conflict. Differences in the acquisition of rights and in the amount of conflict generated will, in turn, affect subsequent political developments. (Bendix, 1964: 55-104; Rokkan, 1966) Looking at economic factors alone would prevent, for example, a full understanding of the struggle of blacks in the United States (Parsons, 1965; Dye, 1971), or an appreciation, as Herbert Gans has observed, that the 'social protest of the 1960's takes the form of the equality revolution.' (Gans, 1971: 610-621)

Political Rights in Canada

Voting

In Western societies, winning the right to vote was a crucial element in the acquisition of political equality. Its importance is substantiated by political observers and by the determined efforts of those seeking enfranchisement. (Shils, 1962: 38; Cole and Filson, 1967: 351) Major restrictions on universal suffrage in Canada have been based on property, ethnicity, and sex. Some form of property qualification was the rule in the early days of Canadian nationhood, based on requirements found in the constituent provinces. (Ermatinger, 1886; Garner, 1969) Such restrictions were eventually eliminated, with Nova Scotia finally taking this move in 1920 and Quebec in 1936. In federal elections, property had ceased to be the basis of voting rights as provinces moved toward manhood suffrage, most by the turn of the century, and this was consolidated with the passage of the Dominion Elections Act, 1920.

Restrictions based on race, language, or religion have been slower to disappear, and in this sense may suggest the greater potential for inequality associated with ethnicity. In various provinces, Chinese, Japanese, Asian Indians, and Doukhobors were prevented from voting up until recently. For example, references to race were not dropped in British Columbia until 1953, and federally, Doukhobors were not enfranchised until 1955. North American Indians and Eskimos have also faced severe difficulties, with Indians on reservations not able to vote federally until 1960, and still unable to vote in Quebec. Other groups, not as easily identifiable by physical characteristics, have also been excluded, most notoriously during the hysteria associated with World War I. In the election of 1917, even naturalized British subjects born in an enemy country who had arrived in Canada prior to 1902 were disenfranchised, as were those whose mother tongue was one associated with an enemy power, regardless of place of birth. (Qualter, 1970: 10-12)

The struggle for woman suffrage took place in Canada during the same period as it was an issue elsewhere in the English-speaking world. Here it was a low-keyed battle, probably hampered to some extent by the apathy of women. It was only in Quebec, granting women the right to vote in provincial elections as late as 1940, that the struggle was truly heated. Curiously enough, there is evidence that women did vote in Quebec in the early years of the nineteenth century, a right that soon became lost. (Cleverdon, 1950)

If universal suffrage can be regarded as one of the conditions of political equality, it follows that everyone's vote should have equal weight. (Rees, 1971: 39) Since votes are aggregated through electoral districts, this means that, at a minimum, districts should be of approximately equal size. This has usually not been the case, however, where the governing party is able to manipulate electoral bourdaries for its own advantage. British politics has had its 'rotten boroughs' while the United States has introduced the term 'gerrymander' to describe the manipulation of boundaries. In Canada, the general conservatism of the political process has enhanced such inequalities by giving undue advantage to rural constituencies, despite the great growth of cities, and more recently, of suburbs. To overcome some of the glaring injustices, Parliament passed the Electoral Boundaries Commissions Act of 1964, which allocated the drawing up of boundaries to ten provincial commissions. These commissions were empowered to make their decisions without regard to partisan considerations, but in no case to exceed their 'electoral quotas' by plus or minus 25 per cent. The quotas themselves are set by the population of the provinces. The results were hardly perfection, but did go a considerable way towards redressing the worst inequities. Instructions to the commissioners regarding the relative weight to be given factors of 'sparsity, density, and accessibility' meant that rural ridings were not as depleted as they might otherwise have been. At the same time, it is clear that urban interests did increase their weight. (Lyons, 1970)

The example of the federal government has led to the setting up of non-partisan redistribution commissions in some provinces, where in general there is evidence of even greater need of them. For example, 49.4 per cent of the voters in Alberta in 1967 were urban, based on residence in Calgary and Edmonton and their suburbs, and were distributed in only 37.7 per cent of the ridings. 'The most extreme case existed between voters in Dunvegan and in Edmonton North East, where Dunvegan voters had 5.78 times the voting power of electors in Edmonton North East.' (Long, 1969: 351) In Quebec, in the 1973 provincial election, the Liberals dominated. Yet, the Parti Québécois, which only won six seats, had about 32 per cent of the popular vote.

A further aspect of vote weighting is related to the electoral system. It is often argued that a simple plurality system, where the candidate who gains the greatest number of votes, even if this is far from a majority, is still the winner, is inherently unjust. Instead, some system of proportional representation is advocated, in which even minority interests have some likelihood of gaining representation. Criticisms of proportional representation generally are based on its presumed relation to the emergence of many small parties and consequently the difficulty of forming a stable government necessarily based on coalitions. Cairns, in examining Canadian elections from 1921 to 1965, is inclined to take a different stance. He sees the plurality system as aggravating sectional interests, since it permits minor parties with a territorial base to emerge, as well as encouraging major parties to concentrate their efforts where there is greatest electoral pay-off. Proportional representation, he feels, would force parties to seek votes in all parts of the country, and would thereby contribute to greater national integration. (Cairns, 1968: 55-80)

We can demonstrate restrictions on political equality from lack of voting rights and from structural barriers to 'one man, one vote.' In addition, not even all those qualified to vote do so. (Table I)

At the individual level, turnout is affected by factors that generally inhibit the acquisition of political information, the opportunity to participate in politically meaningful activities, and to develop a sense of commitment to the political machinery. This often means that the most recently enfranchised are among those with lowest rates of participation. (Lipset, 1960: 179-219; Milbrath, 1965; Verba and Nie, 1972) In Canada low turnout has been associated with low levels of commitment and information (Laponce, 1967: 75-87), fewer years of schooling (Van Loon, 1970: 385), younger age and female sex (Laskin and Baird, 1970: 457-458). In other words, political equality as manifested in the right to vote does not obliterate other continuing sources of inequality.

Table I: Voter Turnout in Provinces, Canadian Federal Elections*

	Average Turnout 1921–1965 (%)
Prince Edward Island	83
Saskatchewan	77
Nova Scotia	77
New Brunswick	76
British Columbia	74
Quebec	73
Manitoba	73
Ontario	72
Alberta	68
Newfoundland[a]	65

[a] Based on seven elections from 1949.

*Source: John Courtney, *Voting in Canada* (Scarborough: Prentice-Hall of Canada, 1967), pp. 200-201.

Representation

Representation as an aspect of political equality is difficult to establish. It raises fundamental questions: to what extent are there formal barriers to seeking representation? Are representatives typical of the people they represent? Are representatives also important decision-makers?

Formal barriers to the attainment of political office are relatively few in Canada, and mainly concern the disqualification of those who derive some direct benefit from government (Qualter, 1970: 46-52). Property qualifications virtually disappeared in 1872, and those related to religion, by Confederation (Ward, 1950: 61-82). This aspect of representation cannot then be viewed as a serious handicap to political equality. What can be considered is the extent to which Canadian representatives are 'typical' of their constituents.

Since Confederation there have been fifteen prime ministers in Canada. With only two exceptions, and these early in Canada's political history, all had university education or its equivalent, even long before this was enjoyed by large numbers of the population. Legal training was acquired by eleven, two were newspaper editors, and one had been the editor of an important journal. Four were Catholics and the remainder Protestant. From the information available, we know that most of these were from the numerically dominant United Church. Three were of French origin, eleven of British, and one of mixed German-United Empire Loyalist heritage. The latter, John Diefenbaker, was also only the second exception to the pattern of birth and usual residence in central Canada. Canadian prime ministers, in other words, can be described as possessing the background characteristics of the groups traditionally dominant in Canadian society, yet not of great wealth themselves, nor intimately tied to aristocratic familial background or the centers of great economic power. (Engelmann and Schwartz, 1975)

The composition of the federal cabinet differs from the characteristics of prime ministers primarily in its geographic distribution, since it is deliberately formed to represent the provinces of Canada. Since the universe from which cabinet members are selected is shaped by population size and party fortunes, some discrepancies in what might be considered an 'equitable' share of cabinet posts is not usual. In particular, Quebec tends to be under-represented and Ontario over-represented in Conservative governments, while Quebec tends to be over-represented and the Prairies under-represented in Liberal governments. (Schwartz, 1974b: 64-79) The coincidence between provincial boundaries and other characteristics means that additional forms of maldistribution will be found. For example, Van Loon and Whittington argue that French- and English-speaking are represented according to their distribution in the population, but this has been the case only in Liberal Cabinets. (Van Loon and Whittington, 1971: 348-349) University education, training at law, high socio-economic status also are general characteristics of cabinet members. (Porter, 1965: 386-398; Engelmann and Schwartz, 1975; Van Loon and Whittington, 1971: 351-352)

With some exceptions, the characteristics of members of parliament faithfully reflect those of the cabinet (Ward, 1950; Kornberg, 1967). What we know about provincial legislators suggests similar trends (Manzer, 1974: 240-243) Up until recently at least, the representation of religious faiths was carefully controlled through the drawing of constituency boundaries in Newfoundland (Rothney, 1962: 557-570), while in Saskatchewan the minor faiths tended to be under-represented (Smith, 1968: 178-206). Women have yet to play a prominent role as representatives, with the first women elected to provincial legislatures in 1961 in Quebec, 1967 in New Brunswick, and 1970 in Prince Edward Island. (Qualter, 1970: 52) Only three women have served as cabinet ministers in Ottawa, Ellen Fairclough in the Diefenbaker government, Judy LaMarsh in the Pearson government and Jeanne Sauvé in the Trudeau government.

Elites, that is, *those who hold positions of power* (Lasswell, Lerner,

Rothwell, 1952: 6) *or those most eminent in their field* (Pareto, 1935: 1423-1424) are subjects of great interest because of their presumed impact on the milieu in which they operate. Observers of political elites with the kind of social characteristics described here have sometimes been led to postulate the existence of a cohesive 'establishment' or monolithic elite group, controlling all signigicant decisions affecting national existence. (For example, Mills, 1956; Domhoff, 1967) An extreme conspiratorial view of elite actions has not been popular in Canada, where social scientists have often been reluctant to make any judgments on the implications of elite characteristics. (Engelmann and Schwartz, 1975; Van Loon and Whittington, 1971: 353) John Porter, on the contrary, takes a much less cautious position. While he too is reluctant to infer any deliberate collusion in terms of the representation of special interests, he is not prepared to end there.

> If we accept Mannheim's persuasive argument that a person's beliefs about social reality are shaped by the social milieu to which he has been exposed, we can see that the definitions of reality which provide the framework for making political decisions depend much on the social background and life experiences of politicians. The predominance of some occupational groups and people of one class background means that limited perspectives are brought to bear on social issues. In Canada, it is the homogeneity of political leaders in terms of education, occupation, and social class which gives the political system its conservative tone. (Porter, 1965: 391)

This leads us to what is probably the most important question of all, the relative influence of representatives as decision-makers. There are some who would argue that, given the complexity of modern government, the most crucial decision-makers are those with the technical knowledge and long-term commitment to office who are typically a part of the governmental bureaucracy. While not going quite this far, Van Loon and Whittington state that 'the upper and middle or technocratic levels of the bureaucracy play a vital part in the decision-making process in Canada.' (1971: 355-356) The recognition of this importance, coupled with the nature of their appointments and their lack of direct responsibility to the electorate, has led to concern about their accurate reflection of political needs. We consequently hear discussions in favor of a more 'representative' bureaucracy. (Porter, 1965: 449-451)

Porter is the most influential spokesman for the position that even cabinet members, that is, the highest echelons of the political elite, are really not the crucial decision-makers. Instead, he gives primacy to the corporate elite, not by suggesting that they subvert the processes of government to their own interest, but because he believes that the actions they take simply have more impact on the life of the country than anything done by government. Moreover, since the political elite is basically middle class and conservative, it has no incentive to challenge the kinds of decisions made by the corporate elite; nor does it pursue actions that the corporate elite finds threatening. The accuracy of this judgment seems to be upheld by recent and continuing debates on the role of American investment and business in Canada. Finally, Porter attributes the weaker role of the political elite to the instability of their career patterns, in which active engagement in politics seems to be a temporary job. (Porter, 1965: 405-415)

Civil Rights in Canada

Religious Freedom

The protection of religious freedom (as well as others) is evident in the history of Canada. For example, the Quebec Act of 1774 conferred rights of citizenship on Roman Catholics long before they won these in Britain. It was not long before there was a Catholic Prime Minister, John Thompson (1892-1894). Canada was also the first member of the British Commonwealth to elect a Jew to public office, in 1807. The oath of office in force at the time prevented him from taking his seat, but this was changed in 1832, when full political and civil rights were accorded Jews, more than two decades earlier than in Britain. The British experience in developing guarantees of human rights took place largely in the eighteenth century, and certainly by the time of Confederation, Canadians could look to the British common law for protection as well. (Schmeisser, 1964: 54-124) More recently, these protections have been made explicit in a Canadian Bill of Rights (1960).

Currently, Canadians reveal little concern about religious freedom. Asked to evaluate the personal importance of four basic human rights — freedom of speech and religion, freedom from fear and want — Canadians gave primary importance to free speech. Religion was placed first by only 11 per cent, resulting in an over-all rank of fourth. Further, there was a steady decline in the importance given to religious freedom by those of younger age. (Gallup Poll Report, July 26, 1972) These results may reflect the growing secularization of Canadian society. It is also possible that freedom of speech incorporates many of the elements also necessary for religious freedom, and hence the selection of speech was made on the understanding that it was a broader and more inclusive guarantee of other fundamental rights.

In light of the history of apparent religious tolerance and the current lack of concern with religious freedom, it might be tempting to ignore religious rights as an aspect of citizen equality. Instead, we must consider the place of religion in Canadian society because of its relation to the question of equality. It demonstrates, in a way to be more fully explored in the following section, the dictum that individual freedoms do not necessarily produce collective equality. As a group property, religion is associated with unequal chances for the acquisition of positions of leadership, and unequal chances for random distribution in the existing social class hierarchy. (Porter, 1965) To understand better why this is the case, we must look at religion as a source of social conflict, an instrument of coercion, and a dimension of social cleavage.

One of the most divisive religious issues occurred early in Canadian history, and also involved the emotionally-charged area of public education. While still a territory, Manitoba had denominational schools protected by the legislative provisions for its entry into Confederation. (*The British North America Act*, 1871, 34-35 Vic., c. 28) When it became a province in 1890, the provincial legislature immediately moved to abolish these schools. After a remarkable series of moves, in which the Judicial Committee of the Privy Council revealed a deep repugnance for denominational schools, Catholic voters in Manitoba appealed to the Macdonald government in Ottawa. The subsequent recommendations, issued as a Remedial Order to the province, compounded issues of religious freedom, educational opportunity, and provincial rights. The Manitoba school question was the principal issue of the 1896 election, and helped bring about the defeat of the Conservatives and the election of the Liberals under Laurier. The bitterness aroused by the issue was not restricted to Manitoba, but also found fertile ground elsewhere, and especially in Quebec, (Schmeisser, 1964: 158-169; Wade, 1968: 435-439; Saywell, 1968: 120-125) where Conservative support for denominational schools confirmed the Catholic clergy in their adherence to that party, and their animosity to the Liberals. Nevertheless, Laurier's candidacy was to break the hold of the Conservative Party on French-speaking voters in Quebec, who were apparently more impressed with Laurier's plea for compromise, his support of provincial rights, and his potential as the first Prime Minister of French origin. (Wade, 1968: 341-382) It was a legacy of rejection that would continue to haunt the Conservatives.

Additional issues emerged to keep Catholics from the Conservative Party and to exacerbate political divisions. These were not necessarily signs of overt anti-Catholicism from Conservative leaders, nor were they even always specifically religious in content on those occasions when they were primarily tied to French-English divisions. Yet whatever the reasons, the end result has been the same. Hence, in the 1920's we find the Ku Klux Klan pursuing a virulently anti-Catholic campaign in western Canada, where it gave active support to Conservatives in Saskatchewan. There is evidence that they in fact contributed to the defeat of the Liberals in the election of 1929. (Kyba, 1968) This was at a period when John Diefenbaker was active in provincial politics, and while there is no evidence linking him with the Klan or welcoming their efforts on behalf of the Conservatives, the historical association was there (Newman, 1963: 21-22). It was a memory that would die hard, and when he assumed the national leadership of the party, opponents attempted to make the connection, apparently with some success in French Canada (Newman, 1963: 289). While not usually prone to violence, or consumed by hatred, the Loyal Orange Order, opposed to Catholicism and favoring the Conservatives, also contributed to continuing cleavages (Senior, 1972).

What we have termed the coerciveness of religion lies in part in the absence of a single religious faith, to which everyone adheres with equal commitment. This means that some faiths, regardless of protection of individual freedom of worship, are subject to restraints. Restrictions on Jehovah's Witnesses, on Doukhobors in British Columbia, Hutterites and Amish in the Prairie Provinces, Jews in Quebec are all cases in point. Similarly, the enforcement of the Lord's Day Act has meant the imposition of a single standard of behavior, regardless of how individuals or groups may feel about the sanctity of Sunday as a day of rest. Uniformity in adherence to the Act has been eroded, as provinces have been permitted to institute opposing or conflicting practices, but not without cost in community civility, and not without the imposition of forms of social control suggestive of an established church. (Schmeisser, 1964: 101-110)

Finally, we must point to the continuing relevance of religious divisions in the political fabric of the country. Lucas, studying about 600 single industry communities, found religion to be the basic division on all major political issues (Lucas, 1971: 342-345). The tie between religion and politics is not exclusively a characteristic of small towns but occurs even in large cities, as a study of Hamilton, Ontario indicates. There researchers found that both the local Catholic Church and the Anglican parish organization provided support and workers to selected candidates. (Jacek, *et. al.*, 1972: 196-197) A twenty-year review of public opinion in Canada found even a simple dichotomy between Protestant and Catholic sufficient to indicate that it was the single most divisive social characteristic for supporters of the *same* political party (Engelmann and Schwartz, 1975). Numerous studies continue to find sharp differentiation among party supporters along religious lines. (For example, Laponce, 1969: 187-216; 1972: 270-286; Meisel, 1972: 3)

Table II demonstrates this from a study done after the 1965 election. Some of the findings are no doubt due to a compounding of religion and national origin, most notably the French-Catholic and British-Anglican-Presbyterian-United Church connection, but also the link in Western Canada between Lutherans and Anabaptist sects and non-British, non-French European origin. (Schwartz, 1974a: 579-583) Yet there is clearly some independent effect from religion, as demonstrated nationally by Alford (1963; 1964: 215), Engelmann and Schwartz (1975), and by Anderson in a single constituency (1966: 27-37). All these confirm, in general, the greater affinity of Catholics for the Liberals and Protestants for the Conservatives.

Increasing secularization is not likely to erode these basic cleavages, since while their roots lie in issues with a strong religious content, their continuity derives from more immediate experiences and interpersonal ties that connect individuals with their coreligionists. For example, in probing current reasons for the typical patterns of voter alignment, found in this instance among Ontario voters in 1968, Lynn MacDonald

Table II: Religion And Vote in 1965*

(percentage)

	Liberal	Conservative	NDP	Social Credit	Crédit .	Total [a]
Roman Catholic	57	22	31	6	100	43
Ukrainian Catholic	1	2	3	—	—	1
United Church	17	35	24	26	—	22
Anglican	10	18	13	21	—	12
Presbyterian	3	9	3	9	—	5
Baptist	3	3	1	—	—	3
Lutheran	1	3	8	11	—	3
Greek Orthodox	**	**	1	4	—	**
Other Protestant	3	5	4	20	—	4
Jewish	2	**	3	—	—	2
None	2	3	5	2	—	3
Number	(1,048)	(676)	(328)	(67)	(65)	(2,727)

[a] Includes other parties, don't knows, etc.
** Less than 1 per cent.

*Source: Mildred A. Schwartz, 'Canadian Voting Behavior,' in Richard Rose (ed.), *Electoral Behavior: A Comparative Handbook,* p. 580. Copyright © by The Free Press, 1974.

(1969) saw no contribution from issues with a religious content, nor from the religion of the candidate. Most effect could be attributed to 'social involvement in the religious community.' The importance of such interpersonal ties was also suggested by an earlier study in Kingston, Ontario (Meisel, 1956: 481-496).

Throughout Canada's history religion has been tied to social conflict, and it continues to divide citizens along partisan lines. These experiences have contributed to the formation of denominational groups unequal in their enjoyment of the resources of the total society.

The Nature of Equality

Throughout our discussion of religious freedom, and of civil rights in general, there was an insinuation that there exists a fundamental dilemma in the conversion of individual freedoms into collective rights. Marx and Engels, for example, were inclined to dismiss the whole concern with civil rights as only an aspect of bourgeois liberalism, which did not get to the heart of major social inequalities. (Lakoff, 1964: 216-224) We cannot proceed then without some evaluation of the *nature of equality* itself, and not just its manifestation in political, civil, or social rights.

Most commonly, equality is understood in terms of opportunity. In its most extreme form, it represents nineteenth century laissez-faire liberalism, a perspective associated with sociology through the work of Herbert Spencer, one of its most famous advocates. (Lakoff 1964: 143-155) 'Rugged individualism' was not, however, a particularly strong theme in political philosophy in Canada (Horowitz, 1968: 3-57). Interpreted more temperately, the great appeal of equality of opportunity lies in the recognition it gives to freedom of choice.

Important limits on full opportunity stem from the handicaps imposed by past and cumulative inequalities. Thus the passage of fair employment practices laws in the United States has not overcome the disadvantages suffered by blacks. (Miller and Roby, 1970: 126-128) Reviewing the situation of the French-speaking in Quebec, which remains far below that of English-speaking with regard to the prestige of their occupations and the rewards of income (Lieberson, 1971), the Royal Commission on Bilingualism and Biculturalism (1969: III, 61-86) noted the difficulties imposed on those who wished to catch up.

> Because of their higher educational level, their position in the occupational structure, and their original position as leaders in Quebec's industrialization, the Anglophones have always been better prepared than the Francophones to enjoy the benefits of the province's economic development. Once socio-

economic patterns have been established, they tend to be self-perpetuating; the momentum favouring the Anglophones was never matched in the Francophone community.*

On the one hand, we can find inequality of opportunity, as in the case of qualified French-speaking workers employed in situations where the language of advancement is English. On the other hand, even where such barriers are not present, the ability to compete may be curtailed by residues of discrimination compounded by low expectations of success, or by inequalities in other areas of life. Thus, in the case of the French-speaking worker, he may begin with educational deficiencies, related to the fact that 'Quebec is below the national average on almost all of such educational criteria as money spent on education, qualifications of teachers, pupil-teacher ratio, and per-pupil expenditure.' (Magnuson, 1969: 4) Vast increases in educational expenditures may have surprisingly little immediate pay-off, particularly in the process of catching up to those already far ahead in the competitive race.

Under such circumstances, compensatory measures for undoing past inequities have appeared most attractive. One such solution, tempting in its simplicity, is the imposition of quotas for redistributing opportunities and rewards. In effect, this is a shift from individual to group rights. The peculiar nature of such demands lies in their more frequent use as mechanisms for *denying* equality. For example, minorities have often been given some opportunity to migrate, obtain entry into universities, obtain jobs in large corporations – but on the basis of a set numerical upper limit. The irony of current demands for quotas, as they are expressed in the United States, lies in their presumed ability to right old wrongs through a process of reverse discrimination. In other words, where the application of universalistic criteria have failed, these are to be replaced by ascriptive ones.

The history of language-use policy in the federal civil service provides evidence that the imposition of a merit system, where positions were filled through competitive examinations, and particularly when recruiting came under the aegis of a central Civil Service Commission in 1918, led to a sharp decline in the participation of French-speaking Canadians. With efficiency and rationality the keystones of bureaucracy, the intention of merit systems is to discriminate between the qualified and the unqualified. But crucial to the form this discrimination takes are the criteria considered relevant to the evaluation process. Thus, despite the existence of two official languages, French was under-represented in the

*Report of the Royal Commission on Bilingualism and Biculturalism, Vol.III (Ottawa: Queen's Printer, 1969). Reproduced by permission of Information Canada.

civil service. This low proportion of French-speaking was publicized in 1946, leading to the appointment of a committee under Solicitor General Joseph Jean (the committee itself created only through the efforts of French-speaking Members of Parliament). Their recommendations were to the point: three French-speaking deputy ministers immediately, and dual deputies, one for each language, in four other crucial departments. Objections were heated, with the recommendations treated as a serious threat to the merit system, and the committee's report was neither tabled nor published. (Royal Commission on Bilingualism and Biculturalism, III, 1969; 97-112) More recent efforts at increasing French-language use have skirted the imposition of numerical quotas, but have viewed proportions as both signs of discrimination and as positive guidelines for overcoming discrimination.

> We do not endorse a 'quota system' or 'representation principle' in the selection of candidates. We do not imply that every sector of the Public Service ought to be 22 per cent Francophone — or 26 per cent, which was the proportion of those of French mother tongue in the Canadian labour force in 1961. Such figures are only gross guidelines for discovering those sectors or groups in the federal administration where Francophones were numerous or few. (Royal Commission on Bilingualism and Biculturalism, III, 1969: 93)

Yet the problem with statements such as the above is the ease with which the use of proportions is converted into fixed rules, and with it, into attacks on the benefits of individual achievement.

Quotas, when taken to an extreme, imply a rigid, caste-like society. Yet they still represent one way of coming to terms with the results of past inequities and should not be completely dismissed without examining their possibility as temporary guidelines. Moreover, it is not inconceivable that there will be social systems in which large numbers prefer quotas, with all their costs, as a way of managing social conflict.

For example, post-World War II Austria has used a system of *Proporz*, where personnel are recruited to the public service on the basis of fixed proportions of members of the two major parties, the People's Party (OeVP) and the Socialist Party (SPOe). One acknowledged consequence has been a lessening of social conflict, as the Socialists, formerly deliberately excluded from non-elective public offices, were now incorporated into all facets of the political system. (Secher, 1958: 791-808; Engelmann, 1966: 260-283)

One should also recognize the rigidities introduced by a rigorous system of merit. Strict adherence to universalistic criteria is often criticized because of the implicit inclusion of characteristics which have themselves been shaped by discriminatory practices. But even if it were possible to move beyond such limitations, consider the nature of a society where everyone got what he truly deserved. Success and failure would be as pre-determined as in any ascriptively-based society.

A more radical form of compensation than quotas was proposed by Marx. We recall that he described equal rights, even in the communist society he desired, as bourgeois rights, since the rewards would be in proportion to an individual's productivity. But since people are neither equal in their abilities nor their needs, rights should actually be unequal. As the higher phase of his ideal society evolves, it should be possible to allocate resources on the basis of 'From each according to his ability, to each according to his needs!' (Marx, 1956: 258) The evidence suggests that this would require not only major changes in social organization, but even more important, major transformations in social and personal values.

This discussion, we hope, has succeeded in demonstrating the complex relation between civil rights and equality, as well as some reasons for the lack of simple solutions to the problems posed. Simultaneous desires for liberty, justice, and equity raise inevitable dilemmas in the development of civil rights. The social definition of the form of equality sought is a normative issue. But its achievement is always constrained by mundane political realities.

Social Rights in Canada

Education

Bendix, among others, gives primacy to education as a basic social right, seeing it as a precondition for acquiring and enjoying other rights, even when the latter are otherwise legally guaranteed. (Bendix, 1964: 87) The unique property of education as a social right is its compulsory nature. It becomes in this way a public duty and not just an individual right. (Marshall, 1964: 90) Equality of citizenship requires, at the least, literacy, for how else can citizens participate in a responsible fashion? The full secrecy of the ballot, for example, depends on a literate voting public. The obligation of the citizen to become educated is matched by the responsibility of the state to see that he has the opportunity. Over time, this has been reflected in demands for increasing amounts of formal schooling to insure a highly skilled and productive work force.

An examination of the provinces indicates that education is one of the important factors for continuing differences among Canadians. It also reveals the slowness with which provincial governments have accepted responsibility for the education of their people (Johnson, 1968: 85).

While secondary schools have a long history in Canada, they were for those who could pay the appropriate fees. Only in the 1930's did free secondary schools become general, and then not even in Quebec or Newfoundland. Post-secondary education did not increase appreciably until the 1960's. For example, in 1951-52, only 5 per cent of the 18- to 24-year-olds were enrolled full-time in universities. By 1965-66 this had risen to 11 per cent. (Economic Council, 1969: 126) Interprovincial differences continue in both areas, but not to the extent formerly true, as all areas share in the recent expansion of educational opportunities. The greatest disadvantage is still felt by the Atlantic provinces, and New-foundland particularly. Some indication of the recency with which disparities have been removed, and educational advantages more gener-ally shared, have been discussed by Rocher in Chapter Five.

One of the sharpest differences that remains is in the quality of teachers employed. While the Canadian average for secondary school teachers with university degrees is 61 per cent, this is exceeded from Ontario westward, with Ontario and British Columbia 14 per cent above the average. Nova Scotia alone of the remaining provinces is somewhat better than the overall average. In contrast, Newfoundland has 46 per cent of its teachers with university degrees, and Quebec only 40 per cent. (Economic Council, 1969: 134-136)

The slowness with which free education has been adopted, the recency of expanded post-secondary education, the continuation of regional disparities, although many of these have been lessened through special efforts beginning in the 1960's, all contribute to the fact that adequate education has only recently come to be a general good. At the same time, while economists have emphasized the relation between increased education, productivity, and material well-being, it would be naive to assume that increases in the educational level of the labor force will alone remove other, more fundamental regional differences. In many instances, provinces have trained their residents for employment elsewhere, some-times elsewhere in Canda, and at least in the past, in the United States. (Porter, 1965: 29-59; Stone, 1969: 83-88)

The recency with which the Province of Quebec imposed compulsory education is a direct result of ethnic and religious tensions. The beginning of English-Protestant settlement in Quebec is associated with the establishment of two separate and distinct school systems, one Protestant and the other Catholic. These systems remained virtually unchanged until the 1960's, and for the most part, operated indepen-dently of each other. But the Catholic school system was opposed to compulsory education, fearing state intervention in what was guarded as a religious prerogative. While the Protestant system, as we indicated, had tried to introduce compulsory education, with the issue debated in the legislature as early as 1892, the French Catholics used their majority position to block what would have been a major divergence from their own school system. The protection of a separate cultural identity has remained a paramount concern for the French-speaking (Royal Commission on Bilingualism and Biculturalism, II, 1968: 23-37), but with growing recognition that some of the mechanisms developed to foster this had at the same time hindered the competitive capacity of those so trained, especially to meet the growing demand for technological skills. The subject was thoroughly investigated by a Royal Commission, the Parent Commission, established in 1961, which went on to recommend a drastic reorganization of education. (*Report of the Royal Commission of Inquiry on Education in the Province of Quebec,* 1963-66) In the 1966 provincial election, rejection of many of the proposed educational changes was a principal theme of the Union Nationale Party, and was successful in defeating the incumbent Liberals. (Dion, 1967) Subsequently, as indicated by Rocher in Chapter Five, the whole temper of the province of Quebec has altered, not the least because of changes introduced in the educational system.

The relevance of religious and ethnic factors is by no means confined to Quebec. The issue of denominational education has been important in all provinces, most prominently in Newfoundland, where by the 1860's, the outline of a three-part division of responsibility among Catholics, Anglicans, and Methodists was firmly established. In 1892, a fourth church, the Salvation Army, was officially recognized as a party to the school system. (Rowe, 1952) Only with the establishment of a Royal Commission in 1964 did Newfoundland too consider the costs of denominationalism in developing a school system appropriate to overcoming a backward and chronically depressed economy. (*Report of the Royal Commission on Education and Youth, Province of Newfoundland and Labrador,* 1967-1968)

We have previously considered the controversy generated by the move to do away with separate schools in Manitoba. In other provinces, the compromises necessary to protect religious control over education, parallel with the development of an extensive public school system, have always produced some measure of conflict, although fortunately not as grave as that generated by the Manitoba crisis.

It is not easy to say what is the best way of organizing education to insure maximum protection of religious, ethnic, and linguistic rights and also actively promote social rights. As we have indicated in the case of the French-speaking, earlier modes of coping with the encroachments of English language and culture may have served an important function for preserving the French language and culture, as well as the strength of Catholicism. But at the same time they left many people unable to compete effectively with those whose principal language was English. This is not to say that many of the continuing disadvantges of French-speaking Canadians do not stem from both deliberate and covert forms of discrimination. In addition, the experiences of a minority people have often encouraged feelings of low self-esteem and general discouragement in the face of the very real obstacles to achievement.

By now, the relation between social class and education, including academic performance, length of schooling, and attendance at university, should be among the best known of sociological generalizations. Continued stress on the importance of class background as a determinant of educational achievement may even have some unfortunate consequences, by hindering the search for educational reform. It should not be forgotten that the existing educational structure is not only the result of the class system, but also an important mechanism for perpetuating it, as has been discussed in Chapters Four and Five. This has been particularly the case of the kinds of school systems developed in Ontario and Quebec. Porter has pointed out how this has prepared and sustained a socially coherent elite.

Apart from trade union leadership, university graduation is becoming a precondition of entrance to leadership roles. The Canadian university system has been small and the chances of groups of people with friendship contacts at universities moving up into various elite structures is considerable.

So, too, are the private fee-paying schools of eastern Canada greatly over-represented in the elites. This common private school educational experience is simply an item within the common experience of class. Because of the importance of the classical colleges this tendency was even greater in French Canada, particularly when some of the colleges stood out as being unusually important in the background of the elite. Collège Sainte-Marie and Le Petit Séminarie of Quebec were as important in the class system of Quebec as are Upper Canada College and Lower Canada College to the class structure of English Canada. (Porter, 1965: 528)

Improving the Quality of Life

The centrality of education in this discussion is a tribute to its multi-faceted consequences. Our objective has been to *conceive of education as a crucial means for enhancing the quality of life.* This effect comes about as one learns the skills for obtaining better-paying and more satisfying employment, experiences the opening up of new ideas and alternatives, and acquires the general knowledge for better coping with varied problems. At the most pragmatic level, education means greater earning power. But, from this perspective, education can only benefit those for whom increased training can be translated into jobs. It is more of a luxury for those with irremediable physical or mental handicaps, (The Senate of Canada, *Report on Aging*. Ottawa: Queen's Printer, 1966) or people severely isolated from a variety of employment opportunities requiring high levels of skill, such as has been general for native peoples and for many in the Atlantic provinces. (Brewis, 1963; Poetschke, 1968: 8-20; Harp, 1971: 174-186; Borovoy, 1966: 13-15) Where education is tied to employment, it serves to enhance the likelihood of individual social mobility. It is not particularly effective for tackling problems of collective disadvantage, such as afflict the aged and those in regions with serious developmental problems. As Miller and Roby point out,

> By itself, the educational strategy for poverty reduction suffers from four major limitations: the strategy neglects many poor people; its goals are difficult to achieve, requiring a radical redistribution of resources and first-rate staffs; the strategy is only partially effective for those youths who do obtain education because discrimination and other factors intervene between education and income; its heavy emphasis on education damages individuals and society by constricting alternative channels of occupational mobility and by restricting the pluralism of social values.*

The importance of broad access to free education cannot be gainsaid; it is not, however, a realistic solution to all problems in inequality.

The enjoyment of a good life, one lived with some measure of dignity, requires access to certain amenities; absence of these spells poverty. There may be some folk wisdom in the saying that money can't buy happiness. Yet to the contrary, social psychological research indicates that income is positively correlated with happiness (Bradburn, 1969), and with greater mental and physical well-being generally. Why not then do away with the worst edges of inequality by providing everyone with a minimum basic income? Aside from moral, economic, and political objections, there are two that have derived from social science research. These are the notions of 'the culture of poverty' and 'relative deprivation,' both of which have served to hamper approaches to poverty reduction that emphasize income reallocation.

The *culture of poverty* is a concept elaborated by the anthropologist Oscar Lewis to describe a particular kind of culture, a complex of norms, values, and blueprints for social existence found among some poor people. It is characterized by a lack of integration with the dominant

---

*S.M. Miller and Pamela Roby, *The Future of Inequality* (New York: Basic Books, 1970), pp. 128-129.

social institutions and strong hostility to these. Persons who identify with this culture express feelings and behavior indicating lack of faith in themselves, in others, and in the future. They feel inferior and helpless, and act in dependent ways. (Lewis, 1966: 215) While Lewis himself did not have this intention, the concept has come to be used as an explanation for poverty rather than an effect, and a rationale for avoiding the restructuring of opportunities. (Roach and Gursslin, 1967: 383-392)

The *concept of relative deprivation* has been used to describe the discrepancy between objective conditions and subjective evaluations of these. (Merton, 1957: 227-236) Its pertinence to discussions of equality relates to the shifting ways in which lines of poverty can be drawn, without ever eliminating some group that can be characterized as relatively poverty-stricken. (Economic Council of Canada, 1968: 104-105; Podoluk, 1971: 119-215) It argues that the use of such economic interventions as income supports for the bottom strata, while necessary and humane, would not contribute to a more equalitarian society, since the bottom would still remain. This objection rightfully recognizes the likelihood that evidence of social differentiation will give rise to feelings of envy and deprivation. The reduction of relative deprivation probably depends on a radical restructuring of the social stratification hierarchy, such that the spread between top and bottom becomes sharply compressed. (Miller and Roby, 1970)

Currently, the importance given to relative deprivation and the culture of poverty has declined. According to a more recent view of the Economic Council of Canada,

> ... poverty is an economic problem to a much greater extent than most people have realized in the past. This is not to denigrate the human and social aspects of poverty. These are of vital importance. But there are also important economic aspects of poverty which have been generally overlooked, or at least underemphasized. We therefore attempt here to focus attention on the economic costs of poverty, on the economic effects of poverty on the poor, and on the need for creating income-earning capacities and opportunities among the poor.*

This perspective, which conceives of poverty in terms of some absolute level of deprivation, takes more easily to solutions based on direct economic intervention. (Cutt, 1971: 337-345)

A third approach to equalizing and improving the quality of life is through the provision of *social welfare services.* The function of welfare

---

*Economic Council of Canada, *Sixth Annual Review* (Ottawa: Queen's Printer, 1969), p. 108. Reproduced by permission of Information Canada.

services, particularly as these are broadly distributed, is quite independent of the effects of educational expansion or income reallocation.

> The extension of the social services is not primarily a means of equalizing incomes. In some cases it may, in others it may not. The question is relatively unimportant; it belongs to a different department of social policy. What matters is that there is a general enrichment of the concrete substance of civilized life, a general reduction of risk and insecurity, and equalization between the more and the less fortunate at all levels — between the healthy and the sick, the employed and the unemployed, the old and the active, the bachelor and the father of a large family. (Marshall, 1965: 113)

The provision of welfare services has a long history, beginning with private acts of charity and local, communal efforts to aid the sick and handicapped. The intervention of organized government, particularly at a national level, is a relatively new phenomenon, although it had its beginnings in the Elizabethan Poor Laws. Up until this century, most efforts to aid the disadvantaged took a minimal form and generally had little regard for the dignity of those who received the services.

It was not until 1927 that the Canadian government assumed responsibility for a major public welfare program with the introduction of the Old Age Pensions Act. This did not herald large-scale governmental efforts in this area, with aid to the blind waiting until 1937. In other words, the worst years of the Depression passed before the federal government was to acknowledge the need for comprehensive programs of social welfare, benefiting all Canadians. Since then, more areas of life have come to be viewed as public responsibilities, more concern has been shown for regional inequalities, and more thought has been given to the provision of services without regard to means. These measures have brought about some heartening amelioration, as exemplified by the greater utilization of health services when these are not dependent on the ability to pay. At the same time, there have been disturbing signs of their ineffectiveness in raising the quality of life. The Special Senate Committee on Poverty, through the first-hand observations of its members and the submissions made before it, was convinced that past measures had done little to undermine the deep-rooted nature of poverty in Canada. (*Senate Report on Poverty*, 1971)

The results of the Senate Committee's deliberations are contained in a series of recommendations that call for a guaranteed annual income tied to work incentives, along with improved public welfare measures. (*Senate Report on Poverty*, 1971) What is left untouched is the very problem the Committee so poignantly argued in confronting the dilemma of poverty in the midst of affluence: the lack of employment. Unless we come to accept the notion that large numbers of able-bodied do not need to work, we are still faced with evidence that not all people are able to find work, no matter how hard they look; that some must do work for which they are over-qualified; and that others are already too old, inadequately educated, or psychologically damaged ever to benefit from retraining programs. (For other criticisms, see Black, 1972: 439-443; Adams, *et. al.,* 1971.)

It is not our intention, and indeed it is beyond our capacities, to present a blueprint for improving the quality of life and introducing greater equality in social rights. We have suggested some typical measures, all of which have drawbacks, particularly if any one is treated as a sole solution. What is most important, particularly in this discussion of social rights, is that we do not lose sight of our central concern with political problems. Social rights are part of the political experience, and their absence reflects a low level of political resources.* The ways in which the disadvantaged may acquire social and other rights is then the last element in our scheme for relating politics and equality.

Acquiring Citizen Rights

The ways in which citizen rights are acquired can be viewed from two perspectives: the pressures exerted by the disadvantaged, and the overtures toward political incorporation made by those with greater resources. The channels of influence or action can be divided into three, following the suggestion of Stein Rokkan (1966). Rokkan describes these as traditional, electoral, and organizational.

Traditional Channels of Influence

Traditional channels of influence are invoked through contracts with traditional leaders, local notables, and ties of kinship. From the perspective of the disadvantaged, such channels will often involve informal petitioning and indirect forms of contact. Under conditions where traditional channels are most common, change is generally slow and more likely to affect small groups, such as kin, rather than general categories of people.

Tradition also plays a role in the actions of those with greater access to power. This is the case when they are prepared to extend citizen rights

---

*The former staff members of the Special Senate Committee on Poverty, who resigned after predicting that the Senators would not get to the heart of the problem of poverty, go so far as to describe poverty as 'the result of inequality of power.' (Adams, *et. al,* 1971: 81) It is not clear what is to be gained from such a definition, which unnecessarily downgrades the patently economic aspects of poverty. But if it is taken as a partial definition, then it accurately reflects the crucial political content of poverty.

from a sense of 'noblesse oblige.' Established elites may also seek allies against the encroachments of rivals who are rapidly acquiring greater resources, and look to disadvantaged groups to aid them in their struggles. Laws favorable to the organization of workers and the extension of the franchise in 1867 by the British Tories can be taken as illustrations of both these motivations. (Mackenzie and Silver, 1968) The economic historian Karl Polyani (1944: 166) even went so far as to argue that the British workers participated little in these changes. The Tories, representing the old landowning class, were under strong pressure from the new industrialists. For both groups, the newly formed working classes appeared as potentially useful allies. But it was the Tories particularly who recognized the value of extending rights to them. As it was said of Disraeli on the anniversary of his death, 'In the inarticulate mass of the English populace, he discerned the Conservative working-man as the sculptor perceives the angel prisoned in a block of marble.' (*The Times,* April 18,1883)

The use of traditional channels seems most appropriate to social settings where formal channels of influence are meagre, but in truth the former never disappear. One thing that often does occur, however, is a rise in the belief that influence exerted through personal ties is of questionable legitimacy. It leads to fears, especially in attempting to understand the behavior and motivation of the most privileged, of conspiracies and collusion (Domhoff, 1967; Mills, 1960). It also leads to attacks on mechanisms for conferring personal favors and sustaining personal loyalties such as the 'political machine,' a form of party organization formerly quite prevalent in large American cities. But without seeing any false virtues in these machines, some social commentators have observed the important functions they performed by their very particularistic approach to political life. For those low in power — the poor, immigrants, ethnic and racial minorities — they often provided those ties to the political community otherwise lacking. (Bell, 1960; Gosnell, 1968)

The emphasis on personal ties is reflected in the widespread use of patronage (Lemieux, 1971: 227). Prior to the 'quiet revolution' in Quebec, patronage was a customary form of political behavior, aided by the fact that the public service was not run on a merit system. In the 1935 provincial election, the Liberals under Premier Taschereau made extensive use of public works in ways that produced tangible and direct results.

> The public works programme provided additional, if temporary employment, and meant sizable government orders for local hardware merchants and shopkeepers in various towns and villages. Whenever the government provided a community with some badly needed public facility it was able to

present itself as a 'benefactor' which had 'done something' for that particular town or district. This was an important consideration for the average Quebec voter when he was trying to decide which party to vote for. Government candidates in most electoral districts also spent fairly large sums of money on the distribution of drinks of 'whisky blanc' and handed out other gifts and favours which helped to convince the voters that the Liberals were 'des bons garçons.' (Quinn, 1963: 64)

This was the first election contested by the Union Nationale and they naturally objected to such practices. On their election, however, they proved themselves even more masterful in the use of patronage, enhancing the hold of traditional ties and styles of politics. (Quinn, 1963; Laporte, 1956; Dion and O'Neill, 1956)

In all societies, a traditional channel that retains special significance is the family. This is because of the family's importance in socializing the young. It is in the family that the child acquires his initial status attributes, those that will have a strong bearing on what he does as an adult. There he obtains, either directly or indirectly, the dispositions that will lead him to assume his adult political postures. (Sigel, 1970) In the most general way, familial experiences are relevant to the acquisition of citizen rights because of the ways that they provide the skills and motives to use existing rights, and to press for additional ones. Families can be more or less successful in the way they socialize members to assume their citizen roles. The more successful they are, the better they will provide the basis for adults actively and effectively to take on full citizenship.

Studies of *political socialization* are still quite rare in Canada, but the few published sources we have indicate that here too the family plays a political role. (Van Loon and Whittington, 1971: 67-71) In a study of school children living in Kingston, about 30 per cent of those in lower grades indicated a party preference, rising to 46 per cent by the eighth grade. These percentages are considerably lower than those of comparable studies in the United States, where 60 per cent had a party preference by the fourth grade. (Pammett, 1971: 139) Through ecological analyses based on census records, vital statistics, and electoral data, Vincent Lemieux has examined the ties between kinship and politics in the Island of Orleans. His results indicate that factors sustaining lines of kinship, including marriages within the community and among social equals, also sustain traditional partisan loyalties. (Lemieux, 1971)

Electoral Channels

BASES FOR GAINING THE VOTE

If we need to look for evidence of the importance attached to full voting rights, we can find it in the efforts made by those lacking these rights. Women, the working classes in those countries where there has been a limited franchise based on wealth, and blacks in the United States have been the major groups fighting for political incorporation in the past two centuries. In all of these instances, no effort has been too great, and no action too dangerous to hinder the struggle for suffrage. To vote is to exercise power. As Julian Bond, a member of the Georgia legislature and a dedicated worker for the cause of black civil rights, recently said in an effort to recruit more black voters, 'If you hit somebody with a vote and hit them right, they'll remember it for the rest of their natural-born life.' (*New York Times*, August 8, 1971)

To the extent that electoral channels are effective means for influencing the behavior of others, and in particular, of furthering the quest for citizen rights, it might be wondered why those without the franchise ever receive it. That is, why are those already enfranchised willing to share their political power? Of course, the extension of the franchise is not always done willingly, but may be the result of seizure of power through superior force, or of fears of revolt. Such motivations do not, however, appear to have played an important role in Canada. Political agitation has not been absent, and in pre-Confederation times, even took the form of outright rebellion. But the franchise was not at issue.

The extension of the franchise may be, as we previously described, a case of searching for allies, on the assumption that the newly enfranchised will be especially grateful to those who gave them their rights. For example, the historian Alan Grimes (1967) describes such a situation with respect to the winning of woman suffrage in the frontier areas of the United States. There, established interests of various sorts felt threatened by the miners, cowboys, railroad workers, and other rootless types that thronged to the western frontier. The conferring of female suffrage years before this was the norm either elsewhere in the country or in national elections was, according to Grimes, premised on the belief that women would be supporters of the established order.

The intent was widely recognized as an effort to disfranchise those who might be opposed to conscription, but at least were recognized as Liberal supporters. The women who were enfranchised were, on the other hand, presumed to have reason to support the Union government. The blatancy of the political appeal was not lost to the Liberals, and was the object of an extravagant complaint by the biographer of Laurier: 'It was frankly a stacking of the cards, a gerrymander on a colossal scale, an attempt without parallel except in the tactics of Lenin or Trotsky to insure the dominance of one party in the state.' (Skelton, 1967: 529-530)

We recall that women did not receive the right to vote in Quebec provincial elections until 1940. Considering Grimes' (1967) thesis on how Mormon settlers in Utah looked to their wives for support of the religious community, particularly in the face of threatened intervention from the federal government and settlement by outsiders, we might have anticipated some parallels in Quebec. That is, while the French-speaking Catholics were the majority in Quebec, they were a minority elsewhere, and might have seen their women as an aid to a stronger voice in Canadian society. It is not altogether clear why this was not so, but we have a few indications from the history of the suffrage movement in that province. To begin with, the agitation for suffrage came from English-speaking women, and it was only in the 1920's that an effort was made to enlist the French. Madame Gérin-Lajoie, who became chairman of the French section of the Provincial Franchise Committee, remained in this post for only a month, resigning apparently under pressure from the Roman Catholic Church (Cleverdon, 1950: 230) Other women emerged to play a leading role in the French community, most notable Thérèse Casgrain and Idola St. Jean, but their struggle was a difficult one, hampered by the active opposition of the Church. Cardinal Villeneuve expressed the official position when he stated that the franchise would disrupt the family, expose women to the seaminess of politics, was not even wanted by the majority of women, and was not an effective agency of reform. (Cleverdon, 1950: 257) Also to contend with was the contempt of many of the province's politicians, and the indifference of the bulk of the women. As one opponent put it, 'to give women the vote meant overturning the social order, and was against the spirit of the Roman Catholic Church, and would bring no advantage.' (Cited in Cleverdon, 1950: 242) Opponents, in other words, could see no advantage to themselves. Meanwhile, for the women in Quebec, barriers to voting rights went hand in hand with restrictions on civil rights.

The extension of the franchise may also stem from an ideology that stresses egalitarian values, as was the case with the French Revolution. Pressures for universal manhood suffrage have derived from a number of ideological themes, including a belief in voting as a 'natural right.' Such views had some currency in nineteenth century colonial British North America, but generally did not carry as much weight as did beliefs in the need for a stake in the community, demonstrated by the ownership of property.* The move toward women's voting rights progressed most smoothly in the Prairie Provinces, and particularly Alberta and Saskatchewan. There, women always had the active support of men in their petitions to the political authorities, a support generated and sustained by the values inherent in the progressive, populist political movements active in the Prairies. (Cleverdon, 1950: 44-83)

*For a summary of the views current at this period, see Garner, 1969: 4-10.

MOBILIZING THE ELECTORATE

Given the right to vote, the effectiveness of electoral channels of influence depends on the mobilization of the electorate in the direction of self-interested actions, and the availability of organizations through which these interests can be expressed. The difficulties posed by these two requirements are illustrated by the relation between social class and voting in Canada. Objectively, class inequalities are important. Yet there is a low level of class-based voting, and class-based parties have a history of long-run instability.

In a comparative study of class-based voting, Britain, Australia, and the United States were all found to have a higher incidence of class voting than Canada. In fact, in Canada there was no appreciable indication of class voting at the federal level.* A follow-up study of these countries found the same rank order, and no increase in class voting in Canada. (Alford, 1967:85) The class-based voting that does occur emerges in particular provinces, being strongest in Ontario and then British Columbia. In contrast, Quebec and the Prairies are almost invariably low. Later studies confirm these patterns and show little evidence of increased class voting. (Schwartz, 1974a: 585-589; Meisel, 1972: 3-5).

We might naturally wonder whether the low level of class voting is related to a lack of class consciousness. Data on working class identification are reported in Table III, derived from a nation-wide study done after the 1965 general election. Identification is related to region of residence and vote in the 1965 election in order to examine both the effects of regional cleavages, and the channelling of class consciousness into partisan directions. The principal finding is that the largest proportions of working class identifiers are in the Atlantic and Prairie Provinces, and the lowest in British Columbia and Quebec. And, as we had previously noted, the level of class voting in these regions is the highest of all Canadian provinces. Secondly, while the differences among the Liberals, Conservatives and NDP are not extreme, the NDP did obtain support from proportionately more working class identifiers than did the major parties. At the time of our study, both the Créditistes and Social Credit drew a majority of supporters from those who considered themselves working class. A similar study of the 1968 election, however, found that the NDP drew 62 per cent of its support from those with working class identification, compared to 49 per cent for the Créditistes.

---

*Robert R. Alford, *Party and Society: The Anglo-American Democracies* (Chicago: Rand McNally, 1963). For details and an evaluation of Alford's procedure, see Mildred A. Schwartz, 'Canadian voting behavior,' in Richard Rose, *Electoral Behavior: A Comparative Handbook,* (New York: The Free Press, 1974), p. 584.

Table III: Percentage Choosing Working Class Identification by Region and 1965 Vote*

Region	Liberal	Conservative	NDP	Social Credit	Total[a]
Atlantic	48 (100)[c]	56 (83)	37 (8)	—	52 (229)
Quebec	37 (357)	52 (97)	20 (70)	59 (65)	40 (793)
Ontario	43 (424)	42 (311)	64 (132)	—	46 (1,054)
Prairies	44 (89)	52 (125)	52 (56)	57 (37)	51 (395)
B.C.	28 (78)	21 (58)	55 (62)	61 (26)	39 (256)
Total	40 (1,048)	45 (674)	49 (328)	58 (67)[b]	45 (2,727)

[a] Column totals include other parties, don't knows, etc.
[b] The total for Social Credit includes four cases in the Atlantic provinces and Ontario, while the Quebec Créditistes are not included.
[c] Figures in parentheses indicate the total number of respondents.

*Source: Mildred A. Schwartz, *Politics and Territory* (Montreal: McGill-Queen's University Press, 1974), p. 135.

(Meisel, 1972: 7) Our most interesting results, in any case, are those associated with particular regions. For example, in the Atlantic provinces, Quebec, and the Prairies, we find a high level of working class identification among Conservative voters. Yet since on the basis of leadership, programs, or traditions, the Conservative Party cannot be considered a working class party, we have an instance where working class consciousness is not translated into class voting.* Conversely, the high level of consciousness among NDP voters in Ontario and British Columbia provides some of the basis for class voting in those provinces. Without providing further evidence at this point, we can conclude that the patterns of class mobilization are related to strong regional and ethnic-religious cleavages, which often cut across but sometimes reinforce class cleavages. Class mobilization as it is reflected in class parties provides some of the subject matter of the following section on organizational channels.

Organizational Channels

THE RIGHT TO ORGANIZE
Without the right to vote, electoral channels of influence are closed. Without the right to organize, organizational channels may be illegal,

---

*For some explanation of these tantalizing findings about the Conservatives, see Mildred A. Schwartz, *Politics and Territory*, 130-134. For a discussion of the working class appeal of the Union Nationale and Le Ralliement des Créditistes, see Pinard, (1959: 87-109; 1971).

but they can still exist. Historically, legal restrictions on the right to organize were often directed against the working class. (Bendix, 1964: 80-87)

Any direct action, such as strikes, has been particularly suspect. For example, the Winnipeg General Strike of 1919, when almost all business, industry, and communication were halted, was treated as a prelude to insurrection, and brought federal intervention. (Masters, 1950) Other serious labor conflicts have involved provincial governments, as with the automobile workers in Ontario, the woodworkers in Newfoundland, and the asbestos workers in Quebec.* During the Depression, the Conservative government in Ottawa revealed its anxiety over pressures from the unemployed, leading to violence in Regina where the On-to-Ottawa march was halted in 1935, and to a strong show of police force in 1932 when the unemployed wished to meet with Prime Minister Bennett. (Neatby, 1972: 34-35, 63-64) Some restrictions on association can always be expected, since they stem from a fear that complete freedom of association would permit the disaffected to challenge constituted authority.

Interestingly enough, restrictions on organization may also proceed from libertarian motives. The ideology of the French Revolution, with its emphasis on individual freedom, considered most forms of association both illegal and undesirable barriers to the free relations between the individual and the state. This concern with the concomitants of individual freedom was examined in our earlier discussion of the dilemmas associated with the extension of civil rights.

WORKING CLASS PARTIES

Just as the absence of the right to organize will not fully prevent associations from emerging, so the presence of the right will not necessarily lead to its utilization. At the most, laws will provide enabling legislation, but they do not guarantee that associations will be formed, or with what effect. (Evan and Schwartz, 1964) Legal authorization will make the founding and continuity of an organization easier, the life of its members less subject to harassment, and its strength more potent in the struggle for influence.

We have already considered the difficulties associated with the development of class consciousness. Such consciousness is, to a degree, present, but it is not directed in a single organizational direction. The problems of organizing the working class do not deny the long history of working class parties and political movements in Canada. (Horowitz,

---

*For an analysis of the latter see Trudeau, 1956.

1968: 58-84; Robin, 1968) While there have been many successes, what we find most relevant is the failure to supplant one of the major parties, as occurred in Britain, with the Labour Party displacing the Liberals, or mobilize workers into a stable electoral force, as in many Continental European countries, such as West Germany and the successful Social Democrats.

The weakness of working class parties in Canada has been attributed to some general characteristics of North American society. (Lipset, 1950: 2) These include the absence of a feudal past, beliefs in unlimited opportunities, and the existence of a western frontier providing an outlet for the disaffected and a life style minimizing status differences. But as we have already suggested, Canadian equalitarianism has not been as strong as that in the United States. Some crucial differences in political experience have fostered different political values, including what Horowitz terms a 'tory touch.' This has led to both a more conservative party than the United States' equivalent, and a viable socialist party. (Horowitz, 1968: 3-57)

Trade unions have everywhere been the stimulus to the formation of workers' parties, as unionists seek a political arm for their own interests. In Canada, trade unions have been slow and uneven in development, as a consequence of variations in internal cohesiveness, economic problems, and relations with governments, all specific to individual provinces. These factors have undoubtedly had some effect on parties, as has the reluctance of trade unions to engage in partisan politics. While the CCF and now the NDP have found strong support in organized labor, this has never been sufficient to make these parties the sole political arm of the working class.

Finally, we find some reluctance in both the CCF and NDP to cast their appeal exclusively in class terms. While a more consistently ideological wing of both parties has always existed, it was usually kept in check. (Horowitz, 1968: 206-207) As is so frequently the case in class parties, the strongest ideologists are intellectuals and other middle class members, not workers. Marx, of course, assigned a special role to intellectuals who, recognizing the changes in the offing, would then cast their lot with the proletariat by providing them with their revolutionary ideology. Yet as the NDP Waffle exemplified, the concern with ideological consistency expressed by middle class intellectuals, no matter how important or relevant to the concerns of the working class, may still not provide the framework necessary for working class political mobilization.*

*Compare the experiences of European workers' parties in Michels, 1962: 238-253, 293-304.

STIMULI TO FORMATION

Whether successful or not, the activities of intellectuals in the mobilization of the working class may be seen as one way in which organizational rights are acquired and organizational channels of influence used: that is, through the recognition by the more powerful of the historic mission awaiting the yet disadvantaged group. As in our previous discussions, here too we find that organizational channels are created and groups mobilized as part of a search for allies by those with greater resources. For example, Marx observed that in the initial phases of factory organization,

> ... the labourers still form an incoherent mass scattered over the whole country, and broken up by their mutual competition. If anywhere they unite to form more compact bodies, this is not yet the consequence of their own active union, but of the union of the bourgeoisie, which class, in order to attain its own political ends, is compelled to set the whole proletariat in motion, and is moreover yet, for a time, able to do so.*

Encouragement of organizational formation, and with it, setting in motion the use of organizational channels of influence, can also come about from a quite different ideological perspective, that found in nationalist syndicalism. This ideology sees society as an organic whole, requiring that the society be organized into groups: workers, students, government functionaries, and so on. Organization takes place from above, or through the infiltration of existing associations, and is subject to strong central control. The needs and demands of the groups are expressed through spokesmen of each group, who in turn are obliged to transmit and enforce the directives of the central authority. This is not an ideology of democratic participation, but a rationale for the kinds of fascism practiced in Italy under Mussolini and in Spain under Franco. (Paine, 1961; 1968; von Beckerath, 1937; Einaudi, 1968)

The value of organizational channels lies in the discipline and coherence organizations bring to a problem. Groups of people have greater visibility than individuals, because of their overall impact. To say, for example, that a disgruntled individual plans to boycott a store is quite different than to threaten such action from an organized group. Organization means the possibility of acting in concert, and this in turn enhances the potency of traditional and electoral channels. That is, informal pressures on leaders or promises of voting mean a great deal more when they come from some organized entity. The existence of a multiplicity of organizations can, as well, lead to situations of irreconcil-

---

*Karl Marx and Frederick Engels, 'Manifesto of the Communist Party,' in Lewis S. Feuer (ed.), *Basic Writings on Politics and Philosophy* (Garden City: Doubleday, 1959), p. 15.

able conflict, since the weapons that appear when individuals become a coherent group make conflicts among groups of serious content. Such conflicts may be encouraged by the activities of a central authority, using them as a technique of 'divide and rule.' And as we have indicated with our example of national syndicalism, the formation of groups can be the tool of a central authority, deliberately to make them agencies of control.

Conclusions

Citizen equality has been treated here as a complex of political goals, achieved through the broad extension of political, civil, and social rights. The acquisition of these rights constitutes exercises in power, as pressure is put on those in authority to reallocate resources, and as authorities choose to make reallocations in the face of shifts in demands and realignments in the loci of pressure. Throughout, we had to recognize the difficulties in achieving equality, since what contributes to a better life for one group, does not necessarily do the same for others. It is often fortunate, in fact, when a particular social policy helps some without actively harming others. In reviewing the Canadian experience, at times we indicated satisfaction with the movement toward equality; at others we noted the barriers to equality affecting particular population groups.

In a sociological discussion of politics, it may be surprising that so much time was spent on basically philosophical issues, for example, on the nature of representation and liberty and the meaning of equality. This was unavoidable since, while the sociologist is concerned with analyzing and explaining the nature of social reality, the desired content of that reality is always a normative issue. Solutions offered to current inequalities include changes in structural arrangements, shifts in values, and alterations in individual perspectives and behavior. Regardless of their ideological orientation, they all involve some judgment of the ethical imperatives for organizing society.

References

Adams, Ian, William Cameron, Brian Hill, Peter Penz, *The Real Poverty Report.* Edmonton: M.G. Hurtig Ltd., 1971.

Alford, Robert R., 'Class voting in the Anglo-American political system,' in S.M. Lipset and Stein Rokkan (eds.), *Party Systems and Voter Alignments.* New York: The Free Press, 1967.

——, *Party and Society.* Chicago: Rand McNally, 1963.

——, 'The Social Bases of Political Cleavage in 1962,' in J. Meisel (ed.), *Papers on the 1962 Election.* Toronto: University of Toronto Press, 1964.

Anderson, Charles H., *Toward a New Sociology: A Critical View.* Homewood, Ill.: Dorsey Press, 1971.

Anderson, Grace, 'Voting Behaviour and the Ethnic-Religious Variable: A Study of a Federal Election in Hamilton, Ontario' *Canadian Journal of Economics and Political Science,* XXXII (February, 1966), 27-37.

Bachrach, Peter, *The Theory of Democratic Elitism.* Boston: Little, Brown, 1967.

Beckerath, Erwin von, 'Fascism,' *Encyclopedia of the Social Sciences,* 3. New York: Macmillan, 1937, pp. 133-135.

Bell, Daniel, *The End of Ideology.* Glencoe, Ill.: The Free Press, 1960.

Bendix, Reinhard, *MaxWeber, An Intellectual Portrait.* Garden City: Doubleday, 1960.

——, *Nation-Building and Citizenship.* New York: John Wiley and Sons, 1964.

Black, Erroll, 'One Too Many Reports on Poverty in Canada,' *Canadian Journal of Political Science,* V (September, 1972), 439-443.

Borovoy, A. Alan, 'Indian Poverty in Canada,' *Canadian Labour,* XII (December, 1966), 13-15.

——, 'Rebuilding a Free Society,' in Rotstein, *Power Corrupted.* Toronto: New Press, 1971, pp. 99-117.

Bradburn, Norman M., *The Structure of Psychological Well-Being.* Chicago: Aldine, 1969.

Breton, Raymond, 'The Socio-Political Dynamics of the October Events,' *Canadian Review of Sociology and Anthropology,* IX (February, 1972).

Brewis, T.N., *Regional Economic Policies in Canada.* Toronto: Macmillan, 1963.

Cairns, Alan C. 'The Electoral and the Party System in Canada,' *Canadian Journal of Political Science,* I, (March, 1968), 55-80.

Canada, Dominion Bureau of Statistics, *Vital Statistics.* Ottawa: Queen's Printer, 1963.

Clark, Terry N. *Community Structure and Decision-Making.* San Francisco: Chandler, 1968.

Cleverdon, Catherine L., *The Woman Suffrage Movement in Canada.* Toronto: University of Toronto Press, 1950.

Cole, G.D.H., and A.W. Filson, *British Working Class Movements.* London: Macmillan, 1967.

Courtney, John, *Voting in Canada.* Scarborough: Prentice-Hall of Canada, 1967.

Cutt, James, 'Selectivity or Universality? Income Support Alternatives for Families with Children,' in John Harp and John R. Hofley (eds.), *Poverty in Canada.* Scarborough: Prentice-Hall of Canada, 1971, pp. 174-186.

Dahrendorf, Ralf, *Class and Class Conflict in Industrial Society.* Stanford: Stanford University Press, 1959.

Dion, Gérard, and Louis O'Neill, *Political Immorality in the Province of Quebec.* Montreal: Civic Action League, 1956.

Dion, Léon, *Le Bill 60 et la Société Québécoise.* Montreal: HMH, 1967.

Domhoff, William, *Who Rules America.* Englewood Cliffs: Prentice-Hall Inc., 1967.

Dye, Thomas R., *The Politics of Equality.* Indianapolis: Bobbs-Merill, 1971.

Economic Council of Canada, *Fifth Annual Report.* Ottawa: Queen's Printer, 1968.

Economic Council of Canada, *Sixth Annual Review, Perspective 1975.* Ottawa: Queen's Printer, 1969.

Einaudi, Mario, 'Fascism,' *International Encyclopedia of the Social Sciences,* 5. New York: Macmillan, 1968, pp. 334-336.

Engelmann, Frederick C., 'Austria: the pooling of opposition,' in Robert Dahl (ed.), *Political Opposition in Western Democracies.* New Haven: Yale University Press, 1966, pp. 260-283.

Engelmann, Frederick C., and Mildred A. Schwartz, *Canadian Political Parties: Origin, Character, Impact.* Scarborough: Prentice-Hall of Canada, 1975.

Ermatinger, C.O., *Canadian Franchise and Election Laws.* Toronto: Carswell, 1886.

Etzioni, Amitai, *The Active Society.* New York: The Free Press, 1968.

Evan, William M., and Mildred A. Schwartz, 'Law and the Emergence of Formal Organizations,' *Sociology and Social Research,* XLVIII (1964), 270-280.

Fletcher, Marsha, 'Judicial Review and the Division of Powers in Canada,' in J. Peter Meekison, *Canadian Federalism: Myth or Reality.* Toronto: Methuen, 1968, pp. 140-158.

Gamson, William, *Power and Discontent.* Homewood, Ill.: Dorsey Press, 1968.

Gans, Herbert J., 'Social Protest of the 1960's Takes the Form of the Equality Revolution,' in Norman R. Yetman and C. Hoy Steele (eds.), *Majority and Minority.* Boston: Allyn and Bacon, 1971, pp. 610-621.

Garner, John, *The Franchise and Politics in British North America 1755-1867.* Toronto: University of Toronto Press, 1969.

Gosnell, Harold, *Machine Politics,* 2nd ed. Chicago: University of Chicago Press, 1968.

Grimes, Alan, *The Puritan Ethic and Woman Suffrage.* New York: Oxford University Press, 1967.

Hagy, J.W.,'Quebec Separatists: The First Twelve Years,' *Queen's Quarterly,* LXXVI (1969), 229-238.

Harp, John, 'Canada's Rural Poor,' in John Harp and John R. Hofley (eds.), *Poverty in Canada.* Scarborough: Prentice-Hall of Canada, 1971, pp. 174-186.

Horowitz, Gad, *Canadian Labour in Politics.* Toronto: University of Toronto Press, 1968.

Irving, J.A., 'Psychological Aspects of the Social Credit Movement in Alberta. Part III: An Interpretation of the Movement,' *Canadian Journal of Psychology,* I (September, 1947).

——, *The Social Credit Movement in Alberta.* Toronto: University of Toronto Press, 1959.

Jacek, Henry, John McDonough, Ronald Shimizu, and Patrick Smith, 'The Consequence of Federal-Provincial Campaign Activity in Party Organizations: The Influence of Recruitment Patterns,' *Canadian Journal of Political Science,* V (June, 1972), 196-197.

Johnson, F. Henry, *A Brief History of Education in Canada.* Toronto: McGraw-Hill, 1968.

Kornberg, Allan, *Canadian Legislative Behavior: A Study of the 25th Parliament.* New York: Holt, Rinehart and Winston, 1967.

Kyba, Patrick, 'Ballots and Burning Crosses — the Election of 1929,' in Norman Ward and D.S. Spafford (eds.), *Politics in Saskatchewan.* Toronto: Longmans, 1968.

Lakoff, Sanford A., *Equality in Political Philosophy.* Cambridge: Harvard University Press, 1964.

Laponce, Jean A., 'Ethnicity, Religion, and Politics in Canada: A comparative Analysis of Survey and Census Data,' in Mattei Dogan and Stein Rokkan (eds.), *Quantitative Ecological Analysis in the Social Sciences.* Cambridge: MIT Press, 1969, pp. 187-216.

——, 'Non-Voting and Non-Voters: A Typology,' *Canadian Journal of Economics and Political Science,* XXXIII (February, 1967), 75-87.

——, 'Post-dicting Electoral Cleavages in Canadian Federal Elections, 1949-68: Material for a Footnote,' *Canadian Journal of Political Science,* V (June, 1972), 270-286.

Laporte, Pierre, 'Les élections ne se font pas avec des prières,' *Le Devoir,* 1 Oct.-7 Dec., 1956.

Laskin, Bora, 'Reflections on the Canadian Constitution after the First Century,' *Canadian Bar Review,* XLV (September, 1967), 395-401.

Laskin, Richard, and Richard Baird, 'Factors in Voter Turnout and Party Preference in a Saskatchewan Town,' *Canadian Journal of Political Science,* III (September, 1970), 457-458.

Lasswell, Harold, Daniel Lerner, C.E. Rothwell, *The Comparative Study of Elites.* Stanford: Stanford University Press, 1952.

Lemieux, Vincent, *Parenté et Politique.* Quebec: Les Presses de l'Université Laval, 1971, p. 227.

Lewis, Oscar, 'The Culture of Poverty,' *Scientific American,* CCXV, 1966.

Lieberson, Stanley, *Language and Ethnic Relations in Canada.* New York: John Wiley and Sons, 1971.

Lipset, S.M., *Agrarian Socialism.* Berkeley: University of California Press, 1950.

——, *Political Man.* Garden City: Doubleday, 1960.

Long, John A., 'Maldistribution in Western Provincial Legislatures: The Case of Alberta,' *Canadian Journal of Political Science,* II (September, 1969), 351.

Lower, A.R.M., F.R. Scott, *et. al., Evolving Canadian Federalism.* Durham: Duke University Press, 1958.

Lucas, Rex H., *Minetown, Milltown, Railtown.* Toronto: University of Toronto Press, 1971.

Lyons, W.E., *One Man — One Vote.* Toronto: McGraw-Hill, 1970.

MacDonald, Lynn, 'Religion and Voting: A Study of the 1968 Canadian Federal Election in Ontario,' *Canadian Review of Sociology and Anthropology,* VI (August, 1969), 129-144.

Mackenzie, Robert, and Alan Silver, *Angels in Marble.* Chicago: University of Chicago Press, 1968.

Macpherson, C.B., *Democracy in Alberta: The Theory and Practice of a Quasi Party System.* Toronto: University of Toronto Press, 1962.

Magnuson, Roger, *Education in the Province of Quebec.* Washington: U.S. Government Printing Office, 1969, p. 4.

Manzer, Ronald, *Canada: A Socio-Political Report.* Toronto: McGraw-Hill Ryerson, 1974.

Marshall, T.H., *Class, Citizenship and Social Development.* Garden City: Doubleday, Anchor, 1964.

Marx, Karl, *Selected Writings in Sociology and Social Philosophy,* ed. by T.B. Bottomore and M. Rubel. New York: McGraw-Hill, 1956.

Marx, Karl, and Frederick Engels, *Basic Writings on Politics and Philosophy,* Lewis S. Feuer, (ed.). Garden City: Doubleday, 1959.

Masters, D.C., *The Winnipeg General Strike.* Toronto: University of Toronto Press, 1950.

Mathias, Peter, *Forced Growth.* Toronto: James Lewis and Samuel, 1971.

Mayo, Henry B., *An Introduction to Democratic Theory.* New York: Oxford University Press, 1960.

Meisel, John, 'Religious Affiliation and Electoral Behavior,' *Canadian Journal of Economics and Political Science,* XXII (1956), 481-496.

——, *Working Papers on Canadian Politics.* Montreal: McGill-Queen's University Press, 1972.

Merton, Robert K., *Social Theory and Social Structure,* revised and enlarged. New York: The Free Press, 1957.

Michels, Robert, *Political Parties.* New York: Collier-Macmillan, 1962.

Milbrath, Lester, *Political Participation.* Chicago: Rand McNally, 1965.

Miller, S.M., and Pamela Roby, *The Future of Inequality.* New York: Basic Books, 1970.

Mills, C. Wright, *The Power Elite.* New York: Oxford University Press, 1956.

Morf, G., *Le Terrorisme Québécois.* Montreal: Les Editions de l'Homme, 1970.

Mosca, Gaetano, *The Ruling Class,* trans. by H. Kahn. New York: McGraw-Hill, 1939.

Neatby, H. Blair, *The Politics of Chaos.* Toronto: Macmillan, 1972.

Newman, Peter, *Renegade in Power: The Diefenbaker Years.* Toronto: McClelland and Stewart, 1963.

Paine, Stanley G., 'Falangism,' *International Encyclopedia of the Social Sciences,* 5. New York: Macmillan, 1968, pp. 289-292.

Pammett, Jon H., 'The development of political orientations in Canadian schoolchildren,' *Canadian Journal of Political Science,* IV (March, 1971), 139.

Pareto, Vilfredo, *The Mind and Society,* trans. by A. Bongiorno and A. Livingston, ed. by Livingston. New York: Harcourt, Brace and World, 1935.

Parsons, Talcott, *Sociological Theory and Modern Society.* New York: The Free Press, 1967.

——, 'The Political Aspect of Social Structure and Process,' in David Easton, (ed.), Varieties of Political Theory. Englewood Cliffs: Prentice-Hall Inc., 1966.

Parsons, Talcott, and Kenneth B. Clark (eds.), *The Negro American.* Boston: Beacon Press, 1965.

Pinard, Maurice, 'Classes sociales et comportement électoral,' in Vincent Lemieux (ed.), *Quatre élections provinciales au Québec.* Quebec: Les Presses de l'Université Laval, 1969.

——, 'Working Class Politics: An Interpretation of the Quebec Case,' *Canadian Review of Sociology and Anthropology,* VII (May, 1970), 87-109.

—— *The Rise of a Third Party.* Englewood Cliffs: Prentice-Hall Inc., 1971.

Podoluk, Jenny R., 'Low Income and Poverty,' in John Harp and John R. Hofley (eds.), *Poverty in Canada.* Scarborough: Prentice-Hall of Canada, 1971, pp. 119-125.

Poetschke, L.E., 'Regional Planning for Depressed Rural Areas – the Canadian Experience,' *Canadian Journal of Agricultural Economics,* I (February, 1968), 8-20.

Polyani, Karl, *The Great Transformation.* New York: Farrar and Rinehart, 1944.

Porter, John, *The Vertical Mosaic.* Toronto: University of Toronto Press, 1965.

Qualter, T.H., *The Election Process in Canada.* Toronto: McGraw-Hill, 1970.

Quinn, Herbert F., *The Union Nationale.* Toronto: University of Toronto Press, 1963.

Rees, John, *Equality.* New York: Praeger, 1971.

Report of the Royal Commission of Inquiry on Education in the Province of Quebec, Vol. 1-5. Quebec: Queen's Printer, 1963-1966.

Report of the Royal Commission on Bilingualism and Biculturalism, II-IV. Ottawa: Queen's Printer, 1968-1969.

Report of the Royal Commission on Education and Youth, Province of Newfoundland and Labrador, Vol. I-II. St. John's: Queen's Printer, 1967-1968.

Report of the Royal Commission on Health Services, Vol. I. Ottawa: Queen's Printer, 1964.

Roach, Jack L., and Orville R. Gursslin, 'An evaluation of the concept "culture of poverty,"' *Social Forces,* XLV (March, 1967), 383-392.

Robin, Martin, *Radical Politics and Canadian Labour, 1880-1930.* Kingston: Queen's University Press, 1968.

Rokkan, Stein, 'Mass Suffrage, Secret Voting and Political Participation,' in Lewis A. Coser (ed.), *Political Sociology.* New York: Harper, 1966.

Rothney, G.O., 'The Denominational Basis of Representation in the Newfoundland Assembly, 1919-1962,' *Canadian Journal of Economics and Political Science,* XXVIII (1962), 557-570.

Rowe, F.W., *The History of Education in Newfoundland.* Toronto: Ryerson, 1952.

Saywell, John, *Quebec 70.* Toronto: University of Toronto Press, 1971.

Saywell, John T., 'The 1890's,' in J.M.S. Careless and R. Craig Brown, *The Canadians 1867-1967.* Toronto: Macmillan, 1968.

Schmeisser, S.A., *Civil Liberties in Canada.* London: Oxford University Press, 1964.

Schwartz, Mildred A.,, 'Canadian Voting Behavior,' in Richard Rose (ed.), *Electoral Behavior: A Comparative Handbook.* New York: The Free Press, 1974, pp. 543-617.

——, *Politics and Territory.* Montreal: McGill-Queen's University Press, 1974.

Secher, Herbert P., 'Coalition Government: The Case of the Second Austrian Republic,' *American Political Science Review,* LII (September, 1958), 791-808.

Senate of Canada, *Report of the Special Committee on Poverty in Canada.* Ottawa: Queen's Printer, 1971.

——, *Report on Aging.* Ottawa: Queen's Printer, 1966.

Senior, Hereward, *Orangeism: The Canadian Phase.* Toronto: McGraw-Hill Ryerson, 1972.

Shils, Edward, *Political Development in New States.* The Hague: Mouton, 1962.

Sigel, Roberta (ed.), *Learning about Politics.* New York: Random House, 1970.

Skelton, O.D., *Life and Letters of Sir Wilfrid Laurier,* Vol. II. London: Century, 1921.

Smith, D.E., 'The Membership of the Saskatchewan Legislative Assembly, 1905-66,' in Norman Ward and Duff Spafford (eds.), *Politics in Saskatchewan.* Toronto: Longmans, 1968, pp. 178-206.

Stone, Leroy O., *Migration in Canada, Some Regional Aspects,* 1961 Census Monograph, Dominion Bureau of Statistics. Ottawa: Queen's Printer, 1969.

Tarnapolsky, W.D., *The Canadian Bill of Rights.* Toronto: Carswell, 1966.

Trudeau, P.E. (ed.), *La Grève de l'Amiante.* Montreal: Cité Libre, 1956.

Van Loon, Richard, 'Political Participation in Canada, The 1965 Election,' *Canadian Journal of Political Science,* III (September, 1970).

Van Loon, Richard J., and Michael D. Whittington, *The Canadian Political System.* Toronto: McGraw-Hill, 1971.

Verba, Sydney, and Norman H. Nie, *Participation in America.* New York: Harper and Row, 1972.

Wade, Mason, *The French Canadians,* rev. ed. Toronto: Macmillan, 1968.

Ward, Norman, *The Canadian House of Commons.* Toronto: University of Toronto Press, 1950.

Weber, Max, *The Theory of Social and Economic Organization,* trans. by A.M. Henderson and Talcott Parsons. New York: The Free Press, 1947.

Winham, Gilbert, 'Attitudes on Pollution and Growth in Hamilton, or "There's an awful lot of talk these days about ecology,"' *Canadian Journal of Political Science,* V (September, 1972).

3 : ISSUES OF INDUSTRIAL SOCIETY

Introduction to Part Three

The four chapters of the previous section emphasized the issue of social inequality, always with reference to possible social changes. The following four chapters take up issues which continue to relate to the theme of inequality in Canada, but more specifically, are oriented to social change in Canadian society.

The changes in basic societal institutions, such as the family, work patterns and organization, social values and norms, and residence patterns, are so pervasive in influence as to both reflect and affect all aspects of Canadian social life, patterns of inequality included. Thus, for example, the changing functions of the family, with the present *relative* unimportance of the family for economic production and even for socialization, permit new definitions of male and female roles. Notably, and obviously affecting the occupational structure and institutionalized inequalities, the contemporary Canadian emphasis upon the nuclear or conjugal family frees women for activity in the labor force where previously the female role was almost exclusively defined with reference to the home and family. Or, to take another example, the characteristic feature of Canadian migration and residence patterns since the end of World War II has been a rural to urban migration, so that today the overwhelming majority of Canadians live in cities. The concentration of resources in the city thereby may be viewed not just as some feature of Canadian society which has changed and continues to change, but also one which affects the distribution of resources and the life styles of Canadians. The contemporary Marxist model which employs the concepts of *metropolis* and *hinterland* illustrates this notion that cities dominate resources, drawing raw materiel from rural areas and concentrating processing, consumption, and occupational opportunities in the urban areas. Hence, urbanization affects the nature of change in a society, and also the nature of inequality.

Sociologists have given prominence to issues such as the changing role and structure of the family; the increasing number and influence of large-scale social, economic, and political organizations; the increasing manifestations of deviant behaviors, and the increasing concentration of urban rather than rural residence. This prominence is justified, for these issues relate to changes which have been experienced not only in Canadian society, but in every industrialized and industrializing society.

All too obviously social change is a complex matter. The new economic demands and benefits of industrialized societies as contrasted to agrarian societies precipitate, even if reciprocally, changes in basic institutions of society. For example, it has been argued that the nuclear family is more compatible with industrial society than is the larger extended kin-system. Industrial societies require to some extent the abandonment of particularistic, kin-based systems of reciprocal obligation and sharing so that contract labor and a money economy may be established. The requirement is not the destruction of extended kinship ties, for they persist in Canadian society and any industrialized society, most markedly in Japan; but the nuclear responsibilities come to be emphasized, and the extended responsibilities atrophy. In part, too, this is related to the necessity for a highly mobile labor force, responsive to occupational supply and demand. An extended family would impede such mobility, where a nuclear family, as testified by the North American experience, is highly mobile. The nation is the job market, not the local community or city.

Industrialization also is associated with increased occupational specialization. In pre-industrial societies it was possible for the kinship system to be the basis of work, education, and political organization. But with sheer increase in population size, technological and organizational complexity, and magnitude of industrial production, such kin organization is all but impossible. The administrative as well as the productive tasks increase, as problems of co-ordination and control proliferate. Large formal organizations take over functions previously performed by the extended family and other simple organizations; some of the responsibility for the socialization of children is assumed by the formal school organizations; production and distribution of commodities are assumed by large-scale corporate organizations; social control and the administration of resource and service distribution are assumed by various levels and agents of large government organizations. In a word, bureaucratization abounds.

So too does deviance. With societal complexity, clear-cut and persistent norms of conduct are no longer apparent. A plethora of subcultures and subgroups exist, often with conflicting criteria of behavior. The social control previously vested in the family and small, tightly knit communities is overcome in the anonymity of large cities; formal agencies of social control, such as the police and the courts, have to assume the control functions previously performed informally within the household and the small town. The *Gemeinschaft* of the somewhat mythical bygone days is replaced by the anomic *Gesellschaft* society of the industrialized twentieth century — a transition exaggerated by those deploring the present and longing for a mythical pastoral past, but a significant and dramatic change nonetheless.

In Chapter Eight, Colette Carisse examines the changing family. The issue which she poses is one which has intrigued social theorists from time immemorial: is the family necessary? Given the changes which have characterized the family, and given the alternative agencies which exist to perform functions previously monopolized by the family, the possibility of the family as an obsolescent institution, destined to wither away, is very much with us in twentieth century Canada. The question is not one of collectivist rhetoric, but one generated by real social changes. (Keller, 1973)

Carisse approaches the issue from a cross-cultural look at family forms and functions. She offers ideal family types, based on their relations to environmental resources and family goals. The basic family types, the maternal (lower class), patriarchal (middle class), and fraternal (middle class) are employed in an examination of Canadian data. She concludes by predicting that it is the last, the fraternal or egalitarian family, which will come to prevail in Canada.

Changes in the family and in society, and the decline in family influence and social control, relate to deviance among young people. In Chapter Nine, Edmund Vaz considers the use of marihuana among Canadian youth as the specific issue illustrating the larger issue of deviance. We should hope it is unnecessary, but will nonetheless point up that the discussion of deviance or marihuana use is not dependent upon any moral judgment. Marihuana use, or any manifestation of deviance, is deemed deviant relative to some collectively understood normative, and sometimes legal system. Therefore, such definitions as well as the behavior are always subject to change.

Taking care to outline how social issues come to be defined as such, Vaz concentrates upon marihuana use as an illustration of sociological outlooks and generalizations relating to deviance and conformity. He estimates the extent of marihuana use in Canada, noting that its use by

Canadian youth seems to extend across class lines, and is more common among males, among students who are low academic achievers, and in urban centers.

He considers marihuana use as social behavior, involving interaction with others, some organization, and norms. As symbolic interactionists would put it, Vaz notes that 'users and non-users are conforming to different definitions of the situation.' Deviance generally is a relative matter; behavior viewed as deviant by some members of society is not so viewed by others. Vaz favors the notion that deviance is behavior defined as deviant by groups in positions of power in Canada. He judges that repressive laws designed to secure conformity to the moral definitions of such groups insure criminal violations. Vaz carefully distinguishes deviance as behavior from deviant roles or self-definitions, the latter a function of the responses of others, and particularly of stigmatization or the labelling process. He also considers specifically why marihuana is used in Canada, and explores explanations derived from the 'anomie theory' adapted by Merton, concluding that Merton's model can only account for a small proportion of marihuana use. The explanation which he favors employs the concept of 'youth culture.' It is the competition for social prestige among peers and in particular the simple participation in the social activities of friends that leads, in Vaz's view, to much marihuana use amongst Canadian young people, in a gradual and routine process of experimentation, social interaction, and finally pleasure.

In Chapter Ten, Charles Gordon discusses the issue of bureaucratization. Theory and research enquiring into the conditions and qualities of effective administration are taken up. But so too are the questions which relate to the impact which large organizations have upon the everyday lives of each of us in an age where we have become accustomed to 'big business' and 'big government.'

Gordon distinguishes the internal and external features and problems of bureaucratic organization. Considering the internal features, he outlines classical approaches to the study of organization, such as Weber's administrative approach and the worker-centered approaches of Taylor and Mayo. These are then contrasted with a contemporary systems approach, that of Etzioni.

The external relations of the organization are considered as a matter of control over and effect on the environment. Citing numerous Canadian illustrations, he discusses organizational benefits, management and ownership, and the predictability of the environment. These in turn are related to internal problems, such as organizational size, the staff-line controversy, and professionals in bureaucracy. In conclusion, he suggests that the issue of bureaucratization is central to any sociological study, given the pervasive influence of such organizations in industrial societies.

The closing chapter in this section of the book deals with the environmental context within which most Canadian families exist, most criminally deviant acts occur, and most Canadian organizations, including universities, are to be found: the city. The issue is urbanization itself, manifested in the exodus from farm to city. Boyd and Mozersky consider the character of the city and its suburbs, the problems of urban population density, problems of residence, transportation, and anomie. The process of urbanization is intrinsically related to fundamental questions regarding the physical and social quality of life in modern Canada, for most of us will spend our lives in a large metropolis.

Throughout the chapter, Boyd and Mozersky concentrate upon three population variables: size, density, and heterogeneity. They open by distinguishing urbanization — the process of urban growth and change — from urbanism — the social and cultural characteristics of urban residents. Using Canadian and cross-cultural measures of urbanization they explore the factors which might explain urban growth and change. In this regard, they use Hauser's division of human ecology into four major variables: population, social organization, environment, and technology (Hauser, 1969).

The classic work by Park and Burgess — the concentric ring model of urban growth — is described and evaluated for Canada. The authors observe that the zones of the city which have attracted most sociological attention have been the zone of transition and the commuter zone. The former is examined in a discussion of 'urban blight' in Canada.

They then look at migration and natural growth as they affect cities, outlining the Canadian experience, especially with regard to ethnic composition. They note, for example, the relatively recent decline in the proportion of persons of British origin, and generally the high degree of ethnic diversity in Canadian cities — strikingly so in Windsor and Winnipeg.

The ethnic composition of Canada leads them into their discussion of urbanism, and the processes of adaptation, integration, and assimilation. Taking up the question of 'social disorganization' in cities, they consider Canadian data regarding participation in voluntary associations, and the role of the family and the neighborhood in the city.

Generally, as they and others must conclude, the growth of Canadian cities is unlikely to be reversed in the near future, and as a consequence, a study of the nature and quality of urban existence is fundamental to an understanding of Canada.

References

Hauser, Philip, 'The Chaotic Society: Product of the Social Morphological Revolution,' *ASR,* XXXIV (February, 1969), 1-19.

Keller, Suzanne, *Does the Family Have a Future?* Andover, Mass.: Warner Modular Publications, 1973, pp. 1-14.

Recommended Readings: Annotated

Beattie, Christopher, Jacques Désy, and Frank Longstaff, *Bureaucratic Careers: Anglophones and Francophones in the Canadian Public Service.* Ottawa: Information Canada, 1972.

Studies of Canadian organizations are rare. This work considers ethnic background or language as they affect career chances in the federal civil service.

Becker, Howard, *Outsiders: Studies in the Sociology of Deviance.* New York: The Free Press, 1963.

Becker initiated an approach to deviance which emphasizes that the deviant is the person so labelled when apprehended and punished, while the non-deviant or 'straight' is the person who has not been caught or punished for committing deviant acts.

Bell, Norman, and Ezra Vogel (eds.), *The Family.* Glencoe, Ill.: The Free Press, 1960.

This is a selection of papers which is rather more contentious than those normally found in a compilation. It is particularly useful as a study of the changing family.

Etzioni, Amitai, *Complex Organizations.* New York: The Free Press, 1961.

This is probably the most innovative contribution by a contemporary sociologist to the theory of organizations. Etzioni analyzes organizations by goal and authority structure.

Ishwaran, K. (ed.), *The Canadian Family: A Book of Readings.* Toronto: Holt, Rinehart and Winston, 1971.

This collection of papers is particularly useful for its explicit comparison of Canadian and American family changes.

Queen, Stuart, and Robert Habenstein, *The Family in Various Cultures,* (3rd edition). Philadelphia: J.P. Lippincott, 1967.

The value of this book rests with the range of family types examined, from simple, agrarian societies, to the kibbutz, to contemporary North America.

Lithwick, N.H., and Gilles Paquet, *Urban Studies: A Canadian Perspective.* Toronto: Methuen, 1968.

For sociologists, this work may be too heavily economic. Yet it is an informed and careful analysis of conditions in Canadian cities.

Merton, Robert K., *Social Theory and Social Structure.* New York: The Free Press, 1957.

This is perhaps the most cited work in American sociology. It contains Merton's elaboration of the concept of anomie and its application to the analysis of deviance.

Stone, Leroy, *Urban Development in Canada.* Ottawa, Dominion Bureau of Statistics Census Monograph, 1967.

The demographic character of the rural to urban transition is clearly documented in this monograph.

Vaz, Edmund, *Middle-class Juvenile Delinquency.* New York: Harper and Row, 1967.

There is some tendency to think of delinquency (juvenile deviance) as a lower class phenomenon, despite the numerous data repudiating such a conception. Vaz's work is among the few explicitly devoted to middle class delinquency.

CHAPTER EIGHT

The Family: The Issue of Change

Colette Carisse
University of Montreal

Introduction

The persistence of the family in changing societies may be viewed as a social issue with marked ideological overtones. Its defenders are conservatives; its opponents utopians. People are not neutral about the family; it stirs deeply rooted feelings of love and hate, contempt or adulation. As with religion, some denounce it as an opium and others glorify it as a symbol of what is to be cherished in life. When its future is questioned, some are convinced that it should be abolished like property; others advocate a government family policy to protect it from being overwhelmed.

From the point of view of its defenders, the family is the basic unit of society. In a recent study, 150 innovative women in different fields of activity were asked what they thought of the family as an institution. They were favorable to the family in a proportion of two to one. The following are a sample of pro-family responses: 'the family is the basic unit of society,' it 'fulfills a basic need in human nature,' 'if we want a well-balanced and work-oriented nation, we must develop family values;' especially 'as one gets older it is a source of satisfaction highly superior to professional realization;' the family 'assures the continuity of generations in the society' and constitutes 'an essential framework for the fulfillment of the children we have created.'

These perspectives lead advocates of the family to the logical conclusion that the 'moral crisis' in the western world is a result of disrupted family life. 'Conflict is breaking out between generations, delinquency is increasing among adolescents, the number of conflicts between husband

and wife are growing as are the number of broken homes. It is vain to believe that the situation *will become normal again* by itself. I would even propose that a mother should be paid to stay in the home if this is necessary.'*

Alternatively, from the radical perspective, Marx concluded that the family was the basic mechanism by which private ownership of property was perpetuated. He referred, however, to a specific type of family, namely the male-dominated *monogamistic* (single mate) family, prescribed and sanctioned by laws. In his *Origin of the Family, Private Property and the State,* Engels repeatedly pointed out that emotional and sexual fulfillment can only be enhanced when property does not motivate family relations. The family need not be repressive.

From this point of view, it is interesting to observe what happens to the family in countries which have undergone a revolution abolishing privilege based upon property. In family-centered China, the socialist revolution broke the old family system at the points where it had been strained. First, young men were freed from subordination to the oldest male. Second, young women were freed from double subordination to their husband and their husband's mother as a result of the revolution's emphasis on the equality of the sexes. 'A social revolution is accelerated change, and as such, it can swiftly sweep away the lags that have been accumulated over a long period of time' concludes Nimkoff.† The family has not been abolished in communist China but its patriarchal structure has been dismantled and different living arrangements have been created according to the type of job the woman has and whether she is involved in a large industrial complex or an agricultural commune.

The Cosers present an interesting study which shows the relationship between ideology and emerging social relations in a revolution; they studied the status of the illegitimate child in four societies that had undergone a social revolution: France, Russia, Cuba, and China. In all four, the stigma of illegitimacy was abolished in the revolution's early fervor. The underlying ideology which these revolutions were implementing was that any child is born a citizen and as such is entitled to all civil rights. However, both France and Russia reinstated inheritance rights, in order to control property transmission, once the new revolutionary elite had established not only its power, but also its wealth. We have yet to see what the second generation of revolutionaries will do in Cuba and China.

But is the family, its existence and its strength, really the issue? In our

*Wilder Penfield, *L'homme et sa Famille* (Montreal: Proops Press Inc., 1967), p. 20.
†Nimkoff, *Comparative Family Systems* (Boston: Houghton Mifflin, 1965), p. 56.

opinion, the family serves too often as a scapegoat. In the face of our failure to replace the receding Protestant ethic with moral values adjusted to conditions of modern life, we accuse the family of 'sickness.' Rigid linear authority, with no structural channel for feedback, is not particular to the family; it is shared by most authority relations in our societies including those in the economic and political spheres (Etzioni, 1968). It is not the demands of family life as such which hinder social development, but rather the competitive consumption that takes place within the family. At least this is the opinion of many social critics.

Thus we share Rodman's opinion. 'When we mix together many discrete facts about families and many vested interests in families, we are bound to come up with varying interpretations ... Do we take the fact that there are few inter-racial marriages and few full-time career women to indicate that these matters are somehow against human nature and therefore best to avoid, or do we take these as indicative of cultural obstacles that should be removed ... The student of family sociology must be on the alert.* The persistence of the family is an ideological issue, but we will try to study it from a basis in facts.

The Family: Universality or Diversity?

We must begin by discussing a theoretical problem which is to be found at the beginning of most family textbooks or readers. 'Is the family universal?' The adventurous theorist must avoid two pitfalls in answering this question: *circular reasoning* and *sociocentrism*. In a *structural-functional* approach, the reasoning would go as follows: We see a structure performing certain functions everywhere; since these functions are a prerequisite for the survival of society, this structure must exist. In a very competent study, Murdock has used this line of reasoning. In every society we can identify a *basic nuclear unit* that we can call family. Everywhere this structure performs four basic functions: *socialization, economic co-operation, reproduction, and sexual relations.* The nuclear unit (mating couple and any children) combines in different ways to form larger family types, but it is always identifiable. (Murdock, 1949)

However, Ira Reiss, in a theoretical paper, presented four cases which indicate that all four functions listed by Murdock are not performed everywhere by the nuclear family. Table I summarizes her evidence.

In the Nayar tribe the women receives a legal nominal husband who never lives with her. She has many lovers and biological *filiation*

---

*Hyman Rodman, 'The Textbook World of Family Sociology,' *Social Problems,* 12:4 (1965), 449. Reprinted by permission of The Society for the Study of Social Problems.

Table I: Functions of the Nuclear Family in Four Societies

Society	Socialization	Economic Responsibility	Reproduction	Sexual Rights
Nayar of the Molabar	yes	no	no	no
Caribbean (lower class)	yes	no	no	no
Kibbutz	yes	no	yes	yes
Trobianders	yes	no	no	yes

(fatherhood) is not established. The family is *matrilineal* (descent traced through mother) and the extended maternal family (maternal relations) is economically responsible for the mother and the children. In the Caribbean lower class, the women very often live for a short time with different men, none of whom assumes permanent responsibilities as a husband or father. With the help of extended kin, the mother is responsible for her children. In these two cases, the basic unit is the mother-child relationship. The man is less attached to a family unit either because his customary role is hunting and fighting or because the society does not provide him with a secure job. To a lesser extent, this family pattern was also to be found in the slave families of colonial America and in some Indian tribes of North America (Driver, 1961).

The Trobiander case is more complex. In this matrilineal society, the man behaves as a husband in the sense that he has a relatively permanent sexual relationship with his wife and in the sense that he is recognized as the father of the children and has a playful, affectionate relationship with them. However, it is the mother's brother who is responsible for the upbringing and physical care of the children.

Some examples of deviation from Murdock's functional scheme may also be found in modern communal living. In the kibbutz, couples are identified and share a common room. Parents are recognized as such and are heavily involved in 'nurturant socialization, i.e., the giving of positive emotional response to infants and young children' (Reiss, 1965: 447). However, the commune has direct economic responsibility for both adults and children and takes physical care of the young. The commune as a group also provides emotional support in that it is small enough to permit face-to-face relationships. Similarly, in the larger Chinese rural communes, the nuclear family unit lives as a separate household but the commune assumes responsibility for sustenance and socialization. Both of these communal types are, in a sense, experimental. 'They want to do away with the patriarchal aspects of the family, to have marriage based on love, easy divorce, and communal upbringing of children' concludes Reiss (1965: 446). However, these two ventures in utopia are based on a common condition: because of the pressure for economic development, women's work is needed outside of the household. While in Russia the grandmother continued to perform traditional household activities, in Israel and China, new structures had to be created. Just as in the case of illegitimacy, we must wait and see whether communal family relations are maintained under conditions of relative abundance. If they are, it would indicate that ways of thinking had really been changed. This indeed would be a cultural revolution.

Reiss' argument leads to the conclusion that there is only one universally found characteristic of the family: *a primary relationship which serves the basic function of nurturant socialization for the child.*

However, Weigert and Thomas argue that to show that this relationship is universal does not mean that it is logically necessary. They warn us against the danger of *sociocentrism:* that is, 'the positing of a past or present social structure as an absolute universal necessary for man, such that other forms are understood as deviations from it.' The authors base their argument on a *voluntaristic* view of man in society; man can shape his fate. Rather than speaking in terms of the social system as self-perpetuating, in the voluntaristic view individuals desire to recreate their group. And they may implement any form of social organization that is theoretically possible in order to do so; they can venture into utopia. Along with Reiss (1965), the authors agree that there is no *necessary* relationship between marriage and the nuclear family unit. Children could be conceived in test tubes, nurtured by a mechanical device and attended by whoever desired to care for them. The future is plastic and not strictly determined by the past or present.

Our view relates to a conception of man in a social system. The defining property of the socio-cultural system is *communication through symbols.* In order to develop a self, to learn, to create goals for himself, man, a social animal, must communicate and share a common system of code perceptions. That is, he must live in a social order, with a shared symbolic or linguistic system (Duncan, 1962).

This process of constant coding and decoding is, of necessity, learned. In order to survive as a human organism, the newborn infant must be fed. In order to become a human being, he must also learn to communicate with symbols in a primary relationship; he must be socialized. The primary relationship between an infant and an adult that is directed toward the goal we will call *nurturing communication,* is the basis for a specific *socio-cultural system.* This basic socio-cultural system is the *family.* By definition, it is inter-generational (extends across several generations), implying a sustained relationship over time. Because of the biological facts of human nurturing, the mother is more likely to be the adult in the system if the adult generation is reduced to one person. The fact that the goal is nurturing communication will determine other properties of the family system, and its relations with its individual members.

The actual structure of the family, namely, the number of persons included, and the range of activities performed, depends on the interplay of the family with its environment. We will develop this point later in the chapter. Here, we wish to stress only that the structure of families varies from one society to another and from one subgroup to another within the same society. Lines of inheritance of property and name, rules of residence, relations with kin and size of household, combine in different ways so that the range of family structures is highly diversified. (See 'Family' in *International Encyclopedia of Social Sciences,* pp. 300-311.) Nimkoff has cross-tabulated the different family structures found in the Human Relations Area Files. The cross-tabulation of rules of residence and rules of descent gives the distribution of family types shown in Table II (1965: 25).

Table II shows a clear relationship between rules of residence and lines of descent, in that matrilocal families tended to evidence matrilineal descent, and patrilocal families were characterized by patrilineal descent. When type of marriage is considered, Nimkoff also found that polygamy was favored in 415 cultures, monogamy in 135 and polyandry in four.

Goode, however, in his study of worldwide family trends, shows clearly that the trend is toward the *conjugal* or *nuclear* family unit, i.e., a married couple responsible for their own children in a separate household. This trend can be demonstrated statistically. In Canada, 90 per cent of the households with children contain two parents and no other kin. However, even this conjugal or nuclear family unit may take many forms. Families will develop different properties over time according to the nature of the social environment. This relationship of the family to its social environment will be the subject of the next section. We will also consider the family as a micro-environment for its members.

It seems clear that when the family emerges from a traditional or archaic past, as the society urbanizes and industrializes, it is likely to adopt a structure similar to the North American nuclear family. Yet, in the most technologically advanced societies, individuals are turning toward alternative forms of the family. However, of all the forms of the family that are theoretically and empirically possible, some forms are more probable or more likely to be preferred, given the social environment in which the family must exist.

Family and Traditional Society

In traditional societies, everyone thinks of himself in relation to others as either a relative or a non-relative. Blood ties define position and relationship as does occupation in our society. The kinship system includes all the relationships of rights and obligations that integrate

Table II: Distribution of Family Types by Rules of Residence and Descent*

Residence	Descent				
	Matri–lineal [1]	*Patri–lineal* [2]	*Double* [3]	*Bila–teral* [4]	*Total*
Matrilocal[5]	38	3	1	43	85
Avunculocal[6]	12	0	0	1	13
Patrilocal[7]	14	202	23	74	313
Duopatrilocal[8]	0	2	1	0	3
Bilocal[9]	0	1	0	29	30
Duolocal[10]	3	1	0	0	4
Neolocal[11]	2	1	0	24	27
Uxoripatrilocal[12]	2	28	1	28	59
Uxorineolocal[13]	0	0	0	5	5
Uxoribilocal[14]	0	1	0	9	10
Viravunculocal[15]	9	0	1	1	11
Total	80	239	27	214	560

[1] Descent traced through mother.
[2] Descent traced through father.
[3] Ritual status from one parent, economic status from the other.
[4] All statuses inherited from both parents.
[5] Residence with wife's mother.
[6] Residence with male's mother's brother.
[7] Residence with husband's father.
[8] Residence alternating between wife's father and husband's father.
[9] Residence is based on a choice between husband's and wife's father.
[10] Residence with either wife's mother or husband's father.
[11] Residence in an entirely separate household.
[12] Residence with wife's father.
[13] Residence near the wife's family.
[14] Residence with wife's father or mother.
[15] Residence with father's brother.

*Source: Based on the World Ethnographic Sample.

people into the society. It is the common denominator of political, legal, and economic relationships.

If the *incest taboo* (rules prohibiting intercourse with blood relations) did not exist, according to Lévi-Strauss the biological would dominate the social, nature would dominate culture; societies would be broken into a multitude of mating couples isolated from effective relations with others. The incest taboo is less a rule which prevents one from marrying one's mother, sister, or daughter than a rule which obliges one to give one's mother, sister or daughter to others. It is the gift *par excellence,* submission to the norm of reciprocity. *Exogamy* (requirement that one marry outside some group, such as a family) is a permanent effort to establish a greater cohesion, a more effective solidarity and a more subtle evolution or social development. The woman becomes the standard value in the exchange but the exchange is worth more than the things exchanged. Exchange, and the rule of exogamy which stems from it, have a social value in themselves: they make it possible to tie men together, to superimpose ties of kinship regulated by rules which are henceforth social. Lévi-Strauss cites Margaret Mead who reports the commentary of an Arapesh informant responding, in an imaginary dialogue, to a friend who wants to marry his own sister: 'What! You want to marry your sister? What has come over you? Don't you want a brother-in-law? Don't you understand that if you marry the sister of another man and another man marries your sister, you will have at least two brothers-in-law and that if you marry your own sister, you won't have any? With whom will you go hunting? With whom will you plant your crops? Who will you have to visit?'* *Marriage is an exchange;* it is the archetype of exchange. It creates the ties without which man cannot rise above his biological organism to attain a social organization. Indeed, *exogamy and language serve the same function: communication with others and the integration of the group.*

Family and Industrial Society

We do not live in a traditional pre-literate society; we live in North American society, a modern world where technology based upon scientific knowledge has replaced simple techniques, where food is commercially produced, where machines supply energy and where the majority of the population lives in urban centers. These characteristics of modern society are accompanied by *structural differentiation: social units are more specialized and more autonomous,* thus changing the mode of

*Claude Lévi-Strauss, 'The Principle of Reciprocity,' in Coser and Rosenberg (eds.), *Sociological Theory.* Copyright© Macmillan Publishing Co., Inc., 1957.

integration. In this social and economic context, family organization cannot be largely synonymous with social organization as in small rural communities closer to an archaic type. The thesis is well known: *The family has lost most of its social functions but has become more exclusive and important in the ones that it does perform.* We will elaborate briefly on this theme:

(1) In subsistence and craft economies the family is the basic unit of production. With industrialization, the family becomes specialized in consumption.

(2) Mechanization brought about a division of labor in the family as well as in the society: the husband exchanges his labor for money, while the wife is expected to specialize in domestic tasks and in consumption.

(3) With the development of the school system, the family lost much of its function of teaching the young and procuring employment for its members (nepotism) because status became based upon competence.

(4) The family unit decreased from large and extended to small and nuclear.

As such, these statements are too simple, but they express the direction of change.

In short, the family, like religion, has receded from the public into the private sphere of life as work and family have become polarized. The family pattern which emerged in the Western world is the conjugal type. As pointed out above, Goode in his study of Islam, Africa, India, China,and Japan came to the conclusion that there is a world-wide trend toward the conjugal family as an ideal type (Goode, 1963). This is a process of orderly social change starting from different points and moving at different paces. This process involves privatization in which the family comes to specialize in the fulfillment of *affective* or emotional needs and in the socialization of small children. Within the family, the wife becomes specialized in affective support (an expressive role); the husband in relating the family to the society (an instrumental role). Parsons and Bales have argued that this form of family best 'fits' an industrial social structure. Since then, many have argued rather that this form of family corresponds to a transitional stage between a society based upon agriculture and a society based on industry (Sussman and Burchinal, 1962).

Family Structure and Systems of Property

Despite the trend toward conjugality, we find it almost impossible to speak of 'one family system.' We have already stated our theoretical position that because the basic goal of family activity is nurturing communication, the one structural invariant in families is a primary relationship between at least one adult and one child. Different family forms have evolved historically within the conjugal type because of differences in the interchange between this system and its environment. We will here develop the hypothesis that *family forms depend on the relationship of the family to property.*

Nimkoff, in his analysis of the 540 cultures included in Murdock's World Ethnographic Sample already referred to, discovered a rough relationship between type of family system and level of subsistence as well as amount of family property. The independent nuclear family system tends to predominate in hunting and gathering societies, the extended family system where there is a more ample and secure food supply (Nimkoff, 1965: 37).

In North American society, many comparative studies have shown that class, defined by some sort of ranking, differentiates family structures. Some years ago (1964), Farber formulated a typology that contrasted two types of relationships within families: an orderly succession of generations through transmission of family culture versus the permanent availability of the individual for different conjugal and family relations. On the one hand, regular transmission of family culture and property logically implies the predominance of the group over the individual, a central authority, effective means to control family members, family stability and rights of succession defined by law. Permanent availability, on the other hand, implies a predominance of the individual over the group, and a system which is open to many influences, having little to preserve. In a society that values personal achievement, staying together thus becomes less a question of control and more a question of personal commitment.

In this theoretical study, Farber had not specifically related his ideal family types to class position as defined by property. He did this later in a study comparing the upper class and the lower class kinship systems of midwestern American families (1971). He postulated that kinship ties lock the individual family into a network of relationships which sustain the class structure by inhibiting the upward mobility of the poor and maintaining the family culture and property of the rich. The two basic family forms of the two classes are linked structurally. Because the dominant form is the family geared to property, a counterform must develop which permits propertyless families to survive and to develop a rationale for remaining in the total social system. This adjustment of dominant values to lower class conditions has been referred to by Rodman (1963), who suggested that the lower class lives according to a pragmatic moralism without rejecting the dominant values of the society.

Three Ideal Family Types

Farber concludes that the lower class kinship organization is a response to an unfavorable social and economic environment. Taking this cue from Farber, we have elaborated three ideal types of families. These *ideal types* (mental constructs exaggerating the features of some social item) have been developed in relationship to three cumulative *goals* that different environments make possible for families (Trist, 1971).

Our ideal types represent three combinations of input and goal:

(1) In a poor environment, supplying only the minimum of energy, only the basic purpose of survival, growth to maturity and self-perpetuation can be realized; subsistence goals.

(2) In a rich environment, supplying a surplus of energy, additional goals incorporating the family into the society can be pursued; group goals.

(3) In an environment which supplies an abundance of information, given a minimum amount of resources, the members can have additional personal goals; individual goals.

These types are *ideal types in the Weberian sense:* they are *mental constructs*. They are not theory, but they can generate hypotheses, direct attention to certain aspects of reality and help integrate diverse data which otherwise would be random.

Type I: The Subsistence Goal and the Maternal Family

Every system aims at surviving. For the family this means providing food, clothing, and shelter for its members. The family also has the elementary goal of nurturing, bringing the infant to maturity. 'Men must eat to survive, and for most persons in their waking hours, activities associated directly or indirectly with the satisfaction of hunger are the most compelling, recurrent and time-consuming pursuits.' (Nimkoff, 1965)

The environment can be scarce in resources. This is the case either in a global society which has a subsistence economy or in a lower class position which restricts economic chances in a class society. In a poor environment, the family receives only a minimum energy input for self-maintenance. The main activities of the family will be related to the biological tasks of the creation and perpetuation of life. *La vie est un allaitement sans fin.* Every role is strongly associated with the nurturing function of 'mothering.' The myth which typifies this type of family is that of the 'good mother.' (Brodeur, 1971) The father is evaluated as a provider, a mother function. The mother transforms resources into food and clothing.

This type of family has been beautifully described by Hoggart (1954) in his study of lower class families in London. His study describes a popular culture that provides a good warm life for the persons involved. This life is founded on care, affection and a sense of membership in the small group (1954: 37). Sin is any act against the ideal of home and family, against the desire to keep the family together (1954: 32). The father is part of the inner life of the home, not someone who spends most of his time miles away. The mother always has too much to do and her thoughts revolve almost entirely around her family room (Hoggart, 1954: 37). These men and women are by no means heroes. Their life is a challenge and they cannot but live up to it.

Lower class daily life in punctuated with incantations: 'don't worry,' 'take it as it comes,' 'make yourself at home,' 'the more the merrier,' 'quand on est né pour un petit pain' or 's'enlever le pain de la bouche.' The persistence of these expressions does not prove that people believe them but they are reassuring and no one asks clearly whether they are valid. Pierre Des Ruisseaux (1971), for example, has made a complete inventory of the beliefs and *mores* which are prevalent among the lower class in French Canada. Their life seems to be made up of countless objects and acts which bring either good or bad luck.

In describing this culture, centered around the home and around a life which is at the same time simple and subtle, disorganized and balanced, and entirely motivated by sentiment, Hoggart and similar writers contradict the theory that middle class cultural models diffuse to the lower class through passive and servile imitation.

Gans proposed the same thesis in his study of a suburb of Boston inhabited by poor Italian immigrants (1962). Certainly as the standard of living and education increases and with massive diffusion of information, a society is evolving in which cultural differences between classes will be less clear-cut. However, working class culture and the kind of family found in it are active systems which reinterpret the new way of life in their own way and according to their own laws of change. In so far as they have been affected by modern conditions, they have changed along the 'lines on which their older traditions made them most open and undefined.' (Hoggart, 1954: 32)

Gans observed that sentiment ties members of this type of family together. In agreement with the myth the good mother is loved, but the bad mother is hated. If the mother fails in her nurturing function, those dependent upon her become hostile toward her because they are frustrated in their basic needs. If the father fails in his function as provider because he cannot keep a job, he may find the situation at home unbearable and be forced to leave, as Komarovsky noted in his analysis of the frustrating experience of unemployed men (1940).

Type II: Group Goals and the Patriarchal Family

'Beyond survival, men are greatly interested in comfort and power, which are not unrelated to the proliferation and accumulation of material goods.' (Nimkoff, 1965: 37) If the family lives in an environment that provides more resources than those needed for nurturing and maintenance, it will be able to develop *additional goals*. These will guide the transformation of the surplus energy or resources provided by the environment. The family will have plans for the future. These goals become a group project directed toward gaining social recognition, power, position, and property for the family. These are goals which must be accomplished outside the family *in society*. Symbolically, the father's role embodies this group project; the father defines the project and leads his family in realizing it. The mythical figure here becomes *the strong and wise father, the patriarch*. In real life, there is a social division of roles in the patriarchal family, the mother fulfilling the nurturing function and the father personifying the group project.

The plans incorporated into the group project are long-range and are related to family property, whether land, a family business in commerce or manufacturing, or holdings in stocks and bonds. The property base can be very large or relatively small. Thus this type of family may be found both in the upper class and in the middle class and in different kinds of societies at different epochs. For example, in Canada, the Molson family has been studied by A. Dubuc (1974). These entrepreneurial families make little distinction between family problems and business problems. Their fate is linked to the development of the economy: from land to trade, to manufacturing, to industry.

These families have characteristics in addition to the affective bond created by nurturing. Family cohesion is based on carrying out the group plan and conflict is usually a conflict of wills based upon different assessments of the relations between means and ends. It is likely to be rebellion against the patriarchal control implied by the realization of the group project.

THE CHANGING PATRIARCHAL FAMILY

However, a modern society is bureaucratic; the means of production and exchange are held anonymously by large trusts. A man's life usually consists of an orderly career in a large corporation. Can this career be defined as a group project? Can it still be the basis of family cohesion and organization? We propose that the characteristics of the family have been changed in the following way. Family property was highly visible and clearly associated with a name, but a salary has to be transformed into consumption in order to become visible and to distinguish a person and his family. The wife transforms the salary into visible consumption, not only in terms of food and clothing, which are taken for granted in this class, but also in terms of a broader life-style (Boudrillard, 1970). Social life, based upon visible consumption (e.g., housing), becomes the group project and the members become related to each other by the pleasure principle in addition to their quest for social placement. An inside view of the resulting family life has been provided by Seeley and his colleagues in their anthropological description of an upper class Toronto community called Crestwood Heights (1961).

The leadership of the father is normal in a family where the members are oriented toward a common goal: he co-ordinates individual efforts. However, who is the 'boss' in modern families where the mother specializes in transforming income into a style of life? Advertisers are well aware that women are responsible for 80 per cent of the purchases made and do not hesitate to direct their publicity to the female decision-maker. When Europeans write about America, they often draw the stereotype of an entrepreneurial, loud mother who makes all the decisions and runs the family. Americans (and Canadians), on the other hand, think of themselves as equalitarian because many household tasks are shared. The father, putting on an apron especially designed for him, washes the dishes or changes diapers. He washes the car while the mother does the ironing. Even if the mother does most of the shopping, decisions to buy, to entertain, or to take a vacation are made jointly. Americans present this kind of conjugal family as an ideal for other societies. It is the model held up in serial drama on television and projected from many advertisements depicting the fun morality of a leisure society.

We have seen that according to Parsons and Bales, there is a functional differentiation of roles in this type of family: The mother plays an affective-supportive role co-ordinating family activity whereas the father plays an instrumental role relating the family to the work situation. Scanzoni (1970), in a recent study, has reinterpreted this model of the division of labor in terms of exchange theory. In our societies, money is the exchange value *par excellence,* as were women in Lévi-Strauss' model of archaic societies. Scanzoni proposes that in the interplay between the work and the family subsystems, money is exchanged for affection. We conclude, however, that this seemingly egalitarian exchange-oriented family is in fact a patriarchal one in which the father directs plans for success not only in his own career but also in his wife's transformation of his income into conspicuous comsumption.

There are economic prerequisites for this kind of family. Chinoy described many years ago (1955) how the automobile worker redirects his mobility aspirations into the kind of private status gained by consumption. Whereas he has little chance of changing jobs, his income is likely to increase through union negotiations thus allowing him vicarious mobility through consumption. In this kind of situation where success is not related to a successful career but only to consumption, the wife has more opportunity to be dominant. We agree here with Scanzoni who concludes that 'the matrifocal family is the result of the husband's being almost totally blocked from the opportunity structure' (1970: 11) but one should not conclude that the opposite patrifocal structure is more desirable. In Scanzoni's model, the prerequisite for the ongoing exchange process is that the father has a relatively favored position in the opportunity structure. He either fails or succeeds in locating himself in a position with opportunities depending on the advantages he is given at birth.

Type III: Individual Plans and the Fraternal Family

We will be dealing here with a type that will emerge mainly among the better educated. We can postulate that technological development has made possible the 'take-off' from a subsistence economy to a more developed and diversified economy based on industrial production. Technological development and new information systems have produced an explosion of knowledge which is entensively and rapidly diffused. This leads to a contemporary cultural mutation, as proposed by Tiryakain (1967) and also Dumazedier (1970), in which the individual wants to assume that his own plans for personal development determine in part societal goals. In what has become a movement, youth, women, and the poor are fighting for their right to decide matters which affect them. It seems to us that this movement could affect family structures. People may try to co-ordinate their own personal goals with the common basic goal of nurturance and some family group project. Some of the family surplus (information, time, and money) in an economy of abundance can be allocated to the fulfillment of individual plans.

The dual career family, studied in England by the Rapoports (1971), is an example of this model. The husband and wife, both well-educated, have their own careers and they pool resources in nurturing the children. A career, however, could be any type of project for personal development or social participation and not simply a paid job.

Some communes could be classified as fraternal families in as much as they are built around the co-ordination of personal projects in addition to the nurturing of children. Their goals would be different from the Hutterite community, for example, which is in fact a group family project, oriented to a collective rather than individual goal.

However, cohesion is problematic in this system because each member has a strong attachment to his own project. Only belief in common values can work as a cohesive force. Exchange of experience through informal communication must be frequent. In this type of family, children soon develop their own independent projects, and are likely to move out on their own sooner than in other family types.

Social Placement or Socialization for a Role

The family, as a system, is controlled by its relation with the outside. We have suggested that its structure is largely determined by the type of environmental input. In addition, like every other system, it must produce *an output* that is acceptable to its surroundings. An example will illustrate what we mean. A social worker attached to a Montreal juvenile court recently investigated the case history of a young boy, aged thirteen, who had spent two years in detention because he continually dropped out of school. She found that he belonged to a family where the mother was warm and loving and the father was a good provider in a somewhat fringe occupation where he was helped by the older sons. Although they all gave lip service to formal education, they created an atmosphere in which the boy felt more comfortable at home than at school. *This family functions well as a unit but does not produce an output which conforms to the society's minimum requirement of schooling.* We find a similar problem at the other end of the social scale in the children of the well-to-do who refuse to maintain the family's social level. They drop out of school long before they have attained the level that is needed to fulfill their parents' high aspirations and desires to maintain the family's social status. They do not see the point of preparing themselves for a competitive career in the 'rat race.' If numerous enough, they may form a dynamic counterculture (Roszak; 1969) where sons and daughters will not inherit their parents' social position even though they benefit from it. But these cases are exceptions to the rule, located at the extremes of the social scale. In general, the family is highly influential in social placement, in bringing its children to have the socially appropriate idea of sex roles and professional aspirations.

Many studies report class differences in child socialization practices. Kohn (1969) relates these differences not only to parental values but also to class defined not in terms of education or income but as differences in occupational environment. 'Middle class occupations characteristically deal more with the manipulation of interpersonal relations, ideas and symbols, while working class occupations deal more with physical objects. Middle class occupations are likely to be free of close supervision, while working class occupations are more subject to standardization and direct supervision. In short, middle class occupations demand a greater degree of self-direction; working class occupations require that the individual conform to rules and procedures established by authority.'*

A Canadian study illustrates this point poignantly by showing that socialization practices changed when Newfoundland fishermen abandoned their occupation which required a high degree of self-control and judgment. When the parents were fishermen, they were extremely permissive, except when a child showed a flaw in his reality assessment at sea which could mean his death. When the ex-fishermen became workers, they began to demand conformity to social norms of their sons who would not work with and succeed them.

Kohn concludes that social class, as defined by occupation, is consistently related to fathers' values for their children (1969: 71). By comparing the American data with data gathered in Turin, France, he also found that differences between classes are more significant than differences between societies. In short, self-direction is associated with an orientation in which one feels one can do what one sets out to do, whereas conformity is associated with an orientation in which one is conscious of the dangers of 'stepping out of line.' (Kohn, 1969: 87) People who live at a subsistence level are afraid of the environment. In an archaic society they are afraid of nature; in the lower class of modern society they are afraid of the dominant middle class society.

There are results consistent with Kohn's theory. Lower class parents are more apt to use physical punishment whereas middle class parents rely more on 'reasoning, isolation, appeals to guilt, and other methods of involving the threat of less love.' (Bronfenbrenner, 1958) Lower class parents are known to be more authoritarian, which is consistent with their desire to maintain the obedience that leads to conformity.

In summary, Kohn's analysis shows that there is coherence between class, perceived as an environment, values, defined as constructs of this environment, and parental behavior, seen here in terms of preparation for social roles. The school usually reinforces the development toward the place in society defined by the family. Children from homes that are well-equipped with all kinds of resources (books, records, educational games, and conversations about a broad range of subjects) usually go to schools that are also well-equipped both with human and material resources. The content and methods of teaching in these schools also produce a 'middle class' and 'proper' product. Children from deprived families can hardly function in this environment (Minuchin, 1967), and children from the lower class soon learn that it is not intended for them.

*Melvin Kohn, *Class and Conformity: A Study of Values* (Homewood, Ill.: The Dorsey Press, 1969).

In the first grades, there is only a low relationship, in the same school, between school performance and class of origin. The difference between children from different classes widens with every additional year, as the school system reinforces original differences between self-images and opportunities. A child enters school for the first time with hopes for success, even if these are tempered with fear. But the specific talents of the lower class child are not valued and with the experience of failure he retreats into a negative image of himself.

Even if equipment were as good in a school in a poor neighborhood as in a rich one, there would still be discrimination if the content of the curriculum was not tailored to the needs of the milieu and the methods of teaching did not rely on the specific talents of the children, which are not verbal. While they do not learn to count, read or even hold a pencil at home, they are superior to their middle class peers in their responsibility for themselves and their younger siblings when their parents are absent. They also excel in 'ghetto' (or slum) survival. (See Chapter Five.)

Many studies have shown a relationship between the student's choice of a career and parental values (a good summary to be found in Osipov, 1968). For example, in Holland's (1966) study of the American national merit sample of 1950, each father ranked nine goals for his child and stated his hopes for his child's eventual income. The boys themselves were categorized according to the content of their aspirations. The results indicate that fathers of boys whose aspirations were realistic valued ambition in their sons and hoped their income would be considerable. Fathers of boys in the intellectual category (scientific career) valued curiosity. Fathers of boys who had an interest in the social sciences valued self-control. Fathers of the boys in the enterprising group wished happiness, adjustment and popularity for their sons. And fathers of boys in the artistic category valued curiosity and independence. Results for daughters were in the same general directions. Ginzberg concluded, in a limited study of Barnard College sophomores, that girls are much more influenced by their fathers than by their non-working mothers in their vocational aspirations (results reported in Osipov, 1968: 54 and 78). Kandel and Lesser (1969) have found that adolescents are more influenced by their parents than by their peers in their plans for the future.

Sex roles, also to be played in the larger society, are first learned at home. Parents teach their children the elementary grammar of cultural models. This process is too well-known to be developed. Differences in the way they are dressed, in the toys they are given, in the reasons they are complimented or reprimanded, mould boys' and girls' personalities differently. Opposite qualities are stressed for boys and girls: carefulness and sensitivity for girls, creativity and initiative for boys. Boys and girls are given tasks around the home which reproduce the sexual division of labor. Boys and girls of sixteen and seventeen have strongly interiorized the cultural image of their sex role. They have a stronger impression of the cultural image of their own sex than of that of the opposite sex. In a recent study of the sex role perception of Montreal French secondary students, it was found that:

> ... boys and girls (N: 379) say that the woman is more sensitive (90% boys, 91% girls), that she has more aesthetic feeling (78% and 79%) and that she is more altruistic (66% and 78%), and that the man is more egotistical (56% and 63%). However, there are conceptual differences on certain personality traits where each sex has a tendency to amplify its own stereotypes. The woman is more reserved (65% boys, 77% girls), the man is more self-sufficient (75% and 48%) and more logical (58% and 35%). In addition, boys see topics of discussion (84% and 68%) and scholastic aptitudes (64% and 48%) as more discrete.

> Most boys adhere more easily than girls to the ideology of the social supremacy of men. Thus, they are more likely to diminish the importance of the pursuit of advanced studies for women (68% and 44%), to consider that given equal competence it is better to vote for a man as a deputy (57% and 36%) and that men make better surgeons, lawyers and doctors (59% and 40%).

> They agree strikingly with regard to family roles ... For a large number of students (84% boys, 86% girls) the wife should cook and clean the house and the husband should take care of the economic needs of the family. They also consider (90% and 88%) that a woman who has children is happier at home than working.*

Just as the school reinforces the family's initial influence toward reproducing this class system in our society, it strengthens sexual segregation and division of labor. In the secondary schools, girls are oriented toward professions that are extensions of their family nurturing and servicing functions: nursing, social work, secretarial work, and lab technology. They are not encouraged to choose a curriculum with math or science. (Komarovsky, 1964)

To be sure, women have attained near parity with men at the four-year bachelor's level in colleges and universities in the U.S.A. and Canada. However, the proportion of women graduates goes down notably when one goes successively from B.A. to M.A. and from M.A. to Ph.D. In 1968,

---

*Robert Ménard, 'Hétérosexualité d'étudiants de onzième année.' Master's thesis, University of Montreal, 1972.

one doctorate in seven was granted to a woman in Quebec, one in ten in Ontario and one in eight in U.S.A. Women continue to be largely a minority group in the scientific fields in spite of their increased presence in the university in general. (See Table XII.)

Extra-Boundary Relations

We will now describe more specifically the interaction between the family and its milieu. We will consider the nuclear family as a group with boundaries, asking ourselves what kind of interaction it has with kin and the wider society.

Relations with Kin

In every type of family, the nuclear unit, consisting of parent(s) and offspring, is clearly identifiable. In order to measure the closeness between the nuclear family and relatives, we can construct a continuum with two poles: total integration and total isolation. The preliterate society is close to the pole of total integration. As we have pointed out, according to Lévi-Strauss, in such societies the family is commensurate with the society (1957). Rights and duties are clearly defined for the living and the dead. Rules of avoidance are specific, and people expect to be punished if they transgress them. In traditional societies, somewhat removed from the integration pole but where social differentiation is low, the corporate kin is the preferred ideal. Goode concludes that 'when an individual attained sufficient wealth and social standing, he succeeded in creating and maintaining a large assemblage of kin under his leadership ... but we must also avoid exaggerating the ties of the extended family which preceded the modern conjugal family. It seems empirically clear that prior to the modern era in the Western world, and in all the cultures that I have been examining, several generations of one family did not live under the same roof.'*

Even if we have no accurate data describing the situation of fifty years ago, we are certain that industrialization and urbanization have changed the way the contemporary family interacts with relatives. Wirth described the isolation of the nuclear family as part of 'urbanism as a way of life.' (1938) For a time, Parsons and Bales' theory that the isolation of the nuclear family is functional for geographical and social mobility was widely accepted. It is now evident that *less overlap and looser*

---

*W. J. Goode, *World Revolution and Family Patterns*, p. 371. Copyright © Macmillan Publishing Co., Inc., 1963.

integration with the kinship structure does not necessarily mean total isolation of the nuclear unit. It is sheer ideology that being born into a certain family and bearing a certain name do not determine one's status.

There is a rather general kinship norm in industrial societies: be helpful and keep in touch. This norm is reciprocal and the strongest rights and obligations are between parents and children. The fourth commandment, 'honor thy father and mother,' is not translated into specific rules except for certain rituals during the Christmas season or on the occasion of marriage, birth or death. Thus regular patterns of behavior have to be discovered and justified. Sussman (1968) has suggested that activities shared by related families provide economic and emotional well-being. Since participation is largely voluntary, it competes with other voluntary organizations. 'The kin network is one of several alternative social structures and becomes preferred when it provides real or perceived pay-offs for participating individuals superior to those offered by other social institutions. But, it is likely that participants cannot totally withdraw from the tradition and commitment laden relationship of the nuclear family and related kin.'*

Since one chooses one's mate oneself, independently of one's relatives and since a family is held together by the conjugal bond, kinship ties can either threaten or help the individual unit. If kinship contacts support the nuclear family, it becomes less concerned with maintaining its exclusiveness and relaxes its boundaries. If kinship contacts threaten the nuclear family, it emphasizes its separateness. Research on the cultural orientation of bi-ethnic marriages in Montreal reveals such a pattern. In these marriages, a choice must be made between the French and English cultures, especially where alternatives are mutually exclusive as in the language of the children's school. Generally, the culture of the male and of the English spouse were favored. In couples where the husband is English, roles are clear-cut: there is an overall winner (English/male) and an overall loser (French/female). However, the situation where the husband is French and the wife is English is highly conflictive because each spouse is a loser and a winner on different grounds. The adaptive reaction of these couples was precisely to close the system's boundaries. They considerably lowered the amount of interaction with relatives because relations with them could disturb their precarious cultural accommodations (Carisse, 1966).

Bert Adams (1970) has extensively reviewed the research on kinship in the United States done in the 1960's. Here are a few highlights. One fact stands out clearly: the level of interaction with relatives is quite high.

*M.B. Sussman, 'Directive and Integrative Behavior in Today's Family,' *Family Process*, 7:2 (1968), 245.

For example in three different studies conducted in urban centers of the United States, the proportion of respondents who interacted with relatives about once a week ranged from 33 to 67 per cent (Axelrod, 1956: Greer, 1956; Bell and Boat, 1957). In the San Francisco study (Bell and Boat, 1957), 42 per cent interacted once a week, 25 per cent more than once a month, 25 per cent occasionally and 8 per cent never. A recent Finnish study also found that nearly every respondent, in all communities, maintained some interaction with his parents and siblings. There were variations in the effective contacts maintained only with regard to more distant relatives (Stolte, Heiskanen, 1967: 39).

If isolation is rare, so is separation. Most family members live close together even if mobility is the accepted myth in a highly industrialized society where one is expected to follow job opportunities from coast to coast. All research results show that to a surprisingly high degree, North Americans live near their relatives. About 62 per cent of the 2,567 old people studied by Shanas (1968) had either a son or a daughter within walking distance. Most of Reiss' (1962) middle class respondents had at least a few relatives in the Boston area. Sixty-eight per cent of the fifty-eight blue collar couples in Komarovsky's (1964) sample of a New York City suburb had parents living in the community and only 7 per cent lived further than two hours by car from their parents. Leichter and Mitchell (1967) found that 86 per cent of their New York Jewish families had 16 or more relatives living in the same area. Sweetser (1969), in a well-documented study of the Finnish family studied the degree to which siblings live near each other in relation to whether or not they had migrated. She found that migrants to town live near each other slightly more frequently. She also found that mobility, whether geographical or social, is a family characteristic. It explains variations not accounted for by the occupation of the father or the level of education of the mobile person.

However, research has uncovered an asymmetry in kinship relations in urban industrial societies, *most ties being matrilateral* (mother's relatives). Adams points out (1970) the factors in the trend toward matrilaterality. First, women participate more in kinship relations; they know more relatives and consider them more important. Second, mother-daughter ties are close. Third, the daughter has a close relationship with both parents.

It may be argued that this 'kinkeeper' role is functional to the performance of female domestic roles. That one maintains kinship relations because they are functional to work performance also explains that Sweetser (1969) found, in Finland, that male farmers have more contact with relatives than do their wives. These contacts help them perform farm work. The relationship between work and kinship relations changes in urban industrialized societies. In these societies, there is a sharp division between the public and private life of an individual. Ideologically, the family is identified with privacy and privacy is the realm of women. Women adapt to these rules of the game by being more active in kinship relations. But they have not necessarily created these rules. Men react to them just as much by forming in-groups in the public sphere. According to Lionel Tiger (1969), in-groupness allows one to maintain power and authority and is identified with work and maleness.

Since the type of work and the closeness of kinship ties are related, we are led to investigate the influence of kin on nuclear family behavior. In the early 1960's, Litwak (1960a, 1960b) was the first to challenge the notion that the family was exclusively a nuclear unit by pointing out that the mobility of urban city dwellers was substantially helped by relatives. Current research is uncovering what is being exchanged in these relationships; money, help, advice, emotional support, and more jobs for relatives (nepotism) than we like to admit. In the common three-generation family, the middle generation is in a postion to give more both to its parents and to its children.

Most research reports that lower class families have relatively more contact with a wider group of relatives than middle class families. This is consistent with Farber's (1971) hypothesis that the lower class family is more open to kin because these provide the family resources in time of crisis. Ethnic or regional minorities also interact with kin more frequently for much the same reasons. The members of the middle class pay lip service to the norm that kin are important but keeping in touch seems to satisfy them. Furthermore, even when kinship relations are intense in the middle class, they are only part of a generally more extensive pattern of social participation in formal organizations as well as in informal friendship networks. The real question is this: *What is the relative importance of kin as opposed to other sources of influence such as friends, the information media and formal organizations?*

Family and Social Network

At this point, we can add further elements to the three ideal types of family developed earlier. We proposed that when energy input from the environment is low, the system's goal can hardly rise above maintenance and the basic mothering relationships of nurture. This family is home-centered and relatives are accepted because they are relatives. Friends are drawn into the private pole of life and treated as part of the family. The relationships with kinship networks are determined by the goals of the system: relatives are potential sources of support, both affective and material, for the survival of the individual family group. It is functional to extend membership.

A second type of family can evolve when the environment provides a surplus. A group project becomes an additional goal which directs group behavior and locates the family in the power structure through the father's activity. This is why we labelled this type 'paternal.' Kinship and friendship relations are structured according to the requirements of the group project just as are nuclear family relations. They are related to the exterior goal of the family and they derive their meaning from the requirements of the work and career of the father and the social placement of the children. The members are attracted less to the home than to life in society and their concern is with the family's place in it.

We proposed that because the culture of post-industrial societies places a high value on personal development and creativity, a third type of family, the fraternal family, where individual goals are served by the family context, might develop. Meaningful communication is another value of post-industrial society. People seemingly rediscover the pleasure of communicating for its own sake. Their relationships are not instrumental but ends in themselves. We thus suggest that an intermediary zone between the private world of the family and the public world of work is developing, at least for families of the fraternal type and for families that have rejected consumption as a family project. Their relationships are based on a consensus which is possible because they are selective. A new concept will have to be introduced: *intimacy*. It is halfway between the privacy of love, hate, or parental devotion on the one hand, and the rationality and instrumentality of relations in the bureaucratic, public sphere, on the other.

This type is not purely hypothetical. One can find concrete examples of it in the contemporary communes which are neither families, as we know them, nor work groups. They are in essence 'communes,' that is, they are based on shared characteristics which are the basis of consensus. Because they are elective, not ascribed, relations are characterized by 'intimacy.' While they are not families, they provide the social environment in which fraternal families can develop. Nor are they modern versions of the extended family because relations are based on shared interest, not on a group goal. Their members determine their own goals rather than have them ascribed to them. However, the various versions of communes are only one concrete form of the intermediary zone of intimacy proposed here. This zone does not need a material base, even if it is likely to express itself in some overt form of informal organization. Figure 1 gives a picture of the differences between family system boundaries in the different ideal types we have been constructing.

Marie Letellier (1971) has vividly described an example of the first type of family, an intimate primary group of relatives with close peer ties along sex and age-group lines. The French Canadian family in a neighborhood of Montreal that she describes resembles the families studied by Gans. According to him, networks of personal relations in the lower class are essentially peer-oriented. Many studies suggest that this is a fairly universal phenomenon in working class groups.

> At marriage a new peer group is formed, consisting of family members and a few friends of each spouse. This group meets after working hours for long evenings of sociability. Although the members of the group are of both sexes, the normal tendency is for the men and women to split up, the men in one room and the women in another.... The mainstay of the adult peer group society is the *family circle* ... made up of bilateral kin: in-laws, siblings, and cousins predominantly.... Family members come together if they are roughly of the same age, socio-economic level, and cultural backgrounds. The hold of the peer group on the individual is very strong ... Each of the marriage partners is pulled out centrifugally toward his or her peers, as compared with the middle class family in which a centripetal push brings husband and wife closer together ... Peer groups are found in all classes, but in the middle and upper class, they play a less important role, especially among adults. In the lower-middle class, for example, peer groups are made up of neighbors and friends, and exist alongside the nuclear family, but usually they do not include members of the family circle. Moreover, dependence on the peer group for sociability and mutual aid is much weaker. In the lower-middle class, and more so in the upper-middle class, people move in a larger number of peer groups, often formed to pursue specific interests and activities. The West End Pattern, of *one* peer group, is not found here. Consequently, the influence of the peer group on the life of the middle class is much less intense.*

We similarly found that working class families in Montreal have a social life that includes mostly (and sometimes exclusively) members of the family: aunts and uncles, brothers and sisters and also cousins (Carisse, 1964 and 1966). M.A. Tremblay (1971) has also described what seems to be a perfect example of a closed community, French Bay, Nova Scotia. Until the nineteen-fifties, this community had lived in isolation with a self-sufficient economy, well above the poverty level, which supported a perfectly balanced family organization in which all social and religious activities took place.

We found the type II family, with emphasis on nuclear family boundaries or identity, largely in the middle class. Here the family as a nuclear group is strongly identified and family activities are highly valued. The people who plan advertisements know this well. They picture the middle class family (with two children in the 1970's as opposed to three in the 1960's) living happily in their carpeted living room, cruising

---

*Herbert J. Gans, *The Urban Villagers: Group and Class in the Life of Italian Americans,* p. 243. Copyright © Macmillan Publishing Co., Inc., 1962.

Figure 1: Three Types of Boundaries for a Family System Typology

(Note: The double line represents the boundaries of the basic system.)

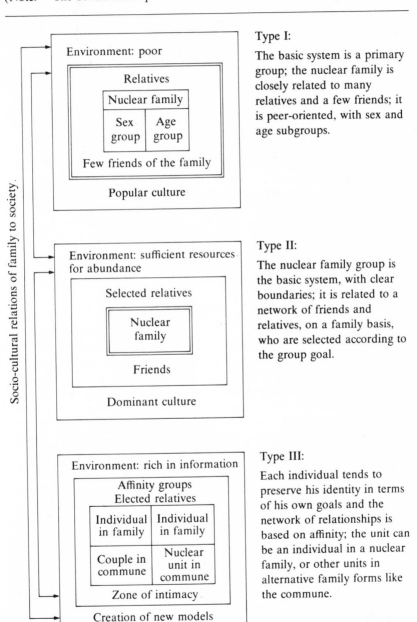

Type I:

The basic system is a primary group; the nuclear family is closely related to many relatives and a few friends; it is peer-oriented, with sex and age subgroups.

Type II:

The nuclear family group is the basic system, with clear boundaries; it is related to a network of friends and relatives, on a family basis, who are selected according to the group goal.

Type III:

Each individual tends to preserve his identity in terms of his own goals and the network of relationships is based on affinity; the unit can be an individual in a nuclear family, or other units in alternative family forms like the commune.

in their new car, or sharing the pleasures of outdoor sports. Professional families in particular include more friends than relatives in their social activities (Carisse, 1964).

In the absence of research, type III communality is harder to depict precisely because the common interest that is shared and the individual goals pursued are quite diverse. Generally, an example could be the co-operative relations formed in many student co-ops.

The Family as a Social Context

We have seen how the family relates to its environment; we will now see how the family system provides an environment, or social context, for its members. The family, as a system in action, has to solve several basic problems. Bell (1971) has proposed that these fall into three dimensions:

(1) *Accomplishment,* or progress or achievement in a given direction. If the essence of interaction within the family is some sharing of attitudes and aspirations, then the meaningfulness which the interaction has for the actors is an index of the degree of goal accomplishment.

(2) *Individuation,* or the ability of the group to stimulate and tolerate distinctiveness in its members.

(3) *Routinization,* or predictability in the behavior of the group's members so that they can act together smoothly.

A family which survives will have solved a number of opposing demands: continuity of goals, yet toleration of innovation brought about by a necessary diversity; stability of behavior, yet mobility that permits individual adaptation to changing inputs; co-operation for achieving group goals, yet independence to achieve individual plans. We will have a better understanding of family life if we do not postulate consensus and harmony as the basis of stability, marital adjustment, and communication between generations. A better conceptual framework is to look at the family as a *negotiated order* between members with conflicting interests.

The most important characteristic of the family from the perspective of an enduring small group is emotional involvement in the group as a whole and in its various subgroups. This involvement gives the individual feelings of belonging, of security and of being loved. These are basic needs of 'psychic survival.' (Maslow, 1954) However, either lack or excess of these feelings can degenerate into violence and hate (Goode, 1971; Strauss, 1971). The anti-psychiatry movement has made this point very clearly (see mainly the work of Laing and Cooper, among others). The organization of the system may become over-rigid as a result of its past functioning. It fails to create alternative behaviors in the face of new challenges (inputs). This is particularly important in periods of transition when the environment is changing rapidly and in societies where individuals themselves are expected to develop throughout their life. The family as a social context can thus either favor the personal development and self-fulfillment of its members or it can frustrate these. If it does the latter, it is useless to look for a scapegoat, whether a difficult child, an unloving mother or an absent father. The system *per se,* or the interpersonal structure it has evolved over time, is where to look for the explanation of so-called 'pathological' behavior.

Furthermore, a family's equilibrium is never permanently reached. As the family system develops over time it has to be redefined constantly. Its goals have to be reassessed. The developmental approach proposed by Hill and Rodgers (1964) points out precisely that a family moves through different cycles defined as role configurations. They argue that levels of maturity have to be attained at each life cycle in order to move successfully to the next one.

In families, as in every small group, basic problems are solved through communication of information and decision-making. We will first deal separately with these two processes. Then we will deal with two facets of the process of becoming socialized and its opposite pathology.

Communication as Family Dynamics

A basic principle agreed on by students of small group interaction is that all communication has two components: *information* (i.e., directed toward goal accomplishment) and *emotion* (i.e., directed towards persons). These two facets of communication are always present, but in any single unit of interaction one or the other clearly dominates. However, researchers have found that information and emotion are not clearly distinguishable in family interaction and that the reliability of direct observation of family interaction is dangerously low. This is because 'the character of family life is such that the degree of affective involvement on the part of its members is probably more intense than in any other system.' (Lennard and Bernstein, 1970: 91) This situation is further complicated by the fact that, unlike most other systems, the family includes members of different generations. We should thus not be surprised that we find that the types and frequencies of communication within the family differ from other primary groups. Research shows first that families express more conflict and disagreement in general and second that they have more expressive acts, or communications directed at persons and expressing sentiments, than any other primary group.

Decisions as Family Process

The family is an ongoing pattern of interactions that are not carried on at random but are highly structured. This ongoing organization is the context of daily lives made up of hundreds of details, each requiring a decision. What to cook for dinner and who will wash the dishes? If we have extra money, should we buy a new model car or a washing machine? If there is an unexpected dentist's bill, should we cut the food or the vacation budget? How late can the children come in at night and how many evenings a week can they stay out late? Should girls and boys have the same or different rules? These are only a few of the well-known (and caricatured) issues to be decided upon in a family context. In fact, family life is a complex of informal decisions.

These decisions are a function of a delicate distribution of power and influence and of subtle bargaining and exchange processes which are extremely difficult to measure, as Turk and Bell (1972) have well established in their Toronto research.

Of course, family communication, like other activities, is highly routinized. Probabilities of what will be done in a given situation can be established by observing families. This type of patterning into an organized system is going on unconsciously. Exchange of information is a preliminary part of the decision process if the decision is to be rational and optimize individual satisfaction.

Decisions may change the system in a variety of ways. Some groups (or individuals) will decide according to past experience and their choices will therefore be highly determined as in systems that have only a memory with no imagination of the future.

The type I families are most likely to be traditional or conformist. Their low access to new information does not favor a habit of decision-making other than following habitual formulae. Because these families are person-oriented, they are reluctant to engage in the discussion necessary to explore alternatives for action. Since their members are non-competitive among themselves, no one would dare show the necessary competence for innovation. If they are moving to a pathological state, these families will show a tendency for early closure, thus making ineffective decisions (Reiss, 1971).

The type II families will more easily explore alternatives because they are more object-oriented. Because they communicate more information, they will more easily judge alternatives according to the system's goal (family project) and shared values. Their position in the society exposes them more to new information which they can use because they are more open to change and able to innovate. On the other hand, the dominance of the family project as a criterion for choice may very well curb the expression of individual needs so that a new criterion for choice will be established only with great difficulty.

In type III families, individual projects (by definition in the model) are superimposed on the group goal. Reformist or innovative decision-making is thus more probable in this type, and revolutionary decisions are possible, based on individuals' bringing new values into the system. However, some conflict in values is probable and there must be a negotiated order if the group is not to break up.

Socialization as a Family Process

Socialization is usually defined as the process of learning a set of norms and values associated with behavior in a certain position. The agent 'teaches' the norms through an interplay of positive and negative controls, namely punishment for bad behavior and rewards for good behavior. Parents are usually conceived as agents, and the children as recipients. The role of socialization is to give the child a social definition of his 'self.' Through it, the child acquires basic skills and habitual behavior. Moreover, socialization is a life-long interaction between the individual and his socio-cultural environment. The family should also be viewed as an exchange relationship, with the child not merely the passive object of socialization. In this sense, we could say that an infant 'teaches' his mother to love. Of course, the mother can learn the proper way to handle a new-born baby in books, but behaving as a mother is *not* reproducing a norm. It means experiencing a process of communication and exchange of information.

For the infant, the 'mother' represents the total environment which is only later enlarged to include the rest of the family. We know that in some animals the very first image determines a fixed reaction in given circumstances. This is known as 'imprinting.' A human being is too flexible to be so determined but we can easily accept Rokeach's hypothesis that the child's experience in the first year gives him a lasting image of the environment as either hostile or co-operative. A hostile environment will not adapt to the child's needs and behavior whereas a co-operative one will answer the child's behavior with messages that can be recognized and are acceptable. A co-operative environment will be 'conversational' (Berger, 1970). When we defined nurturing communication as a basic function of the family we meant precisely that it provides the context in which this self-organizing, self-adapting dialogue takes place.

This approach to 'socialization' seems necessary to us in order to refute the generally accepted notion that the only important aspect of socialization is its content, the culture, and that parents are responsible for transmitting this culture to the children in a one-way process of influence. Skills, images, wisdom, and also stereotypes are transmitted from one generation to another. What we wanted to stress here, is that the family is the first milieu where communication is experienced. It is the first context where an infant will learn to exchange information in a meaningful way. This is the first skill that a human being must learn, as we have pointed out. And it is the one function of the family that cannot be taken over by other organizations.

Family in North America

It is easy to predict the 'death of the family,' especially when one does not have to specify the context in which human beings will be born and live (cf. David Cooper, 1971). A more realistic approach is to ask ourselves if there is any trend toward *change*. We can do this by comparing contemporary societies which represent different levels of development, and also by observing trends over a few decades. Using census data, we will compare the Province of Quebec, which has recently emerged from a traditional past, the Province of Ontario, which is the most developed of the Canadian provinces, and the U.S.A., the first 'new nation' of the world where a post-industrial society is at hand in many regions. In general, we observe that the continuum Quebec-Ontario-U.S.A. follows the 1951-1961- 1971 trend. This means that in the absence of an abrupt change, or specific policy that would curb the trend, the U.S.A.'s near future represents the future state of Canadian society. In this short analysis, we will ask ourselves if the family and the impact of living in a conjugal unit for most individuals is receding as the unique model of private behavior.

Conjugality

All statistics pertinent to marriage indicate that conjugality as a way of life is slightly diminishing. This statement is based on the following observations, from Statistics Canada data. The American statistics are taken from Ferris' Indicators of Change in the American Family and Indicators of Change in the Position of Women.

(a) The number of marriages per 1,000 persons is diminishing in the long run. The increases in the period 1961 to 1964 (Ontario and U.S.A.) and 1966 to 1968 (Quebec) may be explained by the fact that the cohorts of the high birth rates following the depression have arrived at marriage age (Table III).

(b) The median age at first marriage is decreasing and this is true more for men than women, thus diminishing the age gap between

Table III: Marriage Rate, USA, Ontario, Quebec, for Selected Years

(Total marriages per 1,000 unmarried women 15-44 years of age)

Year	USA	Ontario	Quebec
1951	164.9	148.8	92.4
1956	165.6	151.8	93.6
1961	145.4	132.8	83.1
1966	145.0	125.5	86.6
1968	146.6	128.9	85.0

Table IV: Median Age at First Marriage, USA, Ontario, Quebec, for Selected Years

Year	USA		Ontario		Quebec	
	Male	Female	Male	Female	Male	Female
1951	23.7	21.1	24.4	21.9	25.1	22.6
1961	22.9	19.8	23.8	21.0	24.6	21.8
1966	22.3	20.1	23.5	20.9	24.1	21.9
1968	22.1	20.4	23.3	21.2	24.0	21.9
1970	—	—	23.4	21.3	24.0	22.1

Table V: Percentage Married Persons, by Sex, USA, Ontario, Quebec, for Selected Years

Year	USA				ONTARIO		QUEBEC	
	Male		Female		Male	Female	Male	Female
	white	non–white	white	non–white				
1951	71.1	64.1	67.2	62.0	68.8	68.7	61.9	60.8
1961	69.6	62.0	66.8	60.9	69.9	69.2	62.8	61.6
1966	68.9	59.0	65.0	58.3	68.1	67.0	61.9	60.3
1968	68.9	59.8	64.2	54.6	67.7	66.4	67.7	60.2

Table VI: Percentage Two-Parent Families, USA, Ontario, Quebec, for Selected Years

Year	USA	Ontario	Quebec
1951	86.8	90.5	90.0
1956	86.8	91.9	91.1
1961	87.2	92.1	91.3
1966	87.2	92.2	91.5
1968	86.9	—	—

Table VII: Percentage One-Person Households, USA, Ontario, Quebec, for Selected Years

Year	USA	Ontario	Quebec
1951	11.6	6.5	4.5
1956	12.9	7.4	5.0
1961	15.3	9.0	7.0
1966	17.1	10.9	9.0
1968	17.7	—	—

spouses. This may be interpreted as an increased value placed on the conjugal situation which facilitates communication between spouses (Table IV).

(c) In the overall population, the proportion of married persons has decreased slightly, in spite of a temporary increase in 1961 in Canada only (Ontario and Quebec). This trend may be clearly indentified in the U.S.A., whether we take men or women as a basis for comparison (Table V).

(d) There are fewer marriages but people are getting married younger. These two trends are compatible with an increase in the rate of divorce in all three societies. This explains that in the case of single parent families, this person is more often than before someone who is separated rather than widowed.

(e) But generally, the proportion of complete families (father, mother, and children) is very stable in the U.S.A. and is on the increase in

Ontario and Quebec. In nine cases out of ten, children do live with two married adults, whether both or only one of them are their parents (Table VI).

(f) One of the significant trends is the marked and general increase of households of one person, both young and old, men and women. In the U.S.A. one out of five domiciles is inhabited by one person. In Canada, this proportion is one out of ten. We can therefore state that the unmarried more frequently live independently of their family of origin, if they are young, and of their family of procreation, if they are old (Table VII).

Fecundity

It is apparent that there has been a phenomenal decrease in birth rates in Canada. In Quebec for example, the natality rate which had always been superior to that of Ontario has become inferior since 1956 (in 1971, 15.3 per cent in Quebec and 17.6 per cent in Ontario). This decrease is

Table VIII: Live Birth Rates per 1,000 Females, USA, Ontario, Quebec, for Selected Years

Year and Mother's Age Group	USA White	USA Non-white	Ontario	Quebec
1951				
20–24	206.0	252.5	186.4	176.0
25–29	174.2	184.2	181.3	217.3
15–44 (total)	107.7	142.1	99.8	117.2
1961				
20–24	247.9	292.9	239.3	198.6
25–29	194.4	221.9	211.6	216.8
15–44 (total)	112.2	153.5	108.3	108.6
1968				
20–24	162.6	200.8	155.1	128.2
25–29	139.7	144.8	145.0	137.5
15–44 (total)	81.5	114.9	71.7	68.0
1970				
20–24	—	—	150.1	112.0
25–29	—	—	147.5	130.3
15–44 (total)	—	—	71.8	59.5

Table IX: Global Rate of Illegitimate Births, USA, Ontario, Quebec, for Selected Years

Year	White	USA Non–white	Ontario	Quebec
1951	7.9	87.2	1.24	.94
1961	10.5	100.8	1.61	1.13
1968	12.5	89.5	1.94	1.29

Table X: Rate of Illegitimate Births for Selected Age Groups, USA, Ontario, Quebec, 1968

Age Group	White	USA Non–white	Ontario	Quebec
15–19	9.0	80.2	47.9	29.7
20–24	23.1	128.2	38.0	38.3
25–29	22.7	118.4	8.9	12.7
30–34	14.0	97.2	3.4	6.1

particularly dramatic in French Canada because large families were highly valued and presented as an ideal in the recent past (Carisse, 1964).

(a) In all three societies we note a general decline in fecundity (births) starting in 1961. The change in fecundity is recent and sudden. Certainly large families are no longer an ideal and young people today have drastically reduced the number of children they have. A further analysis of fecundity by age groups would show that the family tends to be modelled according to different life aspirations; contemporary young couples have a few children when quite young or rather space births or delay the first birth to the thirties when they are well established (Table VIII).

(b) In the U.S.A. and in Ontario, women of 20-24 are more fecund than are those of the 25-29 age group which reflects the younger age at marriage. On the average, family life may project a younger image.

(c) There is a marked increase in births outside of legal marriage. In the U.S.A., the majority of illegitimate births are situated in the 20 to 30 age group. The illegitimate births are not then due to the inexperience of

**Table XI: Percentage Distribution of the Population, by
Education and Sex, USA, Ontario, Quebec, for
Selected Years**

Level of schooling [a]	USA		Ontario		Quebec	
	1960	*1970*	*1951*	*1961*	*1951*	*1961*
Male						
None	7.4	4.5	1.7	1.2	1.6	1.1
Elementary	32.1	22.7	51.2	45.8	64.3	55.6
Secondary	41.1	35.0	36.2	45.0	26.5	35.8
Some university	9.1	11.3	7.6	3.1	4.8	3.2
University completed	10.3	15.0	3.4	4.9	2.8	4.3
Female						
None	6.0	3.9	1.4	1.1	1.2	0.9
Elementary	29.7	21.2	43.5	39.7	60.2	52.9
Secondary	43.8	56.0	43.4	54.7	34.3	42.4
Some university	9.5	10.1	10.1	2.5	3.7	2.2
University completed	6.0	8.6	1.6	2.0	0.6	1.6

[a] In official publications, the categories describing the levels of schooling are slightly different.

Quebec and Ontario, 1951: none; 1-8 years; 9-12 years; 13-16 years; 17 years and more.

Quebec and Ontario, 1961: none; elementary; secondary; some university; university completed.

USA, 1957, 1962, 1969: 0-4 years; 5-8 years; high school — 1-4 years completed; college — 1-3 years completed; college — 4 years or more.

teenagers. On the other hand, young women of 15 to 19 account for almost half of the illegitimate births in Ontario and almost 30 per cent in Quebec. But the fact remains that four out of ten illegitimate births occur among women between 20 and 24 in Quebec as well as Ontario (Tables IX and X).

The Condition of Women

We have previously pointed out that with increased industrialization, a drastic separation of the different spheres of life occurs. Men live a public life in their careers pursuing remunerated work; women live a private life in their role as mother-wife in the home. But this division of social roles between the instrumental and the affective is being altered.

(a) *Increased level of education.* It is well-known that both men and women are getting more education. But what is important is that the gap between men and women in higher education is gradually being reduced.

Table XII: Percentage of Total Degrees Conferred on Females, by Level, USA, Ontario, Quebec, for Selected Years

Degrees	USA 1951	1961	1968	Ontario 1951	1961	1968	Quebec 1951	1961	1968
Bachelor's	29.6	38.9	44.1	35.0	36.9	40.4	19.5	22.5	31.1
Master's	20.9	30.8	35.7	11.6	16.4	17.5	16.1	23.4	23.3
Doctor's	9.2	10.6	12.2	5.1	4.8	10.1	5.9	14.6	14.0

Table XIII: Labor Force Participation, USA, Ontario, Quebec, for Selected Years

	USA 1951	1961	1969	Ontario 1951	1961	1971	Quebec 1951	1961	1971
Sex									
Male	87.3	83.6	80.9	84.8	81.2	80.3	87.1	80.2	71.4
Female	34.7	38.1	42.7	26.4	32.9	44.3	24.2	28.1	35.2
Marital Status (female)									
Single	50.0	46.5	56.7	62.5	54.7	56.3	58.4	57.9	52.2
Married	30.1	32.5	39.5	15.0	27.4	44.0	7.4	14.4	28.4
Age Group (female)[a]									
20–24	46.6	47.1	56.8	51.0	51.6	66.6	46.1	51.0	61.4
25–34	35.4	36.4	43.8	27.6	33.7	50.1	23.9	26.9	39.9
35–44	39.8	43.8	49.9	25.5	36.1	50.5	20.6	24.7	34.4
45–54	39.7	50.1	53.8	23.8	38.4	50.9	19.1	26.6	33.8

[a] Minimum age for inclusion is 15 years old in Canada, 14 years old in the USA for 1951 and 1961, and 16 years old in the USA for 1969.

There is also a greater tendency for women with higher education to use their knowledge in a profession, either by choosing (in greater proportion) not to get married, or by having a dual career after marriage (Tables XI and XII).

(b) *Labor force participation*. The tendency here is clear and coherent. As a whole, women are increasingly participating in the labor force. In the U.S.A., in 1969, more than four women out of ten were in the labor force. This increase is noticeable in all age groups. It is, however, possibly more accentuated in the 45-54 age group as this is an age when the requirements attached to the role of motherhood become less demanding. However, the increase is also important in the 25-35 year old group, an age which traditionally coincides with the care of young children. This evidence of dual careers is corroborated by an increase in the participation of married women in professional activities (Table XIII).

Conclusion: The Future of the Family

What is the future of the family? Or more realistically, what will the family of the future be like? If we take a hard look at vital statistics, nothing leads us to believe that marriage and the family will collapse in the near (or not so near) future. We feel that forms commensurate with our type III family will be better equipped structurally to break the vicious cycle aimed at 'reproducing the system,' a system geared to more production and more consumption, depleting the resources of the universe and widening the gap between the third world and the 'first world.'

Type III families rest on an orientation to the individual, his right to realize himself and to elaborate personal plans. They represent a context in which the modern problem of 'the proper dialectic of solitude and being with other people' can be worked out (Cooper, 1971: 140). The search for alternative family forms is going on among minorities with a high degree of consciousness. Most of these ventures are a search for utopia. The important thing about them is not their 'success' as defined by stability or even individual happiness. Many ventures in communal living, for example, have not found adequate solutions to old problems regardless of the forms they have taken. Also, as many authors have pointed out, an experimental search for communal living is part of North American tradition and has not succeeded in the past in replacing families. However, we think that the present social context gives a new meaning to this search. It cannot but have a different orientation in a society where the level of technology permits abundance for the majority, and makes possible basic security for all and where both the production and diffusion of knowledge are exploding. The individuals entering the new family arrangements are in fact those who have experienced these privileges. They belong to the younger generation of developed countries who have lived only in post-war prosperity. They are middle class and better educated than the average and, as Roszak (1969) points out with humor, 'they are Dr. Spock's children and have been fed on demand.' In this affluent environment, perhaps it is the fraternal family which will provide the nurturing communication which we believe to be the important function of the modern family.

References

Axelrod, M., 'Urban Structure and Social Participation,' *American Sociological Review,* XXI (1956), 3-18.

Bell, W., and M. Boat, 'Urban Neighborhoods and Informal Social Relations,' *American Journal of Sociology,* LXII (1957), 391-398.

Buckley, Walter, *Modern System Theory.* Englewood Cliffs: Prentice-Hall Inc., 1968.

Buckner, Taylor, 'Social Reality as Process.' Annual Meeting of the Canadian Sociological and Anthropological Association, St. John's, Newfoundland: June 1971 (Mimeo).

Carisse, Colette, 'Accommodation conjugale et réseau social des mariages biethniques au Canada,' *Revue Française de Sociologie,* VII (1966), 472-484.

——, *Planification des naissances en milieu canadien-français.* Montreal: Presses de l'Université de Montréal, 1964.

Chinoy, Ely, *Automobile Workers and the American Dream.* Garden City: Doubleday, 1955.

Clark, L., and J.B. Carney, *Consumer Behavior.* New York: Harper, 1958.

Cooper, David, *The Death of the Family.* New York: Random House, 1971.

Des Ruisseaux, Pierre, 'Croyances et pratiques populaires au Canada français.' Thèse de maîtrise, Département d'Anthropologie, Université de Montréal, 1971.

Dubuc, Alfred, *Thomas Molson, entrepreneur de Montréal, 1780-1863.* Montreal: Presses de l'Université de Québec, 1974.

Dumazedier, J., 'La société post-industrielle et le loisir,' Comité de recherche du loisir et de la culture populaire: Seventh World Congress of Sociology, Varna, Bulgaria, 1970 (Mimeo).

Duncan, Harold, *Indians of North America.* Chicago: University of Chicago Press, 1961, pp. 291-292.

Duncan, Hugh Dalziel, *Communication and the Social Order.* New York: Bedminster Press, 1962.

Edwards, John N., 'Familial Behavior as Social Exchange,' *Journal of Marriage and the Family,* XXXI (April, 1969), 518-526.

——, *The Family and Change.* New York: Knopf, 1969.

Eisenstadt, S.N., *Essays on Comparative Institutions.* New York: John Wiley and Sons, 1965, pp. 22-24.

Engels, F., *L'origine de la famille, de la propriété privée et de l'état.* Paris: Alfred Costes, 1948.

Ehrmann, Winston, 'Marital and Non-Marital Sexual Behavior,' in Harold T. Christensen, *Handbook of Marriage and the Family.* Chicago: Rand McNally, 1964, pp. 585-623.

Etzioni, A., *The Active Society, a Theory of Societal and Political Processes.* New York: The Free Press, 1968.

Farber, Bernard, *Family: Organisation and Interaction.* San Francisco: Chandler, 1964.

——, *Kinship and Class: a Mid-Western Study.* New York: Basic Books, 1971.

Ferreira, J.A., and William D. Winter, 'Information Exchange and Silence in Normal and Abnormal Families,' *Family Process,* VII, 2 (1968), 251-276.

——, 'Decision-Making in Normal and Abnormal Two-Child Families,' *Family Process,* VII, 1 (1968), 17-36.

——, *Research and Family Interaction.* Palo Alto: Science and Behavior Books Inc., 1968.

Ferris, Abbot L., *Indicators of Trends in the Status of American Women.* New York: Russell Sage Foundation, 1971.

——, *Indicators of Trends in the Status of the American Family.* New York: Russell Sage Foundation, 1970.

Fogarty, M.P., R. Rapoport and R.N. Rapoport, *Sex, Career and Family.* London: George Allen and Unwin, 1971.

Gans, Herbert J., *The Urban Villagers: Group and Class in the Life of Italian Americans.* New York: The Free Press, 1962.

Gaugh, Kathleen, 'Is the Family Universal: the Nayar Case,' in Bell and Vogel, *A Modern Introduction to the Family.* Glencoe, Ill.: The Free Press, 1960, pp. 76-92.

Goffman, Irvin, *Asylums.* Chicago: Aldine, 1959.

Goode, William J., 'Force and Violence in the Family,' *Journal of Marriage and the Family,* XXXIII, 4 (November, 1971), 624-635.

——, 'Unigeniture vs. Equal Division,' in R. Bendix and S. Lipset, *Class Status and Power.* New York: The Free Press, 1967.

——, *World Revolution and Family Patterns.* New York: The Free Press, 1963.

Gordon, Michael, *The Nuclear Family in Crisis: The Search for an Alternative.* New York: Harper and Row, 1972.

Hill, Reuben, and Roy H. Rodgers, 'The Developmental Approach,' in H.T. Christensen, *Handbook of Marriage and the Family.* Chicago: Rand McNally, 1964.

Hoggart, Richard, *The Uses of Literacy.* London: Chatto and Windus, 1954.

Holland, L., *The Psychology of Vocational Choice.* Waltham, Mass.: Blaisdeel, 1966.

Jackson, Don D., 'The Individual and the Larger Contexts,' *Family Process,* VI, 2 (1967), 139-147.

Jacobson, P., and A.P. Matheny, 'Mate Selection in Open Marriage Systems,' *International Journal of Comparative Sociology,* III (1962), 98-163.

Kandel, D. and G. Lesser, 'Parental and Peer Influence on Educational Plans of Adolescents,' *American Sociological Review,* XXXIV, 1 (April, 1969), 213-223.

Kohn, Melvin, *Class and Conformity: A Study of Values.* Homewood, Ill.: The Dorsey Press, 1969.

Komarovsky, Mirra, *Blue-Collar Marriage.* New York: Random House, 1964.

——, *The Unemployed Man and his Family.* New York: Dryden Press, 1940.

Laing, R.D., *La politique de l'expérience.* Paris: Stock, 1969.

——, *The Politics of the Family.* Toronto: Canadian Broadcasting Corporation (CBC Learning Systems, Box 500), 1969.

Lapassade, Georges, *L'entrée dans la vie.* Paris: Editions de Minuit, 1963.

Laszlo, Ervin, *System, Structure and Experience.* New York: Gordon and Breach Science Publishers, 1969.

Leichter, Hope J., and William E. Mitchell, *Kinship and Casework.* New York: Russell Sage Foundation, 1967.

Lennard, H.L., and A. Bernstein, *Patterns in Human Interaction.* San Francisco: Jossey-Boss, 1970.

Letellier, Marie, *On est pas des trous de culs.* Montreal: Parti-Pris, 1971.

Lévi-Strauss, Claude, 'The Principle of Reciprocity,' in Coser and Rosenberg, *Sociological Theory.* New York: Macmillan, 1957, pp. 74-84.

Litwak, Eugene, 'Occupational Mobility and Extended Family Cohesion,' *American Sociological Review,* XXV (1960), 9-21.

——, 'Geographic Mobility and Extended Family Cohesion,' *American Sociological Review,* XXV (1960), 385-394.

Litwak, Eugene, E. Shiroi, L. Zimmerman, and J. Bernstein, 'Community Participation in Bureaucratic Organizations: Principles and Srategies,' *Interchange,* 1, 4 (1970).

Marriage, Family and Living, 'Premarital Sexual Behavior: A Symposium,' *Marriage, Family and Living,* XXIV, 3 (1962).

Maslow, Abraham Harold, *Motivation and Personality.* New York: Harper, 1954.

McKinney, John, *Constructive Typology and Social Theory.* New York: Appleton- Century-Crofts, 1966.

Ménard, Robert, 'Hétérosexualité d'étudiants de onzième année.' Thèse de maîtrise, Départment de Sociologie, Université de Montréal, 1972.

Miller, James G., 'The Nature of Living Systems: the Group,' *Behavioral Science,* XVI, 4 (July, 1971), 277-302.

Minuchin, S., *Families of the Slums.* New York: Basic Books, 1967.

Mogey, John, 'Family and Community in Urban-Industrial Societies,' in H.T. Christensen, *Handbook of Marriage and the Family.* Chicago: Rand McNally, 1964.

Morris, R.N., and John Mogey, *The Sociology of Housing.* London: Routledge and Kegan, 1965.

Murdock, George P., *Social Structure.* New York: Macmillan, 1949.

Nimkoff, *Comparative Family Systems.* Boston: Houghton Mifflin Co., 1965.

Olson, David H., 'Marital and Family Therapy: Integrative Review and Critique,' *Journal of Marriage and the Family,* XXXII, 4 (November, 1970), 501-538.

Osipov, Samuel H., *Theories on Career Development.* New York: Appleton-Century-Crofts, 1968.

Parsons, Talcott, 'On the Concept of Influence,' *Public Opinion Quarterly,* XXVII (1963), 40.

Parsons, T., and Robert F. Bales, *Socialization and the Family.* Glencoe, Ill: The Free Press, 1955.

Penfield, Wilder, *L'homme et sa famille.* Montreal: Proops Press Inc., 1967.

Pineo, Peter C., 'The Extended Family in a Working-Class Area of Hamilton,' in Blishen, Jones, Naegele, and Porter, *Canadian Society.* Toronto: Macmillan, 1961, pp. 140-150.

Rapoport, R., and R.N. Rapoport, *Dual Career Families.* Middlesex: Penguin, 1971.

Reiss, David, 'Varieties of Consensual Experience 1: a Theory for Relating Family Interaction to Individual Thinking,' *Family Process,* X, 1971, 28-35.

Reiss, Ira L., 'The Universality of the Family: a Conceptual Analysis,' *Journal of Marriage and the Family,* XXXVII (November, 1965), 443-453.

Reiss, Paul J., 'The Extended Kinship System: Correlates of and Attitudes on Frequency of Interaction,' *Marriage and Family Living,* XXIV (1962), 333-339.

Riskin, Jules, and E. Fauce, 'Family Interaction Scales 1: Theoretical Framework and Method,' *The Archives of General Psychiatry,* XXII (1970), 504-512.

——, 'Family Interaction Scales 3: Discussion of Methodology and Substantive Findings,' *The Archives of General Psychiatry,* XXII (1970), 527-537.

Rodman, Hyman, 'The Lower Class Value Stretch,' *Social Forces,* XLII, 2 (1963), 205-215.

——, *Lower-Class Families: The Culture of Poverty in Negro Trinidad.* New York: Oxford University Press, 1971.

——, 'The Textbook World of Family Sociology,' *Social Problems,* XII, 4,1965.

Rokeach, Milton, *The Open and Closed Mind; Investigation into the Nature of Belief Systems and Personality Systems.* New York: Basic Books, 1960.

Roszak, Theodore, *Making of a Counter Culture.* New York: Doubleday, 1969.

Scanzoni, John H., *Opportunity and the Family.* New York: The Free Press, 1970.

Schatzman, Leonard, and Anselm Strauss, 'Social Class and Modes of Communication,' in Alfred G. Smith, *Communication and Culture.* New York: Holt and Rinehart, 1966, pp. 442-456.

Seeley, John R., R.A. Sim, E. Loosley, 'Crestwood Heights,' in Blishen, Jones, Naegele and Porter, *Canadian Society.* Toronto: Macmillan, 1961, pp. 117-168.

Séminaire International sur la Famille (8 e), Acta Socilogica, VIII, 1-2, Oslo, August, 1963.

Shanas, Ethel, *et al., Old People in Three Industrial Societies.* New York: Aldine Press, 1968.

Sjoberg, Gideon, *The Preindustrial City.* New York: The Free Press, 1960.

Spiro, Melford E., *Children of the Kibbutz.* New York: Schocken Books, Inc., 1965.

Sprey, Jetse, 'On the Institutionalization of Sex,' *Journal of Marriage and the Family,* XXXI (August, 1969), 432-440.

Stolte, Heiskanen, and Veroncia, 'Social Structure, Family Patterns and Interpersonal Influence,' *Transactions of the Westermack Society,* XIV, 1967.

Sussman, Marvin B., 'Directive and Integrative Behavior of Today's Family,' *Family Process,* VII, 2 (September, 1968), 239-250.

Sussman, Marvin B., and L. Burchinal, 'Kin Family Network: Unheralded Structure in Current Conceptualizations of Family Functioning,' *Marriage and Family Living,* August, 1962.

Sussman, Marvin B., and Betty Cogswell, 'Family Influences on Job Movement.' Paper presented at the Eleventh Family Research Seminar, London, 1970. Published in *Social Forces,* Fall, 1971.

Sweetser, D.A., 'Occupational Mobility and Communication Among Primary Relations,' San Francisco, 1969, (Mimeo).

Tiger, Lionel, *Men in Groups,* New York: Random House, 1969.

Tiryakain, Edward, 'Conceptual Issues: a Model of Societal Change and its Indicators,' in Samuel Z. Klausner, *The Study of Total Societies.* New York; Doubleday, 1967, pp. 69-97.

Tremblay, Marc-Adélard and Marc Laplante, 'Famille et parenté en Acadie,' in *Publications in Ethnology,* III, Ottawa, 1971.

Trist, Eric, 'Organisation et système,' *Revue Française de Sociologie,* XI-XII (1971), (Numéro spécial), 123-239.

Turk, James L., and Norman W. Bell, 'Measuring Power in Families,' *Journal of Marriage and the Family,* (May, 1972), 215-222.

Walker, Kathryn E., *Time-Use Patterns for Household Work Related to Homemakers' Employment.* National Agricultural Outlook Conference, Washington, D.C., 1970.

Watzlavick, P., J.H. Beaven, and D. Jackson, *Pragmatics of Human Communication.* New York: Norton and Co., Inc., 1967.

Weigert, Andrew, and Darwin Thomas, 'Family as a Conditional Universal,' *Journal of Marriage and the Family,* XXXIII, 1 (February, 1971), 188-194.

Wilensky, H., 'Mass Society and Mass Culture, Interdependence or Independence,' *American Journal of Sociology,* XXIX (April, 1964), 173-197.

Wirth, L., 'Urbanism as a Way of Life,' *American Journal of Sociology,* XL, I (1938), 24.

CHAPTER NINE

Deviance and Conformity: The Issue of Marihuana Use

Edmund Vaz
University of Waterloo

Introduction

A striking social phenomenon of the past decade has been the enormous increase in the illegal use of drugs (notably marihuana) among young people. Although no systematic count has been undertaken the Governmental Inquiry into the non-medical use of drugs estimated that approximately 215,000 high school and university students use marihuana, and this figure does not include non-student users. This estimate is considerably higher than any previously suggested. (*Interim Report,* 1970: 142)

At one time marihuana use was considered a minor social problem in Canada. Today the marihuana controversy is a major social issue, a source of unrelenting debate that sometimes borders on hysteria. Marihuana use is gradually becoming an acceptable practice in the lives of a growing number of otherwise conforming persons, both young and not-so-young. This suggests that the use of marihuana may be here to stay.

By looking at marihuana use as a social issue we hope to explore and thereby illuminate some aspects of deviant and conforming behavior. Possession of marihuana for non-medical purposes is a criminal offense, but we do not imply that deviance concerns itself only with violations of the law. What we say here about deviance has as much relevance for understanding the violation of norms that occurs within legitimate groups and institutions as with the breach of the criminal code.

Marihuana Use as a Social Issue

A discrepancy between widely shared social standards of conduct and the actual conditions of social life is a basic component of social issues. Because the hiatus between cultural standards and social behavior varies in extent and significance, social problems are not all of equal importance to the society. In what ways then is the use of marihuana a social issue in Canadian society? In what ways is there a major discrepancy between the social criteria for conduct and social actuality?

Social standards are neither randomly distributed nor equally shared throughout the system. This suggests that not everyone perceives social reality in the same way. Differences in social status greatly influence people in their perception and definition of what is proper and moral. It will also make a difference in their definition of what constitutes a social issue. Some lower-middle class groups have always been adamantly opposed to prostitution, gambling, and the use of alcohol, but the large majority of society has learned to live with these practices. The recreational use of marihuana which many young middle class persons consider moral, albeit illegal, is usually perceived by their parents as degrading, something that weakens moral restraints and leads to crime. This does not imply that users are better informed about drugs than non-users; in fact both users and non-users are apt to be poorly informed.

Persons who define social issues do not all carry equal authority nor does each person go about defining social issues for himself. And it is not necessarily the aggregate of separate opinions that defines whether something is a social issue. (Merton, 1971: 803) Persons in strategic positions of authority carry more weight than others. *When drug use was confined largely to lower class groups of society, middle and upper class persons were less prone to make a social issue of such behavior.* Today an important reason for the public drama surrounding marihuana use is that middle and upper class persons are smoking pot, or must face the fact that their children do so and are likely to continue doing so. Many of the parents of these young people occupy positions of power in society, and some are its representatives and law makers. Under these conditions the power holders are forced to see their laws being flagrantly violated by growing numbers of their own kind. This must give them pause to reconsider the traditional explanations of marihuana use and the existing laws for its control. Simultaneously, while many adults cry out against the use of marihuana they seem hamstrung in what action to take. The need for a government appointed Commission of Inquiry (*Interim Report,* 1970) seems clear evidence that a large majority of the adult population and its representatives are ambivalent in their attitudes, and unsure of their knowledge of marihuana use.

It is not only the dangers that drug use entails that turn so many people against it. Drug use and the widespread smoking of marihuana have become identified with a style of life that is anathema to conventional, middle class Canadian society. This often includes a defiance of authority, an almost whimsical indifference to established institutions and traditions, and a search for thrills and exhilerating experiences. The colorful dress, demeanour, and argot often associated with this orientation are thought to symbolize a threat to basic moral values.

The use of drugs has never been consonant with the traditional middle class values of society. The values of hard work, frugality, asceticism and rational practicality have long been part of Canadian society; moreover Canadians generally have always disapproved of acts designed to achieve states of ecstasy unless, perhaps, they were the by-products of religion or hard work. Admittedly the differential distribution and institutionalization of these values is always problematic. But today they seem especially incongruent in a society where major institutions are undergoing transformation, where there is a high standard of living, and where people spend increasingly more time at play and less time at work. The idea that pleasure should be a reward for hard work must seem odd to increasing numbers of young people whose general comportment and attitude reflect their affluent and indulgent upbringing. These values do not fit the peer-group mentality and social ethic typical of today's middle and upper class youth. The unchecked use of marihuana (and other drugs) by young people can only mean that there exists a gross conflict of values and widely different conceptions of relevant group norms. As the basic institutions of society experience change its traditional values are being questioned repeatedly by growing segments of the population.

It seems quite clear that increasing numbers of respected young people are engaging in conduct which despite its general condemnation, they consider neither immoral nor harmful. The risk they run in their use of marihuana reflects partly the strength of their conviction. In these groups marihuana use is socially acceptable conduct; this presents a clearcut challenge to the institutionalization of values, sentiments and attitudes that underly the laws forbidding unauthorized possession of marihuana.

Illegal Use of Marihuana

Hard drug use has been associated usually with prostitutes, slum-rooted criminals and other stigmatized groups, which is perhaps one reason for the prevailing view that any drug use causes crime. In fact there has been an undeniable association between the two. (Mann, 1967: 239-240; Clausen, 1971: 185-226) In addition, its use has been associated with those whose life styles and behavior, although not criminal, have been viewed as deviant by middle class standards. For example, for decades marihuana use has been commonplace among jazz musicians. Some thirty years ago when a name dance band arrived in Montreal for an engagement, marihuana was found stashed in the horns of some of the musicians.*

The subterranean nature of illegal drug use makes it extremely difficult to obtain reliable statistics about the activity, and it also precludes gaining sound knowledge of many aspects of using drugs. Under such conditions statistics should be interpreted with care, and generalizations are best avoided. In Canada official statistics on the illegal use of drugs are unreliable and estimates of the extent of illegal drug use are crude. Such information reveals little about the nature of drug use, e.g., the importance of drugs to the user. More recently survey research has been employed to assess the extent of drug use in the larger population, but even here the results are not always reliable. Generally persons are apt to under-report their use of drugs, except in those groups where drug use is a sign of sophistication, e.g., among certain adolescent groups. (Clausen, 1971: 201)

Although marihuana is undoubtedly the most frequently used illegal drug the extent of its use in Canada is known in only very general terms. Yet there is still reason to believe that a vast increase in the use of marihuana has occurred, especially among young people. Prior to the 1960's there was little evidence of marihuana use in Canada. In 1962, 20 cases of marihuana use were reported by the RCMP. After 1962 marihuana use increased, and by 1968, 2,331 cases were reported to the RCMP. By 1969 this figure had jumped to 4,215. In 1969 the RCMP reported that they had identified 13,500 users of the weed, and they estimated an additional 45,000. (*Interim Report*, 1970: 142-148) However, the Federal Government Inquiry estimated that there were approximately 215,000 student users of marihuana.

Survey research indicates that the gross rates of marihuana use vary widely. A 1968 survey of freshmen at Loyola University in Montreal found that 15 per cent of males and 7 per cent of females had used cannabis at least once. In 1969 a survey conducted at McGill University estimated that 34.6 per cent of students had used marihuana, and that 29.3 per cent had used hashish. Studies limited to the law faculties at the universities of Toronto and British Columbia found levels of cannabis use to be 35 per cent and 45 per cent respectively.

Surveys of high schools conducted in 1968 estimated that marihuana

*Read also Mezz Mezzerow and Bernard Wolfe, *Really the Blues* (New York: Random House, 1946).

usage ranged between 5.7 per cent and 19.7 per cent, and in 1969 between 5.9 per cent and 24 per cent. In Whitehead's study of marihuana use among 1,606 high school students (from grades 7, 9, 11, and 12) in Halifax, Toronto, and Montreal, rates showed little variation, 6.6 per cent in Halifax to 8.5 per cent in Montreal. (Whitehead, 1970: 23)

Concerning the frequency of marihuana use, the general impression is that the majority of high school and university users have taken marihuana only a few times. A study conducted at Bishop's University in 1969 found that about half of those who had used marihuana had done so fewer than five times, and almost 20 per cent had stopped using the drug. A 1968 study of high schools found that 60 per cent of those who had tried marihuana had used it fewer than four times. The 1969 study of 4,500 Montreal high school students found that 55 per cent had used it fewer than five times, and 67 per cent fewer than seven times. (*Interim Report,* 1970: 145) Whitehead's previously mentioned study uncovered 'relatively little frequently repeated use of drugs.' 'Except for tobacco and alcohol for males and tobacco for females the rates of frequent drug use are well under 3 per cent.' (Whitehead, 1970: 19) While the extent of marihuana use is increasing among young people, its frequency seems less noteworthy. Very likely users smoke about once a week.

Among high school students, one study found a positive relationship between social status and the use of pot; also there is a steady increase in rates of using marihuana by grade, from 1.43 per cent for grade seven to 12.45 per cent for grade twelve. An increase in the same direction holds for the use of LSD, but the rates are lower. (Whitehead, 1970: 37-39)*

The higher the scholastic performance, the lower the rates of drug use. When students with an overall average of 'under 40' are compared with those whose average is '75 or over,' the rate of drug use among the lower group is startlingly higher than among the higher performing group. Specifically *the rate of marihuana use is at least eight times as high among the lower than the higher academic category.* (Whitehead, 1970: 44) These data also show that *males more often use most drugs than do females.* However, for tranquilizers there were considerably more female than male users in some cities. For marihuana there are about twice as many male as female users.

A vast increase in drug use is likely to occur first in large urban areas since this is where institutional change and the upheaval of values initially take place. The RCMP reported that the use of pot began to increase after 1962 in Montreal, a year later in Toronto, and in

---

*For American data read Erich Goode, *Drugs in American Society* (New York: Knopf, 1972), pp. 36-37.

Vancouver in 1965. (*Interim Report,* 1970: 142) A study conducted in 1963 among 682 middle class high school students aged from 15 to 19 years from 4 communities in Ontario found that fewer than 1 per cent admitted selling, using or trying to use 'drugs of some kind,' and fewer than .5 per cent admitted doing so more than once or twice. (Vaz, 1965) At the time there was little public discussion concerning the propriety of the marihuana laws, and the 'marihuana problem' did not exist. Marihuana use was not a serious expression of deviance for middle class society.

Conformity, Norms, and Laws

As recently as ten years ago middle and upper class young people obeyed the law against unauthorized possession of marihuana because they wished to, they believed the rule. They found it gratifying to conform, embarrassing to deviate. So it is with most of us. It must seem odd to those who get their 'kicks' from breaking the law to learn that most of us derive pleasure (Cohen, 1966: 3) from doing what is right and avoiding what is wrong. Today matters have changed, and growing numbers of youths smoke 'pot.' This means that large numbers of people disagree with the law, and testifies that the law lacks the moral clout it once had. It is not that marihuana users generally derive special satisfaction from law violation (although some no doubt do), but that *users and non-users are conforming to different definitions of the situation.*

The institutionalization of norms, which refers to behavior that has moral consensus, is always variable in a system. At no time do all members define the norm in the same way, internalize the norm to the same degree or attempt to obey the norm uniformly. Consider the variable behavior and attitudes of young people and those of their parents towards smoking 'grass.' Or the many styles and differential degrees of participation among marihuana users. The vast majority are occasional users, others smoke more regularly, while a small percentage, perhaps, believe in the weed and are psychologically hooked.

The question can always be asked: when has consensus been achieved? At what point can we say that expectations are institutionalized? This can never be answered precisely. Not everyone in the system needs to internalize the norm for it to be institutionalized. But the people who are most closely involved with the particular practice should be aware of the norm and the demands associated with it, while others should generally recognize and accept the rule. (Johnson, 1960: 20; Cohen, 1968: 150) Today many persons closely involved with upholding the marihuana law, and other respectable law-abiding elements in society are ambivalent towards the norm and the demands associated with it, while large segments of the population violate the law. This is clear evidence that *the law against unauthorized possession of marihuana is not institutionalized throughout the society.*

If we could establish objectively which practices and customs are absolutely damaging and disruptive to the society and which are not, it would greatly facilitate our knowing which ones to emphasize. Yet there are always some rules that enjoy more respect and consensus than others, often those circumscribing practices that are considered most important for the society. One criterion is the attempt to equate deviance with danger, i.e., to proscribe those practices that are considered damaging to men and to the society. Admittedly there must be some rules to govern the acquisition, use, and distribution of goods and services. There must also be some provision for the distribution of property and sexual favors, and every society must make some arrangements for the replacement and care of its members. And it seems reasonable to legislate against murder and treason. In the long run wholesale violation of these rules might seriously harm the society. Yet many people are asking whether the use of marihuana for pleasure is so important that it requires prohibition by law. As yet there is little substantial information to suggest that the recreational use of 'pot' would be damaging. The marihuana issue is certainly not a societally strategic problem.

It is extremely difficult to equate deviance in society with the danger that it poses for its members. Some activities are forbidden though they do little or no harm to the society; other customs and practices, e.g., automobile racing, mountain climbing, institutionalization of the cocktail party, that are enthusiastically encouraged, are frightening in their possible consequences for both participants and the society. Usually everyone believes that he knows what practices are dangerous and ought to be proscribed; but to establish objectively what practices really are dangerous is another and more difficult matter.

Not everyone is equally convinced that society is rational in its approach to making laws. Some writers suggest that modern society is a multi-group organization, each group possessing its own values, traditions, and vested interests. Power is also differentially distributed among them which means that some groups are in a better position, and therefore better able, to have their rules enacted into law. Laws are passed in society by those groups who occupy positions of power, who have an interest in the passage of the laws, who can influence others as to the urgency of the legislation, and who can overcome the objections of competing interests. (Cohen, 1966: 34-35) Wheeler suggests that there exists a kind of moral politics whereby competing power blocks are continually struggling and negotiating to have enacted laws to protect their own interests, their own standards of morality and decency, and uphold their own traditions. This suggests that much of *what passes for deviant behavior in society* (e.g., mental illness, homosexuality, drug addiction, prostitution, physical handicaps, etc.), *represents little more than the tastes and attitudes of those groups who occupy positions of power* (Wheeler, 1967: 614; Becker, 1963: 1964; Freidson)

This is evident in the history of narcotics legislation in Canada from 1908 to 1923. In her recent discussion, Shirley Cook (1969) emphasizes three influential factors operating during this period. A number of prominent groups were involved with drugs; there was the medical profession (whose members were commonly prescribing medications containing opiates), the Chinese peddlers of opium, and there was widespread use of medicines containing opiates by the general public. Admittedly the Patent and Proprietary Medicines Act was introduced to control the indiscriminate use of harmful drugs by physicians and others, but the penalties for violation of this Act were much less drastic than those for violation of the Opium and Narcotic Drug Act. In the end it was the Chinese who were the losers; they rather than the physicians were designated deviants. Cook suggests that the decision to consider the narcotic users as criminals clearly reflects the stratification order and power differential between groups at the time.

Secondly, the moral reformers 'had the arena of social legislation-making to themselves.' (Cook, 1969: 40) Because it was largely a 'hidden type conflict' there were no opposing views, their moralistic testimonials and writings went unchallenged, and there was no need to arouse public opinion. They fostered belief in the 'dope fiend' image of the drug user, they condemned the use of drugs as acts which, they alleged, encouraged the 'natural depravity of man,' and they strongly advocated protection for the moral fibre of the citizenry. It is important to note that these views were 'espoused by the superordinate group who made and enforced the rule,' and the absence of public debate successfully neutralized any objection.

A further contributing factor was the long-standing hate and hostility directed against Asian immigrants — especially the Chinese and Japanese in Canada. In the 1922 narcotics debates the 'moral ruin of innocent young people' was attributed to the 'foreign inferior race.' (Cook, 1969: 43) This heightened the moral indignation of the legislators, and the penalties were increased. Cook suggests that had there been no racial hatred between whites and Asians the moral indignation against drug users and stringent enforcement of the law would have waned as it had against the high status manufacturers of tobacco and alcohol, many of whom were of British ancestry. Their high social standing partially immunized them from the kind of intense vilification that was directed against the Chinese. Moreover until after World War II, the Chinese remained a despised social group because of immigration restrictions, their occupational skills, and their high social visibility.

It should be noted here that the efficacy of a *repressive law as a means of social control* depends largely on the behavior it is meant to control. Repressive law is usually least effective in the control of the so-called vices in society, e.g., prostitution, the use of marihuana and drugs of addiction, other forms of sexual deviance, and in some cases, gambling. In Canadian society today the law does not seem to deter increasing numbers of young people from smoking 'pot,' instead it makes criminals of them. Admittedly most countries have some form of legislation affecting these practices, but few try so hard as we to make criminals of people who 'have vices.'

Informal controls and social definitions of behavior are an important means of regulating the conduct of men. Our participation in social activities and our choice of conduct is usually independent of its legal status; for example, it is not the illegality of prostitution that deters so many women from entering such a lucrative occupation. Nor is it the fear of prison that deters us from murder, treason, and rape. For most of us the mere thought of these acts revolts us and violates our sense of morality. 'Shooting heroin' or sniffing glue turns us off, we have neither interest nor appetite for many of these practices. But this is not to suggest that some forms of conduct should not be outlawed, nor does it imply that the legalization of marihuana is necessarily the correct solution to the marihuana issue. However, it does imply that the removal of the repressive law will not automatically open the floodgates for the abuse of marihuana and drugs of addiction. It is also true that repressive law is an extremely costly and inefficient means of regulating the vices of men.

This is very evident in the case of narcotics. Whatever the moral status of drug use in society there is a great demand for drugs. But the use of drugs is prohibited by law, and, especially for addictive drugs, strongly stigmatized. Wherever there exists a widespread demand for goods and services there will likely emerge some business enterprise (legal or illegal) to meet the demand. But the production and provision of drugs (like prostitution) is illegal; this increases the risk of the enterprise and curtails the supply without necessarily reducing the demand. Because there are always some who are willing to pay for their pleasure this provides the opportunity for very high profits; also, the more vigorous the police enforcement the greater the risk in providing the services, and the greater the profits.

Penalties for trafficking in narcotics (especially addictive drugs) are very severe and consequently the cost of drugs is exorbitant. This forces the addict (unless he is wealthy) to steal in order to support his habit. Briefly it makes a criminal of an otherwise law-abiding person. As Cohen writes, 'The zeal to stamp out nonconforming behavior by criminal legislation tends to transform non-crime into crime, foster the creation of illegal forms of business enterprise and to encourage the pursuit of certain forms of crime in order to make others possible.' (Cohen, 1968: 231-243) It seems clear that the most predictable results from enacting repressive laws for the regulation of vices are an increase in crime statistics, and the further social degradation and suffering of an increasing number of citizens.

Another view on the task of defining deviance in society was suggested about seventy years ago by the great French sociologist, Emile Durkheim. He felt that deviant behavior did more than disrupt the stability of the society. He saw the violation of serious rules, e.g., the criminal code, as providing an important service for society. (1949: 70-110; 1950) Briefly, deviant behavior reinforced social cohesiveness. Very often the deviant violates rules about which members of the community feel strongly. This provides them with a target for their collective wrath. In their fervor to 'bear witness against the offender and to express their outrage' the excitement quickens the rate of their interaction; in the process they articulate shared sentiments and recognize common concerns, strengthening the bonds of solidarity and sense of community among them. In this way crime alerts members of the community to their common interests, welds the private consciences of people into a shared sense of morality, and highlights the basic values or collective conscience of the society. Rather than disunity it breeds unity among men.

If Durkheim is correct, it implies that the smooth functioning of society and the stability of its basic values are, to a considerable extent, dependent on periodic threatening acts of deviance. Crime becomes positively functional for society. It has been said that a society 'gets the crime that it deserves.' An implication of Durkheim's views is that, in order to remain intact and preserve its stability, society needs a certain amount of deviance. (Erikson, 1966) If this is correct it may be that the society itself functions in such a way as to generate the volume of deviance that it needs.

But there is more to the matter. Modern industrial society is highly differentiated along social class, ethnic, religious, and occupational lines. These groups seldom share common interests or obey the same rules. The institutionalization of common values and sentiments is therefore problematic. Do acts of crime in contemporary society ordinarily evoke a collective outrage among diverse groups? Is there a collective indignation, a uniform resentment that binds people together and automatically promotes their social cohesion? It is perhaps more likely that widespread acts of crime breed suspicion among men, and fear, uneasiness, and division within society. (Cressey, 1971: 4-17)

Witness the widespread use of marihuana among young people. Instead of integrating society it has inflamed controversy, divided families, generated anxiety and bred dissension. The acute conflict in attitudes and values between younger and older generation has erupted publicly. Common understandings (whatever their previous state) have suffered. Under such conditions the formal agencies of social control are sometimes called upon for assistance. Law courts occasionally serve to reduce ambiguity in the rules, clarify meanings, and reaffirm confidence in the normative order. In this case the government appointed inquiry into the nonmedical use of drugs is designed to bring clarity to the issue, help reconcile divergent attitudes, and spawn a common understanding of the problem. While Durkheim's ideas are exciting, even startling, a considerable amount of research is required before their empirical value is satisfactorily established.

As yet there is no agreement about how society decides what forms of behavior to consider deviant. As Wheeler writes, 'Some forms of conduct appear to be proscribed in just about every society; some forms show the work of special interest groups; and no society has yet managed to eliminate deviant behaviour.' (Wheeler, 1967: 615)

In discussing deviance one must always specify the system of rules or norms that is being violated. Not all rules apply to all groups. Often there are different versions of the rules, with various meanings attributed to them. One's perception of the rules and the degree to which one internalizes them will depend largely on one's personal experiences and position in the social structure.

The differential social location of people provides varying opportunities for reaching the good things in life, but it is also a structural inducement to differing kinds of deviance. Yet upper class crime is not always corporate crime. Although pushers do not peddle drugs among medical practitioners, doctors do get hooked on drugs. The professional discretion given doctors for curing the sick provides them with the opportunity for the illegal use of drugs. (Winick, 1964: 265-266)

The social position of people, and their age, is sometimes reflected in their attitudes towards marihuana use. In contrast to some younger age groups many of the older, conventional groups of the population strongly condemn the use of 'pot.' Yet the much larger number of youthful non-users do not likely condemn the users. In a recent study of persons under thirty and over fifty years of age, Boydell and Grindstaff

(1971) found that their youngest respondents were the most lenient in their attitudes towards applying legal sanctions for marihuana use. More than anything else this suggests the growing institutionalization by young people of marihuana use as a morally acceptable activity. Yet what is morally right conduct includes more than what is legally permitted. The legalization of marihuana will not automatically make its use moral in the eyes of those who presently condemn it. They will continue to sanction, albeit informally, those whose conduct they deplore.

Deviance and roles

Not only must there be some set of rules to guide people's behavior, there must also be some *consensus* about the validity of the rules. This means that a certain segment of the group must agree that these rules are the right rules and they ought to be obeyed. This is reflected in the laws against the possession of marihuana with which the large majority of the population is presently in agreement. Once a person claims membership in a group he immediately becomes subject to its rules regardless of how he feels about them. He must try to conform or be sanctioned, and perhaps forfeit claim to group membership. Since the vast majority of persons agree with the laws governing the possession of marihuana, and because they seldom find themselves in circumstances conducive to its possession, they experience little difficulty in obeying the law.

But to say that deviance is the result of violating institutionalized rules is not quite enough. This is because rules are related to groups and to the social roles that people occupy within them. *Institutionalized rules are those that define the role expectations and obligations to which one becomes subject when joining a group.* This means that deviance is relative to the groups to which one belongs, and to the social roles that one occupies. To occupy the role of Canadian citizen is to become subject to the laws that govern Canadian society, and no exemptions are made to criminal liability because of a person's social status. On the other hand, unless one is a pusher one is not subject to the informal system of rules that articulates such activities. Similarly, to be an insider in a closely-knit group of marihuana users is to be privy to their secrets, and subject to the rules by which their activities are governed.

We all belong to a number of groups and occupy a variety of roles. To lay claim to a role means that we wish to assume a certain *identity* and wish others to define us as a particular kind of person. We should remember that the groups to which we belong and those in which we aspire membership, besides the roles that we claim, largely limit the kinds of person we may be and the attitudes that we assume. This means that social roles are a principal means of social *control*. To be a successful role claimant requires conformity to role obligations, i.e., the expectations of those others with whom one typically interacts as role incumbent. Failure to conform produces strain in social encounters and elicits the disapproval (sanctions) of others. The roles that we claim, whether they are deviant or non-deviant, strongly control the kinds of conduct in which we engage. For example, prerequisites for the role of 'head' among drug users are the values of spontaneity, authenticity, and a manifest contempt for social proprieties. (Carey, 1968: 145-171) It involves a certain orientation towards drugs, considerable frequency and variety of drug use, and minimal association with the customary institutions of society.

Labelling the Deviant

It is one thing to break a rule, e.g., to 'push hash,' to tell a lie, commit a sin. It is something else to have others think of us as a pusher, liar or sinner. These are social roles — socially recognized categories of persons. All social roles include names and *labels* that are part of the language that we use in classifying people. Depending on the role, the terms that we use have relatively precise meanings for us. The roles of mother, father, and school-teacher are well known, but the role of 'twinkie' is perhaps best known in homosexual circles, that of 'plunger-boy' among gamblers, and the roles of 'pothead,' 'junkie,' and 'mellow dude,' among users of drugs.

The labels that we use in categorizing others suggest strongly that they are a particular kind of person. To be labelled a 'head' or a 'speed freak' implies that one possesses a special kind of character, that one *is* that kind of person, that one possesses a certain quantum of deviant stuff that distinguishes one from others. To occupy a role also means that others anticipate that one will *customarily act* in accordance with the definition of the role.

Who we are and what we are depend largely on the culture in which we live and those others with whom we customarily interact. The variety of roles provided by the larger culture will greatly determine the kinds of person we can be. One cannot be a swinger, hipster, mellow dude, or tough guy unless these roles are present to be appropriated in the culture.

The self is a social object and it emerges gradually throughout our daily interaction with others, in those encounters where we are continuously trying on new roles, consolidating old ones and shedding those that no longer become us. Successfully to claim a role means that we must conform to culturally established role obligations and thereby try to convince others that we are a particular kind of person. As others go about evaluating, defining, and categorizing our performances, we attempt to influence their decisions (especially those others whom we like) by saying the right thing and avoiding the wrong moves. Almost every act that we perform is linked to the conception that we hold of our self. *It is only through social encounters and seeing how others respond that we can ever tell if our role claims have been validated.* The youth who claims to smoke pot regularly, but who refuses to try hash and never turns on will have difficulty validating his claim among insiders.

Some kinds of deviance are apt to be efforts at claiming, testing or consolidating a certain kind of self. Much of our sexual behavior is motivated not only by role anxiety, but by wanting others to define us as being a particular kind of person. The university student who wishes to be considered a free-wheeling, cool, swinging type might feel that smoking pot and 'making it' with women are essential to the role. Perhaps it would be difficult to be this type of person and not take a drink, wear the latest fashion, make out with women, or smoke 'pot.' One may not have to smoke pot to be a swinger, but smoking 'pot' proclaims that one is not 'square.' This is *role-expressive behavior,* and it is also a means of achieving status within an increasing radius of persons.

But every role has its costs. To appropriate certain roles largely *precludes* us from assuming other roles. Once we get others to accept our claims to being a certain kind of person, it means that we can more easily offend, disappoint or anger them by violating their expectations of us. Those who make no such claims do not run these risks.

Not all social roles are eagerly cultivated. Some roles we deplore: the roles of traitor, heroin addict, alcoholic or neurotic we shun altogether. One of the consequences of being cast in a disreputably defined mould is that it necessarily has a *self-fulfilling* character. (Wheeler, 1967: 636) Although the drug peddler may deny that the role reflects his 'true' self he soon finds that friends and acquaintances change their manner toward him, he is less socially acceptable, and his world becomes increasingly restricted. For comfort he must look elsewhere, often to other outcasts like himself.

The *visibility* of an act to others is obviously crucial in triggering the process of acquiring a deviant character. To be discovered smoking 'pot' by a friend may result in his joining the group, to be discovered by a policeman may result in being 'busted.' Yet detection by the police is not necessarily more harmful than discovery by others. Depending on the participants, the circumstances surrounding the behavior, and the inclination of the police officer, official action may or may not be taken. However, the next-door neighbor who witnesses the same behavior may be an immediate source of gossip.

Organized denunciation is relatively rare in the production of deviant characters. Highly publicized court cases are an obvious exception, but the diffusion of a socially degrading label is more often an informal process generated by word of mouth. The range of visibility of a deviant act will vary from perhaps only the parties involved to the larger society. In many instances the social visibility of deviant acts is minimal, for example, illicit sex acts, shoplifting, confidence games, illegal drug-taking and call-girl prostitution. The larger the radius of persons who are aware of the deviant act, and the greater the public attention that it evokes, the greater the probability of its damaging a person's character.

STIGMA

To say that activities that are socially discredited are deviant behavior is only a half-truth. There is much behavior that is frowned upon and unwelcome that *does not violate normative rules* and is not considered deviant. To be poor, to be a slum dweller, to be mentally retarded, physically handicapped or a 'suspicious character' are all socially disvalued roles, but they are not deviant roles. To clean the streets, to collect garbage, shine shoes, or strip before an audience are typically disreputable kinds of work. Seldom do parents rear their children for such jobs. Yet these kinds of work do not violate the normative rules of society. People who perform these activities we consider unfortunate, but we seldom blame them for their misfortune. Sanctions are not applied to those who we feel have little or no choice in the matter. Not so with the deviant — the user or pusher of marihuana. Society sanctions these persons because the possession of marihuana is a violation of the criminal code. But there is more than the formal action of a community towards a misbehaving person. In the process we label and brand him, more for having violated the normative rules of society than for having violated the law. And herein lies the seed of the *stigmatization* process.

To be stigmatized is to be marked as a morally undesirable person. Until recently this was inevitably the fate of the marihuana user. It no longer is. However, in the past the 'pot' smoker was called a 'dope fiend,' said to be 'depraved,' 'degraded' and 'morally irresponsible;' he was termed 'dangerous,' 'evil,' 'criminally inclined' and 'liable to kill and indulge in any form of violence.' Stigmatization is this kind of collective process of attaching *pejorative labels,* terms of moral inferiority, to a person. A major part of the process is the 'terrible censure' of opinion that is directed against the person; this necessarily misrepresents the person's activities and attacks his integrity. In the case of marihuana the censure is levelled first against the drug. But it is a short step to denunciation of the drug user. Where the drug is a 'terrible evil' the user is soon defined as 'morally depraved,' driven to vice.

There are a number of requirements for successful denunciation of the deviant (Garfinkel, 1956: 420-424), yet the success of the stigmatization process is judged more by the consequences than by the means employed. At the same time stigma is not an irreversible process. Although it seems always to arouse feelings of injustice it does not fix deviance in the person nor need it result in renewed deviance. For example, smoking 'pot' may be only a temporary activity — a fling at risk-taking, and a 'pothead' may give up drugs forever.

What we have been discussing are the responses of others to a person's real or imagined behavior and their consequences for his *public identity*. Although the responses of others to deviance seem unlimited, such responses and the labels that are applied are never a private matter. Because the *labelling process* itself arises in a social system it is closely circumscribed by rules. How we respond to the deviance of others, who may legitimately sanction or label another, the justification of the label and the severity of the sanctions that are applied are all governed by rules. Moreover, how we react to deviants, whether we are punitive, tolerant, violent or considerate is influenced also by the formal and 'personal' roles that we occupy and their significance for us. The culture often provides us with relatively *ready-made responses* to particular kinds of deviance and deviant persons.

We know in advance how 'civic-minded' Canadians, sophisticates, God-fearing persons, hippies and policemen will feel and respond to many kinds of deviance. Murder, blackmail, robbery, treason will be condemned and there will be almost total denunciation of such acts. However, there is much less consensus concerning the so-called vices such as gambling, the use of marihuana and drugs of addiction, and prostitution. These are activities for which there is widespread demand, and from which persons derive profound satisfaction. The recipients of such services are not victims, but beneficiaries, and one's definition of these activities is apt to be greatly influenced by the professional and informal roles that one occupies. For example, hippies and sophisticates are apt to be relatively tolerant of such activities, but parents of teenage children, 'civic-minded' Canadians, the clergy and senior citizens have often taken a firm stand against prostitution, drug use and various kinds of sexual deviance.

But during a period of rapid social change, clearly established responses to differing kinds of deviance are much less available. This is currently true of marihuana use. Marihuana users no longer suffer the disgrace that previously befell them. It is no less a crime to possess marihuana, but there is much less stigma attached to its use. Not all groups and social roles are equally vulnerable to social change and some groups remain adamantly opposed to marihuana use.

The gradual redefinition of marihuana use is reflected in the operation of the courts. The number of written reports, appellate opinions and discussions concerning the handling of first offenders for possession or marginal trafficking clearly reflects the uncertainty of the courts in this matter. However, the law was amended in August, 1969 to provide the option of proceeding by summary conviction instead of indictment in cases of simple possession of marihuana and hashish. (*Interim Report*, 1970: 185, 187-188) Imprisonment is now rarely resorted to in such cases, the general rule being not to imprison first offenders.

All this does not deny the general vilification of those who use marihuana and other drugs. It does strongly suggest, however, that our folkways and norms are changing, and that increasing numbers of persons are unwilling to stigmatize categorically and irrevocably persons who smoke 'pot.'

A serious result of occupying a visibly low status role and of engaging in socially disreputable activities is that the stigma is often an important ingredient in social encounters. Admittedly the degree to which social interaction is strained as a result of stigma is problematic, but visible cues of physical defects enter into, and usually complicate, social interaction. Ultimately these experiences often leave their mark on the personality of the stigmatized person. This is much less the case with the user of marihuana. Unless he is very high the user exhibits few if any visible cues of his habit. Nor does the knowledge of a person's use of marihuana greatly strain social encounters. Whatever stigma is attached to the marihuana user, there is little evidence to suggest that it will pose serious problems for him in social interaction.

The miniculture of marihuana users, the 'pot parties,' and the social milieux arranged for marihuana use often foster strong inter-personal relationships. The fact that marihuana users limit much of their use of 'pot' and related activities to this web of contacts, and socialize with others similarly circumstanced helps guard against the damaging consequences of stigma and helps prevent a deviant self-image from arising. At the same time most marihuana users strongly reject those who 'shoot' heroin, and the miserable prospects of getting hooked and existing in a tortured, strain-ridden world of hustlers. (Smart and Jackson, 1969) Heroin addicts and 'speed freaks' are frowned upon, and 'cool' drug users look upon them with utter disdain. The labels used in referring to heroin addicts ('burn artists,' 'snitches,' 'punks') suggest the stigma attached to heroin use.

Explanations of Marihuana Use

Until now we have looked at some salient aspects of deviant and conforming behavior in relation to marihuana use as a social issue in Canada. Our next task is to try to explain or account for the use of marihuana in society. Any explanation of behavior (deviant or other-wise) presupposes some underlying theory or general set of rules to which all of the same category of acts are supposed to conform. However, it would be foolhardy to expect more of sociology than it can possibly offer at this time. Rather than highly rigorous, formal kinds of theory, characteristic of the physical sciences, current sociological explanations of deviance are best viewed as 'successive approximations' to this kind of precise theoretical formulation. Perhaps our 'theories' of deviance should be thought of as relatively systematic sociological perspectives on deviant behavior.

One approach to the explanation of deviance, e.g., marihuana use, assumes that the variation in the rates and forms of using marihuana is best explained by looking at the *kinds of people* who smoke 'pot.' The emphasis is on the individual and the processes whereby he acquires the practice of using marihuana. Not everyone uses marihuana, and it is assumed that only certain kinds of people do so. The question to be answered is: What sort of person would do this sort of thing? (Cohen, 1966: 41-47) Ultimately this leads us to categorize the 'kinds of people' variously disposed to using the drug. Next we enquire: How do people become the kinds of people who smoke 'pot'? To answer this question we explore their histories and family backgrounds. This is a *psychological* approach to the problem.

However, acts, whether getting married, attending university, or turning on with marihuana, are not related only to the biographies of the actors. These events can be located also in the society, in a social class, a family, a city, professional group or boys' gang. Varying forms of deviance are differentially distributed throughout the society. For exam-ple, we know that predatory aggressive kinds of delinquency are disproportionately located among the urban lower classes. We know also that the crime-rate in Canada declines as the educational level increases. (Giffen, 1965: 79) There is good reason to believe that proportionately more persons under twenty-five years of age use 'pot' than persons over fifty. Moreover, these facts about society tend to remain remarkably stable over time. This suggests that *while persons come and go in society the kinds and rates of their deviant behavior remain relatively constant.* Clearly the rates and characteristic distributions of this behavior are a property of the systems in which they occur, and can be studied as such. We can ask the question: What is it about the cultural, structural, and organizational make-up of the society that produces the regularities in rates, nature, and distribution of deviant behavior? To answer this question we must concentrate on the properties of the society, not those of the individual. This is the *sociological* approach to the problem of deviance and the one taken in the theories presented in the following section.

In trying to explain the rates of suicide in society Emile Durkheim paid almost exclusive attention to the cultural and social structures of the system. He was not concerned with the idiosyncratic motives of individuals, but he was interested in motives that were common to categories of suicides. Moreover, Durkheim was concerned with motivation as a function of the structural make-up of the system. In this manner he was applying a sociological perspective to the problem. It is to his work that we turn first.

Durkheim, Anomie Theory and Marihuana Use: An Application

Durkheim was interested in the problem of group cohesiveness, and was especially concerned with the fact that specialization in the occupational structure of society resulted in a change in social solidarity and social integration, and produced conflict and tension among men. Confusion resulted, and people worked at cross-purposes. He attributed this to a breakdown in the principal mechanism of social control, the body of common understandings and definitions in society. This condition he termed *anomie or deregulation,* by which he seemed to mean *normlessness.* (Durkheim, 1949; 1951) Moreover, he believed that where normlessness prevailed the behavior and relationships of men reflected a disabling lack of direction which resulted in tendencies towards social disorganization.

Durkheim pursued this idea in his work on suicide and believed that suicide rates were best explained with reference to the properties of the system, not those of the individual. Durkheim believed that there was no 'natural' limit to the desires and social wants of men. What controlled their choice of goals, limited their ambitions, and disciplined their aspirations were the rules in society. One of the functions of these rules is to 'define for each class of men what it is legitimately entitled to ... and thereby create the possibility of a sense of satisfaction and fulfillment.' (Cohen, 1966: 75; Durkheim, 1951: 149) As a product of society, this body of rules is learned and gradually internalized into one's conscience. Durkheim believed that if anything occurred to break down these controls, men were thrown behaviorally off balance. 'Overweening ambition' always exceeds the possibility of fulfillment. Nothing gives satisfaction, and meaning is sapped from life. Under such conditions effort is not rewarded, there is no pay-off. Often men are unable to endure this. Durkheim asks: 'How could the desire to live not be weakened ... ?' (1951; 153) Sometimes this state of affairs leads to suicide.

To employ anomie theory to explain marihuana use primarily, but not exclusively among high school and university students is to consider their behavior a manifestation of a more general social problem. If growing numbers of youths must use 'pot' in order to feel confortable with others, the problem depends upon the properties and functioning of the society. One question is: Does a state of anomie exist in the daily lives of young people? Can we detect a deterioration in the moral and social spheres governing the lives of these youths? Are the lives of young students aimless, without direction, devoid of meaning?

During the past fifty years society has undergone widespread institutional change (Hobart, 1968; Elkin, 1968; Mann, 1970). Population change has produced an increase in the number of young people in the productive years of life, and today we believe that they should remain in school and out of the labor market. Cities continue to benefit from in-migration at the expense of rural areas; family size has decreased and traditional, patriarchally-run families have given way to more democratic units. Yet standards governing parent-child relationships have become blurred, and while the family atmosphere has grown more permissive, relationships are often uneasy. As old certainties undergo transformation in the sphere of social relations and morality, the adolescent role has grown vague, and its expectations and obligations are difficult to teach.

High schools have relaxed their authoritarian structure, and in some cases students seem to run the schools. The vacillation in attitudes and policies of teachers, and the continual revision of curricula and standards reflect the strain being felt in the field of education. Similarly, as religion adapts to the larger transformation taking place, it has grown noticeably sensitive to the social 'needs' of young people, and increasingly concerned with social issues.

Today's moral scene (especially in the vast middle and upper-middle strata) is confused; there has developed a profusion of moralities, new styles of affluent living have emerged, but new justifications and sanctions have yet to take hold. Definitions of authority have been transformed, but remain unclear.

This suggests a normative malaise or quasi-deregulation in many sectors of society. Deprived of clearcut expectations for conduct, perhaps young people do live in a world of partially legitimized rights, of normative uneasiness and moral uncertainty. Perhaps life is a 'bad scene' for these youths, and augurs poorly for the future. Under such conditions their desire to escape from reality seems plausible, even likely. The use of drugs is one form of escape. This implies that marihuana users are plagued with problems of daily living, and that they try to alleviate their difficulties by escaping into the 'never never land of euphoria.' But does smoking 'pot' enable them to escape the problems that bedevil them? How is marihuana functional for the moral uncertainty and semi-normlessness that circumscribe their lives?

In its capacity to produce hallucinations and emotional change, marihuana does not compare with LSD and other hallucinogens. As a means of escape from everyday reality marihuana will seldom produce the aesthetic and mystical experience common to the use of LSD. The occasional use of 'pot' by young people is no solution to their daily problems of adjustment and is likely an unsatisfactory means of escape.

For the relatively small percentage of youths who are psychologically hooked and for whom marihuana use is an integral part of their lives, this may serve as a second-rate means of escape. Ironically, for these youths smoking 'pot' is also a form of bondage since escape is dependent upon its continual use. But marihuana is a poor choice as a means of escape. Hallucinations are seldom a result of marihuana use, but (like alcohol hallucinations) an indication of overdose. Although some users of marihuana do use hallucinogens, there are no data to suggest that the majority of young people who use marihuana are seeking an escape from reality. Whatever their problems, their occasional indulgence in marihuana reflects an involvement in a world that matters to them – the broadening culture of middle and upper-middle class youths. That so many youths pursue their education or seek permanent employment testifies to their participation in the world of today as a preparation for the future. In no way are the majority of these youths truant from life.

Durkheim did not try to develop a general theory of deviant behavior. This task was performed some years later by Robert K. Merton (1957: 131-194) in his well known paper entitled *Social Structure and Anomie,* which was a modification of Durkheim's ideas and which laid a foundation for a general theory of deviant behavior. It provides us with an additional explanation for marihuana use.

Robert K. Merton, Anomie Theory and Marihuana Use: An Application

In attempting to explain differential rates of deviance Merton focused on the cultural and social composition of society. He believed that anomie resulted from *socially structured strain.* In his scheme he distinguishes three conceptual elements: first there are *cultural goals* (things that are worth striving for), secondly he includes *norms* that prescribe the choice of legitimate means for goal attainment, and thirdly he singles out the objective set of facilities and opportunities, i.e., the *institutionalized means* for reaching the cultural goals. A change in any one of these

Table I: A Typology of Modes of Individual Adaptation*

Modes of Adaptation	Culture Goals	Institutionalized Means
Conformity	+	+
Innovation	+	−
Ritualism	−	+
Retreatism	−	−
Rebellion	±	±

*Source: R.K. Merton, *Social Theory and Social Structure,* p. 140. Copyright © 1968 by The Free Press.

elements may produce strain and despair for certain sectors of the society. For example, should the culturally preferred goals suddenly become beyond attainment, strain will ensue; a redefinition of what constitutes the legitimate means for reaching the goals also may create strain because of the possible ambiguity experienced in the substitution of means.

This scheme emphasizes the notion that *the very values that society cherishes and requires to generate conformity among its members also lead them to deviance.* Through the use of two variables — culturally preferred goals and institutional means — Merton shows (see Table I) that acceptance or rejection (two values per variable) of the goals or means can result in a number of logically possible types or modes of adaptation.

CONFORMITY

The first mode of adaptation is *conformity,* the others are the deviant adaptations of innovation, retreatism, ritualism, and rebellion. According to Merton, *conformity results when actors are favorably disposed to strive for the culturally preferred goals, and employ the legitimate means for their attainment.* This is the most common response in a stable society. It is evident that the vast majority of Canadian youths accept the goals of society, conform to the conventional norms and abstain from using marihuana.

INNOVATION

For Merton, the condition of anomie arises from socially structured strain. However, it is not the lack of institutional opportunities for material success that produces anomie. It is the equalitarian beliefs that emphasize economic opportunity for everyone, yet create for some sectors *seemingly insurmountable restrictions to the legitimate means and facilities, breeding strain and frustration and weakening their commitment to the norm.* Under such conditions, men grow ambivalent towards the norms and have second thoughts about conforming to the rules. The gradual attenuation of legitimacy from the norms sometimes leads to *innovation,* i.e., *the use of 'more or less expedient illegitimate means.'* (Clinard, 1964: 18) Merton considered these activities illegitimate innovations that often lead to monetary gain. Thus *deviance constitutes a solution to anomie.*

Perhaps this helps explain the presence and operation of criminal organizations that distribute hard drugs in the lower classes. But it cannot satisfactorily explain the use of marihuana among increasing numbers of Canadian high school and university students. Admittedly, there likely has been an increase in certain forms of delinquency among middle and upper class youths over the past twenty-five years; this may be defined as a certain dissatisfaction with particular aspects of the legitimate order. More recently the increase in student radical groups (that cover a wide spectrum of political views) both in high school and university, may also indicate a certain disenchantment, notably with the academic institutions in the system. Yet there is no evidence to suggest that the majority of these youths have renounced the legitimate means of society. Quite the contrary, often they wish to improve them. The limited scope of their aggressive challenge to the established order, and their continued attendance at school or university reflect their considerable commitment to the institutionalized means and long-range goals. We do not believe that there is a 'number sufficiently large to result in a more frequent disjunction between goals and opportunity' among marihuana users than non-users that are goal-oriented. Equally important, marihuana use does not readily make sense as an alternative means of achieving material success in society, although it might easily symbolize a thumbing of the nose at the conventional idea of success.

RITUALISM

Can *ritualism, conformity to means while rejecting societal goals,* explain marihuana use by young people? In recent years a number of Canadian campuses have been marked by student crises and uprisings that suggested a spreading malaise among many, but by no means all students. Most of the students were allegedly dissatisfied (in varying degree) with the organization of their institutions, a small number were also critical of society and many of its preferred goals. In effect, they declared that the struggle for the 'good things of life' (and all the material objects that this entails) is a 'bad bag.' For them, happiness was not to be found in a materially oriented, largely middle class way of life, and they refused (if only temporarily) to be so consumption oriented.

Yet while they objected to many of society's goals, many of them pursued their education at the universities. Admittedly, they continued their work with little devotion or sense of direction. Their conformity to academic requirements was often ritualistic, almost compulsive behavior. Given such overt conformity, marihuana use is an inconsistent behavior. The notion of retreatism does not aid us in our explanation. Marihuana use is not ritualistic conformity to the legitimate means, as Merton's scheme requires.

RETREATISM

Retreatism is perhaps the least common (though most popularly accepted) form of adaptation among young people. *The rejection of both the legitimate means and ends of society* is likely the final adaptive practice of persons who have suffered a series of socially damaging experiences. Vagrants, chronic drunks, heroin addicts and other social rejects often comprise this group. Do the huge majority of young students who use 'pot' repudiate the cultural goals and institutions in society? Are they rebelling against authority, against their parents, escaping from reality, from boredom, or whatever? Do they look and act as if they are retreating from society?

Admittedly, there are some youths who do express a morbid rebelliousness against authority; sometimes it is only parental relationships that suffer; in other cases youths have poor academic records, personality problems, or undergo other socially painful experiences. Some of these youths do feel alone, alienated, and depressed, and may ultimately gravitate with their problems to the city streets. But in the majority of cases it is the daily hardship and grim quality of street living that alienates the so-called 'street people' from the remainder of society. It is under such conditions that tensions, anxieties, and problems tend to emerge.

In the late sixties the majority of street people were youths of middle class origin, most had completed high school, and had left home. In the summer months (and some continued their street existence throughout the year) they found themselves 'doing their own thing' on the streets of large urban centers. Their efforts at scrounging, begging, panhandling and petty stealing in order to stay alive were circumscribed by a patchwork street culture of esoteric interests, such as Eastern religion, philosophy and witchcraft, characterized by half-baked knowledge and colorful ritualistic displays. They were mostly harmless. The use of 'pot' was and continues to be high among these youths, but it appears neither colorful nor exciting, and is devoid of the ritualistic apparatus often found among other groups. Smoking marihuana has become routine for them, and they sometimes smoke alone and in public places. The alienation and retreatism of these similarly circumstanced youths are an uninspiring source of motivation to encourage the attainment of culturally approved goals. Instead, they tend to breed a collective inertia and to reinforce each other's depression and myopic perspective of society.

REBELLION

The final mode of adaptation is *rebellion*. Like retreatists, rebels are also alienated, and reject the legitimate means and ends of society, but they neither withdraw from, nor adapt to, the society. Through political or more violent action, they try to *create a greatly modified social structure by substituting new means and ends*. When rebellion becomes endemic to large sectors of the system it is potentially dangerous for the outbreak of revolution. When limited to small powerless elements of the society (e.g., unorganized bands of student drop-outs of many political persuasions) this sometimes provides the conditions for the existence of small, relatively alienated groups. But surely this response seems applicable only in a limited way to a fraction of Canadian youths. Rebels feel little commitment to the existing normative structure; to attribute such a lack of commitment to more than a small percentage of marihuana users does not ring true. Understandably, however, there is likely a correlation between marihuana use and student revolutionaries. But the overwhelming majority of high school and university students who have used and continue to use 'pot' are not alienated from society; they have a general idea of where they wish to go and how best to get there.

The Merton scheme is a strong attempt to design a general sociological theory of deviance. It gives short shrift to the characteristics of individuals and concentrates on culture and social structures. What is not emphasized forcefully is the influence of others on the conduct of the actor. (Cohen, 1965: 9-14; Merton, 1964: 213-243) The actions of others always matter, and one tends to act in ways that elicit the support of one's reference groups. To act alone illegally is a difficult road to travel. Deviance, e.g., smoking 'pot,' almost invariably occurs in a social system, and it influences those others with whom one is associated in the system. Early experiences with marihuana are apt to be experimental, but they are no less influenced by the groups to which we belong, the informal roles that we occupy, and the identities that we claim. Differential active involvement in such groups will greatly influence our continued participation and frequency of marihuana use. Similarly, our involvement with marihuana will affect those who comprize our reference group. Finally, the scheme fails to specify those determinants that inform us which of the modes of adaptation will be selected.

Until now we have attempted to account for the use of marihuana by young people by paying special attention to the differential emphases given to the cultural goals and institutionalized means in society. We noted that *each of the four kinds of deviant response helped explain a small proportion of marihuana use. But we were unable to account for marihuana use by the large majority of these youths.*

Perhaps a special set of motives is not required to explain marihuana use among middle and upper class youths. Nor need we posit that these youths turn from legitimate to illegitimate means to reach their goals. Another perspective is to look at the legitimate content and internal structure of the *youth culture* in which the majority of young people participate. The following perspective suggests that differential involvement, i.e., conformity to the legitimate established activities of youth, leads to differential use of marihuana. It may be that the roots of marihuana use, like other forms of deviant behavior, reside in the culturally esteemed patterns themselves.

Marihuana Use and the Middle Class Youth Culture

Notwithstanding its ethnic, religious, and regional diversity, the youth culture is cemented by an inlay of common experience, shared values and interests, and collective behavior patterns (Vaz, 1965; 1971: 174-185). *Middle class youths are strongly peer-oriented, conspicuously non-intellectual, given to socializing; the values of conformity, social prestige, and the pursuit of pleasurable activities rank high* . (Vaz, 1965)

The content of the youth culture is neither rebellious nor delinquent and seldom does it antagonize middle class values. The large majority of its activities and interests receive the blessing of parents and teachers, and the organized opportunities for non-intellectual affairs, and their popularity in high school and university reflect their institutionalization and testify to adult concern for young people.

Among middle class youth prestige is a scarce commodity and the daily competition for social recognition is brisk and pervasive. Seldom does an event occur in which the element of competition is not present, and peers are alert to pass judgment. Gradually competition with 'everyman' becomes internalized and the 'generalized other' becomes an ubiquitous audience always keeping score. Even among strangers a youth's conduct reflects the effort to elicit attention and seek approval.

Yet most of the social activities in and out of high school and university are fun-oriented and ostensibly non-competitive, which helps consolidate social ties and weld group cohesion. This lack of seriousness and competitiveness is reflected in the expressions used to describe these activities, e.g., 'It's all in fun,' 'It's just for kicks,' or 'We were just havin' a few laughs.'

Among young people veiled competition for prestige stimulates behavioral experimentation. This experimentation (Dubin, 1959: 152) usually gains the attention of peers, nourishes competition and takes the form of behavioral nuances sufficiently novel to distinguish them from existing patterns and the competing efforts of peers. All social conduct is partly exploratory and efforts at marginal differentiation (being different, but not too different) tend to be guarded, tentative and ambiguous, and occur in situations characterized by 'mutual exploration and joint elaboration' of behavior. (Cohen, 1955: 60) Because there exist strong motivations to conform to prevailing norms and cultural models, innovation is tolerated only if it falls within the precincts of acceptable interests and cherished values. But since these activities occur in a non-competitive setting, creative efforts are applauded, and behavioral novelty is seldom defined as deviant. As newly developing practices and games become established they acquire their own rules, rituals, and mythologies.

Under such conditions law violation need not emerge from anti-social impulses. Illegal behavior that originates in anti-social impulses is apt to violate acceptable conduct and be disapproved. The common core of motivation for most law violation among these youths is learned through sustained involvement in respectable activities. (Scott and Vaz, 1963) In this manner certain forms of law violation become a routine affair. The more 'normal' an individual, i.e., the greater his active participation in customary legitimate social affairs, the greater the likelihood of his committing deviant acts. (Scott and Vaz, 1963)

MARIHUANA USE AS A NOVEL EXPERIENCE

The practice of smoking 'pot' does not spring full blown among young people, but is linked to the typical activities and social roles available to them. Active involvement in activities like smoking, drinking, dating, going steady, dancing and giving parties is instrumental in gaining social status. In turn this elicits further opportunities for social engagements.

Whether we become interested in something and the amount of time and energy that we devote to its pursuit will depend largely on whether it matters to us. One thing that matters to us is ourselves. The variety of roles in the youth culture greatly influences the acceptable identities that are available for appropriation. These too are an important source of social standing. What happens is that we are motivated to learn and to engage in those acts, adopt those demeanors, employ those behavioral gimmicks that will support the roles that we are playing, and highlight the identities that we risk on display. Deviant behavior readily serves the same functions, and is often selected when it coincides with, communicates, symbolizes or otherwise spotlights the identity being claimed. A youth's choice of roles and identity is crucial in accounting for his conduct at any one moment. As new roles are selected and new identities displayed for validation new attitudes and practices are required. New criteria become applicable according to which youths will be judged by peers, and depending on the degree of their ego involvement in their role, evaluate themselves. (Cohen, 1971)

The use of marihuana is merely a single step in a sequence of increasingly prestigeful social activities. One study of 'pot' smokers reveals that between 83 per cent and 90 per cent reported smoking tobacco, and between 79 per cent and 85 per cent reported using alcohol. (Whitehead, *et al.,* 1970: 10-17; Goode, 1972: 35) For youths who have progressed from tobacco to alcohol to sex the mere knowledge of marihuana and its argot is sufficiently novel to elicit attention and gain recognition from peers. The next step in the developing sequence might be the use of tranquilisers, stimulants, glue, cough syrup or marihuana itself depending on the availability of the stuff, and perhaps the roles being claimed by the youths.

However, an account of marihuana use among middle and upper-middle class youth must explain the opportunity for its use. If mere knowledge of marihuana is sufficient to gain the respect of peers, actually to possess the stuff is more likely to spark attention, arouse excitement, elicit approval. To possess the weed is itself an operating invention. The pushers and dealers are themselves youths (often friends) which lends credence to our perspective (Carey, 1968), while destroying the absurd notion that peddlers introduce marihuana to young people.

The next likely step is experimentation with marihuana, and exploration and elaboration of the process leads to a few drags of the weed until gradually, in the company of friends, the youth learns to derive pleasure from smoking. (Becker, 1973) It is these kinds of unobtrusive acts that lead gradually to unanticipated elaboration beyond the boundaries of legitimacy. *Marihuana use is the outcome of a sequence of routine activities; young people are introduced to marihuana by their friends and they are turned on by their friends. Moreover such activities are socially rewarding, i.e., they receive the approval of peers, and conform to the standards of those groups that matter to them.*

Since smoking 'pot' coincides with recreational activities we should expect continued experimentation in its use. Marihuana use is not a specific drug activity. Whitehead reports that six times as many marihuana users have used glue (an operating invention), nine times as many have used stimulants, and eleven times as many have taken barbiturates as non-marihuana smokers. (Whitehead, 1971: 68) But behavioral differentiation does not stop with the use of 'pot.' Novelty is found also in the kinds of 'grass' and types of 'roach holders' that are used (Smart and Jackson, 1969: 66).

Marihuana use is only one of many kinds of novel experience pursued by young people. One reason for their ready acceptance of 'pot' is that it fails to violate grossly their everyday attitudes and values, nor does it interfere with their customary style of living. However, the use of hard drugs, such as heroin, is harshly condemned since it makes uncontrollable demands on them, and being hooked (unless one is wealthy) inevitably leads to social degradation, psychological distress, and physical hardship. It is a deadly affair.

COMPATIBILITY OF MARIHUANA USE WITH THE YOUTH CULTURE
The compatibility of marihuana use with existing features of the youth culture greatly facilitates its acceptance. Research data show that 'pot' is used predominately in groups, and primarily in a social setting with friends. In one study 94 per cent of regular users reported that their initial use of marihuana occurred mainly among friends while 80.6 per cent reported that mostly friends comprised the social milieu for their customary use of marihuana. (*A Study of Marihuana Users and Usage,* 1970: 28) In 91.8 per cent of cases the group mood was reported to be either happy or relaxed, gay or carefree. (*A Study,* 1970: 9) These data highlight the social, convivial, and leisure oriented conditions in which 'pot' is customarily smoked. Its relaxing, mildly intoxicating characteristics are perfectly congenial with the after-school and weekend activities of many young people. Are these not the typical emotional reactions of young persons engaged in everyday youth culture events?

What we are saying is that smoking 'pot' is remarkably entertaining, relaxing, and enjoyable, and that there is nothing seemingly incompatible or mutually exclusive between smoking 'grass' and normal involvement in legitimate activities of young people. Moreover, marihuana use very likely improves the extent and quality of those very activities and values that are considered desirable and are approved by middle class parents and teachers. Youths who smoke 'pot' will likely augment their circle of friends, be more socially in demand, and, if they are to be believed, very likely increase their sense of aesthetic appreciation (Goode, 1970), besides adding a spark to their sex lives.

PSYCHOLOGICAL EFFECTS OF MARIHUANA USE
The psychological effects of marihuana use vary greatly and are quite difficult to predict (*Interim Report,* 1970: 77). The dose, preparation, type, method of administration, social milieu, besides the expectations and personality of the user all influence the subjective effects of marihuana, especially at the lower dosage levels. The effects are also a function of learning to smoke properly, of being sensitive to and able to recognize and label the effects. However, were marihuana use to produce

regularly a psychologically depressive state that dampened the social activities of young people we should not expect them to use it much.

A marihuana 'high' usually involves several stages (*Interim Report,* 1970: 78-79): the initial reaction is often stimulating and perhaps includes some mild tension; it is usually replaced by a pleasant feeling of well-being; rapid mood changes often occur and considerable hilarity may be replaced by periods of silence. Psychological effects typically reported by users include happiness, contentment, increased conviviality, heightened sensitivity to humor, either increased or decreased verbal fluency, and the lessening of inhibitions among other sensations. (*Interim Report,* 1970: 79) Is it surprising that most marihuana users most of the time like what they experience?

Are these psychological effects not characteristic of parties, socials and other legitimate recreational activities? In fact these events are organized in order to produce many of these kinds of responses. When such reactions are not forthcoming the events are considered failures. The psychological reactions to marihuana are largely compatible with the subjective effects common to other social events and they do not violate the psychological expectations of young people. Is it any wonder that smoking 'pot' is spreading among young people frequently engaged in legitimate social activities?

MOTIVES

Marihuana use is not triggered by deviant motives nor by any special need, but stems from the common core of motivation associated with differential participation in the daily activities of young people. Motives are not starters of action nor are they individually invented, but are learned in the course of interaction, from the community at large, and permit men to act in one way or another. (Mills, 1940: Cressey, 1953: 93-136) The justifications and rationalizations for using 'pot' are appropriated from others in the process of learning to smoke the stuff, distinguish the effects, and enjoy the sensations. An operational vocabulary of motives is learned, gradually internalized and becomes the only one youths possess that can meaningfully express their experiences.

The terms used by youths to recount their experiences with 'pot' mirror their unserious definition of marihuana, and are congruent with its effects and the fun-orientation of their routine activities. For example, they 'smoke a joint,' they 'blow grass,' they 'do dope,' and they 'smoke pot,' (terms that also reflect marginal differentiation in the use of language), because 'it's fun,' because 'I like to,' because 'getting high ... is much better than getting drunk ... you're happier than getting drunk ...,' or because 'I use it the same way I use alcohol,' or 'just for kicks.'

However, there are a multiplicity of groups among young people, which include politically active, socially conscious, intellectual units such as the Maoists, Hippies, Free Thinkers, Bohemians, among others. Whatever these labels mean young people identify with them, they claim prominent roles in these groups, they think of themselves in such terms, and until their claims are successfully challenged (or until they outgrow these roles) much of their everyday life is conducted according to current group standards. The terms used by these youths to explain their use of 'pot' will reflect their group's special interests, yet overlap with the more specific argot of marihuana use. The final product is a rhetoric that enables members to rationalize their conduct, and helps justify the ideology and vested practices of the group.

We should expect them to use terms that are critical, abstract, serious, and idealistic, that deal with topics such as God, values, aesthetics, freedom, equality, and humanity in general. However, distinguishable differences with terms common to the larger youth culture will be evident. Members of these groups often report that they use marihuana because they are 'alienated from society,' because they are 'searching for God,' because it facilitates their 'search for peace,' because they 'seek self-realization' and 'self-integration,' because they wish for 'inner satisfaction,' because they are looking for the 'spirit of love,' or a 'new awareness.' Many state that they are seeking 'new values,' and that 'conventional society is rejected because originality and spontaneity are no longer possible,' (Garvin, 1967) while others report that they are driven to 'search for authentic experience.'

Middle and upper class youths do not experience status deprivation, and seldom are they burdened with common strains and stresses. They do not turn to marihuana because they are alienated from society, rebelling against their parents or because they reject conventional society. Their relative disenchantment with society, their vocal disillusionment with the adult world and their critical attitudes are role expectations typical of a number of student roles. To be an intellectual, to be politically active, to be socially concerned, to be an activist, means to assume these kinds of roles, hold particular attitudes, espouse certain values, use the appropriate vocabulary and make oneself heard. Instead of being driven to marihuana to escape from reality, the narrow circumscribed worlds in which these youths live, the temporary roles that they claim, and the fleeting identities that they assume, require that they embrace the routine marihuana-smoking reality of which they are part architect. (Suchman, 1968: 146-155; Blumer, 1967: 48-52)

SOCIAL CONDITIONS FOR MARIHUANA USE AMONG YOUNG PEOPLE
Here we explore the structure of opportunity (Cloward and Ohlin, 1960; Cohen, 1966: 108-113) for engaging in legitimate social activities that

are required for the illegitimate use of marihuana. One condition that facilitates marihuana use among young people is their having access to the requisite physical objects for engaging in socially approved legitimate affairs. For example, access to a car, pocket money, the latest clothes, alcoholic beverages, are important for being popular and socially active. Yet not all activities attractive to university students will appeal to high school youth, and the more sophisticated roles will be unavailable to them. Also the objects will vary with the social games and activities that prevail. In any case differential access to these objects greatly influences the opportunity to participate in legitimate social affairs and consequently increases the opportunities for using marihuana.

A positive attitude towards socializing and engaging in peer-oriented activities is indispensable. The price for non-participation in peer activities is social pariahdom — an inordinately high cost in the socially oriented world of young people. Is it any wonder, then, that the young person who engages in a social setting where the norms encourage active involvement in social events will have little choice but to experiment with marihuana if the opportunity arises in the *routine* course of events?

The social organization and cultural heterogeneity of urban centers provide greater opportunity for experimentation and innovation in behavior than in rural areas. The built-in obsolescence characteristic of industrial society and predominant in urban areas has helped institution-alize the value of innovation. The cultural nuclei of student life are found in the large universities and high schools in metropolitan centers where the proliferation of groups, and the availability of newly emerging roles help maximize opportunities for innovating practices and games congruent with the leisure activities of young people. Compared to rural youths, city students have a much wider choice of social events and organized opportunities in which to participate and experiment with sophisticated and novel kinds of behavior. We have already noted that the more frequent use of marihuana appeared first in the metropolitan centers of Montreal, Toronto, and Vancouver. Rural youths often take their lead from their urban brothers in their selection of practices, customs, and behavioral fads. We should anticipate that they will also follow suit in the use of 'pot.'

Changing sex roles help explain the differential use of marihuana between the sexes. Research has shown that middle class boys and girls engage in similar delinquent acts. (Wise, 1967: 179-188) This is because boys and girls participate in common activities, which often foster opportunities for deviance. Since marihuana use is compatible with the social affairs of youths, we should anticipate that girls who are most active socially are most apt to smoke 'pot.'

While norms encourage certain forms of heterosexual relationships and activity between the sexes, prevailing restrictions on the general female role help produce differential rates of marihuana use between boys and girls. Except in matters of fashion a girl is still not expected to experiment in behavior; to initiate sensuous activities, to search for kicks or for a new awareness are still largely prohibited to her. However, in contrast to the past, role expectations are that she co-operate more readily with the male initiative in a larger variety of activities. Differential conformity to expectations of this general role will influence marihuana use among girls.

The opportunities that exist for involvement in socially approved activities greatly affect the chances of young people using marihuana. Access to different means for social participation, highly desirable physical and personality characteristics, an enthusiastic attitude towards socializing, residence in or near a metropolitan area, and being socially active — all are important variables influencing the opportunities to smoke 'pot.'

In summary, this perspective states that marihuana use by young people is predominantly social behavior; in the large majority of cases it occurs episodically or occasionally, and is experienced as a pleasurable, relatively harmless activity that is perfectly compatible with the recreational activities of youths. Thus, it is best understood through a knowledge of the structure and content of the legitimate culture of young people and their differential involvement therein.

Conclusion

Whenever the marihuana issue is discussed the question inevitably arises whether it would be easier to legalize marihuana than to continue present policies of control. Or would some half-way measure be the best solution? It is important to remember that the general term 'social control' refers to the social processes and structures that serve to prevent or reduce deviant behavior. These include the formal, specific kinds of control structure such as law enforcement agencies, law courts, correctional institutions, probation officers and the general legal apparatus of society. They also incorporate those forms of social control that are built into the culture structure; these include role prescriptions, and cultural understandings and definitions of how we are to respond appropriately to different kinds of deviance. The optimum means of controlling behavior in society usually depend on the particular kinds of behavior to be regulated. As we have remarked already, legal controls have proven very unsuccessful in regulating the so-called vices of men.

It is unfortunately true that the knowledge required for the prevention and reduction of deviance, e.g., marihuana use, does not always follow obviously from what we know about the causes of the behavior. However, the theories touted to explain deviant conduct do carry implications for its reduction and control. But given the knowledge of all the variables and their inter-relationships which caused marihuana use in society, we might still lack the requisite technical skills for its manipulation in attempting to control use of the drug. Furthermore, knowledge of the causes of marihuana use does not necessarily inform us where in the system it is best to intervene in monitoring the activity. For example, a prominent theory of deviant behavior suggests that the differential distribution of legitimate means in society generates varying kinds of deviance among the lower classes in their efforts to achieve material goals of success. In this case, effectively to reduce deviance requires (among other things) a more equitable distribution of legitimate means throughout the system. The question is: do we possess sufficient knowledge equitably to redistribute legitimate facilities and opportunities throughout the society? Are we able to anticipate the undesirable side effects of such a structural upheaval? Are we willing to pay the cost in values, attitudes, and traditional living patterns?

Efforts to prevent and reduce deviance are apt to be most effective when they are based on scientific knowledge, nevertheless the use of other methods is sometimes rewarding. And society need not always wait until all the evidence has been accumulated. Although the incidence of marihuana use is increasing, only a small minority of the population (especially those aged eighteen to thirty years) is likely to approve legalizing the drug. The belief and fear that smoking 'pot' leads to the use of hard drugs is one variable that likely turns many people against the thought of legalizing marihuana. On this point the evidence is not conclusive, and there will always be some who, if only through daring and bravado, will start 'shooting' the stuff. But especially among the middle and upper classes, the incompatibility of addiction to hard drugs (with its inordinately severe demands on the user) with their long-range goals, values, and daily style of social life militate forcibly against their wide acceptance of opiates.

People sometimes enquire whether we can eliminate the drug problem in society. This is like asking whether it is possible to eliminate crime and delinquency in society. The answer is categorically no. We have already remarked that our responses to deviance are circumscribed by norms. In fact, we are too moral a society to permit the technically most efficient means to be used in solving our social problems. In comparison to other social problems, e.g., poverty and organized crime, smoking 'pot' palls into insignificance. The question is, under what conditions, at what cost, and at the neglect of what other social problems does society wish to deal with the drug problem?

It cannot be over-emphasized that smoking 'pot' is not a solitary undertaking; like sexual intercourse, partying, drinking and other recreational forms, it is endemically a social activity. Its use reflects a particular philosophy of life and an expected part of living. There is good reason to believe that drug use is here to stay, and that we had better get used to the idea. But this is no cause for alarm. Present methods of control exert little impact on the use of drugs. Yet some form of control over their use seems desirable for the younger age groups. Since the sale of liquor is legally forbidden to persons under eighteen years (although there is no law against selling cigarettes — an addictive drug — to children) it is unlikely that marihuana will be made legally available to them. Yet a certain percentage of this age group already smokes 'pot,' thus some kind of non-sensational educational program to alert both young and older users to the facts and consequences of marihuana use seems in order. In the long run, smoking 'pot,' like smoking tobacco, may be found to be harmful to the smoker's health. Conclusive evidence of this sort may take a long time to accumulate, but if marihuana is fully legalized, some form of long-range regulation of physical effects would be in the best interests of society. (Clausen, 1971: 226)

The best argument (based on limited information) for the legalization of marihuana is that it is a non-addictive drug, it is no more damaging than smoking cigarettes or drinking alcohol, that increasingly large numbers of people smoke 'pot,' and most importantly, that the present laws make criminals of persons whose use of the drug is harmless to society. Most marihuana users go undetected, however, many of those persons who are arrested for using 'pot' are distinguished less by their drug use than by their allegedly radical political views, loose morals, and general unconventionality. Thus the marihuana laws contribute to differential enforcement of the law which does nothing to create respect for the law, but further provokes those who are perhaps already socially and economically disadvantaged. Yet is is also true that were the law uniformly enforced, the vast increase in arrests would further handicap the already overburdened operation of the courts.

In sum, the controversy continues over the effects of marihuana, the incidence of its illegal use, and its value for society. Attitudes towards marihuana use are changing appreciably, noticeably faster among the younger age groups. But there is no immediate reason to suspect that complete legalization of marihuana will be enacted. Certainly the public has not reached any consensus on the matter nor is it likely to in the near future. If the time comes when society believes that marihuana is a desirable commodity, and that it should be made legally available to everyone, the drastic transformation in values and attitudes accompanying such a position will have markedly altered the nature of the marihuana issue in society. (Clausen, 1971: 226) In the meantime, a major redefinition of the law (i.e., eliminating all criminal consequences for growing, possessing, and general contact with marihuana) is undoubtedly in the best interests of society. (Brecher, *et al.,* 1972: 523; *Cannabis: A Report,* 1972).

References

A Study of Marihuana Users and Usage (Project F 169), The Alcholism and Drug Addiction Research Foundation, 1970.

Becker, Howard S., 'Becoming a Marijuana User,' *American Journal of Sociology,* LIX, 1953.

——, *Outsiders.* Glencoe, Ill.: The Free Press, 1963.

——, *The Other Side: Perspectives on Deviance.* Glencoe, Ill.: The Free Press, 1964.

Blumer, Herbert, *The World of Youthful Drug Use.* School of Criminology, University of California at Berkeley, 1967, pp. 48-52.

Boydell, Craig L., and Carl F. Grindstaff, 'Public Attitudes toward Legal Sanctions for Drug and Abortion Offences,' *Canadian Journal of Criminology and Corrections,* XIII, 3, 1971.

Brecher, Edward M., *et al.,* (eds.), *Licit and Illicit Drugs,* The Consumers Union Report. Mount Vernon, N.Y., 1972, p. 523.

Cannabis: A Report of the Commission of Inquiry into the Non-Medical Use of Drugs. Ottawa: Information Canada, 1972.

Carey, James J., *The College Drug Scene.* Englewood Cliffs: Prentice-Hall Inc., 1968, pp. 145-171.

Clausen, John A., 'Drug Use,' in Robert K. Merton and Robert Nisbet, *Contemporary Social Problems.* New York: Harcourt, Brace, Jovanovich, 1971, pp. 185-226.

Clinard, Marshall B., *Anomie and Deviant Behavior.* New York: The Free Press, 1964, p. 18.

Cloward, Richard A., and Lloyd E. Ohlin, *Delinquency and Opportunity.* Glencoe, Ill.: The Free Press, 1960.

Cohen, Albert K., *Delinquent Boys.* Glencoe, Ill.: The Free Press, 1955, p. 60.

——, *Deviance and Control.* Englewood Cliffs: Prentice-Hall Inc., 1966.

——, 'Deviant Behavior,' International Encyclopedia of the Social Sciences. New York: Macmillan, 1968, p. 150.

——, 'Deviant Behavior and its Control,' in Talcott Parsons (ed.), *American Sociology: Perspectives, Problems, Methods*. New York: Basic Books, 1968, pp. 231-243.

——, *Stability and Change in Deviance*. 1971.

——, 'The Sociology of the Deviant Act: Anomie Theory and Beyond,' *American Sociological Review*, XXX (1965), 9-14.

Cook, Shirley, 'Canadian Narcotics Legislation 1908-1923: A Conflict Model Interpretation,' *Canadian Review of Sociology and Anthropology*, VI, 1, 1969.

Cressey, Donald (ed.), *Crime and Criminal Justice*. Chicago: Quadrangle Books, 1971, pp. 4-17.

——, *Other People's Money*. Glencoe, Ill.: The Free Press, 1953, pp. 93-136.

Dubin, Robert, 'Deviant Behavior and Social Structure: Continuities in Social Theory,' *American Sociological Review*, XXV (1959), 152.

Durkheim, Emile, *Suicide*, (trans, by John A. Spaulding and George Simpson). Glencoe, Ill.: The Free Press, 1951.

——, *The Division of Labor in Society*, (trans. by George Simpson). Glencoe, Ill.: The Free Press, 1949, pp. 70-110.

——, *The Rules of Sociological Method*, (trans. by S.A. Solovay and John H. Mueller and edited by George E.G. Catlin). Glencoe, Ill.: The Free Press, 1950.

Elkin, F., *Families in Canada*. Ottawa: Vanier Institute of the Family, 1968.

Erikson, Kai T., *Wayward Puritans: A Study in the Sociology of Deviance*. New York: John Wiley and Sons, 1966.

Freidson, Eliot, 'Disability as Social Deviance,' in Marvin B. Sussman (ed.), *Sociology and Rehabilitation*, American Sociological Association in co-operation with the Vocational Rehabilitation Administration, U.S. Department of Health, Education and Welfare.

Gallagher, James E., and Ronald D. Lambert, *Social Process and Institution: Canadian Studies*. Toronto: Holt, Rinehart and Winston, 1971, pp. 174-185.

Garfinkel, Harold, 'Conditions of Successful Degredation Ceremonies,' *American Journal of Sociology*, LXI, 5, 1956, 420-424.

Garvin, Andrew, 'Why They Do It,' *Newsweek*, July 24,1967.

Giffen, P.J., 'Rates of Crime and Delinquency,' in W.T. McGrath (ed.), *Crime and its Treatment in Canada*. Toronto: Macmillan, 1965, p. 79.

Goode, Erich, *Drugs in American Society*. New York: Knopf, 1972, pp. 35-37.

——, *The Marijuana Smokers*. New York: Basic Books, 1970.

Hobart, Charles, 'Growing Up Absurd — Youth and the Changing Canadian Moral Structure,' in B.Y. Card, *Trends and Change in Canadian Society*. Toronto: Macmillan, 1968.

Interim Report of the Commission of Inquiry into the Non-Medical Use of Drugs. Ottawa: Queen's Printer 1970, p. 142.

Johnson, Harry, *Sociology: A Systematic Introduction.* New York: Harcourt, Brace and World, 1960, p. 20.

Mann, W.E., 'Opiate Addiction in Canada,' in W.E. Mann (ed.), *Deviant Behavior in Canada.* Toronto: Social Science Publishers, 1967, pp. 239-240.

——, (ed.), *Social and Cultural Change in Canada.* Toronto: Copp Clark, 1970.

Merton, Robert K., 'Anomie, Anomia, and Social Interaction: Contexts of Deviant Behavior,' in M. Clinard, *Anomie and Deviant Behavior.* New York: The Free Press, 1964, pp. 213-242.

——, 'Social Problems and Sociological Theory,' in Robert K. Merton and Robert Nisbet (eds.), *Contemporary Social Problems.* New York: Harcourt, Brace, Jovanovich, 1971, p. 803. (This is the best book on social problems.)

——, *Social Theory and Social Structure,* revised and enlarged edition. Glencoe, Ill.: The Free Press, 1957, pp. 131-194.

Mills, C Wright, ·'Situated Actions and Vocabularies of Motive,' *American Sociological Review,* V, 6, 1940.

Scott, Joseph W., and Edmund W. Vaz, 'A Perspective on Middle-Class Delinquency,' *Canadian Journal of Economics and Political Science,* XXIX, 3, 1963.

Smart, Reginald G., and David Jackson, *The Yorkville Subculture.* Toronto: Addiction Research Foundation, Jan., 1969.

Suchman, E.A., 'The "Hang-Loose" Ethic and the Spirit of Drug Use,' *Journal of Health and Social Behavior,* IX (1968), 146-155.

Vaz, Edmund W., 'Middle-Class Adolescents: Self-Reported Delinquency and Youth Culture,' *The Canadian Review of Sociology and Anthropology,* II, 1, 1965.

Wheeler, Stanton, 'Deviant Behaviour,' in Neil J. Smelser (ed.), *Sociology: An Introduction.* New York: John Wiley and Sons, 1967.

Whitehead, Paul C., *Drug Use among Adolescent Students in Halifax,* revised edition. Youth Agency, Province of Nova Scotia, March, 1970.

Whitehead, Paul C., Reginald G. Smart, and Lucien Laforest, 'Multiple Drug Use among Marihuana Smokers in Eastern Canada,' revised version of a paper presented to the National Research Council Committee on Problems of Drug Dependence, Washington, D.C., 1970, pp. 10-17.

Winick, Charles, 'Physician Narcotic Addicts,' in Howard S. Becker (ed.), *The Other Side: Perspectives on Deviance.* Glencoe, Ill.: The Free Press, 1964, pp. 265-266.

Wise, Nancy Barton, 'Juvenile Delinquency among Middle-Class Girls,' in Edmund W. Vaz (ed.), *Middle-Class Juvenile Delinquency.* New York: Harper and Row, 1967, pp. 179-188.

CHAPTER TEN

Complex Organizations: The Issue Of Bureaucracy

Charles Gordon
Carleton University

Introduction

Bureaucracy, it seems, has become a principal villain in society, and there are few, from politician to social scientist, who do not enjoy flagellating it. The infamy may or may not be justified; but it creates problems for those who wish to describe and analyze these organizations. And such analysis is necessary to any understanding of the nature of contemporary society.

In the first instance, bureaucratic organizations are essential to the processes of social change. They are tremendous consumers of resources, and distributors of resources. The large buildings of the society, those which require great populations, are built by and for organizations. The physical, as well as the social changes in the cities are being wrought by such as the Toronto Dominion Centre, the Canadian Pacific Railway, and of course, the levels of government. One could argue that the history of Canada has been wrought by organizations — the Hudson's Bay Company, the Canadian Pacific and the Canadian National Railways, the Montreal trading companies and many more.

Since the organizational structure is not a monolith, there is tremendous competition between these organizations for the resources that each needs to survive. This competition consumes resources in itself, and affects in a major way the legal, political, and economic processes of the society. The original battle over who would build the transcontinental railway reached the highest levels of the government. Resources spent by organizations on lobbying, public relations, and advertising to keep them 'competitive' have become a major part of the costs that organizations incur. The recent hearings of the Food Prices Review Committee are a striking example of this.

The very size of these organizations, and their complexity, creates an 'inertial' force in the implementation of social policy — inertia as a barrier to social change, or, equally important, inertia that can make an organization a juggernaut when set in motion. The former is the quality that has led us all to curse bureaucracies; but the force for change must be reckoned with as well. C.D. Howe said that 'nothing is administratively impossible' (Newman, 1963: 36), and he often proved it in the many ministries that he headed. The control of large organizations, to get them to change, or to prevent change, is one of the crucial problems in society. It is at the core of the debate over multinational corporations, the power of developers, and a large number of very pressing political issues.

For a large and increasing portion of the population, a bureaucratic organization is the mechanism whereby they obtain their personal resources, and whereby they are rewarded for their efforts. Put simply, such organizations determine their life style and life chances; as such, they are a crucial part of the stratification system of the country. This is true in large part because bureaucractic organizations function as large employers. Occupation is the key to social status in industrial societies — it is your job that gives you the privileges and the money to buy the goods that indicate social status. Organizations provide many of the occupations. White collar jobs, and service jobs, have grown from around 25 per cent of the labor force of Canada in 1901 to over 50 per cent in 1961 (Ostry, 1967: 12). Thereby, the hierarchy and ranking procedures within the organizations approximate the class system for the society as a whole; an organizational career is a path of social mobility. Thus, major social problems having to do with the social status of disadvantaged groups are problems of access to organizations or discrimination by them. For example, to change the status of women in Canadian society, efforts are made to insure their access to positions in organizations.

Employees are not the only people for whom bureaucratic organizations determine status. A large part of the population is dependent upon people who work in organizations. Further, those who neither have a current occupation nor are dependent on someone who does, often must deal directly with organizations to get their living. For the poor, it is the welfare agency and Manpower and the Unemployment Insurance Commission; for the sick, the hospital and the health insurance commission; for the student, the school; for the felon, the prison; and for the elderly, the deliverer of Social Insurance, and various other aid programs. It is at least arguable that much of the agricultural population is dependent in this way, as well; either upon corporate farms, or upon such bodies as the Saskatchewan Wheat Pool, or the Milk Marketing

Board of Ontario. In fact, Ontario has nineteen such boards, governing thirty-seven different commodities (*Canada Yearbook,* 1971: 567).

Almost everyone acts out much of his life in the context of a bureaucratic organization. During school years, and on through working careers, there is an encounter between the individual personality and the constraints of organizational structure. This encounter, which may be frustrating and alienating, is a major factor in the quality of individual lives in Canada today.

This is true whether we are referring to executives, clerks, or clients. Each of them has spent much of his life in these large organizations, and can expect to continue to do so. For despite the publicity given 'drop-outs,' most people will pursue some sort of career. For such people, an organization not only gives them status, it determines the quality of day-to-day life. Notions about red tape, an alienating 'grind,' having to play 'yes-man' to a hated boss, the encounter with the 'faceless bureaucrat' are not just clichés. They are very real events in people's lives, events that must be coped with if those lives are to be lived. The 'faceless bureaucrat' is himself an individual whose life is being acted out in the setting of a large organization; and the encounter with those who seek his services is as crucial to him as it is to them. Those who are in organizations and those who must deal with them, must develop ways of coping with the situations that the organizations create. These coping strategies tell us a great deal about everyday life in Canadian society. Such a concern may seem mundane; but that is exactly what makes it so important. We cannot let our distaste for the 'bureaucracy' substitute for analysis and understanding. It is, and will remain, too big to go away, and too crucial to ignore. What follows is the conceptual 'tool-kit' that sociology provides to look at these organizations, and to help understand them and the critical issues that the organizations present.

The Matter of Definition

To this point, we have used the term bureaucracy rather loosely, without defining it beyond everyday usage. In fact, the word refers to a quite specific aspect of organization. Bureaucracy is a variable dimension of a category called *complex organization.*

Such organizations have been defined in terms of their establishment to *serve some particular purpose or goal.* As we shall see, that definition is not as simple as it appears on the surface. But it is where we start. It distinguishes complex organizations from families, where 'purposes' are diffuse and encompassing, or from societies, where the goals are also very diffuse.

344 Issues in Canadian Society

Bureaucracy refers to the *administrative machinery* of such organizations — the staff, regulations, and structures that are responsible for *maintaining* the organization as a going concern as opposed to that segment of the organization directly involved in *goal attainment*. In a university, the deans and secretaries, by virtue of their support function, are part of the bureaucracy, while professors are properly viewed as directly engaged in goal activities (transmission of knowledge). It can be seen then, that the extent of bureaucratization can vary from organization to organization, although all complex organizations, no doubt, have a minimum of bureaucracy (Blau and Scott, 1962: 7-8).

There are a number of other characteristics that go with the goal orientations that we have mentioned, and they are best summed up in the following definition. A complex organization consists of:

(1) stable patterns of interaction,
(2) among coalitions of people having a collective identity (e.g., a name and location(s)),
(3) pursuing interests and accomplishing given tasks, and
(4) co-ordinated by power and authority structures. (Corwin, 1967: 167)

It must be remembered that the organization is made up of interacting individuals. It is very easy to 'reify' the organization — to view it as a living, breathing beast in itself. But while it is useful to speak in that way, it must be remembered that it is a form of intellectual shorthand.

The importance of this is clearest when we examine the nature of organizational goals, our defining characteristic. As Silverman (1970) points out, the organization is really the sum total of the meanings that its members (and certain non-members) apply to it. Thus, the goals (or desired future states) are a sum (or more complex product) of goals that various folk have as individuals. And there is a considerable variety of kinds of goals that can be involved. Among these, the following kinds of goals seem particularly important:

(a) *Charter Goals:* These are the express purposes for which the organization is set up. They are often embodied in a legal document, such as letters patent, act of incorporation, or act of parliament. These may well be imposed by persons outside the organization. While explicit, these goals may cover far less explicit purposes. But they are significant in themselves, if only because they often impose legal bounds on an organization. For instance, it is often critical to all sorts of economic and legal benefits for an organization to be defined as profit or non-profit.

(b) *Informal Goals:* These are the interpretations that individuals put on the purposes of the organization. These may resemble the charter goals, but they may vary from them widely. Further, these interpretations may vary within an organization; there may be considerable conflict over whose interpretation will determine the actions of the organization.

(c) *Personal Goals:* These refer to the aspirations that an individual has for himself in his participation in the organization. Those might be prestige, security, or wealth, or any number of things. These may complement the organizational goals, or they may oppose those goals, or they may be irrelevant. For example, in a prison, if we assume that the 'goal' of a prisoner is to escape, his success is antithetical to that of the organization; if his goal is to serve his time and learn a trade, the situation is reversed.

(d) *Ideological Goals:* These are goals that exist beyond the organization as such, and lie in some larger value system. They may serve to justify any of the other sorts of goals. Thus an individual may join the army to 'make the world safe for democracy,' or join a charitable organization to further 'good Samaritan' values.

(e) *Inertial Goals:* This refers simply to the desire for the organization to persist. This may override a number of other considerations, and other goals may be changed to suit this one.

All of these goals may exist in an organization at any time; that is, they form the definitions that people make of what the organization should do. These definitions in turn determine the actions that people take.

Organizations, except in rare cases, have differentiated power structures. As we shall see, there are a number of factors that contribute to having power in the organization. Whatever the basis for the power, it means the ability to impose one's own goals or meanings on others in the organization.

Thus, if I am president of the firm, I have the ability to make the goals of the firm the same as my own, and to make others act accordingly. If I am lower down in the same firm, and have no power, I must act as the boss says; further, I must accept his ideas into the thinking that motivates my own action. The kind of imposition mentioned here may be accepted by the individual; he may accept or 'legitimize' it. But he may not and the result may be conflict or the alienation of the individual forced to act out goals that are not his own.

Classical Perspectives I: Administrative Theories of Organization

The classical theories in the study of complex organizations are of a sort that have justly been termed *'machine theory'* (Worthy, 1950). These theories share a view of organizations operating in an essentially machine-like process for the achievement of a goal. That is, organizations are viewed as a series of inter-related dependent parts, highly specialized, and performing regular and repetitive actions. They do not necessarily view the individual himself as functioning 'mechanically' but they do see organizations as systems designed to function as if he were.

In sociology, these theories are represented in the work of Max Weber (1946). Weber's work has been attacked and modified, but remains a powerful model, nonetheless. Weber developed his model as part of a larger model of how authority or legitimate power works in the society — how and why orders can be given and followed. To understand his work on bureaucracy, we first must recall his conception of authority.

As Schwartz pointed out in Chapter Seven, Weber posited three kinds of authority:

(1) *charismatic authority:* authority based on the personal qualities of the leader;

(2) *traditional authority:* authority based on prior custom and precedent. Things are done as they 'always' have been done;

(3) *rational-legal authority:* authority rests on the choice of means aimed at specific goals with the least use of resources — rationality; and on a set of rules and regulations which govern behavior — legality. *Bureaucracy is the name used to designate the organizational manifestation of rational authority.*

The key point of contrast between these modes of authority lies in the role of individual preference and variability in the exercise of power. Charismatic authority, in particular, is based upon the whim of one individual; the organization is therefore also dependent on his wisdom and stamina. On the other hand, *bureaucracy is designed in its ideal form to control the effects of individual variability upon the smooth functioning of the organizational apparatus.*

Particularly, this restricts the ability of the individual to impose his own set of goals and meanings on the organization. The system accepts its goals from outside, and seeks to meet them efficiently. Thus, it is based upon tying the individual to the organization, getting him to accept and legitimize the structure itself. Charismatic authority requires that the subject give a certain meaning to an individual; rational-legal authority requires that he give a certain meaning to the structure. This being achieved, the structure then defines the situation from then on.

Weber's interest is in the way in which one can ensure that authority will be obeyed, and policies carried out, regardless of the policy or its end product. For that reason, his theory, and theories that share this interest are termed *administrative* theories.

Weber saw the following characteristics of bureaucratic organizations as critical:

(1) The tasks are distributed through the various positions in the organization as official duties. This implies a finely-honed division of labor, and a high degree of specialization. This, in its turn, allows for a high degree of technical skill to be achieved.

(2) The positions are organized into a strict hierarchy of authority. Each person is responsible to someone.

(3) A system of rules and regulations governs all decisions and behavior.

(4) All dealings between individuals are supposed to be impersonal, either official-official or official-client. Clients are dealt with as cases, and any bonds of friendship or such are to be ignored within the organization.

(5) Employment by the organization constitutes a full-time and often life-long career for the official. Career advancement is to be either by seniority or by achievement, or both.

There are two other factors which deserve mention as well. One factor which is a manifestation of the others is the requirement that all transactions and dealings within organizations must be recorded in writing and preserved. The reason for this is to make the continued operation of the system independent of the variable nature of human memory. In practice, some of the most famous symbols of bureaucracy come from this requirement. Particularly, the term 'red tape' derives from the red ribbons used to bind up excess paper at the U.S. state department as it overflowed the filing cabinets during the Civil War.

The second factor which is very important is the exclusion of the 'owner' from the structures of the system. Weber specifically excludes the policy maker, for that is what the 'owner' is, from the bureaucracy. The bureaucracy is the apparatus by which that policy is carried out. By working in the organization, the official accepts that policy as a given.

The 'owner' need not be the economic owner, but may be the cabinet minister who makes the selection of goals for the government organization. In many organizations, there may be many 'owners'; who 'owns' the police, for instance? Even in business, the growth of large corporations has created much controversy over who does indeed own them.

There is also ambiguity in the relations of the technical skills and knowledge required to work in an organization to the policy decisions of the organization. In the Department of the Environment, a highly technical area, the minister is a lawyer. But the decisions he makes are highly dependent on technical knowledge. In such cases, the owner is hard put to be independent of his administrators; it is hard for them not to make policy. This has been a particular problem in government but it is true elsewhere as well (Hodgett, 1957).

Classical Perspectives II: Worker-centered Theories of Organization

In contrast to the administrative theories, there is a body of literature centered around the nature of the industrial worker. This work is based upon in-plant research done by both sociologists and industrial engineers — studies by and large commissioned by management with the end of increasing production. This fact may account for a certain bias in the interpretation of data that form the base of these studies; different sorts of conclusions have been drawn from the same data (Blumberg, 1969).

The origin of this body of theory lies in the 'scientific management' work of Frederick W. Taylor. To Taylor, the worker was not unlike a machine, in that, given the proper input (money) the worker could be asked to perform tasks efficiently. The most efficient task was the simplest; and Taylor and his associates were famous for the time-and-motion studies that broke complex production processes into extremely simple, repetitive processes.

Any task could be broken into components; and then workers could be selected who could perform these components in the least wasteful way. Taylor felt that if his system worked, at its best it would insure both high profits for management and steady high wages for the employee. Employees would earn high wages because they would be working at piece rates on jobs that they could do well.

The 'scientific management' school gave way to studies of the conditions surrounding the work tasks, so as to make their performance more perfect. Out of a series of such studies, particularly the famous 'Hawthorne' studies, an industrial researcher named Elton Mayo started what became the 'human relations' approach to organizations.

The Hawthorne studies started in an analysis of the effects of lighting on worker production in a plant of the Western Electric Company. Two groups of workers were isolated and one group had its lighting changed while the other's was held constant. Production went up in both groups, apparently as a function of the attention the workers were receiving from the researchers. At this point, Mayo and his team entered.

Mayo called into question the kind of motivation assumptions that had been part of scientific management. He felt that workers often operated in terms of subjective, and often non-rational assessments of situations and these should be the subject of management concern, rather than just the objective facts of the situation, such as lighting and pay-rates. Later on, Mayo came to emphasize two other factors as well. One of these was the degree of autonomy and control that the worker held over his own conditions; the other was the importance of the informal relationships between workers, and the social structure of the work group. The latter conclusion has received far more emphasis, particularly in terms of restriction of output and the exercise of social pressure. But recent authors have begun to stress the importance of control.

The *human relations approach,* in its *emphasis on group norms and social sources of satisfaction,* may have underplayed the role of money as a motivation. Studies (Dubin, 1956) suggest that many workers see their jobs only as a source for the money to do the things that they really want to do. Their real interests are not located in the organization, and the organization's goals are irrelevant to their own. Thus, the 'rational' incentives are important.

It also must be noted that the human relations approach is no more an approach to the whole organization than are the administrative theories. It arose initially to look at factors affecting production among the workers. It does not look at similar factors among management; rather, it seems to take management as given.

Also, the human relations model depends, as do the administrative models, on legitimation processes: 'The investigation showed, to quote Mayo, that "management succeeds or fails in proportion as it is accepted without reservations by the group as authority and leader"' (Pugh, 1972:130).

Finally, this approach is dependent on two questionable assumptions. It assumes that a 'happier' worker will produce more; this assumption is necessary to justify reforms to the management that implement them. There is considerable question in research evidence as to the validity of such an assumption (Applewhite, 1965). It also assumes an ultimate identity of interest between the management and the workers. This assumption is questionable, even if you do not adopt the opposite assumption of inevitable conflict.

The Classical Perspectives in Comparison

These perspectives obviously differ in where they focus on the organization. These differences are reflected in the titles we have used to refer to them. But there are other differences that should be pointed out as well:

(1) Whereas the administrative perspective excluded the 'owner' from the model, the worker-centered perspective lumps owner and manager together to the extent that the issue is considered at all.

(2) Whereas the administrative models emphasize the *formal* organization, the worker- centered model focuses on the *informal.* This means that in the latter case, the concern is with interaction at the work place, but in aid of either the informal and/or *personal* goals. The formal organization refers to the prescribed interaction

in pursuit of the *charter* goal, or the charter goal as interpreted by the effective policy-makers of the organization. (In the ideal, the policy is set by the owner.)

These differences are summarized graphically in Figure 1.

The 'informal-administrative' theories which are indicated in the figure, but which we have not discussed, are not really organizational theories in the usual sense. But we will find when we look at the role of the organization in social change, and at the role of professionals in organizations (doctors, lawyers, and so forth), we will be in dire need of such theories. C. Wright Mills, in his important study, *The Power Elite* (1956), discusses the social relations of the organizational elite in the United States. John Porter, while discussing Canadian social stratification in *The Vertical Mosaic* (1965), provides information for this 'box' in Canada. William H. Whyte's *The Organization Man* (1957) is a journalistic and persuasive account of the social relationships of executives. None of these are systematic *organizational* theories; but they provide a basis for some interesting organizational theorizing. We shall get into this later.

The New Synthesis: Systems Theory

The classical theories have tended to adopt a rather narrow focus; either on management, ignoring the worker; or on the worker, in the interest of management. The new theories, based on the concept of the organization as a system, have attempted to look at an organization as a whole, including both management and the workers.

One of the most significant of these theories has been that of Amitai Etzioni (1971). The Etzioni approach has its origins not in the Weberian bureaucracy model, but in the Weberian approach to authority from which the bureaucracy model grew. Etzioni posits three sorts of authority that are exercised by the elite in an organization:

(1) coercive: authority based upon the sanction of force, or the threat of the use of force — 'Do as I say or I'll hit you.'

(2) remunerative: the use of money or similar economic rewards — 'If you do as I say, I'll pay you $400 a week.'

(3) normative: the use of symbolic rewards such as esteem, love, damnation, etc. — 'Do as I say and I'll give you a blue ribbon.'

Along with the kinds of authority that might exist, Etzioni proposes three types of involvement on the part of the non-elite; that is, three sorts of commitment that tie those without authority into the organization. The three types of involvement are:

(1) alienative involvement: the lower participant is not committed to the organization, and stays in it to avoid dire consequences, for example an imprisoned felon,

Figure 1:   Classical Perspectives of Organization

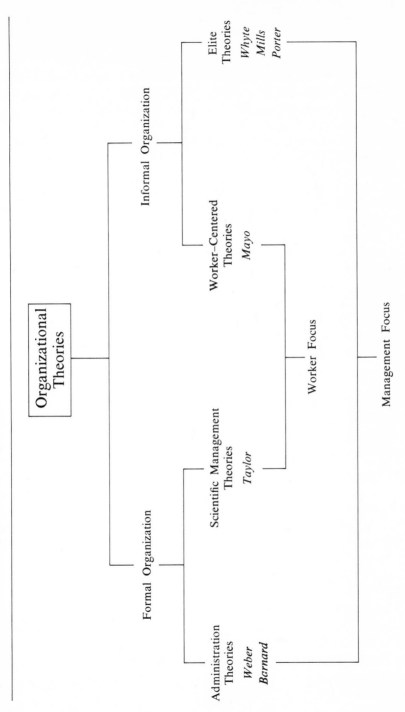

(2) calculative involvement: the commitment here is in terms of economic or status rewards,

(3) moral involvement: commitment in terms of symbolic rewards.

A convert is committed to the church in hopes of the comfort and promise of salvation that it offers.

The basic notion here is a simple one; the elite (the 'owners') offers certain rewards to gain the co-operation of others. The 'others' offer participation in order to gain certain rewards. For an organization to function well, the kinds of rewards offered must be the kinds of rewards sought.

If one combines the three kinds of authority with the three kinds of involvement, one can find nine combinations. These combinations Etzioni terms 'compliance systems;' each compliance system is the way in which an organization operates. Of the nine possible compliance systems, the three identified along the diagonal of Figure 2 are expected to be the most effective, in that the rewards offered and the rewards sought or expected, are congruent.

If the rewards offered and sought are not congruent, the organization will either work poorly or fail; or, the authority or the involvement will change so that the compliance system is workable. The organization can exist with an incongruent system; but that will happen only if it can command sufficient outside resources to prevent its failure. Many schools, for example, offer normative rewards (grades) to children with alienative involvement (held in by school-leaving laws). The school usually does not become coercive; but it will not, cannot, be allowed to fail. So many resources are poured in, instead.

Further, Etzioni feels that each type of compliance structure is appropriate to certain sorts of goals. The coercive system works best in terms of an 'order' goal, such as the control of deviants, as in prisons and mental institutions. Remunerative or utilitarian organizations are most appropriate to 'economic' goals as in business organizations. Finally, the normative organization is best at achieving 'culture' goals — either the preservation of the culture, as in schools, or the creation of new culture, as in research institutes.

Etzioni is able to use the 'compliance' scheme to account for a great many of the structural characteristics of organizations, such as their communications patterns, social control mechanisms, recruitment procedures and socialization.

The problems with the Etzioni scheme lie in two areas. In the first case, few organizations have a 'pure' compliance system — there is apt to be some variability in the means of authority, and a lot of variability in the involvement of individuals in the organization. Etzioni suggests that

Figure 2: Etzioni's Model of Compliance Systems

	Coercive	Remuneration	Normative
INVOLVEMENT			
Alienative	(1) coercive	(2)	(3)
Calculation	(4)	(5) remuneration	(6)
Moral	(7)	(8)	(9) normative

AUTHORITY spans the Coercive, Remuneration, and Normative columns.

there can be some gross variations, but the problem seems to be a bit more complex.

Etzioni makes a distinction between that which an organization must do to survive, and that which it can do to use its resources most wisely. He feels that organizations will strive to be effective in this latter sense, and as they do, they will strain toward the congruence of authority and involvement. The problem is that this focuses on the internal arrangements of the organization, without looking at its relationship to its environment. And in two ways, the environment can negate the dynamic that Etzioni proposes. In the first instance, it can legally, ethically or otherwise constrain the changes in compliance or involvement that an organization makes. For example, at the same time that one law (the school-leaving law) creates an alienative involvement for a number of students, another law diminishing or forbidding corporal punishment may prevent coercive authority. Thus, a basic incongruity is created by external forces.

At the same time, the environment, for whatever reasons, may provide resources sufficient to enable the organization to persevere, even grow, without its either being effective or having a congruent compliance system. If only to keep the children off the street, the schools mentioned above are unlikely to be allowed to close; more resources are just pumped in. Industrial plants, such as the Dosco Steel plant in Nova Scotia, or the Lockheed plants in the U.S., have been kept afloat by massive amounts of public resources. In both cases, the state could not afford to have all those men not working. Etzioni, while differing from the classical theorists in concerning himself with all levels of an organization, resembles them in considering organizations as relatively closed systems, and de-emphasizing their relations with their environment.

In general, Etzioni focuses on the relationship between the existing compliance system and various processes within the organization. The effect of environmental factors is played down. Because of this, Etzioni may be said to be dealing with relatively closed systems.

In the past few years, there has been a group of writings on organizations which see them as relatively open systems; that is, as systems in a relatively constant interchange with their environment. This approach leads to analysis which associates kinds of factors in the environment of organizations with structures within the organizations. Thus, organizational form may be related to technology (Woodward, 1965), geography (Stinchcombe, 1959) or a number of other factors. Organizational structures are viewed as a matter of adaptation to environmental conditions. And organizations are differentiated by their degree of control over the environment.

Theoretical Overview

Given such theories, the key to understanding complex organizations seems to lie in three sorts of factors:

(1) The meanings that individuals, singly and in groups, put on the organization: this refers to the way in which they interpret and plan their own actions in relation to the kinds of goals that we mentioned early in the chapter. The relation of the informal goals to the personal and ideological goals is essentially the legitimation process referred to by Weber, or the involvement process referred to by Etzioni. The way in which an individual interprets informal goals in relation to the actions of his peers is at the core of the human relations approach.

(2) The distribution of power: power is the ability to impose one's own meanings upon others, or to sanction their behavior so as to get them to do something, and short of the use of force, the exercise of power is clearly a matter of legitimation, and the authority vested in individuals. If you obey my order, it is because you accept my sanctions on your behavior. If I threaten you with damnation if you do not learn this chapter, that will be powerful only if you believe in hell.

Within the bounds of an agreed-upon system, I can exercise power and impose a meaning upon you if I am powerful; I can define a situation and thus the context in which you act and the rewards you will receive for acting. Thus, I determine the meaning of that action for you.

(3) The third key sort of variable is the degree to which the organization is affected by environmental factors, or affects and/ or controls that environment. This refers to the power of the

organizational elite, not only over those in the organization, but also over persons who are not part of the organization. We turn to this aspect now.

Organizations and Environment

Many studies of organizations have seen them as dependent upon their environment. But the real point is that organizations struggle with the environment; some do better in the struggle than others. And those that win form a major part of the 'environment' with which the others must struggle. John Porter has stated the problem as follows:

> Capitalist corporate behavior is a theoretically rational form of behavior. The ends of profit-making (or other ends such as firm survival or growth) are arrived at through a series of calculated means. In the environment of the capitalist economy, there are many impediments to the most efficient linking of means and ends. Some impediments, such as oceans or mountains, are natural, and the rational means of overcoming them are supplied by technology. But there are social impediments: taxes are levied for war or welfare; trade unions make demands; foreign governments impose restrictions; nasty dictators take over property (as do not so nasty provincial premiers); and politicians make other unfavorable conditions at home and abroad for the maximization of profit. Technology cannot overcome these social impediments, but various pressures can be applied to reduce their effects and thus to stabilize the capitalistic economy. These pressures may be direct ones on government or less direct ones through public relations schemes. By and large, corporations have been able to exert sufficient pressure on governments, and on social institutions generally, to stabilize the field in their favor. This stabilizing of the environment is the politics of industry (Porter, 1965: 269).

If we realize that the goals of corporations need not be profit maximization; and that other kinds of organizations besides corporations (universities, for example) are also joined in the struggle to control their environments, certain points are clear. *The politics of organizations represent stabilization of the environment in relation to the goals of an organization.* This is a peculiarly interesting question in Canada, where many of these organizations are 'multinational,' that is, with political control that lies outside the country, in the U.S., the U.K., or Japan.

The question of ownership is crucial, since the power over the organization is power in the society as well. But ownership, in the usual sense, and power in the organization are not synonymous.

The relationship between ownership and control has been a matter of concern for many years, going back as far as Burnham (1941) and Berle and Means (1932), and continuing until the present (Galbraith, 1967). The history of the controversy has been part of the history of the business corporation. But it is an issue that arises in non-economic organizations as well.

The concept of the owner is a broad one; it would seem to involve three notions, (1) deriving the benefit from the organization, (2) legal responsibility, (3) decision- and policy-making authority.

Organizations and Benefits

There is one model (Blau and Scott, 1962) which classifies organizations in terms of this first notion. There are, in the typology, four kinds of organizations:

(1) *Mutual Benefit:* these organizations exist for the joint enjoyment of all their members. An example is the Canadian Legion or the United Church.

(2) *Business Concerns:* the prime beneficiary here is the owner, in the economic sense. The examples are industrial firms, either publicly owned, like Bell Canada, or privately owned, like the corner stores.

(3) *Service Organizations:* the prime beneficiary here is the client of the organization, in direct contact with the organization. Examples are hospitals, schools and so forth.

(4) *Commonweal Organizations:* these are organizations which benefit the public at large, as distinct from the people whom they benefit directly. Examples are the Department of External Affairs, or the Canadian Forces.

The key problem that the model introduces is the complex relationship between owner and beneficiary. Only in the case of the business organization are they presumed to be synonymous; in practice, even that presumption may not hold up. The difference is most clear in the service and commonweal organizations. In many of these organizations, the interests of the owner and the clients may be opposed and the prime beneficiary is someone else altogether. The particular case in mind is a welfare agency. The owner is the relevant governmental unit, and through that the public at large. The beneficiary is presumably the client; but in fact, the system does not work that way (Jacobs, 1966; Cloward and Piven, 1971). The prime beneficiary is the elite of the economic structure in that welfare serves to regulate the labor market.

Legal Responsibility and Decision-Making: Owners and Managers

The relationship between financial/legal control of an organization and decision-making control is a complex one. And it is a crucial issue in the exercise of the power of the organization.

When the business organization was viewed as a relatively weak entity within a market system, it was seen as a sort of one-man operation. The same man was owner, manager, and technical operator all in one. But few organizations remain that way; the functions are separated, and themselves separate into subfunctions.

The need for capital, and for an ownership structure that could outlive individuals led to the fragmentation of ownership through the issuing of shares of stock to many buyers. This reinforced the divorce from management, since the gaggle of shareholders could not hope actively to manage the firm. The problem becomes the extent to which this disparate group of owners can effectively control the managers that they have hired to run the firm. The problem becomes more complex as the technology becomes more esoteric: how can the managers, in their own stead, control the technical experts that they have hired to produce goals or services for them?

One major argument holds that the separation of ownership from management is more apparent than real, for the following reasons (Child, 1970):

(1) Through a number of devices such as non-voting shares, and because of the difficulty of getting any unity of action in the great mass of small shareholders, the power concentrates in the hands of a few large shareholders, power sufficient to exercise control over the managers. This is reinforced by the increasing concentration of shareholdings in the portfolios of large institutions such as insurance companies, pension funds and foundations, and even universities, particularly in the U.S.

(2) The strength of these large shareholders is reinforced by the interlocking directorships which allow for influence over a number of organizations, particularly financial ones. Thus, the manager who backs his directors may find himself in trouble with the firms that supply or underwrite his activities, since the same directors may be involved in those firms. The 'pyramiding' of shareholdings (I own control of company A with 40 per cent of its stock; company A controls company B by purchasing 30 per cent of its stock and so forth) may allow for effective control, based on relatively small investment and these interlocked directorships.

(3) The managers may own some of the shares of the business; and while those shares may be peanuts in the corporate structure, they form a large part of the personal wealth of the manager. Thus, he is likely to act in accord with the maximum profit on those shares.

(4) The managers are likely to be of a background similar to that of the big owners, or alternately, socially mobile into a similar social position. The result would be a shared set of aspirations, attitudes

and meanings with the owners. They are, simply put, more likely to be in agreement than to have major conflicts.

(5) The constraints of the environment, such as the market, will cause the managers to pursue the same profit interest as the owners.

For these reasons, some sociologists feel that ' ... top managers and major capital owners are not distinct groups in any sociologically important respect. Managers do not therefore comprise ... a new independent technocratic group.... In short, the development of management does not signify an important modification of traditional social stratification.'*

The above assumption does allow that managers will pursue their own self-interest, expressed in a number of ways. This might be in terms of profit maximization, paralleling the owners. But other possibilities exist — goals such as high sales revenue, growth of assets, or long run profits and growth. In addition to these, which might be said to represent the informal goals of the managers, there are the kinds of career and status ends that the individual may have — the personal goals of the managers. The assumption is that these will be the primary ends that the managers will pursue, more important than either the goals and/or needs of the owners, or the public at large. There is also the fact, noted by Cyert and March (1963), that managers do not have sufficient information to seek the greatest degree of satisfaction of their goals; rather, they will seek some minimum level of achievement that is 'satisfactory,' whether or not it is all that is indeed possible.

Another group of managerial theorists agree that the managers are out from under the control of the owners, but that this is not necessarily a bad thing. The notion is that the manager, freed from the narrow pursuit of profits for the owner, could do more humane sorts of things:

> [*These theorists*] have felt that because managers appeared to be enjoying conditions in which they did not have to maximize returns to ownership — a sectional interest — they could now pursue policies which reflected a more balanced set of goals, in terms of meeting a wide range of social as well as economic requirements. (Child, 1970: 42)

The manager of a corporation would, in this view, be able to take account of such things as potential pollution, or the employment of minority groups, along with making some minimum profit. Kaysen (1957) has referred to this possibility as the 'soulful corporation.' This does not need to assume some sort of conversion from avarice — rather it says that the freedom from the blinkers of profit maximization allows the

---

*John Child, *The Business Enterprise in Modern Society*, p. 40. Copyright © Collier-Macmillan Limited, 1970.

manager to see the welfare of his firm in a longer and wider perspective. It also leads him to react in a different way to the kinds of legal and social restraints that may surround the firm.

Canadian Examples

In Canada, the control has perhaps stayed more with the financial owners rather than managers in Canadian-owned family corporations. The picture is not so clear in the case of foreign-owned companies.

What is clear is a close-knit system of interlocking ownership and concentration in the Canadian economy. John Porter has documented this clearly (Porter, 1965). Aside from the number of family-owned corporations — Molson's for example — there is considerable concentration of ownership.

The mechanism by which this happens is demonstrated in the following summary of the structure of the Power Corporation, which in the past few years has become one of the most powerful firms in Canada.

Gelco Industries Ltd. holds 38.32 per cent of the outstanding convertible preferred stock and 95.93 per cent of the outstanding participating preferred stock, representing 50.01 per cent of the votes represented by voting shares.
Nordex Ltd. has voting control of Gelco; Nordex Ltd. is an association of Paul Desmarais and Jean Parisien.
Year end, December 31, 1971: total assests $382,718,000; total net income $10,024,000.
Investment Portfolio (at December 31,1971)
Argus Corporation 10.4 per cent outstanding common shares

Wholly-owned Subsidiaries:
Trans-Canada Corporation Fund,
Shawinigan Industries Ltd.,
Power Corporation International Ltd.,
C.M. Investments (B.C.) Ltd.

Other Subsidiaries:
Campeau Corporation Ltd. — 52.2 per cent voting interest
Canada Steamship Lines Ltd. — 99.6 per cent common shares outstanding
Dominion Glass Co. Ltd. — 56.7 per cent voting interest
Laurentide Financial Corp. Ltd. — 53.3 per cent voting interest
Liverpool Plains Pastoral Co. Pty. Ltd. — 91.6 per cent voting interest
The Investors Group — 50.2 per cent voting interest
The Imperial Life Assurance Co. of Canada — 51.2 per cent outstanding common stock.
(Main Source: *Financial Post Survey of Industrials,* 1972:376-377, prepared by Wallace Clement.)

Power itself is controlled by a smaller firm, Gelco, which holds 50.1 per cent of the stock. Power in turn controls a large number of firms, by holding anywhere from 50 to 100 per cent of the shares. These firms then hold varying degrees of ownership in other firms. The result is an interest, more or less direct, in companies that range from bus lines to glass manufacture.

In recent years, John Kenneth Galbraith has written that a 'technostructure' has grown up, made of the technically skilled and specially trained, who in fact make key decisions on criteria all their own. Their power is based upon the fact that their skills and knowledge are presumed to be prerequisite for these organizations to produce effectively. But that power is important only to the extent that effective production is the goal of the firm within which the technostructure operates. In a structure as complex and convoluted as the Power Corporation, production may only be one of the goals that the ultimate decision-maker may have in mind for that segment of the corporation. Thus, the position of the technostructure may not be as all-powerful as it seems.

One of the results of this kind of indirect control is to remove policy-making far from the particular organization that must bear its impact and implement its directives, and far from the ownership. The decision may be taken in terms that make little sense for the organization in question, but rather in terms of the whole corporate structure, or of the ultimate profit-maker(s) in the corporation.

The importance of the ownership question lies in the immense power of such corporations in affecting the social structures within which they operate. A corporate decision, taken by financier, manager, or technician, is apt to influence the lives of a great many people. This influence operates at all levels, from the individual through the community, the province, the region, and the nation as a whole.

At the level of the community, corporate decisions may be all-powerful. This is particularly true in the so-called company town, but it is true in other, and larger communities as well. The single industry community is particularly vulnerable to the actions of that industry, since these communities were originally creatures of the company. Indeed, in a community's early stages, the company was so in control of these communities, that they were really part of the organization (Lucas, 1971). Later on, the companies have 'spun-off' the aspects of the community that they previously owned — housing, health services, etc. — but they remain the large employer, the large rate-payer and large consumer of services. Thus the community is quite dependent upon them.

This extends to the deepest aspects of community structure — the stratification system, the demographic make-up of the town. As Lucas points out, both the age distribution and the sex ratio are dependent upon the stage of development of the company. This process, where the community is virtually a reflection of the structure of the firm, is powerful enough when the development of the company continues on an even keel. When there is a major change in the company, for whatever reason, there is a multiplied effect on the community.

For example, in recent years there has been a considerable degree of change in the market for wood pulp products. The effects on the town of Temiscaming, Quebec, which was built by and around a CIP paper plant, were as follows:

> The death sentence was pronounced on this northwestern Quebec town of 2,400 two weeks ago when Canadian International Paper Co. announced the closure on May 31st of its Kipawa plant, the industrial sub-structure of Temiscaming ... Meanwhile, faced with the loss of their jobs, houses, friends and a particular way of life, the townspeople are unbelieving. They cannot admit their town is finished.

> They cannot believe that CIP, which has been for half a century a kind of father and friend as well as employer, will, with a stroke of a pen, and on four months notice, throw them all out.*

In larger communities, where there is more than one company, similar problems may still exist, but in a less obvious fashion. Communities with more than one company may still be based on one industry — for instance, Hamilton on steel, London on insurance — and changes in the external market or internal competitive structure of the industry may greatly affect the community. (Ottawa deserves special mention, having the federal government as its dominant, if not only industry.)

The firms that are dominant in a community supply the basis for the power structure and for decision-making for the community, even in large cities. Floyd Hunter (1953) found that in 'bigtown' (Atlanta, Georgia) the business community dominated the power structure of the city. Business elites may not have the over-riding power that Hunter cites; but when they do not, it often means that there are other organizational elites to compete with them.

To some extent, being a business man is a source of power for the individual. But to a large extent, his power may be *ex offficio*, based upon the organization that he represents, and the weight that it chooses to

*W.W. Johnson, 'Management Theory and Cabinet Government,' *Canadian Public Administration*, XIV, 1 (1971).

swing in the community. (Schulze, 1958) Pellegrin and Coats (1956) found that the executives of the large, absentee-owned firms in the city that they studied could make or break the various civic clubs and projects by participating or not. That participation was determined not by community need, but by company policy — either specific directives, or by the rewards that the company offered to its employees for such participation. In Ottawa, the federal government as chief employer and land-holder wields tremendous influence. Such influence may be direct, as in the decision to move the Royal Mint to Winnipeg; but it may be indirect as well. The largest block of contributions to the United Way comes through collection campaigns among civil servants.

At the level of the province, the various attempts to stimulate industrial development are key examples of the relationship between corporate decision-making and social control. For example, a major forestry project in Manitoba, intended to create thousands of jobs, was financed by a Swiss firm whose principal backers were kept secret. The president of the firm was quoted to the effect that if the Manitoba government insisted on knowing who the backers were, the deal for the project would be cancelled. (Mathias, 1971: 131) Another firm involved in the same project was found to be one of a string of between 20 and 200 firms connected by interlocking directorships and other forms of association, many of which were 'paper' companies with no real existence. The complexity of such corporate arrangements makes it difficult for the state to deal with them, even though these firms are receiving considerable government monies.

The actions of these various firms affected many aspects of life in Manitoba, most directly the employment and land rights of its native peoples. Less directly, the amount of provincial monies invested in these schemes represented resources not used in other aspects of life in the province. But the decisions that seemed really to determine what happened were made at such a distance that the key decision-makers were not even known.

The Public Sector: Who Pays?

Until now, we have, for the most part, discussed the problem of ownership in relation to private industry organizations. In that sector, we can calculate, more or less, the benefit to the owner. The problem there is (a) to identify the real 'owner,' meaning the ultimate beneficiary, and (b) to calculate the effects of his pursuit of his interest (and others' contestation of that pursuit) on the social fabric of the community.

There is an analogous issue to be considered when we examine the public sector, but in the public sector, the kinds of calculations required are of a different sort. The relation between the source of capital and the reaper of the benefits is less clear. In the case of the 'service' organization, the client is almost always someone who cannot pay for the benefit to be offered. In the case of the 'commonweal' organization, the society at large pays, and supposedly reaps the benefit.

The 'service' organizations exist only partially to serve their clients. Indeed, it can be argued that they exist not to serve those individuals, but rather to manipulate them for the benefit of the society at large, to keep a certain order in the society. (Cloward and Piven, 1971)

The clients who are served by such organizations are for the most part those dependent upon the society, because they are not economically self-sustaining. These include the young, the poor, the old, the sick, the deranged, and the criminal. For example, Zigler and Harter (1969) point out that one of the key elements in defining a mental retardate is his economic viability. If he holds a job, he is not institutionalized. If he loses that job, his status as a 'civilian' is in doubt. As Zigler and Harter point out, an economic recession may make an individual retardate. In societies where the key to the value system lies in the relationships to production the person who is dependent is deviant. Thus, the client-centered organization essentially serves two functions: (1) to allocate resources to the dependent, in the absence of family resources, and (2) to maintain the social order in the face of this deviance. The person without resources is in some senses a sinner (Hofley, 1971); the role of the social agency is both to support him and to 'save' him. In the case of the Salvation Army, this 'salvation' is obvious; in the case of the municipal Department of Social Welfare, it is more subtle, but nonetheless essentially similar. Because these organizations are serving a basically similar purpose — the control of deviants by socialization, segregation or sustenance — they tend to be structurally similar as well.

The battle for policy-making control in these organizations between the various power bases is in a way similar to that of the business organizations. There is a struggle between the technical personnel, the administrative personnel, and the 'owners.' The owners in this case are the elected officials.

This is a particular dilemma under the parliamentary system where the heads of many governmental organizations are directly elected officials. Members of parliament tend to be lawyers; the departments that they are presumed to direct and control may have chores that are more or less relevant to the law. Put another way, the reasons for appointment to a government portfolio may or may not relate to the holder's knowledge of the area in question. The minister may be technically skilled but that is a fortuitous circumstance, as much affected by political and regional consideration, as by special training. (The congressional system, with non-elective cabinet selection, need not be any better in this regard: John Kennedy, tongue in cheek, remarked on his brother's appointment to cabinet, 'I see nothing wrong with giving Robert some legal experience as Attorney-General before he goes out to practice law.') (Adler, 1965: 104)

This issue goes deeper than the play of partisan politics; it has important consequences for the existence of representative, democratic government. It is argued on one hand that the government agencies must remain independent, so that they can act for the benefit of the society, free from the whim of partisan politics, and using their particular skills to the utmost. Alternatively, politicians can be argued to be the representatives of the people, in necessary control over the bureaucracy, whose members would otherwise act in terms of self-interest, even if defined in professional terms. The issue has been stated clearly by H.S. Gordon, in a discussion of Canada's most powerful financial institution, The Bank of Canada.

> Can we argue that central bank independence is indeed essential to the functioning of democratic government? It may be argued that if the government controlled the Bank of Canada it could make special financial deals for political purposes. If we assume, however, that the Bank of Canada as it is now constituted never makes special deals of a questionable nature we may be assuming too much. If the Bank of Canada were to engage in such a transaction, it would probably never see the light of day. But if the Bank were a department, or the Auditor General were designated as the Bank's auditor, which he is not, any irregularities of this nature would find their way into the Auditor General's report and would thus be opened to the scrutiny of Parliament and the general public. The independence of the Bank of Canada from the Auditor General does not guarantee the integrity or impartiality of the Bank's practices nearly so much as it guarantees their secrecy. It has often been suggested that central banking activities must be shrouded in secrecy (and kept hidden for many years after the event) if central banks are to do their work effectively, but this is merely a myth that has been perpetuated by the sub-culture of the financial world, and by the Bank of England in particular. Financiers, bankers and central bankers have for a long time regarded themselves as a Pythagorean priesthood possessing the vital mysteries whose power is diminished if they are exposed to vulgar eyes. The desire for central bank independence springs more from this mythology than it does from defensible pragmatic arguments. It is a mythology that strikes at the root of democratic government.*

*H.S. Gordon, 'The Bank of Canada in a System of Responsible Government,' *Canadian Journal of Economics and Political Science*, XXVII, 1 (1961), 22.

The argument is also significant when we look at the role that the organization may play in the implementation of policy. If it goes along with the policy as set out by the minister, or the government of the day, the organization may be vitally (or brutally) effective in the implementation of that policy. To some extent, this is what the Nazis achieved in Germany; a brutally effective, ideologically 'sold' bureaucracy.

It is just as plausible, however, that the wheels of bureaucracy will grind slowly, if at all, in the implementaiton of a policy to which its members are resistant. In addition, the very organization imposed on the situation may serve to slow up those wheels. Take the case of New York City, for example:

> ... Labor troubles have dramatized (Mayor) Lindsay's difficulties in governing New York, but routine management of the city has proved an equally severe test. The ponderous inefficiency of the governing machinery that he has inherited has seriously impeded his effort to reverse the deterioration in municipal services. Many of the road-blocks that now make city government inefficient are the perverse by-product of the various reform movements that have swept through city hall in the past fifty years. In order to forestall deceptions, the reformers installed a series of rigid fiscal checks through the whole network of government. Political job holders were replaced with career civil servants, who were insulated from political pressures. Minute administrative procedures were prescribed by law. Government, as a result, did become more equitable and honest. The price that was paid was that the machinery became frozen and inflexible.*

A process of bureaucratization, begun in pursuit of the best of purposes, has come to neutralize, if not contravene those purposes.

Goal Definition and Predictability

Whether an organization is dependent upon the environment, or has achieved some measure of control over it, it has a relationship with that environment. It has things that it wishes to get from the environment, and other things which it wishes the environment to accept from it. To achieve its desired relationship with the environment, the organization must arrange itself in such a way as to take in some resources, adapt them in some way, and presumably, produce something for the environment.

The organization, in seeking its desired relationship with the environment, must first of course reach some decision as to what it desires, and

*Reichley, 'New York: A Nightmare for Urban Management.' Courtesy of *Fortune* Magazine © 1969 Time Inc.

how best to achieve it. At the broadest level, the selection of goals is involved in the ownership problems of which we wrote previously. At the narrowest level, it is a matter of 'what shall we do for the next hour?' There is thus a range from general goals to specific and often minor tasks. The scope of behavior involved is illustrated with the following examples from the formation of the Company of Young Canadians.

Goal
'The objects of the company are to support, encourage and develop programs for social, economic and community development in Canada or abroad through voluntary service.'

Strategy
'A volunteer is put into a community with no specific purpose, other than to eventually help to cause change.'

Tactics
'He spends his first months establishing himself, talking to people, trying to identify problems that the community presents. Eventually, some problems will become constant and the volunteer will have an idea about community needs. His job is then to help the community organize itself around the problems it has observed, and to help the community arrive at solutions to its own problems.'

Tasks
'The work of Dal and Helen was remarkably unexciting. She babysat, ironed clothes, washed dishes, and ran a recreational program for children. Dal became a home-made probation officer and a parole chief, a book-keeper, a welfare worker and a dance organizer.' (Hamilton, 1970:3)

The goals are matters of the broadest scope — 'community development' in our example of the CYC. Indeed, these broad goals are not far from being statements of values. Because of this, it is not unusual to have these very broad goals imposed from outside the organization, by legislative act in the case of the CYC, in less direct ways by the impact of societal values upon the goal-setters of the organization. The discretion of members of the organization increases with the specificity or narrower scope of behavior.

Organizational structure and goal achievement are dependent upon environmental inputs of two sorts: (1) 'long-run patterns of environmental influence' and (2) 'states of the environment at times of innovation and crisis.' One of the keys to the structure is the relation between the long-run patterns and the crises. Put another way, the key is how many crises the organization is liable to run into, as opposed to dealing with a recurrent, predictable context within which to operate.

The organization with a totally predictable environment is one that can run in the most bureaucratic fashion — it is the situation where a bureaucracy works best. This is the situation where the bureaucratic rules will continually be applicable, where the bureaucrat himself can find comfort in those rules in deciding how to perform his task. A predictable environment need not be one that is always the same; it just needs to be one whose changes are regular, or are in themselves predictable.

The more crises that appear, and the less predictable the environment, the more immediately flexible the organization must be if it is to succeed in interacting with the environment. Etzioni (1961) suggests, for example, that when an army unit shifts from a peace-time to a war-time role, its structure becomes more flexible to the extent that in actual combat, many of the rigidities of rank and uniform are forgotten. On the other hand, there may be no better model for a Weberian ideal-type bureaucracy than a peace-time garrison army.

Burns and Stalker (1967) define two kinds of organizations, each suited to a different 'ratio' of crisis to stability:
(1) the *mechanistic* organization, which corresponds to the Weberian rational- legal bureaucracy, best adapted to relative stability.
(2) the *organic* organization, adapted to continually changing conditions; relying on the continual redefinition of tasks as needs arise. Information passes as advice rather than orders, and throughout the organization, as opposed to conforming to a strict hierarchy.
The notion here is simple enough; if situations are continually changing, the rules must also be changed to deal with them.

It is in such situations that innovation is needed and ideally occurs. But even innovation itself is hard for an organization to cope with. In the first place, innovation is by definition a deviant act; a formal organization, like any organization, seeks initially to continue business as usual; thus the innovator, necessary as he may be, may be resisted by the organization. To some extent, he becomes part of the unpredictability.

The innovator is not and cannot be bound by strict hierarchical rules; so that if the organization seeks to employ his services, they must insure his loyalty. The organization will depend even more than the classic bureaucracy on the way its members legitimize the organization.

Stinchcombe (1959) suggests that one way in which this takes place is through craft or professional norms. Thus, in the construction industry, the builder counts on the craftsmanship of the plumbers, the carpenters and so forth. Graves (1970) writes of pipe-line construction, where the geography and the nature of the chores are such as to prevent regular hiring in a bureaucratic way — there is an irregular work pattern which precludes formal procedures, but requires workers in a hurry when they are needed. 'Crews, about half of which are highly skilled, must be recruited within a few hours, a few days at most. Neither public and private employment agencies nor unions can supply crews with necessary timing. Groups of kinsmen and friends, however, amass crews rapidly and effectively.' Thus another informal network, working by word of mouth, is the key to the organization's meeting its irregular need for manpower. It may not work 'well;' but that is the way it works.

A particularly severe crisis that faces an otherwise structured system often leads to complete innovation in that system, again informally. Perhaps the clearest example is the *Crise d'octobre* in Quebec in 1970. It can be argued whether the crisis was real or perceived – who knows what an 'apprehended insurrection' is? But the reaction was the suspension of the bureaucracy of the law, in favor of a totally non-formal enforcement of arrest and internment procedures.

The stability of the context within which the organization operates is the major factor which determines whether a formal bureaucratic structure is the most effective way for it to operate. The notion implies stability not only in the task demands, but also in terms of the various inputs to the organization. If an organization is not assured of such stability, or at least predictability, in its supplies of material or labor, then the strains on the organization will force it to adapt in ways not unlike those demanded by task irregularity.

The relationship of the organization to other organizations depends upon where it fits in terms of the regularity of its task, and the degree of control it has over its environment. If the organization is well in control, then it can regulate both its input of resources and the output of products and by-products. It need take relatively less heed of those other organizations in its environment. Thus, in the one-industry towns described by Lucas (1971), the company need not by greatly concerned with the municipal government, unless it chooses to be. On the other hand, a dependent organization may change radically to fit the actions and needs of the organizations in its environment. Funding agencies have tremendous power over the organizations that they fund (Maris and Rein, 1967).

The relationships between organizations are often summed up in the relations between their elites. Much of this can be seen in terms of bargaining, using whatever resources are relevant. Indeed, this is the way in which large organizations function to allocate societal resources. The appearance of Bell Canada before the CTC is essentially an inter-organizational bargaining meeting, in the same sense that the meetings between Air Canada and the International Association of Machinists are.

It is usual to think of the environment affecting organizational structure. But in a bargaining environment, the organizational structure becomes a resource in terms of the ability of the elite to deal with other organizations. Thus, the 'democratic' structure of the International Typographers Union (Lipset, Trow and Coleman, 1956) had a distinct effect on its bargaining position. In general the 'political' structure of the organization is what allows the elite to act for it. And when push comes to shove at the bargaining table the backing of the organizational membership is a crucial consideration.

Organizational Ecology

The structure of a formal bureaucracy demands certain patterns of hierarchy and of communications. To meet these demands implies not only a certain social pattern, but certain physical arrangements as well. There are various instances where the ecology of an organization, that is, the arrangement of its activities in physical space, determines its social patterns.

Ideally, the organization, or its leaders, design their space in relation to the design of their management pattern. That ideal assumes (1) that all the activity of the organization goes on within the space that the organization controls, (2) that the organization is in a position to design its space as opposed to taking over an existing building; or (3) can change the space to suit itself (it may be renting, rather than owning); and (4) that it has thought about the problem of physical space in the first place. These assumptions are pretty hard to meet; and to the extent that they are not met, the social patterns of the organization must adapt themselves to imperfect space. (This is not always unintentional; after World War II, Winston Churchill had the House of Commons rebuilt too small to hold all its members, as he felt this had a salutary effect on the operations of the Commons.)

There are a number of organizations which are simply too spread out to maintain strict bureaucratic controls. The two studies cited earlier, of construction (Stinchcombe) and of pipe-line construction (Graves), are both treatments of organizations where not only is the environment irregular, but all the action takes place at a great distance from the managerial offices. Hierarchical communications, the kind of checking-up that hierarchy implies, are almost impossible in such situations. The result is dependency on professional or informal arrangements in lieu of bureaucratic arrangements.

The problems of spatial relationships are also involved in the internal relationships of an organization. For example, Blauner (1964) writes of the difficulties of a textile hand owing to the 'pressures' of his work. These pressures were the result of a 'stretch-out' in the work, that is, each hand had to tend several machines. This was in itself difficult; that difficulty was multiplied by the physical layout of textile work. The carding room in a cotton textile mill, a room at least the size of a football field and filled with machinery, was tended by three men. One of the union grievances in one such textile mill was that the loom fixers, who did continuous repairs on the looms, were not allowed time to go to a central supply to get lubricants. The trip to the oil barrel might be 200 yards; the time came off the rest period of seven minutes that was occasionally allowed to the workers. A textile mill weave room is so noisy that interaction can only be minimal. Thus, the development of informal groups and formal communications is severely limited.

Similarly, Gouldner (1955) in his studies of a gypsum mining operation cites the difficulty of maintaining bureaucratic structure, when many of the workers are separated and working below ground in the mine.

The simple geography of an office can greatly alter the communications pattern of an organization, and thus the way it controls its members. A peculiarly interesting example of this is Carleton University. The buildings at Carleton are connected by underground tunnels, which restrict traffic, and at least face-to-face communication to fixed patterns during the foul Ottawa winters. The distance between academic buildings and the administration building, short above ground, is quite long by tunnel. For this reason, among others, none of the academic officers of the university has chosen to maintain his office in the Administration Building.

Ecological arrangements are expressive of organizational arrangements as well as constraining them. For the most part, placement in an office building and the amount of space allotted is strongly related to position in the organizational hierarchy. The Canadian government maintains an official formula relating status in the civil service to an entitlement to a certain amount of space, the enclosure of that space, and the furnishing of the space. The right to enclosed space, that is, the right to privacy, is definitely part of a high status. That privacy relates to two aspects of organizational structure: (1) privacy means non-observability — the subordinate cannot check up on his superior; and (2) control — the private office can be controlled and arranged by its occupant, whereas general space is planned for the user. The more status, the more power — both over others, and over one's self; this is reflected spatially.

It has also been found that the availability of certain aspects of natural environment is important to the ability of the worker to work. But this relates to status as well:

'Although job and space analysis have brought more efficient patterns to the general office floor in the logical progression of paper work operations and in the physical situation of immediate supervisors to workers, one striking similarity to the office of by-gone days persists —

the brass still gets the glass.' (Forrest, 1969) In some instances, to get a happier work force, translucent panels have been used so that some natural light filters through to the central office as well. But generally, the more attractive work space is allocated to higher status personnel. Toronto City Hall may be the only building in Canada where the brass has enclosed offices, and the staff get the windows.

The Structural Problems of Organizations

The basic problems of structure *within* complex organizations are similar to the problems that exist in all social organizations. The process whereby organizational structures evolve is in essence the same as the processes of societal development that Durkheim writes of the *The Division of Labor in Society*. Briefly, this process involves the development of the organization as a system of differentiated, specialized and independent parts.

As organizations grow, functions previously performed by one man become assigned to specialists, and the specialists themselves are further divided into sub-specialists. For example, consider the changes in the role of the foreman: once the foreman hired, fired, designed production processes, scheduled work and so forth. Now the firm has separate departments for personnel, research and development, and systems analysis. Each of the foreman's functions has become differentiated and specialized. This differentiation has advantages in terms of efficiency, perhaps; but it also leaves the problem of holding the complex together.

How is order maintained in the face of the growing complexity of organizations? The process of differentiation increases the likelihood of departures from the prior order. Thus, a major part of the structure of formal organizations is related to dealing with the real or perceived threats to existing patterns. The task is to maintain order or social control, or conversely, to deter deviance. Figure 3 illustrates the organizational processes that are related to each of the strategies of social control.

Figure 3: Strategies of Organizational Control

Before the fact	Integration	Segregation
	Socialization	Recruitment
	Training	and selection
	Education	procedures
After the fact	Rehabilitation	Expulsion
	Retraining	

The kinds of strategies that the organization applies will depend upon what it is trying to do, and the resources at its command. For example, the church may try to reintegrate the deviant believer through such devices as confession and penance. On the other hand, it may choose to excommunicate. The key to both of these, of course, is the fact of belief in the first place. Excommunication does not mean much to someone who does not believe in the sacraments. In a wider sense, this again points out the crucial part that legitimation plays in the success of any organizational strategies. Basically, unless there is some degree of legitimation, integrative strategies will not work. An organization based on coercion must segregate its deviants.

The Problem of Size: Integration and Differentiation

As the organization grows in size and complexity, the problems of maintaining coherent operation become more difficult and demanding. The result is that more attention must be paid to them; put another way, more people must be involved in maintenance rather than in dealing with the environment. The result is that the proportion of personnel involved in administration rather than production increases as the organization grows.

This can be seen in a common sense fashion. In Figure 4 the 'x's' are production workers, the 'y's' are managers. Assume for the moment that one person supervises two others. And on and on. Obviously, organizations do not operate in such a simplistic way. But the various complex relationships that exist between size and administrative problems (Starbuck, 1965) are seen to point to the general rule that the *number of people involved in co-ordination and support grows faster* than the number of people that are being supported and co-ordinated.

One can argue that more people are required for such duties. But it is true as well that the support of increasing non-productive personnel makes heavy demands on organizations. Lenski (1965) has written that the stratification processes of societies grow more hierarchical and differentiated as the society is able to produce more than is needed for subsistence — that is, when the society can afford a non-producing upper class. The process in organizations is quite analogous. As they grow, they are able to produce enough to insure support for the infra-structure that co-ordination seems to require.

As time goes on, a cycle develops where the maintenance of the administrative personnel requires more production personnel, which require more administration and so on. This kind of growth seems crucial in organizations. They either grow or fold up, or are swallowed by the organizations that are growing. It is to insure the resources needed

Figure 4:   Proportion of Management to Workers

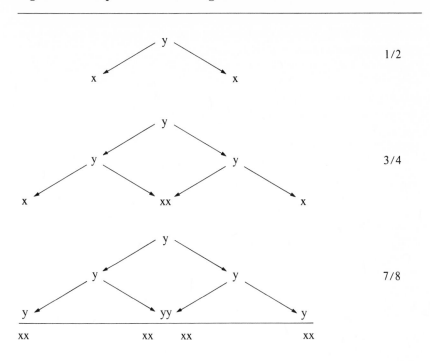

for this growth that large organizations seek to control and manipulate their environment in the ways we spoke of earlier.

The growth in size of the organization is accompanied by a gradual differentiation of the roles within the organization. By this, we mean that jobs previously combined in the activities of one person are separated out as special duties, each assigned to a different individual. This is a process that is, as you will recall, crucial to the nature of a bureaucracy in particular. Thain (1969) has shown diagramatically the patterns of growth in corporations.

Small and Simple		Large and Complex
Stage I	Stage II	Stage III
One Unit	One Unit	Multi-Unit
'One Man Show'	Functionally Specialized Group	General Office and Decentralized Divisions

The organization in Stage I is heavily dependent upon outside support, to get what it needs from the environment. The owner is usually the manager, and everything else, because he cannot afford back-up assistance. He is extremely vulnerable to perturbations in the environment and changes in sources of supply and customers. The company is often highly vulnerable to illness or death of that key man. The result is that 'it is no accident that nearly all bankruptcies occur in Stage I companies.' (Thain, 1969: 34)

The second stage involves functional specialization of individual roles within one unit. The survival problem has usually been licked at this point, and the organization is better able to cope with its environment, although it is not in complete control: 'Nearly all Stage II companies are much less reliant on external factors than Stage I operators and have enough depth in resources that they can afford some planning.... However, many Stage II companies seeking growth, profitability and security and realizing that they are as vulnerable to the life cycle of one product as the Stage I company is to the life cycle of one man, attempt to diversify ...*

The Stage III firm seems, more than anything else, like a feudal society — a king and court maintaining control over a series of baronial fiefdoms. There is a central office, whose functions are supervision and control over the managers of the various divisions, each of which is virtually a firm to itself. Divisions are producing for their own market, rather than combining their efforts for a common product.

By and large, the evolution from stage to stage is accompanied by increasing bureaucratization. For example, Thain lists the following changes in reward systems as part of the differentiation process:

Stage I Informal, personal, subjective, used to maintain control and divide a small pool of resources to provide personal incentives for key performers.

Stage II More structured, usually based to a greater extent on agreed policies as opposed to personal opinion and relationships.

Stage III Allotment by 'due process' of a wide variety of different rewards and punishments on a formal systematic basis. Company-wide policies usually apply to many different classes of managers and workers with a few major exceptions for individual cases.

The key element in the bureaucratization process, the legitimization of the goals and structures, is harder to achieve as the organization becomes a set of semi-autonomous units. The problem of reconciling the various kinds of goals, which is what legitimization is about, is very much like

---

*Donald Thain, 'Stages of Corporate Development,' *The Business Quarterly*, XXXIV, 4(1969), 38.

the problem of maintaining a federal system — is one loyal first to the division (province) or to the organization *in toto* (the nation)?

One attempt to reconcile the units in the organization has been based upon making success in internal competition the criterion for the personal success of the managers. Advertising agencies are prominent examples (Bensman, 1967). These agencies are organized into a series of teams, each of which prepares an advertising campaign for the client. The team whose work is most consistently chosen will win a place in the firm; a team whose work is ignored may not last in the firm. The result is to tie the goals of the individual to success in the company's terms; the internal competition will tend to prevent an informal set of goals from arising among employees.

Differentiation implies a wide variety of ways in which subsections may informally interpret the charter goal of the organization. The various branches of a government ministry, for example, might have quite different interpretations of its proper role. Each of those divisions will attempt to persuade the others of its interpretation, if only to assure the largest possible share of the usually short budget. This kind of sub-unit competition is quite common, and it appears in a number of forms.

THE STAFF-LINE CONTROVERSY
The smoothing of relations between the *staff* (those who perform specialized managerial or other tasks) and the *line* (those involved in production and its administration) has long been a problem in organizations. The root of the conflict has been found to lie in three basic conditions: (1) conspicuous ambitions and 'individualistic' behavior by staff officers; (2) the complications stemming from the efforts of the staff to get acceptance of its non-production function; and (3) promotion into higher staff offices depends upon line approval. (Dalton, 1950)

As long as there is a product sold for profit, contribution to production can always be called upon as the ultimate measuring stick, even more than contribution to sales. The result is that during the economic downturn of the last couple of years, it is the staff that has been hit particularly hard by cut-backs. A recent issue of *Fortune* (1971) describes the heavy personnel cut-backs at United Airlines as part of an attempt to stem losses; the cut-backs are in ancillary personnel. Accompanying the article is a striking picture of a plush carpeted office, empty of people and desks, with phones resting on the floor waiting to be taken out.

PROFESSIONALS IN ORGANIZATIONS
The staff-line problem is particularly acute when the staff is made up of professionals. There are two factors which make professionals hard for

the line administrator to deal with: (1) the esoteric nature of professional knowledge and (2) the stress on a peer-based authority system. Both refer to the fact that only a fellow professional knows what a professional is up to; others have to take things on faith. There is no way that you fully know what your doctor is up to; the key is that you believe in his ability and good will. The organization is, in a similar way, dependent on the professional (or skilled craftsman). (Stinchcombe, 1964) Administration, in the face of this 'faith' relationship, becomes pretty difficult. Two quotes from the administrators of industrial research laboratories are clear examples:

> Don't worry about the time your researchers come to work or whether they wear sneakers. That's about as much as I know about management.

> I don't know the head of any research organization who really knows how to evaluate his own laboratory. He can do it intuitively, but he has no real means of comparison.*

The norms of the professions, which emphasize autonomy and judgment only by peers, violate the basic tenets of bureaucratic organizations. Yet more and more professionals work in, or with, large bureaucratic organizations. Further, many of these are government run or funded organizations (schools, hospitals). This increasing expense has led to attempts by governments to rationalize and control them — usually to make them more bureaucratic, and this leads to problems with the professions.

THE CONSULTANT

Like many of the functions of organizations, the staff functions may be 'contracted out' to persons outside the organization. The growth of consulting has been large, both in private business and in government. (Meredith and Martin, 1970)

There are certain manifest reasons for consulting. It may be cheaper to hire specialized staff only as they are needed, rather than provide continuous employment for the specialists. Indeed, certain specialists may only be available on a consulting basis. Consulting firms in some sense represent a further refinement of the division of labor, in that they specialize in some defined function.

Besides this manifest function, the consultant has some latent functions: (1) *The blessing of the fishing fleet:* Before the fleet went out, the Bishop used to bless it, adding God's help presumably to the skills of the

*Dan Cordtz, 'Bringing the Laboratory Down to Earth,' *Fortune,* LXXXIII, 1 (1971). Reprinted by permission.

fishermen. The consultant, in many cases, may perform the same role. In this case, he is an individual of high standing or professional repute. He is not asked to participate in the project so much as he is asked to approve of it, and lend his reputation to it. Phillip Selznick, writing of the T.V.A., referred to the process as co-optation. This kind of role has in the recent past often fallen to academics — since academics have become of high status, their blessing of a project has come to be quite significant. (2) *The Hired Gun:* The consultant may be brought in to perform some unpopular task, since, once it is over with, he can go away. He does not have to remain in day-to-day informal interaction, and thus bear the consequences of his previous actions. Winn, describing Alcan, notes that 'internal change agents' do not survive very long, and that it is better to have the organization shaken up by an outside consultant (1969). To some extent, it allows for a kind of scapegoating that is often quite useful.

Communications

An alternative dimension to examine in the study of organizational structure is the pattern of communications within the organization. There are those indeed who see communications as the crucial concept in the study of organizations. To some extent this is a truism — organizations are patterns of social relationships, and no such relationship exists without communications. Because of this fact, almost anything said about organizations is a statement about communications. Beyond this fact, however, there are certain statements applying specifically to the flow of information.

There is a notion that many of the problems of a group or organization are due to some inadequacy in communications — that ignorance leads to lack of understanding leads to conflict. The implied solution is an increase in the flow of communications. But such an increase may present as many problems as it solves. A conflict that has lain dormant may flower when everyone learns that it exists — 'If I had known you felt like that, I would never have agreed to your project.' Also, the simple increase in the volume of communications may inundate both the individuals in the organization, and the organizational systems which transmit them. The notorious 'red tape' is, at least in part, a problem of an excess volume of information to be put through a bureaucratic system.

An organization, by definition, sets limits on the flow of communications, and the kind of communications among its members. In a group comprising as few as 30 people, there are 435 possible relationships, 435 possible channels of communications. To speak of those 30 people as an organization is to look at restrictive and regulated patterns of communication. In the ideal type of bureaucracy, a key aspect is the restriction of communications to those of a formal nature between people in a hierarchical relationship.

We have spoken earlier about the organization being made up of a number of people who want to express their own meanings in the organization. The communications process is of course essential to the expression of these meanings.

In the first instance, the individual must put his idea, his meaning, into a form that can be transmitted to others. This is called *encoding*. In the case of face-to-face communications, this seems to be a relatively simple process — one simply speaks his mind. It is, of course, more complicated. There is a lot more conveyed in the words than their 'dictionary' meanings. And, face-to-face there is a lot of communication that is not in the words.

When the relationship is not face-to-face, as with most of the relationships in a large organization, the encoding process is of a different sort. The richness of face-to-face must be compressed and limited. If you send a memo, all the inflection is lost, and the verbal form is limited. In the most limiting case, you are communicating with or through a machine. Then, your message must be put into the special language of the machine — shortened for the Telex, or programmed for the computer.

At the other end of the process, the receiver of the message must somehow extract the meaning, hopefully the meaning that the sender intended. This process, called *decoding*, has its own set of problems. The more abstracted the message, that is, the more compressed and selective the information that it contains, the greater the chance that the decoded message will be different from the original.

Communications, like other aspects of organizations, may be formal or informal, that is, in aid of the aims of the organizations or not. Related to this distinction is that between *instrumental* and *expressive* communications. The former are those that transmit information and knowledge; the latter, those that transmit attitudes, norms and values, and reinforce them. The social networks which transmit these kinds of communications may overlap, but they may differ widely, too, even within the same organization. One way to study an organization is to examine the way in which different kinds of communications are transmitted.

In some cases, instrumental communications may be the only ones that are either desirable or possible. In the classic bureaucracy, communications are supposed to be limited to those which relate to the job and which are passed up and down the chain of command. In a prison, the guards and the inmates share little in the way of norms and attitudes – the only expressive communications would be negative. Thus vertical communications will be limited to the necessary minimum.

In a prison, expressive communications would be horizontal, to maintain peer-group solidarity among the prisoners. By way of contrast, think of a church, where there is a limited amount of instrumental communications, reflecting the relatively limited skills that the congregants have to learn. But the amount of vertical expressive communications will be considerable, to reinforce the belief that is the basis for the perseverance of the church as an organization.

Access to various information networks is another indicator of power, however those networks are organized. The secrecy classifications common in governmental organizations are a manifestation of this. The 'higher' the classification of the material, the more restricted the network of people who can have access to it. And that very restriction is indicative of high status for the people involved.

Looked at another way, narrow communication may present a problem. Knowledge may be limited that needs to reach throughout the organization. Leaders often over-estimate the size of the audience for their messages. The result is that people at the bottom of the organization may not get all the directives – this may mean problems both for the individual (the soldier who does not hear of a coming attack) or for the organization (the soldier who does not receive the order to attack on schedule).

As communications go through a large network of people, they may be modified in transit. Perhaps each person will 'echo' the message onward. But particularly with expressive communications, the message will be translated on the way. This is particularly true of the 'grapevine' that is present in many organizations. There are a number of stories of rumor transmission that show how details of the rumor are changed to fit the previous knowledge of those who are doing the transmitting.

Communications up a hierarchical line will also be subject to modification. This is based on the fact that the hearer can bring sanctions to bear upon the bringer of the message. The extreme form was when despots would behead the bearer of bad news; in a modern counterpart this writer has seen a disc-jockey afraid to announce to an audience that a popular group failed to show up for a concert for fear of his own safety. The antithesis is the stereotyped 'yes man,' hearing only what he wants to hear, saying what others wish to be said. (A famous movie producer was quoted as saying to his aides, 'Don't say yes until you hear what I have to say first.')

If, in fact, the actual handling of communications was identical with power, then secretaries would be the most powerful figures in many organizations. They may or may not initiate messages, but they transmit, encode and decode many of the messages. That they remain relatively subordinate figures attests to the importance of a number of other factors, such as the traditional roles of women, identification and legitimation. Nonetheless, it is interesting to think what it would be like if all secretaries in a firm were to take strike action, if only for a few days.

Organizations and Leaders

There have been numerous references to the burdensome loneliness of power, from Harry Truman's pithy 'If you can't stand the heat, get out of the kitchen' to the famous abdication speech of Edward VIII. Certainly, it seems plausible that the high incidence of divorce, alcoholism and ulcers among executives might be a result of severe pressures. But, obviously, all men who lead organizations do not commit suicide, nor do they all get ulcers. There are coping strategies.

Some people have a greater tolerance for responsibilities than others. To some extent, this is a matter of personalities. For example, there is a quite startling passage in Winston Churchill's diary of World War II where he says that taking office in the face of the fall of Europe actually allowed him to sleep better, knowing that destiny was now in his hands.

One way of dealing with the pressures of office is to appeal to sources of authority outside the organization. This in effect reduces the loneliness of decision-making by imposing some degree of constraint, or of social support for the individual in question. The sources of this authority may lie in some ideology, perhaps in what we termed earlier the ideological goals of the organization. Perhaps it lies in an appeal to class and family (for example, look at Soames in *The Forsyte Saga*). The sources of authority may be more individual and bizarre — this might throw light on Mackenzie King and his spiritualism.

It should be mentioned that, except in rare instances, the power of the organizational elite, while relatively great, is not unlimited. There is at least some extent to which they must obey some sort of rules. These rules may not be the same as for the rest of the organization, often they are special for the leader. But they are rules nonetheless.

There has been considerable debate over the extent to which leaders are expected to follow the norms of their group. One argument is that as the leaders they set the norms; therefore, they are free to do as they like. The other is that as leaders they must be the good example for others to follow. Thus, if Prime Minister Trudeau says 'fuddle duddle' in the House of Commons, people are quite upset, even if they have been known to 'fuddle duddle' themselves.

There is no one answer to this argument. Leaders may be allowed to roam in terms of one set of norms, but kept on a short leash in terms of others. One notion which is useful in considering this dilemma is that of *idiosyncracy credits*. Basically, the idea is that by following the norms the leader can build up a stock of these credits. He can then 'spend' them by doing as he pleases. In other words, when a person has succeeded in having his leadership accepted and legitimized, he can act on his own. What this notion emphasizes is that one cannot 'overspend' his credits; that is, excessive violation of expectations can lose him his legitimacy. If that is lost, it may mean loss of job; it may also mean difficulty in running the organization.

The extent to which the elite has been autonomous means that any change in the distribution of power in the organization will be essentially alienating to them. This is particularly true because their position of power has allowed them to define what is 'right' and 'true' for the organization. Further, the fact that they are an elite means that they have been, for the most part, rewarded by the system as it exists. Their view of the world and the organization has worked, at least for them. Given this, the attempts at change, from within the organization (unions for example) or without (government regulation or public participation) will not only be limitations on behavior: they will be personal challenges, as well as violations of the 'truth.' In some cases, the needed changes will be literally inconceivable to the current elite. Their view of the world cannot encompass the problems that others may be having.

A clear example of the problems engendered by organizational change is the effects upon executives of mergers and acquisitions in industry. Men who were previously able to project their personalities as entrepreneurs are now constrained by a new corporate structure, which may even put them in a subordinate position. This has been found to be a very difficult change to make for these men; indeed, many of them could not make it. The result was that, after such mergers, a number of executives left lucrative positions to go out on their own again. (*Fortune,* 1969)

Organization and Individuals: The Middle Range

What we refer to here are those positions which are in some ways subordinate and in other ways superior. They include middle management and supervisory personnel in industry and government and the so-called semi-professions, such as teaching, social work and nursing. Roughly speaking, we are dealing with the problems of the white collar worker.

The classic picture of such individuals emphasizes their conformity. Dependent upon the bureaucratic system for security and mobility, the individual clings to the rule book and takes no action that the 'book' will not cover. He is a creature of precedents and timidity.

Another version of this individual is conveyed in the notion of 'The Organization.' The junior executive, dependent upon his superiors and on the firm, becomes the classic 'yes' man. The individual submerges all of his choices into the firm — choice of house, neighborhood, clothing, etc. Not only the employee, but his wife as well, must fit a mould exactly. A pointed description of this type of employee was given by a Montreal executive.

> Up to now, all the Brownie points that companies have been giving here have been for long and faithful service. Never mind if the guy has been doing anything creative for you. His compensation, vacation, pension plan have all been based on whether he gave his bosses a warm feeling.*

In general, the constraints upon the employees in this middle range are increasing. This is true for the following reasons:

> 1. centralization in large firms, along with standardization of operations.
> 2. the demographic characteristics of organizations. Organizations remain pyramidal and hierarchical, but many top positions are now occupied by relatively young men, thereby creating mobility blockage that will last a lifetime for subordinates unwilling or unable to move.
> 3. technological changes have rendered many managerial functions redundant and obsolete.
> 4. the combination of the above creates a routinization and trivialization of the managerial jobs.(Hodgson, 1972: 12)

The results of these constraints for the individual are remarkable if we remember the 'bureaucratic personality.'

> 'Three out of three executives now hate their jobs,' one observer stated bluntly.... The biggest schism today in corporations and bureaucracies is not owners and employees, or between management and the union. It is between top and middle management.... The resentment and pent-up rage of middle managers against their bosses would keep top managers awake at night, if they were fully aware of the fierceness of the hostility against them. (Hodgson, 1972: 11)

Hodgson may be overstating the case. And he may be overstating the novelty of the situation. The question is, again, how do people cope with this? The seething anger that Hodgson mentions is a response of a sort, although he begs off what these people do as a consequence of their anger.

---

*R. Hodgson 'The rules of the game have been changed.... The players have not been notified,' *The Business Quarterly*, XXXVII, 2 (1972), 13.

The orientation to upward mobility is only one possible solution for these 'middle people.' And for people in service organizations, the other alternatives are worth examining.

It is as a reaction to this sort of problem that Corwin explains the growth of 'militant professionals.' Corwin's particular example is teachers. Faced with a slackening in the relative authority and prestige of the teaching profession, and thus with a slackening in the mobility to be gained by being a teacher, the teachers become 'militant' in their demands and actions against the school system. This means that they are more willing to unionize, or at least, to adopt the tactics of labor unions that formerly would have been foresworn, such as strikes, working to rule, or other job actions. Teachers do not have the chance for appeal to professional peer groups that are available to doctors or lawyers. And they are willing, because they have lower chances for mobility, to adopt an adversary stance against the administration with whom they formerly would have identified.

The middle range member of the organization does have ways of taking action within the structure of the organization. The key is that, as he is frustrated by the organization, he will pursue his own goals at the expense of the organization's official goals. This has appeared in a number of guises, but it has shown clearly in resistance to organizational change imposed from above. The Glassco Commission Report has occasioned a series of major changes in the management process in the government of Canada, and along with the requirements of bilingualism, has created major problems for members of the civil service. One statement of the results is as follows:

> The reaction of managers to excessive demands made upon their time by innovation has been to conceal their apprehension lest they be considered unprogressive or even reactionary. But now 'motherhood' concepts in management are being resisted. Outright refusals to cooperate with time-consuming innovators are no longer a novelty. Managers are expressing their concern openly, at management meetings, and are finding that their views are widely held among their colleagues. Even among the innovators considerable caution is becoming evident.*

And Air Marshall Sharp (1968), in looking at the results of unification of the forces notes a tendency toward 'regression,' by which he means a return (witting or not) to procedures and attitudes from before the change. Both of these suggest the ability of individuals to resist change to which they are opposed.

It is more difficult for the individual to institute change where the elite does not allow it, since the necessary resources may not be at hand. But it

---

*H.L. Laframboise, 'Administrative Reform in the Federal Public Service,' *Canadian Public Administration,* XIV, 3 (1971), 324.

can and does happen occasionally, at least until the brass catches up. A recent example was the action of the staff of the Senate Committee on Poverty in writing and releasing their own conclusions which contradicted those of the report of the full committee. A more extreme example was the action of a U.S. Air Force general in initiating his own orders to bomb North Vietnam in the light of his own view of how best to prosecute the war.

Organization and the Individual: The Lower Participant

In the framework that we have employed to this point, we should expect that the lower participant will suffer from *alienation* (a sense of helplessness and dissatisfaction), since he is the member of the organization with the least power. The alienation of the industrial worker has long been a theme in social thought, going back to Marx and beyond.

This is a theme that has become particularly significant in recent years, with the increasing introduction of sophisticated automated manufacturing and office procedures. There is considerable debate upon the real effect of automation; there is debate indeed on just what automation is. The key variables are not involved in automation as such, but rather, are things that mediate the encounter of the individual with the technology, or allow him to cope with the technology.

Robert Blauner has studied the relation of different kinds of technology to varieties of worker alienation. Among the things that seemed to relate to the degree of worker alienation were the degree of union solidarity, the availability of a close-knit community outside the plant, and the ability of the worker to structure his own work situation, and to control it to some degree.

Within these alternatives lie the main ways for the lower participant to cope with a highly structured and potentially alienating situation. He can seek help in a collective way, whether (1) by seeking control through collective action (the union) or (2) withdrawing commitment and seeking meaning in non-work activities (the community).

Both of these represent major changes in the way in which the individual goals of the lower participant relate to the organizational goals as defined by the elite. Put another way, the structure of meaning in the organization has changed. Put still another way, the legitimation has changed. In the first case (collective control), the lower participants have adopted an adversary position vis-à-vis the organization, and they pursue personal goals at the expense of the elite. In the second case (community orientation), the investment in the organization exists only to insure the means for outside activities. The job is important only to get the dollars to pay for the cottage or whatever. In both of these cases, the individual goals have become estranged from the charter and informal goals, and the lower participants do not legitimate the organizational authority.

When this lack of legitimation takes place, the consequences can be considerable. The results may be high job turn-over, absenteeism, and in some cases, sabotage. This can be major, or just minor ways of getting back at the firm without doing damage. A description of the new Vega plant in Lordstown, Ohio, is a case in point. Along with things like cut gas lines, smashed dashes, and ruined engine blocks, there is nuisance damage done to shut down the line.

> A favorite trick at Lordstown is locking the keys inside a car as it nears the end of the line, ready to be gassed and driven off to the lot. 'It really doesn't hurt anything,' one man says. 'The foreman just has to run like a scalded dog to get a master key before they shut the line down. And no foreman wants the line shut down on account of him.'*

The alternative is to find fulfillment outside the organization. This is true of the lower participants in many kinds of organizations. It is true, almost by definition, of prisoners. But Dubin found this orientation to be characteristic of many industrial workers. (The author is aware of a plant where there is almost always a strike on the first day of the hunting and fishing season.) The work is purely utilitarian, to supply the means for the outside life. For many workers, this last alternative is what is expected out of work. Whatever else it is, it is not disappointing — it is just a job.

There is the possibility that the lower participant will be given more control of his situation. Paul Blumberg reviewed a vast body of research and reached the following conclusion:

> There is hardly a study in the entire literature which fails to demonstrate that satisfaction in work is enhanced or that other generally acknowledged benefits accrue from a genuine increase in workers' decision-making power. (Blumberg, 1968: 123)

If the 'personalizing' facility of the worker is increased, alienation decreases. It is clear that, along with that decrease, there is a general upgrading of the experience for the worker; it is usually beneficial for the organization as well.

Conclusions

Complex organizations are important because they are power structures. Because they are powerful, they have a call on large portions of the material and social resources of the society, and play a major part in the

*From 'Blue Collar Saboteurs' by Geoffrey Norman. Originally appeared in *Playboy* Magazine; copyright © 1972 by *Playboy.*

distribution of those resources to individuals. Because they are themselves differentiated structures of power, with some persons having more power than others, the individuals who direct those organizations control the distribution of resources, both from the organization to its clients, and within the organization to its members.

These facts have a number of major consequences for the society. It is easy enough to recite the immense power of the large organizations which are characteristic of Canada as an industrial society. It is the contention here that the stratification process is in large measure the product of bargaining and/or conflict between large organizations. For example, the future of a large city, Sydney, Nova Scotia, depended on the results of bargaining between the government and a large British corporation, Hawker-Siddley. The social standing of much of Sydney's population was more or less determined by that bargaining.

But when one reviews the power of large organizations, one must be careful to avoid the pitfalls of reification. The 'organization' acts only insofar as those who have power *within* the organization decide to commit the organization to action, and only insofar as relevant members of the organization legitimate the process and the elite. There are times, of course, when that legitimation is problematic. For example, the membership of a union may reject a contract negotiated in their names by the elite of the union.

What this suggests is that major processes in the society are a product of the particular views of the men who lead large organizations, and the ways by which their leadership is maintained.

Being successful in an organization has consequences for the views of those who have power. Robert Michels (1915) wrote of the *'iron law of oligarchy;'* he was referring to *the tendency for those who obtain leadership positions to direct their activities in terms of maintaining those positions.* But there is more than just wanting to maintain one's own position. If one has had a system work well for oneself, one is going to think it a pretty good system, and worth continuing. One will want to maintain the status quo, not just in terms of personal and inertial goals, but in terms of informal, character and ideological goals.

The kinds of organizations that we have are dependent upon certain kinds of values and assumptions. These notions, about rationality, the nature and worth of work, the nature of motivation and achievement are essential to the hierarchical, large, career-providing organizations that exist at present in Canada. Arthur Stinchcombe (1965) has pointed out the extent to which the nature of a given set of organizations reflects the history of the era in which they emerged. The organizations that are present and powerful at the moment, and the values and norms that underlie them, are the products of a particular set of conditions in the development of industrial societies. The people who lead and succeed in these organizations accept these values, if for no other reason than that they have found them workable.

But a number of changes have taken place, and the questions must be asked: Are those organizations, or the values of their elites, still workable? If not, how do they change? The basis of our organizational stratification process has been relatively limited labor supply and relatively limitless resources. But the development of technology has created a labor surplus, and has also pushed towards the limits of resources. (Catton, 1972)

The leaders of organizations will want to maintain them as is. But some of the members of the organizations, in some cases the bulk of them, will have a very different kind of encounter with society and the organization. The kind of career that an organization offers, for example, may no longer be attractive to members. The result will be lessened legitimation, and increased alienation. Or it will be the emergence of new organizational forms, that reflect the new meanings that individuals will bring to organizations.

There will always be organizations, in the sense of identifiable assemblies of people in pursuit of some set of interests. But as the conditions of life in society, and on the planet change, the interests will change, and so will the organizational forms, and they will react upon the interests.

Such changes will be both a reflection of societal change, and a creator of it. For the organization is, above all, a distributive mechanism — it moves resources, transforms them and passes them on. And distribution is the essential social process — it is the 'reason' why people are social beings. Bureaucratic organizations are at the core of social existence. It should not surprise us that they play such a large role in our lives, as individuals and as a society. It should be our concern to understand and direct their role in our lives.

References

Adler, W., *The Kennedy Wit*. New York: Bantam Books, 1965.

Albrook, R.C., 'The Frustrations of the Acquired Executive,' *Fortune,* LXXX, 6, 1969.

Applewhite, Phillip, *Organizational Behavior*. Englewood Cliffs: Prentice-Hall Inc., 1965.

Argyris, Chris, *Integrating the Individual and the Organization*. New York: John Wiley and Sons, 1964.

Bensman, J., *Dollars and Sense.* New York: Macmillan, 1967.

Berle, A.A., and G.C. Means, *The Modern Corporation and Private Property.* New York: Harcourt, Brace, Jovanovich, 1932.

Blau, Peter, and W.R. Scott, *Formal Organizations.* New York: Chandler, 1962.

Blauner, Robert, *Alienation and Freedom.* Chicago: University of Chicago Press, 1964.

Blumberg, Paul, *Industrial Democracy.* London: Constable, 1968.

Burnham, James, *The Managerial Revolution.* New York: John Day, 1941.

Burns, T., and G. Stalker, *The Management of Innovation.* London: Tavistock, 1967.

Catton, William, 'Sociology in an Age of Fifth Wheels,' *Social Forces,* L, 4, 1972.

Canada Year Book 1970-1971. Ottawa: Dominion Bureau of Statistics, 1971.

Child, John, *The Business Enterprise in Modern Society.* London: Collier-Macmillan, 1970.

Cloward, R., and F. Piven, *Regulating the Poor.* New York: Pantheon, 1971.

Cordtz, Dan, 'Bringing the Laboratory Down to Earth,' *Fortune,* LXXXIII, 1, 1971.

Corwin, Ronald, 'Education and the Sociology of Complex Organizations,' in Donald Hansen and Joel Gustl (eds.), *On Education.* New York: John Wiley and Sons, 1967.

Cyert, R.M., and J.G. March, *A Behavioral Theory of the Firm.* Englewood Cliffs: Prentice-Hall Inc., 1963.

Dalton, Melville, 'Conflicts between Staff and Line Managerial Officers,' *American Sociological Review,* XV (1950), 342-351.

Dill, W.R., 'The Impact of Environment on Organizational Development,' in S. Mailick and W. van Ness (eds.), *Concepts and Issues in Administrative Behavior.* Englewood Cliffs: Prentice-Hall Inc., 1962.

Doern, G.B., 'The National Research Council: The Causes of Goal Displacement,' *Canadian Public Administration,* XIII, 2 (1970), 140-184.

Dubin, Robert, 'Industrial Workers' Worlds: A Study of Central Life Interests of Industrial Workers,' *Social Problems,* III, 1 (1956), 131-142.

Durkheim, E. *The Division of Labor in Society.* New York: The Free Press, 1933.

Etzioni, Amitai, *The Comparative Analysis of Complex Organizations.* New York: The Free Press, 1971.

Gordon, H. Scott, 'The Bank of Canada in a System of Responsible Government,' *Canadian Journal of Economics and Political Science,* XXVII, 1 (1961), 1-22.

Gouldner, A.W., *Patterns of Industrial Bureaucracy.* New York: The Free Press, 1955.

Graves, Benny, 'Particularism, Exchange and Organizational Efficiency: A Case Study of a Construction Industry,' *Social Forces,* XLIX, 1 (1970), 72-81.

Hamilton, Ian, *The Children's Crusade.* Toronto: Peter Martin Associates, 1970.

Hodgson, R., 'The rules of the game have changed ... The players have not been notified,' *The Business Quarterly,* XXXVII, 2 (Summer, 1972), 11-18.

Hofley, John, 'Problems and Perspectives in the Study of Poverty,' in J. Harp and J. Hofley (eds.), *Poverty in Canada.* Scarborough: Prentice-Hall of Canada, 1971.

Hunter, Floyd, *Community Power Structure.* Chapel Hill, N.C.: University of North Carolina Press, 1953.

Inkeles, Alex, *What is Sociology: An Introduction to the Discipline and Profession.* Englewood Cliffs: Prentice-Hall Inc., 1969.

Jacobs, Paul, 'The Welfare Bureau,' in Paul Jacobs, *Prelude to Riot.* New York: Random House, 1966.

Johnson, W.W., 'Management Theory and Cabinet Government,' *Canadian Public Administration,* XIV, 1 (1971), 73-81.

Katz, Daniel, and Robert Kahn, *The Social Psychology of Organizations.* New York: John Wiley and Sons, 1966.

Laframboise, H.L., 'Administrative Reform in the Federal Public Service,' *Canadian Public Administration,* XIV, 3 (1971), 303-325.

Lenski, Gerhard, *Power and Privilege.* New York: McGraw-Hill, 1965.

Levitt, Kari, *Silent Surrender.* Toronto: Macmillan, 1970.

Loving, Rush, Jr., 'How a Hotelman Got the Red Out of United Airlines,' *Fortune,* LXXXV, 3, 1972.

Lucas, Rex, *Minetown, Milltown, Railtown.* Toronto: University of Toronto Press, 1971.

Mathias, P., *Forced Growth.* Toronto: James Lewis and Samuel, 1971.

Meredith, H., and J. Martin, 'Management Consultants in the Public Sector,' *Canadian Public Administration,* XIII, 4 (1970), 383-395.

Michels, Robert, *Political Parties.* Glencoe, Ill.: The Free Press, 1915.

Mills, C. Wright, *The Power Elite.* New York: Oxford University Press, 1956.

——, *White Collar.* New York: Oxford University Press, 1951.

Mooalem, Jack, 'Conducting a Fair and Informative Stockholders' Meeting,' *The Business Quarterly,* XXXVI, 4 (1971), 47-51.

Newman, Peter, C., *Renegade in Power.* Toronto: McClelland and Stewart, 1963.

Ostry, Sylvia, *The Occupational Composition of the Canadian Labour Force.* Ottawa: Queen's Printer, 1967.

Pellegrin, R.J., and C.H. Coates, 'Absentee-Owned Corporations and Community Power Structure,' *American Journal of Sociology,* LXI (1956), 413-419.

Porter, John, *The Vertical Mosaic.* Toronto: University of Toronto Press, 1965.

Pugh, D.S., *et al.,* *Writers on Organizations.* Harmondworth, U.K.: Penguin Books Ltd., 1972.

Roszak, Theodore, *The Making of a Counter Culture.* New York: Doubleday Anchor, 1968.

Schulze, R.O., 'The Role of Economic Dominants in Community Power Structure,' *American Sociological Review,* XXIII (1958), 3-9.

Schurmann, F., *Ideology and Organization in Red China.* Berkeley: University of California Press, 1966.

Sharp, F.R., 'Lessons from Armed Forces Unification,' *The Business Quarterly,* XXXIII (1968), 1,7: 12-15, 19, 23, 83-87.

Silverman, David, *The Theory of Organizations.* London: Heinemann, 1970.

Starbuck, William, 'Organizational Growth and Development,' in J. March (ed.), *Handbook of Organizations.* Chicago: Rand McNally, 1965.

Stinchcombe, Arthur, 'Bureaucratic and Craft Administration of Production: A Comparative Study,' *Administrative Science Quarterly,* IV (1959), 168-187.

Taylor, Frederick W., *Scientific Management.* New York: Harper, 1911.

Thain, Donald, 'Stages of Corporate Development,' *The Business Quarterly,* XXXIV, 4 (1969), 33-45.

Thompson, James, and Arthur Tuden, 'Strategies, Structures and Processes of Organizational Decision,' in Thompson, *et al., Comparative Studies in Administration.* Pittsburgh: University of Pittsburgh Press, 1959.

Weber, Max, 'Bureaucracy,' in H. Gerth and C.W. Mills, *From Max Weber.* New York: Oxford University Press, 1946, pp. 196-244.

Whyte, William H., Jr., *The Organization Man.* Garden City: Doubleday, 1957.

Winn, A., 'Some Aspects of Organization Development in Alcan,' *The Business Quarterly,* XXXIV, 4 (1969), 46-52.

Woodward, Joan, *Industrial Organization: Theory and Practice.* New York: Oxford Unviersity Press, 1965.

Worthy, J.C., 'Organizational Structure and Employee Morale,' *American Sociological Review,* XV (1950), 169-179.

Zigler, E., and S. Harter, 'The Socialization of the Mentally Retarded,' in D. Goslin (ed.), *Handbook of Socialization Theory and Research.* Chicago: Rand McNally, 1969.

CHAPTER ELEVEN

Cities: The Issue of Urbanization

Monica Boyd and Kenneth Mozersky
Carleton University

Introduction

Cities have been of interest to sociologists for a variety of reasons, but a considerable part of this interest has focused on the problems that seem to be generated by cities and urban living. In a negative light, cities have, at various times, been viewed as disorganized, corrupt, dirty, and breeders of crime. Disorganization is the aspect that has probably attracted the most sociological attention because of the fact that many groups of diverse backgrounds were brought together in cities with the consequent uprooting of old traditions, whether ethnic, religious or familial, and the thrusting together of this multitude of differing lifestyles and outlooks. The manner in which the accommodation of these diverse groups to the urban environment occurs is one of the areas of concern in this chapter.

Closely related to this is the question of urban blight and human behavior, or how the physical environment influences, and is influenced by, the social environment. The traditional social problems approach here has examined slums and their effects on those who live in them. This chapter will discuss urban blight and other changes in land use functions as part of the process of growth of the industrial city and the ways in which human groups adapt to these changes. In effect, the central problem is one of the social integration of human groups with each other and with the environment in cities. The key to understanding these issues is through the examination of two concepts: urbanization and urbanism. These concepts refer to separate, though related, aspects of urban growth and change, and are central to the work of urban sociologists.

Urban Sociology

Urban sociology refers to that branch of sociology which examines man's social behavior in an urban setting. Urban sociologists attempt to answer such questions as: what are the patterns of behavior which urban man displays, and what are the causes or factors associated with these observed behaviors and cultural beliefs? In the process of answering these questions, urban sociologists often must answer other questions, such as: what is a city; what do we mean by urban? These questions represent two main areas of investigation found in urban sociology. Studies which focus on the social and cultural characteristics of urbanites are called *urbanism studies* to distinguish them from *urbanization studies,* which investigate the growth of urban centers, and document the change in size and density and number of cities. Both fields are inter-related, however. A student of urbanism frequently must assume certain definitions of a city, which a student of urbanization might question; and conversely a student of urbanization frequently assumes that certain changes in the size and density of an urban settlement will lead to changes in human behavior without testing for the validity of the assumptions, as an investigator of urbanism might.

Urbanization and the Physical Form of Cities

Urbanization refers primarily to the demographic changes involving city growth and the proliferation of new cities through population increases (Tisdale, 1941). Urban settlements occur where and when a human population concentrates as opposed to scattering widely over a geographical area. Thus urbanization can proceed in two ways: by the multiplication of points of concentration and by an increase in the size of individual concentrations.

It should be observed that this definition of urbanization implies a comparative approach: cities are centers of population concentration, which suggests that non-cities are those areas (typically called agrarian) which lack a certain size and density of population. However, these definitions of urban and urbanization are too vague to be useful to urban sociologists. In order to identify and study the urbanization process and the urban population, more specific criteria are used. In Canada, for example, the following localities are considered urban areas (Stone, 1967:5):

(1) Incorporated cities, towns, and villages of at least 1,000 population;

(2) Unincorporated agglomerations of at least 1,000 population;

(3) Built up fringes of incorporated cities and towns, (of at least 5,000 population) with a population density of at least 1,000 per square mile.

Such a definition means that areas defined as urban are not always synonymous with politically defined municipalities (see Jackson, 1973:52). Such a definition also varies by country. In Denmark, for example, urban status is granted to places with as few as 200 inhabitants while in Japan the number is usually a minimum of 30,000 (Hawley, 1971:7). In the United States a place is defined as urban if it contains 2,500 or more inhabitants. These various definitions of urban mean that cross-national studies of urbanization are not always feasible or accurate. For example, one would expect that Denmark's level of urbanization (defined as the proportion of the population living in urban areas) would be inflated compared to the definition used for the United States. Of course sometimes adjustments can be made: it appears that after adjusting the United States definition of urban, both Canada and the United States had similar levels of urbanization in 1961, with at least 70 per cent of their respective populations residing in areas defined as urban (Stone, 1967:17).

In addition to the term 'urban,' the term 'metropolitan area' is used by Statistics Canada to include the main market area of a city. Conceptually, the Census Metropolitan Area (CMA) corresponds to the United States 'Standard Metropolitan Statistical Area,' the English 'conurbation,' the French 'agglomération,' the United Nations 'Urban Agglomeration' and the German 'Stadt Region.' As of the 1971 Census, the following twenty-two agglomerations were considered Census Metropolitan Areas:

Newfoundland:	St. John's
Nova Scotia:	Halifax
New Brunswick:	Saint John
Quebec:	Quebec, Montreal, Chicoutimi-Jonquière
Ontario:	Hamilton, Kitchener, London, Ottawa, Sudbury, Toronto, Windsor, Niagara-St. Catharines, Thunder Bay
Manitoba:	Winnipeg
Saskatchewan:	Regina, Saskatoon
Alberta:	Calgary, Edmonton
British Columbia:	Vancouver, Victoria

The definition of urban and metropolitan areas incorporates the concepts of size and density. Levels of urbanization are measured either by the proportion of the total population that resides in urban centers or alternatively by an increase in the number of urban complexes. Using the percentage of the population residing in urban areas as the measure of urbanization, it is apparent from Figure 1 that within a hundred years Canada has been transformed from a rural country to a highly urbanized one. By 1971, seventy-six per cent of Canada's population was urban. This transformation is associated with the increasing concentration of urban population in the larger urban centers of 100,000 or more and a gradual decrease since 1901 of the concentration in centers of less than 25,000 population. There are also very significant differences between the regions, reflecting the regional concentration of industrial activities and regional disparities in economic development. Ontario, Quebec and British Columbia have been the most highly urbanized provinces since 1881 (Stone, 1967:33). This growth in the population classified as urban has also been accompanied by a growth in the number of urban centers. In the seventy-year period, 1901-1971, the number of incorporated cities, towns and villages of 1,000 population and over has increased six and one-half times from 325 in 1901 to 2120 in 1971.

The increase in the Canadian urban population in part reflects a real expansion as areas are reclassified from rural to urban and as city boundaries are enlarged. The urban population increase also reflects demographic growth, composed of net migration and natural increase. Much of the decennial increase in the urban population from 1871 to 1881 and 1951 to 1961 is due to demographic growth in incorporated areas rather than to reclassification of areas (Stone, 1967:84, 88-89).

An industrialized society is not only characterized by large numbers of urban inhabitants, but also by cities which occupy prominent functional positions. The concentration of population in urban areas is necessary to meet the demands of manufacturing and service industries. Hauser states the relationship most succinctly:

> As Adam Smith noted, the greater the agglomeration [of population in cities], the greater is the division of labor possible; and this permits increased specialization, easier application of technology and the use of non-human energy, economies of scale, external economies, and the minimization of the frictions of space and communication. In brief ... clumpings of people and economic activities constitute the most efficient producer and consumer units yet devised.*

There is a certain efficiency which cities possess by virtue of their size which facilitates an interdependency among their residents through a division of labor. This means that people become specialists in various

---

*P.M. Hauser, 'The Chaotic Society: Product of the Social Morphological Revolution,' *American Sociological Review*, XXXIV, 1 (1969), 4.

Figure 1: Canada 1871-1961: Population by Settlement Categories, as a Percentage of Total Population*

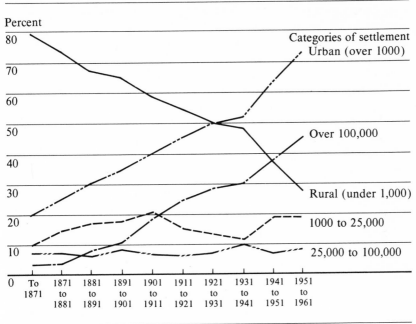

*Source: T.R. Weir, 'Population Changes in Canada, 1867-1967,' in R.L. Gentilcore (ed.), *Geographical Approaches to Canadian Problems* (Scarborough: Prentice-Hall of Canada, 1971), p. 11, Figure 6.

tasks, whether it be assembly-line work or managing a restaurant, and that they are consequently dependent upon specialists in other areas to provide them with their material and cultural needs. It is rare for such specialization within a population to occur in non-urban areas, primarily because such areas do not contain enough people, and usually do not exhibit the marked degree of heterogeneity in population composition that is found in cities.

In addition to the economic and population concentration factors, a related but more theoretically complete framework for understanding the growth of cities is offered by Duncan (1959) who suggests that the four major variables for understanding urban growth and change are: *(1) population; (2) social organization; (3) environment and (4) technology.* Variables of *size, density and heterogeneity* are included in the population category. *The concern with population* leads to analyses of changes in city size and changes in the composition of the urban population. This refers to such things as the *ethnic, racial, religious or occupational distribution of the population,* and the changes that may occur in the proportions of people in various groups. Thus, in addition to studying how many people live in cities, an analysis of population composition would include the number and proportion of white collar workers and blue collar workers or the study of which ethnic groups are most likely to dominate in various occupations or neighborhoods.

Changes in population are usually associated with the introduction of new forms of social organization. The relatively simple society characterized by age and sex grading but which does not contain a major division of labor by task is most often associated with a small population. Durkheim's argument in *The Division of Labor* (1933) is that as population increases in size and density, the social organization becomes more differentiated with people being slotted into jobs because of their expertise, rather than their age, sex or family background — performance rather than quality becomes important.

Durkheim's argument applies to the study of urban centers in its emphasis upon a complex division of labor accompanying an increase in population size and density only if concomitant improvements in technology are made, particularly in transportation and communications. This leads to an increase in the dynamic density of a population, or the potential number of social interactions that it is possible for an urban dweller to have (Schnore, 1958). The net result is a complex form of urban and industrial social organization which must deal with the problem of integrating a diverse population.

Technology is closely related to social organization, in part determining what type of organization will occur, and in part, setting limits on the uses of technology. Technological developments in transportation and communications have played key roles in the formation of urban social structures. They have also shaped urban form to a large extent, in that they have determined the physical boundaries of neighborhoods, suburbs, business districts and other aspects of the spatial structure of cities.

The environment consists of two elements: *the natural and the man-made.* In industrial cities the man-made parts of the environment clearly dominate. The concern with urban renewal and urban blight is aimed at reshaping the buildings, streets, and houses that are part of the man-made environment. The natural environment no longer poses a major problem to be overcome in industrial cities, except for the adverse effects that man has had on it. Thus, the pollution problem is a result of the successful conquering of the natural environment, and because of the roles that industrial technology and social organization have played, the concern has shifted from that of overcoming the environment to that of fear of destroying the environment.

Physical Aspects: The Burgess Hypothesis

Sociologists who seek to understand cities and urban growth as a composite of human behavior, population characteristics, technology and environment frequently are called *human ecologists*. Human ecologists tend to focus on the urban community by asking how human behavior becomes spatially and temporally patterned as a result of man's adaptation to the physical and social environment. Thus human ecologists view land patterns and the physical structure of a city as reflecting social behavior, the city's population characteristics, environment, and technology. Given this approach, two questions can be raised: (1) Is there a universal form or structure to all cities, and specifically to industrial cities? (2) Do Canadian cities conform to this universal structure, or are they unique with different land use patterns and different problems?

The classic statement regarding the spatial structure of industrial cities is that of Ernest W. Burgess who wrote in the 1920's about the city of Chicago (Park and Burgess, 1925). Burgess' theory dealt with the changing land use patterns of the industrial city as it grew and experienced the processes of the invasion and succession of activities competing for city space. His 'concentric zone' hypothesis describes the city as a series of concentric circles, radiating out from the center of the city, each with a predominant activity or function, distinct from the function of the other zones. (Figure 2)

The zones and their major activities are as follows:

Zone I: The inner city, or core area, which consists primarily of business and commercial establishments.

Zone II: Surrounding the core is the area in transition between commercial and residential usages. This zone contains deteriorated buildings, both residential and commercial, in which may be found the skid rows, ethnic ghettos and transient hotels.

Zone III; Burgess labelled this area the zone of working men's homes, characterized by residents who lived close to their places of work in Zone I. The homes in this area are not tenements, but may consist of multiple dwelling units of up to several families living in duplex or triplex housing. It could be considered as a blue collar or working class residential area.

Zone IV: Out from Zone III, Zone IV contains the better residences whose inhabitants would be primarily middle class in origin. The housing in this zone consists of single family dwelling units and a number of better apartment buildings.

Zone V: This is the commuters' zone and contains the most expensive homes. It is considered to be an upper-middle to upper class residential area which serves as dormitory suburbs for the city.

Figure 2:   Concentric Zones of the City*

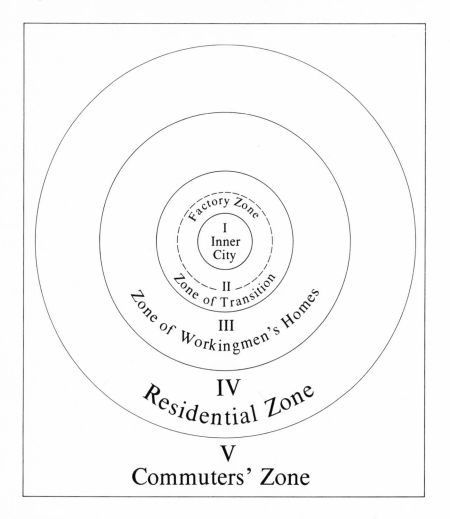

While Burgess meant these descriptions to apply primarily to northern industrial cities in the United States that were experiencing growth through immigration, they have been found to fit a number of industrial cities in other countries including Canada (Schnore, 1965; Guest, 1969). The concentric ring model of cities is more of an ideal type than a close descriptive set of categories, but it demonstrates the following propositions about cities: (1) activities are not randomly distributed throughout a city, but tend to form spatial clusters with other activities of a similar nature; (2) there is a gradient from the center of cities outward along which the predominant activities change from commercial to residential; and (3) there tends to be a direct relationship between residential social status and distance from the center of the city.

In human ecological terms, the areas of cities undergo changes because of the competition for land between various types of activities, such as commercial versus residential; and neighborhoods change their character through invasion and succession whereby new population groups and social or economic activities replace and dominate the older ones (McKenzie, 1968; Park, 1936; Hawley, 1950).

However, the pattern which may be exhibited is to a large extent determined by the age and size of the city. Guest (1969) tested the Burgess hypothesis on a number of Canadian metropolitan areas and reported that the higher socio-economic groups tended not to live in the central city areas, but were concentrated primarily in the suburbs, especially in larger and older cities. This tendency increased from 1951 to 1961 and can be expected to continue. During this ten-year period, smaller and newer cities like Calgary and Edmonton showed only modest changes in the proportions of people with low socio-economic status residing in the central city while older and larger cities like Toronto and Montreal exhibited large shifts in the concentration of these groups, with the suburbs showing heavy concentration of high status groups, and the central city areas undergoing major increases in the proportion of low status residents (Guest, 1969: Table 4). Much smaller cities, like Sudbury and Timmins, Ontario, did not conform to the Burgess pattern at all.

The most characteristic change which the larger cities are undergoing is that of metropolitanization, which involves, partly, 'the relative deconcentration of population "into specialized areal units" ... tied together in a ... "territorial division of labor"' (Schnore and Peterson, 1958:62). In its simplest form, this means that the outer residential area fulfills the shelter functions, while the inner commercial area fulfills the economic and employment functions. Metropolitanization occurs as a city grows in size, and, normally, those cities farthest along on this process are also the oldest cities.

While Burgess' concentric ring model of city growth has some general applicability to Canadian cities, there are exceptions to this rule. Hardwick, reporting on the city of Vancouver, demonstrates that this city is evolving into a 'core-ring' pattern which deviates somewhat from the concentric ring pattern (Hardwick, 1971). He describes Vancouver as having two concentric rings, an inner one which contains the central business district plus residential activities spatially located so as to approximate the Burgess model, and an outer ring which also contains commerce and residences, but which has more circumferential movement between home and work within this outer ring rather than movement of the same kind between this area and the downtown business district.

To some extent the topography of an area sets limiting factors on the 'natural' growth of a city, and Vancouver, being surrounded by mountains and water, may be affected far more by these than Prairie cities like Winnipeg or Regina. One observer has noted that ' ... the supply as well as the quality of open space varies considerably from city to city. The quantity seems to increase from east to west. . . . ' (Rashleigh, 1962:73) In addition to the availability of land, there are normative and zoning differences in its use. For example, most Western Canadian cities separate streets and houses with a back lane that parallels every street, but runs behind houses and buildings. They are used by service vehicles and for refuse collection. Eastern cities, by contrast, rarely have this attribute, even in places that seemingly have land available and are not faced with severe overcrowding. The original pressures against this luxurious use of land in Eastern cities were economic ones, while the same type of pressure did not exist in Western Canada. It had become normative for housing developers in Western cities to include back lanes up until very recently. The newer developments resemble their Eastern counterparts now and the rear yard boundaries of newer houses are no longer separated by laneways. Changing economic circumstances account for this through the increased demand for new housing during the last two decades.

While there are differences between the structure and land use patterns of cities within Canada, overall there appears to be general conformity to the Burgess model for cities of 100,000 or more inhabitants. In this regard, Canadian cities are not unique when they are compared to cities in other industrialized countries. North American cities vary in age by an average of a century, and in relative terms, were all started and kept growing through an age of industrialization. It is not suprising, then, that they tend to more or less resemble each other in their overall land use patterns.

This does not mean that cities throughout the world all conform to the concentric zone pattern. Comparisons between North and South American cities show that in the latter countries the pattern is quite often reversed, with the most expensive and most desirable residences located in or near the centers of the cities (Schnore, 1965; Sjoberg, 1960). Many Latin American cities date from pre-industrial times, and many have experienced the effects of industrialization much later in their development than their North American counterparts. Thus, the proposition stated earlier is reversed for Latin American cities; generally, there tends to be an *inverse* relationship between residential social status and distance from the center of the city. There is no middle class suburban development. Rather, low status areas and slums tend to be located on the outskirts of the cities. In a pre-industrial situation, the centers of cities were not subject to the same type of competition for space that occurred in the Western industrialized countries. City centers were the focus of social, cultural, and intellectual activities. They also contained markets where goods were exchanged or sold, but which did not require intensive and expensive land and facilities. It was advantageous for elites to live close to all of this activity, and consequently the central cores of such cities contained the most desirable and expensive homes.

In reporting on the ecology of Latin American cities Schnore points out that almost all of the studies done in that area describe the changes that are occurring in this traditional pattern. During the last three or four decades there has been a shift toward the North American pattern in the following ways: (1) there has been an increase in the amount and diversity of economic activity in city centers; with (2) a related increase in the amount of automobile traffic plus other forms of transportation; which has led to (3) a decrease in the attractivenesss of such areas as places to live. Hence, elites have moved out of the center and into the periphery. The centers of these cities tend to resemble more and more the Burgess model, with low status housing and commercial activities occupying the core areas, and residential status increasing with distance from the core. Slums and *barriadas* still remain on the outskirts, however, and new development either skips over these, or invades these areas and displaces the former residents.

Several characteristics of Canadian cities emerge from this discussion. The first is that the structure of Canadian cities cannot be considered apart from the larger context of Canada as an industrial country. Canadian cities are urban-industrial areas, and as such, generally conform to the overall structural pattern of cities in other industrial countries. Secondly, this structure approximates the Burgess concentric zone model in its overall characteristics regarding the spatial interrelations of differing types of activities. Finally, the closeness to the Burgess model is related to the size and age of the city. The older and larger cities in Canada most closely resemble the concentric ring model, and it is probable that other cities will also tend to resemble it as they become larger.

Urban Blight

In their examinations of urban life, sociologists have tended to focus on two of the concentric zones discussed above: the zone of transition (zone II) and the commuters' zone (zone V). The zone of transition is studied because it is here that many of the phenomena defined as problematic are found; the commuters' zone is studied because it represents a new form of urban life, that of suburbia. We will look at the social aspects of the zone of transition and the commuters' zone in later discussions of urbanism. But because many of the social features of the zone of transition reflect, although are not necessarily causally derived from, the physical surroundings, a closer look at the areas of urban blight is warranted. *Urban blight refers to that part of the man-made environment which is deemed to be undesirable by a majority of urban residents.* The causes of urban blight are closely related to changes in the population, organization, environment, and technology of a city. And, while blight is most commonly associated with internal changes in a city, it is also closely related to changes in the total population size of the city.

The identifying characteristics of blight are the physical features of buildings within a blighted area. Deterioration of interior and exterior walls, lack of maintenance regarding painting, washing, or repairing broken windows or stairs are the most common physical attributes of blighted buildings. If these buildings serve housing needs, the area is often referred to as a slum whose occupants are of lower and working class status, and who may be members of ethnic or racial minorities. If the buildings serve commercial needs they may be warehouses, wholesale outlets or manufacturing centers, which normally would not require day-to-day contact with the shopping public.

In the industrial cities of North America, the blighted areas are most often found in or near the center of the city, either on the fringe of the central business district or actually forming part of it. Blighted buildings were usually built for purposes that have changed as the city grew, and so were not designed for the purposes which they must presently meet. A city planner has written that ' ... the (city) core tends to have a number of inherited buildings, built originally for housing, manufacturing, or wholesale trade. As these buildings are taken over by central business district functions they may either enjoy a continued life with a new function in an old form or they will, unit by unit normally, be reconstructed in form as well as function.'*

There is no inherent reason for urban blight to accompany urban growth, but it would appear to be closely intertwined with general changes in the industrial order. Cities that experience the largest rates of population growth tend to be those cities that are also experiencing expansion in their industrial, manufacturing, or service sectors. Non-industrial or predominantly agricultural centers have not had the same impetus to grow. Technological changes have almost always been associated with industrial growth, and, therefore, constitute one of the prime causes of city growth.

As cities have moved upward and outward, they have had to adapt to new or differing modes of economic and social activities. This is how the bypassing effect occurs as a cause of urban blight. In residential areas it is caused by the upward social mobility of individuals who vacate lower-cost housing closer to the center of the city for more expensive housing in the suburbs. Those who are upwardly mobile can also afford the increased transportation costs involved in commuting from suburb to downtown.

The lower-cost housing is then occupied by groups of lower socio-economic status who can neither afford the better suburban houses nor the higher transportation costs associated with suburban living. Often, but not always, such neighborhoods become the blighted areas of the city. Residents must rent their housing because they cannot afford to own their own homes, and the buildings may be left to fall into disrepair by absentee landlords.

Most Canadian cities have blighted areas, although the proportions vary from city to city. No single, simple definition of blight exists, although all blighted areas have certain characteristics in common. One is a preponderance of older dwellings. The Census lists dwellings built prior to 1920, and while such dwellings do not automatically fall into the blighted category, there is a higher probability that they would do so than newer dwellings. According to the 1961 Census, of all dwellings in Canadian cities of 100,000 or more inhabitants, 25.3 per cent were built prior to 1920. Selected cities varied in this proportion, as Table I illustrates.

The proportion of pre-1920 dwelling units in these cities is mainly a function of the historical growth rates of each city. Those cities that grew rapidly prior to 1920, and grew more slowly after 1920 would be

*James Vance Jr., 'The Focus on Downtown,' *Community Planning Review,* XVI (1966), 12.

Table I: Percentage Pre-1920 Dwellings in Selected Cities

	Edmonton	Calgary	Winnipeg	Hamilton	Toronto
Dwellings pre-1920	13.3	19.6	51.7	33.1	24.0

Table II: Population of Selected Cities, 1921 and 1961*

Population (000's)	Edmonton	Calgary	Winnipeg	Hamilton	Toronto
1921	87	78	229	154	686
1961	374	290	476	359	1,942
1921 as % of 1961 population	23.2	26.8	48.1	42.8	35.3

*Source: L. Stone, *Urban Development in Canada* (Ottawa: Statistics Canada, 1967), Table L5.
Reproduced by permission of Information Canada.

expected to have higher proportions of pre-1920 dwelling units, since much of the physical development occurred in that period. Table II illustrates this point.

Winnipeg and Hamilton, which had the highest proportion of older dwellings, also had the largest increases in their total growth occuring before 1920. Therefore, the age of a city and the period of rapid growth would appear to be important explanatory variables for determining the potential for blight when age of dwellings is used as such an indicator.

However, there are better indicators of blight than the age of the dwelling unit. Statistics Canada defines a dwelling unit which is in need of major repair as one which ' . . . is in a seriously run-down or neglected condition and shows one or more major structural deficiencies.' The other indicator of blight is overcrowding; an overcrowded dwelling is defined by the Census as ' . . . one in which the number of persons exceeds the number of rooms occupied.' That is, if a three room apartment is occupied by four or more people, it is defined as overcrowded. Table III shows the proportion of overcrowded dwellings and dwellings in need of major repair, for the same selected cities.

Not all overcrowded dwellings are in need of major repair, but it is probable that most of the units needing repair are overcrowded.

Table III: Urban Blight in Selected Cities, 1961*

	Edmonton	Calgary	Winnipeg	Hamilton	Toronto	Canada: cities (100,000+)
Dwellings in need of major repair (%)	4.5	3.5	5.0	3.1	2.2	3.3
Overcrowded dwellings (%)	14.6	10.2	12.1	10.5	9.8	13.0

*Source: *1961 Census of Canada,* adapted from *Urban Renewal Study for the City of Edmonton,* Edmonton City Planning Department, 1963-64, Part 1, p. 3.

Similarly, most of such units were probably built prior to 1920. Thus, an improved definition of urban blight would refer to an area containing buildings which have all three characteristics: *old age, structural defects, and overcrowding.* Using the 1961 Census figures, therefore, approximately 3 to 4 per cent of urban housing could be considered blighted.

While this may not appear to be a large figure, there is evidence that blighted areas contribute disproportionately to a city's problems. An urban renewal study in Edmonton lists the following characteristics of a blighted area in that city. The area itself makes up only 1.4 per cent of the total city area, but accounts for 6 per cent of the city's population; 17.9 per cent of the city's physical assaults and sexual offences; 13.3 per cent of the city's juvenile problems; 18 per cent of the city's tuberculosis cases; 7.2 per cent of the city's infant mortality; 10.4 per cent of the city's residential fire calls; and 4.1 per cent of the city's tax revenue. (*Urban Renewal Study for the City of Edmonton,* 1963/64, 1:22)

There is no doubt that the physical properties of the buildings themselves affect the social behavior of their residents. What is in doubt, however, is *how much* effect the physical environment has. In the 1920's and 1930's it was common in sociological circles to refer to slum areas as being 'disorganized' or lacking in the characteristics most commonly thought of as belonging to the middle class: low crime rates; low rates of school drop-out; low rates of mental illness; visible evidence of personal accomplishment, and so on. Later studies, most notably that of Whyte (1943), have shown that slums are not 'disorganized' but contain very prominent types of social organizations which serve as integrating mechanisms for residents of the slum. Similarly, studies have shown that mental illness occurs among all social classes with only the particular type of illness differing between classes (Hollingshead and Redlich, 1958) and that crime is not a lower class phenomenon only, but also occurs, under the guise of white collar crime, among the middle class. (Broom and Selznick, 1958: 624)

However, this should not minimize the problems that exist in blighted areas. They tend to be serious because they directly affect the quality of life of people living in those areas. Thus, violent crimes directly threaten human life. High infant mortality may be directly related to the environment. It is these kinds of problems which focus our attention on blighted areas. There are, therefore, good reasons for our concern with the relationship between the physical and social environments. Because of this, urban renewal plans are often aimed at providing greater social opportunities by altering the physical environment.

It is important to point out that the preceding discussion is meant to apply to cities in industrialized countries, particularly those in the Western Hemisphere. Urban blight obviously occurs in non-Western and non-industrialized countries, but it may have different causes and different consequences. It is our thesis that urban blight in industrialized countries is closely related to changes in city size and city structure and that the key to this is the shifting land use pattern within the city. The Burgess model predicts that city growth will always be accompanied by a shift in a spatial location of urban activities, and that 'bypassing' occurs as buildings are forced to fulfill functions which are different from those for which they were originally built. Blight may be viewed as an unanticipated consequence of urban growth which produces undesirable social patterns. There is also considerable social and physical mobility for individuals and groups in the industrial city, and the growth of Canadian cities has been accompanied by such mobility. It is the mobility of groups within the city that is partly responsible for the 'bypassing' of areas and the unequal distribution of mobility opportunities which cause blight. Cities in Canada and the United States have experienced these phenomena mainly because of the imperatives of industrial growth in the two countries.

Immigration and Heterogeneity

Since the changes in urban structure reflect in part the high incidence of physical mobility in a population, movements within a city and in and out of cities are often studied by urban sociologists. The most important type of physical movement with respect to changes in urbanization and urban form is *net migration,* or *the difference between the numbers of*

*people migrating to a city from another 'area and the number of people
leaving the city for another area during the same time period.* In addition
to this net migration, natural increase also is an important source of
urban growth; the relationship between these two demographic variables
is important in any discussion of city growth.

In the early days of industrialization, cities in Western countries were
considered to be consumers of people. The death rates from insanitary
and impoverished working and living conditions were so high that they
often exceeded the birth rate of the urban population. The only reason
that the cities did not numerically decline, however, was because of the
very high rates of migration which more than compensated for the
deficit of people caused by high death rates. Today, however, cities grow
in population because of both natural increase and net migration,
although the importance of each factor varies with the size of the city.
Stone (1967: 96) shows that for cities of 100,000 persons and over, net
migration accounted for 50 per cent of the population increase between
1951 and 1961, while for smaller cities the proportion of growth
attributable to migration steadily declined with decreasing size of city.
Such findings undoubtedly reflect the greater economic attractiveness
which the larger cities have for would-be migrants.

Migrants to cities can come from three different places: from non-
urban areas, from other urban areas, and from other countries. Rural to
urban migration is the major type of migration to cities for the less
industrialized nations of the world where the agrarian population is
numerically and proportionately very large. Such relatively heavy
immigration from surrounding rural areas may result in personal, social,
and cultural disorientation as the immigrant groups adjust to city life.
Or, as suggested by Abu-Lughod (1961), heavy, continual streams of
rural immigrants may result in the ruralization of the city.

Today rural to urban migration is less of a factor in the growth of the
Canadian urban population than previously. The dominant streams of
internal migration appear to be inter-urban rather than rural in origin
(George, 1970: 187). In view of the fact that over three-fourths of
Canada's total population reside in areas defined as urban, it would
further appear that rural immigrants to Canadian urban centers would
be small in number and could not form the rural segregated enclaves that
might be expected to form in less urbanized countries where urban and
rural cultures are more dissimilar and where rural immigration
predominates.

However, net international migration has contributed greatly to the
past and present growth of Canadian cities. Table IV shows the
disproportionate attractiveness of urban centers for immigrants. For

each census, beginning in 1921, the foreign-born have been more urbanized than the native-born population. With the movement of post-World War II immigrants into urban areas, the difference has been increasing.

Over two-thirds of the post-war immigrants are located in cities of 100,000 or more, reflecting the attractiveness of metropolitan areas for immigrants. In 1961, for example, the three metropolitan areas of Toronto, Montreal, and Vancouver alone contained 1.2 million foreign immigrants (including pre-World War II immigrants), or 65 per cent of the total foreign-born population (Kasahara, 1963). A study conducted by the Department of Manpower and Immigration in 1968 shows that these trends are continuing. Over one-half of the 1968 immigrants to Canada intended to reside in Montreal, Toronto or Vancouver (Lithwick, 1970:88).

The most important contribution of international migration to the heterogeneity of Canadian cities undoubtedly is the diversity of origin which is associated with both the birthplace and the ethnic-cultural background of the migrant. Without question, post-war immigration has

Table IV: Percentage Urban[a] for Native and Foreign-born Populations, Canada, 1921-1961*

Year	Total Population	Native Born	Foreign Born
1921	49.5[b]	47.6	56.4
1931	53.7[b]	52.0	59.9
1941	54.3[b]	53.0	60.5
1951	61.6	60.0	71.0
1961	69.6	67.5	81.4

[a] Up until the 1951 Census, an urban area was defined as a place which, under the municipal Acts of the Provinces, was incorporated as a city, town or village. All populations residing outside these urban communities were classified as rural. Changes were made in 1951, 1956, and 1961 to encompass more of the population living under urban conditions. For example, in 1951 incorporated cities, towns or villages of under 1,000 population were excluded while unincorporated places of 1,000 or more were included. In addition, the whole metropolitan area of larger cities having built-up suburbs adjacent to the core city was included. Subsequent changes in 1956 and 1961 were designed to improve the measurement of populations living in urbanized areas surrounding the larger cities and towns. For a more detailed discussion of definitional changes and their implications, see DBS 99-512, *1961 Census, Bul.* 7.1-2, pp. 2-1 to 2-3.
[b] Excludes Newfoundland.

*Source: W.E. Kalbach, *The Impact of Immigration on Canada's Population* (Ottawa: Statistics Canada, 1970), p. 87, Table 2.21. Reproduced by permission of Information Canada.

led to considerable changes in the ethnic composition within and between Canadian cities. We have made comparisons of changes between 1941 and 1961 in the ethnic composition of seventeen 1961 Metropolitan Areas based on thirteen ethnic categories. We have found that between 1941 and 1961 the percentage of residents of British origin decreased for all cities; the proportion of residents of French origin increased slightly for all metropolitan areas except Ottawa; and the proportion of other ethnic groups increased as well for all cities. The change over time has been greatest for Toronto, followed by Calgary and Edmonton. We also examined the internal heterogeneity of each city, where the ethnic group composition of a metropolitan area may be said to be heterogeneous to the extent that no single ethnic group is predominant. On the basis of the thirteen ethnic group categories, Winnipeg, Edmonton, and Windsor exhibited the greatest internal diversity in 1941 and 1961, while Quebec City and St. John's were the most homogeneous. Over time, the diversity has increased for all Canadian cities. It should thus be apparent that the cities with the highest attraction for recent immigrants are not necessarily the most ethnically diverse. For example, of the 1951-61 immigrants reported as metropolitan residents in 1961, nearly 40 per cent resided in Toronto (Kasahara, 1963). A high proportion of the immigration to Toronto, however, has been Italian or German, which swells the size of the foreign-born population but may not increase the ethnic diversity as much as would immigration of Italians, Germans, Ukrainians, Polish, Russian, Chinese, Japanese, Jews, and so on.

Given the preference of migrants for urban areas, the differing proportions of foreign-born for various ethnic groups undoubtedly are factors in the differing urban-rural patterns of residence which exist between ethnic groups. Over 90 per cent of the Italians and Jews reside in urban areas, followed by the Polish, British, and French. Foreign-born immigration also appears to have influenced the residential distribution of ethnic populations within Census Metropolitan Areas. For example, nearly three-quarters of the 1961 metropolitan population of Asiatic origin and roughly two-thirds of those of Italian, Ukrainian and Polish origins live in the central cities of Metropolitan Areas. (DBS, 99-516, 4/8/1966:27) These patterns are also associated with the relatively lower levels of educational attainment which characterize central cities. There is some evidence that British immigrants who have relatively high levels of education tend to locate in areas surrounding the central cities. Conversely, the Italian, Ukrainian and Polish groups who have relatively lower educational attainment tend to reside in the central cities (DBS, 99-516, 4/8/1966; Kalbach, 1970).

Urbanism: The Processes of Adaptation and Integration

The ethnic heterogeneity of Canadian cities is of interest to urban sociologists who seek to discover the forms of social organization which emerge in a relatively large settlement of heterogeneous individuals. This focus upon the adaptation of man to an urban setting and the resultant forms of interaction can be traced back to the Chicago School (Sjoberg, 1960), composed of sociologists such as Park, Burgess, McKenzie, and Wirth. One of the most influential North American urban sociologists was Louis Wirth. Drawing upon studies of urbanization, Wirth defined a city as 'a relatively large, dense and permanent settlement of heterogeneous individuals.' (1938:1) He attempted to show that the social organization that most often emerged in a city could be logically related to, although not causally derived from, its size, density, and heterogeneity. His argument begins by noting that the greater the number of individuals, the greater is the potential for interaction and the greater the range of variation with respect to personal traits, occupations, and cultural attributes. In turn, the greater the range of variation in the latter traits, the greater the degree of spatial segregation of individuals according to race, ethnicity, economic and social status, and individual tastes. This greater heterogeneity means both an absence of a common folk tradition with bonds of kinship and a common value structure, and the inability of an individual to know fully all other members of the urban settlement. The increase in numbers and resulting heterogeneity thus mean a change in the character of social relationships. There is a substitution of more formal controls for informal controls and an increased superficiality and anonymity of social contacts. Given the greater superficiality, anonymity and transitory character of social interaction, the urban resident may gain a certain amount of personal freedom from the control of the primary group, but also may become anomic.

Density and heterogeneity are also used by Wirth as factors underlying the nature of urban institutions and urban personalities. Specifically, Wirth argues that an increase in density reinforces the effects of size in diversifying people and their activities and in increasing the complexity of the social structure. Heterogeneity likewise has effects similar to those observed from increases in size and density. The changes associated with increased heterogeneity are especially noticeable in the stratification system, where increased social interaction among a variety of persons tends to break down the rigidity of the caste and class lines which have been observed in smaller and more homogeneous societies. In turn, the increasing geographical and social mobility of the individual leads to even greater contact between people of diverse backgrounds and underlies the sophistication and cosmopolitanism of the urbanite. However, in spite of the presence of a heterogeneous urban population, there is a levelling tendency attributable to mass production of goods and services for an impersonal market. Wirth notes that when large numbers use common services such as libraries, schools, movies and other types of mass media, the needs of the average person determine the kind and quality of the service rather than the needs of particular individuals.

The conclusion of Wirth's argument is that certain characteristics of personality and social organization typify urban settlements and these characteristics are derived from increasing size, density, and heterogeneity. The urbanite is described as possessing any number of the following traits: reserve, blasé outlook, indifference, sophistication, rationality, tolerance of differences; he is competitive, exploitive, nervous, lonely and/or anomic.

It should be noted that many of the attributes of urban life as depicted by Wirth are negative if one values primary rather than secondary relations and personal integration rather than disorganization. The observations of Wirth in part reflect the times in which he wrote. Wirth's conclusions on the nature of urban society were made in the United States during the 1930's, between two world wars, in the middle of a severe economic depression, and with a heavy reliance on the observation of rooming house dwellers and ethnic group colonies who resided in various parts of Chicago, but especially in the zone of transition. Consequently, the heritage of Wirth and his contemporaries was a conceptualization of urban life which stressed the dislocation of the individual, the absence of social solidarity and consensus, and social disorganization. Today's urban sociologists must ask whether such a conceptualization is accurate. Numerous groups in urban society such as the family, voluntary associations, and neighborhoods are studied for their ability or failure to integrate the individual or social group into the larger community. Various sociological studies of slums and suburbs investigate the presence or absence of an integrated community in these specific urban areas. Studies also are often made of ethnic groups on grounds that the factors of ethnicity and migration experience negatively affect the social integration of these groups, which in turn is expressed by high rates of deviancy, anomie and other indicators of social disorganization.

Ethnicity

There are problems of adjustment to a foreign country and linguistic differences that separate many first generation immigrants from people born in Canada. The ethnic group often acts as a buffer between its immigrant members and the larger society. However, the extent to which ethnic communities in a city support and assist new members is a function of the model of ethnic relations which characterizes a given society. A model of Anglo-conformity exists when there is renunciation of previous ethnic ties and a complete acceptance of Anglo-Saxon values and behavior. As opposed to complete conformity to a given standard there is the notion that diverse peoples culturally contribute to the formation of a new way of life and thus form a 'melting pot.' The acceptance of a new way of life nevertheless implies that there is a weakening of specific ethnic identity and an 'assimilation' of various ethnic groups. Only in the case of the model of cultural pluralism are ethnic groups assured of their cultural heritage (Gordon, 1964).

In Canadian cities, there is evidence that these successive ethnic generations have not 'disappeared' into the larger society and have not become completely assimilated. In Montreal, one study has shown that significant ethnic interaction occurs, i.e., that more often people tended to visit or have friends from the same ethnic group as their own (Breton, 1964). Moreover, higher rates of ethnic interaction were found within those ethnic communities that were what Breton called institutionally complete and could provide a range of services and facilities for their members. The degree of institutional completeness within the ethnic communities was measured by the number of churches, newspapers, periodicals, and welfare institutions that were provided specifically by and for each ethnic community. Breton found the following groups to be relatively institutionally complete: Greeks, Germans, French, Hungarians, Italians, Lithuanians, Poles, Russians, and Ukrainians. This list might differ from city to city, representing the differing concentrations of various ethnic groups throughout the country. However, it means that it is possible for significant numbers of people to maintain a majority of their daily interactions with members of their own ethnic group, and a minority of their contacts outside that group.

This raises the question of the notion of the city as a 'melting pot' wherein people from diverse ethnic backgrounds are brought together in relatively dense settlement patterns, resulting in the loss of their ethnic identity and in their blending in with the majority of the population. There are several pieces of evidence that argue against this 'melting pot' idea, and which suggest instead a type of pluralism wherein Canadian society is composed of a number of diverse and persistent ethnic groups.

Total assimilation would mean that the probability of marrying someone from outside one's own ethnic group would be the same as marrying someone from within one's ethnic group, aside from considerations of the respective sizes of the groups. In fact, in Canada there is relatively little intermarriage between many ethnic groups, except for some Northwestern European groups who are culturally similar to the dominant British Isles group in Canada, and Poles and Russians, who may have high rates of intermarriage with other Eastern Europeans. Ethnic origin groups such as the British Isles, French, Italians, Jews, Ukrainians and Asiatics all have high intramarriage rates (Kalbach and McVey, 1971: 279). Given this marital pattern, ethnic loyalties are retained and the maintenance of ethnic subcultures is possible.

Relatedly, the residential patterns of ethnic groups in urban areas reflect this pluralistic condition as well. In most Canadian cities there tends to be residential segregation of ethnic groups. This means that considerable sections of residential areas are inhabited almost exclusively by members of the same ethnic group. This type of residential homogeneity varies from group to group, but it is pronounced enough to be more than accidental. It may be based on a number of factors: inability to afford housing in different areas, prejudice and discrimination, or a preference for living near other members of one's group. Typically, differences in socio-economic status have been used to account for residential segregation. People live where they can afford to live, and any ethnic or racial residential clustering has been attributed to the similarity in socio-economic status among members of the ethnic or racial groups.

Analysis of census data for the city of Toronto suggests that there is a high degree of ethnic residential segregation within that city, but that much of it cannot be accounted for by socio-economic differences between ethnic groups (Darroch and Marston, 1971). Using indices of dissimilarity, which compute the percentage of each ethnic group who would have to move out of their present residence to approximate the residential distribution of the British origin group in Toronto, Darroch and Marston found that, (1) Northwestern European origin groups like Scandinavians and Germans were least segregated and Asiatics, other Europeans, Ukrainians, Poles, Russians, and Italians were most segregated, and (2) that differences in education, occupation, and income accounted for only a small proportion of the residential segregation that exists between these groups. A tentative conclusion is that residential segregation is based on the preference of ethnic group members for living in neighborhoods with other members of their own ethnic group. It may also be, although data on this are lacking, that where there is a high degree of such segregation there will tend to be institutionally complete ethnic communities.

Ethnicity may serve as an integrating device for individuals in urban areas. The strength of ethnic subcultures has been maintained in Canadian cities although some modification or movement toward assimilation has occurred. Nevertheless, specific forms of social organization, like voluntary associations, religious institutions, and a specialized press which all cater to specific ethnic needs are evidence for the importance of ethnicity as a countervailing force to the types of social disorganization that Wirth thought were so characteristic of city life. Although cities may be quite heterogeneous in their entirety, they are composed of homogeneous sections or neighborhoods. These areas may be homogeneous on a social class dimension as well as an ethnic dimension. Since many individuals, while living in a heterogeneous city, restrict a good deal of their interactions to other individuals in their own ethnic group, the degree of disorganization may be exaggerated as it applies to Canadian cities.

The Changing Functions of Voluntary Associations

The concern of urban sociologists with the possible disorganizing effects of urban life also has led to an examination of the integrative functions of the *voluntary association, the family and neighborhood groups in contemporary society*. In particular, investigators into the integrative functions of various social groups ask one of two questions: (1) what are the relationships which exist between a social group and other social units of its environment and (2) what kinds of functions does a particular group perform for its constituent members? The first question is invariably asked in any study of the correlates of urbanization and/or industrialization. For example, with urbanization, the type of voluntary association in existence changes, as does the relationship between any one voluntary association and another social unit. Various lodge halls or volunteer fire brigades which were prevalent in the earlier towns of Canada seldom exist in today's urban areas. Social welfare agencies and the highly organized United Way have taken over the functions once performed by settlement houses, and a variety of new voluntary associations such as pollution groups, tenants' associations and suicide or distress centers have emerged (Olsen, 1971:2). Thus, voluntary organizations are not unique to the urban community, but the emergence of different types of voluntary associations in response to and reflecting the nature of the urban environment may be considered a topic of sociological inquiry.

In addition, the focus upon voluntary organizations in terms of the functions which they perform for their members is part of the general sociological focus on the role which quasi-primary groups play in integrating the individual or social group into the larger social system. Here the assumption is that the individual cannot function as a social animal unless he is, and perceives himself to be, a member of a social group with a common history, norms, values, and behavior. As suggested by Wirth, increasing complexity and geographical mobility which result from urbanization and industrialization tend to lessen the importance of groups, such as the family, which formerly provided this sense of membership. The individual who loses this sense of membership is prone to a loss of identity and a sense of normlessness. Consequently he may suffer alienation and anomia. This anomia is evident at an aggregate level in high rates of crime, high mental illness rates, and high divorce rates. These rates are indicative of social disorganization, which is the weakening or destruction of the relationships which serve to integrate the individual or social group into the larger social system.

Consequently, urban sociologists study voluntary associations as social groups in an urban setting which may provide some sense of group membership and belonging. Generally this association is quite limited in scope; the term 'voluntary association' refers to a group of people who are organized for the pursuit of some specialized activity or goal. This organizing of people involves voluntary participation; members are seldom monetarily remunerated although they may be compensated for their participation in terms of status or prestige. The motives for joining a voluntary association vary. One Canadian study (Hughes, 1943:122) stresses the change associated with urbanization in Canada as a motive:

> In a stable community the French Canadian, like other people so placed, need not and does not actively seek companions and collaborators. They are his by virtue of birth and family community. In Cantonville, where many people are newcomers, where many are engaged in new pursuits, and where new problems are arising, the business of finding associates and of creating instruments for collective action is more active and conscious.*

One can further argue that with the rapid growth of cities in Canada the urban immigrant frequently encounters a life with which he is not familiar and seeks a relationship with those who have similar difficulties. The end result may be the formation of voluntary associations.

In addition to performing an integrative function for various groups in the urban environment, urban voluntary associations are mechanisms through which a variety of urban goals may be achieved. For example, voluntary associations may act as initiators in the area of urban planning. Voluntary associations in urban communities also may function to maintain the cultures of various immigrant groups and/or social groups. Finally, the voluntary associations may provide outlets through which citizens can express their opinions. They thus can act as adaptive

---

*E.C. Hughes, *French Canada in Transition*, p. 122. © 1943 by the University of Chicago.

mechanisms by which urban society can ease tensions and alter its goals and values through its own organizations (Smith, 1966). In his study of the effects of a factory relocation in St. Catherines, Ontario, Crysdale (1968b) notes that the resulting unemployment and downgraded employment of factory employees led to a withdrawal from voluntary recreational, occupational, and cultural associations and an increase in radicalism. This change in political behavior is congruent with the notion that voluntary associations serve a political function through the development and circulation of ideas and information, and the division of community power. Where they are lacking, political behavior tends to be apathetic or extremist (Crysdale, 1968b).

Although voluntary associations may attain specified goals, perpetuate the culture of a given group, and act as adaptive mechanisms, most studies of voluntary organizations in the urban setting focus upon their integrative function (Babchuk and Edwards, 1965). This focus immediately raises two questions: (1) are voluntary associations in fact integrative for individuals and for groups in the urban setting, and (2) to what extent have urban voluntary associations taken over the integrative functions of the family and of neighborhood groups? There is no clear-cut answer to either question. Sills argues (1968:372) that there are enormous difficulties in verifying integrative functions of various voluntary associations. Verification requires the conditions of a controlled experiment, that is, the assigning of population to two situations of membership or non-membership in voluntary associations and holding of other factors constant. Given the complexity of the social milieu, these conditions can almost never be approximated.

A recent study (Curtis, 1971) indicates that over a third of the Canadian population are not members of voluntary associations. Approximately 64 per cent of the adult Canadian population are members of such voluntary associations as trade unions, business or professional organizations, other occupational organizations, fraternal groups, service clubs, charitable, national sports and social organizations, boy scouts, and girl scouts. This rate is roughly comparable to that observed in the United States. Twenty-eight per cent of the Canadian population, however, can be categorized as nominal members, or very occasional participants, who belong to only one voluntary association; a final 36 per cent of the population contains highly active participants and members of two or more associations. This segment of the population also tends to be the most highly ranked with respect to income, education, and occupational prestige. Membership is also associated with age: affiliation with one or more associations and multiple memberships tend to be lowest for young adults; membership rises gradually with age, reaching

Table V: Percentage with Associational Membership and Multiple Affiliations (Unions Excluded) by Size of Community, Canada*

Community Size	Associational Membership	Multiple Affiliations
≤10,000	56	29
10,000 − 30,000	62	38
30,000 − 100,000	52	26
>100,000	56	31

*Source: James Curtis, 'Voluntary Association Joining,' *American Sociological Review*, XXXVI (October, 1971), 876-877.

its peak and levelling off in the late forties and generally declining in the fifties and later years.

With respect to membership rates, Table V shows that there is no clear-cut trend for voluntary associational membership rates to rise with increasing size of community of residence in Canada. Curtis also finds a similar lack of correlation between voluntary associational membership rates and community size in samples from the United States, Great Britain, German, Italy, and Mexico.

The above picture, while based on national rather than urban/rural samples, places a limitation on the claims advanced on behalf of voluntary associations. First, it suggests that the total amount of time spent in voluntary associational activities may be exaggerated; a member need not be an active participant. More importantly, it suggests that the voluntary associations are not mass phenomena: that is, all strata do not equally belong to, or form, voluntary associations. And finally, it appears that a rural-urban, or size of community distinction is not very useful in understanding variations in membership rates. Thus there is no real answer to the question of whether voluntary associations have taken over the functions of the family and local groups.

Although the importance of voluntary associations for the individual in urban society may have been exaggerated, they still permit some insight into the nature of urban life. Specifically, if categories of age, class, religion or race and ethnicity are differentially represented in voluntary associations, and if associations crystallize along these lines, the voluntary associations formed may be integrative for select groups of individuals but may be non-integrative in terms of increasing networks of participation in the larger society. With respect to Canada, Hughes

(1943) has clearly shown that ethnic and religious differences underlie the various types of associations formed in the Cantonville (Drummondsville) community of the 1930's. For example, Hughes noted that the fraternal lodge was very much a part of Catholic life. Yet when one considers French and English Catholics of the same socio-economic status one finds that the latter did not belong to these lodges. One reason appears to be that English Catholics tried to avoid identification with the French even where they had a common religion. Hughes (1943: 128) notes:

> ... they make a good many defensive statements to dissociate themselves from certain features of Quebec Catholicism. Most of them are moving up in the world occupationally and in social connections ... certainly the Cantonville English Catholics have nothing to gain among their English-Protestant colleagues by associating themselves with so French and so Catholic a group. On the other hand, since their careers depend in no way upon public popularity among the French, there is no positive motive to lead them into the order.

The resulting divisions along ethnic and religious lines in turn supported the hierarchical system of stratification in Cantonville. The implication of this finding is that under certain conditions, voluntary associations based on ethnicity may provide a sense of cohesion and belonging for members involved but may be detrimental with respect to the overall position of that ethnic group in the larger society.

The Urban Family

In addition to voluntary associations, urban sociologists view the structure of the urban family and kinship networks as indicative of the effects of increasing size and density on interaction patterns. The family is of sociological interest not only because it serves as a primary group midway between the individual and the larger society, but also because it is modifiable in response to changes in the larger society. Changes resulting from urbanization and industrialization are viewed as having important consequences for the functioning of the family as an integrative unit.

The concern of the urban sociologist with the impact of urbanization and urbanism on family and kinship systems is evidenced by the attention paid to the prevalence and structure of the nuclear family (the group comprising husband, wife, and unmarried children) in urban society. In North America urban growth has been associated with industrial growth, and the resulting organizational complex now performs many of the functions once considered the job of the family. Of course the family is still the procreative agency but publicly-supported schools educate children who are over six years of age, stores provide clothing and food, and hospitals provide medical services. This trend is continuing with the growth of day care centers, which in combination with the above, permit ever-increasing numbers of 'working mothers.' This increased employment of women (36 per cent in 1971 in Canada for all women over fourteen years of age), as well as the changes in the services which the family provides to its members, suggest changes in the distribution of power within the family unit. In a rural economy power is vested in the male head of the household who makes important decisions, and husband and wife perform role-specific tasks. In the urban-industrial setting, power is more evenly distributed between husband and wife. The implications of these changes are not clear-cut. Some social scientists describe this trend as the loss of the husband's power over his wife and children, and they suggest that family solidarity declines. Others have suggested that family solidarity may actually improve as tasks become shared, communication increases, and the family is treated as a goal in itself rather than a means to other goals of child-raising and economic sustenance.

This focus on changes in the family which are correlated with urbanism and/or industrialization needs to be qualified according to social class and ethnicity. With respect to ethnicity, Elkin (1964) points out that the traditional family may not give way to a more egalitarian power structure for some ethnic and minority groups since family life is intertwined with the feeling of ethnic identity and the maintenance of certain traditional customs and values. With respect to social class, role allocation within the nuclear family may be expected to differ depending upon position in the stratification structure. Evidence from industrialized nations suggests that increasingly egalitarian relationships are character-istic of middle class nuclear families rather than of working or lower class families.

Associated with the changes in the family power structure is the emphasis upon the change from an extended family to a smaller nuclear family system and the relative isolation of this latter unit from other kin. According to this view, not only does the increasing size, density, and heterogeneity of the city lead to impersonal, superficial, transient, and segmental relationships, but also, with urbanism, contact with kin declines or becomes nonexistent in the urban setting. Numerous North American studies, however, suggest otherwise. It appears that within the Western context the urban family system can be conceptualized as a modified extended family system. This system consists of nuclear families that are bound together by affection and by a series of activities or provision of services such as kinship visiting, joint recreational family get-togethers, and mutual services such as care of children, helping older family members, assisting at weddings and provision of aid in times of crisis. (See Sussman and Burchinal, 1962.) The frequency of urbanite contact with relatives further supports this contention. Relatively high rates of interaction among kinship members were found by Pineo (1968b) in his study of the extended family in a working class area of Hamilton, and by Crysdale (1968a) in his examination of family and kinship in a blue-collar community. Pineo (1968b) observed that of the persons with parents and parents-in-law living in the Hamilton metropolitan area, between 77 per cent and 88 per cent had contact with their parents at least once a week. Between 55 per cent and 67 per cent of the men in his sample and all of the women had contact with in-laws at least once a week. (See also Chapter Eight.)

Crysdale's (1968a) study of Toronto residents suggests that an important factor which helps account for interaction with family or other primary group members is educational attainment, or the lack of it. People who had gone beyond high school were less active in primary relations than were people with lower education. Higher education and higher job status put people in touch with a wider variety of groups and organizations thereby decreasing the rate of contact with relatives, neighbors and immediate co-workers.

Sociological studies of kinship involvement of urbanites often simultaneously examine contact of urbanites with neighbors. In his study of the extended family in a working class area of Hamilton, Pineo (1968b) noted that the involvement of respondents with friends seemed as intense as their involvement with kin. While 68 per cent reported at least weekly contact with some relative, 63 per cent reported at least weekly contact with 'their best friend in the neighborhood.' However, the nature of the relationship between friend and kin on the part of the respondents may differ. Closest informal associations appear to be those of kin rather than of friend or neighbor, and may reflect the preference of urbanites for the familiarity of a kinship relationship (Schulman, 1971). However, it also may be that the more intense relationships with relatives on the part of various urbanite samples represent the minimal fulfillment of a social obligation to keep in touch, while contact with friends is the expression of a definite preference (Pineo, 1968a: 199).

Neighborhoods in the Urban Setting

In addition to the voluntary association and the family, the neighborhood is also examined by urban sociologists as an adaptive and integrative mechanism for urban dwellers. The term 'neighborhood' is commonly used in two ways: as a voluntary group and as a geographical unit which is compact enough to permit interaction of its members. These two aspects of area and group interaction are frequently intermixed with the result that *neighborhood is frequently defined as an area in which the inhabitants are well acquainted with one another and are in the habit of visiting one another and exchanging services and information.*

The sociological focus on the neighborhood orginated with Cooley's (1909) definition of neighbors as one of the three basic primary groups, the others being the family and the play group. The initial attention to the role of the neighborhood as an integrative mechanism was given further stress during the 1930's and 1940's by urban sociologists and urban planners who saw the neighborhood as counteracting urban social disorganization. Based on the sociological premise of the need for primary social contacts, plans were devised in which a given area was to be physically constructed in such a way as to be conducive to intimate social interaction. As conceived by planners the neighborhood unit is an area of small size and relative self-sufficiency. The area is bounded by arterial streets sufficiently wide to facilitate by-passing the area instead of passing through it. The area also includes schools, small parks, recreational areas, and shopping facilities. The application of the neighborhood unit plan is most clearly seen in the British new town system.

The neighborhood unit plan has been criticized on a number of points. Sociologists note that the neighborhood as it is used in planning is not necessarily the same thing as a small group of people who constitute a neighborhood in an interactional sense. Each cluster of urban neighbors tends to include families who interact with other nearby clusters and who ignore physical boundaries (Keller, 1968). The self-sufficiency aspect of the neighborhood plan is also criticized. Carried to its logical conclusion, the notion of self-sufficiency has the negative effect of failing to integrate the individual with the rest of the city. In addition, a self-contained neighborhood affects not only the individual, but also the performance level of the government. Jane Jacobs (1961) stresses that neighborhoods must be continuous and overlapping to insure effective governmental response to the various needs of a sub-area of a community.

Critics of the neighborhood unit plan also have argued that it is unrealistic for any one primary group to provide a sense of identity or group membership for individuals in a modern society. The integration of individuals is often accomplished through multiple membership not only in the neighborhood or in a particular locality but also in socioeconomic strata, occupational groups and voluntary associations. In keeping with this argument, research in Toronto's East York has shown that close relationships have become despatialized. Very few of those persons toward whom respondents felt close lived in the respondents' immediate neighborhood (Wellman, 1972: 96).

Notwithstanding the criticisms which have been levelled at the neighborhood unit plan, the sociological importance of the plan undoubtedly has been its stress on the potential and actual role of the neighborhood as an integrative mechanism in urban society. Sociological investigations of the neighborhood focus upon two aspects: the importance of neighbors to the urbanite as compared with other informal groups and the quality of the interaction which occurs at the neighborhood level. Rates of contact are frequently used as measures of the importance of neighbors. Investigations into frequency of contact with neighbors generally reveal the much greater importance of relatives as a source of contact for urbanites (Axelrod, 1956; Bell and Boat, 1957; Greer and Kube, 1959; Tomeh, 1964). The relative importance or unimportance of neighbors for urbanites depends somewhat upon social class position and stage of life cycle. With respect to the latter, Wayne's (1972: 90) study of Toronto East York showed that couples with young children do more neighboring than couples with no children. This finding is easily explained by the fact that children frequently are important stimuli for getting to know a neighbor. They need constant surveillance out of which may emerge mutual aid services and reciprocal obligations; also the children themselves may form friendships which in turn lead to contact among the parents. Likewise, in old age there is a dependence upon an area and on neighbors since the elderly very often depend upon those living nearby for certain services and assistance (Mann, 1965). With respect to social class there is some evidence which suggests that middle class and upper class individuals tend to have lower rates of contact with their neighbors than do lower class individuals. These class differences appear to reflect both the alternative networks of participation which are available to people of higher educational and occupational standing and the different definitions of what it is to be a good neighbor.

Investigations into the concept of neighboring have found that to neighbor or to be a neighbor implies reciprocal obligations. A neighbor is expected to help minimally in times of crises such as fires, floods, and epidemics and to offer such assistance as the situation requires. Neighbors also may be expected to help in times of need, ranging from help with a child, exchanging tools, informal visiting and giving advice or exchanging information (gossip). However, the degree of mutal aid and privacy that characterizes the relationship between any two people living near each other varies a great deal. Keller notes (1968: 53-54):

> ... we find that neighboring is more extensive, solidary, and generalized, and in that sense de-individualized in the solid working class areas, the small cohesive villages, and the homogeneous new community, where need

combines with fellowship to make neighbor relations almost as close and nearly as necessary as family relationships. In contrast to these, the middle class areas of solid comfort in greater occupational and cultural heterogeneity are marked by neighboring that is more selective, less intertwined with other aspects of life, and more likely to emphasize personal sociability and compatibility. Less crisis-oriented, it is also less utilitarian than its traditional working class or rural counterpart.*

Slums and Suburbs

As a sociological concept the neighborhood clearly is distinct from voluntary associations, ethnic groups and the family by virtue of its geographic boundary. Having a spatial or physical referrent is also true of two other areas of sociological inquiry: slums and suburbs. As mentioned earlier, two approaches are found with respect to studies of these urban sub-areas. One question frequently asks what changes in the physical nature of the city take place over time, and thus is concerned with the factors underlying the growth of blighted areas and suburbs. Certainly in industrialized countries there are rapid changes in social and economic life styles which may result in the rearrangement of urban land use. The problem of urban blight is partly related to urban buildings being put to uses different from those for which they were designed, while the growth of the suburbs often involves a change in land use from agrarian to residential as the city expands.

The second question asked with respect to suburbs and blighted areas is whether or not these areas are also sociological communities which function to integrate their members. Such a focus is in keeping with Wirth's stress on social organization as changing with city size, density, and heterogeneity. Both slums and suburbs are considered as sub-societies which are characterized by their own values and patterns of interaction which reflect the properties of size, density, and heterogeneity.

What are the characteristics of a slum as a social system? To answer this question we must return to a discussion of the physical properties of a blighted area. Partly because of their high visibility, the physical conditions in a slum tend to be the criteria for definition of an area as a slum. Slums are described as those areas where housing is dilapidated and overcrowded and where adequate social services such as fire, police, and educational services are lacking. Such a definition of course is relative. Many areas described as slums in Toronto might not be defined

---

*Suzanne Keller, *The Urban Neighborhood*, pp. 33-34. Copyright © Random House, 1968.

as such in countries where the standard of living was lower or where cultural definitions of a standard dwelling were different (see Glazer, 1965).

If areas of high density and neglected, overcrowded housing are valid indicators of a slum, it is only because of their association with the social life in a given sub-area of a city. Economically marginal persons tend to reside in physically defined slums because of lower cost of housing. Thus much of the way of life that is associated with the slum is really a culture of the lower class or what can be termed 'the culture of poverty' (Lewis, 1961, 1968). Certainly, all lower class people do not live in slums, but the majority of people who live in physical slums are at the lower end of a status ranking continuum as evidenced by the frequent interchangeability of the term 'low income area' for 'slum.' This predominance of lower class inhabitants with limited opportunity for advancement may create a subculture in which certain values and ways of behavior are stressed. Lewis (1968) characterizes such slum inhabitants as lacking a nurturing, protective childhood, having early sexual experiences and casual liaisons, frequent family desertion and a matriarchal family structure, strong present-time orientation and an absence of planning for the future, fatalism, and resignation. Other characteristics are the notion of male superiority and sexually segregated social lives, the treatment of the job as a means to other goods rather than an end in itself, the view of white collar job holders as not working, and a general hostility towards the outside world (Gans, 1962).

While the above characteristics represent the adaptation and reaction of poor people to their marginality (Lewis, 1968), many of the characteristics such as family desertion are viewed as problematic by members of the larger society. Thus ameliorative efforts designed to eradicate the culture of poverty are made, frequently in the guise of urban renewal and guaranteed income or welfare schemes. The bulk of these efforts are directed toward those individuals defined as 'poor' and in need of assistance and improved living quarters.

There is no official concept of poverty in Canada. The Economic Council of Canada (1968) describes families as poor when most if not all of their income is spent on essentials such as food, clothing, and shelter. Data for 1967 suggest that 55 per cent of Canada's low income families reside in urban municipalities of 1,000 or more, with 35 per cent residing in metropolitan centers (Lithwick, 1971: 20).

Information on low income groups in Canadian urban areas is provided by the 1965 Canadian Welfare Council (Woodsworth, 1965) study of urban need in four Canadian cities: Vancouver, Toronto, Montreal, and Saint John. Data were collected on 201 families with respect to their living conditions and attitudes towards major problems.

While the generalizability of the findings of the Canadian Welfare Council is limited due to the nature of the sampling, the results offer insight into the social organization of urban slum areas as a reflection of the low pay, unskilled status and irregular nature of employment of the inhabitants.

An obvious indication of poverty in the above-mentioned four cities is the 1965 median household income, which for the entire sample is $275 per month or $3,300 per year. The median income per person is $46 a month or $552 per year and reveals that the families selected did represent the financial poor. From this income, nearly 72 per cent is spent on food and housing and the remainder is spent on health care, educational needs, clothing, recreation, and savings. The allocation of the major portion of income to the two basic needs of food and shelter suggests that money planning of a traditional nature becomes not only unrealistic for people of low income, but impossible. Furthermore, debts constitute a serious problem for these individuals. Fifty-seven per cent of the total sample owes over $100 on a median household income of $275 a month.

These financial difficulties both result from and are reflected in educational and occupational standing and housing facilities. Approximately 70 per cent of the Urban Need in Canada (Woodsworth, 1965) sample had less than a grade eight education and 88 per cent were blue collar workers. Forty-six per cent of the adults had been unemployed for over ten weeks.

If levels of education and occupation are seen as underlying low income levels, it is equally true that the low income levels are manifested in housing characteristics. Most of the sample live in multiple housing; only 10 per cent reside in single family, detached dwelling units and most of these live in Vancouver. The condition of the housing is considered bad or unfit in almost half of the cases. Family sizes are large, the median family size is about six, which means that there are roughly 1.28 persons per room compared with an average of .7 for the census population. Ten per cent of the sample had ten or more people in the family. Reflecting poverty and the high rates of residential mobility (56 per cent have lived in their present domicile less than two years), the vast majority of cases (86 per cent) rent rather than own their homes.

Given the above set of socio-economic characteristics for a self-selected sample of urban poor in Canada, the urban sociologist seeks to examine the resultant patterns of behavior, attitudes, values, and aspirations. Both the physical surroundings and the image which the slum or deteriorated area has acquired in the eyes of the larger community have an important impact on the social organization of an urban slum area. A slum dweller's conception of himself may come to reflect the relatively low evaluation that the larger society makes of slums and their inhabitants. Such an attitude frequently is revealed in terms of the low quality services offered to the occupants of a slum, ranging from garbage collection, police protection, and enforcement of housing codes to the availability of hospitals, churches, and schools. As a result of negative evaluations, an individual's perceptions of the world are distorted and his aspirations may be very low (Clinard, 1966; Hunter, 1964). It should be noted, however, that not all slum dwellers have such perceptions. Gans (1962) observes that some blighted areas are predominantly working class areas where employment is low-income but steady. These workers might be less susceptible to negative evaluations than persons who are unemployed and economically marginal.

The self-deprecating and despairing attitudes of slum dwellers are serious not only because of their effects on the behavior of the affected individuals, but also because they tend to be taught to the children. Thus a cycle of poverty is started in which norms and behaviors of a subculture are transmitted from generation to generation. This phenomenon is observed most clearly in the negative attitudes which parents and children express toward formal education, which in industrialized nations provides opportunities for advancement. Parents do not value education highly because it has never helped them and because they often are unfamiliar with the range of social and economic positions which are available with education. Their children readily absorb these values, set their sights on a manual job and drop out of school at an early age. These tendencies are partially revealed in the studies by the Canadian Welfare Council (Woodsworth, 1965), where it is shown that parents desire an educational attainment for their children which is higher than their own but not as high as that desired by middle class parents, who commonly advocate college. Less than half of the respondents interviewed wanted college for their sons and less than a third advocated college for their daughters.

There is some indication that the lack of educational aspirations of slum dwellers relative to those of the middle and upper classes reflects an accurate assessment of reality rather than attributes of laziness or apathy. Data collected on the difference between the occupational levels expected and the occupational levels desired for children of respondents in the *Urban Need in Canada* study (Woodsworth, 1965) reveal at least some realistic assessment on the part of parents. Only 20 per cent expect professional attainment while 31 per cent desire this for their children. Overall, the expectations and desires are fairly low with 69 per cent expecting blue collar work for their children and 58 per cent desiring such.

Lack of aspiration, apathy, and isolation may characterize not only slum children but also adult slum dwellers as a result of the negative assessment by the larger society and the extremely low status position occupied by these individuals. Thus slum dwellers are frequently characterized as having a high degree of isolation and alienation (Clinard, 1966). However, evidence suggests a wide range of variability in the support of this proposition. Mann's (1961) study of a Toronto slum does suggest that the economically marginal situation of many individuals is disruptive. The widespread practice of subletting affects family stability. Borrowing and lending of food and the use of neighborhood grocery stores where credit is provided often leads to strained relationships rather than good neighborhood integration.

However, in the study of *Urban Need in Canada* (Woodsworth, 1965), over 80 per cent of the samples in Vancouver, Montreal, Toronto, and Saint John indicated that they felt they did belong to the community in which they resided, thus implying that they were not isolated or anomic. Participation in formally organized volunteer associations was low with nearly two-thirds of the sample not belonging to any type of organization. But care must be taken in interpreting this statistic since it is based on formal membership in a group and evidence suggests that slum dwellers do have high rates of informal contact with their immediate neighbors and relatives. The prevalence of the feeling of integration into the community is again revealed by the attitudes of the respondents toward leaving their homes. About 70 per cent of the total sample liked their present neighborhood and did not want to leave it in spite of the inadequacies or limitations of their present housing situation. Such findings again suggest that not all slum dwellers feel inferior or rejected. Studies of urban renewal, for example, have shown that residents of a blighted area find many satisfactions in their immediate surroundings and will not be moved from it to areas that offer improved physical conditions (Fried and Gleicher, 1961; Gans, 1962).

If slums have been erroneously conceptualized as fairly homogeneous areas characterized by the low socio-economic status of their inhabitants, social disorganization and individual anomia, the same charge of stereotyping can be made against images of suburbia. Studies conducted in the early 1950's tended to characterize suburbia as the habitat of young executives on the way up, as middle class and homogeneous, as status-conscious, child-centered and female-dominated (Dobriner 1963: 6). This conceptualization is revealed in *Crestwood Heights* (Seeley, *et al.*, 1956), which is a study of Forest Hill, a former independent surburban village near Toronto.

Several reasons seem to underlie this conceptualization of suburbia as a homogeneous socio-economic community. As suggested by Dobriner (1963) and Berger (1966), suburbs have highly visible features such as patios, barbecues, lawn mowers, tricycles, shopping centers, station wagons, which are easily organized into representing a distinct way of life. Furthermore, it appears that the high visibility of the suburbs existed for one particular type of suburb, namely residential. More often than not, during the post-World War II decade, the suburbs were built by developers with the result that their boundaries were highly delineated. These factors, coupled with the fact that many of the suburbs studied in the 1950's were unquestionably middle class, resulted in a stereotyped conceptualization of suburban living. In actuality, many of the comparisons made between urbanites and suburbanites were comparisons between differing socio-economic classes and differing age groups, and to this extent the comparisons are suspect (Gans, 1963).

The interest of urban sociologists in suburbs as representing a new form of social organization in the urban setting was unquestionably stimulated by the massive settlement of areas outside the central city after World War II. One of the spin-offs of World War II was the mass production of cars and trucks with the result that the North American population suddenly became very mobile (Schnore, 1957). Furthermore, not only did the population experience better means of transportation and communication, but it also experienced rapid growth as a result of high rates of marriages and births, which in turn increased demand for single dwelling types of housing. This demand, coupled with the car, meant that an extensive type of land use was feasible. Individuals could reside outside the city yet work within its confines and be the recipients of various goods and services provided by the metropolis. Such residential settlements could be called suburbs to the extent that they were areas adjacent to cities but were economically and socially dependent upon a given metropolis.

In the case of Canada, Figure 3 suggests that it was not until 1921 that adjacent areas surrounding the central city had a higher rate of growth than that of the central city. Figure 3 further shows a rapid increase in the rate of growth for adjacent subdivisions of cities of 30,000 or over following 1941. Table VI also shows the 1951-1961 growth rates for the central city and suburban areas. Given these growth trends for areas outside the central city, it is no wonder that social scientists have been concerned with suburban society. However, although one can talk about a suburban explosion to the extent that the lowest growth rate between 1951 and 1961 occurred in the central city (Table VI), data on metropolitan areas suggest that the majority of the population still reside in the central city.

Figure 3:   Growth Rate of Cities of 30,000 and Over and their Census Subdivisions, 1871-1961*

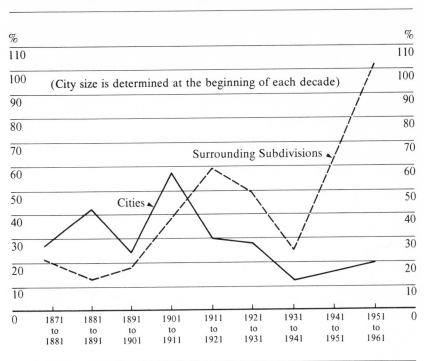

*Source: L. Stone, *Urban Development in Canada,* (Ottawa: Statistics Canada, 1967), p. 135. Reproduced by permission of Information Canada.

The growth of suburbs, however, does not imply that all suburbs are similar in terms of their population composition and in terms of functions which they perform for the city. Suburbs may be characterized as *residential or industrial.* Industrial suburbs are those areas which *serve as centers of employment and which employ a large proportion of their residents. They are a population attracting area* and may result from industry moving out of the city to the periphery or to industrial parks (Schnore, 1965: 155).

The residential suburb is the most common type; it employs relatively few people in its boundaries and is a population dispersing rather than a population gathering area. As noted by Boskoff (1963: 109-110), it is important to realize that residential suburbs differ among themselves in terms of origins, socio-economic strata, political structure, availability of

Table VI: Population Change for Central Cities and Remainder of 1961 Census Metropolitan Areas, 1951-1961*

		Percentage Change in Population[a]		
Areas	*MA*	*Central*[b] *City*	*Other,*[c] *10,000+*	*Remainder*[d] *of MA*
All MA's	44.8	23.8	57.0	110.7
Atlantic	31.9	11.7	78.6	70.6
Quebec	41.1	27.9	53.6	117.7
Ontario	45.8	15.5	54.5	116.3
Prairies	61.6	50.2	70.4	133.0
B.C.	39.9	10.9	29.3	90.7

		Percentage of 1961 MA Population		
Areas	*MA*	*Central City*	*Other 10,000+*	*Remainder*
All MA's	100.0	61.9	5.8	32.3
Atlantic	100.0	57.1	16.4	26.5
Quebec	100.0	75.0	3.8	21.2
Ontario	100.0	53.4	4.4	42.2
Prairies	100.0	72.9	10.9	16.2
B.C.	100.0	46.5	6.1	47.4

[a] The 1961 areas of the MA are held constant.
[b] Groups of incorporated centers are used in some cases (Montreal – all cities of 10,000 and over in 1961 on Montreal Island; Kitchener – Kitchener and Waterloo; Ottawa – Ottawa, Hull and Eastview).
[c] Centers of 10,000 and over in 1951 that were not defined as forming a central city.
[d] Portion of MA outside of cities of 10,000 and over in 1951.

*Source: L. Stone, *Urban Development in Canada* (Ottawa: Statistics Canada, 1967), p. 157, Table 8.1. Reproduced by permission of Information Canada.

institutional facilities, and the current relation to the central city. For example, a suburb may be formed by the slow growth of a community from an automonous village to one which is economically and socially dependent upon a larger city; or, it may result from the conversion of agricultural land to residential uses. Criss-crossing these two dimensions are the origins of a community as unplanned or planned. Suburbs may also differ in terms of their status as incorporated or unincorporated areas, or in terms of the availability of schools, shopping centers, churches, and recreational facilities. Suburbs also vary with respect to the occupational composition of their populations.

All of the above criteria allow us to distinguish between different types of residential suburbs, such as mass-produced suburbs like Levittown in New York, traditional upper class suburbs such as Forest Hill, Toronto or Rockcliffe Park, Ottawa, or even suburban slums. Such a lack of homogeneity in and between suburbs thus makes generalization concerning a suburban way of life very risky. Generalization also is difficult because in North America there is a variation in suburbs due to their age. New suburbs are likely to be extremely homogeneous with respect to age, marital status, and income of the occupants. As suburbs age, there is a turnover which makes the population more heterogeneous; in fact, suburbs may be characterized by a cycle of white collar to blue collar occupancy. This process is apparently underway in one of the better known suburbs, Levittown. In 1950 to 1951 the area was characterized by a 62 per cent white collar population; by 1960 the proportion had gone down to 50 per cent, with a corresponding increase in blue collar occupancy (Dobriner, 1963).

The fact that there is no one categorical type of suburb and that suburbs differ in age, origin, population characteristics, political status and institutional facilities does not invalidate a question asked by urban sociologists as to whether or not suburban settlements form sociological communities. If, in fact, suburbs can be demarcated from the central city not only on the basis of physical distance from the city center, but in terms of social organizational characteristics as well, then one can argue that suburbs in fact do represent new features of urban life. If distinctive features are found, two additional questions must be raised: (1) are these features determined by the characteristics of the population which has moved there; or (2) are the physical features of distance from the city and single dwelling units conducive to the formation of patterns of interaction regardless of the social organizational characteristics of the inhabitants prior to moving to the suburban area?

It is clear that the movement out of the central city into the peripheral areas has been interpreted by some social scientists as representing a flight from urbanism and a search for the rural life. The rural idea is clearly invoked by some of the names given to suburban developments, such as Garden City, Pinewood, and Meadowlands. However, one needs to ask if these names for areas which were purposively developed and primarily residential in character are really indicative of an anti-urban feeling on the part of the suburbanites who went to live there. Without question there are individuals who positively value attributes of rural life, but the bulk of evidence suggests that on the average suburbanites are motivated to move to areas outside the central city for reasons other than an escape from the hypothesized anomie and alienation of city life. S.D. Clark (1966) in his study of Toronto, and Herbert Gans (1963; 1967) in his study of Levittown suggest that the availability of housing plus better value for a given price rather than an active denial of urban society may be the crucial reason underlying the massive growth of the suburbs. In his discussion of fifteen suburban areas of Toronto, Clark argues that people move to suburbs because they are in search of space, notably a house, and the only place where they can find a house which they can afford is in the suburb. He maintains that the views which people hold about suburban versus city life have little to do with their becoming suburbanites. Qualifications of course must be made with respect to types of suburbs. Certain high prestige areas are attractive to some groups regardless of housing and space reasons. Attitudes toward suburban living also appear to vary between suburbs of different social rank. Morgan (1971) observes that residents of lower status suburbs were more likely to stress central city bigness with its congestion as a reason for choosing suburban life, while residents of upper status areas cite reasons of property protection, and tax and property differentials.

Clark's observations concerning the motivations of suburbanites for a move into a given area suggest that if differences are found between people in cities and suburbs these differences may reflect the values, attitudes, and habits which people had before moving and are not the result of living in suburbia *per se*. In addition to Gans' study (1967), this contention is supported by the follow-up study of Levittown by Dobriner (1963), and by Berger's (1959) study of a working class suburb in California. These two studies found that many groups and individuals retained their life styles after moving to areas outside the central city. This does not negate the various findings that certain groups of suburbanites emphasize neighboring, family activities, outdoor leisure activities, and participation in voluntary associations to a greater extent than do urban residents (Bell, 1958; Hendricks, 1971). Rather, these differences may simply represent differences in social class between suburbanites and urbanites. Or, these individuals may have in fact moved to the suburb after their realization of the importance of the family, neighborhood, and voluntary group participation. Thus, rather than undergoing alteration in their life style they may in fact have formed the basis for suburban features of activities centered on the family and one's neighbors.

In addition to the above discussion concerning the selectivity of immigration to the suburbs, the alternative argument stresses that the suburban features of familism and neighboring are due to the locational features of the suburb. As areas which are adjacent to the central city and yet maintain some degree of social and economic dependence on the central city, suburbs have two definitive characteristics; distance from the central city and a high rate of commuting (Martin, 1957). These characteristics are important in terms of structuring the social relationships in suburban communities. The further away people reside from the central city, the less accessible the central city appears to be. This means that suburban residents are not likely to be as active as city residents in various social activities within the central city proper. At the same time the suburbanites have a great deal of accessibility to their immediate communities. In short, ecological position, or distance from the central city, implies the detachment of the suburbanite from central city activities and a great deal of neighboring within the community residential area.

Commuting also represents the response of suburbanites to their distance from the central city. Martin (1957) notes two possible consequences of the extreme reliance on commuting. First, commuters participate less than non-commuters in voluntary associations and in formal groups within the suburban area proper. Presumably this applies to the male memberships since they are actively involved in commuting to the central city. Secondly, as a result of this daily commuting of males, women play a more important role in voluntary associations and other organizing activities within the suburban community. Given the relatively greater importance of women in the organizational activities of the suburban community, such areas become characterized as female-dominated and child-centered. The above observations are limited to residential communities, and obviously these social consequences may not occur (1) if the suburb in question is very large, densely populated and/or characterized by apartment dwelling units rather than single dwelling units, or (2) if the suburb is industrial rather than residential.

These two cultural and ecological explanations of the social organizational features of the suburbs are not contradictory but rather must be seen in combination. A large body of literature suggests that no one factor seems to be operating alone although social scientists differ in their stress on socially and culturally selective immigration or ecological characteristics as the ultimate pre-determining force underlying suburban characteristics. Some social scientists argue that the desire for housing of a certain type and cost plus preferences for various life styles are more important in structuring the nature of social relationships in suburbia than are ecological factors (Gans, 1968). Conversely, others argue that the physical features of the suburban community, notably the distance from the central city and the phenomenon of commuting, initially structure relationships observed in the suburbs. People respond to these ecological features by selectively migrating to suburbs for reasons of age, stage in family life cycle, socio-economic class, and social mobility aspirations. In actuality, both the ecological and culturally selective factors provide the basis for suburban life styles (Tallman and Morgner, 1970).

Distance from the city is an important ecological factor in our understanding of the suburb in yet another way. The growth in the number of suburban areas is part of the low density, haphazard expansion which is known as urban sprawl. Urban sprawl begins when a growing urban population generates an increased demand for single family housing, and this demand is met by the conversion of agricultural land to urban residential and industrial uses. While this conversion of farm land to non-farm activities has been decried by critics of urban growth, the main problem would seem to be the pattern of growth which is associated with urban expansion. Suburban developments tend to be inefficient users of land simply because single family homes use more land than multiple dwelling units. Even given this different intensity of land use, suburbs can be more efficient users of land if they are built in a cluster format rather than developed in the conventional way of a grid subdivision (see Whyte, 1967), and more densely settled (Carver, 1962). There is very little federal, provincial or local control, however, of the ways in which suburbs are developed. Consequently the conventional subdivision method of developing land for residential purposes may be extremely wasteful.

Critics of urban sprawl not only condemn the conversion of agricultural land to urban uses, but also note that the growth of residential and industrial suburbs rob central cities of middle class citizens and tax revenue. In fact, as middle and upper class citizens move out, the central city income may decline while costs increase since low income residents of the central city area pay fewer taxes but still require recreational, medical, educational, and protective services. If property and industry taxes are increased to compensate for these increased costs, cities are likely to find that they lose even more of their middle and upper income groups and industries to areas adjacent to the central city. A working arrangement between the suburbs and the central city is one solution to the central city's revenue problem and to the suburban government's financing of the services which its residents require. Such metropolitan governments exist in Toronto and in Winnipeg, where the central city and suburban areas share in the provision of services such as streets, water mains, and schools. There are, however, many problems associated with metropolitan government. Suburban communities often are reluctant to enter into a reciprocal relationship with a central city because of the resultant loss of political autonomy. And, as Rose (1972) suggests for Toronto, central cities may find that the social benefits of metropolitan government accrue not to them but to the constituent suburban municipalities.

Conclusions

The use of the three variables of size, density, and heterogeneity in explaining urbanism and urbanization constitutes a simplified way of discussing a complex sociological phenomenon. Cities as forms of human organization do not lend themselves readily to a set of simple formulae or easy specifications. This chapter, by discussing such seemingly diverse topics as neighborhoods, slums, ethnicity, migration, suburbs, family, voluntary organizations, and city structure, has expanded upon the immensity of urban phenomena that are subsumed under the concepts of size, density, and heterogeneity.

The necessity for this kind of sociological dissection becomes clear when one wishes to gain knowledge of the determinants and consequences of urban social behavior. To label a person as 'urban,' and then to assume that all his behavior is predictable is too gross a simplification. More must be known about the meaning of the term 'urban,' which implies the coming together of a number of other sociological variables, all of which also are determinants of social behavior. Thus, social class or neighborhood probably have a more immediate effect on behavior than does urban residence. However, it is only in the city that the entire spectrum of human categories is represented in a relatively close proximity. It therefore becomes necessary for urban man to be able to cope with points on this spectrum that are different from his own. The sociologist's concern with integration and adaptation in the urban environment focuses on this necessary ability to handle differences. Failure to accomodate such differences may result in anomie. An anomic condition is one in which the norms become vague or unimportant. The anomic individual is not responsive to any particular reference group which might exert some form of social control over him. That this condition exists in cities may be inferred from the relatively high rates of suicide, homicide and other crimes which, above all else, appear strongly to differentiate urban from rural areas.

Similarly, the family, which has traditionally been the strongest agent of social control, has been modified to adapt to the urban environment. The large, extended family which stretched across generations has been replaced with the nuclear family which is small, and usually consists of no more than two generations. Other institutions such as the urban school, the peer group, or the church to some extent, have increasingly taken over socialization functions that traditionally were the realm of the extended family. We are not entirely sure of all of the consequences of this, but it appears certain that at each stage some measure of social control is lost; that is, what the family loses in its socializing role is only partially gained by these other institutions. This could be what is responsible for urban anomie.

The future of cities in Canada is presently a topic of serious debate among politicians, city planners, and social scientists. There is growing unease over the prospects of unabated metropolitan growth, particularly in and between our largest metropolitan areas like Montreal and Toronto. Some of this concern is with the governability of continuously growing cities and the co-ordination of municipal services for an expanding metropolis. Some of it is with the sociological problem of integrating diverse groups of people in a large city. Some concern is also felt over the urban poor, and over the fact that cities have a way of generating poverty at accelerating rates. Part of this is due to the in-migration of rural poor who are attracted by better urban welfare services, but it is also partly due to the urban economic system which is seen as harsher and more competitive than the rural system, and which may generate a higher economic mortality rate.

By the same token, however, cities continue to be magnets, drawing both people and activities to them, because as Hauser pointed out, these dense agglomerations are efficient users of people, space, and time. People are attracted to, and remain in cities because of the plurality of opportunities that exist therein. These may be social, cultural, economic or political, and nowhere but in cities are they found in such abundance.

This is the feature that is hardest to replicate in the so-called new towns. Planners and politicians, in seeking ways of coping with increasing metropolitanization, often speak of creating new cities, either by building up existing small towns or by creating new cities from scratch. There is more to a city, though, than houses, buildings, factories, sewers, and streets. The perception of opportunities must also exist before people will be attracted to these places. That is why rural Ontarians bypass Carleton Place and move to Ottawa, or why rural Manitobans bypass Gimli and move to Winnipeg. It is also why the Government of Brazil, in creating a new civil-service city in the jungle, found that while several hundred thousand Brazilians were forced to live in Brasilia, very few actually wanted to. Vastly improved technological innovations in transportation may make such out-cities more possible in the coming decades, while still recognizing the importance of links to the existing cities.

It can therefore be expected that our present metropolitan areas in Canada will continue to grow, although a diminished rural population and low demographic vital rates would mean that some of such growth would be the result of foreign immigration. Nevertheless, such growth will probably be in the existing cities. An understanding of the sociological components of an urban area is, therefore, necessary both for the sake of the knowledge itself as well as for attempting to make cities into reasonable places in which to live.

References

Abu-Lughod, Janet, 'Migrant Adjustment to City Life,' *American Journal of Sociology,* LXVII (July, 1961), 22-32.

Axelrod, M. 'Urban Structure and Social Participation,' *American Sociological Review,* XXI (1956), 13-18.

Babchuk, N., and J.N. Edwards, 'Voluntary Associations and the Integration Hypothesis,' *Sociological Inquiry,* XXXV (Spring, 1965), 149-162.

Bell, Wendell, 'Social Choice, Life Styles, and Suburban Residence,' in William Dobriner (ed.), *The Suburban Community.* New York: G.P. Putnam's Sons, 1958, pp. 225-247.

Bell, Wendell, and M.D. Boat, 'Urban Neighborhoods and Informal Social Relations,' *American Journal of Sociology,* LXII (1957), 391-398.

Berger, Bennet M., 'Suburbs, Subcultures and the Urban Future,' in Sam B. Warner, Jr. (ed.), *Planning for a Nation of Cities.* Cambridge, Mass.: MIT Press, 1966, pp. 143-162.

——, *Working Class Suburb.* Berkeley, California: University of California Press, 1959.

Boskoff, Alvin, *The Sociology of Urban Regions.* New York: Appleton-Century-Crofts, 1963.

Breton, Raymond, 'Institutional Completeness of Ethnic Communities and the Personal Relations of Immigrants,' *American Journal of Sociology,* LXX, No. 2, (Sept., 1964), 193-205; reprinted in B. Blishen, *et al.,* (eds.), *Canadian Society,* (3rd edition). Toronto: Macmillan, 1968, pp. 77-94.

Broom, Leonard, and Philip Selznick, *Sociology.* New York: Row, Peterson and Company, 1958.

Carver, Humphrey, *Cities in Suburbs.* Toronto: University of Toronto Press, 1962.

Clark, Samuel Delbert, *The Suburban Society.* Toronto: University of Toronto Press, 1966.

Clinard, Marshall B., *Slums and Community Development.* New York: The Free Press, 1966.

Cooley, Charles H., *Social Organization.* New York: Scribner and Sons, 1909.

Crysdale, Stewart, 'Family and Kinship in Riverdale,' in W.E. Mann (ed.), *Canada: A Sociological Profile.* Toronto: Copp Clark, 1968, pp. 262-276.

——, 'Social Effects of a Factory Relocation,' in W.E. Mann (ed.), *Canada: A Sociological Profile.* Toronto: Copp Clark, 1968b, pp. 262-276.

Curtis, James, 'Voluntary Association Joining: A Cross-National Comparative Note,' *American Sociological Review,* XXXVI (October, 1971), 872-880.

Darroch, A. Gordon, and Wilfred G. Marston, 'The Social Class Basis of Ethnic Residential Segregation: The Canadian Case,' *American Journal of Sociology,* LXXVII, No. 3. (Nov., 1971), 491-510.

Dobriner, William M., *Class in Suburbia.* Englewood Cliffs: Prentice-Hall Inc., 1963.

Dominion Bureau of Statistics, *1961 Census of Canada: Ethnic Origins of the Canadian Population,* 99-516: vol 7, part 1. Ottawa: Queen's Printer, 1966.

Duncan, Otis Dudley, 'Human Ecology and Population Studies,' in P.M. Hauser and O.D. Duncan, (eds.) *The Study of Population.* Chicago: University of Chicago Press, 1959, pp. 678-716.

Durkheim, Emile, *The Division of Labor in Society.* New York: Macmillan, 1933.

Economic Council of Canada, *Fifth Annual Review.* Ottawa: Queen's Printer, 1968.

Elkin, Fred, *The Family in Canada.* Ottawa: The Vanier Institute, 1964.

Fried, M., and P. Gleicher, 'Some Sources of Residential Satisfaction in an Urban Slum,' *Journal of the American Institute of Planners,* XXVII (1961), 305-315.

Gans, Herbert J., *The Urban Villagers.* New York: The Free Press, 1962.

——, 'The Effects of the Move from City to Suburbs,' in Leonard Duhl (ed.), *The Urban Condition.* New York: Basic Books, 1963, pp. 184-198.

——, *The Levittowners.* New York: Pantheon, 1967.

George, M.V., *Internal Migration in Canada.* Ottawa: Dominion Bureau of Statistics, 1970.

Glazer, Nathan, 'Slum Dwellings Do not Make a Slum,' *New York Times Magazine,* November 21, 1965, reprinted in Nathan Glazer (ed.), *Cities in Trouble.* Chicago: Quadrangle Books, 1970.

Gordon, Milton M., *Assimilation in American Life.* New York: Oxford University Press, 1964.

Greer, S., and E. Kube, 'Urbanism and Social Structure: A Los Angeles Study,' in M.B. Sussman (ed.), *Community Structure and Analysis.* New York: Thomas Y. Crowell, 1959, pp. 93-112.

Guest, Avery M., 'The Applicability of the Burgess Zonal Hypothesis to Urban Canada,' *Demography,* VI, 3, (August, 1969), 271-277.

Hardwick, Walter G., 'Vancouver: The Emergence of a "Core-Ring" Urban Pattern,' in R. Louis Gentilcore (ed.), *Geographical Approaches to Canadian Problems.* Scarborough: Prentice-Hall of Canada, 1971, pp. 112-118.

Hauser, Philip M., 'The Chaotic Society: Product of the Social Morphological Revolution,' *American Sociological Review,* XXXIV: 1 (February, 1969), 1-19.

Hawley, Amos, *Human Ecology: A Theory of Community Structure.* New York: The Ronald Press, 1950.

——, *Urban Society.* New York: The Ronald Press, 1971.

Hendricks, Jon, 'Leisure Participation as Influenced by Urban Residential Patterns,' *Sociology and Social Research,* LV (July, 1971), 414-428.

Hollingshead, August B., and Frederick C. Redlich, *Social Class and Mental Illness: A Community Study.* New York: John Wiley and Sons, 1958.

Hughes, Everett C., *French Canada in Transition.* Chicago: University of Chicago Press, 1943.

Hunter, David R., *The Slums: Challenge and Response.* New York: The Free Press, 1964.

Jackson, John N., *The Canadian City.* Toronto: McGraw-Hill Ryerson, 1973.

Jacobs, Jane, *The Death and Life of Great American Cities.* New York: Vintage Books, 1961.

Kalbach, Warren E., *The Impact of Immigration on Canada's Population.* Ottawa: Dominion Bureau of Statistics, 1970.

Kalbach, Warren E., and Wayne E. McVey, *The Demographic Bases of Canadian Society.* Toronto: McGraw-Hill, 1971.

Kasahara, Y., 'A Profile of Canada's Metropolitan Centers,' *Queen's Quarterly,* LXX (Autumn, 1963), 303-313.

Keller, Suzanne, *The Urban Neighborhood.* New York: Random House, 1968.

Lewis, Oscar, *The Children of Sanchez.* New York: Random House, 1961.

——, *A Study of Slum Cultures.* New York: Random House, 1968.

Lithwick, N. Harvey, *Urban Canada: Problems and Prospects.* Ottawa: Central Mortgage and Housing Corporation, 1970.

——, *Research Monograph No. 1: Urban Poverty.* Ottawa: Central Mortgage and Housing Corporation, 1971.

Mann, Peter H., *An Approach to Urban Sociology.* London: Routledge and Kegan Paul, 1965.

Mann, William E., 'The Social System of a Slum: The Lower Ward, Toronto,' in S.D. Clark (ed.), *Urbanism and the Changing Canadian Society.* Toronto: University of Toronto Press, 1961.

Martin, W.T., 'Ecological Changes in Satellite Rural Areas,' *American Sociological Review,* XXII (April, 1957), 173-183.

McKenzie, Roderick D., *On Human Ecology.* Chicago: University of Chicago Press, 1968.

Morgan, David R., 'Community Social Rank and Attitudes toward Surburban Living,' *Sociology and Social Research,* LV (July, 1971), 401-413.

Morris, R.N., *Urban Sociology*. London: George Allen and Unwin, 1968.

Olsen, Dennis C., 'Formal Voluntary Organizations in the Canadian Context.' Unpublished Master's thesis, Carleton University, 1971.

Park, Robert E., 'Human Ecology,' *American Journal of Sociology*, XLII, (July, 1936), 1-15.

Park, Robert E., and Ernest W. Burgess, *The City*. Chicago: University of Chicago Press, 1925. (Heritage of Sociology Series, 1967).

Pineo, Peter C., 'Social Consequences of Urbanization,' in H.H. Lithwick and Gilles Paquet (eds.), *Urban Studies: A Canadian Perspective*. Toronto: Methuen, 1968, pp. 179-203.

——, 'The Extended Family in a Working-Class Area of Hamilton,' in Bernard R. Blishen, *et al.*, (eds.), *Canadian Society*. Toronto: Macmillan, 1968, pp. 140-150.

Rashleigh, E.T., 'Observations on Canadian Cities, 1960-61,' *Plan Canada*, III (Sept., 1962), 60-77.

Rose, Arnold, *Governing Metropolitan Toronto*. Berkeley: University of California Press, 1972.

Schnore, Leo F., 'Metropolitan Growth and Decentralization,' *American Journal of Sociology*, LXIII (September, 1957), 171-180.

——, 'On the Spatial Structure of Cities in the Two Americas,' in Philip M. Hauser and Leo F. Schnore (eds.), *The Study of Urbanization*. New York: John Wiley and Sons, 1965, pp. 347-398.

——, 'Social Morphology and Human Ecology,' in Leo F. Schnore (ed.), *The Urban Scene*. New York: The Free Press, 1965, pp. 152-168.

Schnore, Leo F., and Gene B. Peterson, 'Urban and Metropolitan Development in the United States and Canada,' *Annals of the American Academy of Political and Social Science*, CCXVI (March, 1958), 60-68.

Schulman, Norm, 'Social Networks in an Urban Setting,' paper presented at the Canadian Sociology and Anthropology Association Meeting, St. John's, Newfoundland, 1971.

Seeley, John R., R. Alexander Sim, and Elizabeth W. Loosley, *Crestwood Heights*. Toronto: University of Toronto Press, 1956.

Sills, David L., 'Voluntary Associations: Sociological Aspects,' in David L. Sills (ed.), *The International Encyclopedia of the Social Sciences*, vol. 16. New York: Free Press and Macmillan, 1968, pp. 363-379.

Sjoberg, Gideon, *The Preindustrial City, Past and Present*. New York: The Free Press, 1960.

Smith, David H., 'The Importance of Formal Voluntary Organizations for Society,' *Sociology and Social Research*, L (July, 1966), 483-494.

Stone, Leroy O., *Urban Development in Canada*. Ottawa: Dominion Bureau of Statistics, 1967.

Sussman, Marvin B., and Lee Burchinal, 'Kin Family Network,' *Journal of Marriage and the Family*, XXIV (August, 1962), 231-240.

Tallman, Irving, and Ramona Morgner, 'Life Style Differences Among Urban and Suburban Blue-collar Families,' *Social Forces,* XLVIII (March, 1970), 334-348.

Tisdale, Hope, 'The Process of Urbanization,' *Social Forces,* XX (March, 1941), 311-316.

Tomeh, A.J., 'Informal Group Participation and Residential Patterns,' *American Journal of Sociology,* LXX (1964), 28-35.

Urban Renewal Study for the City of Edmonton, Edmonton City Planning Department, 1963-64.

Vance, James E., Jr., 'Focus on Downtown,' *Community Planning Review,* XVI (Summer, 1966), 9-15.

Wayne, Jack, 'The Case of the Friendless Urbanite,' in Alan Powell (ed.), *The City.* Toronto: McClelland and Stewart, 1972, pp. 80-92.

Wellman, Barry, 'Who Needs Neighborhoods,' in Alan Powell (ed.), *The City.* Toronto: McClelland and Stewart, 1972, pp. 94-100.

Whyte, William Foote, *Street Corner Society.* Chicago: University of Chicago Press, 1943.

Whyte, William H., 'Cluster Development,' in H. Wentworth Eldredge (ed.), *Taming Megalopolis,* vol. I. New York: Doubleday, 1967, pp. 462-477.

Wirth, Louis, 'Urbanism as a Way of Life,' *American Journal of Sociology,* XLIV (July, 1938), 1-24.

Woodsworth, D.E., *Urban Need in Canada: Overview 1965.* Ottawa: Canada Welfare Council, 1965.

4 : SOCIOLOGY AND THE UNIVERSITY

Introduction to Part Four

Sociology is essentially a feature of this century. Its antecedents may be found much earlier, and some of its great contributors worked in the nineteenth century. But it is over the past seven decades that sociology came to be established, largely in the United States. In Canada, formal instruction in sociology and persons engaged in sociological research were unknown prior to the past fifty years. Indeed, only since World War II has there been a sociological establishment in this country, with no great expansion until the 1960's.

The perspectives of modern sociology as they are represented in Canada are not so very different from those of sociology in the United States, the United Kingdom, Germany, or any of the Western nations. In no one of these nations is a theoretical consensus to be found among sociologists. But there are certain assumptions in common, such as the fundamental view that human behavior is learned, patterned, and repetitious. And there is a common vocabulary of shared meanings, concepts which are intended to describe human social behavior whatever the culture. In common too is the basic and necessary commitment to cross-cultural or cross-national generalizations. Such comparative analysis reflects the notion that sociology deals with human social behavior and societies, and not just Canadian, American, French, or Soviet, etc.

However, it would be incorrect to suggest that sociology has thereby realized some form of universalism or internationalism. It seems clear that formal sociology, whatever its aspirations and standards of neutrality, does reflect the ideologies and problems of its national hosts. This would be most strikingly apparent were we to contrast American and Soviet sociology. Thus, whatever the sociological commonalities we may speak of, it is also the case that we must be aware of national sociologies which are derived from and responsive to their particular social, cultural, and political contexts. To believe otherwise because of some commitment to an idealized notion of social scientific value neutrality and scientific objectivity would be to indulge in gross error. Objectivity is to be had in replicable and valid research, and not the selection of research problems.

Sociological enquiry has always been related to the social issues peculiar to particular times and societies. Thereby distinguishable national styles of sociology have emerged. It is unfortunately the case, as we argue in Chapter Twelve, that Canada has lagged behind in developing a sociology particularly suited to national social issues. Rather, Canadian sociology, particularly Anglophone sociology, has yet to emerge from the shadow of its American origins.

Anglophone and Francophone sociology in Canada have in common a conspicuous American influence, and theological influences, Protestant in English Canada and Roman Catholic in Quebec. But the developmental experiences were quite different. In English Canada the development of formal sociology was hindered by two factors: the entrenchment in Anglophone universities of social history which to some extent substituted for an explicit sociology; and the absence of salient social issues which could have stimulated and hastened the emergence of sociological enquiry. In contrast, sociology was more readily incorporated into Francophone university settings, and non-university intellectual activities. We believe that this is attributable to the social action programs of the Roman Catholic Church, and of greater import, to the conspicuous existence of a critical and disruptive social issue: the industrialization of traditional rural Quebec. Related issues such as the rural-urban transition, secularization, and changing family structure served as foci for Francophone sociologists. In retrospect, we see this to be illustrative of the interplay between societal issues and systems of thought and enquiry. Such is the thesis of Chapter Twelve, which is intended to illustrate the nature of sociology, its character in Canada, and the manner in which this discipline, dedicated to the study of man in a social environment, is itself a product of that environment.

Chapter Thirteen continues and concludes the analysis of the Canadian context of sociology. In some sense more speculative than previous chapters, this final chapter invites the very question, why bother to read this book at all? Or, why study sociology? Or, what is the utility of sociology in contemporary industrialized societies such as Canada?

All the contributors to this volume of course believe that they are engaged in a useful activity, and would like to have you believe so as well. Yet, that there are difficulties in establishing an effective sociology, and difficulties in effectively communicating that sociology to the novice, are apparent. Ultimately, we all would take the view, as does Crook, that whether or not the study of sociology in the university realizes professional recruits, its more important function is its role in any liberal arts program, indeed, in any man's or woman's education. If this is arrogance of a sort, so be it; but at least it expresses the view that sociology, in some small way, can help create a more informed Canadian public. Sociology may not be as radical as some people believe or others desire. But every now and then sociologists do challenge misconceptions and stereotypes, and do add to our pool of knowledge of human beings, including those who happen to be Canadians.

What sociology may become is impossible to predict, especially in Canada, so very sensitive to the 'Americanization' of the universities. There is little doubt, however, of our optimism. As we argue in Chapter Twelve, there is good reason to expect that Canadian sociology will develop a style of its own, using the best which is to be had from a sociological literature which has grown up in other societies and avoiding the unthinking importation of assumptions and 'explanations' which may only be artifacts of another society. Such is certainly our aspiration. Additionally, we aspire to a sociology inspired by and sensitive to pertinent social issues, by which we mean real and important Canadian social problems, not fads, fashions, and political rhetoric. The humanistic sense which has characterized the best systems of thought should characterize sociology. We aspire further to a sociology which addresses itself to and employs careful, systematic, and cumulative investigation and fact, and not supposition and ideology. These aspirations must not be taken to be a call for some crude sociological nationalism; rather, they express the view that before good comparative generalizations are to be realized, Canadian sociologists have research to do at home, some of it perhaps unique to Canadian society. Then comparison will be from a sound position of fact and not assumption.

The final chapter in this volume brings together many of the matters which have occupied us earlier, from the role of organizations in modern society to conceptions of equality. In some considerable part the author is offering disputed opinions, but opinions deserving of debate by all those in the university community. Crook's central themes relate to the issue of the modern university in a changing, leisure-oriented society, the meaning and quality of university education, and the nature, utility, and quality of the sociology growing up in our large universities. At times, we hope obviously so, Crook is rather rude and critical in his remarks. We take this to be a very appropriate tenor in which to close, for although we are in the business of education, we are also in the business of sociology: in the latter enterprise, there is no place for the 'true believer,' for sociology by its very nature is an exercise in skepticism.

Recommended Readings: Annotated

Gouldner, Alvin W., *The Coming Crisis in Western Sociology.* New York: Basic Books, 1970.

This widely discussed and debated book is a severe criticism of the dominant persons and styles in American sociology.

Hinkle, R., and G. Hinkle, *The Development of Modern Sociology.* New York: Random House, 1954.

Although published some time ago, this book still stands as a good introduction to the development of sociology. It is particularly valuable for its discussion of early American sociologists and the influences upon them.

Hughes H. Stuart, *Consciousness and Society.* New York: Random House, Vintage, 1961.

This book offers an excellent analysis of the European origins of the major classical theorists whose contributions to theory continue to dominate sociology.

Jencks, Christopher, and David Riesman, *The Academic Revolution.* New York: Doubleday, 1968.

This work is a sociological and historical analysis of American university education, contrasting mass and elitist conceptions of education. It also evaluates the role of the professional scholar and scientist in the university and in American society.

Kerr, Clark, *The Uses of the University.* Cambridge: Harvard University Press, 1963.

In a very perceptive, much criticized work, a former prominent university president analyzes the role of the university in contemporary education.

Madge, John, *The Origins of Scientific Sociology.* New York: The Free Press, 1962.

The particular value of this work is in its analysis of the works of prominent European and American sociologists from an emphasis on the emergence of empirical research styles in sociology.

Mills, C. Wright, *The Sociological Imagination.* New York: Oxford University Press, 1959.

Mills takes the cudgel to two extremes which he finds in sociology; the 'grand theory' of the Parsonians and the 'abstracted empiricism' of the rigid methodologists. He offers as an alternative and more sensitive sociology, one informed by what he calls the 'sociological imagination.'

CHAPTER TWELVE

Social Issues and Sociology in Canada

Dennis Forcese and Stephen Richer
Carleton University

European Origins

Systems of thought arise out of the social conditions confronting men at various periods in history. Sociology is no exception to this generalization. If we consider the social contexts in which sociology developed, two periods of dramatic change may be viewed as having decisively influenced sociology: (1) the French Revolution; and (2) the Industrial Revolution.

The French Revolution of 1789 left a society in a state of acute disorder; the old feudal establishment was in ruin while the new republican society was embryonic and strife-ridden. Many observers of the events in France responded to this issue of apparent social breakdown by attempting to isolate the conditions which would produce a stable society. For example, the man who has come to be known as 'the father of sociology,' Auguste Comte (1798-1857), speculated about the basis of collective consensus and an integrated society, anticipating an ultimate and stable stage of human social evolution (Comte, 1896). This concern with order was to become a major and persisting orientation of sociology as the discipline evolved.

It was manifest, for example, in much of the work of Emile Durkheim (1858-1917) in the late nineteenth and early twentieth centuries, particularly in his analyses of social integration and religion (Durkheim, 1897; 1912). In Germany, Ferdinand Toennies' (1855-1936) famous work, *Gemeinschaft und Gesellschaft,* first published in 1887, contrasted 'folk societies,' small and well-integrated, with urban-complex societies, large and heterogeneous (Toennies, 1940). Structure and order were also the objects of a good deal of Max Weber's (1864-1920) efforts, as witness his studies of social and economic organization, bureaucracy, and authority (Weber, 1946; 1947), works published contemporaneously with those of Durkheim.

Sociologists writing in the nineteenth century were also responding to the issues inherent in a different kind of revolution, the Industrial Revolution which was transforming England. Industrializing England inspired theories harking after stability, such as those of Herbert Spencer (1820-1903), but also theories inviting massive changes in society. The principal thinkers considering the societal ramifications of industrialization were Karl Marx (1818-1883) and Frederick Engels (1820-1895). Their theory of class conflict and social change was premised upon a view of the inherent instability of the relations between the workers, or *proletariat,* and the owners of productive property, the *bourgeoisie* (Marx, 1906). The attention directed by Marx and Engels to the links between the economy, conflict, and social change, gradually obliged sociologists to abandon their exclusive preoccupation with the conditions of order as opposed to the conditions of change. For example, as is now conventionally noted, Max Weber's analysis of the relationship between Calvinist ideology and capitalism was stimulated in no small part by Marxist writings. Weber analyzed the development of capitalism as an interactive function of economic and religious-ideological inputs, and produced what remains the outstanding contribution to the sociological literature dealing with social change (Weber, 1930; Forcese, 1968).

The issues which occupied these European sociologists set the frame for the sociology which has developed since. The dualities of order and change, integration and conflict, settled in as orienting foci for subsequent generations of sociologists. The hotbed of sociological growth was to shift to the United States, but the work of the Europeans would play an integral role.

American Sociology

In the twentieth century the growth of sociology has been characterized by American dominance. In the United States sociology gained a niche in rapidly expanding universities. In these universities American sociologists built upon the work of the Europeans, and produced the distinctive sociological models noted in the first chapter. Also in the United States, there developed a distinct tradition of empirical social research, rich in the techniques of data collection and analysis which were innovative elaborations of the tentative empirical efforts of the European antecedents (Madge, 1962). Yet, as we shall take up, it is very clear that while this sociological explosion was occurring in the United States, very little was happening in Canada.

Sociology as a modern academic discipline grew out of the 'boom and bust' character of the American nation. The huge, sprawling nation of immigrants was a potpourri of cultures congregated in the cauldrons of rapidly growing American cities. This 'melting pot' provided the inspiration and the natural laboratory for a unique breed of social reformers and researchers. Social problems such as urban poverty, delinquency, crime, family breakdown, and mental disorders stimulated enquiry into the social bases of such problems, just as a different kind of disorder stirred Comte and other Europeans a century and a half earlier. American social researchers became intent upon the problems of assimilation of immigrant peoples, and the anamoly of misery in the mythologized 'land of plenty.'

This is by no means to suggest that the early American sociologists were 'radicals' in the sense of being committed to wide-ranging social change. Some were very conservative indeed, and generally the commitment of sociologists to changed conditions was of the sort which might best be described as 'tinkering.' Any dedication to the amelioration of perceived social ills was within the unquestionable context of American democratic capitalism. Interest in social reform in many instances had its basis in religious sentiments, as is illustrated in the person of Albion W. Small of the University of Chicago, a minister and the fourth president of the American Sociological Association.

The perspective of American sociologists in the early twentieth century was reformist, and sometimes patronizing. Most definitely the perspective was not that of Marxist political critique and revolutionary sentiment. In fact, it was only much later in the century, after World War II, that a Marxist input became influential in the sociological literature, and then, ironically enough, not in that literature concerning social change, but rather, that dealing with social stratification.

Yet, however restrained and modest the personal desires of American sociologists for change, they did develop a style of enquiry which was clearly oriented to social issues. This emergent American sociology came initially to be dominated by sociologists at the University of Chicago. The 'Chicago School' established a style which depended upon a notion of the 'natural area' and its inhabitants. The social researcher participated in, literally lived, the life of his subjects, and observed their behavior. Work was done on issues such as patterns of urban growth (Park and Burgess, 1924), delinquent gangs (Thrasher, 1927), the migrant impoverished (Anderson, 1923), and slum districts (Zorbaugh, 1928; Wirth 1928), creating a style of humanistic observation which

Figure 1: Issues and Sociological Development

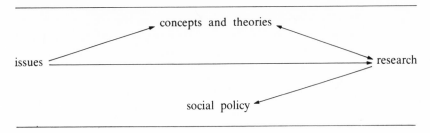

persists in its vividness to the present, some forty-five years later. The problems or social issues which concerned people at the time encouraged sociological research, giving rise to concepts and theories which in time precipitated additional research, and more recently, social policy, such as is illustrated in U.S. Supreme Court decisions regarding integration or education. (See Figure I.)

Also at the University of Chicago, there was emerging a group whose social psychology continues to influence contemporary sociological views on socialization and behavior. The 'symbolic interactionists,' principally represented by Charles Horton Cooley (Cooley, 1902; 1909) emphasized the manner in which people were influenced through the interactive process, with the primary group and the symbolic content of language and behavior shaping personality.

While the University of Chicago established its early ascendency, elsewhere in the United States sociology also was growing, although in a somewhat different direction. Already at Harvard University was the great Russian theorist, Pitirim Sorokin, whose work on social change is one of the most insightful pieces ever published (Sorokin, 1937). In addition, Talcott Parsons, returning from studies in Europe, was soon ensconced at Harvard University. He began to familiarize American sociologists with the work of European theorists such as Weber and Durkheim, translating and interpreting their works, and introducing and integrating into his own writing the European interest in social order (Parsons, 1937). Parsons, in the estimate of friend and foe alike, was to become the dominant figure in American sociology, and perhaps still is (Gouldner, 1970). His systems theory established a less issues-oriented and more abstract style of sociology than that characterizing the Chicago School.

Students of Parsonian sociology were influential in building up many other departments of sociology in the United States. Among those who were to become better known, Robert Merton worked at Columbia

University, Robin Williams at Cornell University, and Seymour Martin Lipset at the University of California at Berkeley.

The pre-World War II period also saw an influx into the United States of European sociologists. For example, Paul Lazarsfeld, who was to make enormous contributions to research techniques, joined the faculty at Columbia University; Reinhard Bendix, who would collaborate on much work with Lipset, went to the University of California at Berkeley. The American universities were not only producing an indigenous style of sociology, meshing classical European and contemporary American influences; they also were attracting and employing brilliant expatriates who were bringing their European training and experience to the United States.

Canadian Sociology

Singling out a few persons and themes, and telescoping seventy years of experience into a few paragraphs, obviously presents a very incomplete history of American sociology. The point which is to be taken from this capsule history is that in the United States sociology developed prodigiously, with distinct, prestigious schools producing research techniques, data, theory, and additional sociologists. The American university system, in its youth less fettered than European universities by traditional and rigid disciplinary boundaries and by budget restraints, was able to accomodate a new and quite unproven social science. This flexibility in the university structure was relatively absent in Canada: the universities and colleges of Anglophone Canada were bounded by traditional British definitions of appropriate university-based subjects, while in Quebec the concept of classical education and the involvement in education of the Roman Catholic Church discouraged the development of secular sociology. The Quebec environment was, however, to prove more congenial to the new social science than was English Canada.

Additionally, in Canada the highly visible social problems associated with huge immigrant populations and burgeoning cities were relatively absent. It is true that Canada was no less a nation of immigrants than the U.S.A., but on a much smaller scale. Moreover, Canada remained essentially a rural nation up to World War II, and the dispersed rural populations did not attract attention in the manner of concentrated urban settlements, where individuals were dependent upon others for production of subsistence items.

Within this context, sociology developed far more slowly in Canada than in the United States, did so differently, and did so subject to the influence of the styles established in the American universities. Where in the United States the early empirical enquiries were urban-centered and tended to focus upon deviance and social disorganization, in Canada, Anglophone and Francophone, rural rather than urban existence was the early object of empirical enquiry. This was appropriate enough given the relatively rural character of Canada: but it tended to render rather incongruous both the Chicago and Parsonian styles which were to be imported into Anglophone Canada, the one intent upon urban social problems and the other upon elaborate and abstract analysis of complex social systems. A better adaptation of alien models was to be realized in Quebec, where the rural-oriented style of the French sociologist Frédéric LePlay was to be adopted.

Sociology in English Canada

In Anglophone Canada there were three principal influences upon sociological development, or its relative absence: (1) the influence of the Protestant religions, or what has been called the 'social gospel' style (Morgan, 1969; Allen, 1971); (2) the influence of established academic history; and (3) the importation of the Chicago and Parsonian emphases.

SOCIAL GOSPEL

As in the United States, so in Canada early interest in social enquiry often derived from a Protestant ethic. Many churchmen found something which Europeans and Americans were beginning to call sociology a logical extension of their missionary and social service interests.

Early efforts in Anglophone Canada to establish formal instruction in sociology were associated with theological backgrounds and faculties. For example, when, in 1914, the University of Toronto inaugurated what was called the Department of Social Service, two people trained at the University of Chicago, one of them a Methodist minister, were hired as lecturers to deal with sociological matters (Allen, 1971: 12).

The religious influence was manifest in other university appointments in Toronto. For example, at Victoria College of the University of Toronto, J.W. MacMillan, a Doctor of Divinity from Manitoba, was hired to teach sociology (*The Yearbook of the Universities of the Empire*, 1925). Generally, across Anglophone Canada, graduates of the Wesley Theological College in Winnipeg were to have a remarkable impact on university-level instruction in sociology.

At McGill University in Montreal the clerical influence was as conspicuous as at Toronto. The Department of Sociology and Social Work, the first such department in Canada, was founded in 1922 by C.A. Dawson, a Baptist minister educated at the University of Chicago. He was outspokenly critical of many features of North American society and was an enthusiastic reformist. His reformist 'social work,' although an approximation of the research-oriented professional sociology developing in the United States, was an approach to social study thoroughly mediated by his religion. Thus, for example, Dawson frequently spoke in terms of 'redeeming men, and altering social conditions such as to favor such redemption.' (Allen, 1971: 289).

Elsewhere in Anglophone Canada, the presence of formal sociology was sporadic and slight. Where sociology was to be found, the Methodist and Baptist impact characteristic of Toronto and McGill cropped up time and time again. At the University of Manitoba, as early as 1910, a Master's degree in sociology was awarded, the only such degree until 1964. The thesis presented for this first graduate degree in sociology was characterized by an inescapable missionary tenor, apparent in its title: 'Are We Spoiling the Natives? An Inquiry into, and a Defence of the Policy of Educating the Subject Native Races of British South Africa.' Despite this early effort, until the 1960's sociology at the University of Manitoba was never represented by more than one instructor at a time, always under the auspices of some senior discipline such as economics, and later, anthropology.

Sociology was represented elsewhere in the province from an early date, but again, never grew to assert itself. Brandon College offered a course in sociology in 1910, and in 1911 sociology was taught at the United Church affiliated United College, now the University of Winnipeg. (Connor and Curtis, 1970: 4)

In British Columbia, there was not a full-time instructor in sociology until the 1930's. At that time a divinity graduate of the Wesley Theological College in Winnipeg was appointed to offer sociology courses (Connor and Curtis, 1970).

In the Maritimes, sociology was first offered at Acadia University in Nova Scotia, where courses in sociology were taught from 1908 (Connor and Curtis, 1970: 4). Dalhousie University in Halifax, Canada's first Anglophone university, did not offer sociology instruction until 1927. At that time they appointed S.H. Price, a minister and a graduate of Columbia University (*The Yearbook of the Universities of the Empire,* 1921). Additionally, at the Roman Catholic-affiliated St. Francis Xavier University in Antigonish, Nova Scotia, by 1928 some formal instruction in sociology was officially being offered.

SOCIAL HISTORY

A second influence upon social analysis and the development of sociology in Canada derived from the traditional academic discipline of history. In some sense, work in Canadian history provided a functional substitute for sociological analysis because there were no conspicuous and pressing social issues that demanded new styles of social analysis such as were developing in the United States. For example, the historian Arthur Lower, teaching at United College in Winnipeg for eighteen years and then for another twenty years at Queen's University in Kingston, is renowned for a style of social-historical analysis that in some part pre-empted sociological investigation, and certainly later influenced those persons working in sociology in English-speaking Canada, and particularly in Ontario.

Also contributing to the strength of social history in Canada was the historian and economist Harold Innis. Innis and Lower influenced one another and collaborated in some of their work (Lower, 1967: 144). The work of people like Lower and Innis was much more than historical narrative, but analysis of the socio-economic conditions of Canadian society, the subject so central to developing sociological theory.

Notably, Innis taught in the Department of Political Economy at the University of Toronto, the department under whose auspices early Canadian sociologists such as S.D. Clark worked. It seems clear that the prestigious influence of social history infiltrated the work of many Canadian scholars, including those committed to the new discipline of sociology. For example, much akin to this style was S.D. Clark's work on the impact of the Protestant religions on the development of Canada (Clark, 1948) and, perhaps more obviously, his major work appraising the rural nature of Canadian society as contrasted to urban America (Clark, 1942).

The affiliation at the University of Toronto of historians, political scientists, economists, and sociologists under the one department, Political Economy, probably made for a stimulating intellectual confluence. But it is quite clear that the junior affiliate, sociology, was thereby deterred from developing a distinctive approach. R.M. MacIver, the American sociologist and political scientist, taught in the University of Toronto Department of Political Economy from 1911 until 1927. Yet, as he was to put it forty years later, 'I had not been able to introduce sociology at Toronto.' (MacIver, 1968) Not until 1933 was there a sociology honors program at the University of Toronto, and not until 1939 did S.D. Clark acquire responsiblity for a semi-autonomous sociology section, still within the Department of Political Economy. Only in the 1960's was there a Department of Sociology at Toronto, S.D. Clark becoming its first chairman.

AMERICAN INFLUENCES

Meanwhile, at McGill University, sociology was having greater success in distinguishing itself from older disciplines. C.A. Dawson, from the time of his appointment in 1922, gradually developed a style of sociology that drew upon his training at the University of Chicago, the hotbed of sociological innovation in the United States. Dawson initiated and encouraged a series of community studies which were after the fashion of the Chicago urban sociologists Robert Park and Ernest Burgess. In the 1930's Dawson's department received a grant of $100,000 from the Rockefeller Foundation in the United States. This grant, the largest ever awarded to that time for social research in Canada, was intended for the study of unemployment and ethnic background, research clearly in the Chicago tradition.

Also from the University of Chicago, Everett Hughes joined Dawson's department at McGill in 1927. While at McGill University, Hughes was to write and publish the only work of Canadian sociological research generally recognized as a classic: *French Canada in Transition,* an analysis of social change in rural Quebec on the eve of urbanization (Hughes, 1943). By the time Hughes left for the United States in 1938, McGill University had a full-fledged Department of Sociology, the first in Canada.

While McGill University developed its sociology, (by the 1940's relatively free of religious ideologies and never as subject as Toronto to the social historical influence), at the University of Toronto development was lagging. Until the 1960's McGill and Toronto were generally conceded to be the uncontested Canadian leaders in sociology, the former in the Chicago tradition, and the latter, insofar as there was an American influence, in the Parsonian tradition. However, it was not until the post-World War II years that this Parsonian tint grew clearly distinguishable at Toronto. In this early post-war period there was an infusion of young American sociologists just beginning their careers.

Several students of Talcott Parsons at Harvard University and Robert Merton at Columbia University took up brief appointments at the University of Toronto, and set the Parsonian stamp upon the program. The Parsonian influence also appeared at the University of British Columbia in the person of Parsons' student, Kaspar Naegele, and at the University of Manitoba with the Harvard University graduate, John Dallyn.

To the University of Toronto there came Dennis Wrong, Ely Chinoy, and Seymour Martin Lipset, bringing with them the systems-functionalist perspectives dominant at Harvard and Columbia Universities. In 1950 Lipset published his Columbia University doctoral dissertation under the title *Agrarian Socialism* (Lipset, 1950), a book which remains a landmark contribution to political sociology, analyzing the development of the CCF party in Saskatchewan.

Given the pre-eminent status and influence of McGill University and the University of Toronto in English Canada, at least up to the late 1950's, it is fair to conclude that the dominant styles of professional sociology which crystallized in Anglophone Canada were modelled on the two dominant American styles: the Chicago School, and structural-functionalist systems theory. It is, of course, oversimplifying to characterize McGill University as exclusively oriented to Chicago-type sociology, and Toronto as exclusively structural-functionalist. By way of exception, for example, Aileen Ross, a student of the interactionist Herbert Blumer at the University of Chicago, spent several years on the faculty of the University of Toronto. Nevertheless, we think it fair to conclude that the emphases in the two departments were distinctly different and were characteristically along the lines which we have described.

Sociology in French Canada

In Quebec, American sociological inputs were also of some influence in Francophone universities, particularly Chicago sociology. But in addition, and initially, sociology gained a foothold in Francophone Quebec in a tradition of European enquiry, particularly that of the French sociologist LePlay. Also, the Roman Catholic Church, the counterpart of Protestant clerical influence in English Canada, fostered a sociological style in encouraging programs of social action and reform (Anand, 1973).

THE FAMILY AND THE WORKER

In nineteenth century France, Frédéric LePlay pioneered methodologically and theoretically in emphasizing the empirical study of the French working class, the rural and the urban worker, in the context of the basic social institution, the family (LePlay, 1855; 1870; 1871). LePlay and his students were particularly interested in the character and social problems of rural social organization, a subject which was relevant to Quebec agrarian society.

Léon Gérin was principally responsible for introducing the LePlay school to Quebec. His work and influence in introducing sociology were largely outside the confines of the university. Gérin never held a university appointment, but he published widely, more than ninety papers and a monograph (Carrier, 1960: 123-124).

Gérin had been formally educated in Quebec, but in 1885, a few months spent at the LePlay School of Social Science in Paris left their mark (Carrier, 1960). When he returned to Canada Gérin sought to apply the LePlay model to social analysis in Quebec. Much of his research was an effort to identify the typical family life of rural Quebec, from which basis he intended to generalize to the wider Quebec society.

His commitment was clearly to empirical social scientific investigation, but equally clearly, he was motivated by some reformist zeal (Anand, 1973). The quality of life in Quebec and the desire to improve this quality characterized Gérin's social science, and in that sense it was clearly issue-derived.

The literature of Gérin and his colleagues remained a rich source of material on rural Quebec, important for the sociology which eventually developed within the contexts of Quebec universities.

CATHOLIC SOCIAL ACTION

The major input into the formal sociology which developed within Francophone universities was the Catholic social action movement. Centered about the universities of Laval and to a lesser extent Montreal, the moral criticism of Roman Catholic social action groups was espoused within the church-dominated colleges. As was the case with the LePlay tradition, those working from the social action perspective were reacting to the issue of social change as Quebec society gradually found itself being transformed from a rural to an industrialized/urban society (Anand, 1973).

In the church-controlled colleges the early social analysis and Church doctrine became inextricably entwined and very distinct from the secular empirical tradition of Gérin. Fundamentally, the Catholic social action movement addressed itself to the social problems caused by a changing society, and to providing an alternative to socialist political action. From these beginnings a secular sociology was eventually to emerge (Anand, 1973).

In 1920 at the University of Montreal, the Jesuits founded l'Ecole des Sciences Sociales, Economiques et Politiques (Anand, 1973). From its inception l'Ecole offered a three-year program in social science, although it was not until twenty-two years later that it was to be granted full faculty status within the University of Montreal. In 1943, within l'Ecole, there was established a research institute for Catholic sociology, l'Institut de Sociologie. Until 1950 its director was Edward Montpetit, who had been a member of l'Ecole from 1920 (Anand, 1973).

At Laval University, there had been study seminars in sociology since 1920. But it was not until 1932 that there was some institutional recognition, when l'Ecole des Sciences Sociales was established. Its explicit purpose was to promote Catholic social doctrine (Anand, 1973). In 1938 it was reorganized within the Faculty of Philosophy and a Catholic priest, Georges-Henri Lévesque, was appointed director of the new school. Lévesque's background was in social and moral philosophy, and the other members of the faculty had similar backgrounds. But by

1943 when the school was upgraded to the status of an independent faculty, instructors were being appointed with training in American postgraduate programs in the social sciences, including formal training in sociology (Falardeau, 1961).

AMERICAN INFLUENCE

From 1943 the Faculty of Social Sciences at Laval University gradually increased its complement of full-time instructors with training in the social sciences rather than theology and philosophy (Fournier, 1973). This meant that the Catholic social action tenor was gradually eroded. Lévesque was directly responsible for this recruitment, for he systematically encouraged his students to go to the United States for postgraduate study, and then brought them home to appointments in his faculty. Thus, for example, in 1943 Jean-Charles Falardeau returned from studies in sociology at the University of Chicago, bringing Chicago-style sociology to Francophone universities. In addition, Martin Tremblay joined the faculty after studies at Harvard University (Anand, 1973: 66).

At the University of Montreal, in 1951 Philippe Garigue was appointed Dean of the Faculty of Social Sciences. Trained in social anthropology at the London School of Economics, Garigue was responsible for appointing persons whose commitment was to a professional and secular sociology, gradually dissipating the Church influence and doctrine. (Fournier, 1973)

Sociology in Canada Today

Presently in English and French Canada departments of sociology have increased in number and size. No university in Canada is without appointments in sociology. In Quebec, Francophone sociology is dominated by Laval and Montreal, although the newer University of Quebec engages in massive instruction in sociology. Among Anglophone universities, the early ascendency of McGill University and the University of Toronto is now rivalled by several major departments, many of which offer doctoral instruction. In Ontario, Frank Jones at McMaster University in Hamilton and John Porter at Carleton University in Ottawa established nuclei about which have grown up large and active departments offering advanced graduate degrees. Similarly, a major program of instruction has developed at York University in Toronto, and at the University of Waterloo.

In the other provinces, it is fair to say that the Anglophone universities have had difficulty in building stable complements of sociologists, but most now have extensive offerings in formal sociology. Particularly distinguished is a major department at the University of Alberta. In addition, doctoral programs are available at the University of British Columbia, Simon Fraser University, and the University of Saskatchewan.

This quantitative increase in sociology is cited because it has important implications for the character of sociology in Canada. It is generally the case, Francophone sociology excepted, that a sociology distinct from American traditions has yet to emerge in Canada. The new appointees to Canadian universities have been Americans or Canadians whose graduate training has been in the United States. That this rapid expansion has occurred only within the past ten years has meant that the sociological perspectives and to some considerable extent the topics examined by sociologists in Canada have not been distinguished from those in the United States. Probably they never should be completely divorced from American sociology, for Canada is inescapably a North American nation. But as distinctive schools of sociology emerged in the United States, so too one would anticipate the eventual emergence of distinctive orientations in English Canada.

In Quebec, sociology has a distinguishable style by virtue of origins less dependent upon American importations, and perhaps also because Quebec has been characterized by a more coherent and cohesive sense of identity or nationhood than has Anglophone Canada (Vallee and Whyte, 1968). French-speaking sociologists have differed from their English-speaking colleagues in their greater willingness to participate in non-university political activities, and in non-university professional activities in civil and political administrations. For example, data from a 1969 survey revealed that 82 per cent of Anglophone sociologists with membership in the Canadian Sociology and Anthropology Association were employed by universities, as contrasted to only 46 per cent of Francophone sociologists. Or to put the contrast differently, only 3 per cent of Anglophone sociologists as opposed to 23 per cent of Francophone sociologists reported government employment (Connor and Curtis, 1970).

Also, we are satisfied to suggest that French Canadian sociologists have been more effective social critics than have sociologists in English Canada. This style of activist French Canadian sociology seems to be perfectly in keeping with its social action origins, now translated into secular political and social interests, and generally an interest in the social issues related to changing Quebec society and Quebec nationalism. We are of the view that the greater issue-awareness of Francophone sociology has made for an identifiable style where the absence of such an awareness and the very recent expansion of the discipline in English Canada has militated against a distinctive sociology.

Also contributing to a distinctive French Canadian sociology is the lesser dependence upon graduates from American sociology programs. Many of the Francophone sociologists have advanced degrees from European universities, especially from France. But very notably, a high proportion of Quebec sociologists have earned their first and their advanced degrees at Quebec universities, principally Laval University. (Table I)

However, in addition to remarking upon the differing influences on Francophone and Anglophone sociology, and the more distinctive Francophone style, it is also worth noting that there is an indication of some convergence. There are some signs of a greater degree of interaction among French-speaking and English-speaking sociologists. As more research is carried out in Canada one would expect this intellectual exchange to increase.

In no small part the amount of contact across linguistic lines has increased because of the recent establishment of an institutional medium for such contact: the Canadian Sociology and Anthropology Association, founded in 1964. English Canadian sociologists, in keeping with the United States orientation of which we spoke earlier, have been proportionately well-represented in the American Sociological Assocation, where French Canadians have not (Connor and Curtis, 1970). The availability of a Canadian professional association has, if nothing else, at least permitted some ties among sociologists inside Canada, and generally a greater reciprocal familiarity with the work being done by Francophone and Anglophone sociologists.

Significantly, when previously the publications of Anglophone and Francophone sociologists tended not to reach beyond the linguistic barrier, a number of works in sociology have had an impact such as to rate as works of Canadian rather than French or English Canadian sociology. For example, in addition to Hughes' classic *French Canada in Transition* (1943), one can point to John Porter's *The Vertical Mosaic* (1965), Marcel Rioux and Yves Martin's *French-Canadian Society* (1964), John Seeley's *Crestwood Heights* (1956), Mildred Schwartz's *Public Opinion and Canadian Identity* (1967), Maurice Pinard's *The Rise of a Third Party* (1971), and Guy Rocher's *A General Introduction to Sociology* (1972).

Whether we will see a Canadian sociological style that effectively integrates the Francophone and Anglophone inputs is impossible to predict, despite the clear indications of communication to an extent which was not the case a decade ago. Should there be a convergence, it is our sincere hope that it consist at least in part of an action-issues orientation such as is already characteristic of sociology in Quebec. The

Table I: Origins of University Training of Sociologists in Canada, 1969*

Education	Mother Tongue			
	French (N = 35)		English (N = 185)	
	N	%	N	%
Location of Institution of B.A. or Equivalent				
French Canada	(23)	66	(—)	—
English Canada	(7)	14	(99)	54
United States	(—)	—	(69)	37
Other	(3)	9	(17)	9
No answer	(4)	11	(—)	—
Location of Institution of M.A.				
French Canada	(23)	66	(—)	—
English Canada	(3)	9	(71)	38
United States	(5)	14	(86)	47
Other	(1)	3	(10)	5
No answer	(3)	9	(18)	10
Location of Institution of Ph.D.				
French Canada	(9)	26	(—)	—
English Canada	(2)	6	(31)	17
United States	(7)	20	(108)	58
Other	(7)	20	(18)	10
No answer	(10)	28	(27)	15
Highest Degree Earned or Expected				
Master's	(9)	26	(28)	15
Doctorate	(26)	74	(157)	85

*Source: Data from a 1967 C.S.A.A. survey, provided by James Curtis. Additional analyses of these and related data are to be found in Connor and Curtis (1970). The data in Table I are cited by Anand (1973).

measure of our aspiration is illustrated by the very character of the text; for though we have endeavoured to present an objective explication of the content and interests of sociology, we have done so with repeated reference to social issues. In its very limited and imperfect way, perhaps such an emphasis will prove prophetic and point to the future character of sociology in Canada.

References

Allen, Richard, *The Social Passion: Religion and Social Reform in Canada 1914-1928.* Toronto: University of Toronto Press, 1971.

Anand, A., 'A Sociological History of French-Canadian Sociology: 1900-1970,' Master's thesis, Carleton University, Ottawa, 1973.

Anderson, Nels, *The Hobo.* Chicago: University of Chicago Press, 1923.

Carrier, H. *Le Sociologue Canadien Léon Gérin, 1863-1951: sa vie, son oeuvre, ses méthodes de recherche.* Cahiers de l'Institut Social Populaire, No. 5, Montreal, 1960.

Clark, S.D., *The Social Development of Canada.* Toronto: University of Toronto Press, 1942.

——, *Church and Sect in Canada.* Toronto: University of Toronto Press, 1948.

Comte, Auguste, *The Positive Philosophy of Auguste Comte,* (trans. by H. Martineau). London: Chapman, 1868.

Connor, Desmond, and James Curtis, *Sociology and Anthropology in Canada.* Montreal: C.S.A.A., 1970.

Cooley, Charles H., *Human Nature and the Social Order.* New York: Charles Scribner and Sons, 1902.

——, *Social Organization.* New York: Charles Scribner and Sons, 1909.

Durkheim, Emile, *Le suicide.* Paris: Alcan, 1897. In translation: (A. Spaulding, G. Simpson) *Suicide.* Glencoe, Ill.: The Free Press, 1951.

——, *Les formes élémentaires de la vie religieuse.* Paris: Alcan, 1912. In translation: (J. Swain) *The Elementary Forms of Religious Life.* London: George Allen and Unwin, 1915.

Falardeau, Jean C., 'La Sociologie au Canada,' *Third International Congress of Sociology,* V, (Amsterdam, 1956).

——, *The Rise of the Social Sciences in French Canada.* Quebec: Department of Cultural Affairs, 1961.

Forcese, Dennis, 'Capitalism, Calvinism, and Confusion: The Weberian Thesis Revisited,' *Sociological Analysis,* XXIX,4, 1968.

Fournier, Marcel, 'L'institutionnalisation des sciences sociales au Québec,' *Sociologie et Sociétés,* V (1973), 27-57.

Gouldner, Alvin, *The Coming Crisis of Western Sociology.* New York: Basic Books, 1970.

Harp, John, and James Curtis, 'A Note on the Role of Language Background,' in Connor and Curtis, *Sociology and Anthropology in Canada.* Montreal: C.S.A.A., 1970, pp. 33-44.

Hughes, Everett, *French Canada in Transition.* Chicago: University of Chicago Press, 1943.

——, 'Teaching as Fieldwork,' *The American Sociologist,* V (February, 1970), 13-18.

LePlay, Frédéric, *Les Ouvriers Européens.* Paris: Imprimerie Impériale, 1855.

——, *L'Organisation du Travail.* Tours: Mame, 1870.

——, *L'Organisation de la Famille.* Paris: Tequi, 1871.

Lipset, Seymour M., *Agrarian Socialism.* San Francisco: University of California Press, 1950.

Lower, Arthur, *My First Seventy-Five Years.* Toronto: Macmillan, 1967.

Madge, John, *The Origins of Scientific Sociology.* New York: The Free Press, 1962.

MacIver, Robert M., *As a Tale that is Told.* Chicago: University of Chicago Press, 1968.

Marx, Karl, *Capital,* (trans. by S. Moore and E. Areling). New York: Modern Library, 1906.

Morgan, J.G., 'The Development of Sociology and the Social Gospel in America,' *Sociological Analysis,* XXX (1969), 42-53.

Park, Robert, and Ernest Burgess, *Introduction to the Science of Sociology.* Chicago: University of Chicago Press, 1924.

Parsons, Talcott, *The Structure of Social Action.* New York: McGraw-Hill, 1937.

Rioux, Marcel, and Y. Martin, *French Canadian Society,* vol. 1. Toronto: McClelland and Stewart, 1964.

Rocher, Guy, *A General Introduction to Sociology.* Toronto: Macmillan, 1972.

Schwartz, Mildred, *Public Opinion and Canadian Identity.* Scarborough; Fitzhenry and Whiteside, 1967.

Seeley, John, R. Sim, and E. Loosley, *Crestwood Heights.* Toronto: University of Toronto Press, 1956.

Sorokin, P., *Social and Cultural Dynamics.* New York: American Book Co., 1937.

Spencer, Herbert, *Social Statics.* London: Appleton, 1865.

Toennies, Ferdinand, *Fundamental Concepts of Sociology* (trans. by C. Loomis). New York: American Book Co., 1940.

Thrasher, Frederick, *The Gang.* Chicago: University of Chicago Press, 1927.

Vallee, F.G., and Donald Whyte, 'Canadian Society: Trends and Perspectives,' in B. Blishen, *et.al.* (eds.), *Canadian Society* (3rd ed.). Toronto: Macmillan, 1968.

Weber, Max, *The Protestant Ethic and the Spirit of Capitalism,* (trans. by T. Parsons). London: George Allen and Unwin, 1930.

—, *From Max Weber: Essays in Sociology,* (trans. by H. Gerth and C.W. Mills). New York: Oxford University Press, 1946.

—, *The Theory of Social and Economic Organization,* (trans. by A. Henderson and T. Parsons). New York: Oxford University Press, 1947.

Wirth, Louis, *The Ghetto.* Chicago: University of Chicago Press, 1928.

Yearbook of the Universities of the Empire, 1925.

Zorbaugh, Harvey, *The Gold Coast and the Slum.* Chicago: University of Chicago Press, 1928.

CHAPTER THIRTEEN

Teaching and Learning Sociology

Rodney K.N. Crook
Carleton University

An interesting if somewhat alarming observation concerning sociologists is the very limited extent to which they typically apply their orientations, knowledge, and skills to the analysis of their own activities. Thus decisions concerning curriculum, teaching, and departmental organization generally appear to be made within the same everyday assumptions as those of non-sociologists. Yet the absence of such analysis, or even of a minimum of sociologically informed comment, renders the sociologist too often an apparently willing victim in the bureaucratization of university organization which has become so destructive of the university community.

This chapter is concerned with the relations between student and professor, and the social context within which sociology may best be approached by the student. The topic is hopefully of interest to both student and professor and is clearly one concerning which extreme variation of opinion may be expected. While the approach taken here is sociological in the sense that social processes and social context are considered throughout, it may be admitted at the outset, without apology, that the particular directions and interpretations express to a great extent the views of the writer. Should the reader find himself disagreeing, this is to be encouraged, since the effect can be to increase the level of awareness and stimulate debate. Such debate is overdue within universities generally, and specifically in departments of sociology.

The University in Modern Society

The major benefits involved in university experience at the undergraduate level are as follows. First, the university as an environment provides an opportunity to read widely and be exposed to a range of alternative interests, allowing the student to become more aware of himself, his society, and the world. Formal courses represent one, and only one, aspect of that exposure. Informal contacts with other students across a variety of interests are an important dimension which tends to be downplayed in many universities.

Within this general purpose the university experience involves learning and expressing a capacity for systematic thought by a degree of specialization and a reasonable mastery of a set of intellectual activities. Such systematization minimally involves the issue of consistency, the nature of evidence (no matter what the discipline), and the processes associated with gaining and using information for specific purposes. I shall have cause to return to these issues later in discussing problems of universities in general and of sociology programs in particular, in providing the type of environment suggested.

In a society dominated by technique, in which universities have become increasingly concerned with skill acquisition, the above comments no doubt have the appearance of being elitist, having little more than rhetorical significance in the context of contemporary North America, including Canada. On the contrary, however, it is my view that under immediate and future conditions, as opposed to the circumstances of the late 1950's and the 1960's, these traditional goals of the university are increasingly relevant and need to be returned to, not merely at the level of rhetoric but in organization and practice.

Under conditions of industrialization, the rapid expansion of higher education occurred in response to the need for technically trained manpower. Frequently, in this development in Canada and elsewhere, the universities resisted this specific job-focused conception of their place in the society, stressing rather the more traditional and diffuse conception of the university. Since the position explicitly taken in the present discussion involves a serious questioning of the specific linkage of university to technical training, it is well at the outset to clarify the basis of the argument, as I am unwilling to have the reader reject my argument on the mistaken grounds of a nostalgic conception of an elitist university system.

A comparative analysis of university enrollments in industrial societies indicates very clearly that the university is not the sole recruiting place for skilled manpower. However, my discussion is not immediately concerned with the analysis of alternative patterns of recruitment, but with the more general issue of the suitability or fit of modern assumptions under the somewhat different conditions posed precisely by technological change itself.

The very speed-up of technological change and its implications for the labor force, given the long period of time required for highly specific technical training, insures an increasing vulnerability of these skills to redundancy. What is, however, required under foreseeable future conditions is an educated and aware population in which the ability to absorb new information becomes ever more important. Such awareness and flexibility are unlikely to develop best under conditions of extreme specialization, but rather in the more general learning environment suggested here as appropriate to the university. Both intellectual breadth and the ability to use information systematically become far more relevant than the continued production of technicians.

Certainly the research functions of the university and related training in graduate studies will continue to express the requirement for highly specialized knowledge and skills. At the level of the undergraduate program, the type of flexibility suggested here becomes increasingly more appropriate the more advanced the level of technological development in the society. This in no way involves the necessity of maintaining elite entry. The basis for entry into university programs, degree and non-credit, can be expanded without in any way reducing the broad intellectual concerns which that environment should and, to some extent, does provide.

Just as the expansion of the university under conditions of rapid industrialization tends to be seen as a direct societal investment, so also, from the students' perspective, attendance at university has become equated with an investment of time and money. The possession of marketable skills has insured differential advantage in the stratification system, in both prestige and economic terms. Thus recruitment into the modern university occurs in considerable measure as a vehicle for personal mobility.

We are already beginning to see the problems which emerge when such expectations are thwarted due to the very rapidity of change noted above. The university will only move towards a re-establishment of social and intellectual concern when this connection with a system of unequal economic rewards changes. Again, it may be suggested that this extreme stress on individual mobility is a distinctly dated carry-over from nineteenth century liberal individualism. *The problem for Canada in the future concerns the better distribution of goods and services and not the mere increasing of opportunity for individuals to compete for unequal economic advantage.* The realities posed by an advanced technological society will tend to break down this direct connection of the university to upward mobility.

Canada as a society is now in a position to move concern away from continued economic expansion measured in terms of G.N.P. and to become much more concerned with issues of well-being or welfare. In other words, the focus is already beginning to shift towards the matter of providing all citizens with access to a way of life and not simply the opportunity to compete. In this movement the role of higher education is critically important and should move in the direction of increased awareness, involvement, and social and political concern. Thus, for entirely pragmatic reasons, the conception suggested here of the under-graduate experience in the university as an environment becomes entirely relevant for a consideration of the future. These opportunities in a variety of different forms can now be made available to Canadians on a far broader base than previously in moving away from the predominant specific concern with individual mobility.

My purpose is not to develop these lines of argument concerning the role of the university now or in the future. However, inasmuch as all issues related to teaching and learning in the university context are affected directly by these pressures, and the processes of unequal rates of change in the institutional structure of society, they are directly relevant to the discussion. If nothing more is achieved than to invite the reader to examine his own assumptions about the place of the university in society, and further, to consider the present situation as essentially short-run and unstable, it will be enough. The beginning of a genuinely sociological orientation involves the attempt to locate particular elements of social life in their societal context. Our discussion occurs precisely in the context of a changing university community in a rapidly changing society.

Sociology and the University Curriculum

I have suggested that university education should provide a context within which the student has the opportunity to develop *a better understanding of himself, of his society, and the world in which he lives.* In addition, the importance of a systematic coming-to-terms with a body of ideas has been stressed as a crucial aspect of higher education. How does sociology fit into this conception of the university experience?

Perhaps the first and most important possibility involved in the study of sociology is to become aware of the assumptions of one's own society, class, etc. *By promoting an understanding of the nature of the cognitive and evaluative framework within which one has been socialized and thus has come to comprehend experience of the world, sociology when properly taught can be a liberating experience which has the effect of increasing awareness of options, both societal and personal.*

This process occurs best through a comparative exposure to the organization of different societies, including at least some knowledge of one or more societies radically different from one's own. By locating the study of man firmly in a comparative perspective, it becomes more possible to be aware of and to question one's own frameworks for interpretation and action.

This continuous attempt to become critically aware of the social world and one's own place in it is not easy. Our own preferences, precisely because they are our own, are guideposts for us in locating ourselves in everyday life. When we do more than simply note with interest and possible amusement the rather esoteric customs of so-called 'primitive' societies, and in fact become more critically aware of our position in history, we are on the way not only to taking over a sociological perspective, but also to becoming educated people.

In teaching sociology, helping the student withhold judgment long enough to gain understanding of social action in its own terms rather than in his own moral terms, is both the first and most difficult objective. No amount of technical discussion, forced feeding of information, or more or less humorous story-telling will achieve this. Because we are modern men, and for the most part North American, we tend to view the world in liberal individualistic terms. Thus students have a built-in bias in the direction of psychologism and find the analysis of social structure and the social determinants of conduct to be in direct conflict with their own preconceptions of individual choice and freedom.

The decision as to how to achieve this result is extremely important for the professor. It is the more difficult because the optimal strategy depends so clearly on the particular situation of the individual student. Yet because it is the first objective, the place to manage the issue is in teaching the introductory course, which in most cases is by far the largest offered in the department. For the most part, the teaching methods are inadequate, in part because of the very difficulties of the situation, about which more will be said, but also because of lack of sensitivity and/or skill on the teacher's part.

Due to the extreme specialization of information, which is an aspect of the knowledge explosion in industrial societies, the integration of knowledge is both difficult and rare. Thus sociology programs tend to become increasingly specialized, involving the examination of highly circumscribed areas of investigation. An examination of most calendars of Canadian universities reveals a fairly similar package of courses dealing with specific issues and processes or segments of society. Courses proliferate in 'the family,' 'work,' 'religion,' 'socialization,' etc. Since the number of possible ways of dissecting social reality and the manner of apprehending that reality is infinitely large, there is clearly an endless supply of possible course titles.

The implication of this chapter needs to be clarified as it bears on the issue of course structure and sequence. First, it is apparent that any undergraduate program in sociology must be balanced by work in other fields. Among these, history (in particular Canadian history), philosophy, and other social sciences are important and should not be looked at as 'electives' but as the type of balance which allows a reasonable education in the social sciences. The distressing tendency for students to take much, if not most, of their work within sociology departments is indefensible on any grounds.

Moreover, a sociology program should be more than merely the accumulation of assorted and discrete credits. Indeed it is only as this occurs that specific information and issues can be treated at other than a descriptive and simplistic level. Unlike many natural science fields in which a rather clear set of assumptions are expected in advanced courses, i.e., there is a progression towards more complex analysis, sociology programs do not typically involve such a development. This is in part due to the absence, or at least scarcity, of generally agreed assumptions, leading to specialization at the level of information, without integration or synthesis.

Most undergraduate programs pay at least lip service to such integration by emphasizing and, in most cases, insisting on a theory course and frequently a course in research methods. Once again, however, the integration is too often problematic. Both theory and methods courses provide at best a bridging between information, interpretation, and implication. Such courses are not distinct bodies of knowledge which must be managed but are a way of providing a focus for the student's own interest in modern society. Once again, the quality of teaching is the critical factor in allowing this integration to occur. Both theory and method should be woven into the fabric of sociology courses at all levels, from the introductory course onwards.

If we are to understand human social action, it is essential to view social organization in comparative terms. It has become common parlance to distinguish 'humanistic' from 'scientific' sociology. This is an unfortunate distinction which when followed in the design of curriculum must of necessity harm the overall effectiveness of sociology programs. *Sociology is certainly a humanistic discipline in the sense that it is concerned with man and with human possibilities. This does not, however, mean that within such a focus of concern we are not faced with issues requiring systematization, precision, and comparison.* When humanism becomes the guise for lack of systematization or evidence, it is bankrupt.

Similarly, when we forget that our focus is man and social reality, due to over-concern with precision and technique, it is unlikely that our analysis will take us far. Teaching and learning sociology is a delicate balance of systematic comparison and social concern. At best it is intellectually exciting and difficult. At worst it is trivial or simply a technical exercise.

A further issue which occurs frequently is the problem of 'relevance.' I trust that the implications of the present discussion are apparent. A sociology which is intellectually alive involves social concern. The tendency to polarize intellectual concerns with practical issues is in all respects unfortunate. However, unless one is satisfied merely to describe any social situation, e.g., poverty or drug abuse, it is necessary to get beyond the 'facts.' Only as we begin to understand such events within a more general context, i.e., to approach their analysis sociologically, is it possible to evaluate alternative possibilities for action. Social policy in this sense requires sociological analysis in order to have any reasonable confidence concerning the probability of reaching desired ends. Without this analysis, there is a very real danger of blunting action through the manipulation of rhetoric.

Without doubt the opposite dangers are important. Sociological research too often can be used as a delaying tactic to avoid change. It is also the case that the activity of sociology itself tends to replace the initial concern which started the enquiry. Enough has been said to indicate my distaste for such a view of the field. The point remains, however, that *only as a specific issue or set of issues are placed in their social context through systematic analysis (itself necessarily involving both theoretical and methodological issues) is it at all possible to change the situation in an effective way*. This is the position taken throughout this volume.

Perhaps in this context it is appropriate to indicate a number of possible mistakes in teaching undergraduate sociology. First, there is what might be called 'sociology as exposé.' Within this approach a cynical unveiling of interests, conflicts, manipulation, and pettiness is presented in the name of objectivity. A favorite target tends to be organized religion. Yet one need not be a sociologist to know that for some people in any classroom religion is important, and an uncritical attack can simply be damaging. Sociology is not best pursued as pseudo-intellectual voyeurism, and people whose identities are so unstable as to require continuous gratification in the form of shock are hardly likely to generate, if only by example, the type of objectivity we seek to develop. Of course, a joke at the frailty of man can assist the teaching process. When it becomes sociology through smear and smut, it is simply harmful.

Another strategy might best be termed 'sociology as fun.' In this strategy, incidents and events in the student's experience are discussed with the possible addition of a few semi-technical terms such as 'role' and 'norm.' Little attempt at a comparative framework is typically made, the stress being essentially descriptive and simplistic. Frequently, the lecturer takes the position that discussion and group projects with a little narrative commentary on his part constitute the best delivery technique.

At the opposite end is the 'hard science' view. In this case, the student is presented with research procedures very early on, and empirical studies of a variety of types become the focus of the course. This approach seeks to be thoroughly 'professional' with all questions of social concern and general intellectual implication safely dismissed in the name of value neutrality. The objective apparently is to get the student as quickly as possible to start to frame hypotheses and the research designs appropriate for their testing.

Interestingly enough, all three strategies exhibit some similar weaknesses. All are anti-intellectual; all are ahistorical; and all are likely to kill off the better and more critically oriented student. Of the three, the last tends at least to be relatively systematic and has the possible, if dubious, virtue of representing most realistically the type of activity likely to be encountered in subsequent courses in many sociology programs.

Yet I have suggested that the immediate objective is to increase the critical awareness of the student, leading him to a better appreciation of his own situation, his society, and the nature of social life. The premature development of pseudo-objectivity by middle class professors teaching middle class students may produce people who are able to handle techniques and thus later enter the labor force in a bureaucratic information-gathering role. It has little to do with the way in which I am suggesting that universities should operate, and indeed, makes only a negative contribution to the university as an intellectually stimulating environment.

Educated and aware people are not neutral, nor should they be. *The meaning of objectivity concerns the handling of information, not the issue of what is worth examining.* The sheer triviality of much contemporary sociology arises from no other reason than intellectual barrenness. There is, in the development of sociology, a critical tradition which has concerned itself with understanding modern society, not simply for reasons of science but because that understanding is a matter of urgent human concern. I am firmly of the opinion that we need to have and to convey that concern and not merely nihilism. Technique does not replace intellectual and social concern but rather needs to be seen clearly as the process of adequately arriving at knowledge.

Sociology has an important place in the curriculum of the modern university, assuming that it is viewed in comparative and historical terms. The field has a contribution to make not only to the education of those students specializing in the social sciences, but as an elective for students in the humanities and natural sciences. Where it is presented in a non-critical, ahistorical and ethnocentric way, through simple description, mere technique, or rhetoric, sociology is only damaging to the university as an intellectual community, and one can have the gravest doubts about its position within the curriculum.* Bad sociology is symptomatic of a naive and intellectually and humanly bankrupt society.

The Student

Students are crucial to the life of the university not merely in the most obvious sense of the financing of Canadian universities, but also because they are the *raison d'être* for many components of university activity. It is thus important to understand the social situation of the student within the university and the relation that involvement has to his other activities, both concurrent and also his life chances. It is similarly important to consider the prior socialization of the student to understand the orientations he brings with him into the university environment which directly affect his expectations and receptivity to that environment.

For full-time students viewing their university experience as the final or at least penultimate stage of their formal education, the university becomes the symbol of a variety of more generalized discontents arising from the situation of young adults in the society. The payment of fees insures that the dependency of many students in relation to their parents continues through the university years, at a period when all possible reasons dictate that the student should be weaned from such dependency and thus be able to take responsibility for his own life. All remarks in this chapter are predicated on the willingness of the university to regard the student as an adult and a reciprocal expectation that the student is able to act in these terms. Again it is apparent on the most obvious sociological grounds that the capacity and willingness to act in this way depend precisely on the more general social context and the more general preparedness of others — parents, teachers, etc. — to release responsibility and autonomy to the student.

*Without considering the arguments directly, I refer the reader to George Grant's essay on 'The University Curriculum' in his *Technology and Empire.* (Toronto: House of Anansi, 1969). Should my own position on the place of sociology appear somewhat critical to many readers, Grant's analysis will serve to place it more clearly as a moderate defense of what is too often intellectually indefensible.

The pressures have always been present for the university to act as an extension of the parent, and it follows clearly from the above comments that any such pressures should be resisted. Yet the rules governing grants and loans serve to maintain paternalism. Similarly, the rapid increase in the size of university administration in the recent past has served to make personal contact more difficult, while the proliferation of rules and the processing of students in keeping with the requirements of overly bureaucratized systems places the student too often in the role of supplicant and dependent rather than an adult autonomous member of a university community. One obvious example is found in the usual registration procedures at most universities, which become encounters with an unreceptive system and serve to alienate the student. It is only as encounters with the university in terms of application, registration, and the details of university life are such as to encourage involvement that the student is likely to move towards the type of further contact with faculty which is essential in maintaining the university as a community. It is a further expression of the over-emphasis of technique and means, and the fundamental misunderstanding of efficiency which has become so problematic in all modern societies, that overbureaucratization has become a galloping sickness in the university.

The student who will get most from the university is likely to be one who makes a decision that indeed he wishes to be in that environment. The student who is in the university by default or because of parental pressure is likely to view the experience in detached terms as a set of requirements which must be met. When the university, because of its own incapacity, encourages this view by providing little in the way of intellectually stimulating and rewarding experiences for the student, the result is an apathetic pursuit of performance minima with a stress on survival.

Part of the difficulty of the student at the present time concerns the very real uncertainty with respect to career possibilities. The university as a clear route to job security and upward mobility is under question, due, if nothing else, to the mounting evidence of the difficulty encountered by highly trained people in many fields in obtaining employment. I have already noted this issue when considering the role of the university under conditions of rapid technological and social change. Yet it has been suggested that it is exactly under these conditions that the university can re-establish the importance of a previously elite tradition of general education and intellectual concern.

The direct route from high school to university has serious difficulties quite apart from the gap between career expectations and the realities of the labor market. Despite modern communications media, the typical student has had access to few social roles in the sense of actually participating in a range of social situations and experiencing what is involved in taking responsibility, in making compromises, and generally coming to terms with the range of impingements of social reality. To take advantage of the university environment to the full, even given the weaknesses within the university itself, such maturity is vitally necessary.

So it is often the case that the student who comes to the university late, or who returns after a period away from formal education, can most successfully manage the problematic elements of the university and take better advantage of the real resources which are available to him. Because his expectations tend to be more realistic and he has made a real choice in entering the role, such a student is able to adapt and work effectively. When dealing with sociology as a field of study, the prior social experience of the student, and not only his intellectual ability, plays an important part.

Another category of undergraduate is the extension or part-time student who continues to hold a position in the labor force while adding to his credits towards a degree. Such students tend to have the great advantage of independence and motivation. Without any doubt, however, their partial participation tends to rule out involvement in the university community to any great extent, apart from attendance at classes. I may say, if only to avoid possible misunderstanding, that the *the opening up of the university via extension programs has been extremely important in serving at least in part to mitigate against the inegalitarianism involved in enrollment in full-time undergraduate programs.*

In thinking about the future, I have stressed the importance of the university as an intellectual community and not merely as a place for technical training. Part of our present difficulty would be resolved by removing *university fees,* which *presently serve to maintain barriers against economically disadvantaged young people.* This could well be accompanied by a general raising of the level of performance expected, not in the sense of more coverage, but rather in the direction of systematization and creativity.

We need to expect more students to move in and out of the university, possibly over an extended period. Many of those students who presently take their work entirely through extension can be encouraged to return to full-time involvement in the university for periods of time, perhaps varying from a few weeks to a year.

This degree of flexibility with respect to the university needs to occur and can be better achieved when we are able to see the university as a social resource. Thus instead of viewing the extension student as paying via fees for the right to claim either promotion or salary increments, we need to see him as seeking to increase both his technical competence and also his level of general awareness. In doing this, it may readily be seen as in the interests of the student and the more general social good, and thus worth making available without serious financial or career costs. In this way, the university can come to play a far more significant role in the life of the community as people move into it as full members at various stages of their life span. These remarks apply not only to credit courses involving work towards a degree but also to allowing very rapid expansion of the university in non-credit areas.

There is little doubt that a combination of factors negatively affects the student's potential receptivity to the university as a significant experience. Anticipatory socialization, generalized discontent, future uncertainties, and the bureaucratic organization of the university itself have been mentioned. In addition, a number of related points may be raised. The very freedom to select widely within available courses, which may be defended strongly on other grounds, has the consequence of isolating the student from a cohort of others in the same life situation. The size and scale of the university organization typically compound this problem.

It is very noticeable that where new programs are developing or where clearly defined programs are relatively small, the involvement with a student cohort provides numerous advantages. First, the cohorts at more advanced stages act as agents of socialization providing information, strategies, and myths which give a sense of involvement in a social unit. Secondly, the cohort itself serves as a basis for membership and solidarity providing benefits at all levels, including the informal intellectual inputs which are so essential in the university experience at its best. The effect of such social relationships is apparent in terms of student academic performance.

In such defined programs, the student also has the opportunity to enter into rather diffuse relationships with professors, extending through time. Again this has the consequence of allowing the emergence of reciprocal trust and concern and increases the likelihood of the professor becoming a significant role model, itself a key element in the emergence and stabilization of genuinely intellectual and social concerns. It is a further commentary on the alienating consequences of liberal individualism that in the name of individual freedom of choice, precisely the social context for the development of interest, involvement, and in the end stable identity itself is undermined.

The student power movement of recent times, although frequently involving a rather naive conception of power, had the real virtue of insisting on the student's involvement in the university community. Such involvement is hardly likely to occur from token membership in university committees, as many activists have discovered. Involvement develops in a social context, as do almost all political and intellectual concerns. The conflict or labor-management model applied to the relationship of students and professors is essentially a bad analogy. It is to problems of size, scale, and bureaucracy that we need to look in analyzing the apathy of students, not to their lack of representation on university senates and department boards.

The increase in bureaucratic rules and procedures is to be understood not so much as a structural necessity but as an increasingly common strategy of social control. It is because diffuse social relationships, with their complexity and taken-for-granted understandings of role shifts, have been undermined that formalization becomes inevitable. Yet the greater the extent of formalization within the university, the greater both the reliance on such rules and the perceived inevitability of such organizational strategies, hence the proliferation of further rules. Yet at each stage the consequence is to undermine further diffuse ties, trust, and commitment, resulting in the further necessity of external controls. As rules replace responsibility so the maintenance of any community becomes tenuous. So also, the structural possibilities for identification and role modelling are removed, increasing the apathy and minimal performance of the student.

My comments on the role of the student are pursued in the subsequent consideration of evaluation and the evaluation of professors. Where the student does not feel a part of an academic community, he should make every effort to approach professors and to discuss both his immediate course work and also matters which are of concern to him. If such efforts do not succeed, i.e., when the faculty prove unresponsive, the student has a right to feel angry and misled. Similarly, when encounters with the university administration become totally counter-productive, the student should complain, since the only justification for the array of administrative staff is in increasing the level of university services. This implies that the university bureaucracy exists to serve the academic community and not to render the continuation of that community problematic.

The Professor

People rarely become university professors because of a dedication to, or even an interest in teaching. The usual process involves increasing specialization of academic interest in the undergraduate years, moving on to graduate programs and culminating in the degree of Ph.D. The research for that degree will tend to be highly specialized. Apart from some exposure in a teaching assistant capacity (and many of the very best graduate students do not have that experience because of the rules governing allocation of funds), the student becomes professor without knowledge or experience of teaching.

Assuming more or less accurately that professors are in most respects like other members of the society (an assumption the reader may wish to question for a variety of reasons) it is apparent that real pressures are exerted which are little different from those operating in other occupational roles. Given the system of academic ranks and salary gradations, *the upward mobility of the professor, both within any given university and also his visibility and opportunities for movement between universities, hinges far more on research output and publication than on other criteria.* Thus in the specific terms of career mobility, the most likely strategy will be to use the maximum of energy in continuing the specialized research work on which the doctorate was granted, viewing other activities as both less important, less rewarding, and indeed, as the routine which has to be managed.

In addition to the problem of pressure — what is termed in American universities 'publish or perish' — the highly specialized nature of many research projects yields quick and often voluminous payoff without any necessary intellectual significance. The further process of specialization at all levels of the education system serves to reduce the probability of the development of general intellectual concerns, including the issues of the meaning and social implication of the research work itself. In other words, the pressures operate towards the development of a technocratic focus which either denies the importance of intellectual concerns or views their analysis as mere dilettantism.

It is thus unfortunate that *in seeking to establish himself securely, an academic may tend to view teaching as a strategy only when his abilities are not particularly strong, or if for other reasons he does not 'inhabit' the prevalent myths of his colleagues.* As a generalization, I would claim that unless an academic has very real intellectual abilities, he simply is not equipped to be a good teacher within the university system. That the teaching 'route' is on occasion used by marginally able people tells us more about the unfortunate state of university instruction than anything else.

However, if in looking back at the 'track record' of an academic, we are able to find evidence of a continuing flow of really good students for whom he has been a significant influence, we have reason to view claims to teaching interest and ability in a different light. For the capacity to generate interest and indeed a continuing commitment to research and intellectual concerns among others is a crucial and rare skill which needs recognition.

The professor of sociology is one case of the more general problem of the professional in an organization. He will tend to have affiliation with the Canadian Sociology and Anthropology Association and also with the American Sociological Association. In the 1960's these associations, taking their impetus from the American scene, have moved towards 'professionalization.' What was previously a Learned Society becomes viewed as a professional association. Graduate training in sociology thus tends to be regarded on this continent as 'professional socialization.' Yet any minimally competent sociologist would have difficulty in justifying the term 'professional' when applied to his activities. Among other things, a professional is one who acts in the public interest via the exercise of some specific skills. It would be naive or nonsensical to claim that sociologists do, or indeed should, act in this way. At the same time, the trend has been to narrow the conception of diffuse social responsibilities involved in holding a university appointment. As noted at the outset, the professor has become a willing victim in the bureaucratization of the universities during the last decade.

A further professional association is the Canadian Association of University Teachers, which again by its very selection of a label allows a definition of its members' activities which is at least problematic. If the university is to be viewed as an environment, the professor is primarily a resource person vis-à-vis the student. The term 'teaching' suggests too clearly the sort of unimaginative 'out of the textbook' and 'into your notebook' mediocrity which typifies the alienated and defeatist performance in many high schools. It leads without much difficulty to the view that university professors should spend much of their time in formal classroom situations and should possibly take instruction from other 'professionals' on teaching technique. This would be the gravest misunderstanding both of the university, and indeed, of the relationship of professor to student.

Yet the apparent willingness with which academics have given up a conception of the generalized and diffuse responsibilities which are the opposite side of the privileges enjoyed by them has led in self-defeating directions. Where faculty define their reponsibilities to undergraduates in the narrowest terms, i.e., regularly meeting their classes, they thereby refuse to make themselves available for the time-consuming business of meeting students outside the classroom. Yet, it is in these other contexts of interaction that a crucial part of the transfer of attitudes, interest, and intellectual concern occurs. Although it is this which makes the university environment significantly different from high schools and other 'plants,' it is the type of underlife of a good department which is hard to measure.

Because of the difficulty of measurement, such diffuse relationships are not amenable to the use of bureaucratic controls, or alternatively to the use of specific rewards. One only discovers that the intellectual life has gone from a university by the generalized apathy of the members and the proliferation of rules which replace commitment by self-defeating regulations governing minimum performance along measurable dimensions.

In commenting on the student situation, I suggested that students who have had the opportunity to enter other social roles are frequently able to deal with the subject matter of sociology more easily than those entering the university directly from high schools. It is similarly the case that *in becoming a sociologist, the experience of numerous social situations of possibly quite different types can be most useful.* This should not be taken as a simplistic formula for sociological training but rather as an observation concerning the relationship of theoretical knowledge to experience. Certainly there is every reason to suppose that periodic movement of personnel between roles in a complex modern society might serve to mitigate against some of the integrative problems of such societies. It would without doubt serve to reduce the tendency for specialization and technique to replace social concern.*

Perhaps the most useful way to look at the university and within it, the department, is in terms of a set of interrelated interests and talents; and it is to the balance between them that one must look when judging the quality of the environment. At the extremes there will be a small number of people defined exclusively in terms of contributions such as research output. One mechanism for handling such appointments is the title 'Research Professor.' Most members of a department will tend to mix, more or less successfully, teaching, research, and general administrative activities. Although it is not of direct concern in this context, it may be noted that the administration of a program is extremely important in mapping out and maintaining the context within which the various aspects of day-to-day life in a department occur. It would be entirely in keeping with the present discussion to view administration by fiat, by default, or by memo to be three strategies which are each likely to be harmful to environmental quality.

In discussing evaluation, I shall suggest the importance of shared meanings. However, in this context it can be noted that departments which work well tend to have a number of reasonably senior academics who share common understandings and who thus are able to manage

---

*The reader will no doubt see similarities between this suggestion and Maoist views relative to the problems of bureaucracy and class interest. Karl Mannheim discussed the uprootedness of the intellectual and his involvement in roles and assumptions of his society at some length. See, e.g., Karl Mannheim, *Ideology and Utopia*, translated by Louis Wirth and Edward Shils, (first published 1936, paperback edition, New York: Harcourt, Brace, and Co.), pp. 153-163 in particular.

situations, new exigencies, and crises in a controlled way. Without such people any department will be unstable, involved in the worst forms of interpersonal conflict, and necessarily a bad environment for students. At its worst, this type of bad tension management involves the students themselves. This core in any department is critical in the socialization of new professors who themselves take over the same skills. In the case of sociology in Canada, the very rapid expansion of the field has meant that there is a scarcity of such experienced academics, and the instability of many departments is rooted in this problem. Clearly it is preferable that they should be experienced in the Canadian academic system with its distinctive blending of American and European patterns.

I have referred on a number of occasions to the importance of diffuse ties and the common more or less taken-for-granted understandings which constitute the basis for an academic community. The rapid expansion of university positions in sociology during the last decade has posed serious problems with respect to these understandings. Academics rightly are concerned about the principle of 'academic freedom' without always clarifying the issues to which that freedom has direct relevance. Thus grading and relationships with students tend on occasion to be viewed as entirely within the individual instructor's freedom of movement. But this is to misunderstand the principle of academic freedom in the name of naive anarchy. Academic standards are indeed matters of mutual concern, involving the university community in general.

Through applying elementary sociological reasoning to the issue, it can readily be noted that such bases of conflict are not merely philosophical differences but represent significant differences of socialization. Under conditions of slow growth, new faculty members, viewed for immediate purposes as recruits into a role, are involved in complex and diffuse relationships within which they locate their own position on appropriate relationships with students and academic standards. Under such conditions there exists a basis for exposure to the wide range of inter-related issues, strategies, and consequences involved in the role of professor. Where the number of recruits increases dramatically, representing great heterogeneity of background, the capacity of any department successfully to absorb new members is threatened. In this situation, the currency of academic freedom may be debased to mean freedom of the individual academic to ignore the minimal social implications of his conduct. Yet I have already noted that where unwritten and diffuse understandings break down, the consequence is necessarily an increase in bureaucratic social control.

The reader might wish to reject my comments as representing an essentially conservative ideology defended by the use of an integrationist perspective on social organization. However, nothing could be further from the truth. Conflict of interest is endemic to social life. The issue is concerned with the mechanisms available to the university as an organization to manage such conflicts, not with the denial of their existence. The reiteration of individual rights without reference to social context and complexity, in a paradoxical way insures only the tyranny of faceless bureaucratic universalism.

The capacity to develop interest and to encourage focused intellectual concern in others is critically important. As a socially useful skill, it is difficult to measure and thus to reward in the more obvious ways. I have noted that the pressures operating within the university tend to down-play this process. Yet this capacity and the provision of a social environment for its development are critical to the intellectual vitality of a university, and beyond to the wider society. People possessing such skills, together with the few who make major intellectual-scientific contributions in their own right, are what the academic role in the university and society is all about.

Grading and Evaluation

One of the most basic lessons to be learned from sociological analysis is that one needs to be constantly aware of what are termed 'the unantici-pated consequences of social action.' It is thus the hallmark of good sociological thought that one seeks to establish what the probable consequences might be of any specific course of action or set of actions, given the inter-relationships which make up the structure of a society or segments of society.

It is fashionable at the present time to argue in the direction of the removal of 'barriers' to learning in the form of examinations, systems of graded evaluation, and formal structures of authority. In seeking to swim against the tide, I ask only that the reader consider the issues and not merely indulge in the rhetoric of the moment.

Under ideal social conditions, there is little doubt that people who are motivated to learn are likely to do so best under conditions which facilitate flexibility with respect to problem definition, approach, and speed and rhythm of development. There exist within universities and outside them social situations in which such 'free' and unstructured approaches are in operation. It is, for example, a common observation that one often learns more over a cup of coffee or a beer than in a formal classroom or lecture theatre situation. My subsequent comments need to be placed firmly in the context of total support for such multi-level contacts. As noted in earlier discussion, the university as an environment should, and to varying degrees does, provide such possibilities.

Faculty and students in a university constitute an intellectual community in which a fundamental equality exists and in which one is free to give prestige to intellectual excellence. One unfortunate implication of the tendency to see the university in entirely job-training and pragmatic terms is that the environment becomes stripped of such contexts and opportunities. Thus a critically important part of the socialization of the student should be to draw him into this community and make it alive and meaningful for him. The fact that this so often does not occur is a total loss to the life, significance, and continuity of the university as a community. In defining the role of the university, it is not too fanciful to believe that the university in the form of its members, student and faculty, can and does make a continuing contribution to the wider community through providing formal and informal situations in which their skills as resource persons can be used. Again the fact that these activities do not occur as frequently and naturally as one would wish leads only to the conclusion that more critical attention needs to be directed towards them.

However, universities are not only environments for the members and indeed the community at large to draw on as necessary. The fact is that universities play multiple roles vis-à-vis the society. The existence of a highly trained manpower pool is essential in any modern society, and the university together with other organizations is involved precisely in the development of such skills. I repeat the earlier point that there has been an unfortunate tendency for other elements of the university environment to be less prevalent and indeed to be ignored, but nevertheless the reality of skill acquisition is unquestionable. Modern societies devote a significant amount of budgetary capacity to ensuring the continued supply of trained manpower.

While it is relatively easier to measure expertise in some areas than others, I take it as given that highly trained people, not only in the most obvious technological skills, have a significant social contribution to make. It has further been argued that even where a direct connection between the specific skills and their application is hardest to arrive at, the very fact of skill acquisition indicates, at least hopefully, the capacity of the person for rapid takeover of new information in areas of problem solving completely unrelated to formal content of program. However, in making this point, it needs to be reaffirmed that it is because of training in systematization, consistency, and evidence that such a carry-over occurs. In other words, where training involves simple technical mastery or memorization, there is no reason to expect the development of a capacity for easy transfer of skill. It is, of course, this view of the university which has been continuously stressed throughout this discussion.

Once information and skills are seen not only as a prerogative of individuals but as a relatively scarce social resource, the matter becomes clearer. The society's 'investment' (in any modern state, not merely capitalist) necessarily involves the selection of those persons who will learn such skills. *Since the costs of skill acquisition are significantly higher than the fees paid in Canadian universities, the effect is clearly to provide a subsidy for all students engaging in higher education.* For easy comparison, we may contrast the situation with that in Britain, where a much smaller percentage of persons receives higher education and does not pay fees in most cases. To argue for ease of entry, e.g., lowering of achievement standards, and further to hold that grading is inappropriate, is in fact to support the establishment and maintenance of a new elite, educated at societal expense, who have no formal obligation to exhibit competence.

In any society, certification of skill increases the likelihood of exercising responsibility in the occupational structure even where the actual knowledge and skill is not itself used directly in that subsequent role. There is thus a minimal obligation to insure that a reasonable level of competence has been attained and exhibited. The removal of formal evaluation from the university could only have the consequence of certifying to nonexistent skills. Such a view of the management of scarce resources in any society is not only self-defeating, it is self-evidently morally bankrupt.

Now the reader may object at this time that in a 'good' society, such differentiation of skill would not be necessary. He might further argue that the university should not contribute to the 'military-industrial complex' or the equivalent. Yet the argument posed here does not hinge on the differential rewards which university education typically opens up. In other words, I am not posing the dicussion in terms of the Davis-Moore view of social stratification in which it is held that unequal rewards are necessary to maintain motivation to enter the more difficult and complex roles in the society. I am merely concerned to show that under any social conditions, ideal or otherwise, there has to be a reasonable probability that the certification of skill accords with the reality of the situation. Otherwise one is left with a society of confidence tricksters who appear to be, and indeed are certified to be, what they in fact are not. Such a problem is in reality far more serious than the more obvious problems of differential reward in a capitalist social system.

An example may serve at this stage. When in need of medical assistance, my first choice would be a physician or other who possesses specific skills and who is dedicated, i.e., is motivated by considerations other than simple economic reward. My second choice would be a person possessing appropriate skills who is not dedicated, and a poor third choice, a person who may well be dedicated (or may not) who has not been required to prove skills at any stage. To follow the medical example a little further, I am suggesting that while there is no doubt that there should be more persons receiving medical training, and while the present rates of remuneration of the profession appear problematic, no possible changes in these areas affect the issue of the necessity of proving competence.

One possible basis for confusion concerns the issue of equality. The fact of a moral and political position in favor of equality does not imply that all members of the society are equally competent in all activities. *A good society is one in which all members have the right, and indeed the social obligation, to develop their abilities as far as possible.* Again, it needs to be stressed that the fact of such differential abilities and interests does not necessarily imply differential access to economic rewards. This distinction is critically important, the more so in a societal context in which competition for economic reward is assumed to be the basis for motivation of all achievement. Thus in rejecting such economic or class inequality, it is possible to assume that all differences need to be removed. This matter is discussed in R.H. Tawney, *Equality* (New York: Capricorn Books, 1961).* Tawney comments 'A society which values equality will attach a high degree of significance to differences of character and intelligence between individuals, and a low degree of significance to economic and social differences between different groups. It will endeavour, in shaping its policy and organization, to encourage the former and to neutralize and suppress the latter, and will regard it as vulgar and childish to emphasize them when, unfortunately, they still exist.' It is not one in which they may claim to have abilities which they do not demonstrate and which thus make no contribution to the social good.

We already have in the university the possibility of non-credit courses and can go much further in opening up the university environment as a community resource. However, such developments do not change the necessity for some areas in which performance is judged. My responsibility as a professor is certainly to engage at different levels with students and to facilitate their own development. However, *one aspect of that responsibility is to insist on the maintenance of some level of performance and to identify and reward in all relevant ways those people who exhibit excellence.*

There is no incompatibility in the position which supports the

*Copyright © George Allen and Unwin, 1931.

expansion of the university in a variety of ways and which wishes to maintain informal opportunities for equal interchange with students, while at the same time acting as an evaluator of performance. It in fact becomes an issue of role shift. Again, an elementary application of a sociological perspective would indicate that such shifts occur most easily where the situation is clearly marked as different, i.e., the activities are separated in time and space. Thus, the university examination as a formal social situation occurring outside the classroom clarifies a shift in role and context. What is important, however, is not the issue of evaluation itself, but rather the question of what should be examined and how it should be examined.

The Basis for Evaluation

It follows from the general orientation throughout this chapter that in my view *the university should stress analytical and synthetic skills rather than the simple mastery or memorization of information.* Just as good teaching provides a mapping within which specific issues, questions, and facts become meaningful, so also one needs to be concerned that the student has developed these skills to some extent at least. Once such capacities are developed the quest for information becomes relatively straightforward, since one has the reasonable expectation that the student can avail himself of library and other materials.

For this reason, I have a strong dislike for multiple choice questions — what are frequently termed in high schools (or experimental psychology laboratories) 'tests.' Unless these are extremely well designed and developed, and they usually are not, the emphasis becomes one of memorization and detail. Of course, the perceived advantage is that teaching assistants are able to 'correct' the test rapidly, or else they can be computer-graded. This achieves a rapid quantification of results with a minimum of effort. It is frequently claimed that such a procedure insures universalism, since all students are evaluated equally. The point is, however, that ease of quantification may or may not be related to the more important issue of the criteria in terms of which it is appropriate to evaluate.

Undergraduate teaching needs to do more than force-feed, and test the memorization and regurgitation capacities of students. Indeed, such an approach to both teaching and evaluation would appear most likely to inhibit precisely the development of those skills which are most appropriate. The responsibility for such evaluation lies squarely with the professor in any course and can only be put into the hands of assistants under the clearest possible controls. I have always found that examinations in the form of short essay answers, perhaps three or four in a three-hour period, give a good indication of the student's abilities, knowledge, and potential. In response to the criticism that such an approach stresses the viewpoint of the professor to too great an extent and is thus not universalistic, I would answer as follows. It is precisely the responsibility of the professor to make such judgments, and ease of quantification via the 'test' does not remove the problem but merely gives an appearance of increased fairness since the evaluative criteria are built into the questions, i.e., what is asked and what is not, the definition of possible answers, and so on.

Of course, professors make judgments, as do all people in all situations; this is a sociological truism. What one needs to have is some reason to believe that such judgments are not arbitrary or totally idiosyncratic. *The criteria for evaluation are precisely social norms and, like other norms, are man-made and man-maintained.* There is, for example, no self-evident meaning in the grade of 60 per cent; its meaning is located within a system of understandings (albeit never total or complete) which we share. In taking a position as university professor, one in fact agrees to enter a system of existing meanings. The socialization of the new professor, although not always made explicit, involves the attempt to locate the understandings concerning grades and relate his conduct to such meanings. It is only as the gap between one's own preconceptions (themselves of course the product of prior social experience) and existing reality in a specific university system becomes so wide as to do violence to one's conception of academic excellence, fairness, etc., that this becomes an unmanageable problem.

Thus there is an on-going tension between one's own criteria and possibly ideal conceptions of the university, and the actual situation in which one finds oneself. The responsibility of the faculty member vis-à-vis the student lies precisely in the management of this tension. This does not, of course, involve the refusal to adopt changes. What it does suggest, however, is the necessity for careful consideration of change within a conception of the possible. After a long period of time, I still exchange papers with other faculty members, both to clarify decisions at the margins and also to insure that the modest level of sharedness referred to above with respect to expectations and meanings is maintained. The professor who comes into a university system from a possibly quite different one, e.g., another society, has the clear responsibility for attempting to identify and adapt to the system in which he voluntarily agrees to locate himself. It is because of the multiple activities of the university, in which the primary dimensions of assessing faculty are of a different type, i.e., the receptivity of professional colleagues to his own scholarship, that this more immediate and local issue of responsibility to students in teaching situations tends to be so rarely discussed.

One aspect of any university concerns a dedication to academic excellence. In a situation of scarce resources,* it is essential to make judgments of relative worth. Thus the perpetuation of the old ideals of scholarship and creativity occur in the same formal system as the overall attempt to develop not scholars, but educated and aware citizens. In giving a student an A grade in the Canadian system, I am making a judgment that on the basis of my evaluation of his work, he has shown a capacity for integration and creativity which is excellent. Thus the grade is a statement — a recommendation. Where no such bases of differentiation occur, the pursuit of excellence is blunted in the name of mediocrity. For this reason, the ambiguity, and at times sheer irresponsibility, of the grading process can have no possible consequences which are other than self-defeating.

A student should have the right to question grading procedures and specific outcomes. In such cases, the usual process of having the work examined by others is well established. Similarly, the faculty person, acting now as evaluator, has some reasonable responsibility for clarifying the basis on which he evaluated.

There are, of course, other bases for evaluation than the examination. However these are selected, the same general guidelines would appear to hold, namely, that the student has the opportunity for indicating his grasp of a body of material and his capacity to work with that material and to 'make it his own.' Thus it would be incorrect to reject my general comments on the grounds of over-intellectualization. Even the most pragmatic and socially relevant issue to which the student addresses his attention provides a context in which a systematic and considered analysis may be undertaken. What is never enough is to reproduce technical knowledge, rules of procedure, or information without showing the applicability and usefulness of such knowledge. I can well support the idea of the student selecting his own projects within a course, yet at the same time, insist that once selected the management of the problem reveal more than a simple capacity for locating information, and certainly more than a capacity and willingness to use rhetoric. This insistence does not do violence to individuality and creativity, but rather concerns the establishment of minimal rules of discourse within which such creativity may develop.

---

*It is important to repeat that the term 'scarce resources' does not refer here to the issue of economic access. It merely insists that intellectual abilities are not equally shared. The university can encourage people to develop their interests and abilities to the maximum without thereby refusing to recognize and reward excellence.

To repeat a point made in another context, part of the difficulty in the teaching of sociology at the present time concerns the absence of systematic analysis. Thus, I have claimed that many students with major concentration in sociology do not develop, and have not been asked to show, the capacity to deal carefully and systematically with a body of knowledge. The grading and evaluation procedures provide the formal context within which this capacity is indicated in a public way. This, I have argued, is essential, not only in developing specialists in the field, but in the more general sense of showing that the student is indeed an educated person capable of learning new skills of a possibly quite different character.

Evaluating Professors: A Note to Students

Evaluation is built into our activities in everyday life. What varies is the basis of that evaluation and the degree to which the criteria are understood and, if not always explicit, at least capable of being made so. Just as professors evaluate students, partly within the formal requirements of the university system, so also it is self-evident that students evaluate professors. In this section, I hope to explore the implications of the present discussion in suggesting appropriate bases for such evaluation. Unless these criteria become reasonably explicit, the more diffuse criteria of evaluation imported from other roles and other settings tend to become dominant and thus distort the evaluation.

It will be obvious to the reader that the most general issue of 'liking' has little place. University teaching is not, and cannot be, a popularity contest in which the professor is predominantly concerned with his acceptance as a human being. In attempting to achieve this all too often, the necessary elements of social distance are removed — what I might term the 'we are all really orphans together' game. Thus, when the professor is forced, simply because of his social situation, to make evaluation judgments of a formal type, he is left with the appearance of simple arbitrariness, destroying the very trust he is presumably so concerned to create. Alternatively, he may seek to subvert the evaluation system itself, either through giving the same grade to all students, or leaving the evaluation in students' hands. This approach again is self-defeating since the abnegation of responsibility insures that the better student is literally cheated of his formal recognition and the weaker student is not required to make the effort to reach his potential. The worst possible variant is found in the 'not only are we all orphans together, but we are all equally powerless in the face of an inhuman and bureaucratized system' game.

Rather than 'liking,' the student should be able to trust the professor. The issue becomes: Does the professor clarify, and preferably give the reasons for, his view of the situation and does he follow through on assurances he gives? Is he available for discussion outside the classroom situation? When you go to see him with a problem, does he treat you with respect and understanding of your situation?

Trust and confidence are critically important in a good student-professor relationship, and they do not hinge on personal liking. Within this context, however, the important issue becomes that of honestly trying to assess the learning experience itself. It is very often only possible to do this after a course is over, and indeed possibly long after, but the question is not so much 'what information did I learn?' but rather 'was this overall experience a worthwhile one?' *If, after completing a course in sociology, your view of the social world, your orientation to yourself and others has not changed in the direction of increased awareness, the course is likely to have been inadequate.* That you may have picked up an easy credit or have had 'fun' will, looking back, appear both less important and also a reason for feeling you were cheated.

Professors vary in their approach to the subject and their manner of delivery. Lecturing skill does not unfortunately always accompany ability. You have a right as a university student to encounter excellence in the classroom. *In some cases, it may be worth the effort to listen carefully to a not very stimulating lecture or set of lectures and to think about the material on your own.* At that time, should it appear that this is indeed a worthwhile 'product' in a poor 'package,' you should go and talk with the professor concerned. Once you make the effort to understand and get beyond the delivery style, you may end up with a really worthwhile experience. Similarly, the brilliant public speaker may or may not have anything to say. Again the same rule applies. Did the professor raise critical issues? Did he provide you with a basis for seeing relationships and organizing and interpreting the material you are reading? If not, you did not have the learning experience you have the right to expect.

I noted earlier that professors have multiple roles. So also the social situation of the student is not a simple one. Of course, you feel under pressure both to get good grades and also in allocating time and effort. Thus one strategy for survival tends to be to select at least some courses which are low key and easily managed. It is pointless to engage in a moral discussion on the merits of such a strategy. It follows from everything discussed in the chapter that I regret the trend which has made what should be a learning environment too often resemble an obstacle course in which one must survive. Nevertheless, I repeat the earlier point that the student has a right to be exposed to excellence in the classroom. When the experience is simply one of mediocre people going through the routine of information-giving without excitement, without flair, without apparent awareness of alternatives, the student has been deceived and should be angry, even when it is relatively easy to do well in the course.

There is no possible excuse in university teaching for mere repetition of well-known information which anyone can read for himself. Spoon-feeding is bad teaching technique at any level of the education system; at the university level, it is completely unacceptable. Just as you are not there to be spoon-fed, so also you are not watching Sesame Street. While humor is a great asset in the teaching process for purposes of tension release, 'reductio ad absurdum,' and simple spacing, the experience is not to be judged as entertainment. The clown in the classroom is probably a menace who is insecure enough to need your laughter and applause. It could be that he is an idiosyncratic genius and on reflection you may decide so, but it is very unlikely. You have the right to be treated as adult and serious people who want to think.

An Approach to Course Organization and Teaching

Some further comment is in order on the appropriate strategies for teaching. I have already both explicitly and implicitly rejected a number of approaches, both to students and to the subject matter of sociology. What then are reasonable alternatives? The use of the term 'teaching' itself is somewhat problematic in the university context since the university constitutes an environment for the student to learn. The professor represents essentially a resource within that environment. As already noted, formal lecturing is to be located firmly within a more general conception of the university, involving both relations with other students and also less formal discussion with the professor.

The lecture is not best viewed as a vehicle for information presentation. It is rather a situation in which issues are raised, and alternatives evaluated. The lecturer should be concerned to demonstrate sociological reasoning. Within the course structure provided by the reading material, he is concerned to indicate assumptions, provide a synthesis, and above all to present for his students a model for sociological analysis. The student is in the university to think and 'discover;' the lecture provides a setting, a context for encouraging that creative process to develop. In the end, learning (as opposed to simple memorization) always requires that creative synthesis on the part of the student himself. The professor's objective is to provide the environment which will best encourage such learning.

Max Weber's statement on the responsibility of the lecturer remains highly relevant. The classroom is not a context for political indoctrination, although such issues may well be discussed in more informal situations in which the responsibilities of the professor are rather different from those of the formal classroom. Yet it is equally necessary to repeat the earlier point that this conception of formal responsibility does not constitute an excuse for avoidance of controversy or relevance. It is similarly the case that indoctrination is not merely political. The classroom is not a place for the establishment of orthodoxy, i.e., while the professor presents his own conclusions and synthesis, his purpose should not be to pressure the student into the same conclusions. In other words, it is the process of sociological thought and the nature and use of evidence which he should be concerned to establish — what might be termed the parameters for creativity, allowing always for alternative possibilities and implications.

It has been suggested that sociology is best pursued in comparative terms. The purpose from the outset in an introductory course is to expand intellectual horizons and develop an awareness of the institutional structure of human societies. Rather than provide a survey of discrete areas of investigation or 'substantive fields,' the purpose is to begin to exhibit the structure behind apparently diverse and discrete units of action, through an examination of linkages and interdependencies. Thus the analysis of religion, kinship, stratification, etc., can be approached initially through the exhibition of their inter-connectedness with evidence drawn on a comparative basis. An evolutionary focus provides a central theme which allows these linkages to be pursued into the analysis of complex modern societies.

Once the basic frame of reference is established and the student begins to adopt a systematic approach to the analysis of social reality, specific problems, theoretical, methodological, and substantive, can be approached more readily. The first and hardest part of learning sociology is to discover and use the cognitive framework, with its linked assumptions. Far too frequently, students are able to take undergraduate degrees without in fact doing this. Once this is achieved, the problem of building on the framework becomes relatively straightforward.

The good lecturer is one who is able to present his discussion in such a way that students with a variety of backgrounds, information, and intellectual abilities are able to learn. Thus he must of necessity be aware of his audience and be able, through illustration and alternative presentation of the same critical points, to adapt to the class. The use of the lecture for the simple reading of carefully prepared notes fails to allow this immediacy of the classroom situation to be used productively.

Similarly, the endless use of illustrations which illustrate nothing, involving unending details of studies, personal experience, or simple digression, adds nothing to a lecture. The bad lecturer is always concerned to get through the hour without incident and hopefully with a sense of minimal rapport. The good lecturer continuously returns to the key issues and while responding to his audience, remains firmly in control of the situation. He seeks through his own enthusiasm and ability to move the student towards discovery, and his satisfaction is to see this occur.

Given this conception of the role of the professor as lecturer and his relation to the learning process of the student, it becomes clear that the teaching process is extremely complex and difficult. It is a total misunderstanding to view the introductory course as easy and relatively straightforward. Thus the practice in many American universities of having teaching assistants handle such courses, teaching from a lock-step text, is to be rejected on all possible grounds. Good teaching at the university level is not easy, and only through experience and very real efforts to change and improve can a professor become more than merely adequate.

Canadian Content

An issue which has become politically volatile is the Canadianization of universities. The social sciences, and probably sociology in particular, are viewed by some nationalists as hotbeds of American orientations and models, and indeed there is strong resistance to continued hiring of non-Canadians for university positions. Some minimal comment in the context of of this chapter appears appropriate as it bears on the issue of teaching.

I have strongly suggested that the primary benefit to be derived from university education is the possibility of being involved in an environment which aids in the development of awareness. Since awareness of self is necessarily an awareness of the society, i.e., the determinants of one's being are precisely social determinants, this involves an understanding of Canadian society. *It is meaningless to think of an educated person living in Canada who has no conception of Canadian history and the mix of pressures, power, and traditions which map the complex fabric of Canadian society.*

Sociology as an academic discipline plays a difficult, and indeed delicate, part in the process of gaining that understanding. While it is without doubt essential to have specific courses dealing with the society, it is also critically important, if only in achieving that end, to view Canada in comparative terms. If we are to avoid merely describing characteristics of any society (sociography), the social processes need to be removed for analytical purposes from their specific cultural locus and considered at a different level — one admitting of comparison and generalization. Only as this is done is it possible then to move back to the specific social-cultural context of present-day Canada both to inform our present awareness and to speak meaningfully about future possibilities. Just as awareness of self involves coming to terms with one's personal biography and present alternatives, so also understanding any society involves some awareness of the trajectory of that society — its institutional history — and also its present situation in terms of internal and external forces impinging and the range of alternatives available.

The difficulty in social science so often has been the strong tendency for its practitioners to remain at one level or the other, either at the descriptive level including institutional history, or so enamoured of the processes of abstraction and generalization that the results seldom inform actual analyses of social processes. The thrust for Canadian content should not be taken at the naive level of meaning that all studies and courses should be oriented to the social structure of Canadian society. This would be self-defeating if for no other reason than its empiricist bias. *Only as observers of social life have at their disposal the categories and conceptual apparatus and the logic for using such frameworks via systematic comparison can our actual knowledge of Canada increase.* Because of proximity and history, comparison with the United States appears tactically a most useful procedure.

What is not appropriate, however, is the simple importation of American problems and American data onto the Canadian scene with the uncritical assumption of their direct applicability. The very fact that a vast amount of American sociology has not been comparative in orientation or conceptualization insures that such simplistic carry-overs are likely to be fruitless and thus have no possible implication for social action in Canada. It may be noted in passing that a sociology which does not inform social action in fact of necessity merely supports the status quo, even, interestingly enough, when its proponents claim to be precisely concerned with social change.

However, it is not merely specific American problems and their uncritical importation into this society which is the issue in sociology. I have noted throughout that sociology itself is to be seen as a form of social activity located temporally and spatially in the social matrix within which it occurs. Thus it is naive in the extreme to suppose that by the simple substitution of Canadian data for American, the problem of a Canadian sociology is solved. It is the assumptions underlying the activity itself which are too often problematic, representing as they do the taken-for-granted world of a society committed to liberal individualism and manifest destiny. That such everyday assumptions become viewed as potentially law-like statements about social reality in general is best viewed as the mythical or ideological basis of uncritical and self-confirming research.

It is all too easy to explain the difficulties in English Canadian sociology on the grounds of cultural imperialism from the United States. However, in order to understand why this has occurred, it is also necessary to examine the cultural context into which that imperialism fitted so well. Sociology was never integrated into the conservative political tradition which historically expressed the Canadian fact, nor did it develop within the assumptions of a radically different political position. Sociology in English Canada tended towards those uncritical empiricist assumptions operating within an often implicit progressive liberal framework which fitted into the technocratic ethos of North America. Sociology expresses, I have argued, the cultural and social reality of the society within which it develops; it does not merely objectively analyze that society. *The problem of a distinct English Canadian sociology is precisely an expression of the problem of Canadian nationhood itself.*

Similarly, the fact that Canadian universities, in terms of organization and curriculum, have increasingly come to resemble the State universities of the United States does not merely stem from the influx of American professors. The structural facts of modern Canada and the absence of understanding, let alone legitimation of a distinct Canadian tradition, have insured the take-over of patterns of activity which are indistinguishable from their American counterparts.*

We should resist the emotional appeal to Canadian content when such an appeal operates within assumptions which would deny the possibility of increasing our knowledge and thereby our range of meaningful alternatives. It would be self-evidently foolish to imagine that Canadian music could be developed by ignoring the essentials of composition. Rather I would argue that as a significant number of Canadians become musically informed, so inevitably they will go on to develop possibly distinct forms of musical composition. In sociology we tread a most difficult path in which we need to develop our theoretical and procedural awareness in order to then increase our knowledge of this society. There can be no short-cut to achieving this result.

In case of possible misunderstanding, let me clarify that this should

---

*This general point is brilliantly argued in George Grant, *Lament For a Nation,* (Toronto: McClelland and Stewart, 1965).

not be viewed as an apology for American cultural imperialism. Such imperialism arises precisely when the attitudes and assumptions of one society are simply and uncritically applied to another — for whatever reason. It is argued that the attempt to develop a Canadian sociology which is not historically informed, theoretically sophisticated, and comparatively oriented, will merely be an alternative ideology.

We come back again to our point of departure. Only as we expand our awareness beyond our everyday assumptions can we develop what C. Wright Mills termed 'sociological imagination.' Yet in attempting this our political situation and concern with Canadian society should not operate to move us towards anti-intellectual and emotional short-cuts, but rather to insure that the foci of our concern remain the possibilities of this society, and indeed, of all societies. At this period of history, the increased mutual awareness and interdependence of societies means that a capacity to come to terms with other conceptions of the world and other modes of social organization is essential. Sociology at its best provides some of the intellectual tools for achieving this end without denying our concern for societal and personal identity.

References

Davis, Kingsley, and Wilbert E. Moore, ' Some Principles of Stratification,' *American Sociological Review,* X (April, 1945), 242-247.

Mills, C. Wright, *The Sociological Imagination.* New York: Oxford University Press, 1959.

Tawney, R.H., *Equality.* New York: Capricorn Books, 1961.

Weber, Max, 'The Meaning of Ethical Neutrality,' in *Methodology of the Social Sciences,* trans. and ed. by Edward Shils and Henry Finch. Glencoe, Ill.: The Free Press, 1949, particularly pp. 6-8.

Author Index

Subject Index

Equality *(cont.)*
 nature of, 223-26
 of opportunity:
  and education, 155-56
  not of ability, 487
  as political issue, 203-5
  and religion, 220-23
Eskimos, 192, 195-96
 Canadian and Danish compared,
  149-50
Ethnic, defined, 164-65
Ethnic group(s):
 in Canada, 171
 in Canadian cities, 257, 408-9, 411-
  14
 conflict as key factor in maintenance
  of, 181-85, 190-91
 conflicting cultural traditions, 183-84
 defined, 167
 degrees of closure, 174
 endogamy, tendency toward, 412-13
 faulty ethnic group model, 177
 identification, 184-85
 impersonal variables affecting
  maintenance of, 179-81
 individualism-voluntarism model,
  178
 inequalities between, in Canada, 194
 maintenance of identity, 163
 racialist view of, 177
 redefinition of stigmatized traits, 192
 relative deprivation, 192-94
 rotten society model, 178
 social-psychological models, 191-94
 stereotypes, 191-92
 structural-functional model, 185-91
 and territoriality, 172
 types of, 173-76
 voting restrictions, 213-14
Ethnic identity, and inequality, 88,
  162-200
Ethnicity: *see also* Multi-ethnic
  societies
 approaches to study of, 168-69, 176-
  94
 defined, 165-66
 and family life, urban, 419

Ethnocentrism, 14
Exchange theory, 18, 43
Exogamy, 174, 267

F

Fairclough, Ellen, 217
Family:
 adaptation to urban life, 435-36
 as basic socio-cultural system, 264-
  65
 birth rates, changing, 293-95
 changing, in North America, 290-97
 changing functions of, 253, 254,
  255, 260-97
 changing role configurations, 287
 communication, 287
 conjugal, 265, 268
 conjugality, changing rates of, 290-
  93
 decisions, 288-89
 demands to be met, 286
 early sociological study of, 458
 effect of industrialization, 254
 form of:
  and class, 269
  and goals, 270-75
  and property system, 268-69
 future of, 297
 ideal types of, 255
  decision-making, 288-89
  fraternal, 274-75
  and the future, 297
  maternal, 270-71
  patriarchal, 272-74
  and social network, 282-86
 in industrial society, 265, 267-68
 lower class mores, 271
 nuclear:
  continuity of institution, 13
  relations with kin, 279-82
 nuturing communication, 264-65,
  269, 289-90
 perspectives on, 260-61
 power, distribution of, 419
 in Quebec, early study of, 458-59
 relations with kin: conflict situations,
  280